THE
GEORGIA
ALMANAC

AND BOOK OF FACTS
1989—1990

THE GEORGIA ALMANAC

AND BOOK OF FACTS
1989—1990

Edited by

James A. Crutchfield

Project Editor
Julia M. Pitkin

Assistant
Mary Ann Drewry McNeese

RUTLEDGE HILL PRESS
Nashville, Tennessee

Copyright © 1986, 1988 by Rutledge Hill Press

All rights reserved. Written permission must be secured from the publisher to use or reproduce any part of this book, except for brief quotations in critical reviews or articles.

Published in Nashville, Tennessee, by Rutledge Hill Press, Inc., 513 Third Avenue South, Nashville, Tennessee 37210

Typography by Bailey Typography, Nashville, Tennessee

Library of Congress Cataloging-in-Publication Data

The Georgia almanac and book of facts, 1989-1990 / edited by James A. Crutchfield; project editor, Julia
    M. Pitkin, assistant, Mary Ann Drewry McNeese.
        p.   cm.
    Includes index.
    ISBN 1-558-53003-7   ISBN 1-558-53002-9 (pbk.)
    1. Georgia—Miscellanea.   2. Almanacs, American—Georgia.
I. Crutchfield, James Andrew, 1938-
F286.G35   1988
975:8'043—dc19
                                                                                88-29841
                                                                                CIP

Manufactured in the United States of America
1 2 3 4 5—93 92 91 90 89

PREFACE

The successful publication of *The Georgia Almanac and Book of Facts* in 1986 has proven the need for an accurate, up-to-date, inexpensive handbook containing vital information about Georgia. In that edition we expressed our desire to update the almanac regularly; its wide acceptance has made that vision a reality.

To my knowledge, *The Georgia Almanac and Book of Facts* represents the first effort to put between two covers a compendium of facts about Georgia. While there are volumes of statistical data and scores of lists, descriptions, and information about individual subjects of interest to Georgians, what makes *The Georgia Almanac and Book of Facts* unique is that all these figures, tables, charts, essays, and other information have been synthesized into one easy-to-read volume.

The Georgia Almanac and Book of Facts is sure to become one of the most used volumes in homes, libraries, and offices. Since Rutledge Hill Press plans to update this book regularly, the publisher would be happy to hear from you, the reader, regarding information you believe future editions should include. In fact, numerous suggestions from readers of the first edition have been incorporated into this edition of what we hope will become known as "the Encyclopedia of Georgia."

—James A. Crutchfield

Dedicated to the citizens of Georgia,
especially those who helped in compiling this almanac

CONTENTS

ACKNOWLEDGEMENTS

In compiling *The Georgia Almanac and Book of Facts*, many books, institutions, departments of state government, and individuals were consulted. We would like to acknowledge these sources for providing the information that made this almanac possible.

Sources used for each section are as follows:*

Agriculture: *Georgia County Guide;* Mike Hammer, State Statistician, Georgia Agriculture Data Center.

Airlines: *Rand McNally 1987 Commercial Atlas and Marketing Guide.*

Airports: *Georgia Airport Directory,* Bureau of Aeronautics, Georgia Department of Transportation.

Alcohol: Department of Revenue, Alcohol and Tobacco Tax Division; *Georgia County Guide;* Herman Oliver.

Area Planning and Development Commissions: Atlanta Regional Commission; Harry West.

Arts: Georgia Council for the Arts; Martha Evans; Frank Ratka.

Banking: Federal Reserve Bank of Atlanta, Statistical Reports Department; George Briggs.

Boundaries: *Georgia Official and Statistical Register, 1983–84,* Office of the Secretary of State.

Chambers of Commerce: *Worldwide Chamber of Commerce Directory,* Worldwide Chamber of Commerce Directory, Inc.

Climate: *Annual Climate Summary,* National Weather Service; National Weather Service, Atlanta, Columbus and Savannah.

Coastline and Shoreline: *Georgia Official and Statistical Register, 1983–84,* Office of the Secretary of State; *Reader's Digest Almanac and Yearbook, 1984.*

Congressional Districts: *Georgia Official Directory of United States Congressmen, State and County Officers, February 1, 1988,* Office of the Secretary of State.

Congressional Medal of Honor: *America's Medal of Honor Recipients.*

Constitution: *Constitution of the State of Georgia* (Revised January 1987), Office of Secretary of State.

Corps of Engineers Lakes: U.S. Army Corps of Engineers; Jack Wilson.

County Name Origins: *The American Counties,* Joseph Nathan Kane; *Georgia Official and Statistical Register, 1983–84,* Office of Secretary of State; Jack Sinks.

County Seats: *Georgia Official Directory of United States Congressmen, State and County Officers, February 1, 1988,* Office of the Secretary of State.

Courts: Administrative Office of the Courts; *Georgia Official Directory of United States Congressmen, State and County Officers, February 1, 1988,* Office of the Secretary of State.

Crime: *Georgia County Guide;* Department of Pardons & Parole, Silas Moore; Fred Steeple, Department of Corrections.

Cyclorama: Georgia Department of Tourism.

Day Care Facilities: Day Care Licensing Division, Family and Childrens Services; Don Garner.

Economics: Bureau of Economic Analysis, U.S. Department of Commerce; *Construction Reports—Housing Authorized by Building Permits and Public Contracts, 1976–1986,* Bureau of the Census, U.S. Department of Commerce; *Georgia County Guide; 1986 Statistical Report,* Georgia Department of Revenue.

Education: Georgia Department of Education, Statistical Services Unit; *Georgia County Guide; Georgia Official Directory of United States Congressmen, State and County Officers, February 1, 1988,* Office of the Secretary of State.

Elections: Elections and Campaign Disclosure, Office of the Secretary of State; Bill Crane; Kim Hutcheson.

Electoral Vote: Office of the Secretary of State.

Elevations, Latitudes and Longitudes: *Georgia Official and Statistical Register, 1983–84,* Office of the Secretary of State.

Employment: Labor Information Systems, Georgia Department of Labor; Amelia Butts.

Endangered Species: U.S. Department of the Interior, Fish and Wildlife Service; Dr. George Drewry.

Energy: *Electrical Power Plants: 1988,* Georgia Power Company; *Georgia County Guide.*

Famous Georgians: *The Encyclopedia of the South; Great Georgians,* Zell Miller; *They Heard Georgia Singing,* Zell Miller.

Flora and Fauna: *The Encyclopedia Americana International Edition,* Grolier, Inc.; The U.S. Department of the Interior, Fish and Wildlife Service.

Forts: *American FORTS Yesterday and Today,* Bruce Grant.

Geographic Center: *Georgia Official and Statistical Register, 1983–84,* Office of the Secretary of State.

Gold: Georgia Department of Tourism.

Gone With the Wind: James A. Crutchfield.

Governors: *Georgia Official and Statistical Register, 1983–84,* Office of the Secretary of State; *This Is Your Georgia,* Bernice McCullar; *Colonial Georgia—A History,* Kenneth Coleman; Dorothy Olson, State Capitol.

Higher Education: *Georgia County Guide;* Georgia State Board of Postsecondary Vocational Education; Office of Research and Planning, University Systems of Georgia.

Highways: *Georgia County Guide; Mileage of Public Roads by Surface Type, 1987,* Division of Planning and Programming, Georgia Department of Transportation.

ACKNOWLEDGEMENTS

Historical Societies: *Directory of Historical Agencies in North America,* Betty Pease Smith.

Historic Sites: Georgia Department of Natural Resources, Parks, Recreation and Historic Sites Division.

History: *Colonial Georgia—A History,* Kenneth Coleman; *The Encyclopedia of Southern History,* David C. Roller and Robert W. Twyman, editors; *Georgia—A Short History,* E. Merton Coulter; *Georgia History Calendar, 1986,* Zell Miller; *Historical Statistics of the South, 1790–1970,* Donald B. Dodd and Wynelle S. Dodd.

Holidays and Days of Special Observance: Office of the Secretary of State.

Housing: *Georgia County Guide; 1980 Census of Housing: Detailed Housing Characteristics,* Bureau of the Census, U.S. Department of Commerce.

Indians: *The Indians of the Southeastern United States,* John R. Swanton.

Labor: *General Social and Economic Characteristics: 1980,* Bureau of the Census, U.S. Department of Commerce; *Georgia County Guide.*

Land Area: *1980 Area Measurement Report,* Bureau of the Census, Geography Division, U.S. Department of Commerce.

Legislature: *Georgia Official Directory of United States Congressmen, State and County Officers, February 1, 1988,* Office of the Secretary of State.

Libraries: *Georgia County Guide; 1987 Georgia Public Library Statistics,* Division of Public Library Services, Georgia Department of Education.

License Plate Identification: *The License Plate Book,* Thompson C. Murray.

Little White House: Georgia Department of Tourism.

Manufacturing: *Georgia County Guide; Georgia Manufacturing Directory, 1987–88,* Research Division, Georgia Department of Industry and Trade; Charlotte Bush.

Medical Resources: *Georgia County Guide; 1985 Inventory of General and Specialized Hospitals in Georgia,* State Health Planning Agency; *1985 Inventory of General and Specialized Nursing Homes in Georgia,* State Health Planning Agency; *Physicians Characteristics and Distribution in the U.S., 1984, 1986, 1987,* American Medical Association.

Mileage Chart: Georgia Department of Transportation.

Military Posts: *Georgia Department of Transportation Official Highway and Transportation Map.*

Miss Georgia: Miss Georgia Pageant Office.

Museums: *The Official Museum Directory,* The American Association of Museums.

National Forests: Division of Forest Service, U.S. Department of Agriculture.

National Historic Landmarks: *Catalogue of National Historic Landmarks,* U.S. Department of the Interior.

National Parks: *Georgia Department of Transportation Official Highway and Transportation Map.*

National Wildlife Refuges: Fish and Wildlife Service, U.S. Department of the Interior.

Natural Resources: *Minerals Yearbook,* Bureau of the Mines, U.S. Department of the Interior.

Newspapers: *1988 Georgia Newspaper Directory,* Georgia Press Association.

Occupations: Bureau of the Census, U.S. Department of Commerce.

Peanuts: Delta Airlines; *The Original Tennessee Homecoming Cookbook,* Daisy King, Editor.

Population: *Georgia County Guide,* Georgia State Office of Planning and Budget; *Georgia Vital Statistics Report: 1986,* Georgia Department of Human Resources; Bureau of the Census, U.S. Department of Commerce.

Public Assistance: *Georgia County Guide; Indicators of Needs for Human Services in Georgia, 1985–1987,* Georgia Department of Human Resources.

Radio Stations: *Broadcasting/Cablecasting Yearbook, 1987.*

Railroads: Public Transportation Division, Department of Transportation.

Religion: *The World Almanac and Book of Facts, 1988.*

Revolutionary War: Mary Ann McNeese.

Rivers: Water Resources Development in Georgia, 1987, Savannah District, U.S. Army Corps of Engineers.

Senators, U.S.: *Georgia Official Directory of U.S. Congressmen, State and County Officers, February 1, 1988,* Office of the Secretary of State.

Sherman's March: *The American Soldier in the Civil War.*

Sports: *CBS News Almanac; Reader's Digest Almanac and Yearbook;* Beverly Bennett, Georgia Sports Hall of Fame; Mike Finn, Georgia Tech Sports Information Department; John Franks, Nashville Sounds Baseball Club.

State Forests: Georgia Forestry Commission.

State Government: *Georgia Official Directory of U.S. Congressmen, State and County Officers, February 1, 1988,* Office of the Secretary of State.

State Parks: Parks, Recreation, and Historic Sites Division, Georgia Department of Natural Resources.

State Patrol Phone Numbers: Department of Transportation.

Taxes: Sales and Use Tax Division, State of Georgia Department of Revenue.

Television Stations: *Broadcasting/Cablecasting Yearbook, 1987.*

Tourist Attractions: *Georgia on My Mind,* Georgia Tourist Division, Department of Industry and Trade.

ACKNOWLEDGEMENTS

Tourist Information: Tourist Division, Georgia Department of Industry and Trade.

Vehicle Registration: *1986 Georgia Type Vehicle Classification by County,* Motor Vehicle Unit, Georgia Department of Revenue.

Voters, Registered: *Georgia County Guide; Registered Voters: 1984–1986,* Elections Division, Office of the Secretary of State.

War Between the States: James A. Crutchfield.

Waterfalls: Department of Industry and Trade.

Wildlife Areas: Department of Natural Resources; Triece Gignilliat; Jane Griess.

Women's Rights: James A. Crutchfield.

Zip Codes: *1988 National Five-Digit Zip Code and Post Office Directory,* U.S. Postal Service.

*Because of its frequent use, *The Georgia County Guide,* Seventh Edition, 1988, Cooperative Extension Service, College of Agriculture, the University of Georgia, is listed as *Georgia County Guide.*

INDEX

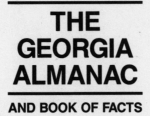

THE
GEORGIA
ALMANAC

AND BOOK OF FACTS

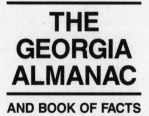

THE
GEORGIA
ALMANAC

AND BOOK OF FACTS

AGRICULTURE

Georgia leads the nation as the largest producer of peanuts and pecans. The state ranked second in poultry sales (eggs and broilers), third in peaches and fourth in egg production.

The most important cash field crops of 1987 were peanuts, tobacco, corn, cotton and soybeans in that order.

Sales of commercial broilers led the livestock market as the top money maker by a wide margin. Second to fifth places were taken by cattle, eggs, hogs, and milk.

Lists of County Extension Directors, Experiment Stations, and a chart showing the number of farms, the average farm size, and the 1982 totals of harvested cropland for all Georgia counties, follow.

County Extension Directors

Appling
James R. Clark
County Office Complex
400 East Park
Baxley 31513
912-367-8130

Atkinson
Philip R. Torrance
County Agriculture Bldg.
Cogdell Road
Pearson 31642
912-422-3277

Bacon
Danny Stanaland
County Office Bldg.
Alma 31510-1985
912-632-5601

Baker
Lanier Jordan
Agriculture Bldg.

Hwy. 37
Newton 31770
912-734-5252

Baldwin
Keith G. Lassiter
Federal Bldg.
114 East Hancock St.
Milledgeville 31061
912-453-4394

Banks
John W. Mitchell
Courthouse Annex
Jolly Street
Homer 30547
404-677-2245

Barrow
Douglas H. Garrison
213 McElroy St.
Winder 30680
404-867-7581

Bartow
Edward P. Hornyak
320 West Cherokee St.
Cartersville 30120
404-382-2324

Ben Hill
Duren E. Bell
515 West Magnolia St.
Fitzgerald 31750
912-423-2360

Berrien
William A. Roberts
County Farm Rd.
Nashville 31639
912-686-5431

Bibb
Rose A. Simmons
145 First St.
Macon 31201
912-751-6338

Bleckley
John P. Parks
Post Office Bldg.
Second St.
Cochran 31014
912-934-6917

Brantley
Robert T. Boland, Jr.
County Office Bldg.
Burton St.
Nahunta 31553
912-462-5724

Brooks
Sonny Winter
Agriculture Bldg.
Moultrie Hwy. #33
Quitman 31643
912-263-4103

Bryan
J. Rastus Byrd
Courthouse Annex
Pembroke 31321
912-653-2231

Bulloch
Gary L. Lee
28 Hill St.
Statesboro 30458
912-764-6101

Burke
W. H. Craven, Jr.
Burke County Office Park
Waynesboro 30830
404-554-2119

Butts
Carl F. Varnadoe
County Courthouse
Jackson 30233
404-775-2601

Calhoun
Paul D. Wigley
County Office Bldg.
Highway 37
Morgan 31766
912-849-2685

Camden
Alice Sue Crews
Bedell Ave. & 15th St.—
End
Woodbine 31569
912-576-3219

Candler
Brad Phillips
310 West Broad St.
Metter 30439
912-685-2408

Carroll
Carl E. Brack
Agriculture Bldg.
102 City Hall Ave.
Carrollton 30117
404-836-8605

Catoosa
Steve Moraitakis
105 Maple St.
Ringgold 30736
404-935-4211

Charlton
R. Terry Thigpen
107-A South Third St.
Folkston 31537
912-496-2040

Chatham
Billy Myers
Old County Courthouse
2nd Floor
130 Bull St.
Savannah 31412
912-651-2291

Chattahoochee
Extension Office
Broad St.
Cusseta 31805
404-989-3055

Chattooga
Ted M. Clark
Post Office Bldg.
Summerville 30747
404-857-1410

Cherokee
George E. Jones
100 North St., B-3
Canton 30114
404-479-1953

Clarke
Dan K. Gunnels
2152 West Broad St.
Athens 30606
404-354-2940

Clay
William O. Kenyon
Killingsworth Bldg.
South Washington
Fort Gaines 31751
912-768-2247

Clayton
Kathleen Wages
1262 Government Circle,
Suite 40
Jonesboro 30236
404-473-5450

Clinch
Audrey B. James
Courthouse Annex
Homerville 31634
912-487-2169

Cobb
Bruce E. Beck
County Bldg.
10-East Park Square
Marietta 30060
404-429-3330

Coffee
Rick Reed
105 South Tanner St.
2nd Floor
Douglas 31533
912-384-1402

Colquitt
R. Douglas Durham
County Government Bldg.
Highway 319
Moultrie 31768
912-985-1321

Columbia
Wendell T. Stubbs
Hwy. 47 North
Appling 30802
404-541-0557

Cook
Glenn Beard
Courthouse Annex
North Parrish Ave.
Adel 31620
912-896-7456

Coweta
Donald J. Morris
215 Federal Office Bldg.

Newnan 30264
404-253-2450

Crawford
Sandra G. Williams
234 Wright Ave.
Roberta 31078
912-836-3121

Crisp
George B. Lee
County Courthouse
Cordele 31015
912-273-1217

Dade
Betty W. Gass
Extension Bldg.
Case Ave.
Trenton 30752
404-657-4116

Dawson
William L. Carlan
Courthouse
Dawsonville 30534
404-265-2442

Decatur
D. Eddie McGriff
Agriculture Bldg.
Vada Highway 97 N.
Bainbridge 31717
912-246-4528

DeKalb
W. A. Steagall
101 Court Square
East Ponce DeLeon
Decatur 30030
404-371-2821

Dodge
Garlon E. Rogers
Agriculture Bldg.
Anson Ave.
Eastman 31023
912-374-4702

Dooly
Charlie E. Ellis
County Agriculture Bldg.
Union St.
Vienna 31092
912-268-4171

Dougherty
Rhen Bishop

County Agriculture Bldg.
1016 Lowe Rd.
Albany 31706
912-436-7216

Douglas
Joan H. Douglas
8501 Bowden St.
Douglasville 30134
404-949-2000

Early
Mickey O. Fourakers
Agriculture Bldg.
114 Magnolia
Blakely 31723
912-723-3072

Echols
R. Larry Corbett
Courthouse
Statenville 31648
912-559-5562

Effingham
Susan Epling
Truetlen Bldg.
403 Pine Street
Springfield 31329
912-754-6071

Elbert
Robert G. Perkins
10 Cloverleaf Dr.
(Fairground)
Elberton 30635
404-283-3001

Emanuel
Carl W. Tankersley
County Office Bldg.
Swainsboro 30401
912-237-9933

Evans
Joan Strickland
Courthouse Annex
3 Freeman St.
Claxton 30417
912-739-1292

Fannin
Mary Jane Jones
EMA Bldg.
West Main St.
Blue Ridge 30513
404-632-3061

Fayette
Emma J. Thornton
100 McDonough Rd.
Fayetteville 30214
404-461-4580

Floyd
Louie C. Canova
201 North 5th St.
Rome 30161-5815
404-295-6210

Forsyth
Patricia E. Kilmark
County Government Bldg.
101 Maple St.
Cumming 30130
404-887-2418

Franklin
Mickey P. Cummings
Cole Building
Hwy. 145
Carnesville 30521
404-384-2843

Fulton
Hal E. Tatum
Suite 560
1718 Peachtree St., N.W
Atlanta 30303
404-572-3261

Gilmer
Ronnie H. Gheesling
9 Dalton St.
Ellijay 30540
404-635-4426

Glascock
Frank M. Watson
Courthouse
Main St.
Gibson 30810
404-598-2811

Glynn
J. Rudolph Beggs
Office Park Bldg.
Room 232
1803 Gloucester St.
Brunswick 31521-9999
912-267-5656

Gordon
Jack N. Dyer
Northwest Branch

3

Experiment Station
Calhoun 30701
404-629-8685

Grady
Donald W. Clark
Agri-Center
65 11th Avenue
Northeast
Cairo 31728
912-377-1312

Greene
Barbara J. Torbet
Extension Bldg.
502 S. Walnut St.
Greensboro 30642
404-453-2083

Gwinnett
John W. Baughman, Jr.
Lawrenceville Square
Suite 10
140 Clayton St.
Lawrenceville 30245
404-995-6650

Habersham
Helen Barrett
Market Bldg.
Habersham Ave.
Clarkesville 30523
404-754-2318

Hall
Robert H. Lowe
220 Green St. SE
Gainesville 30501
404-536-6681

Hancock
Earnest Carswell, Jr.
Federal Bldg.
Broad St.
Sparta 31087
404-444-6596

Haralson
John C. Callaway, Jr.
County Office Bldg.
Buchanan 30113
404-646-5288

Harris
Winifred Parker
Courthouse
Hamilton 31811
404-628-4824

Hart
B. Edward Page
Courthouse Annex
Hartwell 30643
404-376-3134

Heard
Render T. Ward, Jr.
Courthouse
Franklin 30217
404-675-3513

Henry
Millard F. Daniel
345 Phillips Dr.
McDonough 30253
404-957-1533

Houston
David P. Mills
Agriculture Bldg.
733 Carroll St.
Perry 31069
912-987-2028

Irwin
Gary C. Tankersley
Courthouse
Ocilla 31774
912-468-7409

Jackson
Patricia Bell
117 Athens St.
Jefferson 30549
404-367-1199

Jasper
Hiram Frank Sears, Jr.
Post Office Bldg.
Washington St.
Monticello 31064
404-468-6479

Jeff Davis
James R. Reid
County Agriculture Bldg.
Hazlehurst 31539
912-375-5526

Jefferson
Johnnie G. Dekle
7th & Walnut Sts.
Louisville 30434
912-625-3046

Jenkins
Joanne R. Chance

209 Daniel Street
Millen 30442
912-982-4408

Johnson
Beeman C. Keen, Jr.
County Office Bldg.
109 E. College St.
Wrightsville 31096
912-864-3373

Jones
Diane W. Annis
Zackary Bldg.
Atlanta Rd. and Jackson
St.
Gray 31032
912-986-3958

Lamar
John H. Pope
212 Gordon Rd.
Barnesville 30204
404-358-0281

Lanier
J. Benjamin Tucker
Courthouse
Lakeland 31635
912-482-3895

Laurens
Paul Riddle
Telfair St.
Dublin 31021
912-272-2277

Lee
Roy D. Goodson
Governmental Bldg.
120 Courthouse Ave.
Leesburg 31763
912-759-6426

Liberty
Shawn McClellan
100 W. South St.
Hinesville 31313
912-876-2133

Lincoln
Robert L. Powell
Extension Bldg.
Peachtree St.
Lincolnton 30817
404-359-3233

Long
Virginia K. Perdue
Courthouse Annex
Highway 57
Ludowici 31316
912-545-9549

Lowndes
John A. Baker
Civic Center
Highway 84 East
Valdosta 31601
912-242-1858

Lumpkin
G. Kenneth Beasley
112-A W. Hill St.
Dahlonega 30533
404-864-2275

Macon
N. Stewart Newberry
Courthouse Annex
100 Sumter St.
Oglethorpe 31068
912-472-7588

Madison
Larry E. Pierce
Agriculture Service Bldg.
Danielsville 30633
404-795-2281

Marion
James T. Howell
County Office Bldg.
 Basement
Baker St.
Buena Vista 31803
912-649-2625

McDuffie
Howell R. Roberts
116 Main St.
Thomson 30824
404-595-1815

McIntosh
John V. Bryson
Courthouse Bldg.
Highway 17
Darien 31305
912-437-6651

Meriwether
Willis A. Godowns
Extension Bldg.

Talbotton St.
Greenville 30222
404-672-4235

Miller
William A. Inglett
Agriculture Center
406 West Crawford St.
Colquitt 31737
912-758-3416

Mitchell
Clifford E. Lee
28 Court St.
Camilla 31730
912-336-8464

Monroe
J. Cecil Daniels
County Office Bldg.
90 Culloden Rd.
Forsyth 31029
912-994-1118

Montgomery
David Currey
County Office Bldg.
Mt. Vernon 30445
912-583-2240

Morgan
C. Wayne Tankersley
434 Hancock St.
Madison 30650
404-324-2214

Murray
Louis Dykes
Old County Home Bldg.
Highway 52 East
Chatsworth 30705
404-695-3031

Muscogee
Richard Smith
Columbus Government
 Center
Ground Floor
Columbus 31993
404-571-4791

Newton
Michael R. Welborn
1115 Usher St. NE
Covington 30209
404-786-2574

Oconee
Henry E. Bibbs
Courthouse Annex
Water St.
Watkinsville 30677
404-769-5207

Oglethorpe
Multi-Purpose Bldg.
Lexington 30648
404-743-8341

Paulding
G. Scott Daniel
251 W. Memorial Dr.
Dallas 30132
404-445-3885

Peach
Joseph W. Chapman
107 Everett Square
Fort Valley 31030
912-825-6466

Pickens
Richard Jasperse
108-1 Court Street
Jasper 30143
404-692-2531

Pierce
John Ed Smith
County Agriculture Bldg.
Blackshear 31516
912-449-4733

Pike
Judith Reid
Pike County Office Bldg.
Gwyn St.
Zebulon 30295
404-567-8948

Polk
Paul E. Thompson
Courthouse Annex Bldg.
Cedartown 30125
404-748-3051

Pulaski
W. Timothy Hall
County Extension Bldg.
Lumpkin St.
Hawkinsville 31036
912-783-1171

Putnam
David B. Lowe

5

302 West Marion St.
Eatonton 31024
404-485-4151

Quitman
Edward L. Ayers
Old Bank Bldg.
Georgetown 31754
912-334-4303

Rabun
Peter Marziliano
Main St.
Clayton 30525
404-782-3113

Randolph
Mike Matthews
County Office Bldg.
Church & Webster St.
Cuthbert 31740
912-732-2311

Richmond
Clyde E. Lester
Room 211 City-County
   Bldg.
Greene St.
Augusta 30911-3099
404-821-2351

Rockdale
Barbara McCarthy
920-A Main St.
Conyers 30207
404-929-4005

Schley
M. Wilson Weathersby
Extension Bldg.
Highway 19 North
Ellaville 31806
912-937-2601

Screven
Lamar E. Zipperer
Rocky Ford Road
Sylvania 30467
912-564-2064

Seminole
Wallace Gordon
Courthouse Annex
Donalsonville 31745
912-524-2326

Spalding
William L. Wages, Jr.

Courthouse Annex
119 East Soloman
Griffin 30224
404-228-9900

Stephens
James E. Peeples
Courthouse Annex
Tugalo St.
Toccoa 30577
404-886-4046

Stewart
Irene G. DuBose
Courthouse
Broad St.
Lumpkin 31815
912-838-4908

Sumter
Timothy L. Lawson
350 Rucker St.
Americus, 31709
912-924-4476

Talbot
Paul M. Bulloch
Courthouse
Talbotton 31827
404-665-3230

Taliaferro
Courthouse
Second Floor
Crawfordville 30631
404-456-2282

Tattnall
William W. Rahn
301-S City Hall
Glennville 30427
912-654-2593

Taylor
James H. Willis
Community Service Center
Highway 137 West
Butler 31006
912-862-5496

Telfair
Wm. A. McKinnon
713 Telfair Ave.
McRae 31055
912-868-6489

Terrell
E. Harold Wilson, Jr.

Highway 118
Metalworks Bldg.
Dawson 31742
912-995-2165

Thomas
H. Glynn Griner
County Agriculture Bldg.
207 North Madison
Thomasville 31792
912-226-3954

Tift
Lamar G. Martin
County Administration
   Bldg.
225 Tift Ave.
Tifton 31794
912-386-7870

Toombs
Rick Hartley
Courthouse Square
W. Broad St.
Lyons 30436
912-526-3101

Towns
C. Moye Walker
Senior Citizens Bldg.
Lake View Circle
Hiawassee 30546
404-896-2024

Treutlen
Mickey R. Palmer
206 Third St.
Soperton 30457
912-529-3766

Troup
James W. Williams
900 Dallis St.
LaGrange 30240
404-883-1675

Turner
James C. Griffeth
County Agriculture Bldg.
Industrial Blvd.
Ashburn 31714
912-567-3448

Twiggs
J. Mike Isbell
Courthouse Annex
Magnolia St.

Jeffersonville 31044
912-945-3391

Union
R. Neal Moon
Haralson Memorial Civic
  Center
Blairsville 30512
404-745-2524

Upson
Donnie W. Tyler
County Extension Bldg.
321 North Hightower St.
Thomaston 30286
404-647-8989

Walker
Michael O. Bunn
102 E. Napier St.
LaFayette 30728
404-638-2548

Walton
E. Eugene Anderson
Courthouse Annex
126 Court St.
Monroe 30655
404-267-4571

Ware
Tony A. Otts
County Office Bldg.
Waycross 31502-1425
912-285-6161

Warren
Patrick B. Todd
Post Office Bldg.
104 Allen St.
Warrenton 30828
404-465-2136

Washington
Gerald D. Andrews
Courthouse
Sandersville 31082
912-552-2011

Wayne
Randy W. Franks
341 Walnut St.
Jesup 31545
912-427-6865

Webster
David J. Wagner
Courthouse Annex
Preston 31824
912-828-2325

Wheeler
Michael D. Hayes
Neighborhood Service
  Center
Alamo 30411
912-568-7138

White
J. Michael Harris
Courthouse
South Main St.

Cleveland 30528
404-865-2832

Whitfield
Larry W. Thomas
420 North Hamilton St.
Dalton 30720
404-278-8207

Wilcox
W. Tom Jennings
County Agriculture Bldg.
2nd St.
Rochelle 31079
912-365-2323

Wilkes
Courthouse
Rm. B-02
23 Court St.
Washington 30673
404-678-2332

Wilkinson
Mary D. Reece
Courthouse Annex
Main St.
Irwinton 31042
912-946-2367

Worth
Thomas E. Cary
County Government Bldg.
Franklin St.
Sylvester 31791
912-776-8216

Experiment Stations

Map on following page.

1. **College Station, Athens**
   Clive Donoho, Jr., Associate Dean
     and Director
   College of Agriculture
   Experiment Stations
   107 Conner Hall
   The University of Georgia
   Athens 30602, 404-542-2151

2. **Georgia Station, Experiment**
   Associate Director (no current
     director)
   Experiment 30212, 404-228-7263

3. **Coastal Plain Station, Tifton**
   Gale Buchanan, Associate Director
   Tifton 31793, 912-386-3338

4. **Georgia Mountain Branch Station,
   Blairsville**
   James W. Dobson, Superintendent
   Rt. 1, Box 1005
   Blairsville 30512, 404-745-2655

5. **Northwest Georgia Branch Station,
   Calhoun**
   Edward G. Worley, Superintendent
   Calhoun 30701, 404-629-2696

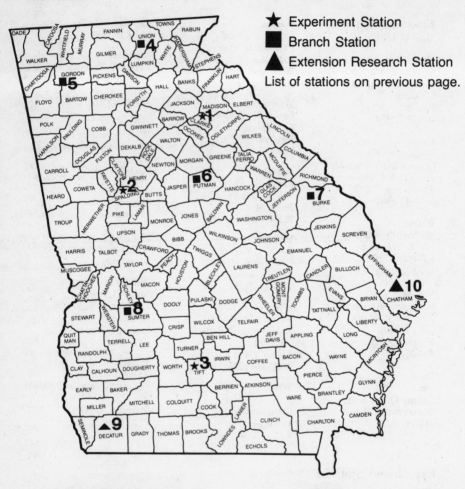

★ Experiment Station
■ Branch Station
▲ Extension Research Station
List of stations on previous page.

6. **Central Georgia Branch Station, Eatonton**
Grady V. Calvert, Superintendent
1508 Godfrey Rd., NW
Eatonton 32024, 404-485-6015

7. **Southeast Georgia Branch Station, Midville**
Charles E. Perry, Superintendent
Midville 30441, 912-589-7472

8. **Southwest Georgia Branch Station, Plains**
Robert B. Moss, Superintendent
Plains 31780, 912-824-4375

9. **Attapulgus Extension & Research Center, Attapulgus**
Dr. Wayne McLaurin,
Superintendent
Extension Research Center
Attapulgus 31715, 912-465-3421

10. **Coastal Area Extension & Research Center, Savannah "Bamboo Station"**
Charles M. Bruce, Superintendent
Rt. 4, Box 433
Savannah 31419, 912-925-1056

Farms

The following chart shows the number of farms and average size as per the 1980 census, as well as the 1982 totals of harvested cropland for the state.

County	Number of farms	Average size (in acres)	Harvested Cropland (in acres) 1982	County	Number of farms	Average size (in acres)	Harvested Cropland (in acres) 1982
Georgia Total	49,630	248	4,761,260	Dooly	304	539	114,366
Appling	653	205	40,223	Dougherty	199	544	42,617
Atkinson	267	341	23,106	Douglas	151	97	2,264
Bacon	422	216	34,123	Early	389	495	93,295
Baker	178	863	53,911	Echols	110	163	4,361
Baldwin	148	300	7,994	Effingham	293	254	29,627
Banks	414	113	5,378	Elbert	368	171	19,888
Barrow	421	94	6,848	Emanuel	519	328	79,064
Bartow	463	224	37,043	Evans	211	264	28,215
Ben Hill	232	282	27,178	Fannin	233	91	3,275
Berrien	556	282	56,226	Fayette	253	126	6,198
Bibb	167	144	8,561	Floyd	504	186	24,946
Bleckley	249	294	45,369	Forsyth	631	78	6,892
Brantley	345	116	7,114	Franklin	665	122	15,134
Brooks	521	379	93,039	Fulton	379	112	7,881
Bryan	93	270	7,051				
Bulloch	702	336	133,730	Gilmer	272	116	3,903
Burke	390	698	153,038	Glascock	96	295	11,409
Butts	171	176	6,284	Glynn	55	180	506
Calhoun	135	836	60,331	Gordon	578	147	29,082
Camden	59	577	605	Grady	625	259	63,888
Candler	261	269	35,840	Greene	236	244	8,167
Carroll	868	112	12,203	Gwinnett	492	68	5,661
Catoosa	315	125	8,662	Habersham	409	103	6,345
Charlton	130	284	1,766	Hall	874	76	9,105
Chatham	59	216	3,128	Hancock	151	316	5,800
Chattahoochee	18	283	—	Haralson	321	120	5,269
Chattooga	292	213	14,040	Harris	255	244	5,263
Cherokee	611	75	5,875	Hart	548	124	26,452
Clarke	102	148	6,082	Heard	190	189	3,874
Clay	94	588	23,233	Henry	426	138	18,452
Clayton	81	88	1,249	Houston	295	345	56,500
Clinch	115	182	3,358	Irwin	419	363	79,180
Cobb	264	66	2,412	Jackson	782	111	14,670
Coffee	833	241	83,150	Jasper	232	291	9,203
Colquitt	867	250	98,634	Jeff Davis	394	270	53,512
Columbia	222	187	6,003	Jefferson	391	403	93,142
Cook	380	238	44,794	Jenkins	251	427	59,059
Coweta	376	179	15,236	Johnson	304	279	42,986
Crawford	153	296	19,954	Jones	184	217	7,267
Crisp	226	545	72,627	Lamar	238	176	9,469
Dade	183	192	2,943	Lanier	172	301	14,543
Dawson	192	94	2,753	Laurens	803	265	114,837
Decatur	484	402	92,248	Lee	186	900	81,530
DeKalb	95	54	641	Liberty	61	327	1,534
Dodge	482	274	60,570	Lincoln	182	241	4,209

County	Number of farms	Average size (in acres)	Harvested Cropland (in acres) 1982	County	Number of farms	Average size (in acres)	Harvested Cropland (in acres) 1982
Long	104	156	4,567	Spalding	262	158	10,598
Lowndes	548	223	42,944	Stephens	221	77	2,814
Lumpkin	289	102	2,891	Stewart	111	610	18,625
Macon	267	522	81,771	Sumter	360	538	110,426
Madison	582	110	19,404	Talbot	144	289	4,250
Marion	147	305	13,010	Taliaferro	82	271	1,959
McDuffie	216	246	9,975	Tattnall	631	205	57,790
McIntosh	29	176	—	Taylor	204	441	31,927
Meriwether	380	240	15,342	Telfair	425	235	43,785
Miller	342	366	62,501	Terrell	229	675	80,442
Mitchell	578	409	121,897	Thomas	540	399	83,073
Monroe	172	341	10,491	Tift	393	279	49,615
Montgomery	274	305	26,846	Toombs	407	242	48,450
Morgan	355	310	27,291	Towns	176	77	2,526
Murray	310	127	12,299	Treutlen	195	278	19,958
Muscogee	49	242	—	Troup	291	190	6,703
Newton	286	177	11,886	Turner	324	354	54,264
Oconee	295	205	20,697	Twiggs	149	270	15,557
Ogelthorpe	351	199	18,504	Union	307	92	5,439
Paulding	296	97	2,844	Upson	243	205	8,618
Peach	179	304	34,358	Walker	584	180	21,449
Pickens	228	96	2,353	Walton	462	174	27,702
Pierce	491	209	39,609	Ware	394	172	15,957
Pike	292	191	15,971	Warren	168	356	15,383
Polk	327	145	13,347	Washington	379	351	62,883
Pulaski	188	476	54,841	Wayne	416	166	30,915
Putnam	167	271	6,853	Webster	106	557	20,962
Quitman	34	687	4,895	Wheeler	260	302	32,005
Rabun	143	81	1,706	White	320	73	4,626
Randolph	162	763	54,537	Whitfield	422	112	11,766
Richmond	139	179	11,292	Wilcox	304	374	49,755
Rockdale	128	111	2,413	Wilkes	382	317	16,046
Schley	111	341	11,451	Wilkinson	162	292	8,086
Screven	409	450	104,865	Worth	557	353	99,398
Seminole	232	428	55,499				

AIRLINES

Listed below are the air carriers which operate within the State of Georgia.

Aeromexico
Airborne Express (air freight only)
Air Jamaica Limited
Air Wisconsin (air freight only)
American Airlines
Bahamasair
Bankair, Inc.
British Caledonian Airways

Cayman Airways, Ltd.
Continental Airlines
Continental Express-Presidential Air
Delta Air Lines
Delta Connection
DHL Airlines, Inc.
Direct Air, Inc.
Eastern Air Lines, Inc.

Eastern Atlantis Express
Eastern Metro Express
Federal Express (air freight only)
Flying Tiger Line (air freight only)
Japan Air Lines
KLM-Royal Dutch Airlines
Lufthansa German Airlines
Metro Airlines
Midway Airlines, Inc.
Midwest Express Airlines, Inc.
New York Air
Northwest Airlines, Inc.

Pan American World Airways, Inc.
Piedmont Aviation, Inc.
Piedmont Commuter System
Sabena Belgian World Airlines
Southern Express
Summit Airlines, Inc. (air freight only)
Swissair
Trans World Airlines, Inc.
US Air
United Airlines
Zantop International Airlines, Inc.
   (air freight only)

AIRPORTS

County	Number	Location	Longest Runway (feet)	Runway Lights	Radio Communications	Instrument Approach
Appling	1	Baxley	3,800	yes	Unicom	yes
Bacon	1	Alma	5,000	yes	Unicom	yes
Baldwin	1	Milledgeville	5,000	yes	Unicom	yes
Barrow	1	Winder	5,000	yes	Unicom	yes
Bartow	1	Cartersville	4,000	yes	Unicom	yes
Ben Hill	1	Fitzgerald	5,000	yes	Unicom	yes
Berrien	1	Nashville	3,000	yes	—	no
Bibb	2	Macon	6,500	yes	Tower	yes
Bleckley	1	Cochran	3,200	yes	Unicom	yes
Brantley	1	Nahunta	3,000	no	no	no
Brooks	1	Quitman	3,600	no	no	no
Bulloch	2	Statesboro Brooklet (t)	5,000	yes	Unicom	yes
Burke	1	Waynesboro	3,200	yes	Unicom	yes
Camden	1	St. Marys	5,000	yes	Unicom	yes
Candler	1	Metter	3,100	yes	no	yes
Carroll	1	Carrollton	5,000	yes	Unicom	yes
Charlton	1	Folkston	2,500	yes	no	no
Chatham	1	Savannah	9,000	yes	Tower	yes
Cherokee	1	Canton	3,400	yes	Unicom	no
Clarke	1	Athens	4,992	yes	Unicom	yes
Clay	1	Fort Gaines (t)	2,900	no	no	no
Clayton	1	Jonesboro	2,980	yes	no	no
Clinch	1	Homerville	4,000	yes	no	yes
Cobb	1	Marietta	4,580	yes	Unicom	yes
Coffee	1	Douglas	5,000	yes	Unicom	yes
Colquitt	2	Moultrie	8,000	yes	Unicom	yes
Cook	1	Adel	4,000	yes	Unicom	no
Coweta	1	Newnan	4,000	yes	Unicom	yes
Crisp	1	Cordele	5,000	yes	Unicom	yes
Decatur	1	Bainbridge	5,100	yes	Unicom	yes
DeKalb	2	Atlanta, Stone Mountain	5,000	yes	Tower	yes
Dodge	1	Eastman	4,500	yes	no	yes
Dougherty	1	Albany	6,600	yes	Tower	yes
Early	1	Blakely	3,200	yes	no	no
Elbert	1	Elberton	3,400	yes	Unicom	yes
Emanuel	1	Swainsboro	4,180	yes	Unicom	yes
Evans	1	Claxton	4,000	yes	Unicom	no

County	Number	Location	Longest Runway (feet)	Runway Lights	Radio Communications	Instrument Approach
Fayette	2	Peachtree City, Woolsey (t)	4,600	yes	Unicom	yes
Floyd	1	Rome	6,000	yes	Unicom	yes
Forsyth	1	Cumming	2,500	no	no	no
Franklin	1	Canon	3,500	yes	no	no
Fulton	3	Atlanta, Fairburn	11,889	yes	Tower	yes
Gilmer	1	Ellijay	3,500	yes	Unicom	no
Glynn	3	Brunswick, Jekyll Island, St. Simons	8,000	yes	Unicom	yes
Gordon	2	Calhoun, Resaca (t)	4,600	yes	Unicom	yes
Grady	1	Cairo	3,000	yes	Unicom	yes
Greene	1	Greensboro	3,300	yes	no	no
Gwinnett	1	Lawrenceville	4,000	yes	Unicom	yes
Habersham	1	Cornelia	3,750	yes	Unicom	yes
Hall	1	Gainesville	5,000	yes	Unicom	yes
Harris	1	Pine Mountain	5,000	yes	Unicom	yes
Henry	2	Hampton, Stockbridge	3,375	yes	Unicom	no
Houston	1	Perry	5,000	yes	Unicom	yes
Irwin	1	Irwinville	3,000	no	no	no
Jackson	1	Jefferson	4,100	yes	Unicom	yes
Jeff Davis	1	Hazlehurst	4,500	yes	no	yes
Jefferson	2	Louisville, Wrens	3,500	yes	Unicom	no
Jenkins	1	Millen	3,000	yes	no	no
Laurens	1	Dublin	5,000	yes	Unicom	yes
Liberty	1	Hinesville	3,700	yes	no	yes
Lowndes	1	Valdosta	6,302	yes	Unicom	yes
Lumpkin	1	Dahlonega	3,000	no	no	no
Macon	1	Montezuma	3,200	yes	no	yes
Marion	1	Buena Vista	3,200	yes	no	no
McDuffie	1	Thomson	5,000	yes	Unicom	yes
McIntosh	1	Darion	3,000	no	no	no
Meriwether	1	Warm Springs	3,000	yes	no	no
Mitchell	1	Camilla	4,000	yes	Unicom	yes
Morgan	1	Madison	3,800	yes	Unicom	yes
Muscogee	1	Columbus	7,000	yes	Tower	yes
Newton	1	Covington	3,000	yes	Unicom	yes
Peach	1	Fort Valley (t)	3,370	yes	Unicom	no
Pickens	1	Jasper	3,600	yes	Unicom	no
Pike	2	Williamson (t), Zebulon (t)	3,300	no	no	no
Polk	1	Cedartown	4,000	yes	Unicom	yes
Pulaski	1	Hawkinsville	3,000	no	no	no
Putnam	1	Eatonton	3,000	yes	no	no
Randolph	1	Cuthbert	3,000	yes	no	no
Richmond	2	Augusta	8,000	yes	Tower	yes
Screven	1	Sylvania	5,000	yes	Unicom	yes
Seminole	1	Donalsonville	5,000	yes	Unicom	yes
Spalding	1	Griffin	3,300	yes	Unicom	yes
Stephens	1	Toccoa	4,000	yes	Unicom	yes
Sumter	1	Americus	5,000	yes	Unicom	yes
Tattnall	1	Reidsville	3,800	yes	no	yes
Taylor	1	Butler	2,700	yes	no	no
Telfair	1	McRae	4,000	yes	no	yes
Terrell	1	Dawson	2,790	yes	Unicom	no
Thomas	1	Thomasville	5,000	yes	Unicom	yes
Tift	1	Tifton	5,000	yes	Unicom	yes

County	Number	Location	Longest Runway (feet)	Runway Lights	Radio Communications	Instrument Approach
Toombs	1	Vidalia	5,000	yes	Unicom	yes
Treutlen	1	Soperton	3,000	no	no	no
Troup	1	LaGrange	5,600	yes	Unicom	yes
Turner	1	Ashburn	3,250	yes	no	no
Union	1	Blairsville	3,200	yes	Unicom	no
Upson	1	Thomaston	3,000	yes	Unicom	yes
Walker	1	LaFayette	4,080	yes	Unicom	no
Walton	1	Monroe	3,300	yes	Unicom	yes
Ware	1	Waycross	5,000	yes	Unicom	yes
Washington	1	Sandersville	3,800	yes	no	yes
Wayne	1	Jesup	3,800	yes	Unicom	yes
Whitfield	1	Dalton	5,000	yes	Unicom	yes
Wilkes	1	Washington	3,400	yes	Unicom	yes
Worth	1	Sylvester	3,400	yes	Unicom	no

(t) Turf runway

ALCOHOL

The following list shows the counties in which liquor sales are legal only in certain cities, and the "wet" cities.

County	Town	County	Town
Appling	Baxley		Lawrenceville,
Barrow	Winder		Lilburn, Suwanee
Calhoun	Edison, Leary	Habersham	Mt. Airy
Camden	Kingsland	Hall	Gainesville
Chattahoochee	Cusseta	Hancock	Sparta
Cherokee	Woodstock	Haralson	Buchanan
Clay	Fort Gaines	Henry	Locust Grove
Clayton	Riverdale	Irwin	Ocilla
Colquitt	Moultrie	Jackson	Arcade
Columbia	Grovetown	Jasper	Monticello
Coweta	Grantville	Jefferson	Louisville
Dooly	Unadilla, Vienna	Johnson	Wadley, Wrightsville
Douglas	Douglasville (Package Liquor)	Marion	Buena Vista
		Meriwether	Greenville, Luthersville, Woodbury
Elbert	Elberton		
Emanuel	Swainsboro	Monroe	Forsyth (Package Liquor)
Evans	Claxton	Montgomery	Uvalda
Fayette	Peachtree City	Morgan	Madison, Rutledge
Floyd	Rome	Newton	Covington
Forsyth	Cumming	Paulding	Hiram, Braswell, Dallas
Franklin	Canon, Lavonia	Peach	Byron
Fulton	Atlanta	Pickens	Nelson
Gordon	Calhoun	Pike	Zebulon
Grady	Cairo	Rabun	Sky Valley
Greene	Siloam, White Plains	Randolph	Coleman
Gwinnett	Duluth,	Schley	Ellaville

ALCOHOL

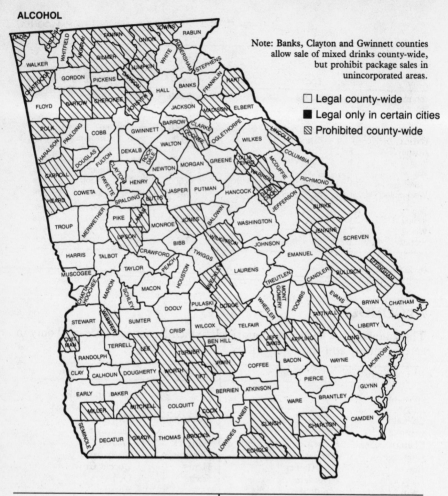

Note: Banks, Clayton and Gwinnett counties allow sale of mixed drinks county-wide, but prohibit package sales in unincorporated areas.

☐ Legal county-wide
■ Legal only in certain cities
▨ Prohibited county-wide

County	Town	County	Town
Screven	Hiltonia, Newington	Treutlen	Soperton
Stephens	Martin, Toccoa	Troup	LaGrange, West Point
Stewart	Lumpkin, Richland	Twiggs	Jeffersonville
Sumter	Americus	Walker	Lookout Mountain
Talbot	Talbotton, Geneva, Woodland	Walton	Walnut Grove
		Washington	Tennelle, Sandersville
Tattnall	Reidsville	Wheeler	Glenwood
Taylor	Reynolds	White	Helen
Telfair	Scotland, Lumber City, McRae	Whitfield	Dalton
		Wilcox	Abbeville
Thomas	Meigs, Thomasville	Wilkes	Washington

Clinch, Jasper: Private club referendum to issue licenses to private clubs only in a normally all dry area. County commissioner can issue letter of approval for license.

The sale of beer is prohibited in Cook, Echols, and Union counties. The counties in which the sale of beer is allowed in certain cities only are: Atkinson, Bartow, Effingham, Fannin, Forsyth, Glascock, Habersham, Jackson, Lumpkin, Murray, Screven, Stephens, Wheeler, White, and Wilcox.

On page 14 is a map showing which counties prohibit the sale of liquor and which allow it only in certain cities, as well as those which allow it countywide.

AREA PLANNING AND DEVELOPMENT COMMISSIONS

The first publicly-supported, multi-county planning agency in the nation was created in 1947. It served the city of Atlanta, DeKalb and Fulton counties, and was called the Metropolitan Planning Commission.

The Georgia General Assembly passed an act in 1957 which allowed the remaining counties in the state to form Area Planning and Development Commissions, or APDCs.

The Georgia legislature passed a law in 1970 that required that APDC boundaries be redrawn by June 30, 1972, so each county would be within the boundary of one of these commissions. As a result, 18 area planning and development commissions were formed.

The commissions are not a government but rather a forum of local government officials working together to solve mutual problems and deciding important issues that affect the whole region, in such areas as human services, aging, environmental services, land use, and transportation. While the commissions do not have the authority to implement plans, they can help through a review and comment process to steer local governments and state agencies on plans that have regional impact.

These commissions, the counties they serve, their addresses, telephone numbers, and directors follow.

Altamaha Georgia Southern APDC
(Appling, Bulloch, Candler, Evans, Jeff Davis, Tattnall, Toombs, and Wayne counties)
P.O. Box 328, 505 W. Parker Street
Baxley 31513, 912-367-3648
Ted Fortino, Executive Director

Atlanta Regional Commission
(Clayton, Cobb, DeKalb, Douglas, Fulton, Gwinnett, and Rockdale counties)
Suite 1801, 100 Edgewood Avenue, NE
Atlanta 30335, 404-656-7700
Harry West, Executive Director

Central Savannah River APDC
(Burke, Columbia, Emanuel, Glascock, Jefferson, Jenkins, Lincoln, McDuffie, Richmond, Screven, Taliaferro, and Warren counties)
P.O. Box 2800, 2123 Wrightsboro Road
Augusta 30904, 404-737-1823
Tim R. Maund, Executive Director

Chattahoochee-Flint APDC
(Carroll, Coweta, Heard, Meriwether, and Troup counties)
P.O. Box 2308, 6 Shenandoah Blvd.
Newnan 30264, 404-253-8521
David T. Barrow, Executive Director

Coastal APDC
(Bryan, Camden, Chatham, Effingham,
  Glynn, Liberty, Long, and McIntosh
  counties)
P.O. Box 1917
Brunswick 31521, 912-264-7363
Vernon D. Martin, Executive Director

Coosa Valley APDC
(Bartow, Chattooga, Dade, Floyd, Gordon,
  Haralson, Paulding, Polk, and Walker
  counties)
P.O. Drawer H, Jackson Hill Drive
Rome 30163, 404-295-6485
C. D. Rampley, Executive Director

Georgia Mountains APDC
(Banks, Dawson, Forsyth, Franklin,
  Habersham, Hall, Hart, Lumpkin,
  Rabun, Stephens, Towns, Union, and
  White counties)
P.O. Box 1720
Gainesville 30503, 404-536-3431
Dr. Sam Dayton, Executive Director

Heart of Georgia APDC
(Bleckley, Dodge, Laurens, Montgomery,
  Pulaski, Telfair, Treutlen, Wheeler, and
  Wilcox counties)
501 Oak Street
Eastman 31023, 912-374-4771
Nicky Cabero, Executive Director

Lower Chattahoochee APDC
(Chattahoochee, Clay, Harris, Muscogee,
  Quitman, Randolph, Stewart, and Talbot
  counties)
P.O. Box 1908, 930 2nd Avenue
Columbus 31994, 404-324-4221
Ron Starnes, Executive Director

McIntosh Trail APDC
(Butts, Fayette, Henry, Lamar, Newton,
  Pike, Spalding, and Upson counties)
P.O. Drawer A
Barnesville 30204, 404-358-3647
Lanier E. Boatwright, Executive Director

Middle Flint APDC
(Crisp, Dooly, Macon, Marion, Schley,
  Sumter, Taylor, and Webster counties)
P.O. Box 6, 203 East College Street
Ellaville 31806, 912-937-2561 or GIST
  345-1204
Bobby L. Lowe, Executive Director

Middle Georgia APDC
(Bibb, Crawford, Houston, Jones, Monroe,
  Peach, and Twiggs counties)

600 Grand Building
Macon 31201, 912-744-6160 or GIST
  321-6160
James Tonn, Executive Director

North Georgia APDC
(Catoosa, Cherokee, Fannin, Gilmer,
  Murray, Pickens, and Whitfield
  counties)
503 West Waugh Street
Dalton 30720, 404-272-2300 or GIST
  234-2300
George Sutherland, Executive Director

Northeast Georgia APDC
(Barrow, Clarke, Elbert, Greene, Jackson,
  Madison, Morgan, Oconee, Oglethorpe,
  and Walton counties)
305 Research Drive
Athens 30610, 404-548-3141
James R. Dove, Executive Director

Oconee APDC
(Baldwin, Hancock, Jasper, Johnson,
  Putnam, Washington, and Wilkinson
  counties)
P.O. Box 707, 3014 Heritage Road
Milledgeville 31061, 912-453-5237 or GIST
  404-324-5372
J. E. Gentry, Executive Director

South Georgia APDC
(Ben Hill, Berrien, Brooks, Cook, Echols,
  Irwin, Lanier, Lowndes, Tift, and
  Turner counties)
P.O. Box 1233, 327 West Savannah Ave.
Valdosta 31601, 912-333-5277 or GIST
  349-5277
Hal Davis, Executive Director

Southeast Georgia APDC
(Atkinson, Bacon, Brantley, Charlton,
  Clinch, Coffee, Pierce, and Ware
  counties)
P.O. Box 2049, 3243 Harris Road
Waycross 31501, 912-285-6097
Nash Williams, Executive Director

Southwest Georgia APDC
(Baker, Calhoun, Colquitt, Decatur,
  Dougherty, Early, Grady, Lee, Miller,
  Mitchell, Seminole, Terrell, Thomas,
  and Worth counties)
P.O. Box 346, Broad Street
Camilla 31730, 912-336-5616 or GIST
  341-4315
Carroll C. Underwood, Executive Director

16

ARTS

The Georgia Council for the Arts (GCA), a division of the Office of Planning and Budget, works to improve and preserve the quality of the arts by providing programming, funding, and other services such as the Georgia Art Bus Program and the Governor's Awards in the Arts Program.

The GCA consists of 24 members, governor appointed to serve 3-year rotating terms. There are 4 at-large members, plus 2 members appointed from each congressional district, backed up by a professional staff, that administers Council decisions.

The GCA also participates in programming available through the Southern Arts Federation, a regional arts organization governed by a board of directors made up of the executive director and chairman of each member state agency. Member states include Alabama, Florida, Georgia, Kentucky, Louisiana, Mississippi, North Carolina, South Carolina, and Tennessee.

The GCA's total budget for fiscal year 1989 is $3.87 million, supported by funding from state General Assembly appropriation, the National Endowment for the Arts, local match and other funds. Grant funding is budgeted at $3.2 million to support Georgia arts organizations.

The Artists-in-Education Program of the GCA places professional artists in residencies of 3 to 18 weeks in Georgia schools or other full-time educational programs. These artists use their talents and resources to provide instruction and cultural enrichment for students and area citizens.

The Georgia Art Acquisition Program of the GCA makes juried artwork available for purchase by eligible nonprofit, tax-exempt organizations. The intent of this program to help establish and expand local collections of quality original works of art by Georgia artists.

The Georgia Art Bus Program of the GCA offers a choice of three professionally designed art exhibits of works by Georgia artists from the State Art collection. These are delivered by rainbow-colored buses to schools and communities state-wide.

The Governor's Awards in the Arts Program is sponsored by the GCA and the National Endowment for the Arts. Georgia individuals or organizations are recognized for their significant influence on the arts, natural environment, or general cultural life of Georgia through distinguished service or creative accomplishment. The 1988 recipients include: Arts Festival of Atlanta; Ulysses Davis, Savannah; Vincent A. Keesee, Tifton; Barbara Lebow, Atlanta; Jill Jayne Read, Athens; Elizabeth Schleicher, Blue Ridge; Theatre in the Square, Marietta; and University of Georgia Sea Grant College Program, Athens, Ben W. Fortson, Jr. Award for Civic Beautification and Conservation.

Following is a list of arts organizations that have been awarded grants for fiscal year 1989, listed by discipline.

Community Dance

ATLANTA
Arts Festival of Atlanta
Carl Ratcliff Dance Theatre
Celeste Miller & Company
Lee Harper & Dancers
Moving in the Spirit Dance Company
Room To Move Dance Company
Ruth Mitchell Dance Company
Terpsicorps Theater
Young Audiences of Atlanta

AUGUSTA
Augusta Ballet

DECATUR
Beacon Dance Company

GAINESVILLE
Gainesville Ballet Company

LILBURN
Gwinnett Ballet Theatre

MARIETTA
Georgia Ballet

Community Literature

ATLANTA
Atlanta Writing Resource Center
Georgia State Poetry Society
Joel Chandler Harris Association
Poetry Atlanta
Southeastern Arts, Media & Education
  Project

AUGUSTA
Sandhills Writers' Conference/Augusta
  College

DECATUR
Dixie Council of Authors & Journalists

MACON
Georgia Poetry Circuit/Mercer University
Wesleyan College Center for Emerging
  Writers

Community Music

ALBANY
Albany Symphony Association

ATLANTA
Arts Festival of Atlanta
Artwood Winds Plus
Atlanta Bach Choir
Atlanta Boy Choir
Atlanta Brass Society

Atlanta Chamber Players
Atlanta Meistersingers
Atlanta Music Club
Atlanta Repertory Opera Company
Atlanta Singers
Atlanta Songwriters Association
Atlanta Virtuosi Foundation
Choral Guild of Atlanta
Composers' Resources
Georgia State University School of Music/
  Summer Opera Workshop
Sandy Springs Chamber Orchestra
Southeastern Savoyards
Young Audiences of Atlanta
Young Singers of Callanwolde

AUGUSTA
Augusta Choral Society
Augusta Symphony Orchestra

BRUNSWICK
Brunswick Community Orchestra

COLUMBUS
Columbus Civic Chorale
Columbus Symphony Orchestra
Southeastern Music Center

GAINESVILLE
Lanier Orchestra League

MACON
Macon Civic Chorale
Macon Symphony Orchestra

MARIETTA
Cobb Symphony Orchestra
Cobb Youth Chorale
Pandean Players

NORCROSS
Gwinnett Festival Singers

ROME
Boys Club Choir of Rome
Rome Symphony Guild

SAVANNAH
Armstrong State College
Savannah Arts Commission/Office of
  Cultural Affairs

STATESBORO
Statesboro-Georgia Southern Symphony Association

TOCCOA
Toccoa Orchestra Guild

TUCKER
DeKalb Symphony Orchestra

Community Parks and Recreation Departments/Arts Councils and Agencies/Service Organizations

ALBANY
Albany Area Arts Council

ATHENS
Clarke County Community Relations Division

ATLANTA
Callanwolde Foundation
Georgia Volunteer Accountants for the Arts
Georgia Volunteer Lawyers for the Arts
Southeast Community Cultural Center
Special Audiences

AUGUSTA
Augusta Mini Theatre
Greater Augusta Arts Council

BLUE RIDGE
Fannin County Arts Program

CARROLLTON
Carrollton Parks, Recreation & Cultural Arts Department

CARTERSVILLE
Etowah Creative Arts Council

CUMMING
Sauwnee Community Center

DAHLONEGA
North Georgia College Fine Arts Department

DALTON
Creative Arts Guild

DECATUR
Arts in South DeKalb

DOUGLASVILLE
Douglas County Cultural Arts Council

DUNWOODY
DeKalb North Arts Center

ELLIJAY
Gilmer County Arts Council

GAINESVILLE
Arts Council

LAWRENCEVILLE
Gwinnett Council for the Arts

MABLETON
South Cobb Arts Alliance

MACON
Macon Arts Alliance

MADISON
Madison-Morgan Cultural Center

MILLEDGEVILLE
Georgia Assembly of Community Arts Agencies
Milledgeville-Baldwin County Allied Arts

MOULTRIE
Colquitt County Arts Council

ROME
Rome Area Council for the Arts

ST. SIMONS ISLAND
Coastal Alliance for the Arts

STATESBORO
Georgia Southern College Art Department

STONE MOUNTAIN
A.R.T. Station

SWAINSBORO
Emanuel Arts Council

THOMASTON
Thomaston-Upson Arts Council

TIFTON
Arts Experiment Station/Abraham Baldwin College

VALDOSTA
Lowndes-Valdosta Arts Commission

WAYCROSS
Okefenokee Heritage Center

Community Presenters

ALBANY
Albany Concert Association

ATLANTA
Dancer's Collective of Atlanta
Martin Luther King, Jr. Center for Nonviolent Social Change
More Productions
Nexus Contemporary Art Center
Pro-Mozart Society of Atlanta
Quantum Productions
Radio Free Georgia Broadcasting Foundation
WABE-FM/Atlanta Board of Education

BLAKELY
Court Square Arts Council

CEDARTOWN
Cedartown Civic Auditorium

DECATUR
J. Arc & Company

MACON
Georgia Trust for Historic Preservation

MARIETTA
Mostly Chamber Music

SAVANNAH
Coastal Jazz Association

ST. SIMONS ISLAND
Island Concert Association

TOCCOA
Currahee Arts Council

Community Theatre

ALBANY
Albany Little Theatre

ATLANTA
Alternate Roots
Arts Festival of Atlanta
Atlanta New Play Project
Atlanta Shakespeare Company
Atlanta Street Theatre
Atlanta Theatre Coalition
Georgia Shakespeare Festival
Great American Mime Experiment
Horizon Theatre Company
Jomandi Productions
Just Us Theater Company
Onstage Atlanta
Open City
Performance Gallery
Production Values
Seven Stages
Southeastern Arts, Media & Education Project
Southern Theater Conspiracy
Stage Hands
Theatre Gael
Young Audiences of Atlanta

AUGUSTA
Augusta Players

COLUMBUS
Springer Opera House Arts Association

DECATUR
Neighborhood Playhouse
Piccadilly Puppets Company

DUNWOODY
Dunwoody Stage Door Players

GAINESVILLE
Gainesville Children's Theatre
Gainesville Theatre Alliance

JEFFERSON
Tumbling Waters Society of Jackson County

MACON
Theatre Macon

MARIETTA
Theatre in the Square

ROME
Rome Little Theatre

SAVANNAH
City Lights Theater Company
Savannah Theatre Company

WARNER ROBINS
Warner Robins Little Theatre

WAYCROSS
Waycross Area Community Theatre

Community Visual Arts

ATHENS
Georgia Museum of Art/University of Georgia
Lyndon House Art Center/Athens Recreation & Park Department

ATLANTA
Arts Festival of Atlanta
Atlanta Art Papers
Georgia Association/American Institute of Architects
IMAGE Film/Video Center
Nexus Contemporary Art Center

AUGUSTA
Gertrude Herbert Institute of Art

GAINESVILLE
Georgia Mountain Crafts
Quinlan Arts

LAGRANGE
Chattahoochee Valley Art Association

MARIETTA
Marietta-Cobb Fine Arts Center

RABUN GAP
Hambidge Center for Creative Arts & Sciences

SAVANNAH
Savannah Art Association

Major Dance

ATLANTA
Atlanta Ballet

Major Music

ATLANTA
Atlanta Opera
Atlanta Symphony Orchestra

AUGUSTA
Augusta Opera Association

SAVANNAH
Savannah Symphony Society

Major Presenters

ATLANTA
Theater of the Stars

SAVANNAH
Georgia Public Radio

Major Theatre

ATLANTA
Academy Theatre
Alliance Theatre Company
Center for Puppetry Arts
Theatrical Outfit

Major Visual Arts

ALBANY
Albany Museum of Art

ATLANTA
Atlanta College of Art
High Museum of Art

COLUMBUS
Columbus Museum

MACON
Museum of Arts and Sciences

SAVANNAH
Telfair Academy of Arts and Sciences

BANKING

According to the Federal Reserve Bank's regional office in Atlanta, Georgia, as of June 30, 1987, there was a total of 366 commercial banks in Georgia with total assets of $49,754,138,000 and total deposits of $38,471,258,000. There were 68 savings and loan associations with total assets of $17,204,547 and $13,324,642 deposits.

Commercial Banks

The following chart shows the number of commercial banks headquartered in Georgia by county, with total assets and deposits as of June 30, 1987, as reported by the Federal Reserve Bank.

County	Banks	Assets	Total Deposits
Appling	1	2,084,000	1,863,900
Atkinson	2	205,890	180,080
Bacon	2	644,310	555,940
Baker	1	1,086,700	892,300
Baldwin	3	2,481,500	2,215,600
Banks	1	2,632,800	2,430,500
Barrow	1	5,424,400	4,767,100

County	Banks	Assets	Total Deposits
Bartow	3	1,057,650	969,560
Ben Hill	2	918,670	797,080
Berrien	3	738,450	653,010
Bibb	3	738,226	6,237,090
Bleckley	2	525,430	465,560
Brooks	3	483,590	429,270
Bryan	1	3,876,200	3,215,300
Bulloch	3	2,327,070	2,102,600
Burke	3	812,050	715,420
Butts	1	3,726,900	3,384,300
Calhoun	3	430,280	383,650
Camden	2	241,090	212,560
Candler	2	648,790	585,600
Carroll	6	3,811,720	3,435,340
Catoosa	2	1,061,340	945,770
Charlton	1	8,264,000	7,016,500
Chatham	6	109,141,140	78,560,260
Chattooga	2	1,027,010	908,370
Cherokee	4	3,687,660	3,328,740
Clarke	3	3,559,070	2,889,800
Clayton	2	1,614,100	1,459,650
Clinch	1	2,529,200	2,300,300
Cobb	9	10,516,490	8,520,900
Coffee	5	2,055,570	1,845,500
Colquitt	2	1,514,900	1,230,180
Columbia	2	652,240	576,740
Cook	3	616,130	554,250
Coweta	3	1,879,130	1,725,960
Crawford	1	1,941,100	1,754,100
Crisp	2	988,250	903,970
Dade	1	3,020,300	2,724,100
Dawson	1	3,129,900	2,804,300
Decatur	1	4,015,500	3,558,400
DeKalb	4	14,233,180	11,962,580
Dodge	3	1,110,280	996,110
Dooly	3	683,310	603,860
Dougherty	3	5,315,450	4,724,140
Douglas	3	2,185,370	1,994,050
Early	2	630,580	527,390
Elbert	2	1,815,020	1,636,920
Emanuel	4	1,406,760	1,274,620
Evans	2	554,130	491,610
Fannin	1	1,684,100	1,423,100
Fayette	3	1,246,150	1,101,300
Floyd	4	4,266,690	3,726,770
Forsyth	2	725,180	610,130
Franklin	3	1,391,590	1,250,000
Fulton	16	174,445,690	120,327,640
Gilmer	2	1,049,670	952,580
Glascock	1	468,500	403,500
Glynn	3	5,690,220	4,899,870
Gordon	1	11,727,800	10,656,200
Grady	3	963,740	855,920
Greene	3	1,287,240	1,155,380
Gwinnett	6	4,156,120	3,668,270

County	Banks	Assets	Total Deposits
Habersham	3	2,839,510	2,589,030
Hall	3	5,910,770	5,061,370
Hancock	2	395,690	348,040
Haralson	2	637,240	580,490
Harris	1	4,054,700	3,673,000
Hart	1	3,443,600	3,143,800
Heard	1	1,846,000	1,602,500
Henry	3	1,901,400	1,697,530
Houston	3	1,479,350	1,337,780
Irwin	2	540,000	466,830
Jackson	4	1,309,400	1,187,220
Jasper	2	522,460	473,290
Jeff Davis	1	2,343,800	2,126,300
Jefferson	4	1,079,570	952,650
Jenkins	2	413,000	364,190
Johnson	1	2,737,300	2,432,100
Jones	2	326,620	284,280
Lamar	2	800,580	713,010
Lanier	1	3,502,500	3,010,100
Laurens	5	2,125,860	1,885,140
Lee	2	1,174,240	1,023,000
Lincoln	1	3,170,800	2,771,700
Lowndes	5	2,964,230	2,614,140
Lumpkin	2	1,119,850	1,015,960
Madison	2	421,490	345,440
McDuffie	1	9,023,900	7,257,400
McIntosh	1	2,956,100	2,581,600
Meriwether	3	464,180	415,190
Miller	1	2,751,500	2,411,800
Mitchell	3	1,060,320	890,490
Monroe	2	614,850	561,850
Montgomery	3	883,480	803,070
Morgan	2	477,630	424,590
Murray	2	1,105,520	996,600
Muscogee	3	13,364,540	11,225,970
Newton	3	1,939,810	1,682,520
Oconee	2	651,680	584,920
Oglethorpe	2	357,920	314,140
Paulding	2	1,498,730	1,372,930
Peach	3	1,390,110	1,230,900
Pickens	2	973,300	882,560
Pierce	3	651,620	593,360
Pike	2	461,800	415,340
Polk	1	594,410	5,238,700
Pulaski	2	717,320	630,310
Putnam	2	812,040	704,800
Rabun	2	1,264,460	1,157,540
Randolph	1	2,540,500	2,181,500
Richmond	2	10,483,340	8,370,140
Rockdale	2	2,182,920	1,956,640
Schley	1	1,883,200	1,645,000
Screven	3	873,480	769,750
Seminole	2	536,830	479,380
Spalding	3	3,091,680	2,704,490
Stephens	3	1,292,960	1,139,250
Stewart	2	214,780	185,420

County	Banks	Assets	Total Deposits
Sumter	2	1,166,340	1,060,350
Talbot	2	299,180	274,270
Taliaferro	1	1,898,700	1,697,700
Tattnall	4	990,580	884,890
Taylor	2	432,900	375,430
Telfair	4	610,050	501,830
Terrell	2	900,700	799,300
Thomas	3	1,444,400	1,264,000
Tift	3	1,581,380	1,378,490
Toombs	4	1,412,010	1,238,180
Towns	2	646,000	568,790
Treutlen	1	2,567,900	2,205,000
Troup	5	2,435,910	2,113,400
Turner	2	737,960	667,610
Twiggs	1	843,500	756,400
Union	2	988,910	885,560
Upson	2	950,210	846,750
Walker	3	1,631,480	1,396,590
Walton	3	1,331,760	1,173,370
Ware	2	1,687,520	1,524,220
Warren	1	2,133,800	1,935,500
Washington	3	1,182,330	1,058,010
Wheeler	1	1,369,800	1,236,300
White	2	1,429,680	1,263,140
Whitfield	3	5,288,970	4,556,540
Wilcox	5	347,140	296,700
Wilkes	1	6,580,300	5,667,400
Wilkinson	3	473,670	416,640
Worth	1	3,472,500	3,126,200

Top 50 Commercial Banks

Listed below are the top 50 commercial banks in Georgia ranked by deposits as of June 30, 1987 as reported by the Federal Reserve Bank.

Name	City	Assets	Deposits
Citizens & Southern NB	Atlanta	9,940,523	7,039,188
First NB of Atlanta	Atlanta	6,811,909	4,669,547
Trust Co Bk	Atlanta	5,210,511	3,274,083
Bank South NA	Atlanta	2,974,178	2,265,887
National Bk of Georgia	Atlanta	1,524,066	1,084,566
First Union NB of Georgia	Clarkston	1,051,476	933,849
Columbus Bk Co	Columbus	720,118	598,457
First Union Bk Augusta	Augusta	758,738	589,826
First Union Bk Savannah	Savannah	495,783	412,849
First NB of Gainesville	Gainesville	469,191	395,153
First NB of Cobb City	Marietta	501,280	387,616
First Union NB Columbus	Columbus	410,173	344,558
Trust Co Bk of Middle Ga NA	Macon	421,200	343,908
Heritage Bk Gwinnett City	Atlanta	295,344	251,821
Trust Co Bk of SE Ga NA	Brunswick	294,645	250,885

Name	City	Assets	Deposits
Trust Co Bk of Cobb City NA	Smyrna	270,462	249,519
First Union Bk Dalton	Dalton	285,944	247,634
Trust Co Bk—Augusta NA	Augusta	289,596	247,188
Trust Co Bk Savannah NA	Savannah	270,464	234,586
First ST B & TC	Albany	253,376	222,550
Bank South Macon	Macon	252,051	220,073
Trust Co Bk of Northeast Ga	Athens	242,578	201,360
First Union Bk Griffin	Griffin	204,114	180,329
Trust Co Bk Columbus NA	Columbus	206,163	179,582
American NB of Brunswick	Brunswick	195,198	170,993
Trust Co Bk of NW Ga NA	Rome	190,821	169,998
Trust Co Bk of S Ga NA	Albany	182,991	164,294
First Union NB Rome	Rome	178,922	151,547
Hardwick B & TC	Dalton	173,882	145,127
Trust Co Bk of Rockdale	Conyers	157,673	140,794
Trust Co Bk of Gwinnett City	Lawrenceville	146,756	135,820
Roswell Bk	Roswell	171,193	130,977
Fidelity NB	Decatur	139,903	129,417
Bank of Canton	Canton	131,355	117,811
First Bk of Savannah	Savannah	145,777	114,779
Bank South of Waycross	Waycross	127,235	114,586
Commercial Bk	Thomasville	126,080	111,518
Brand Bkg Co	Lawrenceville	132,332	111,417
Central & Southern Bk of Ga	Milledgeville	123,358	111,095
Bank of Covington	Covington	126,696	107,349
Calhoun First NB	Calhoun	117,278	106,562
Etowah Bk	Canton	118,572	106,453
First Union NB Valdosta	Valdosta	117,532	103,310
First Bulloch B & TC	Statesboro	110,950	101,064
Habersham Bk	Clarkesville	110,807	100,916
Trust Co Bk of Clayton City	Jonesboro	107,440	96,525
Citizens Bk	Gainesville	104,193	95,427
Commercial Bk	Douglasville	102,611	94,395
North Carolina Nat Bk	Atlanta	188,974	93,711
Bank of Clayton	Clayton	96,897	89,055

Top 50 Savings and Loan Associations

Listed below are the top 50 savings and loan associations in Georgia ranked by deposits as of June 30, 1987 as reported by the Federal Reserve Bank.

Name	City	Assets	Deposits
Georgia FSB	Atlanta	3,602,921	2,458,825
Decatur FS & LA	Decatur	1,935,425	1,671,358
Fulton FS & LA	Atlanta	2,361,536	1,648,320
Great Southern FSB	Savannah	974,427	768,525
Liberty Svg Bk FSB	Macon	986,631	603,593
Bankers First FS & LA	Augusta	648,865	510,951
Athens FSB	Athens	430,161	359,649
First FS & LA	Atlanta	350,037	297,143

Name	City	Assets	Deposits
DeKalb FS & LA	Decatur	375,840	288,709
First FS & LA	Columbus	291,828	242,969
Home FSB of Ga	Gainesville	258,266	227,310
Carrollton FS & LA	Carrollton	242,926	220,646
Southeast FSB	Rossville	225,241	208,405
Albany First FS & LA	Albany	211,312	191,037
Tucker FS & LA	Tucker	292,473	188,273
Gwinnett FS & LA	Lawrenceville	205,819	182,165
First FS & LA	Warner Robins	183,725	170,546
First FSB	Brunswick	208,648	167,527
Home FS & LA	Atlanta	223,922	158,615
Home FS & LA	Rome	158,693	140,222
Citizens FS & LA	Rome	126,543	116,373
West Essex Bk SLA	Winder	146,064	111,061
First FS & LA	LaGrange	128,968	105,423
Fidelity FSB	Dalton	111,758	103,452
United FS & LA	Smyrna	115,740	95,535
Charter FS & LA	West Point	124,312	92,717
First FS & LA	Valdosta	100,236	92,243
Newnan FS & LA	Newnan	113,445	89,782
Southern FS & LA of Georgia	Atlanta	120,132	89,072
Thomas County FS & LA	Thomasville	93,224	84,819
Cherokee FS & LA	Canton	90,743	80,136
Clayton County FS & LA	Jonesboro	77,649	73,481
Vidalia FS & LA	Vidalia	71,847	66,211
Cartersville Fed Svg of Ga	Cartersville	64,714	62,041
First FS & LA	Calhoun	65,478	60,891
Baxley FS & LA	Baxley	64,909	59,740
Moultrie FSB	Moultrie	67,553	59,408
Southern FS & LA of Thomas C	Thomasville	78,153	58,193
Newton FS & LA	Covington	65,710	57,518
Federal Svg Bk	Atlanta	67,254	54,594
First FS & LA	Dallas	70,353	54,529
First FS & LA	Americus	57,083	53,539
Griffin FSB	Griffin	59,473	53,491
First Georgia Svg Bk FSB	Brunswick	69,463	53,468
Valdosta FS & LA	Valdosta	62,380	53,400
Habersham FSB	Cornelia	69,655	52,876
First FS & LA	Cedartown	59,956	52,836
First FS & LA	Griffin	54,456	52,495
First FS & LA	Milledgeville	56,567	49,507
Douglas County FS & LA	Douglasville	52,026	46,621

BOUNDARIES

Georgia is bounded on the north by Tennessee and North Carolina; on the east by South Carolina, the Chattooga, Tugaloo, and Savannah rivers, and the Atlantic Ocean; on the south by Florida and the St. Marys River; and on the west by Florida, Alabama, and the Chattahoochee River.

The total number of miles around the state's boundary is 1,051.

A brief history of each of the five states that touch Georgia follows.

Alabama. Derived from a Creek Indian phrase meaning "Here We Rest."

In the early 1700s several Spanish expeditions visited the state. In 1702 the French founded Mobile and settled near Tallapoosa. Alabama became a territory in 1817, a state in 1819. Montgomery was the first capital of the Confederacy.

Florida. According to Herrera, historian to the King of Spain, Ponce de Leon "Believing that land to be an island, they named it *Florida,* because it appeared very delightful, having many pleasant groves . . . the Spaniards call *Pasqua de Flores,* or Florida."

South Carolina. Named alternatively after French King Charles IX and English kings Charles I and II. In 1690 North and South Carolina became separate entities, and in 1712 they became separately known as North and South Carolina.

North Carolina. *See* South Carolina.

Tennessee. Originally part of North Carolina, Tennessee became a territory of the United States in 1790 and later, in 1796, achieved statehood as the 16th state in the Union.

CHAMBERS OF COMMERCE

A Chamber of Commerce is a voluntary organization of the business community. It unites business and professional individuals and firms, thus creating a central agency which lends itself to improving business and building a better community.

The major responsibility of the Chamber of Commerce is the community's economic well-being. It works to increase wealth and prosperity by facilitating the growth of existing businesses and fostering new ones. This new wealth can be directed toward establishing and improving educational and cultural facilities in order to create the proper business climate for attracting more business and industry.

The Chamber of Commerce meets this responsibility in three steps:

1. It examines community needs to determine what must be done to make it a better place to live and do business.

2. It channels community resources to the fulfillment of these needs.

3. It organizes and develops the necessary leadership to guarantee that the organization will become an effective force for expansion and improvement.

The following list includes all Chambers of Commerce in Georgia, along with their principal contact person.

CHAMBERS OF COMMERCE

Adel
See Cook County Chamber of Commerce

Albany
Albany Chamber of Commerce
P.O. Box 308
Albany 31702, 912-883-6900
C. Lamar Clifton, Executive Vice President

Alma
Alma-Bacon County Chamber of Commerce
P.O. Box 450
Alma 31510, 912-632-5859
Bobby A. Wheeler, Sr., Executive Director

Americus
Americus-Sumter County Chamber of Commerce
P.O. Box 724, 400 West Lamar Street
Americus 31709, 912-924-2646
Yvonne D. DeVane, Executive Vice President

Ashburn
See Turner County Chamber of Commerce

Athens
Athens Area Chamber of Commerce
P.O. Box 948, 300 North Thomas St.
Athens 30603, 404-549-6800
Tom Glaser, Executive Director

Atlanta
Atlanta Chamber of Commerce
235 International Blvd.
Atlanta 30301, 404-586-8400
Gerald L. Bartels, Executive Vice President

Business Council of Georgia
233 Peachtree St. NE, Suite 200
Atlanta 30303, 404-223-2264
Gene Dyson, CAE President

Chamber of Commerce of the United States
223 Perimeter Center Parkway, Suite 115
Atlanta 30346, 404-393-0140
James Vaughan, Manager/Southeastern Region

Women's Chamber of Commerce of Atlanta
1776 Peachtree St., 634 South Tower
Atlanta 30309, 404-892-0538
Marilyn J. Somers, Executive Director

Augusta
Greater Augusta Chamber of Commerce
P.O. Box 657, 600 Broad St. Plaza
Augusta 30913, 404-821-1300
Charles H. Bellmann, Executive Vice President

Bainbridge
Bainbridge-Decatur County Chamber of
  Commerce
P.O. Box 736
Bainbridge 31717, 912-246-4774
David W. Booker, Executive Director

Banks County
Banks County Chamber of Commerce
Rt. 1, Box 10A
Homer 30547, 404-677-2108
John J. Thompson, Jr., President

Barnesville
Barnesville-Lamar County Chamber of
  Commerce
109 Forsyth Street
Barnesville 30204, 404-358-2732
Sue Bankston, Executive Secretary

Barrow County
Barrow County Chamber of Commerce
P.O. Box 456—Old Railroad Station
Winder 30680, 404-867-9444
Cora Lou Nix, Executive Director

Baxley
Baxley-Appling County Chamber of Commerce
P.O. Box 413, 301 West Parker Street
Baxley 31513, 912-367-7731
Jerry Bange, Executive Director

Berrien County
Berrien County Chamber of Commerce
P.O. Box 217, 108 S. Jefferson Street
Nashville 31639, 912-686-5123
Sue G. Browning, Executive Secretary

Blackshear
See Pierce County Chamber of Commerce

Blairsville
Blairsville-Union County Chamber of Commerce
P.O. Box 727
Blairsville 30512, 404-745-5789
Louise M. Sprayberry, Executive Secretary

Blakely
Blakely-Early County Chamber of Commerce
P.O. Box 189, 52 Court Square
Blakely 31723, 912-723-3741
Steve Singletary, Executive Directory

Blue Ridge
See Copper Basin-Fannin Chamber of Commerce

Brantley County
Brantley County Chamber of Commerce
P.O. Drawer B, Highway 301
Nahunta 31553, 912-462-6282
Barbara Chancey, Executive Secretary

Brunswick
Brunswick-Golden Isles Chamber of Commerce
P.O. Box 250, 4 Glynn Avenue
Brunswick 31520, 912-265-0620
M. H. Woodside, Jr., Executive Director

Burke County
Burke County Chamber of Commerce
536 Liberty Street

Waynesboro 30830, 404-554-5451
Jayne F. Brinson, Executive Vice President

Business Council of Georgia
1280 South Omni International
Atlanta 30335, 404-223-2264
Gene Dyson, CAE, President

Butts County
Butts County Chamber of Commerce
P.O. Box 147
Jackson 30233, 404-775-4839
Don Earnhart, President

Cairo
Cairo-Grady County Chamber of Commerce
P.O. Box 387, 961 North Broad Street
Cairo 31728, 912-377-3663
Peggy Chapman, Executive Vice President

Calhoun
See Gordon County Chamber of Commerce

Camden
Camden-Kings Bay Area Chamber of Commerce
P.O. Box 1797, Highway 40
Kingsland 31548, 912-729-5840

Camilla
Camilla Chamber of Commerce
P.O. Box 226
Camilla 31730, 912-336-5255
Phyllis S. Weathersby, Executive Director

Canton
See Cherokee County Chamber of Commerce

Carnesville
See Franklin County Chamber of Commerce

Carroll County
Carroll County Chamber of Commerce
435 North Park Street
Carrollton 30117, 404-832-2446
Ken O'Neill, Executive Director

Carrollton
See Carroll County Chamber of Commerce

Cartersville
Cartersville-Bartow County Chamber of
 Commerce
P.O. Box 307
Cartersville 30120, 404-382-1466
Tim L. Chason, Executive Vice President

Cedartown
Cedartown Chamber of Commerce, Inc.
201 East Avenue
Cedartown 30125, 404-748-3220, Ext. 23
Jean B. Brumby, Executive Secretary

Chatsworth
Chatsworth-Murray County Chamber of
 Commerce

P.O. Box 327, Fort Street
Chatsworth 30705, 404-695-6060
Jimmy Kirkpatrick, Executive Director

Chattooga County
Chattooga County Chamber of Commerce
P.O. Box 217, 106 W. Washington Ave.
Summerville 30747, 404-857-4033
Suzan B. Spivey, Executive Vice President

Cherokee County
Cherokee County Chamber of Commerce
P.O. Box 757, 101 West Main Street
Canton 30114, 404-479-1994 or 1995
Nancy J. Kinsey, Executive Vice President

Claxton
Claxton-Evans County Chamber of Commerce &
 Industrial Development Authority
P.O. Box 655
Claxton 30417, 912-739-2281
Becky Leggett, Secretary

Clayton
See Rabun County Chamber of Commerce

Clayton County
Clayton County Chamber of Commerce
P.O. Box 774, 8712 Tara Blvd.
Jonesboro 30237, 404-478-6549
Phil Mellor, Executive Vice President

Clinch County
Clinch County Chamber of Commerce
604 East Dame Avenue
Homerville 31634, 912-487-2360
Harry James, Executive Director

Cobb County
Cobb Chamber of Commerce
P.O. Box Cobb
Marietta 30065-2429, 404-980-2000
Phil Sanders, Executive Vice President

Cochran
Cochran-Bleckley Chamber of Commerce
P.O. Box 305, 401 Second Street
Cochran 31014, 912-934-2965
Mary Y. Brown, Executive Secretary

College Park
See South Fulton Chamber of Commerce

Columbus
Columbus Chamber of Commerce
P.O. Box 1200, 901 Front Avenue
Columbus 31902, 404-327-1566
Joe F. Ragland, President

Commerce
See Jackson County Chamber of Commerce

Conyers
Conyers-Rockdale Chamber of Commerce
P.O. Box 483, 1186 Scott Street

29

Conyers 30207, 404-483-7049
Alan Long, Executive Vice President

Cook County
Cook County Chamber of Commerce
P.O. Box 481, 120 North Burwell Avenue
Adel 31620, 912-896-2281
Ms. Willie Paulk, Executive Vice President

Copper Basin-Fannin
Copper Basin-Fannin Chamber of Commerce
P.O. Box 875
Blue Ridge 30513, 404-632-5680
Dale Huddleson, Executive Director

Cordele
Cordele-Crisp Chamber of Commerce
P.O. Box 158, 302 East 16th Avenue
Cordele 31015, 912-273-1668
Don Sims, Executive Vice President

Cornelia
See Habersham County Chamber of Commerce

Covington
See Newton County Chamber of Commerce

Cumming
Cumming-Forsyth County Chamber of
Commerce
P.O. Box 711, 877 Buford Road
Cumming 30130, 404-887-6461
Mark Jennette, Executive Director

Cuthbert
Cuthbert-Randolph Chamber of Commerce, Inc.
P.O. Box 31, Plum Street on the Square
Cuthbert 31740, 912-732-2683
Roderick M. Glen, Executive Director

Dahlonega
Dahlonega-Lumpkin County Chamber of
Commerce
Box 2037
Dahlonega 30533, 404-864-3711
Betty Wilson-Wojcik, Executive Director

Dallas
See Paulding County Chamber of Commerce

Dalton
Dalton-Whitfield Chamber of Commerce
P.O. Box 99, 504 Holiday Avenue
Dalton 30722-0099, 404-278-7373
George A. Hanson, Executive Vice President

Darien
See McIntosh County Chamber of Commerce

Dawson
See Terrell County Chamber of Commerce

Dawson County
Dawson County Chamber of Commerce
P.O. Box 299

Dawsonville 30534, 404-265-6278 or 2667
Johnnie E. Sweatte, President

Dawsonville
See Dawson County Chamber of Commerce

Decatur
See DeKalb Chamber of Commerce

DeKalb County
DeKalb Chamber of Commerce
750 Commerce Dr., Suite 201
Decatur 30030, 404-378-8000
James W. Dunn, President

Donalsonville
Donalsonville-Seminole County Chamber of
Commerce
P.O. Box 713, Highway 84 East
Donalsonville 31745, 912-524-2588
Carolyn McLeod, Executive Secretary

Douglas
Douglas-Coffee County Chamber of Commerce
Lock Drawer 1607
Douglas 31533, 912-384-1873
Max Lockwood, Executive Vice President

Douglas County
Douglas County Chamber of Commerce
P.O. Box 395, 2145 Slater Mill Road
Douglasville 30133, 404-942-5022
David Jones, Executive Director

Douglasville
See Douglas County Chamber of Commerce

Dublin
Dublin-Laurens County Chamber of Commerce
P.O. Box 818, 1009 Bellevue Avenue
Dublin 31021, 912-272-5546
W. L. Wilkes, Executive Director

Eastman
Eastman-Dodge County Chamber of Commerce
P.O. Drawer 550, 201 2nd Avenue
Eastman 31023, 912-374-4723
Judy A. Hemphill, Executive Director

East Point
See South Fulton County Chamber of Commerce

Eatonton
Eatonton-Putnam Chamber of Commerce
P.O. Box 656, 105 Sumter Street
Eatonton 31024, 404-485-7701
Roddie Anne Blackwell, Executive Vice President

Elbert County
Elbert County Chamber of Commerce, Inc.
P.O. Box 537, 148 College Avenue
Elberton 30635, 404-283-5651
Dorothy L. McDonald, Executive Vice President

Elberton
See Elbert County Chamber of Commerce

Ellijay
Ellijay-Gilmer County Chamber of Commerce
P.O. Box 818, Broad Street
Ellijay 30540, 404-635-7400
W. E. "Gene" Wright, Executive Director

Fannin County
See Copper Basin-Fannin Chamber of Commerce

Fayette County
Fayette County Chamber of Commerce
P.O. Box 276, 695 Jeff Davis Drive
Fayetteville 30214, 404-461-9983
Bryan Edwards, President

Fayetteville
See Fayette County Chamber of Commerce

Fitzgerald
Fitzgerald Chamber of Commerce
P.O. Box 218, 805 South Grant Street
Fitzgerald 31750, 912-423-9357
Mrs. Joni L. Pigg, Executive Director

Folkston
Folkston-Charlton County Chamber of
   Commerce
P.O. Box 756, 202 W. Main St.
Folkston 31537, 912-496-2536
Jean O. Higginbotham, Director

Forsyth
See Monroe County Chamber of Commerce

Fort Gaines
Fort Gaines Chamber of Commerce
P.O. Box 298, 203 Washington St.
Fort Gaines 31751, 912-768-2934
James E. Coleman, President

Fort Oglethorpe
Fort Oglethorpe Area Chamber of Commerce
P.O. Box 2263, Battlefield Parkway
Fort Oglethorpe 30742, 404-866-0036
Bryan Dantzler, President

Fort Valley
See Peach County Chamber of Commerce

Fulton County
See North Fulton County or South Fulton
   County or Sandy Springs Chamber of
   Commerce

Franklin
Franklin Chamber of Commerce
P.O. Box 265
Franklin 30217, 404-675-3301
Bryan Owensby, President

Franklin County
Franklin County Chamber of Commerce
P.O. Box 151, Athens Street
Carnesville 30521, 404-384-4659
Peggy Vaughan, Secretary

Gainesville-Hall County
Gainesville-Hall County Chamber of Commerce
P.O. Box 374, 230 Sycamore Street
Gainesville 30503, 404-532-6206
Clifton McDuffie, Executive Vice President

Glennville
Glennville Area Chamber of Commerce
134 South Main Street
Glennville 30427, 912-654-2000
Ken King, President

Gordon County
Gordon County Chamber of Commerce
300 S. Wall St.
Calhoun 30701, 404-625-3200
Phillip E. Overton, Executive Vice President

Greater Valley
Greater Valley Area Chamber of Commerce
P.O. Box 584
West Point 31833, 404-645-8877
David R. Echols, Executive Director

Greene County
Greene County Chamber of Commerce
201 N. Main St.
Greenesboro 30642, 404-453-7592
Ana S. Anest, Executive Director

Greensboro
See Greene County Chamber of Commerce

Greenville
See Meriwether County Chamber of Commerce

Griffin
Griffin Area Chamber of Commerce
P.O. Box 73, 1315 West Taylor Street
Griffin 30224, 404-227-6264
Mildred C. Sawyer, Executive Vice President

Gwinnett County
Gwinnett County Chamber of Commerce
P.O. Box 1245, 1230 Atkinson Road
Lawrenceville 30246, 404-963-5128
Jack Sawyer, Executive Vice President

Habersham County
Habersham County Chamber of Commerce
P.O. Box 366, Railroad Depot
Cornelia 30531, 404-778-4654
Russ Spangler, Executive Vice President

Hapeville
Hapeville Chamber of Commerce
P.O. Box 82489
Hapeville 30354, 404-767-4244
James E. Clay, Executive Secretary

Hart County
Hart County Chamber of Commerce, Inc.
P.O. Box 793, Carolina Street
Hartwell 30643, 404-376-8590
Mrs. Teresa B. Shirley, Executive Secretary

Hartwell
See Hart County Chamber of Commerce

Hawkinsville
Hawkinsville-Pulaski County Chamber of
Commerce
P.O. Box 447, Lumpkin & Broad Streets
Hawkinsville 31036, 912-783-1717
Betty Smyth, Executive Secretary

Hazlehurst
Hazlehurst-Jeff Davis County Chamber of
Commerce
P.O. Box 124, 6 Jeff Davis Office Ct.
Hazlehurst 31539, 912-375-4543
Verle L. Thigpen, Executive Vice President

Helen
Greater Helen Area Chamber of Commerce
P.O. Box 192
Helen 30545, 404-878-2181
Helen D. Fincher, Executive Director

Henry County
Henry County Chamber of Commerce
1310 Highway 20, West
McDonough 30253, 404-957-5786
Nettye V. Clifton, Executive Vice President

Hinesville
Hinesville-Liberty County Chamber of
Commerce
P.O. Box 405, 100 Commerce Street
Hinesville 31313, 912-368-4445
Betty M. Slater, Executive Director

Hogansville
Hogansville Chamber of Commerce
P.O. Box 572, 100 Maple Drive
Hogansville 30230, 404-637-8623
John McKibben, Secretary/Treasurer

Homer
See Banks County Chamber of Commerce

Homerville
See Clinch County Chamber of Commerce

Irwin County
Irwin County Chamber of Commerce
P.O. Box 104, Irwin Avenue
Ocilla 31774, 912-468-9114
Mary Nelms, Executive Director

Jackson
See Butts County Chamber of Commerce

Jackson County
Jackson County Area Chamber of Commerce
P.O. Box 399, 117 Athens Street
Jefferson 30549, 404-367-9090
Claude Fullerton, Jr., Executive Director

Jasper
See Pickens County Chamber of Commerce

Jefferson
See Jackson County Chamber of Commerce

Jefferson County
Jefferson County Chamber of Commerce
P.O. Box 630, 211 E. 7th Street
Louisville 30434, 912-625-8134
Patty Zettler, Executive Director

Jeffersonville
See Twiggs County Chamber of Commerce

Jenkins County
Jenkins County Chamber of Commerce and
Development Auth.
200 Southside Cotton Avenue
Millen 30442, 912-982-5595
Caren Oglesby, Executive Vice President

Jesup
See Wayne County Chamber of Commerce

Jonesboro
See Clayton County Chamber of Commerce

LaFayette
LaFayette Area Chamber of Commerce
P.O. Box 985, 304 North Main Street
LaFayette 30728, 404-638-1930
Mrs. Katherine C. Derrick, Executive Secretary

LaGrange
LaGrange Area Chamber of Commerce
P.O. Box 636, 228 Main St.
LaGrange 30241, 404-884-8671
Jane L. Fryer, Executive Director

Lavonia
Lavonia Chamber of Commerce
Old Railroad Depot, General Delivery
Lavonia 30553, 404-356-8202
Joyce D. Parsons, Executive Secretary

Lawrenceville
See Gwinnett County Chamber of Commerce

Louisville
See Jefferson County Chamber of Commerce

Lumpkin
See Stewart County Chamber of Commerce

Lyons
Lyons-Toombs County Chamber of Commerce
P.O. Box 49, 417 North State Street
Lyons 30436, 912-526-6216
Betty Bazemore, Secretary

Macon
Greater Macon Chamber of Commerce
P.O. Box 169, 305 Coliseum Drive
Macon 31298, 912-741-8000
Glenn E. West, CCE, Executive Vice President

Macon County
Macon County Chamber of Commerce

P.O. Box 308, 316 South Dooley Street
Montezuma 31063, 912-472-2391
Peggy H. Williams, Executive Vice President

Madison
Madison-Morgan County Chamber of Commerce
P.O. Box 826, 120 Main Street
Madison 30650, 404-342-4454
Cindy Baldwin, Executive Director

Manchester
See Meriwether County Chamber of Commerce

Marietta
See Cobb Chamber of Commerce

McDonough
See Henry County Chamber of Commerce

McIntosh County
McIntosh Chamber of Commerce
P.O. Box 1497, Fort King George & US 17
Darien 31305, 912-437-4192 or 6684
Robert Walczak, President

McRae
See Telfair County Chamber of Commerce

Meriwether County
Meriwether County Chamber of Commerce
P.O. Box 9
Warm Springs, 31830-0009, 404-655-2558
Allen G. Nicas, Executive Director

Metter
Metter-Candler County Chamber of Commerce
P.O. Box 497, 410 S.W. Broad Street
Metter 30439, 912-685-2159
Buch Lane, President

Millen
See Jenkins County Chamber of Commerce

Milledgeville
Milledgeville-Baldwin County Chamber of
  Commerce
P.O. Box 751, 130 S. Jefferson Street
Milledgeville 31061, 912-453-9311
Linda Southerland, Executive Vice President

Monroe
See Walton County Chamber of Commerce

Monroe County
Monroe County Chamber of Commerce
P.O. Box 811, 102 E. Johnston Street
Forsyth 31029, 912-994-9239
James A. Vaughn, President

Montezuma
See Macon County Chamber of Commerce

Monticello
Monticello-Jasper County Chamber of Commerce
P.O. Box 133

Monticello 31064, 404-468-2116
Joyce McDonald, President

Moultrie
Moultrie-Colquitt County Chamber of Commerce
P.O. Box 487, 329 North Main Street
Moultrie 31776, 912-985-2131
Sam Lofton, Executive Vice President

Nahunta
See Brantley County Chamber of Commerce

Nashville
See Berrien County Chamber of Commerce

Newnan
Newnan-Coweta Chamber of Commerce, Inc.
P.O. Box 1103, 1 Savannah Street
Newnan 30264, 404-253-2270
Inez W. Slaton, Executive Director

Newton County
Newton County Chamber of Commerce
P.O. Box 168, 1121 Floyd Street
Covington 30209, 404-786-7510
Richard L. James, Executive Director

North Fulton
North Fulton Chamber of Commerce
1025 Old Roswell Road
Roswell 30076, 404-993-8808
Delouis J. West, Executive Director

Ocilla
See Irwin County Chamber of Commerce

Oconee County
Oconee County Chamber of Commerce
P.O. Box 338, 55 Nancy Dr.
Watkinsville 30677, 404-769-7947
Barbara Venable, Director

Oglethorpe
Oglethorpe Chamber of Commerce
P.O. Box 178, 214 Sumter Street
Oglethorpe 31068, 912-472-7733
John Coogle, President

Paulding County
Paulding County Chamber of Commerce
150 East Memorial Drive
Dallas 30132, 404-445-6016
Charles Kinney, Executive Director

Peach County
Peach County Chamber of Commerce
P.O. Box 1238, 114 Vineville Street
Fort Valley 31030, 912-825-3733
Robert Turk, Executive Director

Pearson
Pearson Chamber of Commerce
P.O. Box 601
Pearson 31642, 912-422-3277
Phil Torrance, Secretary

Pelham
Pelham Chamber of Commerce
P.O. Box 151, Park Plaza #2
Pelham 31779, 912-294-4924
Amelia Lodge, Executive Director

Perry
Perry Area Chamber of Commerce
P.O. Box 592, 1105 Washington Street
Perry 31069, 912-987-1234
Ann H. Conner, Executive Vice President

Pickens County
Pickens County Chamber of Commerce
P.O. Box 327
Jasper 30143, 404-692-5600
Marsha Brendel, Executive Secretary

Pierce County
Pierce County Chamber of Commerce
P.O. Box 47, South Central Avenue
Blackshear, 31516, 912-449-4741
Dick Ulm, Executive Director

Pike County
Pike County Chamber of Commerce, Inc.
P.O. Box 317, Pike County Courthouse
Zebulon 30295, 404-567-8734
Grover Anderson, Secretary/Treasurer

Pine Mountain
Pine Mountain Chamber of Commerce, Inc.
P.O. Box 483
Pine Mountain 31822, 404-628-4171
Martha F. M. Chewning, Secretary/Treasurer

Quitman
Quitman-Brooks County Chamber of Commerce
900 East Screvan Street
Quitman 31643, 912-263-4841
Grady W. Williams, Executive Director

Rabun County
Rabun County Chamber of Commerce
P.O. Box 761, Highway 441 North
Clayton 30525, 404-782-4812
Marge Striggow, Executive Director

Reidsville
See Tattnall County Chamber of Commerce

Ringgold-Catoosa County
Ringgold-Catoosa County Chamber of Commerce
P.O. Box 52, Rte. 5 Battle Field Pkwy.
Ringgold 30736, 404-937-4250
Richard Parrott, Director

Rockmart
Rockmart Chamber of Commerce
P.O. Box 636, 200 South Marble Street
Rockmart 30153, 404-684-5454, Ext. 18
Ann E. Beck, Executive Director

Rome
Rome Area Chamber of Commerce

P.O. Box 406, 424 Broad Street
Rome 30162, 404-291-7663
Bruce S. Schlosberg, Executive Vice President

Roswell
See North Fulton Chamber of Commerce

Royston
Royston-Franklin Springs Chamber of Commerce
P.O. Box 304, Depot Street
Royston 30662, 404-245-9293
C. Donald Johnson, Jr., President

Saint Simons Island
Saint Simons Island Chamber of Commerce
Neptune Park
St. Simons Island 31522, 912-638-9014
Mrs. Jean S. Alexander, Executive Secretary

Sandersville
See Washington County Chamber of Commerce

Sandy Springs
Sandy Springs Chamber of Commerce, Inc.
P.O. Box 28561, 6021 Sandy Springs Cir.
Sandy Springs 30328, 404-847-9583
Raymond L. Higgins, Executive Director

Savannah
Savannah Area Chamber of Commerce
301 West Broad Street
Savannah 31499, 912-233-3067
David A. Young, President

Screven County
Screven County Chamber of Commerce
101 South Main Street
Sylvania 30467, 912-564-7878
Sara S. Greene, Executive Director

Soperton
Soperton-Treutlen Chamber of Commerce
P.O. Box 296
Soperton 30457, 912-529-6868
John N. Smith, President

South Fulton
South Fulton Chamber of Commerce
6400 Shannon Parkway
Union City 30291, 404-964-1984 or 1985
Otis D. Viall, Executive Director

South Georgia
See Thomasville

Sparta
Sparta-Hancock County Chamber of Commerce
P.O. Box 452
Sparta 31087, 404-444-5715
Marian A. Davis, Executive Director

Statesboro
Statesboro-Bulloch County Chamber of
   Commerce
323 South Main Street

Statesboro 30458, 912-764-6111
George A. Hanson, Executive Director

Stewart County
Stewart County Chamber of Commerce
P.O. Box 1021
Lumpkin 31815, 912-838-4326
Ms. Gina Mathis, Secretary-Treasurer

Summerville
See Chattooga County Chamber of Commerce

Swainsboro
Swainsboro-Emanuel County Chamber of
  Commerce
124 North Main Street
Swainsboro 30401, 912-237-6426
Richard L. James, CCE, Executive Vice
  President

Sylvania
See Screven County Chamber of Commerce

Sylvester
See Worth County Chamber of Commerce

Tattnall County
Tattnall County Chamber of Commerce
P.O. Box 769, Brazell Street
Reidsville 30453, 404-577-6323
Ralph Stewart, Executive Secretary

Telfair County
Telfair County Chamber of Commerce
120 East Oak Street
McRae 31055, 912-868-6365
Walt Thigpen, President

Terrell County
Terrell County Chamber of Commerce
P.O. Box 405, 158 E. Lee Street
Dawson 31742, 912-995-2011
Ima A. Rude, Executive Secretary

Thomaston
Thomaston-Upson County Chamber of
  Commerce
P.O. Box 827, 310 North Church Street, Ste. C
Thomaston 30286, 404-647-9686
Tina Gresham, Manager

Thomasville
Thomasville-Thomas County Chamber of
  Commerce
P.O. Box 560, 401 South Broad Street
Thomasville 31799, 912-226-9600
Lloyd E. Eckberg, CCE, Executive Vice
  President

South Georgia Chamber of Commerce
P.O. Box 2036
Thomasville 31799, 912-226-9600
Lloyd E. Eckberg, CCE, President

Thomson
Thomson-McDuffie Chamber of Commerce
136 Railroad Street
Thomson 30824, 404-595-5963
William E. Drew, Executive Vice President

Tift County
Tift County Chamber of Commerce
P.O. Box 165, 100 Central Avenue
Tifton 31793, 912-382-6200
Kenneth J. O'Neill, Executive Vice President

Tifton
See Tift County Chamber of Commerce

Toccoa
Toccoa-Stephens County Chamber of Commerce
P.O. Box 577, 901 E. Currahee St.
Toccoa 30577, 404-886-2132
Robert H. Evans, Executive Vice President

Turner County
Turner County Chamber of Commerce
P.O. Drawer 608, 121 College St.
Ashburn 31714, 912-567-2541
Marvin Raines, Executive Director

Twiggs County
Twiggs County Chamber of Commerce
P.O. Box 231
Jeffersonville 31044, 912-945-3915
Ms. J. E. Beck, Sr., President

Tybee Island
Tybee Island Chamber of Commerce
P.O. Box 491, 209 Butler Avenue
Tybee Island 31328, 912-786-5444
Chris Simon, Director

Unadilla
Unadilla Chamber of Commerce
P.O. Box 176
Unadilla 31091, 912-627-3207
Charles Goodroe, President

Union City
See South Fulton Chamber of Commerce

United States Chamber of Commerce
See Atlanta

Valdosta
Valdosta-Lowndes County Chamber of
  Commerce
P.O. Box 790, 416 N. Ashley St.
Valdosta 31603, 912-247-8100
John B. Lastinger, Executive Vice President

Vidalia
Vidalia Chamber of Commerce
P.O. Box 306, 104 East First Street
Vidalia 30474, 912-537-4466
Victor Cross, Executive Vice President

Vienna
Vienna-Dooly County Chamber of Commerce
P.O. Box 394
Vienna 31092, 912-268-4554
Lanier Browning, Executive Director

Walton County
Walton County Chamber of Commerce
P.O. Box 89, 323 W. Spring Street
Monroe 30655, 404-267-6594
Frances E. Enslen-Jones, Executive Director

Warm Springs
See Meriwether County Chamber of Commerce

Warner Robins
Warner Robins Chamber of Commerce
1420 Watson Boulevard
Warner Robins 31093, 912-922-8585
Dick Walden, Executive Vice President

Warrenton
Warren County Chamber of Commerce
P.O. Box 27
Warrenton 30828, 404-465-2680
Diane Raley, President

Washington
See Wilkes County Chamber of Commerce

Washington County
Washington County Chamber of Commerce
P.O. Box 582
Sandersville 31082, 912-552-3288
Sandra M. Willis, Executive Secretary

Watkinsville
See Oconee County Chamber of Commerce

Waycross
Waycross-Ware County Chamber of Commerce
424 Hicks Street

Waycross 31501, 912-283-3742
Tom Boland, Executive Vice President

Wayne County
Wayne County Chamber of Commerce
P.O. Box 70, 124 NW Broad Street
Jesup 31545, 912-427-2028
William E. Durrett, Executive Director

Waynesboro
See Burke County Chamber of Commerce

West Point
See Greater Valley Chamber of Commerce

Wilkes County
Wilkes County Chamber of Commerce
P.O. Box 661, 25 E. Square
Washington 30673, 404-678-2013
William E. Boyd, Executive Vice President

Winder
See Barrow County Chamber of Commerce

Women's Chamber
See Atlanta

Worth County
Worth County-Sylvester Chamber of Commerce
P.O. Box 768, 301 E. Franklin Street
Sylvester 31791, 912-776-7718
Angie Hoover, Assistant

Wrightsville
Wrightsville-Johnson County Chamber of
    Commerce
P.O. Box 189
Wrightsville 31096, 912-964-9693
Danny O. Evans, President

Zebulon
See Pike County Chamber of Commerce

CLIMATE

Georgia's climate is mild, with 65°F. (18°C) being the average annual temperature. For the most part the winters are short and mild and the summers warm and humid. Average annual rainfall ranges from approximately 76 inches in the northeast Georgia mountains to 40 inches in the Augusta area. The Atlanta area receives between 48 and 52 inches.

Weather Normals, Means, and Extremes

Following are charts reflecting temperatures and precipitation for Atlanta, Columbus, and Savannah as reported by the National Weather Service.

Month	Weather Station	Temperatures					
		Daily Maximum	Daily Minimum	Record High	Year	Record Low	Year
January	Atlanta	51.2	32.6	79	1949	−8	1985
	Columbus	56.9	35.4	83	1949	−2	1985
	Savannah	60.3	37.9	84	1957	3	1985
February	Atlanta	55.3	34.5	79	1980	5	1958
	Columbus	60.6	37.0	83	1962	11	1973
	Savannah	63.1	40.0	86	1962	14	1958
March	Atlanta	63.2	41.7	85	1982	10	1960
	Columbus	68.0	43.9	89	1982	16	1980
	Savannah	69.9	46.8	91	1974	20	1980
April	Atlanta	73.2	50.4	93	1986	26	1973
	Columbus	77.4	51.9	93	1986	28	1950
	Savannah	77.8	54.1	95	1986	32	1962
May	Atlanta	79.8	58.7	95	1953	37	1971
	Columbus	83.8	60.2	97	1962	39	1963
	Savannah	84.2	62.3	100	1953	39	1963
June	Atlanta	85.6	65.9	101	1952	46	1956
	Columbus	89.4	67.6	104	1978	44	1956
	Savannah	88.6	68.5	104	1985	51	1984
July	Atlanta	87.9	69.2	105	1980	53	1967
	Columbus	91.1	71.0	104	1986	59	1967
	Savannah	90.8	71.5	105	1986	61	1972
August	Atlanta	87.6	68.7	102	1980	55	1986
	Columbus	90.8	70.5	103	1986	57	1952
	Savannah	90.1	71.4	104	1954	57	1986
September	Atlanta	82.3	63.6	98	1954	36	1967
	Columbus	86.0	65.9	99	1957	38	1967
	Savannah	85.6	67.6	98	1986	43	1967
October	Atlanta	72.9	51.4	95	1954	28	1976
	Columbus	77.0	53.1	96	1954	24	1952
	Savannah	77.8	55.9	97	1986	28	1952
November	Atlanta	62.6	41.3	84	1961	3	1950
	Columbus	67.0	42.7	86	1961	10	1950
	Savannah	69.5	45.5	89	1961	15	1970
December	Atlanta	54.1	34.8	77	1971	0	1983
	Columbus	59.5	37.2	82	1977	4	1962
	Savannah	62.5	39.4	83	1971	9	1983

Month	Weather Station	Precipitation						
		Water Equivalent					Snow, Ice Pellets	
		Normal	Maximum Monthly	Year	Minimum Monthly	Year	Maximum Monthly	Year
January	Atlanta	4.91	10.82	1936	.84	1981	8.3	1940
	Columbus	4.52	10.22	1947	.87	1954	2.0	1982
	Savannah	3.09	8.87	1984	.51	1985	2.0	1977
February	Atlanta	4.43	12.77	1961	.77	1978	4.4	1979
	Columbus	4.52	9.41	1961	1.22	1951	14.0	1973
	Savannah	3.17	7.92	1964	1.16	1968	3.6	1968
March	Atlanta	5.91	11.66	1980	1.86	1985	7.9	1983
	Columbus	5.96	12.53	1952	1.38	1985	1.0	1980
	Savannah	3.83	9.57	1959	.18	1955	1.1	1986
April	Atlanta	4.43	11.86	1979	.49	1986	T	1987
	Columbus	4.50	11.67	1953	.10	1986	T	1971
	Savannah	3.16	7.74	1961	.38	1986		
May	Atlanta	4.02	8.37	1980	.32	1936		
	Columbus	4.44	8.45	1959	.22	1962		
	Savannah	4.62	10.08	1957	.51	1953		
June	Atlanta	3.41	7.52	1939	.74	1984		
	Columbus	4.16	10.83	1967	.83	1986		
	Savannah	5.69	14.39	1963	.84	1954		
July	Atlanta	4.73	11.26	1948	.76	1980		
	Columbus	5.50	13.24	1971	1.74	1957		
	Savannah	7.37	20.10	1964	1.35	1972		
August	Atlanta	3.41	8.69	1967	.50	1976		
	Columbus	4.02	10.07	1977	.96	1956		
	Savannah	6.65	14.94	1971	1.02	1980		
September	Atlanta	3.17	7.52	1983	.04	1984		
	Columbus	3.59	6.94	1951	.22	1984		
	Savannah	5.19	13.47	1953	.36	1972		
October	Atlanta	2.53	7.53	1966	T.	1963		
	Columbus	2.07	8.09	1964	0.00	1963		
	Savannah	2.27	8.54	1959	.02	1963		
November	Atlanta	3.43	15.72	1948	.41	1939	1.0	1968
	Columbus	3.06	12.45	1948	.31	1956	T	1975
	Savannah	1.89	4.91	1972	.15	1966		
December	Atlanta	4.23	9.92	1961	.69	1979	2.5	1963
	Columbus	4.75	9.39	1953	.43	1955	T	1981
	Savannah	2.77	5.80	1977	.12	1984	T	1980

T = Trace—an amount too small to measure.

COASTLINE & SHORELINE

General coastline figures represent lengths of the seacoast outline. The coastlines of sounds and of bays are included to a point where they narrow to the width of 30 minutes of latitude, and the distance across at such point is included. Total shorelines include the outer coast, offshore islands, sounds, bays, and rivers to the head of tidewater or to a point where tidal waters narrow to a width of 100 feet.

Coastline	*Shoreline*
100 miles	2,344 miles

CONGRESSIONAL DISTRICTS

Georgia is divided into ten Congressional districts, as shown on the accompanying map on page 32. The representatives are listed with their Washington, D.C. addresses and telephone numbers.

United States
Congressional Districts

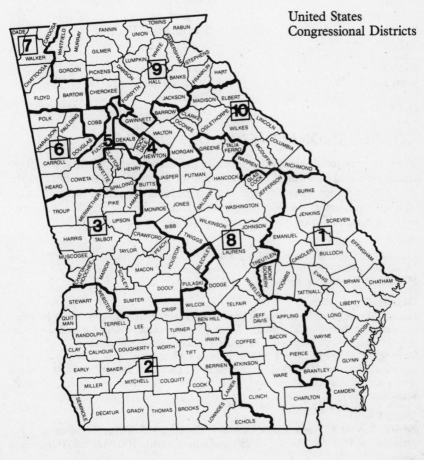

District 1
Lindsay Thomas (D)
Washington, D.C. 20515
202-225-5831

District 2
Charles Hatcher (D)
Washington, D.C. 20515
202-225-3631

District 3
Richard Ray (D)
Washington, D.C. 20515
202-225-5901

District 4
Pat Swindall (R)
Washington, D.C. 20515
202-225-4272

District 5
John Lewis (D)
Washington, D.C. 20515
202-225-3801

District 6
Newt Gingrich (R)
Washington, D.C. 20515
202-225-4501

District 7
George (Buddy) Darden (D)
Washington, D.C. 20515
202-225-2931

District 8
J. Roy Rowland (D)
Washington, D.C. 20515
202-225-6531

District 9
Ed Jenkins (D)
Washington, D.C. 20515
202-225-5211

District 10
Doug Barnard, Jr. (D)
Washington, D.C. 20515
202-225-4101

CONGRESSIONAL MEDAL OF HONOR

The Congressional Medal of Honor is the highest United States military decoration and is awarded in the name of Congress to members of the Armed Forces for gallantry and bravery beyond the call of duty in action against the enemy. Georgia recipients of the Congressional Medal of Honor, their rank, units, and hometowns follow.

War Between the States
Leland, George W. *Rank and organization:* Gunner's Mate, U.S. Navy. *Born:* 1834, Savannah, Ga. *G.O. No.:* 32, 16 April 1864. *Place and date:* Charleston Harbor, 16 November 1863.

Western Indian Wars
Carter, Mason. *Rank and organization:* First Lieutenant, 5th U.S. Infantry. *Place and date:* At Bear Paw Mountain, Mont., 30 September 1877. *Entered service at:* Augusta, Ga. *Birth:* Augusta, Ga. *Date of issue:* 27 November 1894.
Garlington, Ernest A. *Rank and organization:* First Lieutenant, 7th U.S. Cavalry. *Place and date:* At Wounded Knee Creek, S. Dak., 29 December 1890. *Entered service at:* Athens, Ga. *Born:* 20 February 1853, Newberry, S.C. *Date of issue:* 26 September 1893.

World War II
Brown, Bobbie E. *Rank and organization:* Captain, U.S. Army, Company C, 18th Infantry, 1st Infantry Division. *Place and date:* Crucifix Hill, Aachen, Germany, 8

October 1944. *Entered service at:* Atlanta, Ga. *Born:* 2 September 1903, Dublin, Ga. *G.O. No.:* 74, 1 September 1945.

*Dyess, Aquilla James: *Rank and organization:* Lieutenant Colonel, U.S. Marine Corps Reserve. *Born:* 11 January 1909, Augusta, Ga. *Place and date:* Namur Island, Kwajalein Atoll, Marshall Islands, 1 and 2 February 1944.

*Elrod, Henry Talmage. *Rank and organization:* Captain, U.S. Marine Corps. *Born:* 27 September 1905, Rebecca, Ga. *Entered service at:* Ashburn, Ga. *Place and date:* Wake Island, 8 to 23 December 1941.

Lee, Daniel W. *Rank and organization:* First Lieutenant, U.S. Army, Troop A, 117th Cavalry Reconnaissance Squadron. *Place and date:* Montreval, France, 2 September 1944. *Entered service at:* Alma, Ga. *Born:* 23 June 1919, Alma, Ga. *G.O. No.:* 14, 4 February 1946.

McKinney, John R. *Rank and organization:* Sergeant (then Private), U.S. Army, Company A, 123d Infantry, 33d Infantry Division. *Place and date:* Tayabas Province, Luzon, Philippine Islands, 11 May 1945. *Entered service at:* Woodcliff, Ga. *Birth:* Woodcliff, Ga. *G.O. No.:* 14, 4 February 1946.

*Nininger, Alexander R., Jr. *Rank and organization:* Second Lieutenant, U.S. Army, 57th Infantry, Philippine Scouts. *Place and date:* Near Abucay, Bataan, Philippine Islands, 12 January 1942. *Entered service at:* Fort Lauderdale, Fla. *Birth:* Gainesville, Ga. *G.O. No.:* 9, 5 February 1942.

Pharris, Jackson Charles. *Rank and organization:* Lieutenant, U.S. Navy, U.S.S. *California.* *Place and date:* Pearl Harbor, Territory of Hawaii, 7 December 1941. *Entered service at:* California. *Born:* 26 June 1912, Columbus, Ga.

*Thomason, Clyde. *Rank and organization:* Sergeant, U.S. Marine Corps Reserve. *Born:* 23 May 1914, Atlanta, Ga. *Place and date:* Island of Makin, 17 through 18 August 1942.

Korea

Davis, Raymond G. *Rank and organization:* Lieutenant Colonel, U.S. Marine Corps, commanding officer, 1st Battalion, 7th Marines, 1st Marine Division (Rein). *Place and date:* Vicinity Hagaru-ri, Korea, 1 through 4 December 1950. *Entered service at:* Atlanta, Ga. *Born:* 13 January 1915, Fitzgerald, Ga.

*Phillips, Lee H. *Rank and organization:* Corporal, U.S. Marine Corps, Company E, 2d Battalion, 7 Marines, 1st Marine Division (Rein). *Place and date:* Korea, 4 November 1950. *Entered service at:* Ben Hill, Ga. *Born:* 3 February 1930, Stockbridge, Ga.

*Story, Luther H. *Rank and organization:* Private First Class, U.S. Army, Company A, 9th Infantry Regiment, 2d Infantry Division. *Place and date:* Near Agok, Korea, 1 September 1950. *Entered service at:* Georgia. *Born:* 20 July 1931, Buena Vista, Ga. *G.O. No.:* 70, 2 August 1951.

Vietnam

*Bowen, Hammett L., Jr. *Rank and organization:* Staff Sergeant, U.S. Army, Company C, 2d Battalion, 14th Infantry, 25th Infantry Division. *Place and date:* Binh Duong Province, Republic of Vietnam, 27 June 1969. *Entered service at:* Jacksonville, Fla. *Born:* 30 November 1947, LaGrange, Ga.

*Bryant, William Maud. *Rank and organization:* Sergeant First Class, U.S. Army, Company A, 5th Special Forces Group, 1st Special Forces. *Place and date:* Long Khanh Province, Republic of Vietnam, 24 March 1969. *Entered service at:* Detroit, Mich. *Born:* 16 February 1933, Cochran, Ga.

*Davis, Rodney Maxwell. *Rank and organization:* Sergeant, U.S. Marine Corps, Company B, 1st Battalion, 5th Marines, 1st Marine Division. *Place and date:* Quang Nam Province, Republic of Vietnam, 6 September 1967. *Entered service at:* Macon, Ga. *Born:* 7 April 1942, Macon, Ga.

*Durham, Harold Bascom, Jr. *Rank and organization:* Second Lieutenant, U.S. Army, Battery C, 6th Battalion, 15th Artillery, 1st Infantry Division. *Place and date:* Republic of Vietnam, 17 October 1967. *Entered service at:* Atlanta, Ga. *Born:* 12 October 1942, Rocky Mount, N.C.

Jackson, Joe M. *Rank and organization:* Lieutenant Colonel, U.S. Air Force, 311th Air Commando Squadron, Da Nang, Republic of Vietnam. *Place and date:* Kham Duc, Republic of Vietnam, 12 May 1968. *Entered service at:* Newman, Ga. *Born:* 14 March 1923, Newman, Ga.

*Johnston, Donald R. *Rank and organization:* Specialist Fourth Class, U.S. Army, Company D, 1st Battalion, 8th Cavalry, 1st Cavalry Division. *Place and date:* Tay Ninh Province, Republic of Vietnam, 21 March 1969. *Entered service at:* Columbus, Ga. *Born:* 19 November 1947, Columbus, Ga.

Livingston, James E. *Rank and organization:* Captain, U.S. Marine Corps, Company E, 2d Battalion, 4th Marines. 9th Marine Amphibious Brigade. *Place and date:* Dai Do, Republic of Vietnam, 2 May 1968. *Entered service at:* McRae, Ga. *Born:* 12 January 1940, Towns, Telfair County, Ga.

*McKibben, Ray. *Rank and organization:* Sergeant, U.S. Army, Troop B, 7th Squadron (Airmobile), 17th Cavalry. *Place and date:* Near Song Mao, Republic of Vietnam, 8 December 1968. *Entered service at:* Atlanta, Ga. *Born:* 27 October 1945, Felton, Ga.

Pless, Stephen W. *Rank and organization:* Major (then Capt.), U.S. Marine Corps, VMD-6, Mag-36, 1st Marine Aircraft Wing. *Place and date:* Near Quang Nai, Republic of Vietnam, 19 August 1967. *Entered service at:* Atlanta, Ga. *Born:* 6 September 1939, Newman, Ga.

Ray, Ronald Eric. *Rank and organization:* Captain (then 1st Lt.), U.S. Army, Company A, 2d Battalion, 35th Infantry, 25th Infantry Division. *Place and date:* Ia Drang Valley, Republic of Vietnam, 19 June 1966. *Entered service at:* Atlanta, Ga. *Born:* 7 December 1941, Cordele, Ga.

Sprayberry, James M. *Rank and organization:* Captain (then 1st Lt.), U.S. Army, Company D. 5th Battalion, 7th Cavalry, 1st Cavalry Division (Airmobile). *Place and date:* Republic of Vietnam, 25 April 1968. *Entered service at:* Montgomery, Ala. *Born:* 24 April 1947, LaGrange, Ga.

*Wilbanks, Hilliard A. *Rank and organization:* Captain, U.S. Air Force, 21st Tactical Air Support Squadron, Nha Trang AFB, RVN. *Place and date:* Near Dalat, Republic of Vietnam, 24 February 1967. *Entered service at:* Atlanta, Ga. *Born:* 26 July 1933, Cornelia, Ga.

*Posthumous award

It is noteworthy that the first Medals of Honor ever bestowed were awarded to the nineteen Union Army volunteers who in 1862 captured the locomotive, *General*, at Big Shanty, Georgia and sabotaged vital Confederate facilities between Atlanta and Chattanooga. All nineteen men were captured, and eight were tried and executed. Eventually, all in the party were awarded medals, some posthumously.

CONSTITUTION

Since 1777, Georgia has had eight constitutions. The last, adopted in 1945, is one of the few in the United States that require a state to operate on a "pay-as-you-go" basis. Amendments to the constitution can be proposed by the legislature, or by a special convention called by the legislature, but become effective only after being approved by a majority of Georgia's voters in a statewide election.

PREAMBLE

To perpetuate the principles of free government, insure justice to all, preserve peace, promote the interest and happiness of the citizen and of the family, and transmit to posterity the enjoyment of liberty, we the people of Georgia, relying upon the protection and guidance of Almighty God, do ordain and establish this Constitution.

ARTICLE I.
BILL OF RIGHTS
Section I.
Rights of Persons

Paragraph I. **Life, liberty, and property.** No person shall be deprived of life, liberty, or property except by due process of law.

Paragraph II. **Protection to person and property; equal protection.** Protection to person and property is the paramount duty of government and shall be impartial and complete. No person shall be denied the equal protection of the laws.

Paragraph III. **Freedom of conscience.** Each person has the natural and inalienable right to worship God, each according to the dictates of that person's own conscience; and no human authority should, in any case, control or interfere with such right of conscience.

Paragraph IV. **Religious opinions; freedom of religion.** No inhabitant of this state shall be molested in person or property or be prohibited from holding any public office or trust on account of religious opinions; but the right of freedom of religion shall not be construed as to excuse acts of licentiousness or justify practices inconsistent with the peace and safety of the state.

Paragraph V. **Freedom of speech and of the press guaranteed.** No law shall be passed to curtail or restrain the freedom of speech or of the press. Every person may speak, write, and publish sentiments on all subjects but shall be responsible for the abuse of that liberty.

Paragraph VI. **Libel.** In all civil or criminal actions for libel, the truth may be given in evidence; and, if it shall appear to the trier of fact that the matter charged as libelous is true, the party shall be discharged.

Paragraph VII. **Citizens, protection of.** All citizens of the United States, resident in this state, are hereby declared citizens of this state; and it shall be the duty of the General Assembly to enact such laws as will protect them in the full enjoyment of the rights, privileges, and immunities due to such citizenship.

Paragraph VIII. **Arms, right to keep and bear.** The right of the people to keep and bear arms shall not be infringed, but the General Assembly shall have power to prescribe the manner in which arms may be borne.

Paragraph IX. **Right to assemble and petition.** The people have the right to assemble peaceably for their common good and to apply by petition or remonstrance to those vested with the powers of government for redress of grievances.

Paragraph X. **Bill of attainder; ex post facto laws; and retroactive laws.** No bill of attainder, ex post facto law, retroactive law, or laws impairing the obligation of contract or making irrevocable grant of special privileges or immunities shall be passed.

Paragraph XI. **Right to trial by jury; number of jurors; selection and compensation of jurors.**

(a) The right to trial by jury shall remain inviolate, except that the court shall render judgment without the verdict of a jury in all civil cases where no issuable defense is filed and where a jury is not demanded in writing by either party. In criminal cases, the defendant shall have a public and speedy trial by an impartial jury; and the jury shall be the judges of the law and the facts.

(b) A trial jury shall consist of 12 persons; but the General Assembly may prescribe any number, not less than six, to constitute a trial jury in courts of limited jurisdiction and in superior courts in misdemeanor cases.

(c) The General Assembly shall provide by law for the selection and compensation of persons to serve as grand jurors and trial jurors.

Paragraph XII. **Right to the courts.** No person shall be deprived of the right to prosecute or defend, either in person or by an attorney, that person's own cause in any of the courts of this state.

Paragraph XIII. **Searches, seizures, and warrants.** The right of the people to be secure in their persons, houses, papers, and effects against unreasonable searches and seizures shall not be violated; and no warrant shall issue except upon probable cause supported by oath or affirmation particularly describing the place or places to be searched and the persons or things to be seized.

Paragraph XIV. **Benefit of counsel; accusation; list of witnesses; compulsory process.** Every person charged with an offense against the laws of this state shall have the privilege and benefit of counsel; shall be furnished with a copy of the accusation or indictment and, on demand, with a list of the witnesses on whose testimony such charge is founded; shall have compulsory process to obtain the testimony of that person's own witnesses; and shall be confronted with the witnesses testifying against such person.

Paragraph XV. **Habeas corpus.** The writ of habeas corpus shall not be suspended unless, in case of rebellion or invasion, the public safety may require it.

Paragraph XVI. **Self-incrimination.** No person shall be compelled to give testimony tending in any manner to be self-incriminating.

Paragraph XVII. **Bail; fines; punishment; arrest, abuse of prisoners.** Excessive bail shall not be required, nor excessive fines imposed, nor cruel and unusual punishments inflicted; nor shall any person be abused in being arrested, while under arrest, or in prison.

Paragraph XVIII. **Jeopardy of life or liberty more than once forbidden.** No person shall be put in jeopardy of life or liberty more than once for the same offense except when a new trial has been granted after conviction or in case of mistrial.

Paragraph XIX. **Treason.** Treason against the State of Georgia shall consist of insurrection against the state, adhering to the state's enemies, or giving them aid and comfort. No person shall be convicted of treason except on the testimony of two witnesses to the same overt act or confession in open court.

Paragraph XX. **Conviction, effect of.** No conviction shall work corruption of blood or forfeiture of estate.

Paragraph XXI. **Banishment and whipping as punishment for crime.** Neither banishment beyond the limits of the state nor whipping shall be allowed as a punishment for crime.

Paragraph XXII. **Involuntary servitude.** There shall be no involuntary servitude within the State of Georgia except as a punishment for crime after legal conviction thereof or for contempt of court.

Paragraph XXIII. **Imprisonment for debt.** There shall be no imprisonment for debt.

Paragraph XXIV. **Costs.** No person shall be compelled to pay costs in any criminal case except after conviction on final trial.

Paragraph XXV. **Status of the citizen.** The social status of a citizen shall never be the subject of legislation.

Paragraph XXVI. **Exemptions from levy and sale.** The General Assembly shall protect by law from levy and sale by virtue of any process under the laws of this state a portion of the property of each person in an amount of not less than $1,600.00 and shall have authority to define to whom any such additional exemptions shall be allowed; to specify the amount of such exemptions; to provide for the manner of exempting such property and for the sale, alienation, and encumbrance thereof; and to provide for the waiver of said exemptions by the debtor.

Paragraph XXVII. **Spouse's separate property.** The separate property of each spouse shall remain the separate property of that spouse except as otherwise provided by law.

Paragraph XXVIII. **Enumeration of rights not denial of others.** The enumeration of rights herein contained as a part of this Constitution shall not be construed to deny to the people any inherent rights which they may have hitherto enjoyed.

Section II.
Origin and Structure of Government

Paragraph I. **Origin and foundation of government.** All government, of right, originates with the people, is founded upon their will only, and is instituted solely for the good of the whole. Public officers are the trustees and servants of the people and are at all times amenable to them.

Paragraph II. **Object of government.** The people of this state have the inherent right of regulating their internal government. Government is instituted for the protection, security, and benefit of the people; and at all times they have the right to alter or reform the same whenever the public good may require it.

Paragraph III. **Separation of legislative, judicial, and executive powers.** The legislative, judicial, and executive powers shall forever remain separate and distinct; and no person discharging the duties of one shall at the same time exercise the functions of either of the others except as herein provided.

Paragraph IV. **Contempts.** The power of the courts to punish for contempt shall be limited by legislative acts.

Paragraph V. **What acts void.** Legislative acts in violation of this Constitution or the Constitution of the United States are void, and the judiciary shall so declare them.

Paragraph VI. **Superiority of civil authority.** The civil authority shall be superior to the military.

Paragraph VII. **Separation of church and state.** No money shall ever be taken from the public treasury, directly or indirectly, in aid of any church, sect, cult, or religious denomination or of any sectarian institution.

Paragraph VIII. **Lotteries.** All lotteries, and the sale of lottery tickets, are hereby prohibited; and this prohibition shall be enforced by penal laws, except that the General Assembly may by law provide that the operation of a nonprofit bingo game shall not be a lottery and shall be legal in this state. The General Assembly may by law define a nonprofit bingo game and provide for the regulation of nonprofit bingo games.

Paragraph IX. **Sovereign immunity of the state from suit.**

(a) Sovereign immunity extends to the state and all of its departments and agencies. However, the defense of sovereign immunity is waived as to any action ex contractu for the breach of any written contract now existing or hereafter entered into by the state or its departments and agencies. Also the defense of sovereign immunity is waived as to those actions for the recovery of damages for any claim against the state or any of its departments and agencies for which liability insurance protection for such claims has been provided but only to the extent of any liability insurance provided. Moreover, the sovereign immunity of the state or any of its departments and agencies may hereafter be waived further by Act of the General Assembly which specifically provides that sovereign immunity is hereby waived and the extent of the waiver. No waiver of sovereign immunity shall be construed as a waiver of any immunity provided to the state or its departments and agencies by the United States Constitution. The provisions of this paragraph shall not have the effect of permitting the state or any of its departments or agencies to interpose the defense of sovereign immunity as to any action against the state or any of its departments or agencies filed prior to January 1, 1983, if such defense could not have been interposed on December 31, 1982.

(b) The General Assembly may provide by law for the processing and disposition of claims against the state which do not exceed such maximum amount as provided therein.

Section III.
General Provisions

Paragraph I. **Eminent domain.**

(a) Except as otherwise provided in this Paragraph, private property shall not be taken or damaged for public purposes without just and adequate compensation being first paid.

(b) When private property is taken or damaged by the state or the counties or municipalities of the state for public road or street purposes, or for public transportation purposes, or for any other public purposes as determined by the General Assembly, just and adequate compensation therefor need not be paid until the same has been finally fixed and determined as provided by law; but such just and adequate compensation shall then be paid in preference to all other obligations except bonded indebtedness.

(c) The General Assembly may by law require the condemnor to make prepayment against adequate compensation as a condition precedent to the exercise of the right of eminent domain and provide for the disbursement of the same to the end that the rights and equities of the property owner, lien holders, and the state and its subdivisions may be protected.

(d) The General Assembly may provide by law for the payment by the condemnor of reasonable expenses, including attorney's fees, incurred by the condemnee in determining just and adequate compensation.

(e) Notwithstanding any other provision of the Constitution, the General Assembly may provide by law for relocation assistance and payments to persons displaced through the exercise of the power of eminent domain or because of public projects or programs; and the powers of taxation may be exercised and public funds expended in furtherance thereof.

Paragraph II. **Private ways.** In case of necessity, private ways may be granted upon just and adequate compensation being first paid by the applicant.

Paragraph III. **Tidewater titles confirmed.** The Act of the General Assembly approved December 16, 1902, which extends the title of ownership of lands abutting on tidal water to low water mark, is hereby ratified and confirmed.

ARTICLE II.
VOTING AND ELECTIONS
Section I.
Method of Voting; Right to Register and Vote

Paragraph I. **Method of voting.** Elections by the people shall be by secret ballot and shall be conducted in accordance with procedures provided by law.

Paragraph II. **Right to register and vote.** Every person who is a citizen of the United States and a resident of Georgia as defined by law, who is at least 18 years of age and not disenfranchised by this article, and who meets minimum residency requirements as provided by law shall be entitled to vote at any election by the people. The General Assembly shall provide by law for the registration of electors.

Paragraph III. **Exceptions to right to register and vote.**

(a) No person who has been convicted of a felony involving moral turpitude may register, remain registered, or vote except upon completion of the sentence.

(b) No person who has been judicially determined to be mentally incompetent may register, remain registered, or vote unless the disability has been removed.

Section II.
General Provisions

Paragraph I. **Procedures to be provided by law.** The General Assembly shall provide by law for a method of appeal from the decision to allow or refuse to allow any person to register or vote and shall provide by law for a procedure whereby returns of all elections by the people shall be made to the Secretary of State.

Paragraph II. **Run-off election.** A run-off election shall be a continuation of the general election and only persons who were entitled to vote in the general election shall be entitled to vote therein; and only those votes cast for the persons designated for the runoff shall be counted in the tabulation and canvass of the votes cast.

Paragraph III. **Persons not eligible to hold office.** No person who is not a registered voter or who has been convicted of a felony involving moral turpitude, unless that person's civil rights have been restored, or who is the holder of public funds illegally shall be eligible to hold any office or appointment of honor or trust in this state. Additional conditions of eligibility to hold office for persons elected on a write-in vote and for persons holding offices or appointments of honor or trust other than elected offices created by this Constitution may be provided by law.

Paragraph IV. **Recall of public officials holding elective office.** The General Assembly is hereby authorized to provide by general law for the recall of public officials who hold elective office. The procedures, grounds, and all other matters relative to such recall shall be provided for in such law.

Paragraph V. **Vacancies created by elected officials qualifying for other office.** The office of any state, county, or municipal elected official shall be declared vacant upon such elected official qualifying, in a general primary or general election, or special primary or special election, for another state, county, or municipal elective office or qualifying for the House of Representatives or the Senate of the United States if the term of the office for which such official is qualifying for begins more than 30 days prior to the expiration of such official's present term of office. The vacancy created in any such office shall be filled as provided by this Constitution or any general or local law. This provision shall not apply to any elected official seeking or holding more than one elective office when the holding of such offices simultaneously is specifically authorized by law.

Section III.
Suspension and Removal
of Public Officials

Paragraph I. **Procedures for and effect of suspending or removing public officials upon felony indictment.**

(a) As used in this Paragraph, the term "public official" means the Governor, the Lieutenant Governor, the Secretary of State, the Attorney General, the State School Superintendent, the Commissioner of Insurance, the Commissioner of Agriculture, the Commissioner of Labor, and any member of the General Assembly.

(b) Upon indictment for a felony by a grand jury of this state, which felony indictment relates to the performance or activities of the office of any public official, the Attorney General or district attorney shall transmit a certified copy of the indictment to the Governor or, if the indicted public official is the Governor, to the Lieutenant Governor who shall, subject to subparagraph (d) of this Paragraph, appoint a review commission. If the indicted public official is the Governor, the commission shall be composed of the Attorney General, the Secretary of State, the State School Superintendent, the Commissioner of Insurance, the Commissioner of Agriculture, and the Commissioner of Labor. If the indicted public official is the Attorney General, the commission shall be composed of three other public officials who are not members of the General Assembly. If the indicted public official is not the Governor, the Attorney General, or a member of the General Assembly, the commission shall be composed of the Attorney General and two other public officials who are not members of the General Assembly. If the indicted public official is a member of the General Assembly, the commission shall be composed of the Attorney General and one member of the Senate and one member of the House of Representatives. If the Attorney General brings the indictment against the public official, the Attorney General shall not serve on the commission. In place of the Attorney General, the Governor shall appoint a retired Supreme Court Justice or a retired Court of Appeals Judge. The commission shall provide for a speedy hearing, including notice of the nature and cause of the hearing, process for obtaining witnesses, and the assistance of counsel. Unless a longer period of time is granted by the appointing authority, the commission shall make a written report within 14 days. If the commission determines that the indictment relates to and adversely affects the administration of the office of the indicted public official and that the rights and interests of the public are adversely affected thereby, the Governor or, if the Governor is the indicted public official, the Lieutenant Governor shall suspend the public official immediately and without further action pending the final disposition of the case or until the expiration of the officer's term of office, whichever occurs first. During the term of office to which such officer was elected and in which the indictment occurred, if a nolle prosequi is entered, if the public official is acquitted, or if after conviction the conviction is later overturned as a result of any direct appeal or application for a writ of certiorari, the officer shall be immediately reinstated to the office from which he was suspended. While a public official is suspended under this Paragraph and until final conviction, the officer shall continue to receive the compensation from his office.

(c) Unless the Governor is the public officer under suspension, for the duration of any suspension under this Paragraph, the Governor shall appoint a replacement officer except in the case of a member of the General Assembly. If the Governor is the public officer under suspension, the provisions of Article V, Section I, Paragraph V of this Constitution shall apply as if the Governor were temporarily disabled. Upon a final conviction with no appeal or review pending, the office shall be declared vacant and a successor to that office shall be chosen as provided in this Constitution or the laws enacted in pursuance thereof.

(d) No commission shall be appointed for a period of 14 days from the day the indictment is received. This period of time may be extended by the Governor. During this period of time, the indicted public official may, in writing, authorize the Governor or, if the Governor is the indicted public official, the Lieutenant Governor to suspend him from office. Any such voluntary suspension shall be subject to the same conditions for review, reinstatement, or declaration of vacancy as are provided in this Paragraph for a nonvoluntary suspension.

(e) After any suspension is imposed under this Paragraph, the suspended public official may petition the appointing authority for a review. The Governor or, if the indicted public official is the Governor, the Lieutenant Governor may reappoint the commission to review the suspension. The commission shall make a written report within 14 days. If the commission recommends that the public official be reinstated, he shall immediately be reinstated to office.

(f) The report and records of the commission and the fact that the public official has or has not been suspended shall not be admissible in evidence in any court for any purpose. The report and record of the commission shall not be open to the public.

(g) The provisions of this Paragraph shall not apply to any indictment handed down prior to January 1, 1985.

(h) If a public official who is suspended from office under the provisions of this Paragraph is not first tried at the next regular or special term following the indictment, the suspension shall be terminated and the public official shall be reinstated to office. The public official shall not be reinstated under this subparagraph if he is not so tried based on a continuance granted upon a motion made only by the defendant.

Paragraph II. **Suspension upon felony conviction.** Upon initial conviction of any public official designated in Paragraph I of this section for any felony in a trial court of this state or the United States, regardless of whether the officer has been suspended previously under Paragraph I of this section, such public official shall be immediately and without further action suspended from office. While a public official is suspended from office under this Paragraph, he shall not be entitled to receive the compensation from his office. If the conviction is later overturned as a result of any direct appeal or application for a writ of certiorari, the public official shall be immediately reinstated to the office from which he was suspended and shall be entitled to receive any compensation withheld under the provisions of this Paragraph. Unless the Governor is the public official under suspension, for the duration of any suspension under this Paragraph, the Governor shall appoint a replacement official except in the case of a member of the General Assembly. If the Governor is the public officer under suspension, the provisions of Article V, Section I, Paragraph V of this Constitution shall apply as if the Governor were temporarily disabled. Upon a final conviction with no appeal or review pending, the office shall be declared vacant and a successor to that office shall be chosen as provided in this Constitution or the laws enacted in pursuance thereof. The provisions of this Paragraph shall not apply to any conviction rendered prior to January 1, 1987.

ARTICLE III.
LEGISLATIVE BRANCH
Section I.
Legislative Power

Paragraph I. **Power vested in General Assembly.** The legislative power of the state shall be vested in a General Assembly which shall consist of a Senate and a House of Representatives.

Section II.
Composition of General Assembly

Paragraph I. **Senate and House of Representatives.**

(a) The Senate shall consist of not more than 56 Senators, each of whom shall be elected from single-member districts.

(b) The House of Representatives shall consist of not fewer than 180 Representatives apportioned among representative districts of the state.

Paragraph II. **Apportionment of General Assembly.** The General Assembly shall apportion the Senate and House districts. Such districts shall be composed of contiguous territory. The apportionment of the Senate and of the House of Representatives shall be changed by the General Assembly as necessary after each United States decennial census.

Paragraph III. **Qualifications of members of General Assembly.**

(a) At the time of their election, the members of the Senate shall be citizens of the United States, shall be at least 25 years of age, shall have been citizens of this state for at least two years, and shall have been legal residents of the territory embraced within the district from which elected for at least one year.

(b) At the time of their election, the members of the House of Representatives shall be citizens of the United States, shall be at least 21 years of age, shall have been citizens of this state for at least two years, and shall have been legal residents of the territory embraced within the district from which elected for at least one year.

Paragraph IV. **Disqualifications.**

(a) No person on a branch of the armed forces of the United States shall have a seat in either house unless otherwise provided by law.

(b) No person holding any civil appointment or office having any emolument annexed thereto under the United States, this state, or any other state shall have a seat in either house.

(c) No Senator or Representative shall be elected by the General Assembly or appointed by the Governor to any office or appointment having any emolument annexed thereto during the time for which such person shall have been elected unless the Senator or Representative shall first resign the seat to which elected; provided, however, that, during the term for which elected, no Senator or Representative shall be appointed to any civil office which has been created during such term.

Paragraph V. **Election and term of members.**

(a) The members of the General Assembly shall be elected by the qualified electors of their respective districts for a term of two years and shall serve until the time fixed for the convening of the next General Assembly.

(b) The members of the General Assembly in office on June 30, 1983, shall serve out the remainder of the terms to which elected.

(c) The first election for members of the General Assembly under this Constitution shall take place on Tuesday after the first Monday in November, 1984, and subsequent elections biennially on that day until the day of election is changed by law.

Section III.
Officers of the General Assembly

Paragraph I. President and President Pro Tempore of the Senate.

(a) The presiding officer of the Senate shall be styled the President of the Senate.

(b) A President Pro Tempore shall be elected by the Senate from among its members. The President Pro Tempore shall act as President in case of the temporary disability of the President. In case of the death, resignation, or permanent disability of the President or in the event of the succession of the President to the executive power, the President Pro Tempore shall become President and shall receive the same compensation and allowances as the Speaker of the House of Representatives. The General Assembly shall provide by law for the method of determining disability as provided in this Paragraph.

Paragraph II. Speaker and Speaker Pro Tempore of the House of Representatives.

(a) The presiding officer of the House of Representatives shall be styled the Speaker of the House of Representatives and shall be elected by the House of Representatives from among its members.

(b) A Speaker Pro Tempore shall be elected by the House of Representatives from among its members. The Speaker Pro Tempore shall become Speaker in case of the death, resignation, or permanent disability of the Speaker and shall serve until a Speaker is elected. Such election shall be held as provided in the rules of the House. The General Assembly shall provide by law for the method of determining disability as provided in this Paragraph.

Paragraph III. Other officers of the two houses. The other officers of the two houses shall be a Secretary of the Senate and a Clerk of the House of Representatives.

Section IV.
Organization and Procedure of the General Assembly

Paragraph I. Meeting, time limit, and adjournment.

(a) The Senate and House of Representatives shall organize each odd-numbered year and shall be a different General Assembly for each two-year period. The General Assembly shall meet in regular session on the second Monday in January of each year, or otherwise as provided by law, and may continue in session for a period of no longer than 40 days in the aggregate each year. By concurrent resolution, the General Assembly may adjourn any regular session to such later date as it may fix for reconvening. Separate periods of adjournment may be fixed by one or more such concurrent resolutions.

(b) Neither house shall adjourn during a regular session for more than three days or meet in any place other than the state capitol without the consent of the other. Following the fifth day of a special session, either house may adjourn not more than twice for a period not to exceed seven days for each such adjournment. In the event either house, after the thirtieth day of any session, adopts a resolution to adjourn for a specified period of time and such resolution and any amendments thereto are not adopted by both houses by the end of the legislative day on which adjournment was called for in such resolution, the Governor may adjourn both houses for a period of time not to exceed ten days.

(c) If an impeachment trial is pending at the end of any session, the House shall adjourn and the Senate shall remain in session until such trial is completed.

Paragraph II. Oath of members. Each Senator and Representative, before taking the seat to which elected, shall take the oath or affirmation prescribed by law.

Paragraph III. Quorum. A majority of the members to which each house is entitled shall constitute a quorum to transact business. A smaller number may adjourn from day to day and compel the presence of its absent members.

Paragraph IV. **Rules of procedure; employees; interim committees.** Each house shall determine its rules of procedure and may provide for its employees. Interim committees may be created by or pursuant to the authority of the General Assembly or of either house.

Paragraph V. **Vacancies.** When a vacancy occurs in the General Assembly, it shall be filled as provided by this Constitution and by law. The seat of a member of either house shall be vacant upon the removal of such member's legal residence from the district from which elected.

Paragraph VI. **Salaries.** The members of the General Assembly shall receive such salary as shall be provided for by law, provided that no increase in salary shall become effective prior to the end of the term during which such change is made.

Paragraph VII. **Election and returns; disorderly conduct.** Each house shall be the judge of the election, returns, and qualifications of its members and shall have power to punish them for disorderly behavior or misconduct by censure, fine, imprisonment, or expulsion; but no member shall be expelled except by a vote of two-thirds of the members of the house to which such member belongs.

Paragraph VIII. **Contempts, how punished.** Each house may punish by imprisonment, not extending beyond the session, any person not a member who shall be guilty of a contempt by any disorderly behavior in its presence or who shall rescue or attempt to rescue any person arrested by order of either house.

Paragraph IX. **Privilege of members.** The members of both houses shall be free from arrest during sessions of the General Assembly, or committee meetings thereof, and in going thereto or returning therefrom, except for treason, felony, or breach of the peace. No member shall be liable to answer in any other place for anything spoken in either house or in any committee meeting of either house.

Paragraph X. **Elections by either house.** All elections by either house of the General Assembly shall be by recorded vote, and the vote shall appear on the respective journal of each house.

Paragraph XI. **Open meetings.** The sessions of the General Assembly and all standing committee meetings thereof shall be open to the public. Either house may by rule provide for exceptions to this requirement.

Section V.
Enactment of Laws

Paragraph I. **Journals and laws.** Each house shall keep and publish after its adjournment a journal of its proceedings. The original journals shall be the sole, official records of the proceedings of each house and shall be preserved as provided by law. The General Assembly shall provide for the publication of the laws passed at each session.

Paragraph II. **Bills for revenue.** All bills for raising revenue, or appropriating money, shall originate in the House of Representatives.

Paragraph III. **One subject matter expressed.** No bill shall pass which refers to more than one subject matter or contains matter different from what is expressed in the title thereof.

Paragraph IV. **Statutes and sections of Code, how amended.** No law or section of the Code shall be amended or repealed by mere reference to its title or to the number of the section of the Code; but the amending or repealing Act shall distinctly describe the law or Code section to be amended or repealed as well as the alteration to be made.

Paragraph V. **Majority of members to pass bill.** No bill shall become law unless it shall receive a majority of the votes of all the members to which each house is entitled, and such vote shall so appear on the journal of each house.

Paragraph VI. **When roll-call vote taken.** In either house, when ordered by the presiding officer or at the desire of one-fifth of the members present or a lesser number if so provided by the rules of either house, a roll-call vote on any question shall be taken and shall be entered on the journal. The yeas and nays in each house shall be recorded and entered on the journal upon the passage or rejection of any bill or resolution appropriating money and whenever the Constitution requires a vote of two-thirds of either or both houses for the passage of a bill or resolution.

Paragraph VII. **Reading of general bills.** The title of every general bill and of every resolution intended to have the effect of general law or to amend this Constitution or to propose a new Constitution shall be read three times and on three separate days in each house before such bill or resolution shall be voted upon; and the third reading of such bill and resolution shall be in their entirety when ordered by the presiding officer or by a majority of the members voting on such question in either house.

Paragraph VIII. **Procedure for considering local legislation.** The General Assembly may provide by law for the procedure for considering local legislation. The title of every local bill and every resolution intended to have the effect of local law shall be read at least once before such bill or resolution shall be voted upon; and no such bill or resolution shall be voted upon prior to the second day following the day of introduction.

Paragraph IX. **Advertisement of notice to introduce local legislation.** The General Assembly shall provide by law for the advertisement of notice of intention to introduce local bills.

Paragraph X. **Acts signed.** All Acts shall be signed by the President of the Senate and the Speaker of the House of Representatives.

Paragraph XI. **Signature of Governor.** No provision in this Constitution for a two-thirds' vote of both houses of the General Assembly shall be construed to waive the necessity for the signature of the Governor as in any other case, except in the case of the two-thirds' vote required to override the veto or to submit proposed constitutional amendments or a proposal for a new Constitution.

Paragraph XII. **Rejected bills.** No bill or resolution intended to have the effect of law which shall have been rejected by either house shall again be proposed during the same regular or special session under the same or any other title without the consent of two-thirds of the house by which the same was rejected.

Paragraph XIII. **Approval, veto, and override of veto of bills and resolutions.**

(a) All bills and all resolutions which have been passed by the General Assembly intended to have the effect of law shall become law if the Governor approves or fails to veto the same within six days from the date any such bill or resolution is transmitted to the Governor unless the General Assembly adjourns sine die or adjourns for more than 40 days prior to the expiration of said six days. In the case of such adjournment sine die or of such adjournment for more than 40 days, the same shall become law if approved or not vetoed by the Governor within 40 days from the date of any such adjournment.

(b) During sessions of the General Assembly or during any period of adjournment of a session of the General Assembly, no bill or resolution shall be transmitted to the Governor after passage except upon request of the Governor or upon order of two-thirds of the membership of each house. A local bill which is required by the Constitution to have a referendum election conducted before it shall become effective shall be transmitted immediately to the Governor when ordered by the presiding officer of the house wherein the bill shall have originated or upon order of two-thirds of the membership of such house.

(c) The Governor shall have the duty to transmit any vetoed bill or resolution, together with the reasons for such veto, to the presiding officer of the house wherein it originated within three days from the date of veto if the General Assembly is in session on the date of transmission. If the General Assembly adjourns sine die or adjourns for more than 40 days, the Governor shall transmit any vetoed bill or resolution, together with the reasons for such veto, to the presiding officer of the house wherein it originated within 60 days of the date of such adjournment.

(d) During sessions of the General Assembly, any vetoed bill or resolution may upon receipt be immediately considered by the house wherein it originated for the purpose of overriding the veto. If two-thirds of the members to which such house is entitled vote to override the veto of the Governor, the same shall be immediately transmitted to the other house where it shall be immediately considered. Upon the vote to override the veto by two-thirds of the members to which such other house is entitled, such bill or resolution shall become law. All bills and resolutions vetoed during the last three days of the session and not considered for the purpose of overriding the veto and all bills and resolutions vetoed after the General Assembly has adjourned sine die may be considered at the next session of the General Assembly for the purpose of overriding the veto in the manner herein provided. If either house shall fail to override the Governor's veto, neither house shall again consider such bill or resolution for the purpose of overriding such veto.

(e) The Governor may approve any appropriation and veto any other appropriation in the same bill, and any appropriation vetoed shall not become law unless such veto is overridden in the manner herein provided.

Paragraph XIV. **Jointly sponsored bills and resolutions.** The General Assembly may provide by law for the joint sponsorship of bills and resolutions.

Section VI.
Exercise of Powers

Paragraph I. **General powers.** The General Assembly shall have the power to make all laws not inconsistent with this Constitution, and not repugnant to the Constitution of the United States, which it shall deem necessary and proper for the welfare of the state.

Paragraph II. **Specific powers.**

(a) Without limitation of the powers granted under Paragraph I, the General Assembly shall have the power to provide by law for:

(1) Restrictions upon land use in order to protect and preserve the natural resources, environment, and vital areas of this state.

(2) A militia and for the trial by courts-martial and nonjudicial punishment of its members, the discipline of whom, when not in federal service, shall be in accordance with law and the directives of the Governor acting as commander in chief.

(3) The participation by the state and political subdivisions and instrumentalities of the state in federal programs and the compliance with laws relating thereto, including but not limited to the powers, which may be exercised to the extent and in the manner necessary to effect such participation and compliance, to tax, to expend public money, to condemn property, and to zone property.

(4) The continuity of state and local governments in periods of emergency resulting from disasters caused by enemy attack including but not limited to the suspension of all constitutional legislative rules during such emergency.

(5) The participation by the state with any county, municipality, nonprofit organization, or any combination thereof in the operation of any of the facilities operated by such agencies for the purpose of encouraging and promoting tourism in this state.

(6) The control and regulation of outdoor advertising devices adjacent to federal and interstate and primary highways and for the acquisition of property or interest therein for such purposes and may exercise the powers of taxation and provide for the expenditure of public funds in connection therewith.

(b) The General Assembly shall have the power to implement the provisions of Article I, Section III, Paragraph I(b.); Article IV, Section VIII, Paragraph II; Article IV, Section VIII, Paragraph III; and Article X, Section II, Paragraph XII of the Constitution of 1976 in force and effect on June 30, 1983; and all laws heretofore adopted thereunder and valid at the time of their enactment shall continue in force and effect until modified or repealed.

Paragraph III. **Powers not to be abridged.** The General Assembly shall not abridge its powers under this Constitution. No law enacted by the General Assembly shall be construed to limit its powers.

Paragraph IV. **Limitations on special legislation.**

(a) Laws of a general nature shall have uniform operation throughout this state and no local or special law shall be enacted in any case for which provision has been made by an existing general law, except that the General Assembly may by general law authorize local governments by local ordinance or resolution to exercise police powers which do not conflict with general laws.

(b) No population bill, as the General Assembly shall define by general law, shall be passed. No bill using classification by population as a means of determining the applicability of any bill or law to any political subdivision or group of political subdivisions may expressly or impliedly amend, modify, supersede, or repeal the general law defining a population bill.

(c) No special law relating to the rights or status of private persons shall be enacted.

Paragraph V. **Specific limitations.**

(a) The General Assembly shall not have the power to grant incorporation to private persons but shall provide by general law the manner in which private corporate powers and privileges may be granted.

(b) The General Assembly shall not forgive the forfeiture of the charter of any corporation existing on August 13, 1945, nor shall it grant any benefit to or permit any amendment to the charter of any corporation except upon the condition that the acceptance thereof shall operate as a novation of the charter and that such corporation shall thereafter hold its charter subject to the provisions of this Constitution.

(c) The General Assembly shall not have the power to authorize any contract or agreement which may have the effect of or which is intended to have the effect of defeating or lessening competition, or encouraging a monopoly, which are hereby declared to be unlawful and void.

(d) The General Assembly shall not have the power to regulate or fix charges of public utilities owned and operated by any county or municipality of this state, except as authorized by this Constitution.

(e) No municipal or county authority which is authorized to construct, improve, or maintain any road or street on behalf of, pursuant to a contract with, or through the use of taxes or other revenues of a county or municipal corporation shall be created by any local Act or pursuant to any general Act nor shall any law specifically relating to any such authority be amended unless the creation of such authority or the amendment of such law is conditioned upon the approval of a majority of the qualified voters of the county or municipal corporation affected voting in a referendum thereon. This subparagraph shall not apply to or affect any state authority.

Paragraph VI. **Gratuities.**

(a) Except as otherwise provided in the Constitution, (1) the General Assembly shall not have the power to grant any donation or gratuity or to forgive any debt or obligation owing to the public, and (2) the General Assembly shall not grant or authorize extra compensation to any public officer, agent, or contractor after the service has been rendered or the contract entered into.

(b) All laws heretofore adopted under Article III, Section VIII, Paragraph XII of the Constitution of 1976 in force and effect on June 30, 1983, shall continue in force and effect and may be amended if such amendments are consistent with the authority granted to the General Assembly by such provisions of said Constitution.

(c) The General Assembly may provide by law and may expend or authorize the expenditure of public funds for a health insurance plan or program for persons and the spouses and dependent children of persons who are retired former employees of public schools or public school systems of this state.

(d) The General Assembly may provide by law for indemnification with respect to publicly employed emergency medical technicians who are or have been killed or permanently disabled in the line of duty on or after January 1, 1987.

(e) The General Assembly may provide by law for a program of indemnification with respect to the death or permanent disability of any law enforcement officer, fireman, prison guard, or publicly employed emergency medical technician who is or at any time in the past was killed or permanently disabled in the line of duty. Funds shall be appropriated as necessary for payment of such indemnification or for the purchase of insurance for such indemnification or both.

Section VII.
Impeachments

Paragraph I. **Power to impeach.** The House of Representatives shall have the sole power to vote impeachment charges against any executive or judicial officer of this state or any member of the General Assembly.

Paragraph II. **Trial of impeachments.** The Senate shall have the sole power to try impeachments. When sitting for that purpose, the Senators shall be on oath, or affirmation, and shall be presided over by the Chief Justice of the Supreme Court. Should the Chief Justice be disqualified, then the Presiding Justice shall preside. Should the Presiding Justice be disqualified, then the Senate shall select a Justice of the Supreme Court to preside. No person shall be convicted without concurrence of two-thirds of the members to which the Senate is entitled.

Paragraph III. **Judgments in impeachment.** In cases of impeachment, judgments shall not extend further than removal from office and disqualification to hold and enjoy any office of honor, trust, or profit with in this state or to receive a pension therefrom, but no such judgment shall relieve any party from any criminal or civil liability.

Section VIII.
Insurance Regulation

Paragraph I. **Regulation of insurance.** Provision shall be made by law for the regulation of insurance.

Paragraph II. **Issuance of licenses.** Insurance licenses shall be issued by the Commissioner of Insurance as required by law.

Section IX.
Appropriations

Paragraph I. **Public money, how drawn.** No money shall be drawn from the treasury except by appropriation made by law.

Paragraph II. **Preparation, submission, and enactments of general appropriations bill.**

(a) The Governor shall submit to the General Assembly within five days after its convening in regular session each year a budget message and a budget report, accompanied by a draft of a general appropriations bill, in such form and manner as may be prescribed by statute, which shall provide for the appropriation of the funds necessary to operate all the various departments and agencies and to meet the current expenses of the state for the next fiscal year.

(b) The General Assembly shall annually appropriate those state and federal funds necessary to operate all the various departments and agencies. To the extend that federal funds received by the state for any program, project, activity, purpose, or expenditure are changed by federal authority or exceed the amount or amounts appropriated in the general appropriations Act or supplementary appropriation Act or Acts, or are not anticipated, such excess, changed or unanticipated federal funds are hereby continually appropriated for the purposes authorized and directed by the federal government in making the grant. In those instances where the conditions under which the federal funds have been made available do not provide otherwise, federal funds shall first be used to replace state funds that were appropriated to supplant federal funds in the same state fiscal year. The fiscal year of the state shall commence on the first day of July of each year and terminate on the thirtieth of June following.

(c) The General Assembly shall by general law provide for the regulation and management of the finance and fiscal administration of the state.

Paragraph III. **General appropriations bill.** The general appropriations bill shall embrace nothing except appropriations fixed by previous laws; the ordinary expenses of the executive, legislative, and judicial departments of the government; payment of the public debt and interest thereon; and for support of the public institutions and educational interests of the state. All other appropriations shall be made by separate bills, each embracing but one subject.

Paragraph IV. **General appropriations Act.**

(a) Each general appropriations Act, now of force or hereafter adopted with such amendments as are adopted from time to time, shall continue in force and effect for the next fiscal year after adoption and it shall then expire, except for the mandatory appropriations required by this Constitution and those required to meet contractual obligations authorized by this Constitution and the continued appropriation of federal grants.

(b) The General Assembly shall not appropriate funds for any given fiscal year which, in aggregate, exceed a sum equal to the amount of unappropriated surplus expected to have accrued in the state treasury at the beginning of the fiscal year together with an amount not greater than the total treasury receipts from existing revenue sources anticipated to be collected in the fiscal year, less refunds, as estimated in the budget report and amendments thereto. Supplementary appropriations, if any, shall be made in the manner provided in Paragraph V of this section of the Constitution; but in no event shall a supplementary appropriations Act continue in force and effect beyond the expiration of the general appropriations Act in effect when such supplementary appropriations Act was adopted and approved.

(c) All appropriated state funds, except for the mandatory appropriations required by this Constitution, remaining unexpended and not contractually obligated at the expiration of such general appropriations Act shall lapse.

Paragraph V. **Other or supplementary appropriations.** In addition to the appropriations made by the general appropriations Act and amendments thereto, the General Assembly may make additional appropriations by Acts, which shall be known as supplementary appropriation Acts, provided no such supplementary appropriation shall be available unless there is an unappropriated surplus in the state treasury or the revenue necessary to pay such appropriation shall have been provided by a tax laid for such purpose and collected into the general fund of the state treasury. Neither house shall pass a supplementary appropriation bill until the general appropriations Act shall have been finally adopted by both houses and approved by the Governor.

Paragraph VI. **Appropriations to be for specific sums.**

(a) Except as hereinafter provided, the appropriation for each department, officer, bureau, board, commission, agency, or institution for which appropriation is made shall be for a specific sum of money; and no appropriation shall allocate to any object the proceeds of any particular tax or fund or a part or percentage thereof.

(b) An amount equal to all money derived from motor fuel taxes received by the state in each of the immediately preceding fiscal years, less the amount of refunds, rebates, and collection costs authorized by law, is hereby appropriated for the fiscal year beginning July 1, of each year following, for all activities incident to providing and maintaining an adequate system of public roads and bridges in this state, as authorized by laws enacted by the General Assembly of Georgia, and for grants to counties by law authorizing road construction and maintenance, as provided by law authorizing such grants. Said sum is hereby appropriated for, and shall be available for, the aforesaid purposes regardless of whether the General Assembly enacts a general appropriations Act; and said sum need not be specifically stated in any general appropriations Act passed by the General Assembly in order to be available for such purposes. However, this shall not preclude the General Assembly from appropriating for such purposes an amount greater than the sum specified above for such purposes. The expenditure of such funds shall be subject to all the rules, regulations, and restrictions imposed on the expenditure of appropriations by provisions of the Constitution and laws of this state, unless such provisions are in conflict with the provisions of this paragraph. And provided, however, that the proceeds of the tax hereby appropriated shall not be subject to budgetary reduction. In the event of invasion of this state by land, sea, or air or in case of a major catastrophe so proclaimed by the Governor, said funds may be utilized for defense or relief purposes on the executive order of the Governor.

(c) A trust fund for use in the reimbursement of a portion of an employer's workers' compensation expenses resulting to an employee from the combination of a previous disability with subsequent injury incurred in employment may be provided for by law. As authorized by law, revenues raised for purposes of the fund may be paid into and disbursed from the trust without being subject to the limitations of subparagraph (a) of this Paragraph or of Article VII. Section III, Paragraph II.

(d) As provided by law, additional penalties may be assessed in any case in which any court in this state imposes a fine or orders the forfeiture of any bond in the nature of the penalty for all offenses against the criminal and traffic laws of this state or of the political subdivisions of this state. The proceeds derived from such additional penalty assessments may be allocated for the specific purpose of meeting any and all costs, or any portion of the cost, of providing training to law enforcement officers and to prosecuting officials.

(e) The General Assembly may by general law approved by a three-fifths' vote of both houses designate any part or all of the proceeds of any state tax now or hereafter levied and collected on alcoholic beverages to be used for prevention, education, and treatment relating to alcohol and drug abuse.

(f) The General Assembly is authorized to provide by law for the creation of a State Children's Trust Fund from which funds shall be disbursed for child abuse and neglect prevention programs. The General Assembly is authorized to appropriate moneys to such fund and such moneys paid into the fund shall not be subject to the provisions of Article III, Section IX, Paragraph IV(c), relative to the lapsing of funds.

Paragraph VII. **Appropriations void, when.** Any appropriation made in conflict with any of the foregoing provisions shall be void.

Section X.
Retirement Systems

Paragraph I. **Expenditure of public funds authorized.** Public funds may be expended for the purpose of paying benefits and other costs of retirement and pension systems for public officers and employees and their beneficiaries.

Paragraph II. **Increasing benefits authorized.** Public funds may be expended for the purpose of increasing benefits being paid pursuant to any retirement or pension system wholly or partially supported from public funds.

Paragraph III. **Retirement systems covering employees of county boards of education.** Notwithstanding Article IX, Section II, Paragraph III(a)(14), the authority to establish or modify heretofore existing local retirement systems covering employees of county boards of education shall continue to be vested in the General Assembly.

Paragraph IV. **Firemen's Pension System.** The powers of taxation may be exercised by the state through the General Assembly and the counties and municipalities for the purpose of paying pensions and other benefits and costs under a firemen's pension system or systems. The taxes so levied may be collected by such firemen's pension system or systems and disbursed therefrom by authority of the General Assembly for the purposes therein authorized.

Paragraph V. **Funding standards.** It shall be the duty of the General Assembly to enact legislation to define funding standards which will assure the actuarial soundness of any retirement or pension system supported wholly or partially from public funds and to control legislative procedures so that no bill or resolution creating or amending any such retirement or pension system shall be passed by the General Assembly without concurrent provisions for funding in accordance with the defined funding standards.

Paragraph V-A. **Limitations on involuntary separation benefits for Governor of the State of Georgia.** Any other provisions of this Constitution to the contrary notwithstanding, no past, present, or future Governor of the State of Georgia who ceases or ceased to hold office as Governor for any reason, except for medical disability, shall receive a retirement benefit based on involuntary separation from employment as a result of ceasing to hold office as Governor. The provisions of any law in conflict with this Paragraph are null and void effective January 1, 1985.

Paragraph VI. **Involuntary separation; part-time service.**

(a) Any public retirement or pension system provided for by law in existence prior to January 1, 1985, may be changed by the General Assembly for any one or more of the following purposes:

(1) To redefine involuntary separation from employment; or

(2) To provide additional or revise existing limitations or restrictions on the right to qualify for a retirement benefit based on involuntary separation from employment.

(b) The General Assembly by law may define or redefine part-time service, including but not limited to service as a member of the General Assembly, for the purposes of any public retirement or pension system presently existing or created in the future and may limit or restrict the use of such part-time service as creditable service under any such retirement or pension system.

(c) Any law enacted by the General Assembly pursuant to subparagraph (a) or (b) of this Paragraph may affect persons who are members of public retirement or pension systems on January 1, 1985, and who became members at any time prior to that date.

(d) Any law enacted by the General Assembly pursuant to subparagraph (a) or (b) of this Paragraph shall not be subject to any law controlling legislative procedures for the consideration of retirement or pension bills, including, but not limited to, any limitations on the sessions of the General Assembly at which retirement or pension bills may be introduced.

(c) No public retirement or pension system created on or after January 1, 1985, shall grant any person whose retirement is based on involuntary separation from the employment a retirement or pension benefit more favorable than the retirement or pension benefit granted to a person whose separation from employment is voluntary.

ARTICLE IV.
CONSTITUTIONAL BOARDS AND COMMISSIONS
Section I.
Public Service Commission

Paragraph I. **Public Service Commission.**

(a) There shall be a Public Service Commission for the regulation of utilities which shall consist of five members who shall be elected by the people. The Commissioners in office on June 30, 1983, shall serve until December 31 after the general election at which the successor of each member is elected. Thereafter, all succeeding terms of members shall be for six years. Members shall serve until their successors are elected and qualified. A chairman shall be selected by the members of the commission from its membership.

(b) The commission shall be vested with such jurisdiction, powers, and duties as provided by law.

(c) The filling of vacancies and manner and time of election of members of the commission shall be as provided by law.

Section II.
State Board of Pardons and Paroles

Paragraph I. **State Board of Pardons and Paroles.** There shall be a State Board of Pardons and Paroles which shall consist of five members appointed by the Governor, subject to confirmation by the Senate. The members of the board in office on June 30, 1983, shall serve out the remainder of their respective terms, provided that the expiration date of the term of any such member shall be December 31 of the year in which the member's term expires. As each term of office expires, the Governor shall appoint a successor as herein provided. All such terms of members shall be for seven years. A chairman shall be selected by the members of the board from its membership.

Paragraph II. **Powers and authority.**

(a) Except as otherwise provided in this Paragraph, the State Board of Pardons and Paroles shall be vested with the power of executive clemency, including the powers to grant reprieves, pardons, and paroles; to commute penalties; to remove disabilities imposed by law; and to remit any part of a sentence for any offense against the state after conviction.

(b) When a sentence of death is commuted to life improsonment, the board shall not have the authority to grant a pardon to the convicted person until such person has served at least 25 years in the penitentiary; and such person shall not become eligible for parole at any time prior to serving at least 25 years in the penitentiary. When a person is convicted of armed robbery, the board shall not have the authority to consider such person for pardon or parole until such person has served at least five years in the penitentiary.

(c) Notwithstanding the provisions of subparagraph (b) of this Paragraph, the General Assembly, by law, may prohibit the board from granting and may prescribe the terms and conditions for the board's granting a pardon or parole to:

(1) An person incarcerated for a second or subsequent time for any offense for which such person could have been sentenced to life imprisonment; and

(2) Any person who has received consecutive life sentences as the result of offenses occurring during the same series of acts.

(d) The chairman of the board, or any other member designated by the board, may suspend the execution of a sentence of death until the full board shall have an opportunity to hear the application of the convicted person for any relief within the power of the board.

(e) Notwithstanding any other provisions of this Paragraph, the State Board of Pardons and Paroles shall have the authority to pardon any person convicted of a crime who is subsequently determined to be innocent of said crime.

Section III.
State Personnel Board

Paragraph I. **State Personnel Board.**

(a) There shall be a State Personnel Board which shall consist of five members appointed by the Governor, subject to confirmation by the Senate. The members of the board in office on June 30, 1983, shall serve out the remainder of their respective terms. As each term of office expires, the Governor shall appoint a successor as herein provided. All such terms of members shall be for five years. Members shall serve until their successors are appointed and qualified. A member of the State Personnel Board may not be employed in any other capacity in state government. A chairman shall be selected by the members of the board from its membership.

(b) The board shall provide policy direction for a State Merit System of Personnel Administration and may be vested with such additional powers and duties as provided by law. State personnel shall be selected on the basis of merit as provided by law.

Paragraph II. **Veterans preference.** Any veteran who has served as a member of the armed forces of the United States during the period of a war or armed conflict in which any branch of the armed forces of the United States engaged, whether under United States command or otherwise, and was honorably discharged therefrom, shall be given such veterans preference in any civil service program established in state government as may be provided by law. Any such law must provide at least ten points to a veteran having at least a 10 percent service connected disability as rated and certified by the Veterans Administration, and all other such veterans shall be entitled to at least five points.

Section IV.
State Transportation Board

Paragraph I. **State Transportation Board; commissioner.**

(a) There shall be a State Transportation Board composed of as many members as there are congressional districts in the state. The member of the board from each congressional district shall be elected by a majority vote of the members of the House of Representatives and Senate whose respective districts are embraced or partly embraced within such congressional district meeting in caucus. The members of the board in office on June 30, 1983, shall serve out the remainder of their respective terms. The General Assembly shall provide by law the procedure for the election of members and for filling vacancies on the board. Members shall serve for terms of five years and until their successors are elected and qualified.

(b) The State Transportation Board shall select a commissioner of transportation, who shall be the chief executive officer of the Department of Transportation and who shall have such powers and duties as provided by law.

Section V.
Veterans Service Board

Paragraph I. **Veterans Service Board; commissioner.**

(a) There shall be a State Department of Veterans Service and Veterans Service Board which shall consist of seven members appointed by the Governor, subject to confirmation by the Senate. The members in office on June 30, 1983, shall serve out the remainder of their respective terms. As each term of office expires, the Governor shall appoint a successor as herein provided. All such terms of members shall be for seven years. Members shall serve until their successors are appointed and qualified.

(b) The board shall appoint a commissioner who shall be the executive officer of the department. All members of the board and the commissioner shall be veterans of some war or armed conflict in which the United States has engaged. The board shall have such control, duties, powers, and jurisdiction of the State Department of Veterans Service as shall be provided by law.

Section VI.
Board of Natural Resources

Paragraph I. **Board of Natural Resources.**

(a) There shall be a Board of Natural Resources which shall consist of one member from each congressional district in the state and five members from the state at large, one of whom must be from one of the following named counties: Chatham, Bryan, Liberty, McIntosh, Glynn, or Camden. All members shall be appointed by the Governor, subject to confirmation by the Senate. The members of the board in office on June 30, 1983, shall serve out the remainder of their respective terms. As each term of office expires, the Governor shall appoint a successor as herein provided. All such terms of members shall be for seven years. Members shall serve until their successors are appointed and qualified. Insofar as it is practicable, the members of the board shall be representative of all areas and functions encompassed within the Department of Natural Resources.

(b) The board shall have such powers and duties as provided by law.

Section VII.
Qualifications, Compensation, Removal from Office,
and Powers and Duties of Members of
Constitutional Boards and Commissions

Paragraph I. **Qualifications, compensation, and removal from office.** The qualifications, compensation, and removal from office of members of constitutional boards and commissions provided for in this article shall be as provided by law.

Paragraph II. **Powers and duties.** The powers and duties of members of constitutional boards and commissions provided for in this article, except the Board of Pardons and Paroles, shall be as provided by law.

ARTICLE V.
EXECUTIVE BRANCH
Section I.
Election of Governor and Lieutenant Governor

Paragraph I. **Governor: term of office; compensation and allowances.** There shall be a Governor who shall hold office for a term of four years and until a successor shall be chosen and qualified. Persons holding the office of Governor may succeed themselves for one four-year term of office. Persons who have held the office of Governor and have succeeded themselves as hereinbefore provided shall not again be eligible to be elected to that office until after the expiration of four years from the conclusion of their term as Governor. The compensation and allowances of the Governor shall be as provided by law.

Paragraph II. **Election for Governor.** An election for Governor shall be held on Tuesday after the first Monday in November of 1986, and the Governor-elect shall be installed in office at the next session of the General Assembly. An election for Governor shall take place quadrennially thereafter on said date unless another date be fixed by the General Assembly. Said election shall be held at the places of holding general elections in the several counties of this state, in the manner prescribed for the election of members of the General Assembly, and the electors shall be the same .

Paragraph III. **Lieutenant Governor.** There shall be a Lieutenant Governor, who shall be elected at the same time, for the same term, and in the same manner as the Governor. The Lieutenant Governor shall be the President of the Senate and shall have such executive duties as prescribed by the Governor and as may be prescribed by law not inconsistent with the powers of the Governor or other provisions of this Constitution. The compensation and allowances of the Lieutenant Governor shall be as provided by law.

Paragraph IV. **Qualifications of Governor and Lieutenant Governor.** No person shall be eligible for election to the office of Governor or Lieutenant Governor unless such person shall have been a citizen of the United States 15 years and a legal resident of the state six years immediately preceding the election and shall have attained the age of 30 years by the date of assuming office.

Paragraph V. **Succession to executive power.**

(a) In case of the temporary disability of the Governor as determined in the manner provided in Section IV of this article, the Lieutenant Governor shall exercise the powers and duties of the Governor and receive the same compensation as the Governor until such time as the temporary disability of the Governor ends.

(b) In case of the death, resignation, or permanent disability of the Governor or the governor-elect, the Lieutenant Governor or the Lieutenant Governor-elect, upon becoming the Lieutenant Governor, shall become the Governor until a successor shall be elected and qualified as hereinafter provided. A successor to serve for the unexpired term shall be elected at the next general election; but, if such death, resignation, or permanent disability shall occur within 30 days of the next general election or if the term will expire within 90 days after the next general election, the Lieutenant Governor shall become Governor for the unexpired term. No person shall be elected or appointed to the office of Lieutenant Governor for the unexpired term in the event the Lieutenant Governor shall become Governor as herein provided.

(c) In case of the death, resignation, or permanent disability of both the Governor or the Governor-elect and the Lieutenant Governor or the Lieutenant Governor-elect or in case of the death, resignation, or permanent disability of the Governor and there shall be no Lieutenant Governor, the Speaker of the House of Representatives shall exercise the powers and duties of the Governor until the election and qualification of a Governor at a special election, which shall be held within 90 days from the date on which the Speaker of the House of Representatives shall have assumed the powers and duties of the Governor, and the person elected shall serve out the unexpired term.

Paragraph VI. **Oath of office.** The Governor and Lieutenant Governor shall, before entering on the duties of office, take such oath or affirmation as prescribed by law.

Section II.
Duties and Powers of Governor

Paragraph I. **Executive powers.** The chief executive powers shall be vested in the Governor. The other executive officers shall have such powers as may be prescribed by this Constitution and by law.

Paragraph II. **Law enforcement.** The Governor shall take care that the laws are faithfully executed and shall be the conservator of the peace throughout the state.

Paragraph III. **Commander-in-chief.** The Governor shall be the commander-in-chief of the military forces of this state.

Paragraph IV. **Veto power.** Except as otherwise provided in this Constitution, before any bill or resolution shall become law, the Governor shall have the right to review such bill or resolution intended to have the effect of law which has been passed by the General Assembly. The Governor may veto, approve, or take no action on any such bill or resolution. In the event the Governor vetoes any such bill or resolution, the General Assembly may, by a two-thirds' vote, override such veto as provided in Article III of this Constitution.

Paragraph V. **Writs of election.** The Governor shall issue writs of election to fill all vacancies that may occur in the Senate and in the House of Representatives.

Paragraph VI. **Information and recommendations to the General Assembly.** At the beginning of each regular session and from time to time, the Governor may give the General Assembly information on the state of the state and recommend to its consideration such measures as the Governor may deem necessary or expedient.

Paragraph VII. **Special sessions of the General Assembly.**

(a) The Governor may convene the General Assembly in special session by proclamation which may be amended by the Governor prior to the convening of the special session or amended by the Governor with the approval of three-fifths of the members of each house after the special session has convened; but no laws shall be enacted at any such special session except those which relate to the purposes stated in the proclamation or in any amendment thereto.

(b) The Governor shall convene the General Assembly in special session for all purposes whenever three-fifths of the members to which each house is entitled certify to the Governor in writing, with a copy to the Secretary of State, that in their opinion an emergency exists in the affairs of the state. The General Assembly may convene itself if, after receiving such certification, the Governor fails to do so within three days, excluding Sundays.

(c) Special sessions of the General Assembly shall be limited to a period of 40 days unless extended by three-fifths' vote of each house and approved by the Governor or unless at the expiration of such period an impeachment trial of some officer of state government is pending, in which event the House shall adjourn and the Senate shall remain in session until such trial is completed.

Paragraph VIII. **Filling vacancies.**

(a) When any public office shall become vacant by death, resignation, or otherwise, the Governor shall promptly fill such vacancy unless otherwise provided by this Constitution or by law; and persons so appointed shall serve for the unexpired term unless otherwise provided by this Constitution or by law.

(b) In case of the death or withdrawal of a person who received a majority of votes cast in an election for the office of Secretary of State, Attorney General, State School Superintendent, Commissioner of Insurance, Commissioner of Agriculture, or Commissioner of Labor, the Governor elected at the same election, upon becoming Governor, shall have the power to fill such office by appointing, subject to the confirmation of the Senate, an individual to serve until the next general election and until a successor for the balance of the unexpired term shall have been elected and qualified.

Paragraph IX. **Appointments by Governor.** The Governor shall make such appointments as are authorized by this Constitution or by law. If a person whose confirmation is required by the Senate is once rejected by the Senate, that person shall not be renominated by the Governor for appointment to the same office until the expiration of a period of one year from the date of such rejection.

Paragraph X. **Information from officers and employees.** The Governor may require information in writing from constitutional officers and all other officers and employees of the executive branch on any subject relating to the duties of their respective offices or employment.

Section III.
Other Elected Executive Officers

Paragraph I. **Other executive officers, how elected.** The Secretary of State, Attorney General, State School Superintendent, Commissioner of Insurance, Commissioner of Agriculture, and Commissioner of Labor shall be elected in the manner prescribed for the election of members of the General Assembly and the electors shall be the same. Such executive officers shall be elected at the same time and hold their offices for the same term as the Governor.

Paragraph II. **Qualifications.**

(a) No person shall be eligible to the office of the Secretary of State, Attorney General, State School Superintendent, Commissioner of Insurance, Commissioner of Agriculture, or Commissioner of Labor unless such person shall have been a citizen of the United States for ten years and a legal resident of the state for four years immediately preceding election or appointment and shall have attained the age of 25 years by the date of assuming office. All of said officers shall take such oath and give bond and security, as prescribed by law, for the faithful discharge of their duties.

(b) No person shall be Attorney General unless such person shall have been an active-status member of the State Bar of Georgia for seven years.

Paragraph III. **Powers, duties, compensation, and allowances of other executive officers.** Except as otherwise provided in this Constitution, the General Assembly shall prescribe the powers, duties, compensation, and allowances of the above executive officers and provide assistance and expenses necessary for the operation of the department of each.

Paragraph IV. **Attorney General; duties.** The Attorney General shall act as the legal advisor of the executive department, shall represent the state in the Supreme Court in all capital felonies and in all civil and criminal cases in any court when required by the Governor, and shall perform such other duties as shall be required by law.

Section IV.
Disability of Executive Officers

Paragraph I. **"Elected constitutional executive officer," how defined.** As used in this section, the term "elected constitutional executive officer" means the Governor, the Lieutenant Governor, the Secretary of State, the Attorney General, the State School Superintendent, the Commissioner of Insurance, the Commissioner of Agriculture, and the Commissioner of Labor.

Paragraph II. **Procedure for determining disability.** Upon a petition of any four of the elected constitutional executive officers to the Supreme Court of Georgia that another elected constitutional executive officer is unable to perform the duties of office because of a physical or mental disability, the Supreme Court shall by appropriate rule provide for a speedy and public hearing on such matter, including notice of the nature and cause of the accusation, process for obtaining witnesses, and the assistance of counsel. Evidence at such hearing shall include testimony from not fewer than three qualified physicians in private practice, one of whom must be a psychiatrist.

Paragraph III. **Effect of determination of disability.** If, after hearing the evidence on disability, the Supreme Court determines that there is a disability and that such disability is permanent, the office shall be declared vacant and the successor to that office shall be chosen as provided in this Constitution or the laws enacted in pursuance thereof. If it is determined that the disability is not permanent, the Supreme Court shall determine when the disability has ended and when the officer shall resume the exercise of the powers of office. During the period of temporary disability, the powers of such office shall be exercised as provided by law.

ARTICLE VI.
JUDICIAL BRANCH
Section I.
Judicial Power

Paragraph I. **Judicial power of the state.** The judicial power of the state shall be vested exclusively in the following classes of courts: magistrate courts, probate courts, juvenile courts, state courts, superior courts, Court of Appeals, and Supreme Court. Magistrate courts, probate courts, juvenile courts, and state courts shall be courts of limited jurisdiction. In addition, the General Assembly may establish or authorize the establishment of municipal courts and may authorize administrative agencies to exercise quasi-judicial powers. Municipal courts shall have jurisdiction over ordinance violations and such other jurisdiction as provided by law. Except as provided in this paragraph and in Section X, municipal courts, county recorder's courts and civil courts in existence on June 30, 1983, and administrative agencies shall not be subject to the provisions of this article.

Paragraph II. **Unified judicial system.** All courts of the state shall comprise a unified judicial system.

Paragraph III. **Judges; exercise of power outside own court; scope of term "judge."** Provided the judge is otherwise qualified, a judge may exercise judicial power in any court upon the request and with the consent of the judges of that court and of the judge's own court under rules prescribed by law. The term "judge," as used in this article, shall include Justices, judges, senior judges, magistrates, and every other such judicial office of whatever name existing or created.

Paragraph IV. **Exercise of judicial power.** Each court may exercise such powers as necessary in aid of its jurisdiction or to protect or effectuate its judgments; but only the superior and appellate courts shall have the power to issue process in the nature of mandamus, prohibition, specific performance, quo warranto, and injunction. Each superior court, state court, and other courts of record may grant new trials on legal grounds.

Paragraph V. **Uniformity of jurisdiction, powers, etc.** Except as otherwise provided in this Constitution, the courts of each class shall have uniform jurisdiction, powers, rules of practice and procedure, and selection, qualifications, terms, and discipline of judges. The provisions of this Paragraph shall be effected by law within 24 months of the effective date of this Constitution.

Paragraph VI. **Judicial circuits; courts in each county; court sessions.** The state shall be divided into judicial circuits, each of which shall consist of not less than one county. Each county shall have at least one superior court, magistrate court, a probate court, and, where needed, a state court and a juvenile court. The General Assembly may provide by law that the judge of the probate court may also serve as the judge of the magistrate court. In the absence of a state court or a juvenile court, the superior court shall exercise that jurisdiction. Superior courts shall hold court at least twice each year in each county.

Paragraph VII. **Judicial circuits, courts, and judgeships, law changed.** The General Assembly may abolish, create, consolidate, or modify judicial circuits and courts and judgeships; but no circuit shall consist of less than one county.

Paragraph VIII. **Transfer of cases.** Any court shall transfer to the appropriate court in the state any civil case in which it determines that jurisdiction or venue lies elsewhere.

Paragraph IX. **Rules of evidence; law prescribed.** All rules of evidence shall be as prescribed by law.

Section II.
Venue

Paragraph I. **Divorce cases.** Divorce cases shall be tried in the county where the defendant resides, if a resident of this state; if the defendant is not a resident of this state, then in the county in which the plaintiff resides, provided that any person who has been a resident of any United States army post or military reservation within the State of Georgia for one year next preceding the filing of the petition may bring an action for divorce in any county adjacent to said United States army post or military reservation.

Paragraph II. **Land titles.** Cases respecting titles to land shall be tried in the county where the land lies, except where a single tract is divided by a county line, in which case the superior court of either county shall have jurisdiction.

Paragraph III. **Equity cases.** Equity cases shall be tried in the county where a defendant resides against whom substantial relief is prayed.

Paragraph IV. **Suits against joint obligors, copartners, etc.** Suits against joint obligors, joint tort-feasors, joint promisors, copartners, or joint trespassers residing in different counties may be tried in either county.

Paragraph V. **Suits against maker, endorser, etc.** Suits against the maker and endorser of promissory notes, or drawer, acceptor, and endorser of foreign or inland bills of exchange, or like instruments, residing in different counties, shall be tried in the county where the maker or acceptor resides.

Paragraph VI. **All other cases.** All other civil cases, except juvenile court cases as may otherwise be provided by the Juvenile Court Code of Georgia, shall be tried in the county where the defendant resides; venue as to corporations, foreign and domestic, shall be as provided by law; and all criminal cases shall be tried in the county where the crime was committed, except cases in the superior courts where the judge is satisfied that an impartial jury cannot be obtained in such county.

Paragraph VII. **Venue in third-party practice.** The General Assembly may provide by law that venue is proper in a county other than the county of residence of a person or entity impleaded into a pending civil case by a defending party who contends that such person or entity is or may be liable to said defending party for all or part of the claim against said defending party.

Paragraph VIII. **Power to change venue.** The power to change the venue in civil and criminal cases shall be vested in the superior courts to be exercised in such manner as has been, or shall be, provided by law.

Section III.
Classes of Courts of Limited Jurisdiction

Paragraph I. **Jurisdiction of classes of courts of limited jurisdiction.** The magistrate, juvenile, and state courts shall have uniform jurisdiction as provided by law. Probate courts shall have such jurisdiction as now or hereafter provided by law, without regard to uniformity.

Section IV.
Superior Courts

Paragraph I. **Jurisdiction of superior courts.** The superior courts shall have jurisdiction in all cases, except as otherwise provided in this Constitution. They shall have exclusive jurisdiction over trials in felony cases, except in the case of juvenile offenders as provided by law; in cases respecting title to land; in divorce cases; and in equity cases. The superior courts shall have such appellate jurisdiction, either alone or by circuit or district, as may be provided by law.

Section V.
Court of Appeals

Paragraph I. **Composition of Court of Appeals; Chief Judge.** The Court of Appeals shall consist of not less than nine judges who shall elect from among themselves a Chief Judge.

Paragraph II. The Court of Appeals may sit in panels of not less than three Judges as prescribed by law or, if none, by its rules.

Paragraph III. **Jurisdiction of Court of Appeals; decisions binding.** The Court of Appeals shall be a court of review and shall exercise appellate and certiorari jurisdiction in all cases not reserved to the Supreme Court or conferred on other courts by law. The decisions of the Court of Appeals insofar as not in conflict with those of the Supreme Court shall bind all courts except the Supreme Court as precedents.

Paragraph IV. **Certification of question to Supreme Court.** The Court of appeals may certify a question to the Supreme Court for instruction, to which it shall then be bound.

Paragraph V. **Equal division of court.** In the event of an equal division of the Judges when sitting as a body, the case shall be immediately transmitted to the Supreme Court.

Section VI.
Supreme Court

Paragraph I. **Composition of Supreme Court; Chief Justice; Presiding Justice; quorum; substitute judges.** The Supreme Court shall consist of not more than nine Justices who shall elect from among themselves a Chief Justice as the chief presiding and administrative officer of the court and a Presiding Justice to serve if the Chief Justice is absent or is disqualified. A majority shall be necessary to hear and determine cases. If a Justice is disqualified in any case, a substitute judge may be designated by the remaining Justices to serve.

Paragraph II. **Exclusive appellate jurisdiction of Supreme Court.** The Supreme Court shall be a court of review and shall exercise exclusive appellate jurisdiction in the following cases:

(1) All cases involving the construction of a treaty or of the Constitution of the State of Georgia or of the United States and all cases in which the constitutionality of a law, ordinance, or constitutional provision has been drawn in question; and

(2) All cases of election contest.

Paragraph III. **General appellate jurisdiction of Supreme Court.** Unless otherwise provided by law, the Supreme Court shall have appellate jurisdiction of the following classes of cases:

(1) Cases involving title to land;

(2) All equity cases;

(3) All cases involving wills;

(4) All habeas corpus cases;

(5) All cases involving extraordinary remedies;

(6) All divorce and alimony cases;

(7) All cases certified to it by the Court of Appeals; and

(8) All cases in which a sentence of death was imposed or could be imposed. Review of all cases shall be as provided by law.

Paragraph IV. **Jurisdiction over questions of law from state or federal appellate courts.** The Supreme Court shall have jurisdiction to answer any question of law from any state or federal appellate court.

Paragraph V. **Review of cases in Court of Appeals.** The Supreme Court may review by certiorari cases in the Court of Appeals which are of gravity or great public importance.

Paragraph VI. **Decisions of Supreme Court binding.** The decisions of the Supreme Court shall bind all other courts as precedents.

Section VII.
Selection, Term, Compensation, and Discipline of Judges

Paragraph I. **Election; term of office.** All superior court and state court judges shall be elected on a nonpartisan basis for a term of four years. All Justices of the Supreme Court and the Judges of the Court of Appeals shall be elected on a nonpartisan basis for a term of six years. The terms of all judges thus elected shall begin the next January 1 after their election. All other judges shall continue to be selected in the manner and for the term they were selected on June 30, 1983, until otherwise provided by local law.

Paragraph II. **Qualifications.**

(a) Appellate and superior court judges shall have been admitted to practice law for seven years.

(b) State and juvenile court judges shall have been admitted to practice law for five years.

(c) Probate and magistrate judges shall have such qualifications as provided by law.

(d) All judges shall reside in the geographical area in which they are selected to serve.

(e) The General Assembly may provide by law for additional qualifications, including, but not limited to, minimum residency requirements.

Paragraph III. **Vacancies.** Vacancies shall be filled by appointment of the Governor except as otherwise provided by law in the magistrate, probate, and juvenile courts.

Paragraph IV. **Period of service of appointees.** An appointee to an elective office shall serve until a successor is duly selected and qualified and until January 1 of the year following the next general election which is more than six months after such person's appointment.

Paragraph V. **Compensation and allowances of judges.** All judges shall receive compensation and allowances as provided by law; county supplements are hereby continued and may be granted or changed by the General Assembly. County governing authorities which had the authority on June 30, 1983, to make county supplements shall continue to have such authority under this Constitution. An incumbent's salary, allowance, or supplement shall not be decreased during the incumbant's term of office.

Paragraph VI. **Judicial Qualifications Commission; power; composition.** The power to discipline, remove, and cause involuntary retirement of judges shall be vested in the Judicial Qualifications Commission. It shall consist of seven members, as follows:

(1) Two judges of any court of record, selected by the Supreme Court;

(2) Three members of the State Bar of Georgia who shall have been active status members of the state bar for at least ten years and who shall be elected by the board of governors of the state bar; and

(3) Two citizens, neither of whom shall be a member of the state bar, who shall be appointed by the Governor.

Paragraph VII. **Discipline, removal, and involuntary retirement of judges.**

(a) Any judge may be removed, suspended, or otherwise disciplined for willful misconduct in office, or for willful and persistent failure to perform the duties of office, or for habitual intemperance, or for conviction of a crime involving moral turpitude, or for conduct prejudicial to the administration of justice which brings the judicial office into disrepute. Any judge may be retired for disability which constitutes a serious and likely permanent interference with the performance of the duties of office. The Supreme Court shall adopt rules of implementation.

(b) (1) Upon indictment for a felony by a grand jury of this state or by a grand jury of the United States of any judge, the Attorney General or district attorney shall transmit a certified copy of the indictment to the Judicial Qualifications Commission. The commission shall, subject to subparagraph (b)(2) of this Paragraph, review the indictment, and, if it determines that the indictment relates to and

67

adversely affects the administration of the office of the indicted judge and that the rights and interests of the public are adversely affected thereby, the commission shall suspend the judge immediately and without further action pending the final disposition of the case or until the expiration of the judge's term of office, whichever occurs first. During the term of office to which such judge was elected and in which the indictment occurred, if a nolle prosequi is entered, if the public official is acquitted, or if after conviction the conviction is later overturned as a result of any direct appeal or application for a writ of certiorari, the judge shall be immediately reinstated to the office from which he was suspended. While a judge is suspended under this subparagraph and until final conviction, the judge shall continue to receive the compensation from his office. For the duration of any suspension under this subparagraph, the Governor shall appoint a replacement judge. Upon a final conviction with no appeal or review pending, the office shall be declared vacant and a successor to that office shall be chosen as provided in this Constitution or the laws enacted in pursuance thereof.

(2) The commission shall not review the indictment for a period of 14 days from the day the indictment is received. This period of time may be extended by the commission. During this period of time, the indicted judge may, in writing, authorize the commission to suspend him from office. Any such voluntary suspension shall be subject to the same conditions for review, reinstatement, or declaration of vacancy as are provided in this subparagraph for a nonvoluntary suspension.

(3) After any suspension is imposed under this subparagraph, the suspended judge may petition the commission for a review. If the commission determines that the judge should no longer be suspended, he shall immediately be reinstated to office.

(4) The findings and records of the commission and the fact that the public official has or has not been suspended shall not be admissible in evidence in any court for any purpose. The findings and records of the commission shall not be open to the public.

(5) The provisions of this subparagraph shall not apply to any indictment handed down prior to January 1, 1985.

(6) If a judge who is suspended from office under the provisions of this subparagraph is not first tried at the next regular or special term following the indictment, the suspension shall be terminated and the judge shall be reinstated to office. The judge shall not be reinstated under this provision if he is not so tried based on a continuance granted upon a motion made only by the defendant.

(c) Upon initial conviction of any judge for any felony in a trial court of this state or the United States, regardless of whether the judge has been suspended previously under subparagraph (b) of this Paragraph, such judge shall be immediately and without further action suspended from office. While a judge is suspended from office under this subparagraph, he shall not be entitled to receive the compensation from his office. If the conviction is later overturned as a result of any direct appeal or application for a writ of certiorari, the judge shall be immediately reinstated to the office from which he was suspended and shall be entitled to receive any compensation withheld under the provisions of this subparagraph. For the duration of any suspension under this subparagraph, the Governor shall appoint a replacement judge. Upon a final conviction with no appeal or review pending, the office shall be declared vacant and a successor to that office shall be chosen as provided in this Constitution or the laws enacted in pursuance thereof. The provisions of this subparagraph shall not apply to any conviction rendered prior to January 1, 1987.

Paragraph VIII. **Due process; review by Supreme Court.** No action shall be taken against a judge except after hearing and in accordance with due process of law. No removal or involuntary retirement shall occur except upon order of the Supreme Court after review.

Section VIII.
District Attorneys

Paragraph I. **District attorneys; vacancies; qualifications; compensation; duties; immunity.**

(a) There shall be a district attorney for each judicial circuit, who shall be elected circuit-wide for a term of four years. The successors of present and subsequent incumbents shall be elected by the electors of their respective circuits at the general election held immediately preceding the expiration of their respective terms. District attorneys shall serve until their successors are duly elected and qualified. Vacancies shall be filled by appointment of the Governor.

(b) No person shall be a district attorney unless such person shall have been an active-status member of the State Bar of Georgia for three years immediately preceding such person's election.

(c) The district attorneys shall receive such compensation and allowances as provided by law and shall be entitled to receive such local supplements to their compensation and allowances as may be provided by law.

(d) It shall be the duty of the district attorney to represent the state in all criminal cases in the superior court of such district attorney's circuit and in all cases appealed from the superior court and the juvenile courts of that circuit to the Supreme Court and the Court of Appeals and to perform such other duties as shall be required by law.

(e) District attorneys shall enjoy immunity from private suit for actions arising from the performance of their duties.

Paragraph II. **Discipline, removal, and involuntary retirement of district attorneys.** Any district attorney may be disciplined, removed or involuntarily retired as provided by general law.

Section IX.
General Provisions

Paragraph I. **Administration of the judicial system; uniform court rules; advice and consent of councils.** The judicial system shall be administered as provided in this Paragraph. Not more than 24 months after the effective date hereof, and from time to time thereafter by amendment, the Supreme Court shall, with the advice and consent of the council of the affected class or classes of trial courts, by order adopt and publish uniform court rules and record-keeping rules which shall provide for the speedy, efficient, and inexpensive resolution of disputes and prosecutions. Each council shall be comprised of all of the judges of the courts of that class.

Paragraph II. **Disposition of cases.** The Supreme Court and the Court of Appeals shall dispose of every case at the term for which it is entered on the court's docket for hearing or at the next term.

Section X.
Transition

Paragraph I. **Effect of ratification.** On the effective date of this article:

(1) Superior courts shall continue as superior courts.

(2) State courts shall continue as state courts.

(3) Probate courts shall continue as probate courts.

(4) Juvenile courts shall continue as juvenile courts.

(5) Municipal courts not otherwise named herein, of whatever name, shall continue as and be denominated municipal courts, except that the City Court of Atlanta shall retain its name. Such municipal courts, county recorder's courts, and Civil Courts of Richmond and Bibb counties, and administrative agencies having quasi-judicial powers shall continue with the same jurisdiction as such courts and agencies have on the effective date of this article until otherwise provided by law.

(6) Justice of the peace courts, small claims courts, and magistrate courts operating on the effective date of this Constitution and the County Court of Echols County shall become and be classified as magistrate courts. The County Court of Baldwin County and the County Court of Putnam County shall become and be classified as state courts, with the same jurisdiction and powers as other state courts.

Paragraph II. **Continuation of judges.** Each judge holding office on the effective date of this article shall continue in office until the expiration of the term of office, as a judge of the court having the same or similar jurisdiction. Each court not named herein shall cease to exist on such date or at the expiration of the term of the incumbent judge, whichever is later; and its jurisdiction shall automatically pass to the new court of the same or similar jurisdiction, in the absence of which court it shall pass to the superior court.

ARTICLE VII.
TAXATION AND FINANCE
Section I.
Power of Taxation

Paragraph I. **Taxation; limitations on grants of tax powers.** The state may not suspend or irrevocably give, grant, limit, or restrain the right of taxation and all laws, grants, contracts, and other acts to effect any of these purposes are null and void. Except as otherwise provided in this Constitution, the right of taxation shall always be under the complete control of the state.

Paragraph II. **Taxing power limited.**

(a) The annual levy of state ad valorem taxes on tangible property for all purposes, except for defending the state in an emergency, shall not exceed one-fourth mill on each dollar of the assessed value of the property.

(b) So long as the method of taxation in effect on December 31, 1980, for the taxation of shares of stock of banking corporations and other monied capital coming into competition with such banking corporations continues in effect, such shares and other monied capital may be taxed at an annual rate not exceeding five miles on each dollar of the assessed value of the property.

Paragraph III. **Uniformity; classification of property; assessment of agricultural land; utilities.**

(a) All taxes shall be levied and collected under general laws and for public purposes only. Except as otherwise provided in subparagraph (c), all taxation shall be uniform upon the same class of subjects within the territorial limits of the authority levying the tax.

(b) (1) Except as otherwise provided in this subparagraph (b), classes of subjects for taxation of property shall consist of tangible property and one or more classes of intangible personal property including money.

(2) Subject to the conditions and limitations specified by law, each of the following types of property may be classified as a separate class of property for ad valorem property tax purposes and different rates, methods, and assessment dates may be provided for such properties:

(A) Motor vehicles, including trailers.

(B) Mobile homes other than those mobile homes which qualify the owner of the home for a homestead exemption from ad valorem taxation.

(c) Tangible real property, but no more than 2,000 acres of any single property owner, which is devoted to bona fide agricultural purposes shall be assessed for ad valorem taxation purposes at 75 percent of the value which other tangible real property is assessed. No property shall be entitled to receive the preferential assessment provided for in this subparagraph if the property which would otherwise receive such assessment would result in any person who has a beneficial interest in such property, including any interest in the nature of stock ownership, receiving the benefit of such preferential assessment as to more than 2,000 acres. No property shall be entitled to receive the preferential assessment provided for in this subparagraph unless the conditions set out below are met:

(1) The property must be owned by:

(A) (i) One or more natural or naturalized citizens;

(ii) An estate of which the devisee or heirs are one or more natural or naturalized citizens; or

(iii) A trust of which the beneficiaries are one or more natural or naturalized citizens; or

(B) A family-owned farm corporation, the controlling interest of which is owned by individuals related to each other within the fourth degree of civil reckoning, or which is owned by an estate of which the devisee or heirs are one or more natural or naturalized citizens, or which is owned by a trust of which the beneficiaries are one or more natural or naturalized citizens, and such corporation derived 80 percent or more of its gross income from bona fide agricultural pursuits within this state within the year immediately preceding the year in which eligibility is sought.

(2) The General Assembly shall provide by law:

(A) For a definition of the term "bona fide agricultural purposes," but such term shall include timber production;

(B) For additional minimum conditions of eligibility which such properties must meet in order to qualify for the preferential assessment provided for herein, including, but not limited to, the requirement that the owner be required to enter into a covenant with the appropriate taxing authorities to maintain the use of the properties in bona fide agricultural purposes for a period of not less than ten years and for appropriate penalties for the breach of any such covenant.

(3) In addition to the specific conditions set forth in this subparagraph (c), the General Assembly may place further restrictions upon, but may not relax, the conditions of eligibility for the preferential assessment provided for herein.

(d) The General Assembly may provide for a different method and time of returns, assessments, payment, and collection of ad valorem taxes of public utilities, but not on a greater assessed percentage of value or at a higher rate of taxation than other properties, except that property provided for in subparagraph (c).

Section II.
Exemptions from Ad Valorem Taxation

Paragraph I. **Unauthorized tax exemptions void.** Except as authorized in or pursuant to this Constitution, all laws exempting property from ad valorem taxation are void.

Paragraph II. **Exemptions from taxation of property.**

(a) (1) Except as otherwise provided in this Constitution, no property shall be exempted from ad valorem taxation unless the exemption is approved by two-thirds of the members elected to each branch of the General Assembly in a roll-call vote and by a majority of the qualified electors of the state voting in a referendum thereon.

(2) Homestead exemption from ad valorem taxation levied by local taxing jurisdictions may be granted by local law conditioned upon approval by a majority of the qualified electors residing within the limits of the local taxing jurisdiction voting in a referendum thereon.

(3) Laws subject to the requirement of a referendum as provided in this subparagraph (a) may originate in either the Senate or the House of Representatives.

(4) The requirements of this subparagraph (a) shall not apply with respect to a law which codifies or recodifies an exemption previously authorized in the Constitution of 1976 or an exemption authorized pursuant to this Constitution.

(b) The grant of any exemption from ad valorem taxation shall be subject to the conditions, limitations, and administrative procedures specified by law.

Paragraph III. **Exemptions which may be authorized locally.**

(a) (1) The governing authority of any county or municipality, subject to the approval of a majority of the qualified electors of such political subdivision voting in a referendum thereon, may exempt from ad valorem taxation, including all such taxation levied for educational purposes and for state purposes, inventories of goods in the process of manufacture or production, and inventories, of finished goods.

(2) Exemptions granted pursuant to this subparagraph (a) may only be revoked by a referendum election called and conducted as provided by law. The call for such referendum shall not be issued within five years from the date such exemptions were first granted and, if the results of the election are in favor of the revocation of such exemptions, then such revocation shall be effective only at the end of a five-year period from the date of such referendum.

(3) The implementation, administration, and revocation of the exemptions authorized in this subparagraph (a) shall be provided for by law. Until otherwise provided by law, the grant of the exemption shall be subject to the same conditions, limitations, definitions, and procedures provided for the grant of such exemption in the Constitution of 1976 on June 30, 1983.

(b) That portion of Article VII, Section I, Paragraph IV of the Constitution of 1976 which authorized local exemptions for certain property used in solar energy heating or cooling systems and in the manufacture of such systems is adopted by this reference as a part of this Constitution as completely as though incorporated in this Paragraph verbatim. This subparagraph (b) is repealed effective July 1, 1986.

Paragraph IV. **Current property tax exemptions preserved.** Those types of exemptions from ad valorem taxation provided for by law on June 30, 1983, are hereby continued in effect as statutory law until otherwise provided for by law. Any law which reduces or repeals any homestead exemption in existence on June 30, 1983, or created thereafter must be approved by two-thirds of the members elected to each branch of the General Assembly in a roll-call vote and by a majority of the qualified electors of the state or the affected local taxing jurisdiction voting in a referendum thereon. Any law which reduces or repeals exemptions granted to religious or burial grounds or institutions of purely public charity must be approved by two-thirds of the members elected to each branch of the General Assembly.

Paragraph V. **Disabled veteran's homestead exemption.** Except as otherwise provided in this paragraph, the amount of the homestead exemption granted to disabled veterans shall be the greater of $32,500.00 or the maximum amount which may be granted to a disabled veteran under Section 802 of Title 38 of the United States Code as hereafter amended. Such exemption shall be granted to: those persons eligible for such exemption on June 30, 1983; to disabled American veterans of any war or armed conflict who are disabled due to loss or loss of use of one lower extremity together with the loss or loss of use of one upper extremity which so affects the functions of balance or propulsion as to preclude locomotion without the aid of braces, crutches, canes, or a wheelchair; and to disabled veterans hereafter becoming eligible for assistance in acquiring housing under Section 801 of the United States Code as hereafter amended. The General Assembly may by general law provide for a different amount or a different method of determining the amount of or eligibility for the homestead exemption granted to disabled veterans. Any such law shall be enacted by a simple majority of the votes of all the members to which each house is entitled and may become effective without referendum. Such law may provide that the amount of or eligibility for the exemption shall be determined by reference to laws enacted by the United States Congress.

Section III.
Purposes and Method of State Taxation

Paragraph I. **Taxation; purposes for which powers may be exercised.**

(a) Except as otherwise provided in this Constitution, the power of taxation over the whole state may be exercised for any purpose authorized by law. Any purpose for which the powers of taxation over the whole state could have been exercised on June 30, 1983, shall continue to be a purpose for which such powers may be exercised.

(b) Subject to conditions and limitations as may be provided by law, the power of taxation may be exercised to make grants for tax relief purposes to persons for sales tax paid and not otherwise reimbursed on prescription drugs. Credits or relief provided hereunder may be limited only to such reasonable classifications of taxpayers as may be specified by law.

Paragraph II. **Revenue to be paid into general fund.**

(a) Except as otherwise provided in this Constitution, all revenue collected from taxes, fees, and assessments for state purposes, as authorized by revenue measures enacted by the General Assembly, shall be paid into the general fund of the state treasury.

(b) (1) As authorized by law providing for the promotion of any one or more types of agricultural products, fees, assessments, and other charges collected on the sale or processing of agricultural products need not be paid into the general fund of the state treasury. The uniformity requirement of this article shall be satisfied by the application of the agricultural promotion program upon the affected products.

(2) As used in this subparagraph, "agricultural products" includes, but is not limited to, registered livestock and livestock products, poultry and poultry products, timber and timber products, fish and seafood, and the products of the farms and forests of this state.

Paragraph III. **Grants to counties and municipalities.** State funds may be granted to counties and municipalities within the state. The grants authorized by this Paragraph shall be made in such manner and form and subject to the procedures and conditions specified by law. The law providing for any such grant may limit the purposes for which the grant funds may be expended.

Section IV.
State Debt

Paragraph I. **Purposes for which debt may be incurred.** The state may incur:

(a) Public debt without limit to repel invasion, suppress insurrection, and defend the state in time of war.

(b) Public debt to supply a temporary deficit in the state treasury in any fiscal year created by a delay in collecting the taxes of that year. Such debt shall not exceed, in the aggregate, 5 percent of the total revenue receipts, less refunds, of the state treasury in the fiscal year immediately preceding the year in which such debt is incurred. The debt incurred shall be repaid on or before the last day of the fiscal year in which it is incurred out of taxes levied for that fiscal year. No such debt may be incurred in any fiscal year under the provisions of this subparagraph (b) if there is then outstanding unpaid debt from any previous fiscal year which was incurred to supply a temporary deficit in the state treasury.

(c) General obligation debt to acquire, construct, develop, extend, enlarge, or improve land, waters, property, highways, buildings, structures, equipment, or facilities of the state, its agencies, departments, institutions, and of those state authorities which were created and activated prior to November 8, 1960.

(d) General obligation debt to provide educational facilities for county and independent school systems and to provide public library facilities for county and independent school systems, counties, municipalities, and boards of trustees of public libraries or boards of trustees of public library systems, and, when the construction of such educational or library facilities has been completed, the title to such facilities shall be vested in the respective local boards of education, counties, municipalities, or public library boards of trustees for which such facilities were constructed.

(e) General obligation debt in order to make loans to counties, municipal corporations, political subdivisions, local authorities, and other local government entities for water or sewerage facilities or systems. It shall not be necessary for the state or a state authority to hold title to or otherwise be the owner of such facilities or systems. General obligation debt for these purposes may be authorized and incurred for administration and disbursement by a state authority created and activated before, on, or after November 8, 1960.

(f) Guaranteed revenue debt by guaranteeing the payment of revenue obligations issued by an instrumentality of the state if such revenue obligations are issued to finance:

(1) Toll bridges or toll roads.

(2) Land public transportation facilities or systems.

(3) Water facilities or systems.

(4) Sewage facilities or systems.

(5) Loans to, and loan programs for, citizens of the state for educational purposes.

Paragraph II. **State general obligation debt and guaranteed revenue debt; limitations.**

(a) As used in this Paragraph and Paragraph III of this section, "annual debt service requirements" means the total principal and interest coming due in any state fiscal year. With regard to any issue of debt incurred wholly or in part on a term basis, "annual debt service requirements" means an amount equal to the total principal and interest payments required to retire such issue in full divided by the number of years from its issue date to its maturity date.

(b) No debt may be incurred under subparagraphs (c), (d), and (e) of Paragraph I of this section or Paragraph V of this section at any time when the highest aggregate annual debt service requirements for the then current year or any subsequent year for outstanding general obligation debt and guaranteed revenue debt, including the proposed debt, and the highest aggregate annual payments for the then current year or any subsequent fiscal year of the state under all contracts then in force to which the provisions of the second paragraph of Article IX, Section VI, Paragraph I(a) of the Constitution of 1976 are applicable, exceed 10 percent of the total revenue receipts, less refunds of the state treasury in the fiscal year immediately preceding the year in which any such debt is to be incurred.

(c) No debt may be incurred under subparagraphs (c) and (d) of Paragraph I of this section at any time when the term of the debt is in excess of 25 years.

(d) No guaranteed revenue debt may be incurred to finance water or sewage treatment facilities or systems when the highest aggregate annual debt service requirements for the then current year or any subsequent fiscal year of the state for outstanding or proposed guaranteed revenue debt for water facilities or systems or sewage facilities or systems exceed 1 percent of the total revenue receipts less refunds, of the state treasury in the fiscal year immediately preceding the year in which any such debt is to be incurred.

(e) The aggregate amount of guaranteed revenue debt incurred to make loans for educational purposes that may be outstanding at any time shall not exceed $18 million, and the aggregate amount of guaranteed revenue debt incurred to purchase, or to lend or deposit against the security of, loans for educational purposes that may be outstanding at any time shall not exceed $72 million.

Paragraph III. **State general obligation debt and guaranteed revenue debt; conditions upon issuance; sinking funds and reserve funds.**

(a) (1) General obligation debt may not be incurred until legislation is enacted stating the purposes, in general or specific terms, for which such issue of debt is to be incurred, specifying the maximum principal amount of such issue and appropriating an amount at least sufficient to pay the highest annual debt service requirements for such issue. All such appropriations for debt service purposes shall not lapse for any reason and shall continue in effect until the debt for which such appropriation was authorized shall have been incurred, but the General Assembly may repeal any such appropriation at any time prior to the incurring of such debt. The General Assembly shall raise by taxation and appropriate each fiscal year, in addition to the sum necessary to make all payments required under contracts entitled to the protection of the second paragraph of Paragraph I(a), Section VI, Article IX of the Constitution of 1976, such amounts as are necessary to pay debt service requirements in such fiscal year on all general obligation debt.

(2)(A) The General Assembly shall appropriate to a special trust fund to be designated "State of Georgia General Obligation Debt Sinking Fund" such amounts as are necessary to pay annual debt service requirements on all general obligation debt. The sinking fund shall be used solely for the retirement of general obligation debt payable from the fund. If for any reason the monies in the sinking fund are insufficient to make, when due, all payments required with respect to such general obligation debt, the first revenues thereafter received in the general fund of the state shall be set aside by the appropriate state fiscal officer to the extent necessary to cure the deficiency and shall be deposited by the fiscal officer into the sinking fund. The appropriate state fiscal officer may be required to set aside and apply such revenues at the suit of any holder of any general obligation debt incurred under this section.

(B) The obligation to make sinking fund deposits as provided in subparagraphs (2)(A) shall be subordinate to the obligation imposed upon the fiscal officers of the state pursuant to the provisions of the second paragraph of Paragraph I(a) of Section VI of Article IX of the Constitution of 1976.

(b) (1) Guaranteed revenue debt may not be incurred until legislation has been enacted authorizing the guarantee of the specific issue of revenue obligations then proposed, reciting that the General Assembly has determined such obligations will be self-liquidating over the life of the issue (which determination shall be conclusive), specifying the maximum principal amount of such issue and appropriating an amount at least equal to the highest annual debt service requirements for such issue.

(2) (A) Each appropriation made for the purposes of subparagraph (b)(1) shall be paid upon the issuance of said obligations into a special trust fund to be designated "State of Georgia Guaranteed Revenue Debt Common Reserve Fund" to be held together with all other sums similarly appropriated as a common reserve for any payments which may be required by virtue of any guarantee entered into in connection with any issue of guaranteed revenue obligations. No appropriations for the benefit of guaranteed revenue debt shall lapse unless repealed prior to the payment of the appropriation into the common reserve fund.

(B) If any payments are required to be made from the common reserve fund to meet debt service requirements on guaranteed revenue obligations by virtue of an insufficiency of revenues, the amount necessary to cure the deficiency shall be paid from the common reserve fund by the appropriate state fiscal officer. Upon any such payment, the common reserve fund shall be reimbursed from the general funds of the state within ten days following the commencement of any fiscal year of the state for any amounts so paid; provided, however, the obligation to make any such reimbursements shall be subordinate to the obligation imposed upon the fiscal officers of the state pursuant to the second paragraph of Paragraph I(a) of Section VI, Article IX of the Constitution of 1976 and shall also be subordinate to the obligation to make sinking fund deposits for the benefit of general obligation debt. The appropriate state fiscal officer may be required to apply such funds as provided in this subparagraph (b)(2)(B) at the suit of any holder of any such guaranteed revenue obligations.

(C) The amount to the credit of the common reserve fund shall at all times be at least equal to the aggregate highest annual debt service requirements on all outstanding guaranteed revenue obligations entitled to the benefit of the fund. If at the end of any fiscal year of the state the fund is in excess of the required amount, the appropriate state fiscal officer, as designated by law, shall transfer the excess amount to the general funds of the state free of said trust.

(c) The funds in the general obligation debt sinking fund and the guaranteed revenue debt common reserve fund shall be as fully invested as is practicable, consistent with the requirements to make current principal and interest payments. Any such investments shall be restricted to obligations constituting direct and general obligations of the United States government or obligations unconditionally guaranteed as to the payment of principal and interest by the United States government, maturing no longer than 12 months from date of purchase.

Paragraph IV. **Certain contracts prohibited.** The state, and all state institutions, departments and agencies of the state are prohibited from entering into any contract, except contracts pertaining to guaranteed revenue debt, with any public agency, public corporation, authority, or similar entity if such contract is intended to constitute security for bonds or other obligations issued by any such public agency, public corporation, or authority and, in the event any contract between the state, or any state institution, department or agency of the state and any public agency, public corporation, authority or similar entity, or any revenues from any such contract, is pledged or assigned as security for the repayment of bonds or other obligations, then and in either such event, the appropriation or expenditure of any funds of the state for the payment of obligations under any such contract shall likewise be prohibited.

Paragraph V. **Refunding of debt.** The state may incur general obligation debt or guaranteed revenue debt to fund or refund any such debt or to fund or refund any obligations issued upon the security of contracts to which the provisions of the second paragraph of Paragraph I(a), Section VI, Article IX of the Constitution of 1976 are applicable. The issuance of any such debt for the purposes of said funding or refunding shall be subject to the 10 percent limitation in Paragraph II(b) of this section to the same extent as debt incurred under Paragraph I of this section; provided, however, in making such computation the annual debt service requirements and annual contract payments remaining on the debt or obligations being funded or refunded shall not be taken into account. The issuance of such debt may be accomplished by resolution of the Georgia State Financing and Investment Commission without any action on the part of the General Assembly and any appropriation made or required to be made with respect to the debt or obligation being funded or refunded shall immediately attach and inure to the benefit of the obligations to be issued in connection with such funding or refunding. Debt incurred in connection with any such funding or refunding shall be the same as that originally authorized by the General Assembly, except that general obligation debt may be incurred to fund or refund obligations issued upon the security of contracts to which the provisions of the second paragraph of Paragraph I(a), Section VI, Article IX of the Constitution of 1976 are applicable and the continuing appropriations required to be made under this Constitution shall immediately attach and inure to the benefit of the obligation to be issued in connection with such funding or refunding with the same force and effect as though said obligations so funded or refunded had originally been issued as a general obligation debt authorized hereunder. The term of a funding or refunding issue pursuant to this Paragraph shall not extend beyond the term of the original debt or obligation and the total interest on the funding or refunding issue shall not exceed the total interest to be paid on such original debt or obligation. The principal amount of any debt issued in connection with such funding or refunding may exceed the principal amount being funded or refunded to the extent necessary to provide for the payment of any premium thereby incurred.

Paragraph VI. **Faith and credit of state pledged debt may be validated.** The full faith, credit, and taxing power of the state are hereby pledged to the payment of all public debt incurred under this article and all such debt and the interest on the debt shall be exempt from taxation. Such debt may be validated by judicial proceedings in the manner provided by law. Such validation shall be incontestable and conclusive.

Paragraph VII. **Georgia State Financing and Investment Commission; duties.**

(a) There shall be a Georgia State Financing and Investment Commission. The commission shall consist of the Governor, the President of the Senate, the Speaker of the House of Representatives, the State Auditor, the Attorney General, the director, Fiscal Division, Department of Administrative Services, or such other officer as may be designated by law, and the Commissioner of Agriculture. The commission shall be responsible for the issuance of all public debt and for the proper application, as provided by law, of the proceeds of such debt to the purposes for which it is incurred; provided, however, the proceeds from guaranteed revenue obligations shall be paid to the issuer thereof and such proceeds and the application thereof shall be the responsibility of such issuer. Debt to be incurred at the same time for more than one purpose may be combined in one issue without stating the purpose separately but the proceeds thereof must be allocated, disbursed and used solely in accordance with the original purpose and without exceeding the principal amount authorized for each purpose set forth in the authorization of the General Assembly and to the extent not so used shall be used to purchase and retire public debt. The commission shall be responsible for the investment of all proceeds to be administered by it and, as provided by law, the income earned on any such investments may be used to pay operating expenses of the commission or placed in a common debt retirement fund and used to purchase and retire any public debt, or any bonds or obligations issued by any public agency, public corporation or authority which are secured by a contract to which the provisions of the second paragraph of Paragraph I(a) of Section VI, Article IX of the Constitution of 1976 are applicable. The commission shall have such additional responsibilities, powers, and duties as are provided by law.

(b) Notwithstanding subparagraph (a) of this Paragraph, proceeds from general obligation debt issued for making loans to local government entities for water or sewerage facilities or systems as provided in Paragraph I(e) of this section shall be paid or transferred to and administered and invested by the unit of state government or state authority made responsible by law for such activities, and the proceeds and investment earnings thereof shall be applied and disbursed by such unit or authority.

Paragraph VIII. **State aid forbidden.** Except as provided in this Constitution, the credit of the state shall not be pledged or loaned to any individual, company, corporation, or association. The state shall not become a joint owner or stockholder in or with any individual, company, association, or corporation.

Paragraph IX. **Construction.** Paragraphs I through VIII of this section are for the purpose of providing an effective method of financing the state's needs and their provisions and any law now or hereafter enacted by the General Assembly in furtherance of their provisions shall be liberally construed to effect such purpose. Insofar as any such provisions or any such law may be inconsistent with any other provisions of this Constitution or of any other law, the provisions of such Paragraphs and laws enacted in furtherance of such Paragraphs shall be controlling; provided, however, the provisions of such Paragraphs shall not be so broadly construed as to cause the same to be unconstitutional and in connection with any such construction such Paragraphs shall be deemed to contain such implied limitations as shall be required to accomplish the foregoing.

Paragraph X. **Assumption of debts forbidden; exceptions.** The state shall not assume the debt, or any part thereof, of any county, municipality, or other political subdivision of the state, unless such debt be contracted to enable the state to repel invasion, suppress civil disorders or insurrection, or defend itself in time of war.

Paragraph XI. **Section not to unlawfully impair contracts or revive obligations previously voided.** The provisions of this section shall not be construed so as to:

(a) Unlawfully impair the obligation of any contract in effect on June 30, 1983.

(b) Revive or permit the revival of the obligation of any bond or security declared to be void by the Constitution of 1976 or any previous Constitution of this state.

ARTICLE VIII.
EDUCATION
Section I.
Public Education

Paragraph I. **Public education; free public education prior to college or postsecondary level; support by taxation.** The provision of an adequate public education for the citizens shall be a primary obligation of the State of Georgia. Public education for the citizens prior to the college or postsecondary level shall be free and shall be provided for by taxation. The expense of other public education shall be provided for in such manner and in such amount as may be provided by law.

Section II.
State Board of Education

Paragraph I. **State Board of Education.**

(a) There shall be a State Board of Education which shall consist of one member from each congressional district in the state appointed by the Governor and confirmed by the Senate. The Governor shall not be a member of said board. The ten members in office on June 30, 1983, shall serve out the remainder of their respective terms. As each term of office expires, the Governor shall appoint a successor as herein provided. The terms of office of all members appointed after the effective date of this Constitution shall be for seven years. Members shall serve until their successors are appointed and qualified. In the event of a vacancy on the board by death, resignation, removal, or any reason other than expiration of a member's term, the Governor shall fill such vacancy; and the person so appointed shall serve until confirmed by the Senate and, upon confirmation, shall serve for the unexpired term of office.

(b) The State Board of Education shall have such powers and duties as provided by law.

(c) The State Board of Education may accept bequests, donations, grants, and transfers of land, buildings, and other property for the use of the state educational system.

(d) The qualifications, compensation, and removal from office of the members of the board of education shall be as provided by law.

Section III.
State School Superintendent

Paragraph I. **State School Superintendent.** There shall be a State School Superintendent, who shall be the executive officer of the State Board of Education, elected at the same time and in the same manner and for the same term as that of the Governor. The State School Superintendent shall have such qualifications and shall be paid such compensation as may be fixed by law. No member of the State Board of Education shall be eligible for election as State School Superintendent during the time for which such member shall have been appointed.

Section IV.
Board of Regents

Paragraph I. **University System of Georgia; board of regents.**

(a) There shall be a Board of Regents of the University System of Georgia which shall consist of one member from each congressional district in the state and five additional members from the state at large, appointed by the Governor and confirmed by the Senate. The Governor shall not be a member of said board. The members in office on June 30, 1983, shall serve out the remainder of their respective terms. As each term of office expires, the Governor shall appoint a successor as herein provided. All such terms of members shall be for seven years. Members shall serve until their successors are appointed and qualified. In the event of a vacancy on the board by death, resignation, removal, or any reason other than the expiration of a member's term, the Governor shall fill such vacancy; and the person so appointed shall serve until confirmed by the Senate and, upon confirmation, shall serve for the unexpired term of office.

(b) The board of regents shall have the exclusive authority to create new public colleges, junior colleges, and universities in the State of Georgia, subject to approval by majority vote in the House of Representatives and the Senate. Such vote shall not be required to change the status of a college, institution or university existing on the effective date of this Constitution. The government, control, and management of the University System of Georgia and all of the institutions in said system shall be vested in the Board of Regents of the University System of Georgia.

(c) All appropriations made for the use of any or all institutions in the university system shall be paid to the board of regents in a lump sum, with the power and authority in said board to allocate and distribute the same among the institutions under its control in such way and manner and in such amounts as will further an efficient and economical administration of the university system.

(d) The board of regents may hold, purchase, lease, sell, convey, or otherwise dispose of public property, execute conveyances thereon, and utilize the proceeds arising therefrom; may exercise the power of eminent domain in the manner provided by law; and shall have such other powers and duties as provided by law.

(e) The board of regents may accept bequests, donations, grants, and transfers of land, buildings, and other property for the use of the University System of Georgia.

(f) The qualifications, compensation, and removal from office of the members of the board of regents shall be as provided by law.

Section V.
Local School Systems

Paragraph I. **School systems continued; consolidation of school systems authorized; new independent school systems prohibited.** Authority is granted to county and area boards of education to establish and maintain public schools within their limits. Existing county and independent school systems shall be continued, except that the General Assembly may provide by law for the consolidation of two or more county school systems, independent school systems, portions thereof, or any combination thereof into a single county or area school system under the control and management of a county or area board of education, under such terms and conditions as the General Assembly may prescribe; but no such consolidation shall become effective until approved by a majority of the qualified voters voting thereon in each separate school system proposed to be consolidated. No independent school system shall hereafter be established.

Paragraph II. **Boards of education.** Each school system shall be under the management and control of a board of education, the members of which shall be elected or appointed as provided by law. School board members shall reside within the territory embraced by the school system and shall have such compensation and additional qualifications as may be provided by law.

Paragraph III. **School superintendents.** There shall be a school superintendent of each system who shall be the executive officer of the board of education and shall have such qualifications, powers, and duties as provided by general law.

Paragraph IV. **Changes in school boards and superintendent.**

(a) The composition of school boards, the term of office, and the methods of selecting board members and school superintendents, including whether elections shall be partisan or nonpartisan, shall be as provided by law applicable thereto on June 30, 1983, but may be changed thereafter only by local law, conditioned upon approval by a majority of the qualified voters voting thereon in the system affected. It shall not be necessary for a local law which reapportions election districts from which members of a local board of education are elected to be conditioned on the approval of the voters as herein required.

(b) School systems which are authorized on June 30, 1983, to make the changes listed in subparagraph (a) of this Paragraph by local law without a referendum may continue to do so.

Paragraph V. **Power of boards to contract with each other.**

(a) Any two or more boards of education may contract with each other for the care, education, and transportation of pupils and for such other activities as they may be authorized by law to perform.

(b) The General Assembly may provide by law for the sharing of facilities or services by and between local boards of education under such joint administrative authority as may be authorized.

Paragraph VI. **Power of boards to accept bequests, donations, grants, and transfers.** The board of education of each school system may accept bequests, donations, grants, and transfers of land, buildings, and other property for the use of such system.

Paragraph VII. **Special schools.**

(a) The General Assembly may provide by law for the creation of special schools in such areas as may require them and may provide for the participation of local boards of education in the establishment of such schools under such terms and conditions as it may provide; but no bonded indebtedness may be incurred nor a school tax levied for the support of special schools without the approval of a majority of the qualified voters voting thereon in each of the systems affected. Any special schools shall be operated in conformity with regulations of the State Board of Education pursuant to provisions of law. The state is authorized to expend funds for the support and maintenance of special schools in such amount and manner as may be provided by law.

(b) Nothing contained herein shall be construed to affect the authority of local boards of education or of the state to support and maintain special schools created prior to June 30, 1983.

Section VI.
Local Taxation for Education

Paragraph I. **Local taxation for education.**

(a) The board of education of each school system shall annually certify to its fiscal authority or authorities a school tax not greater than 20 mills per dollar for the support and maintenance of education. Said fiscal authority or authorities shall annually levy said tax upon the assessed value of all taxable property within the territory served by said school system, provided that the levy made by an area board of education, which levy shall not be greater than 20 mills per dollar, shall be in such amount and within such limits as may be prescribed by local law applicable thereto.

(b) School tax funds shall be expended only for the support and maintenance of public schools, public vocational-technical schools, public education, and activities necessary or incidental thereto, including school lunch purposes.

(c) The 20 mill limitation provided for in subparagraph (a) of this Paragraph shall not apply to those school systems which are authorized on June 30, 1983, to levy a school tax in excess thereof.

(d) The method of certification and levy of the school tax provided for in subparagraph (a) of this Paragraph shall not apply to those systems that are authorized on June 30, 1983, to utilize a different method of certification and levy of such tax; but the General Assembly may be law require that such systems be brought into conformity with the method of certification and levy herein provided.

Paragraph II. **Increasing or removing tax rate.** The mill limitation in effect on June 30, 1983, for any school system may be increased or removed by action of the respective boards of education, but only after such action has been approved by a majority of the qualified voters voting thereon in the particular school system to be affected in the manner provided by law.

Paragraph III. **School tax collection reimbursement.** The General Assembly may by general law require local boards of education to reimburse the appropriate governing authority for the collection of school taxes, provided that any rate established may be reduced by local act.

Section VII.
Educational Assistance

Paragraph I. **Educational assistance programs authorized.**

(a) Pursuant to laws now or hereafter enacted by the General Assembly, public funds may be expended for any of the following purposes:

(1) To provide grants, scholarships, loans, or other assistance to students and to parents of students for educational purposes.

(2) To provide for a program of guaranteed loans to students and to parents of students for educational purposes and to pay interest, interest subsidies, and fees to lenders on such loans. The General Assembly is authorized to provide such tax exemptions to lenders as shall be deemed advisable in connection with such program.

(3) To match funds now or hereafter available for student assistance pursuant to any federal law.

(4) To provide grants, scholarships, loans, or other assistance to public employees for educational purposes.

(5) To provide for the purchase of loans made to students for educational purposes who have completed a program of study in a field in which critical shortages exist and for cancellation of repayment of such loans, interest, and charges thereon.

(b) Contributions made in support of any educational assistance program now or hereafter established under provisions of this section may be deductible for state income tax purposes as now or hereafter provided by law.

Paragraph II. **Guaranteed revenue debt.** Guaranteed revenue debt may be incurred to provide funds to make loans to students and to parents of students for educational purposes, to purchase loans made to students and to parents of students for educational purposes, or to lend or make deposits of such funds with lenders which shall be secured by loans made to students and to parents of students for educational purposes. Any such debt shall be incurred in accordance with the procedures and requirements of Article VII, Section IV of this Constitution.

Paragraph III. **Public authorities.** Public authorities or public corporations heretofore or hereafter created for such purposes shall be authorized to administer educational assistance programs and, in connection therewith, may exercise such powers as may now or hereafter be provided by law.

Paragraph IV. **Waiver of tuition.** The Board of Regents of the University System of Georgia shall be authorized to establish programs allowing attendance at units of the University System of Georgia without payment of tuition or other fees, but the General Assembly may provide by law for the establishment of any such program for the benefit of elderly citizens of the state.

ARTICLE IX.
COUNTIES AND MUNICIPAL CORPORATIONS
Section I.
Counties

Paragraph I. **Counties a body corporate and politic.** Each county shall be a body corporate and politic with such governing authority and with such powers and limitations as are provided in this Constitution and as provided by law. The governing authorities of the several counties shall remain as prescribed by law on June 30, 1983, until otherwise provided by law.

Paragraph II. **Number of counties limited; county boundaries and county sites; county consolidation.**

(a) There shall not be more than 159 counties in this state.

(b) The metes and bounds of the several counties and the county sites shall remain as prescribed by law on June 30, 1983, unless changed under the operation of a general law.

(c) The General Assembly may provide by law for the consolidation of two or more counties into one or the division of a county and the merger of portions thereof into other counties under such terms and conditions as it may prescribe; but no such consolidation, division, or merger shall become effective unless approved by a majority of the qualified voters voting thereon in each of the counties proposed to be consolidated, divided, or merged.

Paragraph III. **County officers; election; term; compensation.**

(a) The clerk of the superior court, judge of the probate court, sheriff, tax receiver, tax collector, and tax commissioner, where such office has replaced the tax receiver and tax collector, shall be elected by the qualified voters of their respective counties for terms of four years and shall have such qualifications, powers, and duties as provided by general law.

(b) County officers listed in subparagraph (a) of this Paragraph may be on a fee basis, salary basis, or fee basis supplemented by salary, in such manner as may be directed by law. Minimum compensation for said county officers may be established by the General Assembly by general law. Such minimum compensation may be supplemented by local law or, if such authority is delegated by local law, by action of the county governing authority.

(c) The General Assembly may consolidate the offices of tax receiver and tax collector into the office of tax commissioner.

Paragraph IV. **Civil service systems.** The General Assembly may by general law authorize the establishment by county governing authorities of civil service systems covering county employees or covering county employees and employees of the elected county officers.

Section II.
Home Rule for Counties and Municipalities

Paragraph I. **Home rule for counties.**

(a) The governing authority of each county shall have legislative power to adopt clearly reasonable ordinances, resolutions, or regulations relating to its property, affairs, and local government for which no provision has been made by general law and which is not inconsistent with this Constitution or any local law applicable thereto. Any such local law shall remain in force and effect until amended or repealed as provided in subparagraph (b). This, however, shall not restrict the authority of the General Assembly by general law to further define this power or to broaden, limit, or otherwise regulate the exercise thereof. The General Assembly shall not pass any local law to repeal, modify, or supersede any action taken by a county governing authority under this section except as authorized under subparagraph (c) hereof.

(b) Except as provided in subparagraph (c), a county may, as an incident of its home rule power, amend or repeal the local acts applicable to its governing authority by following either of the procedures hereinafter set forth:

(1) Such local acts may be amended or repealed by a resolution or ordinance duly adopted at two regular consecutive meetings of the county governing authority not less than seven nor more than 60 days apart. A notice containing a synopsis of the proposed amendment or repeal shall be published in the official county organ once a week for three weeks within a period of 60 days immediately preceding its final adoption. Such notice shall state that a copy of the proposed amendment or repeal is on file in the office of the clerk of the superior court of the county for the purpose of examination and inspection by the public. The clerk of the superior court shall furnish anyone, upon written request, a copy of the proposed amendment or repeal. No amendment or repeal hereunder shall be valid to change or repeal an amendment adopted pursuant to a referendum as provided in (2) of this subparagraph or to change or repeal a local act of the General Assembly ratified in a referendum by the electors of such county unless at least 12 months have elapsed after such referendum. No amendment hereunder shall be valid if inconsistent with any provision of this Constitution or if provision has been made therefor by general law.

(2) Amendments to or repeals of such local acts or ordinances, resolutions, or regulations adopted pursuant to subparagraph (a) hereof may be initiated by a petition filed with the judge of the probate court of the county containing, in cases of counties with a population of 5,000 or less, the signatures of at least 25 percent of

the electors registered to vote in the last general election; in cases of counties with a population of more than 5,000 but not more than 50,000, at least 20 percent of the electors registered to vote in the last general election; and, in cases of a county with a population of more than 50,000, at least 10 percent of the electors registered to vote in the last general election, which petition shall specifically set forth the exact language of the proposed amendment or repeal. The judge of the probate court shall determine the validity of such petition within 60 days of its being filed with the judge of the probate court. In the event the judge of the probate court determines that such petition is valid, it shall be his duty to issue the call for an election for the purpose of submitting such amendment or repeal to the registered electors of the county for their approval or rejection. Such call shall be issued not less than ten nor more than 60 days after the date of the filing of the petition. He shall set the date of such election for a day not less than 60 nor more than 90 days after the date of such filing. The judge of the probate court shall cause a notice of the date of said election to be published in the official organ of the county once a week for three weeks immediately preceding such date. Said notice shall also contain a synopsis of the proposed amendment or repeal and shall state that a copy thereof is on file in the office of the judge of the probate court of the county for the purpose of examination and inspection by the public. The judge of the probate court shall furnish anyone, upon written request, a copy of the proposed amendment or repeal. If more than one-half of the votes cast on such question are for approval of the amendment or repeal, it shall become of full force and effect; otherwise, it shall be void and of no force and effect. The expense of such election shall be borne by the county, and it shall be the duty of the judge of the probate court to hold and conduct such election. Such election shall be held under the same laws and rules and regulations as govern special elections, except as otherwise provided herein. It shall be the duty of the judge of the probate court to canvass the returns and declare and certify the result of the election. It shall be his further duty to certify the result thereof to the Secretary of State in accordance with the provisions of subparagraph (g) of this Paragraph. A referendum on any such amendment or repeal shall not be held more often than once each year. No amendment hereunder shall be valid if inconsistent with any provision of this Constitution or if provision has been made therefor by general law.

In the event that the judge of the probate court determines that such petition was not valid, he shall cause to be published in explicit detail the reasons why such petition is not valid; provided, however, that, in any proceeding in which the validity of the petition is at issue, the tribunal considering such issue shall not be limited by the reasons assigned. Such publication shall be in the official organ of the county in the week immediately following the date on which such petition is declared to be not valid.

(c) The power granted to counties in subparagraphs (a) and (b) above shall not be construed to extend to the following matters or any other matters which the General Assembly by general law has preempted or may hereafter preempt, but such matters shall be the subject of general law or the subject of local acts of the General Assembly to the extent that the enactment of such local acts if otherwise permitted under this Constitution:

(1) Action affecting any elective county office, the salaries thereof, or the personnel thereof, except the personnel subject to the jurisdiction of the county governing authority.

(2) Action affecting the composition, form, procedure for election or appointment, compensation, and expenses and allowances in the nature of compensation of the county governing authority.

(3) Action defining any criminal offense or providing for criminal punishment.

(4) Action adopting any form of taxation beyond that authorized by law or by this Constitution.

(5) Action extending the power of regulation over any business activity regulated by the Georgia Public Service Commission beyond that authorized by local or general law or by this Constitution.

(6) Action affecting the exercise of the power of eminent domain.

(7) Action affecting any court or the personnel thereof.

(8) Action affecting any public school system.

(d) The power granted in subparagraphs (a) and (b) of this Paragraph shall not include the power to take any action affecting the private or civil law governing private or civil relationships, except as is incident to the exercise of an independent governmental power.

(e) Nothing in subparagraphs (a), (b), (c), or (d) shall affect the provisions of subparagraph (f) of this Paragraph.

(f) The governing authority of each county is authorized to fix the salary, compensation, and expenses of those employed by such governing authority and to establish and maintain retirement or pension systems, insurance, workers' compensation, and hospitalization benefits for said employees.

(g) No amendment or revision of any local act made pursuant to subparagraph (b) of this section shall become effective until a copy of such amendment or revision, a copy of the required notice of publication, and an affidavit of a duly authorized representative of the newspaper in which such notice was published to the effect that said notice has been published as provided in said subparagraph has been filed with the Secretary of State. The Secretary of State shall provide for the publication and distribution of all such amendments and revisions at least annually.

Paragraph II. **Home rule for municipalities.** The General Assembly may provide by law for the self-government of municipalities and to that end is expressly given the authority to delegate its power so that matters pertaining to municipalities may be dealt with without the necessity of action by the General Assembly.

Paragraph III. **Supplementary powers.**

(a) In addition to and supplementary of all powers possessed by or conferred upon any county, municipality, or any combination thereof, any county, municipality, or any combination thereof may exercise the following powers and provide the following services:

(1) Police and fire protection.

(2) Garbage and solid waste collection and disposal.

(3) Public health facilities and services, including hospitals, ambulance and emergency rescue services, and animal control.

(4) Street and road construction and maintenance, including curbs, sidewalks, street lights, and devices to control the flow of traffic on streets and roads constructed by counties and municipalities or any combination thereof.

(5) Parks, recreational areas, programs, and facilities.

(6) Storm water and sewage collection and disposal systems.

(7) Development, storage, treatment, purification, and distribution of water.

(8) Public housing.

(9) Public transportation.

(10) Libraries, archives, and arts and sciences programs and facilities.

(11) Terminal and dock facilities and parking facilities.

(12) Codes, including building, housing, plumbing, and electrical codes.

(13) Air quality control.

(14) The power to maintain and modify heretofore existing retirement or pension systems, including such systems heretofore created by general laws of local application by population classification, and to continue in effect or modify other benefits heretofore provided as a part of or in addition to such retirement or pension systems and the power to create and maintain retirement or pension systems for any

elected or appointed public officers and employees whose compensation is paid in whole or in part from county or municipal funds and for the beneficiaries of such officers and employees.

(b) Unless otherwise provided by law,

(1) No county may exercise any of the powers listed in subparagraph (a) of this Paragraph or provide any service listed therein inside the boundaries of any municipality or any other county except by contract with the municipality or county affected; and

(2) No municipality may exercise any of the powers listed in subparagraph (a) of this Paragraph or provide any service listed therein outside its own boundaries except by contract with the county or municipality affected.

(c) Nothing contained within this Paragraph shall operate to prohibit the General Assembly from enacting general laws relative to the subject matters listed in subparagraph (a) of this Paragraph or to prohibit the General Assembly by general law from regulating, restricting, or limiting the exercise of the powers listed therein; but it may not withdraw any such powers.

(d) Except as otherwise provided in subparagraph (b) of this Paragraph, the General Assembly shall act upon the subject matters listed in subparagraph (a) of this Paragraph only by general law.

Paragraph IV. **Planning and zoning.** The governing authority of each county and of each municipality may adopt plans and may exercise the power of zoning. This authorization shall not prohibit the General Assembly from enacting general laws establishing procedures for the exercise of such power.

Paragraph V. **Eminent domain.** The governing authority of each county and of each municipality may exercise the power of eminent domain for any public purpose.

Paragraph VI. **Special districts.** As hereinafter provided in this Paragraph, special districts may be created for the provision of local government services within such districts; and fees, assessments, and taxes may be levied and collected within such districts to pay, wholly or partially, the cost of providing such services therein and to construct and maintain facilities therefor. Such special districts may be created and fees, assessments, or taxes may be levied and collected therein by any one or more of the following methods:

(a) By general law which directly creates the districts.

(b) By general law which requires the creation of districts under conditions specified by such general law.

(c) By municipal or county ordinance or resolution, except that no such ordinance or resolution may supersede a law enacted by the General Assembly pursuant to subparagraphs (a) or (b) of this Paragraph.

Paragraph VII. **Community redevelopment.**

(a) The General Assembly may authorize any county, municipality, or housing authority to undertake and carry out community redevelopment, which may include the sale or other disposition of property acquired by eminent domain to private enterprise for private uses.

(b) In addition to the authority granted by subparagraph (a) of this Paragraph, the General Assembly is authorized to grant to counties or municipalities for redevelopment purposes and in connection with redevelopment programs, as such purposes and programs are defined by general law, the power to issue tax allocation bonds, as defined by such law, and the power to incur other obligations, without either such bonds or obligations constituting debt within the meaning of Section V of this article, and the power to enter into contracts for any period not exceeding 30 years with private persons, firms, corporations, and business entities. Notwithstanding the grant of these powers pursuant to general law, no county or municipality may exercise these powers unless so authorized by local law and unless such powers are exercised in conformity with those terms and conditions for such exercise as established by that local law. The provisions of any such local law shall conform to those requirements established by general law regarding such powers. No such local law, or any amendment thereto, shall become effective unless approved in a referendum by a majority of the qualified voters voting thereon in the county or municipality directly affected by that local law.

Paragraph VIII. **Limitation on the taxing power and contributions of counties, municipalities, and political subdivisions.** The General Assembly shall not authorize any county, municipality, or other political subdivision of this state, through taxation, contribution, or otherwise, to appropriate money for or to lend its credit to any person or to any nonpublic corporation or association except for purely charitable purposes.

Paragraph IX. **Immunity of counties, municipalities, and school districts.** The General Assembly may waive the immunity of counties, municipalities, and school districts by law.

Section III.
Intergovernmental Relations

Paragraph I. **Intergovernmental contracts.**

(a) The state, or any institution, department, or other agency thereof, and any county, municipality, school district, or other political subdivision of the state may contract for any period not exceeding 50 years with each other or with any other public agency, public corporation, or public authority for joint services, for the provision of services, or for the joint or separate use of facilities or equipment; but such contracts must deal with activities, services, or facilities which the contracting parties are authorized by law to undertake or provide. By way of specific instance and not limitation, a mutual undertaking by a local government entity to borrow and an undertaking by the state or a state authority to lend funds from and to one another for water or sewerage facilities or systems pursuant to law shall be a provision for services and an activity within the meaning of this Paragraph.

(b) Subject to such limitations as may be provided by general law, any county, municipality, or political subdivision thereof may, in connection with any contracts authorized in this Paragraph, convey any existing facilities or equipment to the state or to any public agency, public corporation, or public authority.

(c) Any county, municipality, or any combination thereof, may contract with any public agency, public corporation, or public authority for the care, maintenance, and hospitalization of its indigent sick and may as a part of such contract agree to pay for the cost of acquisition, construction, modernization, or repairs of necessary land, buildings, and facilities by such public agency, public corporation, or public authority and provide for the payment of such services and the cost to such public agency, public corporation, or public authority of acquisition, construction, modernization, or repair of land, buildings, and facilities from revenues realized by such county, municipality, or any combination thereof from any taxes authorized by this Constitution or revenues derived from any other source.

Paragraph II. **Local government reorganization.**

(a) The General Assembly may provide by law for any matters necessary or convenient to authorize the consolidation of the governmental and corporate powers and functions vested in municipalities with the governmental and corporate powers and functions vested in a county or counties in which such municipalities are located; provided, however, that no such consolidation shall become effective unless separately approved by a majority of the qualified voters of the county or each of the counties and of the municipality or each of the municipalities located within such county or counties containing at least 10 percent of the population of the county in which located voting thereon in such manner as may be prescribed in such law. Such law may provide procedures and requirements for the establishment of charter commissions to draft proposed charters for the consolidated government, and the General Assembly is expressly authorized to delegate its powers to such charter commissions for such purposes so that the governmental consolidation proposed by a charter commission may become effective without the necessity of further action by the General Assembly; or such law may require that the recommendation of any such charter commission be implemented by a subsequent local law.

(b) The General Assembly may provide by general law for alternatives other than governmental consolidation as authorized in subparagraph (a) above for the reorganization of county and municipal governments, including, but not limited to, procedures to establish a single governing body as the governing authority of a county and a municipality or municipalities located within such county or for the redistribution of powers between a county and a municipality or municipalities located within the county. Such law may require the form of governmental reorganization authorized by such law to be approved by the qualified voters directly affected thereby voting in such manner as may be required in such law.

(c) Nothing in this Paragraph shall be construed to limit the authority of the General Assembly to repeal municipal charters without a referendum.

Section IV.
Taxation Power of County and Municipal Governments

Paragraph I. **Power of taxation.**

(a) Except as otherwise provided in this Paragraph, the governing authority of any county, municipality, or combination thereof may exercise the power of taxation as authorized by this Constitution or by general law.

(b) In the absence of a general law:

(1) County governing authorities may be authorized by local law to levy and collect business and occupational license taxes and license fees only in the unincorporated areas of the counties. The General Assembly may provide that the revenues raised by such tax or fee be spent for the provision of services only in the unincorporated areas of the county.

(2) Municipal governing authorities may be authorized by local law to levy and collect taxes and fees in the corporate limits of the municipalities.

(c) The General Assembly may provide by law for the taxation of insurance companies on the basis of gross direct premiums received from insurance policies within the unincorporated areas of counties. The tax authorized herein may be imposed by the state or by counties or by the state for county purposes by law. The General Assembly may further provide by law for the reduction, only upon taxable property within the unincorporated areas of counties, of the ad valorem tax millage rate for county or county school district purposes or for the reduction of such ad valorem tax millage rate for both such purposes in connection with imposing or authorizing the imposition of the tax authorized herein or in connection with providing for the distribution of the proceeds derived from the tax authorized herein.

Paragraph II. **Power of expenditure.** The governing authority of any county, municipality, or combination thereof may expend public funds to perform any public service or public function as authorized by this Constitution or by law or to perform any other service or function as authorized by this Constitution or by general law.

Paragraph III. **Purposes of taxation; allocation of taxes.** No levy need state the particular purposes for which the same was made nor shall any taxes collected be allocated for any particular purpose, unless otherwise provided by this Constitution or by law.

Section V.
Limitation on Local Debt

Paragraph I. **Debt limitations of counties, municipalities, and other political subdivisions.**

(a) The debt incurred by any county, municipality, or other political subdivision of this state, including debt incurred on behalf of any special district, shall never exceed 10 percent of the assessed value of all taxable property within such county, municipality, or political subdivision; and no such county, municipality, or other political subdivision shall incur any new debt without the assent of a majority of the qualified voters of such county, municipality, or political subdivision voting in an election held for that purpose as provided by law.

(b) Notwithstanding subparagraph (a) of this Paragraph, all local school systems which are authorized by law on June 30, 1983, to incur debt in excess of 10 percent of the assessed value of all taxable property therein shall continue to be authorized to incur such debt.

Paragraph II. **Special district debt.** Any county, municipality, or political subdivision of this state may incur debt on behalf of any special district created pursuant to Paragraph VI of Section II of this article. Such debt may be incurred on behalf of such special district where the county, municipality, or other political subdivision shall have, at or before the time of incurring such debt, provided for the assessment and collection of an annual tax within the special district sufficient in amount to pay the principal of and interest on such debt within 30 years from the incurrence thereof; and no such county, municipality, or other political subdivision shall incur any debt on behalf of such special district without the assent of a majority of the qualified voters of such special district voting in an election held for that purpose as provided by law. No such county, municipality, or other political subdivision shall incur any debt on behalf of such special district in an amount which, when taken together with all other debt outstanding incurred by such county, municipality, or political subdivision and on behalf of any such special district, exceeds 10 percent of the assessed value of all taxable property within such county, municipality, or political subdivision. The proceeds of the tax collected as provided herein shall be placed in a sinking fund to be held on behalf of such special district and used exclusively to pay off the principal of and interest on such debt thereafter maturing. Such moneys shall be held and kept separate and apart from all other revenues collected and may be invested and reinvested as provided by law.

Paragraph III. **Refunding of outstanding indebtedness.** The governing authority of any county, municipality, or other political subdivision of this state may provide for the refunding of outstanding bonded indebtedness without the necessity of a referendum being held therefor, provided that neither the term of the original debt is extended nor the interest rate of the original debt is increased. The principal amount of any debt issued in connection with such refunding may exceed the principal amount being refunded in order to reduce the total principal and interest payment requirements over the remaining term of the original issue. The proceeds of the refunding issue shall be used solely to retire the original debt. The original debt refunded shall not constitute debt within the meaning of Paragraph I of this section; but the refunding issue shall constitute a debt such as will count against the limitation on debt measured by 10 percent of assessed value of taxable property as expressed in Paragraph I of this section.

Paragraph IV. **Exceptions to debt limitations.** Notwithstanding the debt limitations provided in Paragraph I of this section and without the necessity for a referendum being held therefor, the governing authority of any county, municipality, or other political subdivision of this state may, subject to the conditions and limitations as may be provided by general law:

(1) Accept and use funds granted by and obtain loans from the federal government or any agency thereof pursuant to conditions imposed by federal law.

(2) Incur debt, by way of borrowing from any person, corporation, or association as well as from the state, to pay in whole or in part the cost of property valuation and equalization programs for ad valorem tax purposes.

Paragraph V. **Temporary loans authorized.** The governing authority of any county, municipality, or other political subdivision of this state may incur debt by obtaining temporary loans in each year to pay expenses. The aggregate amount of all such loans shall not exceed 75 percent of the total gross income from taxes collected in the last preceding year. Such loans shall be payable on or before December 31 of the calendar year in which such loan is made. No such loan may be obtained when there is a loan then unpaid obtained in any prior year. No such county, municipality, or other political subdivision of this state shall incur in any one calendar year an aggregate of such temporary loans or other contracts, notes, warrants, or obligations for current expenses in excess of the total anticipated revenue for such calendar year.

Paragraph VI. **Levy of taxes to pay bonds; sinking fund required.** Any county, municipality, or other political subdivision of this state shall at or before the time of incurring bonded indebtedness provide for the assessment and collection of an annual tax sufficient in amount to pay the principal and interest of said debt within 30 years from the incurring of such bonded indebtedness. The proceeds of this tax, together with any other moneys collected for this purpose, shall be placed in a sinking fund to be used exclusively for paying the principal of and interest on such bonded debt. Such moneys shall be held and kept separate and apart from all other revenues collected and may be invested and reinvested as provided by law.

Paragraph VII. **Validity of prior bond issues.** Any and all bond issues validated and issued prior to June 30, 1983, shall continue to be valid.

Section VI.
Revenue Bonds

Paragraph I. **Revenue bonds; general limitations.** Any county, municipality, or other political subdivision of this state may issue revenue bonds as provided by general law. The obligation represented by revenue bonds shall be repayable only out of the revenue derived from the project and shall not be deemed to be a debt of the issuing political subdivision. No such issuing political subdivision shall exercise the power of taxation for the purpose of paying any part of the principal or interest of any such revenue bonds.

Paragraph II. **Revenue bonds; special limitations.** Where revenue bonds are issued by any county, municipality, or other political subdivision of this state in order to buy, construct, extend, operate, or maintain gas or electric generating or distribution systems and necessary appurtenances thereof and the gas or electric generating or distribution system extends beyond the limits of the county in which the municipality or other political subdivision is located, then its services rendered and property located outside said county shall be subject to taxation and regulation in the same manner as are privately owned and operated utilities.

Paragraph III. **Development authorities.** The development of trade, commerce, industry, and employment opportunities being a public purpose vital to the welfare of the people of this state, the General Assembly may create development authorities to promote and further such purposes or may authorize the creation of such an authority by any county or municipality or combination thereof under such uniform terms and conditions as it may deem necessary. The General Assembly may exempt from taxation development authority obligations, properties, activities, or income and may authorize the issuance of revenue bonds by such authorities which shall not constitute an indebtedness of the state within the meaning of Section V of this article.

Paragraph IV. **Validation.** The General Assembly shall provide for the validation of any revenue bonds authorized and shall provide that such validation shall thereafter be incontestable and conclusive.

Paragraph V. **Validity of prior revenue bond issues.** All revenue bonds issued and validated prior to June 30, 1983, shall continue to be valid.

Section VII.
Community Improvement Districts

Paragraph I. **Creation.** The General Assembly may by local law create one or more community improvement districts for any county or municipality or provide for the creation of one or more community improvement districts by any county or municipality.

Paragraph II. **Purposes.** The purpose of a community improvement district shall be the provision of any one or more of the following governmental services and facilities:

(1) Street and road construction and maintenance, including curbs, sidewalks, street lights, and devices to control the flow of traffic on streets and roads.

(2) Parks and recreational areas and facilities.

(3) Storm water and sewage collection and disposal systems.

(4) Development, storage, treatment, purification, and distribution of water.

(5) Public transportation.

(6) Terminal and dock facilities and parking facilities.

(7) Such other services and facilities as may be provided for by general law.

Paragraph III. **Administration.**

(a) Any law creating or providing for the creation of a community improvement district shall designate the governing authority of the municipality or county for which the community improvement district is created as the administrative body or otherwise shall provide for the establishment and membership of an administrative body for the community improvement district. Any such law creating or providing for the creation of an administrative body for the community improvement district other than the municipal or county governing authority shall provide for representation of the governing authority of each county and municipality within which the community improvement district is wholly or partially located on the administrative body of the community improvement district.

(b) Any law creating or providing for the creation of a community improvement district shall provide that the creation of the community improvement district shall be conditioned upon:

(1) The adoption of a resolution consenting to the creation of the community improvement district by:

(A) The governing authority of the county if the community improvement district is located wholly within the unincorporated area of a county;

(B) The governing authority of the municipality if the community improvement district is located wholly within the incorporated area of a municipality; or

(C) The governing authorities of the county and the municipality if the community improvement district is located partially within the unincorporated area of a county and partially within the incorporated area of a municipality; and

(2) Written consent to the creation of the community improvement district by:

(A) A majority of the owners of real property within the community improvement district which will be subject to taxes, fees, and assessments levied by the administrative body of the community improvement district; and

(B) The owners of real property within the community improvement district which constitutes at least 75 percent by value of all real property within the community improvement district which will be subject to taxes, fees, and assessments levied by the administrative body of the community improvement district; and for this purpose value shall be determined by the most recent approved county ad valorem tax digest.

(c) The administrative body of each community improvement district may be authorized to levy taxes, fees, and assessments within the community improvement district only on real property used nonresidentially, specifically excluding all property used for residential, agricultural, or forestry purposes and specifically excluding tangible personal property and intangible property. Any tax, fee, or assessment so levied shall not exceed 2½ percent of the assessed value of the real property or such lower limit as may be established by law. The law creating or providing for the creation of a community improvement district shall provide that taxes, fees, and assessments levied by the administrative body of the community improvement district shall be equitably apportioned among the properties subject to such taxes, fees, and assessments according to the need for governmental services and facilities created by the degree of density of development of each such property. The law creating or providing for the creation of a community improvement district shall provide that taxes, fees, and assessments levied by the administrative body of the community improvement district shall be equitably apportioned among the properties subject to such taxes, fees, and assessments according to the need for governmental services and facilities created by the degree of density of development of each such property. The law creating or providing for the creation of a community improvement district shall provide that the proceeds of taxes, fees, and assessments levied by the administrative body of the community improvement district shall be used only for the purpose of providing governmental services and facilities which are specially required by the degree of density of development within the community improvement district and not for the purpose of providing those governmental services and facilities provided to the county or municipality as a whole. Any tax, fee, or assessment so levied shall be collected by the county or municipality for which the community improvement district is created in the same manner as taxes, fees, and assessments levied by such county or municipality. The proceeds of taxes, fees, and assessments so levied, less such fee to cover the costs of collection as may be specified by law, shall be transmitted by the collecting county or municipality to the administrative body of the community improvement district and shall be expended by the administrative body of the community improvement district only for the purposes authorized by this Section.

Paragraph IV. **Debt.** The administrative body of a community improvement district may incur debt, as authorized by law, without regard to the requirements of Section V of this Article, which debt shall be backed by the full faith, credit, and taxing power of the community improvement district but shall not be an obligation of the State of Georgia or any other unit of government of the State of Georgia other than the community improvement district.

Paragraph V. **Cooperation with local governments.** The services and facilities provided pursuant to this Section shall be provided for in a cooperation agreement executed jointly by the administrative body and the governing authority of the county or municipality for which the community improvement district is created. The provisions of this section shall in no way limit the authority of any county or municipality to provide services or facilities within any community improvement district; and any county or municipality shall retain full and complete authority and control over any of its facilities located within a community improvement district. Said control shall include but not be limited to the modification of, access to, and degree and type of services provided through or by facilities of the municipality or county. Nothing contained in this Section shall be construed to limit or preempt the application of any governmental laws, ordinances, resolutions, or regulations to any community improvement district or the services or facilities provided therein.

Paragraph VI. **Regulation by general law.** The General Assembly by general law may regulate, restrict, and limit the creation of community improvement districts and the exercise of the powers of administrative bodies of community improvement districts.

ARTICLE X.
AMENDMENTS TO THE CONSTITUTION
Section I.
Constitution, How Amended

Paragraph I. **Proposals to amend the Constitution; new Constitution.** Amendments to this Constitution or a new Constitution may be proposed by the General Assembly or by a constitutional convention, as provided in this article. Only amendments which are of general and uniform applicability throughout the state shall be proposed, passed, or submitted to the people.

Paragraph II. **Proposals by the General Assembly; submission to the people.** A proposal by the General Assembly to amend this Constitution or to provide for a new Constitution shall originate as a resolution in either the Senate or the House of Representatives and, if approved by two-thirds of the members to which each house is entitled in a roll-call vote entered on their respective journals, shall be submitted to the electors of the entire state at the next general election which is held in the even-numbered years. A summary of such proposal shall be prepared by the Attorney General, the Legislative Counsel, and the Secretary of State and shall be published in the official organ of each county and, if deemed advisable by the "Constitutional Amendments Publication Board," in not more than 20 other newspapers in the state designated by such board which meet the qualifications for being selected as the official organ of a county. Said board shall be composed of the Governor, the Lieutenant Governor, and the Speaker of the House of Representatives. Such summary shall be published once each week for three consecutive weeks immediately preceding the day of the general election at which such proposal is to be submitted. The language to be used in submitting a proposed amendment or a new Constitution shall be in such words as the General Assembly may provide in the resolution or, in the absence thereof, in such language as the Governor may prescribe. A copy of the entire proposed amendment or of a new Constitution shall be filed in the office of the judge of the probate court of each county and shall be available for public inspection; and the summary of the proposal shall so indicate. The General Assembly is hereby authorized to provide by law for additional matters relative to the publication and distribution of proposed amendments and summaries not in conflict with the provisions of this Paragraph. If such proposal is ratified by a majority of the electors qualified to vote for members of the General Assembly voting thereon in such general election, such proposal shall become a part of this Constitution or shall become a new Constitution, as the case may be. Any proposal so approved shall take effect as provided in Paragraph VI of this article. When more than one amendment is submitted at the same time, they shall be so submitted as to enable the electors to vote on each amendment separately, provided that one or more new articles or related changes in one or more articles may be submitted as a single amendment.

Paragraph III. **Repeal or amendment of proposal.** Any proposal by the General Assembly to amend this Constitution or for a new Constitution may be amended or repealed by the same General Assembly which adopted such proposal by the affirmative vote of two-thirds of the members to which each house is entitled in a roll-call vote entered on their respective journals, if such action is taken at least two months prior to the date of the election at which such proposal is to be submitted to the people.

Paragraph IV. **Constitutional convention; how called.** No convention of the people shall be called by the General Assembly to amend this Constitution or to propose a new Constitution, unless by the concurrence of two-thirds of the members to which each house of the General Assembly is entitled. The representation in said convention shall be based on population as near as practicable. A proposal by the convention to amend this Constitution or for a new Constitution shall be advertised, submitted to, and ratified by the people in the same manner provided for advertisement, submission, and ratification of proposals to amend the Constitution by the General Assembly. The General Assembly is hereby authorized to provide the procedure by which a convention is to be called and under which such convention shall operate and for other matters relative to such constitutional convention.

Paragraph V. **Veto not permitted.** The Governor shall not have the right to veto any proposal by the General Assembly or by a convention to amend this Constitution or to provide a new Constitution.

Paragraph VI. **Effective date of amendments or of a new Constitution.** Unless the amendment or the new Constitution itself or the resolution proposing the amendment or the new Constitution shall provide otherwise, an amendment to this Constitution or a new Constitution shall become effective on the first day of January following its ratification.

ARTICLE XI.
MISCELLANEOUS PROVISIONS
Section I.
Miscellaneous Provisions

Paragraph I. **Continuation of officers, boards, commissions, and authorities.**

(a) Except as otherwise provided in this Constitution, the officers of the state and all political subdivisions thereof in office on June 30, 1983, shall continue in the exercise of their functions and duties, subject to the provisions of laws applicable thereto and subject to the provisions of this Constitution.

(b) All boards, commissions, and authorities specifically named in the Constitution of 1976 which are not specificaly named in this Constitution shall remain as statutory boards, commissions, and authorities; and all constitutional and statutory provisions relating thereto in force and effect on June 30, 1983, shall remain in force and effect as statutory law unless and until changed by the General Assembly.

Paragraph II. **Preservation of existing laws; judicial review.** All laws in force and effect on June 30, 1983, not inconsistent with this Constitution shall remain in force and effect; but such laws may be amended or repealed and shall be subject to judicial decision as to their validity when passed and to any limitations imposed by their own terms.

Paragraph III. **Proceedings of courts and administrative tribunals confirmed.** All judgments, decrees, orders, and other proceedings of the several courts and administrative tribunals of this state, heretofore made within the limits of their several jurisdictions, are hereby ratified and affirmed, subject only to reversal or modification in the manner provided by law.

Paragraph IV. **Continuation of certain constitutional amendments for a period of four years.**

(a) The following amendments to the Constitution of 1877, 1945, and 1976 shall continue in force and effect as part of this Constitution until July 1, 1987, at which time said amendments shall be repealed and shall be deleted as a part of this Constitution unless any such amendment shall be specifically continued in force and effect without amendment either by a local law enacted prior to July 1, 1987, with or without a referendum as provided by law, or by an ordinance or resolution duly adopted prior to July 1, 1987, by the local governing authority in the manner provided for the adoption of home rule amendments to its charter or local act: (1) amendments to the Constitution of 1877 and the Constitution of 1945 which were continued in force and effect as a part of the Constitution of 1976 pursuant to the provisions of Article XIII, Section I, Paragraph II of the Constitution of 1976 which are in force and effect on the effective date of this Constitution; (2) amendments to the Constitution of 1976 which were ratified as general amendments but which by their terms applied principally to a particular political subdivision or subdivisions which are in force and effect on the effective date of this Constitution; (3) amendments to the Constitution of 1976 which were ratified not as general amendments which are in force and effect on the effective date of this Constitution; and (4) amendments to the Constitution of 1976 of the type provided for in the immediately preceding two subparagraphs (2) and (3) of this Paragraph which were ratified at the same time this Constitution was ratified.

(b) Any amendment which is continued in force and effect after July 1, 1987, pursuant to the provisions of subparagraph (a) of this Paragraph shall be continued in force and effect as a part of this Constitution, except that such amendment may thereafter be repealed but may not be amended.

(c) All laws enacted pursuant to those amendments to the Constitution which are not continued in force and effect pursuant to subparagraph (a) of this Paragraph shall be repealed on July 1, 1987. All laws validly enacted on, before, or after July 1, 1987, and pursuant to the specific authorization of an amendment continued in force and effect pursuant to the provisions of subparagraph (a) of this Paragraph shall be legal, valid, and constitutional under this Constitution. Nothing in this subparagraph (c) shall be construed to revive any law not in force and effect on June 30, 1987.

(d) Notwithstanding the provisions of subparagraphs (a) and (b), the following amendments to the Constitutions of 1877 and 1945 shall be continued in force as a part of this Constitution: amendments to the Constitution of 1877 and the Constitution of 1945 which created or authorized the creation of metropolitan rapid transit authorities, port authorities, and industrial areas and which were continued in force as a part of the Constitution of 1976 pursuant to the provisions of Article XIII, Section I, Paragraph II of the Constitution of 1976 and which are in force on the effective date of this Constitution.

Paragraph V. **Special commission created.** Amendments to the Constitution of 1976 which were determined to be general and which were submitted to and ratified by the people of the entire state at the same time this Constitution was ratified shall be incorporated and made a part of this Constitution as provided in this Paragraph. There is hereby created a commission to be composed of the Governor, the President of the Senate, the Speaker of the House of Representatives, the Attorney General, and the Legislative Counsel, which is hereby authorized and directed to incorporate such amendments into this Constitution at the places deemed most appropriate to the commission. The commission shall make only such changes in the language of this Constitution and of such amendments as are necessary to incorporate properly such amendments into this Constitution and shall complete its duties prior to July 1, 1983. The commission shall deliver to the Secretary of State this Constitution with those amendments incorporated therein, and such document shall be the Constitution of the State of Georgia. In order that the commission may perform its duties, this Paragraph shall become effective as soon as it has been officially determined that this Constitution has been ratified. The commission shall stand abolished upon the completion of its duties.

Paragraph VI. **Effective date.** Except as provided in Paragraph V of this section, this Constitution shall become effective on July 1, 1983; and, except as otherwise provided in this Constitution, all previous Constitutions and all amendments thereto shall thereupon stand repealed.

CORPS OF ENGINEERS LAKES

Since the late 1940s, the Corps of Engineers has constructed nine large multi-purpose reservoirs on the major rivers of Georgia. These dams and lakes, built to provide flood control, hydroelectric power, and navigation to the people of the Southeast, have also found their place through the years among the major recreation attractions in the state. The latest figures show visitations at these lakes exceeded 51 million annually. Four of the State's lakes are among the eight most popular Corps-built lakes in the nation. Lake Lanier, northeast of Atlanta, currently holds the Corps' national record for annual visitations with 13 million.

Although Georgia is blessed with many lakes, six of the Corps-operated lakes—Hartwell, Clark Hill, Lanier, Seminole, Walter George, and West Point—are the largest in the state. Total area of all nine publicly-owned lakes is 289,000 acres, with a combined shoreline length of 4,300 miles.

Because of the popularity of these lakes, the Corps of Engineers is deeply involved in the field of outdoor recreation. Development includes a wide variety of recreational facilities, including marinas, boat launching ramps, picnic and camping facilities, hiking trails, swimming beaches, fish attractors, and much more. Some of the lakes, such as newly developed West Point Lake on the Chattahoochee River near LaGrange, have special fishing piers and other features designed for the elderly and the handicapped. In addition, West Point, as a recreation demonstration project, is designed to have such extra features as basketball and tennis courts, a children's fishing pond, and a rifle and pistol range.

For more information on facilities at individual lakes, contact the Resource Manager.

Allatoona Lake. Resource Manager, U.S. Army, Corps of Engineers, P.O. Box 487, Cartersville 30120. On the Etowah River northwest of Atlanta, the 12,000-acre lake has over 270 miles of shoreline. The Etowah Indian Mounds and Kennesaw Mountain Battlefield are within a few miles of the lake.

Carters Lake. Resource Manager, U.S. Army, Corps of Engineers, P.O. Box 42, Oakman 30732. In North Georgia's Blue Ridge, 2 hours north of Atlanta. This 400-foot-deep lake is one of Georgia's newest lakes.

Clark Hill Lake. Resource Manager, U.S. Army, Corps of Engineers, Clark Hill Lake, Clark Hill, S.C. 29821. This 70,000-acre lake, on the Georgia-South Carolina border near Augusta is the largest Corps-managed lake in the state. It is especially known for its fine fishing and has some of the state's best publicly-owned hunting lands.

Hartwell Lake. Resource Manager, U.S. Army, Corps of Engineers, P.O. Box 278, Hartwell 30643. Located on the Savannah River in the rolling country of the upper Piedmont Plateau. Hartwell Lake is easily accessible from Interstate 85. There are 4 marinas and 3 state parks on the lake, as well as 68 other developed public areas.

Lake George W. Andrews. Resource Manager, U.S. Army, Corps of Engineers, P.O. Box 281, Fort Gaines 31751. This lake is the smallest Corps-built lake in Georgia. In spite of its small size, it has a wide range of facilities, including boat ramps and provisions for tent camping.

Lake Seminole. Resource Manager, U.S. Army, Corps of Engineers, P.O. Box 96, Chattahoochee, FL 32324. A renowned fishing hole (specialty, large mouth bass), 5,000-acre Lake Seminole is located in the warm subtropical lowlands of South Georgia where Alabama, Georgia, and Florida join. Its 37,000 acres offer year-round fishing, boating, and camping opportunities.

Lake Sidney Lanier. Resource Manager, U.S. Army, Corps of Engineers, P.O. Box 567, Buford 30518. A 38,000-acre lake with 550 miles of shoreline, including Lanier Islands, a developed outdoor recreation facility.

Walter F. George Lake. Resource Manager, U.S. Army, Corps of Engineers, P.O. Box 281, Fort Gaines 31751. South of Columbus, this lake has long been recognized as one of Georgia's finest fishing lakes. The Eufala National Wildlife Refuge for migratory birds is also located on project lands.

West Point Lake. Resource Manager, U.S. Army, Corps of Engineers, P.O. Box 574, West Point 31833. Located on the Chattahoochee River, about 3 miles north of West Point. The lake is 25,900 acres, with 37 recreational areas and 11 parks, and a public overlook.

COUNTY NAME ORIGINS

Georgia contains 159 counties. Each county name, the year of its establishment, and a brief biographical sketch (when available) of the person for whom it was named, follow.

Appling County. Established 1818; named in honor of DANIEL APPLING. Served as Lieutenant Colonel in War of 1812. He was awarded the sword by the legislature of Georgia; but he died in 1818, before it was presented to him.

Atkinson County. Established 1918; named in honor of WILLIAM YATES ATKINSON. Served as fifty-third governor of Georgia. Also served in Georgia assembly.

Bacon County. Established 1914; named in honor of AUGUSTUS OCTAVIUS BACON. Confederate Army officer. Served in State House of Representatives, 1871–86; serving 2 years as Speaker pro tempore and 8 years as Speaker. U.S. Senator, 1895–1914.

Baker County. Established 1825; named in honor of COLONEL JOHN BAKER. Revolutionary War hero.

Baldwin County. Established 1803; named in honor of ABRAHAM BALDWIN. Educator, president of University of Georgia. Served in State House of Representatives, 1785; Continental Congress, 1785–88; federal constitutional convention, 1787; U.S. representative, 1789–99 and senator, 1799–1807. Signer of U.S. Constitution.

Banks County. Established 1858; named in honor of RICHARD BANKS. A noted physician.

Barrow County. Established 1914; named in honor of DAVID CRENSHAW BARROW. A University of Georgia professor who later served as Chancellor of the university, 1907–25.

Bartow County. Established 1832; named in honor of FRANCIS S. BARTOW. An army general who was killed July 21, 1861 at Manassas Plains. (Bartow County was formerly Cass County. The name was changed December 6, 1861.)

Ben Hill County. Established 1906; named in honor of BENJAMIN HARVEY HILL. Served in State House of Representatives, 1851; State Senate, 1859–60; delegate to Confederate Provisional Congress, 1861; senator, Confederate Congress, 1861–65; U.S. Representative, 1875–77; and senator, 1877–82.

Berrien County. Established 1856; named in honor of JOHN MACPHERSON BERRIEN. After serving as a lawyer, judge and officer of the cavalry, he served in the State Senate, 1822–23; U.S. Senate, 1825–29. He was U.S. Attorney General in President Andrew Jackson's cabinet, 1829–31, before serving 3 more terms in the U.S. Senate, 1841–52.

Bibb County. Established 1822; named in honor of WILLIAM WYATT BIBB. A physician who served as a state representative, 1803–05; U.S. representative, 1807–13; senator, 1813–16, before becoming territorial governor of Alabama, 1817–19, and later first governor of the State of Alabama, 1819–20.

Bleckley County. Established 1912; named in honor of LOGAN EDWIN BLECKLEY. After serving as solicitor general of Atlanta, 1852–56, he fought in the War Between the States. Later he became Supreme Court reporter, 1864–67; associate justice of the South Carolina Supreme Court, 1875–80; chief justice, 1887–94; secretary to the governor.

Brantley County. Established 1920; named in honor of WILLIAM GORDON BRANTLEY.

Brooks County. Established 1858; named in honor of PRESTON SMITH BROOKS.

Bryan County. Established 1793; named in honor of JONATHAN BRYAN.

Bulloch County. Established 1796; named in honor of ARCHIBALD BULLOCH. The first governor of Georgia under American rule, 1776–77, was also a lieutenant in the South Carolina regiment, 1757; Speaker of the Georgia Royal Assembly, 1775–76; and Continental Congress.

Burke County. Established 1777; named in honor of EDMUND BURKE. A member of British Parliament in 1765 who urged the repeal of the Stamp Act and advised conciliation with the American colonies.

Butts County. Established 1825; named in honor of SAM BUTTS. An army officer killed January 27, 1814 at the Battle of Chalibee.

Calhoun County. Established 1854; named in honor of JOHN CALDWELL CALHOUN. A South Carolina legislator who served in their House of Representatives, 1808–09, and represented his state in the U.S. House of Representatives, 1811–17 and Senate, 1832–43, 1845–50. He served in President Monroe's cabinet, 1817–25, as secretary of war, and President Tyler's cabinet, 1844–45, as secretary of state. He served as vice president under presidents John Quincy Adams and Andrew Jackson, 1825–32.

Camden County. Established 1777; named in honor of CHARLES LORD PRATT, EARL OF CAMDEN. A member of British Parliament who opposed as unconstitutional the Stamp Act and tax of American colonies as unconstitutional. He was Lord Chancellor, 1766–70, and Lord President of Council, 1782, 1784–94.

Candler County. Established 1914; named in honor of ALLEN DANIEL CANDLER. A Civil War soldier who was injured at Kennesaw Mountain and lost an eye at Jonesboro. After serving as an educator he became mayor of Gainesville, 1872; was in State House of Representatives, 1873–77; Senate, 1878–79; U.S. representative, 1883–91; secretary of state for Georgia, 1894–98; governor, 1899–1902.

Carroll County. Established 1826; named in honor of CHARLES CARROLL. Signer of the Declaration of Independence who served as senator from Maryland, 1777–1800.

Catoosa County. Established 1853; named in honor of CHIEF CATOOSA. Indian chief.

Charlton County. Established 1854; named in honor of ROBERT MILLEDGE CHARLTON. State legislator, 1829; U.S. District Attorney, 1830; Superior Court judge, eastern district, 1832; U.S. senator, 1852–53; mayor of Savannah.

Chatham County. Established 1777; named in honor of WILLIAM LORD PITT, EARL OF CHATHAM. English nobleman, entered Parliament, 1735. Secretary of state and leader of House of Commons, 1756.

Chattahoochee County. Established 1854; named for the Chattahoochee River, an Indian word which translates "painted stone."

Chattooga County. Established 1838; named for the CHATTOOGA RIVER.

Cherokee County. Established 1830; named in honor of the CHEROKEE INDIAN TRIBE.

Clarke County. Established 1801; named in honor of ELIJAH CLARKE. Twice wounded Georgia militia officer who fought at Alligator Creek, 1778; Wofford's Iron Works, 1780; Musgrove's Mill, 1780; Augusta, 1780; and Long Cane, S.C., 1780.

Clay County. Established 1854; named in honor of HENRY CLAY. Kentucky congressman, 1803; U.S. senator, 1806–07, 1810–11; representative from Kentucky, 1811–14, 1815–21, and 1823–25; secretary of state to President Adams. Ran unsuccessfully three times for the presidency, 1824, 1832 and 1844.

Clayton County. Established 1858; named in honor of AUGUSTIN SMITH CLAYTON. Member and clerk of House of Representatives, 1810–15; Superior Court judge, 1819–25; and U.S. representative, 1832–35.

Clinch County. Established 1850; named in honor of DUNCAN LAMONT CLINCH. Third Infantry Army officer who fought in first and second Seminole Wars. U.S. representative, 1844–45.

Cobb County. Established 1832; named in honor of THOMAS WILLIS COBB. U.S. representative, 1817–21, 1823–24; U.S. senator, 1824–28; Superior Court judge, 1828.

Coffee County. Established 1854; named in honor of JOHN COFFEE. Georgia militia officer wounded in Creek Indian Battle, 1814; state senator, 1819–27; U.S. Representative, 1833–36.

Colquitt County. Established 1856; named in honor of WALTER TERRY COLQUITT. Chattahoochee circuit court judge, 1826; Methodist clergyman, 1827; Senate, 1834 and 1837; U.S. representative, 1839–40, 1842–43; U.S. Senator, 1843–48.

Columbia County. Established 1790; named in honor of CHRISTOPHER COLUMBUS. Italian navigator who sailed from Spain and discovered San Salvador in 1492.

Cook County. Established 1918; named in honor of PHILLIP COOK. Senator, 1859, 1860, 1863 and 1864; Confederate Army officer; U.S. representative, 1873–83; secretary of state, 1890–94.

Coweta County. Established 1825; named in honor of WILLIAM McINTOSH, general, chief of the Cowetas.

Crawford County. Established 1822; named in honor of WILLIAM HARRIS CRAWFORD. Representative, 1803–07; U.S. senator, 1807–13; Senate president pro tempore, 1812; U.S. minister to France, 1813–15; U.S. secretary of war in President Madison's cabinet, 1815–16; secretary of the Treasury in President Madison's cabinet, 1816–25; circuit judge, 1827–34.

Crisp County. Established 1905; named in honor of CHARLES FREDERICK CRISP. Confederate soldier held as prisoner of war, 1864–65; circuit court solicitor general, 1872–77; Superior Court judge, 1877–82; U.S. representative, 1883–96.

Dade County. Established 1837; named in honor of FRANCIS LANGHORNE DADE. Officer in U.S. Infantry, killed in ambush by Seminole chiefs Micanope and Jumper, December 28, 1835.

Dawson County. Established 1857; named in honor of WILLIAM CROSBY DAWSON. Representative, compiler, laws of Georgia, 1820–30; fought in Creek War, 1836; U.S. representative, 1836–41; Superior Court judge, Ocmulgee Circuit, 1845; U.S. senator, 1849–55.

Decatur County. Established 1823; named in honor of STEPHEN DECATUR. Commander of schooner Enterprise in Tripolitan War and United States in War of 1812; forced Barbary Pirates to submit to terms. Killed in a duel with Commodore James Barrow, 1820.

DeKalb County. Established 1822; named in honor of JOHANN DEKALB. French army officer who aided American colonists; was commissioned major general in Continental Army, 1777; died of injury at Battle of Camden, N.J., 1780.

Dodge County. Established 1870; named in honor of WILLIAM EARL DODGE. Delegate to peace convention to prevent Civil War in 1861; U.S. representative from New York, 1866–67.

Dooly County. Established 1821; named in honor of JOHN DOOLY. Georgia militia officer who was killed with his family by Tories in 1780.

Dougherty County. Established 1853; named in honor of CHARLES DOUGHERTY. Judge of the western circuit.

Douglas County. Established 1870; named in honor of STEPHEN ARNOLD DOUGLAS. Illinois House of Representatives, 1836–37; land office registrar; Illinois Secretary of State, 1840–41; representative and senator from Illinois. Defeated by Abraham Lincoln for the presidency, 1860.

Early County. Established 1818; named in honor of PETER EARLY. Twenty-fifth governor of Georgia, 1813–15; U.S. representative, 1803–07; Superior Court judge; state senator, 1815–17.

Echols County. Established 1858; named in honor of ROBERT M. ECHOLS. Georgia assembly; infantry officer U.S. Regiment, 1847; killed at Natural Bridge, Mexico, Dec. 3, 1847.

Effingham County. Established 1777, named in honor of FRANCIS LORD HOWARD, Earl of Effingham, 1763; officer of British army, favored colonists in struggle for independence.

Elbert County. Established 1790; named in honor of SAMUEL ELBERT. Governor of Georgia, 1785; grenadier company officer; expedition against English in east Florida; defended Savannah; wounded and taken prisoner Briar Creek, 1779.

Emanuel County. Established 1812; named in honor of DAVID EMANUEL. Twentieth governor of Georgia, 1801; Revolutionary War; Georgia legislature; president Georgia Senate.

Evans County. Established 1914; named in honor of CLEMENT ANSELM EVANS. Judge; state senator, 1859; Army officer wounded at Gettysburg; Methodist minister, 1866.

Fannin County. Established 1854; named in honor of JAMES WALKER FANNIN. War hero killed, March 27, 1836.

Fayette County. Established 1821; named in honor of MARQUIS DE LAFAYETTE. Resigned from French military service to aid American cause of independence; commissioned Major General in Continental Army, 1777; returned to Paris, 1781; became commander-in-chief of the National Guard, 1789; captured by Austrians, 1792; revisited U.S. in 1784 and 1824–25.

Floyd County. Established 1832; named in honor of JOHN FLOYD. Officer of the Georgia militia; fought Creek and Choctaw Indians; State House of Representatives, 1820–27; U.S. representative, 1827–29.

Forsyth County. Established 1832; named in honor of JOHN FORSYTH. Attorney general of Georgia, 1808; U. S. representative; U.S. senator; U.S. minister to Spain, 1819–23; thirty-first governor of Georgia, 1827–29; U.S. secretary of state under presidents Jackson and Van Buren, 1834–41.

Franklin County. Established 1784; named in honor of BENJAMIN FRANKLIN. Printer; founded Pennsylvania "Gazette," 1728; clerk of Pennsylvania General Assembly; postmaster of Philadelphia; provincial assembly; deputy postmaster general of the British North American Colonies; Continental Congress; signed the Declaration of Independence, 1776; Pennsylvania constitutional convention, 1776; commissioner and minister to France, 1776–85; governor of Pennsylvania, 1785–88; federal constitutional convention, 1787.

Fulton County. Established 1853; named in honor of ROBERT FULTON. Inventor, experimented with a submarine boat in France, 1801; built the Clermont, a steamboat, which sailed up the Hudson River, 1807. Campbell and Milton counties merged with Fulton, January 1, 1932.

Gilmer County. Established 1832; named in honor of GEORGE ROCKINGHAM GILMER. Officer in campaign against Creek Indians; House of Representatives, 1818, 1819 and 1824; U.S. representative, 1827–29, 1833–35; governor, 1829–31, 1837–39.

Glascock County. Established 1857; named in honor of THOMAS GLASCOCK. Georgia constitutional convention; officer in War of 1812; Seminole War, 1817; House of Representatives, 1821, 1823, 1831, 1834 and 1839; U.S. representative, 1835–39.

Glynn County. Established 1777; named in honor of JOHN GLYNN. Member of Parliament.

Gordon County. Established 1850; named in honor of WILLIAM WASHINGTON GORDON. Graduated West Point, 1814; Third Lieutenant, 1815; aide to General Gaines, resigned 1815; first president of Georgia Central Railroad.

Grady County. Established 1905; named in honor of HENRY WOODFIN GRADY. Newspaperman; Georgia representative of *New York Herald*, 1871; editor and part owner of *Atlanta Constitution*, 1880.

Greene County. Established 1786; named in honor of NATHANIEL GREENE. Officer Continental Army, 1775; commanded Army of the South, 1780; president of the court of inquiry for Major Andre.

Gwinnett County. Established 1818; named in honor of BUTTON GWINNETT. Second president of Georgia Provisional Council; signer of the Declaration of Independence, 1776; Georgia constitutional convention, 1777; acting president and commander-in-chief of Georgia, 1777; killed in a duel with General Lachlan McIntosh.

Habersham County. Established 1818; named in honor of JOSEPH HABERSHAM. Served as officer of the First Georgia Regiment, 1776; Continental Congress, 1785–86; postmaster general, 1795–1801.

Hall County. Established 1818; named in honor of LYMAN HALL. Ninth governor of Georgia Provisional Council, 1774–75; signer of Declaration of Independence, 1776; physician; governor of Georgia, 1783.

Hancock County. Established 1793; named in honor of JOHN HANCOCK. First governor of Massachusetts (Commonwealth). Massachusetts provincial legislature, 1766–72; served three terms in Continental Congress, was president one term; first signer of the Declaration of Independence, 1776; major general of Massachusetts Militia; Massachusetts constitutional convention, 1780; governor of Massachusetts; 1780–85 and 1787–93.

Haralson County. Established 1856; named in honor of HUGH ANDERSON HARALSON. Representative, 1831–32; Senator, 1837–38; major general Georgia militia, 1838–50; U.S. Representative, 1843–51.

Harris County. Established 1827; named in honor of CHARLES HARRIS. Lawyer, alderman or mayor of Savannah, Georgia for about 30 years; offered many judicial posts but declined them.

Hart County. Established 1853; named in honor of NANCY MORGAN HART. Married Benjamin Hart of Kentucky, moved to Elbert County, Georgia. Mother of six sons and two daughters; a sharpshooter and patriot reported to have routed and captured many Tories.

Heard County. Established 1830; named in honor of STEPHEN HEARD. Sixth governor; Battle of Kettle Creek, 1781; president of Georgia council, 1782; chief justice inferior court.

Henry County. Established 1821; named in honor of PATRICK HENRY. Virginia House of Burgesses, 1765; Continental Congress, 1774–76; governor of Virginia, 1776–79 and 1784–86; Virginia constitutional convention, 1788.

Houston County. Established 1821; named in honor of JOHN HOUSTON. Chairman of Georgia Sons of Liberty, 1774; Continental Congress, 1775–76; executive council, 1777; governor, 1778 and 1784.

Irwin County. Established 1818; named in honor of JARED IRWIN. Officer of Georgia militia; constitutional convention, 1789; representative, 1790; governor, 1796–98 and 1806–09; permanent constitutional convention, 1798.

Jackson County. Established 1796; named in honor of JAMES JACKSON. Served as lieutenant in Revolutionary War, wounded at Midway, Georgia; brigadier general, 1778; U.S. representative, 1789–91; U.S. senator, 1793–95; governor, 1798–1801; U.S. senator, 1801–06.

Jasper County. Established 1807; named in honor of WILLIAM JASPER. Officer in Colonel William Moultrie's Second South Carolina Infantry, 1775; distinguished himself during attack on Fort Moultrie, June 28, 1776; killed while planting South Carolina flag at battle of Savannah, October 9, 1779. Originally Randolph County, name changed in 1812.

Jeff Davis County. Established 1905; named in honor of JEFFERSON DAVIS. Graduated U.S. Military Academy, 1828; Black Hawk War, 1830–31; representative from Mississippi, 1845–46; commanded Mississippi Riflemen, 1846; with General Taylor in Mexico, 1846; declined appointment as brigadier general, 1847; senator from Mississippi, 1847–51; U.S. secretary of war in cabinet of President Pierce, 1853–57; senator from Mississippi, 1857–61; major general of Mississippi militia, 1861; president of provisional Confederate congress, 1861; president of the Confederacy, 1862; captured, 1865; indicted for treason, 1866; paroled, 1867.

Jefferson County. Established 1796; named in honor of THOMAS JEFFERSON. Virginia House of Burgesses, 1769–74; signer of Declaration of Independence, 1776; governor of Virginia, 1779–81; Virginia house of delegates, 1782; Continental Congress, 1783–85; U.S. Minister to France, 1784–87; U.S. Secretary of State in cabinet of President Washington, 1790–93; vice president of the U.S., 1797–1801; President of the United States, 1801–09.

Jenkins County. Established 1905; named in honor of CHARLES JONES JENKINS. State legislature, 1830; Georgia attorney, 1831; solicitor general middle circuit, 1831; elected ten times to legislature, 1836–49; speaker of the house, 1840, 1843 and 1845; senator, 1856; supreme court, 1860; governor, 1865–68; president constitutional convention, 1877.

Johnson County. Established 1858; named in honor of HERSCHEL VESPASIAN JOHNSON. U.S Senator, 1848–49; Superior court judge of Ocmulgee circuit, 1849–53; governor, 1853–57; senator in Second Confederate Congress, 1862–65; president of constitutional convention, 1865; elected senator but not permitted to qualify, 1866; judge of the middle circuit, 1873–80.

Jones County. Established 1807; named in honor of JAMES JONES. First lieutenant Georgia militia, 1790; House of Representatives, 1796–98; constitutional convention, 1798; U.S. representative, 1799–1801.

Lamar County. Established 1920; named in honor of LUCIUS QUINTUS CINCINNATUS LAMAR. Georgia House of Representatives, 1853; representative from Mississippi, 1857–60 and 1873–77; lieutenant colonel and colonel 18th Mississippi regiment; diplomatic mission to

Russia, France and England for the Confederate States, 1863; professor, University of Mississippi, 1866–67; senator from Mississippi, 1877–85; secretary of the Interior in President Cleveland's cabinet, 1885–88; U.S. Supreme Court justice, 1888–93.

Lanier County. Established 1920; named in honor of SIDNEY LANIER. Tutor, Oglethorpe College, 1860–61; private in Macon volunteers, 1861; wrote "Tiger Lilies" and many other poems; practiced law at Macon, 1868–72; lecturer in English literature at Johns Hopkins University.

Laurens County. Established 1807; named in honor of JOHN LAURENS. Served in Revolutionary War under General George Washington; wounded at battle of Germantown, October 4, 1777; captured one of the redoubts at Yorktown, Virginia; received Cornwallis' sword. Killed in skirmish, Combahee River, South Carolina, 1782.

Lee County. Established 1825; named in honor of RICHARD HENRY LEE. Justice of the peace Westmoreland County, Virginia, 1757; Virginia House of Burgesses, 1758–75; Continental Congress, 1774–80; signer of the Declaration of Independence, 1776; Virginia House of Delegates, 1777, 1780 and 1785; Continental Congress, 1784–87; senator from Virginia, 1789–92.

Liberty County. Established 1777; descriptive.

Lincoln County. Established 1796; named in honor of BENJAMIN LINCOLN. Major general in Continental Army, 1776; at siege of Yorktown, received sword of Cornwallis, 1781; secretary of war, 1781–83; stopped Shay's Rebellion, 1787; lieutenant governor of Massachusetts, 1788; Collector of the Port, Boston, Massachusetts, 1789–1808.

Long County. Established 1920; named in honor of CRAWFORD WILLIAMSON LONG. Physician; used sul-ether in surgical operation at Jefferson, 1841.

Lowndes County. Established 1825; named in honor of WILLIAM JONES LOWNDES. South Carolina House of Representatives, 1806–10; captain of militia, 1807; representative from South Carolina, 1811–22; died at sea, 1822.

Lumpkin County. Established 1832; named in honor of WILSON LUMPKIN. House of Representatives, 1808–12; Senate, 1812–15; U.S. representative, 1815–17 and 1827–31; governor, 1831–35; U.S. senator, 1837–41.

Macon County. Established 1837; named in honor of NATHANIEL MACON. Revolutionary War; North Carolina senate, 1780–82, 1784 and 1785; representative from North Carolina, 1791–1815; Speaker House of Representatives, 1801–07; senator from North Carolina, 1815–28; president North Carolina constitutional convention, 1835.

Madison County. Established 1811; named in honor of JAMES MADISON. First general assembly of Virginia, 1776; Continental Congress, 1780–83 and 1786–88; federal constitutional convention, 1787; representative from Virginia, 1789–97; U.S. secretary of state in cabinet of President Jefferson, 1801–09; President of the U.S., 1809–17.

Marion County. Established 1827; named in honor of FRANCIS MARION. Brigadier general, commander of Marion's brigade, known as "the Swamp Fox"; harassed English troops in the Revolutionary War; won battle of Eutaw Springs; served in South Carolina state Senate, 1782–90.

McDuffie County. Established 1870; named in honor of GEORGE McDUFFIE. South Carolina House of Representatives, 1818–20; Representative from South Carolina, 1821–34; governor of South Carolina, 1834–36; senator from South Carolina, 1842–46.

McIntosh County. Established 1793; named in honor of WILLIAM McINTOSH. Creek Indian chief, leader of Lower Creeks served in Seminole War, 1817–18; brigadier general U.S. Army, killed by his tribesmen who considered him a traitor.

Meriwether County. Established 1877; named in honor of DAVID MERIWETHER. Elected thirteen times to Kentucky legislature, 1832–83; Kentucky constitutional convention, 1849;

Kentucky secretary of state, 1851; senator from Kentucky, 1852; governor of New Mexico territory, 1853–55; Kentucky House of Representatives, 1858–85; Speaker, Kentucky House of Representatives, 1859.

Miller County. Established 1856; named in honor of ANDREW JACKSON MILLER. House of Representatives, 1836; Senate, 1838–56; Superior Court judge.

Mitchell County. Established 1857; named in honor of HENRY MITCHELL. General.

Monroe County. Established 1821; named in honor of JAMES MONROE. Revolutionary War; Virginia legislature; Continental Congress, 1783–86; Virginia senator, 1790–94; served two terms as governor of Virginia (Commonwealth); U.S. secretary of state under President James Madison; President of the U.S., 1817–25.

Montgomery County. Established 1793; named in honor of RICHARD MONTGOMERY. Provincial Congress, 1775; brigadier general Continental Army; killed leading assault against Quebec, 1775.

Morgan County. Established 1807; named in honor of DANIEL MORGAN. Teamster under General Braddock, 1755; lieutenant in Pontiac's War, 1764; captain in Dunmore's War, 1774; captain Virginia riflemen, 1775; captured at Quebec, December 31, 1775; colonel of Virginia regiment, 1776; brigadier general at battle of Saratoga, 1780; defeated General Tarleton at battle of Cowpens, 1781; commanding Virginia militia suppressed Whiskey Insurrection in Pennsylvania, 1794; Representative from Virginia, 1797–99.

Murray County. Established 1832; named in honor of THOMAS W. MURRAY. Legislature, 1818, speaker of the house; nominated for U.S. Congress but died before election.

Muscogee County. Established 1826; named in honor of MUSCOGEE INDIAN TRIBE.

Newton County. Established 1821; named in honor of JOHN NEWTON. Sergeant who, with William Jasper, captured ten British soldiers who were taking colonial prisoners to Savannah to be hanged.

Oconee County. Established 1875. Indian word for "the place of springs" or "the water eyes of the hills."

Oglethorpe County. Established 1793; named in honor of JAMES EDWARD OGLETHORPE. First governor under the trustees. Colonizer; landed at Charleston, 1733; returned to England, 1734; second trip, 1736; advocated religious freedom; returned to England, 1743; surrendered charter of Georgia, 1752; general commander of English forces, 1765.

Paulding County. Established 1832; named in honor of JOHN PAULDING. One of the captors of Major John André, 1780; received silver medal from Congress and pension of $200.

Peach County. Established 1924. Descriptive, Georgia peach.

Pickens County. Established 1853; named in honor of ANDREW PICKENS. Fought Cherokee Indians, 1760; captain to brigadier general, Revolutionary War, 1779–81; awarded sword by Congress for victory at Cowpens, 1781; fought Cherokee Indians, 1782; South Carolina House of Representatives, 1781–94; South Carolina constitutional convention, 1790; representative from South Carolina, 1793–95; major general of militia, 1795; South Carolina House of Representatives, 1800–12.

Pierce County. Established 1857; named in honor of FRANKLIN PIERCE. New Hampshire House of Representatives, 1829–33; representative from New Hampshire, 1833–37; senator from New Hampshire, 1837–42; colonel in Mexican war; brigadier general, 1847; New Hampshire constitutional convention, 1850; president of the U.S., 1853–57.

Pike County. Established 1822; named in honor of ZEBULON MONTGOMERY PIKE. Soldier and explorer; Pike's peak (first sighted by him) bears his name; colonel in War of 1812, was killed in Toronto, Canada.

Polk County. Established 1851; named in honor of JAMES KNOX POLK. Chief clerk Tennessee senate, 1821–23; Tennessee House of Representatives, 1823–25; representative from Tennessee, 1825–39; governor of Tennessee, 1839–41; President of the U.S., 1845–49.

Pulaski County. Established 1808; named in honor of CASIMIRE PULASKI. Polish nobleman who came to America in 1777 to aid American independence; fought at Brandywine and Germantown; mortally wounded at siege of Savannah, 1779.

Putnam County. Established 1807; named in honor of ISRAEL PUTNAM. Served in French and Indian War, 1754–63; Pontiac's War, 1764; major general Continental Army, 1775–79; commanded at New York and Philadelphia.

Quitman County. Established 1858; named in honor of JOHN ANTHONY QUITMAN. Mississippi House of Representatives, 1826–27; chancellor of Mississippi, 1828–35; president Mississippi senate, 1835–36; acting governor of Mississippi, 1835–36; judge high court of errors and appeals, 1838; brigadier general volunteers, 1846; major general regular army, 1847; governor of Mississippi, 1850–51; representative from Mississippi, 1855–58.

Rabun County. Established 1819; named in honor of WILLIAM RABUN. State assembly; president of Senate; governor, 1817–19; died in office, 1819.

Randolph County. Established 1828; named in honor of JOHN RANDOLPH. Representative from Virginia, 1799–1813, 1815–17, 1819– 25, 1827–29 and 1833; senator from Virginia, 1825–27; Virginia constitutional convention, 1829; U.S. minister to Russia, 1830–31; fought duel with Henry Clay, 1826.

Richmond County. Established 1777; named in honor of CHARLES LENNOX, THIRD DUKE OF RICHMOND. Third son of second Duke of Richmond; British Minister Extraordinary in Paris, 1765; secretary of state for Southern Department, 1766; resigned, 1767; favored American colonies and wanted troops withdrawn, 1778.

Rockdale County. Established 1870. Descriptive of the vein of rock located throughout the county.

Schley County. Established 1857; named in honor of WILLIAM SCHLEY. Superior Court judge, 1825–28; House of Representatives, 1830; U.S. representative, 1833–35; governor, 1835–37.

Screven County. Established 1793; named in honor of JAMES SCREVEN. Served as officer of 3rd Georgia Rangers, 1776; resigned, 1778; brigadier general Georgia militia; killed at Midway Church, Liberty County, Georgia.

Seminole County. Established 1920; named in honor of the SEMINOLE INDIAN TRIBE.

Spalding County. Established 1851; named in honor of THOMAS SPALDING. House of Representatives, 1794; constitutional convention, 1798; Senate, 1805–06; commissioner to determine Georgia-Florida boundary line.

Stephens County. Established 1905; named in honor of ALEXANDER HAMILTON STEPHENS. House of Representatives, 1836–41; Senate, 1842; U.S. representative, 1843–59; vice president of Confederate provisional government, 1861; imprisoned for five months, 1865; elected senator by Georgia, but did not present his credentials as Georgia was not readmitted to representation, 1866; U.S. representative, 1873–82; governor, 1882–83.

Stewart County. Established 1830; named in honor of DANIEL STEWART. Brigadier general, Continental Army.

Sumter County. Established 1831; named in honor of THOMAS SUMTER. Lieutenant colonel Sixth Continental Regiment; brigadier general of militia, 1780; voted the thanks of Congress, 1781; South Carolina state senate, 1781–82; Representative from South Carolina, 1789–93 and 1797–1801; Senator from South Carolina, 1801–10.

Talbot County. Established 1827; named in honor of MATTHEW TALBOT. Member state constitutional convention, 1798; Senator, 1808; president of Senate, 1818–23; ex officio governor, 1819.

Taliaferro County. Established 1825; named in honor of BENJAMIN TALIAFERRO. Officer in Revolutionary War; president state senate; delegate state constitutional convention, 1798; U.S. representative, 1799–1802; Superior Court judge.

Tattnall County. Established 1801; named in honor of JOSIAH TATTNALL. In Revolutionary War under General Anthony Wayne, 1782; colonel of Georgia regiment promoted to brigadier general, 1801; House of Representatives, 1795 and 1796; U.S. senator, 1796–99; governor, 1801–02.

Taylor County. Established 1852; named in honor of ZACHARY TAYLOR. Twelfth president of the U.S., 1849–50.

Telfair County. Established 1807; named in honor of EDWARD TELFAIR. Member of state council of safety in 1775 and 1776; delegate to the Provincial Congress at Savannah in 1776; member of the Continental Congress, 1777–79 and 1780–83; one of the signers of the Articles of Confederation and delegate to constitutional convention; governor, 1786 and 1790–93.

Terrell County. Established 1856; named in honor of WILLIAM TERRELL. Physician; House of Representatives, 1810–13; U.S. representative, 1817–21.

Thomas County. Established 1825; named in honor of JETT THOMAS. Captain of artillery under General John Floyd; major general, state militia; built state capitol at Milledgeville, 1807.

Tift County. Established 1905; named in honor of NELSON TIFT. Founded Augusta guards, 1835; Baker County inferior court, 1840–41 and 1849; colonel militia Baker County, 1840; House of Representatives, 1841, 1847, 1851–52; editor Albany "Patriot," 1845–58; captain in Confederate Navy, 1861; U.S. representative, 1868–69.

Toombs County. Established 1905; named in honor of ROBERT TOOMBS. Commanded a company in Creek War serving under General Scott, 1836; House of Representatives, 1837–40 and 1841–44; U.S. representative, 1845–53; U.S. senator, 1853–61; Confederate provisional congress; secretary of state of the Confederate States; brigadier general Confederate Army.

Towns County. Established 1856; named in honor of GEORGE WASHINGTON BONAPARTE TOWNS. House of Representatives, 1829–30; Senate, 1832–34; U.S. representative, 1835–36, 1837–39 and 1846–47; governor, 1847–51.

Treutlen County. Established 1918; named in honor of JOHN ADAM TREUTLEN. Provincial Congress, 1775; first governor under the constitution, 1777–78.

Troup County. Established 1825; named in honor of GEORGE MICHAEL TROUP. House of Representatives, 1803–05; U.S. Representative, 1807–15; U.S. Senator, 1816–18; governor, 1823–27; U.S. Senator, 1829–33.

Turner County. Established 1905; named in honor of HENRY GRAY TURNER. Private Confederate Army, 1861; advanced to captain; wounded at battle of Gettysburg; House of Representatives, 1874–76, 1878 and 1879; U.S. representative, 1881–97; associate justice Supreme Court, 1903.

Twiggs County. Established 1809; named in honor of JOHN TWIGGS. Major general, 1781; aide of General Greene; commissioner to negotiate treaty with the Creek Indians, 1783.

Union County. Established 1832. Descriptive.

Upson County. Established 1824; named in honor of STEPHEN UPSON. Born in Connecticut, 1786; lawyer; graduated from Yale; moved south because of ill health; established law practice in Georgia, 1808. Died at age 40, August 1824.

Walker County. Established 1833; named in honor of FREEMAN WALKER. House of Representatives, 1807–11; mayor of Augusta, 1818–19; U.S. senator, 1819–21; mayor of Augusta, 1823.

Walton County. Established 1818; named in honor of GEORGE WALTON. Secretary Provisional Congress, 1774; delegate Continental Congress, 1776–81; signer Declaration of Independence, 1776; colonel of militia captured at battle of Savannah; held prisoner until 1779; governor, 1779–80; chief justice, 1783–86; governor, 1789; judge of Superior Courts of eastern judicial circuit, 1790; chief justice, 1793; U.S. senator, 1795–96; judge of the middle circuit 1799–1804.

Ware County. Established 1824; named in honor of NICHOLAS WARE.

Warren County. Established 1793; named in honor of JOSEPH WARREN. Physician; president of Provincial Congress, 1775; major general Continental Army, 1775; killed at battle of Breed's Hill (Bunker Hill), June 17, 1775.

Washington County. Established 1784; named in honor of GEORGE WASHINGTON. Successfully led Continental Armies to victory in Revolutionary War, 1781; presided over federal constitutional convention, 1787; first President of the U.S., 1789–97.

Wayne County. Established 1803; named in honor of ANTHONY WAYNE. Nicknamed "Mad Anthony"; army officer wounded at Three Rivers Battle, 1776; captured at Stony Point; awarded thanks and gold medal from Congress, 1779; after serving in Pennsylvania was U.S. Representative, 1791–92; returned to lead Army to victory over Indians at Fallen Timbers, 1793.

Webster County. Established 1853; named in honor of DANIEL WEBSTER. Served as a New Hampshire Representative, 1813–17; Massachusetts Representative, 1823–27; Senator, 1827–41, 1845–50; was Secretary of State in the cabinets of Presidents Tyler, 1841–43, and Fillmore, 1850–52. Originally Kinchafoonee County, named changed in 1856.

Wheeler County. Established 1912; named in honor of JOSEPH WHEELER. Army officer; U.S. Representative from Alabama, 1881–82, 1883 and 1885–1900; returned to Army; helped negotiate surrender of Spanish Army in Cuba, 1898; authored many books.

White County. Established 1857; named in honor of DAVID T. WHITE.

Whitfield County. Established 1851; named in honor of GEORGE WHITEFIELD. A clergyman of the Church of England who arrived in Savannah, 1738; built an orphanage there in 1740; was compiler of hymnbook, 1753.

Wilcox County. Established 1857; named in honor of MARK WILCOX. Army officer.

Wilkes County. Established 1777; named in honor of JOHN WILKES. A member of England's House of Commons who, during the American Revolution, favored the colonies.

Wilkinson County. Established 1803; named in honor of JAMES WILKINSON. Army officer in Revolutionary War; fought against Indians; was representative of U.S. in Louisiana Territory take -over; served there as first governor, 1805–07; led attacks by troops against Canadian border, War of 1812.

Worth County. Established 1853; named in honor of WILLIAM JAMES WORTH. Much honored military officer who served as commandant at U.S. Military Academy, 1820–28; and following numerous other awards was presented sword by Congress, 1847.

COUNTY SEATS

County	County Seat	County Seat[1] Population	County	County Seat	County Seat[1] Population
Appling	Baxley	3,610	Baker	Newton	710
Atkinson	Pearson	2,050	Baldwin	Milledgeville	13,850
Bacon	Alma	3,940	Banks	Homer	930

COUNTY SEATS

County	County Seat	County Seat[1] Population	County	County Seat	County Seat[1] Population
Barrow	Winder	7,360	Glynn	Brunswick	19,190
Bartow	Cartersville	9,860	Gordon	Calhoun	6,450
Ben Hill	Fitzgerald	10,940	Grady	Cairo	8,720
Berrien	Nashville	4,860	Greene	Greensboro	3,190
Bibb	Macon	117,980	Gwinnett	Lawrenceville	15,360
Bleckley	Cochran	4,990	Habersham	Clarkesville	1,240
Brantley	Nahunta	1,010	Hall	Gainesville	16,300
Brooks	Quitman	5,190	Hancock	Sparta	1,820
Bryan	Pembroke	1,370	Haralson	Buchanan	1,100
Bulloch	Statesboro	15,670	Harris	Hamilton	590
Burke	Waynesboro	6,080	Hart	Hartwell	4,950
Butts	Jackson	4,230	Heard	Franklin	830
Calhoun	Morgan	400	Henry	McDonough	3,950
Camden	Woodbine	1,230	Houston	Perry	10,880
Candler	Metter	3,550	Irwin	Ocilla	3,170
Carroll	Carrollton	18,760	Jackson	Jefferson	2,010
Catoosa	Ringgold	2,250	Jasper	Monticello	2,410
Charlton	Folkston	2,320	Jeff Davis	Hazlehurst	4,400
Chatham	Savannah	146,800	Jefferson	Louisville	2,800
Chattahoochee	Cusseta	1,550	Jenkins	Millen	3,660
Chattooga	Summerville	4,750	Johnson	Wrightsville	2,660
Cherokee	Canton	4,230	Jones	Gray	2,600
Clarke	Athens	43,100	Lamar	Barnesville	4,890
Clay	Ft. Gaines	1,100	Lanier	Lakeland	2,630
Clayton	Jonesboro	4,870	Laurens	Dublin	16,570
Clinch	Homerville	3,220	Lee	Leesburg	1,600
Cobb	Marietta	42,810	Liberty	Hinesville	16,480
Coffee	Douglas	12,300	Lincoln	Lincolnton	1,550
Colquitt	Moultrie	15,410	Long	Ludowici	1,440
Columbia	Appling	—	Lowndes	Valdosta	36,970
Cook	Adel	5,560	Lumpkin	Dahlonega	3,060
Coweta	Newnan	15,150	Macon	Oglethorpe	1,490
Crawford	Knoxville	—	Madison	Danielsville	390
Crisp	Cordele	11,170	Marion	Buena Vista	1,670
Dade	Trenton	1,630	McDuffie	Thomson	7,410
Dawson	Dawsonville	560	McIntosh	Darien	1,780
Decatur	Bainbridge	10,900	Meriwether	Greensville	1,230
DeKalb	Decatur	18,470	Miller	Colquitt	2,070
Dodge	Eastman	5,100	Mitchell	Camilla	5,500
Dooly	Vienna	2,760	Monroe	Forsyth	4,960
Dougherty	Albany	84,950	Montgomery	Mt. Vernon	1,920
Douglas	Douglasville	9,550	Morgan	Madison	3,420
Early	Blakely	5,790	Murray	Chatsworth	2,750
Echols	Statenville	—	Muscogee	Columbus	180,180
Effingham	Springfield	1,220	Newton	Covington	12,670
Elbert	Elberton	5,700	Oconee	Watkinsville	2,060
Emanuel	Swainsboro	7,940	Oglethorpe	Lexington	280
Evans	Claxton	2,400	Paulding	Dallas	3,980
Fannin	Blue Ridge	1,330	Peach	Ft. Valley	8,760
Fayette	Fayetteville	4,430	Pickens	Jasper	1,840
Floyd	Rome	30,910	Pierce	Blackshear	3,790
Forsyth	Cumming	2,780	Pike	Zebulon	870
Franklin	Carnesville	490	Polk	Cedartown	8,870
Fulton	Atlanta	382,760	Pulaski	Hawkinsville	4,190
Gilmer	Ellijay	1,720	Putnam	Eatonton	6,640
Glascock	Gibson	720	Quitman	Georgetown	990

County	County Seat	County Seat[1] Population	County	County Seat	County Seat[1] Population
Rabun	Clayton	1,750	Treutlen	Soperton	2,780
Randolph	Cuthbert	3,990	Troup	LaGrange	27,150
Richmond	Augusta	45,440	Turner	Ashburn	4,790
Rockdale	Conyers	7,600	Twiggs	Jeffersonville	1,520
Schley	Ellaville	1,770	Union	Blairsville	690
Screven	Sylvania	4,120	Upson	Thomaston	9,800
Seminole	Donalsonville	3,190	Walker	Lafayette	6,220
Spalding	Griffin	22,810	Walton	Monroe	9,170
Stephens	Toccoa	8,670	Ware	Waycross	18,870
Stewart	Lumpkin	1,440	Warren	Warrenton	2,070
Sumter	Americus	16,110	Washington	Sandersville	6,250
Talbot	Talbotton	1,080	Wayne	Jesup	9,850
Taliaferro	Crawfordville	710	Webster	Preston	390
Tattnall	Reidsville	2,460	Wheeler	Alamo	1,020
Taylor	Butler	2,050	White	Cleveland	1,710
Telfair	McRae	3,370	Whitfield	Dalton	21, 220
Terrell	Dawson	5,410	Wilcox	Abbeville	990
Thomas	Thomasville	18,510	Wilkes	Washington	4,700
Tift	Tifton	14,220	Wilkinson	Irwinton	860
Toombs	Lyon	4,270	Worth	Sylvester	5,970
Towns	Hiawassee	540			

[1]1986 Estimates.
—Data not available.

COURTS

Supreme Court

The court holds three terms of court each year, beginning in September, January and April, and hears no oral arguments in August or December. Court is virtually always held in Atlanta, although the court is authorized to sit and may schedule sessions in other locations such as at an accredited law school in order to demonstrate its procedure to students.

To qualify for office as a justice, a person must be at least 30 years of age, a citizen of the state for three years and a practicing attorney for seven years. Justices are elected to six-year terms in statewide nonpartisan elections. Any vacancies on the court are filled by appointment of the governor.

Supreme Court
244 Washington St., S.W.
Atlanta 30334
404-656-3470

Thomas O. Marshall
Chief Justice
Harold G. Clarke
Presiding Justice

George T. Smith
Hardy Gregory, Jr.
Charles L. Weltner
Richard Bell
Willis B. Hunt, Jr.

COURTS

SUPREME COURT
7 Justices
Jurisdiction:
—Appellate jurisdiction over cases of constitutional issue, title to land, validity of and construction of wills, habeas corpus, extraordinary remedies, convictions of capital felonies, equity, divorce, alimony, election contest.
—Certified questions and certiorari from Court of Appeals.

COURT OF APPEALS (3 divisions)
9 judges
Jurisdiction:
—Appellate jurisdiction over lower courts in cases in which Supreme Court has no exclusive appellate jurisdiction.

SUPERIOR COURT (45 circuits)
127 judges
Jurisdiction:
—Exclusive jurisdiction over cases of divorce, title to land, equity.
—Exclusive felony jurisdiction. Misdemeanors, felony preliminaries.
Jury trials.

Capital felonies.
Constitutional issues.
Title to land.
Wills, equity, divorce.

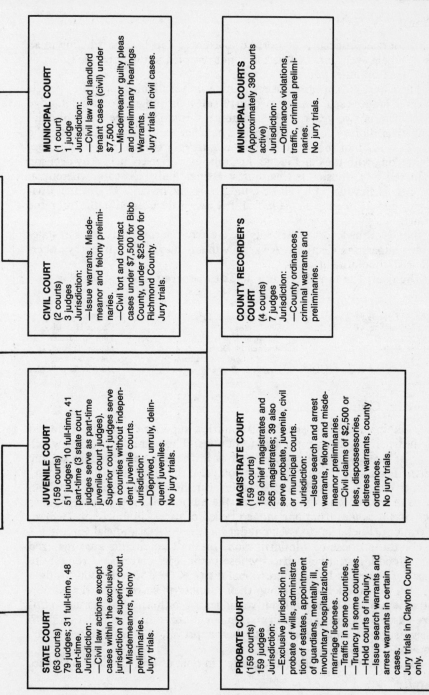

MUNICIPAL COURT
(1 court)
1 judge
Jurisdiction:
—Civil law and landlord tenant cases (civil) under $7,500.
—Misdemeanor guilty pleas and preliminary hearings.
Warrants.
Jury trials in civil cases.

MUNICIPAL COURTS
(Approximately 390 courts active)
Jurisdiction:
—Ordinance violations, traffic, criminal preliminaries.
No jury trials.

CIVIL COURT
(2 courts)
3 judges
Jurisdiction:
—Issue warrants. Misdemeanor and felony preliminaries.
—Civil tort and contract cases under $7,500 for Bibb County, under $25,000 for Richmond County.
Jury trials.

COUNTY RECORDER'S COURT
(4 courts)
7 judges
Jurisdiction:
—County ordinances, criminal warrants and preliminaries.

JUVENILE COURT
(159 courts)
51 judges; 10 full-time, 41 part-time (3 state court judges serve as part-time juvenile court judges). Superior court judges serve in counties without independent juvenile courts.
Jurisdiction:
—Deprived, unruly, delinquent juveniles.
No jury trials.

MAGISTRATE COURT
(159 courts)
159 chief magistrates and 265 magistrates; 39 also serve probate, juvenile, civil or municipal courts.
Jurisdiction:
—Issue search and arrest warrants, felony and misdemeanor preliminaries.
—Civil claims of $2,500 or less, dispossessories, distress warrants, county ordinances.
No jury trials.

STATE COURT
(63 courts)
79 judges; 31 full-time, 48 part-time.
Jurisdiction:
—Civil law actions except cases within the exclusive jurisdiction of superior court.
—Misdemeanors, felony preliminaries.
Jury trials.

PROBATE COURT
(159 courts)
159 judges
Jurisdiction:
—Exclusive jurisdiction in probate of wills, administration of estates, appointment of guardians, mentally ill, involuntary hospitalizations, marriage licenses.
—Traffic in some counties.
—Truancy in some counties.
—Hold courts of inquiry.
—Issue search warrants and arrest warrants in certain cases.
Jury trials in Clayton County only.

Court of Appeals

The Court of Appeals is authorized to exercise appellate jurisdiction in all cases where exclusive jurisdiction is not reserved to the Supreme Court or conferred on other vourts.

The Court of Appeals consists of nine judges divided into three panels of three judges each. Under the court's rules, the judges elect a chief judge for a term of two years, with an automatic rotation of the office of chief judge based on seniority of service. The chief judge is responsible for the administration of the court and appoints three divisional presiding judges who, along with the chief judge, form the executive council. Any decision rendered by a division is final unless a single judge dissents, whereupon the case is considered by all nine judges. In the instance of an equal division of judges hearing a case in full, the case is transferred to the Supreme Court.

Judges of the Court of Appeals are elected to terms of six years in statewide nonpartisan elections. A vacancy in any judgeship is filled by gubernatorial appointment.

The court sits in Atlanta and holds three terms of court per year.

Court of Appeals
Judicial Building, 4th floor
Atlanta 30334
404-656-3450

A. W. Birdsong, Jr.
Chief Judge
Presiding Judges:
Braswell D. Deen, Jr.
William LeRoy McMurray, Jr.
Harold R. Banke

Judges:
George H. Carley
John W. Sognier
Marion T. Pope, Jr.
Robert Benham
Dorothy Toth Beasley

Superior Courts

Located in each of the state's 159 counties, superior courts are organized by judicial circuits, or groups of counties. There are 45 circuits, which vary in size and population, as well as in the number of judges serving them. From one to eight counties comprise the circuits, with the single-county circuits generally located in or near the several large metropolitan areas of the state. In the 45 circuits, the number of superior court judges per circuit ranges from one judge in each of three circuits (Appalachian, Piedmont, Rockdale) to twelve judges in the Atlanta Judicial Circuit.

For the purpose of administration, the judicial circuits are organized into 10 administrative districts whose boundaries correspond roughly to those of Georgia's U.S. congressional districts. The superior court judges of each district elect one among their number to serve as district administrative judge. The administrative judges are authorized by statute to utilize caseload and other information for management purposes and to assign superior court judges, with their approval, to other counties or circuits as needed.

All superior court judges are elected in nonpartisan elections by voters of each circuit to terms of four years. Certain vacancies and new judgeships may be filled by appointment of the governor.

Below is a list of each county name, superior court circuit, and the telephone number of each superior court judge.

County	Superior Court Circuit	Judge Superior Court Telephone	County	Superior Court Circuit	Judge Superior Court Telephone
Appling	Brunswick	912-375-3359	Douglas	Douglas	404-942-8777
Atkinson	Alapaha	912-686-2180	Early	Pataula	912-723-3126
Bacon	Waycross	912-384-0587	Echols	Southern	912-985-1598
Baker	South Georgia	912-246-1111	Effingham	Ogeechee	912-764-6095
Baldwin	Ocmulgee	404-485-7530	Elbert	Northern	404-283-8363
Banks	Piedmont	404-367-1199	Emanuel	Middle	912-552-3227
Barrow	Piedmont	404-367-1199	Evans	Atlantic	912-653-2027
Bartow	Cherokee	404-386-3714	Fannin	Appalachian	404-632-2225
Ben Hill	Cordele	912-273-7950	Fayette	Griffin	404-277-7539
Berrien	Alapaha	912-686-2180	Floyd	Rome	404-291-5121
Bibb	Macon	912-749-6530	Forsyth	Blue Ridge	404-479-2302
Bleckley	Oconee	912-374-7731	Franklin	Northern	404-283-8363
Brantley	Waycross	912-384-0587	Fulton	Atlanta	404-283-8363
Brooks	Southern	912-985-1598	Gilmer	Appalachian	404-632-2225
Bryan	Atlantic	912-653-2027	Glascock	Toombs	404-595-3982
Bulloch	Ogeechee	912-764-6095	Glynn	Brunswick	912-375-3359
Burke	Augusta	404-821-2357	Gordon	Cherokee	404-386-3714
Butts	Flint	404-358-2300	Grady	South Georgia	912-246-1111
Calhoun	South Georgia	912-246-1111	Greene	Ocmulgee	912-485-7530
Camden	Brunswick	912-375-3359	Gwinnett	Gwinnett	404-962-1422
Candler	Middle	912-552-3227	Habersham	Mountain	404-754-6274
Carroll	Coweta	404-832-0525	Hall	Northeastern	404-535-5332
Catoosa	Lookout Mtn.	404-857-2017	Hancock	Ocmulgee	404-485-7530
Charlton	Waycross	912-384-0587	Haralson	Tallapoosa	404-748-2515
Chatham	Eastern	912-944-4771	Harris	Chattahoochee	404-571-4920
Chattahoochee	Chattahoochee	404-571-4920	Hart	Northern	404-283-8363
Chattooga	Lookout Mtn.	404-857-2017	Heard	Coweta	404-832-0525
Cherokee	Blue Ridge	404-479-2302	Henry	Flint	404-358-2300
Clarke	Western	404-354-2767	Houston	Houston	912-987-4448
Clay	Pataula	912-723-3126	Irwin	Tifton	912-382-1556
Clayton	Clayton	404-477-3436	Jackson	Piedmont	404-367-1199
Clinch	Alapaha	912-686-2180	Jasper	Ocmulgee	912-485-7530
Cobb	Cobb	404-429-3164	Jeff Davis	Brunswick	912-375-3359
Coffee	Waycross	912-384-0587	Jefferson	Middle	912-552-3227
Colquitt	Southern	912-985-1598	Jenkins	Ogeechee	912-764-6095
Columbia	Augusta	404-821-2357	Johnson	Dublin	912-272-4131
Cook	Alapaha	912-686-2180	Jones	Ocmulgee	912-485-7530
Coweta	Coweta	404-832-0525	Lamar	Flint	404-358-2300
Crawford	Macon	912-749-6530	Lanier	Alapaha	912-686-2180
Crisp	Cordele	912-273-7950	Laurens	Dublin	912-272-4131
Dade	Lookout Mtn.	404-857-2017	Lee	Southwestern	912-924-2269
Dawson	Northeastern	404-535-5332	Liberty	Atlantic	912-653-2027
Decatur	South Georgia	912-246-1111	Lincoln	Toombs	404-595-3982
DeKalb	Stone Mtn.	404-371-2226	Long	Atlantic	912-653-2027
Dodge	Oconee	912-374-7731	Lowndes	Southern	912-985-1598
Dooly	Cordele	912-273-7950	Lumpkin	Northeastern	404-535-5332
Dougherty	Dougherty	912-431-2114	Macon	Southwestern	912-924-2269

County	Superior Court Circuit	Judge Superior Court Telephone	County	Superior Court Circuit	Judge Superior Court Telephone
Madison	Northern	912-283-8363	Stewart	Southwestern	912-924-2269
Marion	Chattahoochee	404-571-4920	Sumter	Southwestern	912-924-2269
McDuffie	Toombs	404-595-3982	Talbot	Chattahoochee	404-571-4920
McIntosh	Atlantic	912-653-2027	Taliaferro	Toombs	404-595-3982
Meriwether	Coweta	404-832-0525	Tattnall	Atlantic	912-653-2027
Miller	Pataula	912-723-3126	Taylor	Chattahoochee	912-571-4920
Mitchell	South Georgia	912-246-1111	Telfair	Oconee	912-374-7731
Monroe	Flint	912-358-2300	Terrell	Pataula	912-723-3126
Montgomery	Oconee	912-374-7731	Thomas	Southern	912-985-1598
Morgan	Ocmulgee	404-485-7530	Tift	Tifton	912-382-1556
Murray	Conasauga	404-278-0047	Toombs	Middle	912-552-3227
Muscogee	Chattahoochee	404-571-4920	Towns	Mountain	404-754-6274
Newton	Alcovy	404-267-2141	Treutlen	Dublin	912-272-4131
Oconee	Western	404-354-2767	Troup	Coweta	404-832-0525
Oglethorpe	Northern	404-283-8363	Turner	Tifton	912-382-1556
Paulding	Tallapoosa	404-748-2515	Twiggs	Dublin	912-272-4131
Peach	Macon	912-749-6530	Union	Mountain	404-754-6274
Pickens	Appalachian	404-632-2225	Upson	Griffin	404-227-7539
Pierce	Waycross	912-384-0587	Walker	Lookout Mtn.	404-857-2017
Pike	Griffin	404-227-7539	Walton	Alcovy	404-267-2141
Polk	Tallapoosa	404-748-2515	Ware	Waycross	912-384-0587
Pulaski	Oconee	912-374-7731	Warren	Toombs	404-595-3982
Putnam	Ocmulgee	404-485-7530	Washington	Middle	912-552-3227
Quitman	Pataula	912-723-3126	Wayne	Brunswick	912-375-3359
Rabun	Mountain	404-754-6274	Webster	Southwestern	912-924-2269
Randolph	Pataula	912-723-3126	Wheeler	Oconee	912-374-7731
Richmond	Augusta	404-821-2357	White	Northeastern	404-535-5332
Rockdale	Rockdale	404-922-7750	Whitfield	Conasauga	404-278-0047
Schley	Southwestern	912-924-2269	Wilcox	Cordele	912-273-7950
Screven	Ogeechee	912-764-6095	Wilkes	Toombs	404-595-3982
Seminole	Pataula	912-723-3126	Wilkinson	Ocmulgee	912-485-7530
Spalding	Griffin	404-227-7539	Worth	Tifton	912-382-1556
Stephens	Mountain	404-754-6274			

State Courts

State courts retain jurisdiction over trials of nonfelony (misdemeanor, traffic) criminal cases and exercise civil jurisdiction over all general civil actions regardless of the amount claimed, unless exclusive jurisdiction is vested in the superior court. Uniform state court jurisdiction also includes hearing applications for and issuing search and arrest warrants, holding courts of inquiry and punishing contempts by fine ($500 or less) and/or imprisonment (20 days or less). State courts have also been granted constitutional jurisdiction to review decisions of lower courts as may later be provided by statute.

Like superior court judges, state court judges are selected in nonpartisan elections by voters of the respective counties and serve terms of four years. Vacancies and new judgeships may be filled by appointment of the governor in certain instances.

Juvenile Courts

The express purpose of Georgia's juvenile courts, as construed by the state's codified proceedings, is to protect the well-being of children, to provide guidance and control conducive to a child's welfare and the best interests of the state and to serve as nearly as possible care equivalent to parental care for a child removed from the home.

The juvenile court's exclusive original jurisdiction extends to cases involving delinquent children alleged to have committed noncapital offenses and unruly children under the age of 17, deprived children under the age of 18 and juvenile traffic offenders under 16 years of age. In addition, the juvenile court has jurisdiction over custody and child support proceedings referred from the superior court and in cases involving termination of parental rights and enlistment in the military services and consent to marriage for minors. Appeals from the juvenile court in all cases of final judgement are to the Court of Appeals or the Supreme Court.

Juvenile court judges are required by statute to participate in annual training programs sponsored by the Institute of Continuing Judicial Education.

Judges serving separate juvenile courts serve terms of four years. Upon judicial appointment, a person must be over 30 years of age and a citizen of the state for three years, as well as having practiced law for at least three years.

The Council of Juvenile Court Judges is composed of all judges of the courts exercising jurisdiction over juveniles. The membership includes 51 full or part-time juvenile court judges and 58 superior court judges exercising juvenile court jurisdiction. The primary concern of the council is contributing to more effective administration and operation of the state's juvenile courts.

Council of Juvenile Court Judges
244 Washington St., S.W.
Atlanta 30334
404-656-6411

J. Chris Perrin
Executive Director
Mike Sanford
Juvenile Court Specialist

Additional information about Georgia courts can be obtained from:

Judicial Council of Georgia
Administrative Office of the Courts
244 Washington Street, S.W.
Suite 550
Atlanta 30334

Max Cleland
Secretary of State
Elections Division
110 State Capitol
Atlanta 30334

Probate Courts

The probate court exercises exclusive jurisdiction in the probate of wills, the administration of estates, the appointment of guardians and the involuntary hospitalization of incapacitated adults and other dependent individuals. Probate judges are also authorized to perform certain administrative functions such as issuing marriage licenses, pistol permits and delayed birth certificates.

Depending on the particular county, probate judges may be responsible for holding habeas corpus hearings, supervising local elections or presiding over criminal preliminaries. Probate courts may also hear traffic cases and try violations of state game and fish laws, unless there is a demand for a jury trial, in which instance a case would be transferred to the superior court.

One probate judge serves in each of Georgia's 159 counties. Probate judges are elected in partisan elections by the voters of each county to a term of four years. In most counties, a vacancy in office is filled through special election ordered by an official serving as interim judge. In other counties, designated or appointed persons fill the particular vacancy until the next succeeding general election.

Candidates for the office of probate judge must be a county resident for at least two years, have attained the age of 25 and have obtained a high school diploma or its equivalent. In counties with a population of more than 100,000, candidates must be 30 years of age and either a practicing attorney for three years or have served as probate court clerk for at least five years prior to election as judge.

State law requires probate judges to fulfill initial and annual training requirements by attending seminars conducted by the Institute of Continuing Judicial Education and planned together with the Executive Probate Judges Council. The council is a nonfunded state agency charged with the responsibility of advising and coordinating with the Institute concerning matters of continuing education for probate judges.

Magistrate Courts

The statewide system of magistrate courts replaced justice of the peace, small claims and other existing, similar courts as courts with uniform jurisdiction in 1983.

A chief magistrate and one or more magistrates serve each county. The chief magistrate makes appointments to fill vacancies in the office of magistrate (with concurrence of superior court judges), assigns cases among and decides disputes between other magistrates and sets court sessions as necessary.

Chief magistrates are elected in partisan elections. The term of an appointed magistrate runs concurrently with the four year term of the chief magistrate.

Magistrates are required by law to be residents of the county for one year preceding the beginning of their term of office, to be at least 25 years of age and to have a high school education. Judges of courts replaced by magistrate courts who become magistrates by virtue of a statutory grand-father clause are exempt from these qualifications, but additional qualifications may be imposed for any county through local law. All non-lawyer magistrates are required to successfully complete initial certification courses and annual recertification programs approved by the Georgia Magistrate Courts Training Council and conducted by the Institute of Continuing Judicial Education. Attorney magistrates are exempt from the initial training requirements.

As provided by law, judges of other limited jurisdiction courts may also serve as judge of a magistrate court.

Other Courts

Along with the two appellate and five trial courts, approximately 400 local courts form the Georgia court system. Several special courts and numerous courts serving incorporated municipalities operate under a variety of names with varying jurisdictions.

Originally created by statute or constitutional provision, certain special courts have limited civil and criminal jurisdiction throughout the county. Such courts are the civil courts located in Bibb and Richmond counties and the Municipal Court of Columbus. Special courts authorized to exercise criminal jurisdiction only are the county recorder's courts of Chatham, DeKalb and Gwinnett counties and the consolidated government of Columbus-Muscogee County.

The 1983 constitution classified existing and future local city, mayor's, municipal, recorder's and police courts under the umbrella term "municipal courts" to designate them as a group of courts having jurisdiction over ordinance violations and other matters as may be statutorily provided. (One exception is the City Court of Atlanta which retains its original name.) Numbering approximately 390, active municipal courts try local traffic offenses, exercise criminal jurisdiction of magistrate courts and may have concurrent jurisdiction over cases involving one ounce or less of marijuana.

CRIME

Number of crimes reported, 1986.

| County | Total | Violent Crimes | | | | Property Crimes | | | |
		Murder	Rape	Robbery	Aggravated Assault	Burglary	Larceny	Motor Vehicle Theft	Arson
Appling	415	1	3	4	17	148	224	16	2
Atkinson	45	0	2	0	14	16	12	1	0
Bacon	324	0	4	15	15	109	164	13	4

CRIME

| County | Total | Violent Crimes | | | | Property Crimes | | | |
		Murder	Rape	Robbery	Aggravated Assault	Burglary	Larceny	Motor Vehicle Theft	Arson
Baker	56	0	1	0	3	20	31	1	0
Baldwin	1,828	4	19	43	174	639	878	64	7
Banks	101	0	0	1	2	42	42	13	1
Barrow	1,017	3	8	12	54	278	586	71	5
Bartow	1,381	8	3	37	46	425	699	154	9
Ben Hill	889	2	13	26	57	295	460	27	9
Berrien	277	1	3	4	18	92	147	10	2
Bibb	9,305	21	79	254	330	2,261	5,725	617	18
Bleckley	95	1	0	4	11	27	47	5	0
Brantley	116	0	0	1	10	38	57	10	0
Brooks	98	0	2	4	9	23	49	9	2
Bryan	363	2	6	6	17	84	215	30	3
Bulloch	1,302	1	8	27	77	272	872	43	2
Burke	755	2	5	21	88	252	334	50	3
Butts	232	1	3	9	8	110	84	17	0
Calhoun	120	2	1	6	18	36	55	1	1
Camden	800	1	4	28	52	226	441	45	3
Candler	119	0	2	4	2	31	68	10	2
Carroll	2,740	11	27	33	142	616	1,747	149	15
Catoosa	723	0	0	8	23	214	383	91	4
Charlton	7	0	0	0	0	3	4	0	0
Chatham	17,396	41	138	737	669	4,580	10,436	703	92
Chattahoochee	45	0	0	0	5	18	18	3	1
Chattooga	648	0	3	6	38	177	374	43	7
Cherokee	1,277	3	8	18	74	420	650	96	8
Clarke	5,726	4	57	99	326	1,350	3,589	278	23
Clay	38	1	0	2	7	9	15	4	0
Clayton	9,307	5	50	228	372	2,312	5,490	823	27
Clinch	57	0	1	0	2	31	23	0	0
Cobb	17,919	23	107	562	393	4,281	10,446	2,012	95
Coffee	1,292	3	7	34	95	326	757	58	12
Colquitt	1,458	3	13	44	88	503	721	73	13
Columbia	1,352	2	7	14	70	457	726	70	6
Cook	371	2	4	18	51	100	176	19	1
Coweta	1,356	3	9	20	50	467	722	79	6
Crawford	160	0	0	5	9	67	69	10	0
Crisp	1,725	3	10	53	173	477	953	50	6
Dade	221	0	0	3	13	78	97	25	5
Dawson	215	1	0	1	7	76	111	18	1
Decatur	765	1	10	17	71	202	438	25	1
DeKalb	40,824	33	253	1,529	867	10,653	22,992	4,395	102
Dodge	80	0	0	2	4	22	49	3	0
Dooly	13	0	0	3	1	2	4	3	0
Dougherty	5,639	16	63	301	419	1,991	2,645	184	20
Douglas	2,290	3	12	38	108	580	1,301	230	18
Early	287	0	4	3	33	94	138	13	2
Echols	4	0	0	0	0	3	1	0	0
Effingham	384	0	6	9	18	137	182	28	4
Elbert	522	3	2	2	70	141	285	19	0
Emanuel	457	3	8	14	39	145	209	35	4
Evans	47	0	0	1	2	18	23	3	0
Fannin	264	0	4	5	20	138	73	16	8
Fayette	1,246	2	3	8	39	369	750	73	2
Floyd	3,269	12	15	52	145	943	1,825	248	29

County	Total	Violent Crimes				Property Crimes			
		Murder	Rape	Robbery	Aggravated Assault	Burglary	Larceny	Motor Vehicle Theft	Arson
Forsyth	1,294	0	8	5	27	444	680	121	9
Franklin	296	2	2	10	28	94	127	31	2
Fulton	88,182	209	939	6,575	7,691	19,881	42,333	10,480	74
Gilmer	155	0	0	0	3	66	73	13	0
Glascock	3	0	0	0	0	0	2	1	0
Glynn	5,577	7	42	180	635	1,483	2,955	257	18
Gordon	1,047	0	9	23	42	282	599	87	5
Grady	304	2	4	3	12	110	165	8	0
Greene	185	1	5	1	14	84	74	6	0
Gwinnett	13,510	5	65	189	415	3,516	7,999	1,201	120
Habersham	90	0	0	1	9	22	51	7	0
Hall	3,470	2	25	51	178	800	2,097	298	19
Hancock	47	0	0	0	1	22	18	6	0
Haralson	651	1	5	10	69	203	294	64	5
Harris	359	0	4	4	26	160	141	20	4
Hart	201	0	1	0	29	70	90	9	2
Heard	81	0	0	0	5	48	24	4	0
Henry	1,592	3	9	15	74	507	854	124	6
Houston	3,715	8	33	76	230	1,137	2,040	182	9
Irwin	273	1	5	5	14	99	133	13	3
Jackson	744	4	7	12	70	231	359	56	5
Jasper	97	3	0	5	1	50	37	1	0
Jeff Davis	261	1	1	4	11	112	109	20	3
Jefferson	182	2	4	1	31	54	81	9	0
Jenkins	265	3	4	1	19	97	139	2	0
Johnson	21	1	0	0	9	1	9	1	0
Jones	236	1	3	1	10	119	81	21	0
Lamar	294	2	4	5	24	108	140	10	1
Lanier	148	0	3	3	26	35	71	8	2
Laurens	1,294	3	11	25	106	265	839	41	4
Lee	64	0	0	1	11	14	30	8	0
Liberty	1,593	2	18	42	91	426	932	78	4
Lincoln	116	2	1	0	12	33	64	4	0
Long	15	0	0	0	1	7	6	0	1
Lowndes	6,155	8	82	110	248	2,030	3,398	270	9
Lumpkin	165	1	0	1	6	58	86	12	1
Macon	229	1	1	3	20	98	99	3	4
Madison	330	0	0	1	34	116	142	31	6
Marion	51	0	0	2	4	24	17	2	2
McDuffie	180	0	0	1	3	66	104	6	0
McIntosh	179	1	0	2	8	75	85	8	0
Meriwether	60	0	0	0	2	27	28	3	0
Miller	37	0	1	0	2	9	22	3	0
Mitchell	644	4	4	22	89	174	329	17	5
Monroe	569	1	5	5	42	162	313	35	6
Montgomery	12	0	0	0	0	2	9	1	0
Morgan	272	1	0	5	7	135	107	15	2
Murray	461	0	0	4	29	147	219	56	6
Muscogee	9,570	28	96	349	327	2,173	5,990	533	74
Newton	1,853	8	14	25	143	574	996	72	21
Oconee	100	0	0	0	2	47	39	11	1
Oglethorpe	181	0	1	2	5	83	78	12	0
Paulding	793	3	2	8	47	264	399	63	7

County	Total	Violent Crimes				Property Crimes			
		Murder	Rape	Robbery	Aggravated Assault	Burglary	Larceny	Motor Vehicle Theft	Arson
Peach	279	1	3	8	31	87	137	12	0
Pickens	113	1	2	1	5	41	55	8	0
Pierce	122	0	1	1	11	37	64	7	1
Pike	87	1	0	0	19	32	27	8	0
Polk	841	0	5	10	39	296	418	70	3
Pulaski	224	1	2	4	25	83	95	10	4
Putnam	233	0	2	3	21	114	82	11	0
Quitman	3	0	1	0	1	1	0	0	0
Rabun	343	0	0	0	27	150	143	18	5
Randolph	107	0	2	2	16	38	46	2	1
Richmond	11,125	23	96	465	408	3,565	5,841	677	50
Rockdale	1,990	1	11	20	143	490	1,191	131	3
Schley	72	0	0	0	10	28	29	2	3
Screven	257	3	2	6	23	102	104	13	4
Seminole	203	1	0	7	30	46	111	8	0
Spalding	2,880	5	24	59	225	750	1,639	162	16
Stephens	568	2	9	10	26	138	340	35	8
Stewart	67	0	1	1	13	29	20	3	0
Sumter	1,571	2	15	35	146	360	971	35	7
Talbot	93	0	0	2	0	46	35	10	0
Taliaferro	30	1	0	2	1	7	15	4	0
Tattnall	216	1	1	4	10	109	77	12	2
Taylor	104	0	1	3	23	31	40	4	2
Telfair	68	0	0	1	2	27	35	3	0
Terrell	191	2	2	2	14	65	85	11	10
Thomas	1,610	6	11	41	115	462	898	67	10
Tift	1,964	6	20	52	200	452	1,113	110	11
Toombs	261	3	3	2	18	89	140	6	0
Towns	24	0	0	0	0	10	11	2	1
Treutlen	98	1	0	1	2	45	48	1	0
Troup	3,312	12	18	44	258	747	2,069	155	9
Turner	223	0	0	6	23	65	117	11	1
Twiggs	65	0	0	0	9	35	16	5	0
Union	18	0	1	0	0	6	8	0	3
Upson	683	5	3	8	96	231	303	31	6
Walker	1,420	2	18	14	71	542	640	118	15
Walton	811	7	8	13	30	293	413	45	2
Ware	1,984	3	14	86	104	592	1,079	92	14
Warren	11	0	0	0	0	3	5	3	0
Washington	507	4	3	5	44	158	273	14	6
Wayne	556	1	2	19	53	176	267	35	3
Webster	9	0	0	0	3	2	4	0	0
Wheeler	14	0	0	0	2	7	5	0	0
White	194	1	0	1	7	67	100	17	1
Whitfield	3,163	6	12	34	160	689	1,922	333	7
Wilcox	59	1	0	0	5	29	19	4	1
Wilkes	235	0	1	4	15	105	98	9	3
Wilkinson	129	1	3	1	14	55	46	7	2
Worth	474	0	8	9	16	170	241	28	2
State Agency	1,568	0	117	166	177	649	287	89	83
Georgia	329,144	653	2,827	13,315	19,098	86,619	177,440	27,868	1,324

NOTE: These figures solely reflect reports of incidence of crime by law enforcement agencies in each county to the Georgia Crime Information Center.

State Prison Inmates Home County: 1987
Full Time Law Enforcement Employees: 1986

For 1987 the total number of out-of-state prison inmates was 832 males and 30 females. There was a total of 2,755 males and 185 females whose home county was not reported. Excluding the inmates, and those incarcerated in county jails awaiting transfer to a state prison as of December 1987, the state inmate total was 16,746 males and 876 females, for a combined total of 17,622.

In 1986 the state agency total number of sworn officers was 1,098 and 1,338 civilian employees. The state totals were 10,111 sworn officers and 4,084 civilian employees, for a grand total of 14,195.

	Prison Inmates Home County			Full Time Law Enforcement Employees			
County	Male Total	Female Total	Rank of[1] 1987 Total	Sworn Officers[2]	Civilian	1986 Total	Employees Per 100,000 Persons
Appling	20	1	97	—	—	—	—
Atkinson	8	0	146	7	6	13	187
Bacon	18	1	108	15	7	21	209
Baker	7	0	149	6	0	6	152
Baldwin	63	4	40	29	14	43	111
Banks	16	0	117	—	—	—	—
Barrow	55	3	50	21	0	21	88
Bartow	118	6	21	79	23	102	230
Ben Hill	56	4	47	32	11	43	241
Berrien	19	1	102	21	41	32	222
Bibb	467	24	5	383	76	459	292
Bleckley	21	0	97	10	1	11	100
Brantley	10	0	142	6	5	11	107
Brooks	28	1	81	27	5	32	197
Bryan	19	2	97	19	7	26	202
Bulloch	80	6	32	80	22	102	276
Burke	66	4	38	4	0	4	19
Butts	23	0	92	27	8	35	229
Calhoun	20	0	102	15	1	16	287
Camden	33	2	69	47	19	66	449
Candler	19	0	108	16	0	16	201
Carroll	144	7	18	72	26	98	157
Catoosa	27	0	85	62	5	67	164
Charlton	14	0	126	4	0	4	48
Chatham	593	30	3	187	43	230	108
Chattahoochee	2	0	156	2	1	3	13
Chattooga	46	0	57	30	11	41	185
Cherokee	78	4	33	80	16	96	145
Clarke	186	11	12	267	47	314	400
Clay	8	0	146	6	5	11	293
Clayton	281	15	9	207	77	284	162
Clinch	11	0	135	11	4	15	219
Cobb	430	30	7	744	191	935	272
Coffee	54	3	51	34	7	41	141
Colquitt	92	3	29	60	18	78	210
Columbia	29	1	77	12	8	20	38

County	Prison Inmates Home County			Full Time Law Enforcement Employees			
	Male Total	Female Total	Rank of[1] 1987 Total	Sworn Officers [2]	Civilian	1986 Total	Employees Per 100,000 Persons
Cook	17	1	111	26	5	31	219
Coweta	124	2	20	77	9	86	199
Crawford	11	0	135	3	0	3	32
Crisp	64	6	38	40	12	52	251
Dade	22	3	88	5	0	5	38
Dawson	10	1	135	10	4	14	261
Decatur	68	4	37	47	18	65	237
DeKalb	767	36	2	297	79	356	69
Dodge	32	0	76	—	—	—	—
Dooly	18	0	111	5	0	5	44
Dougherty	337	24	8	245	36	281	256
Douglas	115	7	22	32	59	141	195
Early	36	0	66	9	8	17	123
Echols	2	0	156	—	—	—	—
Effingham	31	2	72	25	9	34	160
Elbert	36	1	63	35	6	41	209
Emanual	55	4	49	33	8	41	184
Evans	19	1	102	11	8	19	211
Fannin	21	2	92	11	5	16	105
Fayette	25	1	86	25	1	26	63
Floyd	161	10	14	106	26	132	161
Forsyth	61	2	45	32	11	50	145
Franklin	33	0	72	24	9	33	205
Fulton	2,819	149	1	1,620	409	2,129	343
Gilmer	16	2	111	11	5	16	132
Glascock	6	0	153	1	0	1	41
Glynn	198	9	11	123	25	148	255
Gordon	60	2	46	53	16	69	209
Grady	57	3	47	27	13	40	190
Greene	21	0	97	16	8	24	195
Gwinnett	240	8	10	292	110	402	164
Habersham	37	0	63	41	0	41	152
Hall	153	7	16	181	30	211	253
Hancock	15	0	122	12	7	19	188
Haralson	29	1	77	37	4	41	212
Harris	20	0	102	18	6	24	133
Hart	22	1	92	13	6	19	97
Heard	14	2	117	10	5	15	207
Henry	52	3	53	19	5	24	51
Houston	104	2	26	20	5	25	29
Irwin	29	1	77	14	5	19	199
Jackson	73	2	35	12	4	16	58
Jasper	20	1	97	15	8	23	261
Jeff Davis	18	1	108	8	4	12	96
Jefferson	27	2	81	22	3	25	130
Jenkins	36	2	62	9	0	9	96
Johnson	13	2	122	5	1	6	66
Jones	12	3	122	4	0	4	21
Lamar	20	0	102	20	1	21	161
Lanier	13	0	129	4	4	8	134
Laurens	73	7	34	39	14	53	133
Lee	8	1	144	41	2	13	82
Liberty	52	2	54	41	9	50	103

County	Prison Inmates Home County			Full Time Law Enforcement Employees			
	Male Total	Female Total	Rank of 1987 Total	Sworn Officers[2]	Civilian	1986 Total	Employees Per 100,000 Persons
Lincoln	16	2	111	3	0	3	41
Long	10	1	135	8	4	12	229
Lowndes	142	11	17	137	48	185	249
Lumpkin	13	1	126	—	—	—	—
Macon	25	1	86	3	4	7	47
Madison	32	1	72	9	7	16	80
Marion	7	0	149	2	4	6	109
McDuffie	36	0	66	—	—	—	—
McIntosh	12	0	133	16	5	21	247
Meriwether	56	0	52	37	7	44	196
Miller	13	0	129	17	2	19	255
Mitchell	87	2	30	22	6	28	123
Monroe	24	0	90	—	—	—	—
Montgomery	9	3	133	2	0	2	27
Morgan	18	0	111	17	6	23	182
Murray	30	0	77	31	5	36	153
Muscogee	511	30	4	443	513	956	535
Newton	108	3	24	31	16	47	121
Oconee	12	1	129	3	0	3	19
Oglethorpe	16	0	117	10	0	10	104
Paulding	45	1	57	28	12	40	128
Peach	44	0	60	41	17	58	273
Pickens	22	3	88	14	8	22	176
Pierce	22	1	92	15	5	20	150
Pike	9	2	135	11	2	13	126
Polk	49	2	55	53	17	70	208
Pulaski	22	0	96	14	5	19	201
Putnam	33	1	70	26	20	46	400
Quitman	3	0	155	2	0	2	81
Rabun	15	0	122	21	1	22	195
Randolph	35	2	63	3	0	3	29
Richmond	458	15	6	410	33	443	224
Rockdale	71	2	36	92	25	117	231
Schley	7	0	149	6	0	6	164
Screven	26	2	83	17	0	17	112
Seminole	22	2	90	15	6	21	208
Spalding	151	10	15	107	15	122	234
Stephens	48	1	56	29	11	40	180
Stewart	8	0	146	9	5	14	242
Sumter	85	4	30	70	14	84	269
Talbot	14	0	126	7	3	10	148
Taliaferro	0	0	159	3	0	3	154
Tattnall	45	1	57	22	15	37	187
Taylor	16	0	117	14	2	16	198
Telfair	34	2	66	15	6	21	180
Terrell	27	1	83	15	15	30	236
Thomas	98	7	27	27	11	38	93
Tift	98	6	28	—	—	—	—
Toombs	59	6	44	42	4	46	188
Towns	4	0	154	2	0	2	33
Treutlen	16	1	116	4	5	9	142
Troup	130	12	19	69	15	84	158

County	Prison Inmates Home County			Full Time Law Enforcement Employees			
	Male Total	Female Total	Rank of 1987 Total	Sworn Officers[2]	Civilian	1986 Total	Employees Per 100,000 Persons
Turner	19	1	102	15	6	21	208
Twiggs	7	0	149	5	3	8	79
Union	9	1	142	5	1	6	57
Upson	62	4	42	58	0	58	216
Walker	64	2	42	81	15	96	164
Walton	116	5	23	61	21	81	226
Ware	105	5	25	23	14	37	94
Warren	12	1	129	6	0	6	89
Washington	61	6	40	20	8	28	140
Wayne	32	2	70	19	0	19	85
Webster	1	0	158	2	5	7	289
Wheeler	11	0	135	—	—	—	—
White	9	0	144	12	9	21	189
Whitfield	178	8	13	108	37	145	205
Wilcox	14	2	117	—	—	—	—
Wilkes	32	1	72	19	8	27	234
Wilkinson	11	0	135	14	7	21	189
Worth	40	0	61	23	11	34	170

NOTE: Data excludes those incarcerated in a county jail awaiting transfer to a state prison as of December 1987.
[1]Rank: 1 = highest (range, 1–159)
When counties share the same rank, the next lower rank is omitted. Because of rounded data, counties may have identical values shown, but different ranks.
—Ten counties not submitting data
[2]Sworn Officers are authorized to exercise the power of arrest.

CYCLORAMA

The most moving and impressive memorial of the battle which sealed the fate of the Confederacy is the Cyclorama of the Battle of Atlanta which occurred on July 22, 1864. It is more than a painting; it is a three-dimensional panorama with narration, music and sound effects.

Measuring 50 feet in height, 400 feet in circumference, and weighing over 18,000 pounds, it was painted in 1885-6 by a group of German and Polish artists brought to America for this purpose by Mr. William Wehner, owner of the Milwaukee studio where it was set up and completed. First exhibited in Detroit in 1887, the painting traveled all over the United States before coming to its final resting place in the city whose destruction it commemorates. After several changes in ownership and many locations, the painting was brought to Atlanta in 1891 and exhibited in a building on the north side of Edgewood Avenue, near Piedmont Avenue. It was bought at auction in 1893 by Mr. George V. Gress, an Atlanta citizen, who presented it to the City of Atlanta in 1898. In 1921 the painting was transferred from an old, wooden structure at a location in Grant Park to its present location in the imposing marble building on a hillsite in the central part of the park. In 1936, by means of a WPA grant, the painting was made three-dimensional by the addition of blasted tree stumps, bushes and shrubbery that are shell-torn in effect, broken rails and cross-ties, life-like plaster figures of Confederate and Federal soldiers, and other fragments of war which form the battlefield surrounding the canvas. In viewing the painting it is difficult to determine the ending of the real and the beginning of the illusion. The special light and sound effects give the painting a realism which is startling.

The facility was re-opened in 1982 after 2 years extensive conservation of the painting/diorama and renovation of the building, which now includes a revolving seating platform.

> Grant Park, in southeast Atlanta
> 800 Cherokee Ave. S.E.
> Atlanta, Georgia 30315
> 404-624-1071

DAY CARE FACILITIES

Within the state of Georgia are 1,586 licensed Day Care Centers (DCC) with 19 or more children, 222 licensed Group Day Care Homes (GDCH) with 7 to 18 children, and 3,270 registered Family Day Care Homes (FDCH) with 3 to 6 children for a grand total of 5,078 facilities. Following is a list showing the number of each type of facility per county.

Licensed and Registered Day Care by County: 1987

County	DCC	GDCH	FDCH	County	DCC	GDCH	FDCH
Appling	3	16	5	Chatham	75	10	163
Atkinson	0	0	3	Chattahoochee	0	0	0
Bacon	2	0	17	Chattooga	2	4	10
Baker	1	0	3	Cherokee	14	6	58
Baldwin	13	2	17	Clarke	27	0	30
Banks	1	0	5	Clay	0	0	0
Barrow	7	1	9	Clayton	47	1	88
Bartow	6	5	22	Clinch	2	0	1
Ben Hill	1	6	17	Cobb	112	2	135
Berrien	2	0	5	Coffee	8	1	2
Bibb	54	5	55	Colquitt	9	2	7
Bleckley	2	3	4	Columbia	11	2	25
Brantley	0	0	3	Cook	2	2	1
Brooks	4	0	4	Coweta	13	1	38
Bryan	2	0	2	Crawford	1	0	2
Bulloch	11	7	10	Crisp	4	2	8
Burke	6	0	13	Dade	1	0	2
Butts	4	0	2	Dawson	2	1	3
Calhoun	0	0	0	Decatur	5	0	12
Camden	5	1	3	DeKalb	156	4	409
Candler	1	2	2	Dodge	6	0	3
Carroll	15	10	40	Dooly	2	1	2
Catoosa	7	1	10	Dougherty	46	3	19
Charlton	0	0	1	Douglas	18	0	19

DAY CARE FACILITIES

County	DCC	GDCH	FDCH	County	DCC	GDCH	FDCH
Early	2	0	1	Murray	3	2	24
Echols	0	0	0	Muscogee	49	4	64
Effingham	3	0	1	Newton	6	0	4
Elbert	2	4	15	Oconee	5	3	2
Emanuel	4	6	13	Oglethorpe	1	0	2
Evans	2	1	4	Paulding	5	3	9
Fannin	2	0	35	Peach	3	1	8
Fayette	11	0	18	Pickens	3	3	17
Floyd	20	3	57	Pierce	2	0	7
Forsyth	8	1	8	Pike	3	0	0
Franklin	5	0	4	Polk	5	3	14
Fulton	237	11	405	Pulaski	1	1	0
Gilmer	3	0	6	Putnam	1	0	7
Glascock	0	0	0	Quitman	0	0	0
Glynn	14	3	43	Rabun	1	0	10
Gordon	6	1	32	Randolph	1	0	0
Grady	5	1	17	Richmond	39	3	82
Greene	4	1	1	Rockdale	16	1	15
Gwinnett	87	1	149	Schley	1	1	0
Habersham	8	0	16	Screven	3	2	0
Hall	19	4	39	Seminole	1	0	2
Hancock	1	0	0	Spalding	10	0	5
Haralson	4	1	16	Stephens	4	2	4
Harris	0	1	6	Stewart	0	0	1
Hart	3	0	18	Sumter	9	2	8
Heard	1	0	18	Talbot	0	0	0
Henry	11	2	9	Taliaferro	0	0	0
Houston	22	3	33	Tattnall	4	1	8
Irwin	1	0	3	Taylor	0	1	5
Jackson	7	5	20	Telfair	3	0	4
Jasper	3	0	6	Terrell	2	0	1
Jeff Davis	2	1	14	Thomas	13	0	19
Jefferson	1	0	13	Tift	8	3	28
Jenkins	0	4	6	Toombs	10	1	12
Johnson	1	0	25	Towns	1	0	6
Jones	1	0	14	Treutlen	1	1	13
Lamar	3	0	3	Troup	16	0	214
Lanier	1	0	4	Turner	1	3	1
Laurens	16	3	29	Twiggs	0	0	1
Lee	1	0	0	Union	1	1	11
Liberty	7	0	0	Upson	3	1	12
Lincoln	1	1	2	Walker	12	0	16
Long	0	0	2	Walton	5	1	3
Lowndes	18	2	33	Ware	8	0	10
Lumpkin	3	2	2	Warren	2	0	0
Macon	6	2	5	Washington	2	1	18
Madison	3	1	2	Wayne	3	1	20
Marion	1	0	2	Webster	0	0	0
McDuffie	5	1	4	Wheeler	1	0	0
McIntosh	0	0	0	White	4	0	4
Meriwether	4	0	14	Whitfield	14	10	59
Miller	3	1	3	Wilcox	0	1	1
Mitchell	7	3	9	Wilkes	2	5	9
Monroe	4	0	20	Wilkinson	0	0	2
Montgomery	0	0	1	Worth	3	0	5
Morgan	2	0	3	Georgia	1,586	222	3,270

LEGEND: DCC—Day Centers 19+ children—Licensed
GDCH—Group Day Care Home 7–18 children—Licensed
FDCH—Family Day Care Home 3–6 children—Registered

ECONOMICS

The component of greatest importance in today's economy in Georgia is manufacturing, being the leading source of jobs.

The state's labor force is broken down approximately in the following order from the greatest to the least: manufacturing industries; wholesale and retail trade; government, at federal, state, and local levels; agriculture; lumbering; mining; fishing.

An important sector of the state economy is finance, as evidenced by the mass of corporate headquarters in Atlanta. The Southeast's center for communications and transportation is Atlanta, which is also the chief distributor of goods for the area.

More than $2 billion per year is amassed from tourism in Georgia, with its urban convention centers and coastal resorts as the primary sources.

Following are charts showing the number of housing units authorized in 1985–86 (the construction rate is one measuring stick to the economy), the master economic rate for 1985–86, and per capita income 1980 and 1984.

New Privately Owned Housing Units Authorized in Permit Issuing Places: 1985, 1986

County	1985	1986	County	1985	1986
Appling	13	69	Clay	0	1
Atkinson	—	—			
Bacon	32	6	Clayton	2,959	3,638
Baker	—	—	Clinch	29	9
Baldwin	50	55	Cobb	10,685	10,825
Banks	6	6	Coffee	89	384
Barrow	91	108	Colquitt	32	71
Bartow	39	156	Columbia	1,486	1,501
Ben Hill	132	71	Cook	10	7
Berrien	0	13	Coweta	536	730
			Crawford	43	41
Bibb	764	779	Crisp	62	133
Bleckley	30	—			
Brantley	0	0	Dade	6	28
Brooks	123	10	Dawson	—	—
Bryan	172	316	Decatur	47	65
Bulloch	306	152	DeKalb	7,093	6,896
Burke	0	0	Dodge	34	0
Butts	97	109	Dooly	0	0
Calhoun	—	—	Dougherty	399	651
Camden	334	751	Douglas	1,132	1,368
			Early	0	7
Candler	16	8	Echols	—	—
Carroll	781	694			
Catoosa	63	17	Effingham	113	155
Charlton	0	1	Elbert	0	1
Chatham	2,630	2,446	Emanuel	15	43
Chattahoochee	0	0	Evans	10	5
Chattooga	1	6	Fannin	0	0
Cherokee	1,736	2,816	Fayette	1,281	1,522
Clarke	1,185	1,017	Floyd	298	454

County	1985	1986	County	1985	1986
Forsyth	808	902	Paulding	716	1,087
Franklin	37	11	Peach	110	39
Fulton	7,658	9,134	Pickens	180	207
Gilmer	4	6	Pierce	12	4
Glascock	0	0	Pike	81	122
Glynn	667	368	Polk	199	200
Gordon	200	129	Pulaski	39	0
Grady	18	25	Putnam	0	0
Greene	1	30	Quitman	—	—
Gwinnett	11,904	9,562	Rabun	173	143
Habersham	212	223	Randolph	2	1
Hall	1,032	1,317	Richmond	2,903	2,351
Hancock	1	4	Rockdale	879	1,343
Haralson	183	225	Schley	—	—
Harris	0	0	Screven	14	17
Hart	1	24	Seminole	0	0
Heard	6	0	Spalding	275	540
Henry	1,252	1,471	Stephens	82	34
Houston	839	1,363	Stewart	0	2
Irwin	0	3	Sumter	113	47
Jackson	173	160	Talbot	0	0
Jasper	4	0	Taliaferro	—	—
Jeff Davis	25	64	Tattnall	36	16
Jefferson	0	32	Taylor	16	14
Jenkins	5	20	Telfair	11	6
Johnson	2	1	Terrell	34	28
Jones	4	3	Thomas	97	78
Lamar	63	74	Tift	167	166
Lanier	5	1	Toombs	83	89
Laurens	68	128	Towns	0	0
Lee	181	163	Treutlen	8	6
Liberty	262	504	Troup	591	601
Lincoln	20	26	Turner	9	0
Long	—	—	Twiggs	4	0
Lowndes	489	509	Union	—	—
Lumpkin	19	33	Upson	263	102
Macon	11	2	Walker	142	225
Madison	2	6	Walton	374	345
Marion	0	0	Ware	178	85
McDuffie	53	26	Warren	27	0
McIntosh	0	0	Washington	25	12
Meriwether	0	3	Wayne	17	14
Miller	40	0	Webster	—	—
Mitchell	22	31	Wheeler	0	0
Monroe	24	118	White	25	69
Montgomery	0	0	Whitfield	640	767
Morgan	69	0	Wilcox	0	0
Murray	7	24	Wilkes	14	5
Muscogee	1,329	1,062	Wilkinson	—	—
Newton	427	609	Worth	29	54
Oconee	198	237	Georgia	73,141	76,896
Oglethorpe	—	—			

—Data not available

Master Economic Rank: 1985-1986

County	Master[1] Economic Rank	1986[2] Taxable Sales x $1000	1985[3] Adjusted Gross Income x $1000	1986 Net Property & Utility Digest x $1000	1986[4] Millage Rates
Appling	65	86,954	85,851	554,490	17.23
Atkinson	145	20,923	27,593	56,610	21.28
Bacon	110	77,670	47,033	91,799	19.10
Baker	149	10,186	14,990	71,644	17.08
Baldwin	39	234,405	252,658	267,966	26.00
Banks	116	28,785	43,592	96,533	18.48
Barrow	47	153,052	181,282	228,018	24.49
Bartow	22	299,378	352,047	652,450	19.30
Ben Hill	79	97,185	99,865	139,642	21.25
Berrien	95	62,601	73,518	136,577	15.70
Bibb	8	1,689,012	1,268,251	1,445,027	36.35
Bleckley	113	42,686	67,890	73,301	25.52
Brantley	122	29,505	46,024	98,697	24.12
Brooks	101	43,011	53,697	151,597	18.46
Bryan	99	58,974	75,753	120,687	16.82
Bulloch	37	223,566	204,048	343,579	16.88
Burke	53	80,569	113,267	1,709,273	12.11
Butts	81	97,928	87,374	113,937	24.39
Calhoun	144	15,035	27,474	77,671	17.76
Camden	63	91,380	103,600	250,222	23.14
Candler	127	58,255	36,125	70,925	16.31
Carroll	20	427,232	456,789	432,542	23.62
Catoosa	40	191,599	223,688	285,312	16.21
Charlton	125	30,192	34,300	127,592	18.37
Chatham	5	2,168,626	1,606,432	2,635,137	30.70
Chattahoochee	154	8,658	13,093	15,054	9.99
Chattooga	66	90,468	127,080	171,022	22.68
Cherokee	19	276,822	584,685	686,703	28.45
Clarke	15	857,016	549,206	819,413	35.32
Clay	152	15,466	12,668	35,543	17.78
Clayton	6	1,394,716	1,485,029	2,043,636	32.36
Clinch	137	30,323	32,783	82,606	27.89
Cobb	3	3,925,944	4,436,809	5,476,371	27.50
Coffee	48	181,663	149,452	236,309	24.68
Colquitt	38	240,980	199,369	336,495	15.69
Columbia	28	138,285	440,823	549,596	20.84
Cook	102	65,600	68,725	112,937	20.06
Coweta	26	284,823	375,804	541,033	26.28
Crawford	136	13,386	39,508	71,222	22.25
Crisp	57	193,810	106,858	211,370	14.58
Dade	111	47,576	53,166	84,878	23.73
Dawson	107	23,594	52,231	159,396	18.76
Decatur	51	134,126	128,459	297,777	11.89
DeKalb	2	6,772,895	5,171,237	7,136,127	40.93
Dodge	91	71,920	86,594	101,927	27.25
Dooly	108	53,450	50,891	136,631	15.66
Dougherty	11	997,371	731,925	960,667	28.55
Douglas	18	382,787	559,980	581,562	34.00
Early	92	57,563	64,368	217,844	12.99
Echols	156	1,800	7,727	51,210	17.63

127

County	Master[1] Economic Rank	1986[2] Taxable Sales x $1000	1985[3] Adjusted Gross Income x $1000	1986 Net Property & Utility Digest x $1000	1986[4] Millage Rates
Effingham	60	74,625	139,577	209,621	23.00
Elbert	67	117,887	112,230	155,856	26.26
Emanuel	72	97,539	102,817	178,361	22.80
Evans	115	73,650	47,319	70,601	17.53
Fannin	83	85,973	75,579	121,214	19.54
Fayette	25	178,205	532,419	611,270	31.12
Floyd	12	690,647	610,304	826,810	32.47
Forsyth	29	236,053	303,761	436,225	24.49
Franklin	75	102,725	102,221	133,985	18.56
Fulton	1	10,306,890	7,005,915	10,803,671	35.07
Gilmer	88	92,443	74,595	116,464	22.91
Glascock	155	3,124	13,387	28,441	16.06
Glynn	16	700,823	470,892	977,562	27.33
Gordon	36	165,696	241,334	393,319	19.51
Grady	73	96,408	94,527	197,516	17.76
Greene	105	56,900	63,335	113,512	25.18
Gwinnett	4	2,289,426	2,936,008	3,781,846	33.90
Habersham	45	188,593	181,133	237,709	19.63
Hall	10	782,547	740,949	1,106,760	20.65
Hancock	130	17,944	38,462	112,701	38.09
Haralson	62	85,692	130,918	177,138	24.94
Harris	70	68,137	108,539	230,167	14.26
Hart	71	91,306	108,975	163,488	25.97
Heard	119	11,041	38,223	201,372	19.07
Henry	27	211,918	411,990	445,054	34.23
Houston	14	502,175	662,928	681,740	14.99
Irwin	124	31,484	42,378	99,663	16.86
Jackson	46	211,666	175,122	216,351	23.86
Jasper	126	22,904	46,053	95,008	21.59
Jeff Davis	98	66,854	70,497	137,907	12.46
Jefferson	74	104,964	96,716	177,611	15.78
Jenkins	132	35,396	40,354	76,189	23.11
Johnson	135	24,632	41,130	51,692	25.66
Jones	76	53,011	118,980	176,025	14.18
Lamar	100	56,241	75,546	112,953	20.04
Lanier	147	21,988	23,357	42,568	20.47
Laurens	31	290,122	240,767	408,420	17.83
Lee	97	23,557	92,917	153,216	21.92
Liberty	50	137,998	117,560	227,442	17.55
Lincoln	138	17,302	37,774	63,864	19.94
Long	150	5,628	19,990	62,640	25.94
Lowndes	17	651,125	432,314	697,105	20.13
Lumpkin	94	53,952	70,264	158,265	17.91
Macon	93	57,006	62,706	184,009	15.59
Madison	80	30,097	122,931	150,758	18.57
Marion	148	14,556	24,816	59,634	17.64
McDuffie	64	102,718	119,888	163,665	16.20
McIntosh	129	36,742	39,310	77,995	26.93
Meriwether	59	110,939	115,933	186,661	16.45
Miller	134	25,716	33,475	99,220	17.71
Mitchell	68	99,318	103,341	209,705	13.90
Monroe	56	102,063	100,729	592,906	11.71
Montgomery	141	14,489	31,594	67,880	14.48

County	Master[1] Economic Rank	1986[2] Taxable Sales x $1000	1985[3] Adjusted Gross Income x $1000	1986 Net Property & Utility Digest x $1000	1986[4] Millage Rates
Morgan	90	80,703	79,656	132,705	19.29
Murray	58	80,337	149,485	212,615	17.97
Muscogee	9	1,600,744	1,138,288	1,342,734	23.37
Newton	33	212,531	296,839	369,657	26.15
Oconee	82	37,427	117,472	145,734	25.43
Oglethorpe	121	23,457	50,273	90,592	20.20
Paulding	44	124,624	233,975	228,184	35.73
Peach	69	92,058	131,433	157,902	21.43
Pickens	78	137,609	87,307	150,772	25.15
Pierce	103	44,440	65,889	117,221	19.23
Pike	120	15,527	59,510	91,332	19.50
Polk	43	163,698	218,682	235,479	24.25
Pulaski	118	40,182	50,111	86,451	20.58
Putnam	87	56,756	81,290	204,048	21.50
Quitman	159	5,061	6,453	19,073	25.75
Rabun	86	58,316	63,068	212,985	16.60
Randolph	133	41,308	34,814	76,428	14.32
Richmond	7	1,784,090	1,309,513	1,629,201	24.91
Rockdale	21	349,956	432,143	525,169	33.37
Schley	153	11,407	17,416	36,301	20.75
Screven	85	71,001	76,532	161,250	21.01
Seminole	114	56,790	45,848	102,941	18.28
Spalding	24	373,886	371,010	417,169	30.11
Stephens	52	161,303	151,369	198,503	20.02
Stewart	143	20,292	22,923	73,901	15.96
Sumter	42	193,647	182,005	302,861	15.37
Talbot	142	14,951	30,320	62,307	22.78
Taliaferro	158	4,009	9,128	33,679	13.38
Tattnall	84	72,364	81,141	148,559	21.05
Taylor	117	93,985	42,029	73,758	18.20
Telfair	109	52,365	57,146	101,571	17.23
Terrell	112	50,202	54,666	93,863	14.28
Thomas	30	286,153	247,265	391,424	23.93
Tift	35	255,163	215,314	348,215	14.13
Toombs	55	191,998	141,582	177,217	17.46
Towns	131	36,891	29,236	82,853	7.55
Treutlen	146	16,441	26,048	43,320	19.13
Troup	23	423,652	386,474	487,749	16.91
Turner	123	32,042	46,383	93,905	17.89
Twiggs	128	10,606	45,452	109,545	20.66
Union	104	54,319	48,665	131,106	13.80
Upson	49	134,940	160,516	232,905	21.99
Walker	32	193,156	345,021	366,369	16.70
Walton	41	189,365	240,288	290,106	20.79
Ware	34	303,448	228,066	325,607	20.84
Warren	139	17,643	30,527	74,142	19.73
Washington	61	111,867	110,215	223,276	18.43
Wayne	54	137,916	129,507	275,029	20.20
Webster	157	3,652	9,819	36,986	18.10
Wheeler	151	13,263	20,929	51,093	18.11
White	89	69,741	73,928	157,663	18.25
Whitfield	13	773,739	598,951	921.267	20.49
Wilcox	140	15,036	33,298	65,492	20.39

129

County	Master[1] Economic Rank	1986[2] Taxable Sales x $1000	1985[3] Adjusted Gross Income x $1000	1986 Net Property & Utility Digest x $1000	1986[4] Millage Rates
Wilkes	96	82,968	64,075	129,051	19.04
Wilkinson	106	40,026	68,935	130,107	20.63
Worth	77	67,625	100,754	192,168	18.20
Other		5,553	992,672		
Georgia		51,903,136	49,028,044	71,780,852	

[1]Master Economic Rank is determined by using the information of personal income, sales tax receipts, motor vehicle tags, and assessed property value.
[2]Based on sales tax
[3]Reported on Georgia Returns
[4]The rate of taxation per thousand (one mill equals one tenth of a cent).

Per Capita Income: 1980, 1984

	Per Capita Income		1984[1] Rank	Percent of Georgia Total 1984	Percent of U.S. Total 1984	Percent Change in Income 1980-84
	1980	1984				
Appling	5,936	9,720	59	84.2	76.1	63.7
Atkinson	5,151	9,266	83	80.2	72.5	79.9
Bacon	5,523	8,091	127	70.1	63.3	46.5
Baker	4,323	8,658	104	75.0	67.8	100.3
Baldwin	6,744	9,244	84	80.0	72.4	37.1
Banks	5,981	9,685	64	83.9	75.8	61.9
Barrow	7,143	10,180	40	88.2	79.7	42.5
Bartow	7,149	10,085	47	87.3	79.0	41.1
Ben Hill	6,082	8,769	100	75.9	68.7	44.2
Berrien	6,084	9,134	88	79.1	71.5	50.1
Bibb	8,017	11,091	22	96.0	86.8	38.3
Bleckley	6,372	9,458	74	81.9	74.1	48.4
Brantley	5,074	7,804	138	67.6	61.1	53.8
Brooks	4,568	7,390	149	64.0	57.9	61.8
Bryan	6,187	8,446	112	73.1	66.1	36.5
Bulloch	6,026	8,597	109	74.4	67.3	42.7
Burke	5,334	8,314	118	72.0	65.1	55.9
Butts	6,683	8,984	95	77.8	70.3	34.4
Calhoun	4,884	9,977	50	86.4	78.1	104.3
Camden	7,789	10,473	30	90.7	82.0	34.5
Candler	5,345	7,720	140	66.9	60.4	44.4
Carroll	7,167	10,381	35	89.9	81.3	44.8
Catoosa	6,909	9,117	90	78.9	71.4	32.0
Charlton	5,536	7,644	141	66.2	59.8	38.1
Chatham	8,483	11,589	13	100.4	90.7	36.6
Chattahoochee	5,553	7,812	137	67.6	61.2	40.7
Chattooga	5,985	8,046	130	69.7	63.0	34.4
Cherokee	7,667	11,229	20	97.2	87.9	46.5
Clarke	7,446	11,170	21	96.7	87.5	50.0
Clay	3,222	6,861	158	59.4	53.7	112.9
Clayton	8,851	11,937	10	103.4	93.5	34.9

	Per Capita Income		1984[1] Rank	Percent of Georgia Total 1984	Percent of U.S. Total 1984	Percent Change in Income 1980-84
	1980	1984				
Clinch	5,820	8,295	119	71.8	64.9	42.5
Cobb	10,775	15,410	2	133.4	120.7	43.0
Coffee	5,517	8,254	121	71.5	64.6	49.6
Colquitt	6,085	9,101	91	78.8	71.3	49.6
Columbia	8,164	12,019	9	104.1	94.1	47.2
Cook	5,040	7,425	146	64.3	58.1	47.3
Coweta	8,020	11,275	19	97.6	88.3	40.6
Crawford	6,414	9,560	68	82.8	74.9	49.0
Crisp	6,081	8,622	107	74.7	67.5	41.8
Dade	5,890	7,901	135	68.4	61.9	34.1
Dawson	6,959	11,355	17	98.3	88.9	63.2
Decatur	6,295	9,177	85	79.5	71.9	45.8
DeKalb	10,610	15,161	3	131.3	118.7	42.9
Dodge	5,692	8,342	117	72.3	65.3	46.6
Dooly	5,670	10,302	39	89.2	80.7	81.7
Dougherty	7,408	10,095	44	87.4	79.0	36.3
Douglas	7,953	10,946	23	94.8	85.7	37.6
Early	5,233	8,620	108	74.6	67.5	64.7
Echols	4,884	7,188	156	62.2	56.3	47.2
Effingham	6,709	9,623	67	83.3	75.3	43.4
Elbert	7,079	10,006	49	86.6	78.3	41.3
Emanuel	5,469	7,644	141	66.2	59.8	39.8
Evans	5,801	8,428	114	73.0	66.0	45.3
Fannin	5,738	8,629	106	74.7	67.6	50.4
Fayette	10,998	15,851	1	137.3	124.1	44.1
Floyd	8,082	11,422	15	98.9	89.4	41.3
Forsyth	8,418	12,358	6	107.0	96.8	46.8
Franklin	6,533	10,932	24	94.7	85.6	67.3
Fulton	10,196	14,203	5	123.0	111.2	39.3
Gilmer	6,416	9,712	61	84.1	76.0	51.4
Glascock	6,985	10,343	36	89.6	81.0	48.1
Glynn	8,792	11,421	16	98.9	89.4	29.9
Gordon	6,999	10,787	27	93.4	84.5	54.1
Grady	5,888	8,808	99	76.3	69.0	49.6
Greene	5,765	8,763	101	75.9	68.6	52.0
Gwinnett	10,262	14,704	4	127.3	115.1	43.3
Habersham	6,356	9,177	85	79.5	71.9	44.4
Hall	8,297	12,183	7	105.5	95.4	46.8
Hancock	4,909	7,201	155	62.4	56.4	46.7
Haralson	7,220	10,745	29	93.0	84.1	48.8
Harris	6,213	9,127	89	79.0	71.5	46.9
Hart	6,473	10,094	45	87.4	79.0	55.9
Heard	6,658	10,066	48	87.2	78.8	51.2
Henry	8,522	11,858	11	102.7	92.8	39.1
Houston	8,088	11,316	18	98.0	88.6	39.9
Irwin	4,994	9,693	63	83.9	75.9	94.1
Jackson	6,482	10,318	38	89.3	80.8	59.2
Jasper	6,883	10,386	34	89.9	81.3	50.9
Jeff Davis	6,848	9,486	73	82.1	74.3	38.5
Jefferson	5,648	8,407	115	72.8	65.8	48.8
Jenkins	4,845	7,525	144	65.2	58.9	55.3
Johnson	5,346	8,196	125	71.0	64.2	53.3

131

	Per Capita Income		1984[1] Rank	Percent of Georgia Total 1984	Percent of U.S. Total 1984	Percent Change in Income 1980-84
	1980	1984				
Jones	6,969	9,863	54	85.4	77.2	41.5
Lamar	6,209	9,553	69	82.7	74.8	53.9
Lanier	5,032	7,782	139	67.4	60.9	54.7
Laurens	6,617	9,291	82	80.5	72.7	40.4
Lee	6,369	9,714	60	84.1	76.1	52.5
Liberty	5,996	8,518	111	73.8	66.7	42.1
Lincoln	5,807	8,647	105	74.9	67.7	48.9
Long	5,621	7,307	154	63.3	57.2	30.0
Lowndes	6,666	9,382	77	81.2	73.5	40.7
Lumpkin	5,827	9,372	78	81.2	73.4	60.8
Macon	5,609	7,912	134	68.5	61.9	41.1
Madison	6,426	9,790	57	84.8	76.7	52.3
Marion	5,098	8,347	116	72.3	65.4	63.7
McDuffie	6,557	9,084	92	78.7	71.1	38.5
McIntosh	4,938	7,037	157	60.9	55.1	42.5
Meriwether	5,487	8,058	128	69.8	63.1	46.9
Miller	4,428	8,545	110	74.0	66.9	93.0
Mitchell	5,269	7,983	132	69.1	62.5	51.5
Monroe	6,789	9,552	70	82.7	74.8	40.7
Montgomery	5,503	8,047	129	69.7	63.0	46.2
Morgan	6,978	10,466	31	90.6	81.9	50.0
Murray	6,421	9,335	79	80.8	73.1	45.4
Muscogee	7,892	10,785	28	93.4	84.4	36.7
Newton	7,334	10,429	33	90.3	81.7	42.2
Oconee	7,473	11,572	14	100.2	90.6	54.9
Oglethorpe	6,024	9,809	56	84.9	76.8	62.8
Paulding	6,831	9,527	72	82.5	74.6	39.5
Peach	7,280	10,159	43	88.0	79.5	39.5
Pickens	7,192	10,444	32	90.4	81.8	45.2
Pierce	5,405	7,954	133	68.9	62.3	47.2
Pike	6,807	9,780	58	84.7	76.6	43.7
Polk	6,858	9,819	55	85.0	76.9	43.2
Pulaski	6,175	9,933	51	86.0	77.8	60.9
Putnam	6,633	8,875	97	76.9	69.5	33.8
Quitman	4,699	7,314	153	63.3	57.3	55.7
Rabun	5,660	8,186	126	70.9	64.1	44.6
Randolph	4,364	7,328	151	63.5	57.4	67.9
Richmond	7,365	10,854	26	94.0	85.0	47.4
Rockdale	8,900	12,134	8	105.1	95.0	36.3
Schley	5,481	9,076	93	78.6	71.1	65.6
Screven	5,620	8,243	122	71.4	64.5	46.7
Seminole	5,463	8,968	96	77.7	70.2	64.2
Spalding	7,489	10,174	42	88.1	79.7	35.9
Stephens	6,722	9,449	75	81.8	74.0	40.6
Stewart	4,846	7,466	145	64.7	58.5	54.1
Sumter	6,574	9,656	66	83.6	75.6	46.9
Talbot	5,035	7,317	152	63.4	57.3	45.3
Taliaferro	6,583	9,535	71	82.6	74.7	44.8
Tattnall	5,078	8,035	131	69.6	62.9	58.2
Taylor	6,021	8,435	113	73.0	66.0	40.1
Telfair	6,039	9,440	76	81.7	73.9	56.3
Terrell	4,788	7,581	143	65.6	59.4	58.3
Thomas	6,913	10,180	40	88.2	79.7	47.3

	Per Capita Income		1984[1] Rank	Percent of Georgia Total 1984	Percent of U.S. Total 1984	Percent Change in Income 1980-84
	1980	1984				
Tift	6,771	10,333	37	89.5	80.9	52.6
Toombs	5,771	8,220	123	71.2	64.4	42.4
Towns	4,980	7,844	136	67.9	61.4	57.5
Treutlen	5,133	7,398	147	64.1	57.9	44.1
Troup	7,435	10,905	25	94.4	85.4	46.7
Turner	5,948	8,873	98	76.8	69.5	49.2
Twiggs	5,158	7,395	148	64.0	57.9	43.4
Union	4,499	6,574	159	56.9	51.5	46.1
Upson	6,595	9,295	81	80.5	72.8	40.9
Walker	6,919	9,657	65	83.6	75.6	39.6
Walton	6,763	9,890	52	85.6	77.4	46.2
Ware	7,093	10,087	46	87.3	79.0	42.2
Warren	5,586	8,275	120	71.7	64.8	48.1
Washington	6,394	9,160	87	79.3	71.7	43.3
Wayne	6,546	9,023	94	78.1	70.6	37.8
Webster	5,003	9,701	62	84.0	76.0	93.9
Wheeler	5,036	7,377	150	63.9	57.8	46.5
White	5,580	8,754	102	75.8	68.5	56.9
Whitfield	8,081	11,650	12	100.9	91.2	44.2
Wilcox	5,029	8,202	124	71.0	64.2	63.1
Wilkes	6,769	9,866	53	85.4	77.2	45.8
Wilkinson	6,610	9,324	80	80.7	73.0	41.1
Worth	5,486	8,748	103	75.8	68.5	59.5
Georgia	8,041	11,548			90.4	43.6
U.S.	9,494	12,772				34.5

[1]Rank: 1 = highest (range, 1–159)
  When counties share the same rank, the next lower rank is omitted. Because of rounded data, counties may have identical values shown, but different ranks.

EDUCATION

The state of Georgia has 159 county school systems, plus 28 independent city school systems. Charts reflect the number of schools, enrollment, attendance, dropouts, and graduates; also number of teachers, advanced degrees, beginning salary, cost per pupil, and school lunch program data for both systems follow.

A list of the County Boards of Educations, their addresses and phone numbers follow the charts.

For the State Department of Education see the State Government Chapter.

County Systems; Number of Schools, Enrollment, Average Daily Attendance, Graduates, Dropouts: 1985-86

County	Number of Schools	Total Enroll-ment	% Change Enrollment 1984-85 to 1985-86	Average Daily Atten-dance	Total Dropouts	Total Graduates
Appling	7	3,672	−4.6	3,380	83	202
Atkinson	4	1,421	−1.6	1,301	47	88
Bacon	3	2,225	1.9	2,023	36	120
Baker	1	404	1.3	387	0	0
Baldwin	11	6,184	2.8	5.619	119	251
Banks	4	1,675	5.5	1,429	40	76
Barrow	8	5,051	5.1	4,484	164	181
Bartow	13	7,937	4.2	6,986	216	386
Ben Hill	1	1,204	3.6	1,133	1	0
Berrien	7	2,891	−1.0	2,615	63	155
Bibb	40	25,461	0.2	23,021	472	1,235
Bleckley	3	2,012	−1.6	1,877	38	125
Brantley	3	2,475	4.6	2,258	42	134
Brooks	7	2,978	0.4	2,666	90	102
Bryan	5	2,846	3.5	2,582	87	113
Bulloch	14	6,807	1.5	6,187	149	391
Burke	9	4,467	4.5	4,102	107	179
Butts	4	2,691	2.0	2,467	102	114
Calhoun	3	1,311	−1.7	1,218	17	74
Camden	5	4,495	16.0	3,722	79	173
Candler	3	1,574	−1.2	1,473	45	66
Carroll	15	9,863	4.4	8,866	251	456
Catoosa	13	8,313	1.0	7,228	218	370
Charlton	4	1,802	2.2	1,593	42	83
Chatham	54	33,197	1.9	28,786	792	1,521
Chattahoochee	1	347	−4.9	316	0	0
Chattooga	7	3,270	−3.3	2,854	141	147
Cherokee	19	13,696	4.9	11,960	358	637
Clarke	15	11,660	3.9	9,557	239	524
Clay	1	398	−1.0	376	0	0
Clayton	43	34,235	2.9	29,766	480	1,858
Clinch	4	1,514	−3.9	1,387	36	90
Cobb	70	62,352	3.1	54,886	1,099	3,814
Coffee	9	6,268	2.5	5,697	159	360
Colquitt	14	7,840	2.4	7,183	137	415
Columbia	13	11,565	6.6	10,159	280	643
Cook	5	2,840	0.9	2,498	83	159
Coweta	18	9,322	1.2	8,375	199	448
Crawford	3	1,537	1.9	1,402	35	100
Crisp	7	4,418	0.2	4,017	114	230
Dade	4	2,387	3.5	2,033	64	134
Dawson	3	1,462	8.8	1,348	25	84
Decatur	9	6,135	4.0	5,534	148	223
DeKalb	103	75,215	1.2	67,289	922	5,480
Dodge	7	3,614	0.2	3,346	49	211
Dooly	4	2,047	−0.2	1,877	48	91
Dougherty	32	20,090	−0.1	18,023	629	964
Douglas	18	13,768	2.6	12,220	343	741
Early	3	2,877	0.9	2,653	48	188
Echols	1	547	−0.7	499	13	28

County	Number of Schools	Total Enroll- ment	% Change Enrollment 1984-85 to 1985-86	Average Daily Atten- dance	Total Dropouts	Total Graduates
Effingham	7	5,025	4.9	4,513	112	191
Elbert	7	3,713	-0.5	3,440	76	209
Emanuel	7	4,529	2.9	4,167	144	227
Evans	3	1,800	0.5	1,702	27	112
Fannin	8	2,968	1.1	2,614	62	170
Fayette	12	10,065	8.3	9,096	138	653
Floyd	18	9,125	-1.9	8,256	205	555
Forsyth	11	6,797	3.9	6,147	149	324
Franklin	5	3,314	-1.4	2,978	81	185
Fulton	77	40,297	4.2	35,140	475	2,283
Gilmer	4	2,328	-0.4	2,071	56	114
Glascock	1	724	0.4	673	4	52
Glynn	13	10,412	-3.7	9,289	300	536
Gordon	9	5,009	13.1	4,545	129	125
Grady	7	4,279	-0.8	3,930	50	241
Greene	5	2,404	1.2	2,197	58	111
Gwinnett	51	51,298	8.5	45,863	661	2,435
Habersham	11	4,744	-0.4	4,299	93	257
Hall	19	12,696	2.8	11,465	255	647
Hancock	4	1,987	-4.0	1,848	15	124
Haralson	6	2,819	-1.1	2,526	93	146
Harris	7	2,709	2.5	2,429	51	128
Hart	7	3,428	-3.5	3,189	82	195
Heard	4	1,538	4.6	1,393	37	68
Henry	12	8,417	6.7	7,554	141	343
Houston	24	15,274	2.7	13,746	381	874
Irwin	4	1,739	0.9	1,592	33	104
Jackson	7	2,704	7.4	2,514	64	116
Jasper	2	1,425	3.8	1,293	31	67
Jeff Davis	4	2,664	-0.4	2,398	59	117
Jefferson	6	3,631	-0.7	3,344	111	110
Jenkins	4	1,829	-0.1	1,704	37	89
Johnson	4	1,606	0.8	1,487	44	81
Jones	4	3,656	1.1	3,334	41	227
Lamar	3	2,230	-0.2	2,025	59	110
Lanier	3	1,276	-3.7	1,143	26	62
Laurens	8	4,452	0.7	4,099	104	264
Lee	3	3,536	3.2	3,174	88	142
Liberty	7	7,401	4.0	6,190	108	328
Lincoln	2	1,420	1.7	1,322	14	86
Long	2	1,096	5.2	910	19	40
Lowndes	9	7,053	0.6	6,246	167	388
Lumpkin	3	2,120	3.5	1,900	43	106
Macon	7	2,704	-1.3	2,528	43	167
Madison	7	3,734	-2.0	3,405	104	183
Marion	2	1,633	-3.5	1,519	54	145
McDuffie	6	4,065	1.8	3,731	82	209
McIntosh	3	1,879	-1.2	1,670	61	96
Meriwether	10	4,474	-0.8	4,163	99	230
Miller	3	1,366	-0.9	1,266	31	80
Mitchell	4	3,370	0.7	3,044	64	137
Monroe	3	2,762	4.8	2,508	59	139
Montgomery	3	1,204	-3.4	1,107	13	85

County	Number of Schools	Total Enroll- ment	% Change Enrollment 1984-85 to 1985-86	Average Daily Atten- dance	Total Dropouts	Total Graduates
Morgan	3	2,517	0.0	2,323	44	125
Murray	6	4,846	4.1	4,371	114	198
Muscogee	55	32,420	0.4	28,156	698	1,582
Newton	11	8,025	2.5	7,236	261	366
Oconee	3	2,952	8.2	2,654	62	171
Oglethorpe	3	1,803	0.6	1,658	73	92
Paulding	9	6,723	2.9	5,830	187	267
Peach	4	3,986	−2.6	3,709	75	210
Pickens	3	2,472	4.5	2,229	60	122
Pierce	5	2,897	−0.4	2,633	58	154
Pike	4	1,888	2.5	1,714	49	126
Polk	10	6,633	−2.3	6,028	179	330
Pulaski	3	1,671	−1.2	1,546	24	105
Putnam	3	2,040	1.5	1,839	78	118
Quitman	1	225	−5.1	204	0	0
Rabun	4	1,965	−0.7	1,751	29	132
Randolph	3	1,838	0.3	1,664	35	138
Richmond	51	34,286	−0.3	29,605	954	1,657
Rockdale	10	9,625	4.9	8,838	187	539
Schley	1	452	2.0	419	0	0
Screven	5	3,057	2.8	2,813	50	146
Seminole	3	1,942	1.3	1,756	26	114
Spalding	16	10,231	0.3	9,451	376	462
Stephens	7	4,138	−3.7	3,759	91	242
Stewart	3	1,182	−10.4	1,060	33	99
Sumter	3	1,980	5.4	1,767	66	78
Talbot	2	1,066	−1.7	1,006	10	63
Taliaferro	1	176	−7.9	164	0	0
Tattnall	6	3,198	0.0	2,856	113	136
Taylor	3	1,677	0.2	1,567	34	99
Telfair	6	2,423	−1.5	2,212	56	99
Terrell	4	2,050	−2.1	1,910	62	103
Thomas	5	4,416	1.1	3,907	83	258
Tift	10	7,491	1.8	6,892	107	402
Toombs	4	2,484	2.0	2,203	66	116
Towns	2	831	1.2	732	10	52
Treutlen	3	1,342	−3.0	1,253	24	84
Troup	8	4,181	−0.1	3,765	84	204
Turner	4	2,185	−1.6	1,980	55	112
Twiggs	4	1,821	2.8	1,666	24	69
Union	4	1,786	−0.7	1,647	27	111
Upson	6	3,386	1.8	3,151	67	143
Walker	23	10,210	−1.0	8,854	383	352
Walton	8	5,990	−0.5	5,555	146	306
Ware	8	4,084	1.4	3,724	77	181
Warren	2	1,137	−0.7	1,037	29	55
Washington	6	3,500	−1.2	3,209	85	168
Wayne	8	4,550	−0.9	4,127	114	211
Webster	1	263	−1.1	253	0	0
Wheeler	3	1,168	−0.9	1,052	21	81
White	4	2,078	6.7	1,897	27	129
Whitfield	16	10,055	1.3	8,892	312	435

County	Number of Schools	Total Enroll- ment	% Change Enrollment 1984-85 to 1985-86	Average Daily Atten- dance	Total Dropouts	Total Graduates
Wilcox	4	1,376	0.3	1,268	26	71
Wilkes	4	2,111	-0.3	1,967	35	127
Wilkinson	4	2,164	0.0	2,020	45	125
Worth	6	3,951	-0.1	3,607	97	208
County Total	1,514	981,932	2.1	876,730	20,510	51,450
Georgia	1,771	1,123,172	1.8	1,004,781	23,376	59,082

Independent City Systems; Number of Schools, Enrollment, Average Daily Attendance, Graduates, Dropouts: 1985–1986

County	Number of Schools	Total Enroll- ment	% Change Enrollment 1984-85 to 1985-86	Average Daily Atten- dance	Total Dropouts	Total Graduates
Americus	5	3,785	0.5	3,380	74	216
Atlanta	117	68,236	0.3	62,112	1,341	3,775
Bremen	2	1,229	0.9	1,140	19	70
Buford	3	1,505	1.9	1,320	29	82
Calhoun	3	1,805	-23.4	1,655	53	213
Carrollton	6	3,075	0.7	2,804	27	204
Cartersville	3	2,210	3.9	2,029	86	115
Chickamauga	2	1,150	2.8	1,069	10	106
Commerce	3	1,186	0.6	1,104	18	70
Dalton	9	4,119	-1.3	3,719	83	234
Decatur	9	2,416	-2.6	2,174	44	112
Dublin	7	3,682	1.4	3,384	57	154
Fitzgerald	3	2,562	6.4	2,296	88	148
Gainesville	4	3,100	5.1	2,783	49	172
Hogansville	3	966	-3.1	867	15	63
Jefferson	3	1,557	-0.6	1,371	43	95
LaGrange	10	4,975	0.3	4,525	163	206
Marietta	9	5,026	3.2	4,294	91	179
Pelham	3	1,753	-2.4	1,601	48	98
Rome	13	5,018	2.1	4,608	132	211
Social Circle	2	1,015	2.8	950	28	56
Thomaston	4	1,583	-3.3	1,470	26	96
Thomasville	8	3,647	-0.3	3,358	20	204
Trion	2	1,160	3.4	1,071	13	69
Valdosta	9	7,475	0.5	6,629	157	358
Vidalia	5	2,736	0.8	2,481	55	129
Waycross	7	3,552	-2.2	3,201	93	164
West Point	3	712	-4.6	656	4	33
Georgia	257	141,235	0.1	128,051	2,866	7,632

County Systems; Number of Teachers, Advanced Degrees, Beginning Salary, Cost Per Pupil, School Lunch Program: 1985–1986

County	Number of Teachers	Teachers[1] With Advanced Degrees	Beginning[2] Teacher Salary	Cost Per Pupil (Dollars)	School Lunch Program	
					Percent Participating	Percent Free
Appling	213	106	17,462	2,767	88	44
Atkinson	86	30	16,120	2,435	91	71
Bacon	117	44	—	2,131	89	43
Baker	29	9	—	3,255	98	92
Baldwin	346	191	16,000	2,614	85	48
Banks	85	32	16,100	2,191	81	41
Barrow	254	105	16,200	2,182	81	33
Bartow	441	196	16,700	2,648	85	30
Ben Hill	60	22	—	1,913	93	35
Berrien	175	83	—	2,683	82	40
Bibb	1,379	775	17,200	2,864	88	52
Bleckley	114	60	—	2,393	89	40
Brantley	131	49	16,800	1,993	86	42
Brooks	179	58	—	2,524	92	79
Bryan	152	60	—	2,139	87	44
Bulloch	391	256	16,250	2,476	88	49
Burke	235	75	16,600	2,523	89	71
Butts	140	71	16,800	2,268	80	45
Calhoun	77	43	16,000	2,689	94	68
Camden	202	71	17,433	2,138	80	42
Candler	87	42	16,000	2,267	94	58
Carroll	501	296	16,600	2,486	82	34
Catoosa	402	165	16,840	2,113	78	23
Charlton	102	26	16,500	2,508	85	54
Chatham	1,843	829	17,263	3,285	71	71
Chattahoochee	26	15	16,360	2,759	99	73
Chattooga	178	85	16,700	2,343	89	49
Cherokee	662	294	17,505	2,142	76	16
Clarke	636	409	17,379	3,822	78	52
Clay	25	14	—	2,363	98	87
Clayton	1,857	1,043	18,400	2,700	86	19
Clinch	97	41	16,750	2,798	90	59
Cobb	3,063	1,533	18,150	2,555	76	8
Coffee	344	146	—	2,260	90	53
Colquitt	429	206	—	2,519	87	48
Columbia	542	206	16,600	2,134	77	20
Cook	161	75	16,330	2,488	86	52
Coweta	515	277	17,253	2,645	81	38
Crawford	85	40	—	2,411	91	56
Crisp	253	122	16,960	2,506	94	60
Dade	118	41	16,390	2,279	89	37
Dawson	90	36	—	2,581	82	32
Decatur	335	147	17,500	2,147	91	59
DeKalb	4,099	2,973	19,272	3,573	69	31
Dodge	199	115	—	2,398	93	54
Dooly	120	64	16,800	2,617	93	86
Dougherty	1,088	554	—	2,816	86	57
Douglas	690	376	17,192	2,315	79	18
Early	161	94	16,100	2,335	87	70
Echols	35	15	16,350	2,699	82	46
Effingham	267	92	—	2,109	83	32

County	Number of Teachers	Teachers[1] With Advanced Degrees	Beginning[2] Teacher Salary	Cost Per Pupil (Dollars)	School Lunch Program	
					Percent Participating	Percent Free
Elbert	221	93	16,000	2,303	81	50
Emanuel	247	107	—	2,584	95	67
Evans	105	55	—	2,090	88	54
Fannin	165	93	16,350	2,382	83	40
Fayette	533	270	—	2,454	58	6
Floyd	515	286	—	2,782	84	23
Forsyth	384	185	—	2,482	77	16
Franklin	176	73	16,325	2,279	76	33
Fulton	2,446	1,216	18,504	3,530	71	29
Gilmer	123	70	16,300	2,347	79	36
Glascock	35	12	—	1,935	76	28
Glynn	596	292	17,488	3,111	88	38
Gordon	261	161	—	2,214	88	28
Grady	251	107	16,000	2,302	80	56
Greene	139	63	16,400	2,516	87	81
Gwinnett	2,349	1,274	18,597	2,522	65	6
Habersham	262	147	—	2,461	78	31
Hall	645	406	17,320	2,405	83	24
Hancock	116	41	—	2,458	93	98
Haralson	154	86	16,800	2,423	85	33
Harris	158	81	16,200	2,540	89	51
Hart	193	101	16,424	2,292	83	41
Heard	102	46	17,200	3,488	87	39
Henry	395	154	17,200	2,282	78	25
Houston	823	482	17,300	2,580	79	35
Irwin	98	47	16,200	2,448	92	58
Jackson	159	64	—	2,575	89	36
Jasper	83	37	16,731	2,621	87	61
Jeff Davis	137	64	—	1,967	88	44
Jefferson	200	61	—	2,002	93	76
Jenkins	108	50	—	2,315	90	63
Johnson	94	39	—	2,294	91	65
Jones	185	106	—	1,957	80	31
Lamar	126	45	—	2,568	84	55
Lanier	70	25	—	2,317	92	58
Laurens	257	124	16,700	3,240	84	59
Lee	168	99	16,880	2,107	83	32
Liberty	331	109	—	1,984	82	52
Lincoln	81	37	—	2,350	92	51
Long	55	19	—	2,306	87	59
Lowndes	403	221	—	2,637	75	43
Lumpkin	116	79	—	2,500	73	34
Macon	160	78	—	2,502	95	80
Madison	206	103	—	2,205	90	30
Marion	93	51	—	1,384	89	64
McDuffie	226	85	—	2,297	76	55
McIntosh	112	42	—	2,543	75	65
Meriwether	255	115	16,500	2,185	87	66
Miller	84	38	—	2,608	96	52
Mitchell	194	73	16,600	2,440	87	74
Monroe	151	58	17,011	2,686	92	40
Montgomery	69	33	16,000	2,376	85	71
Morgan	143	63	16,650	2,298	86	54
Murray	241	114	17,000	2,079	75	30
Muscogee	1,840	1,212	17,512	3,079	80	52

County	Number of Teachers	Teachers[1] With Advanced Degrees	Beginning[2] Teacher Salary	Cost Per Pupil (Dollars)	School Lunch Program	
					Percent Participating	Percent Free
Newton	440	196	—	2,329	88	36
Oconee	154	96	—	2,246	80	19
Oglethorpe	104	48	16,300	2,422	79	56
Paulding	320	140	—	2,132	79	20
Peach	220	116	—	2,304	87	55
Pickens	129	68	—	2,593	82	35
Pierce	147	73	—	2,049	91	45
Pike	101	44	16,500	2,260	84	41
Polk	339	217	16,390	2,199	87	39
Pulaski	90	46	16,500	2,234	92	59
Putnam	118	74	—	2,801	95	63
Quitman	17	7	—	3,390	99	96
Rabun	117	54	—	2,570	90	42
Randolph	110	46	16,000	2,245	93	86
Richmond	1,702	593	16,900	2,670	79	59
Rockdale	491	277	17,630	2,544	80	15
Schley	26	15	—	2,373	95	52
Screven	197	94	—	2,683	87	55
Seminole	102	42	—	2,304	89	57
Spalding	546	238	17,180	2,349	77	48
Stephens	230	127	—	2,265	73	40
Stewart	75	35	16,320	1,598	98	92
Sumter	99	61	—	2,559	96	80
Talbot	65	30	16,300	2,520	100	90
Taliaferro	13	3	—	2,881	99	94
Tattnall	175	82	16,050	2,251	87	59
Taylor	98	57	—	2,409	87	68
Telfair	142	83	—	2,579	81	69
Terrell	120	61	—	2,246	97	88
Thomas	246	116	16,300	2,492	87	58
Tift	384	181	16,600	2,067	86	50
Toombs	134	55	16,000	2,220	88	57
Towns	46	21	16,000	2,647	81	41
Treutlen	73	33	—	2,059	90	58
Troup	221	113	—	2,736	87	26
Turner	126	67	—	2,289	88	69
Twiggs	102	41	—	2,403	82	78
Union	105	47	16,100	2,487	93	43
Upson	172	70	16,200	1,968	88	50
Walker	519	197	16,700	2,536	83	33
Walton	335	144	—	2,110	85	36
Ware	216	94	16,850	2,207	90	30
Warren	63	15	—	2,483	82	90
Washington	208	79	16,500	2,585	85	68
Wayne	234	105	—	2,218	85	42
Webster	18	13	—	3,132	95	84
Wheeler	67	29	16,000	2,437	96	74
White	117	67	—	2,777	89	22
Whitfield	510	288	16,900	2,351	82	25
Wilcox	85	58	16,000	2,530	85	65
Wilkes	124	42	16,400	2,336	89	58
Wilkinson	121	56	—	2,566	84	50
Worth	214	111	16,750	2,230	88	55
Total	52,566	26,952				

County	Number of Teachers	Teachers[1] With Advanced Degrees	Beginning[2] Teacher Salary	Cost Per Pupil (Dollars)	School Lunch Program Percent Participating	School Lunch Program Percent Free
City Systems	7,942	4,369				
Georgia	60,509	31,321	16,000	2,744	80	43

Tri-County High (Marion, Schley and Webster) included in Marion; Baker High included in Mitchell; Quitman High included in Stewart.
— Data not available
[1] Masters Degree or higher
[2] For the 1985–1986 school year, the base salary for beginning teachers was $16,000. Some school systems supplement the base salary.

Independent City Systems; Number of Teachers, Advanced Degrees, Beginning Salary, Cost Per Pupil, School Lunch Program: 1985–1986

Independent City System	Number of Teachers	Teachers[1] With Advanced Degrees	Beginning[2] Teacher Salary	Cost Per Pupil (Dollars)	School Lunch Program Percent Participating	School Lunch Program Percent Free
Americus	205	132	16,600	2,062	87	63
Atlanta	3,842	2,098	18,504	4,195	83	80
Bremen	66	48	—	2,270	84	17
Buford	81	40	17,800	2,624	84	28
Calhoun	113	68	17,020	2,866	78	21
Carrollton	161	114	—	2,480	78	35
Cartersville	127	70	—	2,631	64	34
Chickamauga	54	26	—	1,606	60	13
Commerce	67	27	—	2,058	82	34
Dalton	244	181	—	3,560	82	26
Decatur	163	135	17,500	3,698	86	68
Dublin	179	98	17,200	2,021	80	54
Fitzgerald	134	66	—	2,009	78	57
Gainesville	172	118	17,741	2,795	73	42
Hogansville	53	15	16,000	2,025	91	53
Jefferson	84	41	16,300	1,845	86	30
LaGrange	293	177	16,610	2,505	89	52
Marietta	281	172	19,000	4,254	76	43
Pelham	91	35	—	1,959	85	72
Rome	292	161	—	2,602	86	54
Social Circle	61	20	—	2,155	76	47
Thomaston	93	40	16,200	2,339	73	51
Thomasville	213	85	—	3,090	90	59
Trion	54	28	16,700	1,621	70	12
Valdosta	407	192	16,350	2,566	77	69
Vidalia	151	68	—	2,022	85	44
Waycross	215	87	—	2,578	94	70
West Point	50	28	—	2,674	93	80
City Totals	7,942	4,369				

—Data not available
[1] Masters Degree or higher
[2] For the 1985–1986 school year, the base salary for beginning teachers was $16,000. Some school systems supplement the base salary.

County Boards of Education

Appling
Rt. 7, Box 36
Baxley 31513
912-367-8600

Atkinson
P.O. Box 608
Pearson 31642
912-422-7373

Bacon
601 N. Pierce St., Alma
31510
912-632-7363

Baker
P.O. Box 40, Newton 31770
912-734-5346

Baldwin
P.O. Box 1188,
Milledgeville 31061
912-453-4176

Banks
Box 1657, Homer 30547
404-677-2224

Barrow
P.O. Box 767, Winder
30680
404-867-4527

Bartow
P.O. Box 569, Cartersville
30120
404-382-3813

Ben Hill
Courthouse, Fitzgerald
31750
912-423-3320

Berrien
P.O. Box 625, Nashville
31639
912-686-2081

Bibb
Board of Public Education
and Orphanage for Bibb
County
Box 6157, Macon 31213
912-741-8502

Bleckley
Cochran 31014

912-934-2821

Brantley
P.O. Box 613, Nahunta
31553
912-462-6176

Brooks
P.O. Box 511, Quitman
31643
912-263-7531

Bryan
P.O. Box 768, Pembroke
31321
912-653-4381

Bulloch
P.O. Box 877, Statesboro
30458
912-764-6201

Burke
P.O. Box 908, Waynesboro
30830
404-554-5101

Butts
P.O. Box 3819, Jackson
30233
404-775-7532

Calhoun
P.O. Box 38, Morgan 31766
912-849-2765

Camden
P.O. Box 1329, Kingsland
31548
912-729-5687

Candler
P.O. Box 536, Metter 30439
912-685-5713

Carroll
164 Independence Dr.
Carrollton 30117
404-832-3568

Catoosa
Box 130, Ringgold 30736
404-935-2297

Charlton
500 S. Third St., Folkston
31537
912-496-2596

Chatham
Board of Public Education
for the City of Savannah
and County of Chatham
208 Bull St., Savannah
31401
912-651-7000

Chattahoochee
P.O. Box 189, Cusseta
31805
404-989-3678

Chattooga
P.O. Box 30, Summerville
30747
404-857-3447

Cherokee
P.O. Box 769, Canton
30114
404-479-1871

Clarke
P.O. Box 1708, Athens
30603
404-546-7721

Clay
P.O. Box 219, Fort Gaines
31751
912-768-2232

Clayton
120 Smith St., Jonesboro
30236
404-478-9991

Clinch
P.O. Box 177, Homerville
31634
912-487-5370

Cobb
P.O. Box 1088, Marietta
30061
404-422-9171

Coffee
Box 959, Douglas 31533
912-384-2086

Colquitt
P.O. Box 1806, Moultrie
31776
912-890-6206

Columbia
P.O. Box 10, Appling 30802
404-541-0650

Cook
P.O. Box 152, Adel 31620
912-896-2294

Coweta
P.O. Box 280, Newnan
30263
404-253-3530

Crawford
P.O. Box 8, Roberta 31078
912-836-3131

Crisp
P.O. Box 729, Cordele
31015
912-273-1611

Dade
P.O. Box 188, Trenton
30752
404-657-4361

Dawson
P.O. Box 208, Courthouse,
Dawsonville 30534
404-265-3246

Decatur
100 West St., Bainbridge
31717
912-246-5898

DeKalb
3770 N. Decatur Road,
Decatur 30032
404-297-2300

Dodge
P.O. Box 647, Eastman
31023
912-374-3783

Dooly
202 Cotton Street, Vienna
31092
912-268-4761

Dougherty
P.O. Box 1470, Albany
31703
912-431-1285

Douglas
P.O. Box 1077, Douglasville
30133

404-942-5411

Early
503 Columbia Rd., Blakely
31723
912-723-4337

Echols
P.O. Box 207, Statenville
31648
912-559-5734

Effingham
P.O. Box 346, Springfield
31329
912-754-6491

Elbert
50 Laurel Dr., Elberton
30635
404-283-1904

Emanuel
P.O. Box 130, Swainsboro
30401
912-237-6674

Evans
P.O. Box 826, Claxton
30417
912-739-3544

Fannin
P.O. Box 606, Blue Ridge
30513
404-632-3771

Fayette
210 Stonewall Ave.,
Fayetteville 30214
404-461-8171

Floyd
171 Riverside Pkwy., N.E.,
Rome 30161
404-234-1031

Forsyth
101 School St., Cumming
30130
404-887-2461

Franklin
P.O. Box 99, Carnesville
30521
404-384-4556

Fulton
786 Cleveland Ave., Atlanta
30315
404-768-3600

Gilmer
5 West Side Square, Ellijay
30540
404-276-1100

Glascock
P.O. Box 205, Gibson
30810
404-598-2291

Glynn
P.O. Box 1677, Brunswick
31521
912-267-4100

Gordon
P.O. Box 127, Calhoun
30701
404-629-7366

Grady
P.O. Box 300, Cairo 31728
912-377-3701

Greene
P.O. Box 209, Greensboro
30642
404-453-7859

Gwinnett
52 Gwinnett Dr.,
Lawrenceville 30245
404-963-8651

Habersham
P.O. Box 467, Clarkesville
30523
404-754-2118

Hall
711 Green St., Suite 100,
Gainesville 30501
404-536-1080

Hancock
P.O. Box 488, Sparta 31087
404-444-5775

Haralson
P.O. Box 508, Buchanan

143

30113
404-646-3882

Harris
P.O. Box 388, Hamilton
31811
404-628-4206

Hart
P.O. Box 696, Hartwell
30643
404-376-5141

Heard
P.O. Box 98, Franklin
30217
404-675-3320

Henry
P.O. Box 479, McDonough
30253
404-957-6601

Houston
P.O. Drawer N., Perry
30169
912-987-1929

Irwin
P.O. Box 225, Ocilla 31774
912-468-7485

Jackson
P.O. Box 279, Jefferson
30549
404-367-5151

Jasper
126 Courthouse, Monticello
31064
404-468-6350

Jeff Davis
P.O. Box 571, Hazlehurst
31539
912-375-4286

Jefferson
P.O. Box 449, Louisville
30434
912-625-7626

Jenkins
P.O. Box 660, Millen 30442
912-982-4305

Johnson
P.O. Box 110, Wrightsville
31096
912-864-3302

Jones
P.O. Box 517, Gray 31032
912-986-6580

Lamar
204 Gordon Rd.,
Barnesville 30204
404-358-1159

Lanier
P.O. Box 258, Lakeland
31635
912-482-3966

Laurens
P.O. Box 2128, Dublin
31040
912-272-4767

Lee
P.O. Box 236, Leesburg
31763
912-759-6414

Liberty
P.O. Box 70, Hinesville
31313
912-876-2161

Lincoln
P.O. Box 39, Lincolnton
30817
404-359-3742

Long
P.O. Box 428, Ludowici
31316
912-545-2367

Lowndes
P.O. Box 1227, Valdosta
31603-1227
912-242-8760

Lumpkin
101 Mountain View Dr.,
Dahlonega 30533
404-864-3611

Macon
P.O. Box 488, Oglethorpe
31068
912-472-8188

Madison
P.O. Box 37, Danielsville
30633
404-795-2191

Marion
P.O. Box 391, Buena Vista

31803
912-649-2234

McDuffie
P.O. Box 957, Thomson
30824
404-595-1918

McIntosh
P.O. Box 495, Darien 31305
912-437-6645

Meriwether
P.O. Box H, Greenville
30222
404-672-4297

Miller
P.O. Box 188, Colquitt
31737
912-758-5592

Mitchell
P.O. Box 588, Camilla
31730
912-336-5648

Monroe
P.O. Box 1308, Forsyth
31029
912-994-2031

Montgomery
P.O. Box 315, Mt. Vernon
30445
912-583-2740

Morgan
1065 East Ave., Madison
30650
404-342-0752

Murray
P.O. Box 40, Chatsworth
30705
404-695-4531

Muscogee
P.O. Box 2427, Columbus
31994
404-324-5661

Newton
P.O. Box 1469, Covington
30209
404-787-1330

Oconee
P.O. Box 146, Watkinsville
30677
404-769-5130

Oglethorpe
P.O. Box 190, Lexington
30648
404-743-8128

Paulding
522 Hardee St., Dallas
30132
404-443-8000

Peach
P.O. Box 1120, Ft. Valley
31030
912-825-5933

Pickens
211 N. Main, Jasper 30143
404-692-2532

Pierce
P.O. Box 349, Blackshear
31516
912-449-5564

Pike
P.O. Box 386, Zebulon,
30295
404-567-8489

Polk
P.O. Box 128, Cedartown
30125
404-748-3821

Pulaski
P.O. Box 148, Hawkinsville
31036
912-892-9191

Putnam
P.O. Box 31, Eatonton
31024
404-485-5381

Quitman
P.O. Box 248, Georgetown
31754
912-334-4189

Rabun
P.O. Box 468, Clayton
30525
404-746-5376

Randolph
309 N. Webster St.,
Cuthbert 31740
912-732-2641

Richmond
2083 Heckle St., Augusta

30910-2999
404-737-7200

Rockdale
P.O. Drawer 1199, Conyers
30207
404-483-4713

Schley
P.O. Box 66, Ellaville 31806
912-937-2405

Screven
P.O. Box 1668, Sylvania
30467
912-564-7114

Seminole
P.O. Box 188,
Donalsonville 31745
912-524-2433

Spalding
P.O. Drawer N, Griffin
30224
404-227-9478

Stephens
P.O. Box 1427, Toccoa
30577
404-886-9415

Stewart
P.O. Box 547, Lumpkin
31815
912-838-4329

Sumter
P.O. Box 967, Americus
31709
912-924-6949

Talbot
P.O. Box 515, Talbotton
31827
404-665-8528

Taliaferro
Route 2, Box 154,
Crawfordsville 30631
404-456-2575

Tattnall
P.O. Box 157, Reidsville
30453
912-557-4726

Taylor
P.O. Box 1937, Butler
31006
912-862-5224

Telfair
P.O. Box 240, McRae
31055
912-868-5661

Terrell
P.O. Box 151, Dawson
31742
912-995-4425

Thomas
P.O. Box 2300, Thomasville
31799
912-226-7102

Tift
P.O. Box 389, Tifton 31793
912-382-4000

Toombs
P.O. Box 440, Lyons 30436
912-526-3141

Towns
P.O. Box 386, Hiawassee
30546
404-896-2279

Treutlen
202 Third Street, Soperton
30457
912-529-4228

Troup
P.O. Box 1228, LaGrange
30240
404-884-8634

Turner
P.O. Box 518, Ashburn
31714
912-567-3338

Twiggs
P.O. Box 232, Jeffersonville
31044
912-945-3127

Union
Rt. 2, Box 5000, Blairsville
30512
404-745-2322

Upson
P.O. Box 831, Thomaston
30286
404-647-9621

Walker
P.O. Box 29, LaFayette
30728

145

404-638-1240

Walton
115 Oak St., Monroe 30655
404-267-6544

Ware
P.O. Box 1789, Waycross
31502
912-283-8656

Warren
P.O. Box 228, Warrenton
30828
404-465-3383

Washington
P.O. Box 716, Sandersville
31082
912-552-3981

Wayne
555 S. Sunset Blvd., Jesup
31545
912-427-4244

Webster
P.O. Box 149, Preston
31824
912-828-3315

Wheeler
P.O. Box 427, Alamo 30411
912-568-7198

White
P.O. Box 295, Cleveland
30528
404-865-2315

Whitfield
P.O. Box 2167, Dalton
30722

404-278-8070

Wilcox
Courthouse, Abbeville
31001
912-467-2141

Wilkes
P.O. Box 279, Washington
30673
404-678-2718

Wilkinson
P.O. Box 206, Irwinton
31042
912-946-5521

Worth
P.O. Box 359, Sylvester
31791
912-776-8600

ELECTIONS

Presidential Election Results, 1984

County	1984 Walter Mondale	Ronald Reagan	County	1984 Walter Mondale	Ronald Reagan
Appling	1,958	2,929	Cherokee	3,499	11,146
Atkinson	901	944	Clarke	10,132	11,503
Bacon	1,010	1,778	Clay	750	419
Baker	691	675	Clayton	11,763	31,553
Baldwin	3,853	5,717	Clinch	625	862
Banks	1,063	1,549	Cobb	28,414	97,429
Barrow	2,367	4,123	Coffee	2,633	4,200
Bartow	4,780	7,104	Colquitt	3,208	5,815
Ben Hill	1,859	2,313	Columbia	3,727	12,294
Berrien	1,670	2,395	Cook	1,510	1,860
Bibb	26,427	24,170	Coweta	3,650	7,981
Bleckley	1,465	1,912	Crawford	1,423	1,298
Brantley	1,517	1,679	Crisp	2,128	2,895
Brooks	1,661	2,229	Dade	1,150	2,750
Bryan	1,398	2,265	Dawson	643	1,322
Bulloch	3,644	6,117	Decatur	2,656	4,134
Burke	3,127	3,137	DeKalb	77,329	104,697
Butts	1,820	2,141	Dodge	2,513	2,765
Calhoun	1,077	776	Dooly	1,726	1,435
Camden	2,164	2,841	Dougherty	12,904	16,920
Candler	1,014	1,497	Douglas	4,371	12,428
Carroll	5,590	11,436	Early	1,494	2,239
Catoosa	3,089	7,908	Echols	227	453
Charlton	1,111	1,368	Effingham	2,055	4,266
Chatham	28,271	38,482	Elbert	2,670	3,366
Chattahoochee	428	459	Emanuel	2,458	3,920
Chattooga	2,576	2,953			

| County | 1984 | | County | 1984 | |
	Walter Mondale	Ronald Reagan		Walter Mondale	Ronald Reagan
Evans	1,193	1,601	Oconee	1,467	3,471
Fannin	1,965	4,159	Oglethorpe	1,238	2,122
Fayette	2,861	12,575	Paulding	2,621	6,048
Floyd	8,873	15,437	Peach	3,369	2,652
Forsyth	2,275	6,841	Pickens	1,329	2,801
Franklin	1,838	2,549	Pierce	1,501	1,978
Fulton	125,567	95,149	Pike	1,203	1,855
Gilmer	1,234	2,972	Polk	3,262	5,435
Glascock	317	827	Pulaski	1,440	1,509
Glynn	6,574	11,724	Putnam	1,336	1,830
Gordon	2,607	5,566	Quitman	490	361
Grady	2,261	3,886	Rabun	1,267	2,191
Greene	1,992	1,599	Randolph	1,454	1,578
Gwinnett	14,139	54,749	Richmond	21,208	29,869
Habersham	2,125	4,647	Rockdale	3,291	10,121
Hall	7,421	15,076	Schley	403	614
Hancock	2,109	644	Screven	1,747	2,583
Haralson	1,938	3,945	Seminole	1,350	1,636
Harris	2,096	3,138	Spalding	4,878	8,571
Hart	2,496	2,842	Stephens	2,272	4,057
Heard	810	1,492	Stewart	1,308	805
Henry	4,096	9,142	Sumter	3,725	4,607
Houston	9,226	14,255	Talbot	1,494	778
Irwin	905	1,330	Taliaferro	550	318
Jackson	2,717	4,202	Tattnall	1,954	3,641
Jasper	1,122	1,431	Taylor	1,340	1,292
Jeff Davis	1,380	2,233	Telfair	2,049	1,980
Jefferson	2,816	2,999	Terrell	1,598	1,744
Jenkins	1,108	1,399	Thomas	4,039	6,427
Johnson	1,199	1,733	Tift	2,736	4,429
Jones	2,781	3,401	Toombs	2,385	4,470
Lamar	1,605	2,198	Towns	1,007	1,960
Lanier	741	852	Treutlen	843	1,086
Laurens	5,471	7,181	Troup	5,272	9,340
Lee	1,284	2,972	Turner	1,270	1,329
Liberty	2,803	3,229	Twiggs	1,755	1,143
Lincoln	1,115	1,357	Union	1,112	1,914
Long	816	1,099	Upson	2,943	4,803
Lowndes	6,167	10,437	Walker	5,000	10,734
Lumpkin	1,110	1,991	Walton	2,481	4,995
Macon	2,521	1,515	Ware	4,435	5,547
Madison	1,690	3,768	Warren	1,258	1,087
Marion	951	846	Washington	3,034	2,887
McDuffie	2,006	3,284	Wayne	2,434	3,698
McIntosh	1,796	1,512	Webster	534	402
Meriwether	2,864	3,195	Wheeler	774	833
Miller	526	1,348	White	1,090	2,369
Mitchell	2,791	2,737	Whitfield	5,284	11,957
Monroe	2,189	2,420	Wilcox	1,212	1,218
Montgomery	950	1,365	Wilkes	1,586	1,837
Morgan	1,714	2,301	Wilkinson	2,102	1,756
Murray	1,649	3,521	Worth	1,685	2,910
Muscogee	20,835	23,816	Georgia	706,628	1,068,722
Newton	3,389	5,810			

General Election: 1986

In the 1986 general election there were 1,225,009 total votes cast for U.S. senator—623,707 Democratic votes and 601,241 Republican votes, plus 61 write-in votes.

For governor 1,175,114 votes were cast—828,465 Democratic votes, 346,512 Republican votes, and 137 write-in votes.

There was a total of 2,575,819 registered voters, indicating that 47.56% of the estimated voting age population who were registered (29.14% of the voting age population) voted in the 1986 general election.

Gubernatorial Election Results, 1986

County	Democrat Joe Frank Harris	Republican Guy Davis	County	Democrat Joe Frank Harris	Republican Guy Davis
Appling	1,725	422	Coweta	5,738	3,199
Atkinson	936	200	Crawford	1,127	270
Bacon	1,062	204	Crisp	2,065	673
Baker	1,031	256	Dade	1,194	427
Baldwin	4,194	1,549	Dawson	1,031	480
Banks	1,458	454	Decatur	2,635	927
Bartow	3,709	1,385	DeKalb	77,549	47,148
Barrow	6,918	2,083	Dodge	2,223	525
Ben Hill	2,170	446	Dooly	1,624	343
Berrien	1,689	428	Dougherty	16,093	5,283
Bibb	24,405	5,905	Douglas	7,393	4,424
Bleckley	1,659	434	Early	2,033	575
Brantley	1,414	199	Echols	243	44
Brooks	1,696	426	Effingham	2,676	586
Bryan	1,756	404	Elbert	2,833	642
Bullock	5,513	1,465	Emanuel	2,209	706
Burke	2,696	556	Evans	1,196	201
Butts	2,382	796	Fannin	1,999	1,279
Calhoun	959	226	Fayette	6,769	5,401
Camden	1,729	374	Floyd	12,425	4,116
Candler	1,040	238	Forsyth	4,384	2,487
Carroll	8,284	4,085	Franklin	1,960	563
Catoosa	6,761	2,228	Fulton	102,358	47,377
Charlton	737	158	Gilmer	1,844	868
Chatham	31,456	10,003	Glascock	578	146
Chattahoochee	307	78	Glynn	10,142	4,025
Chattooga	3,793	784	Gordon	3,573	1,698
Cherokee	6,097	3,720	Grady	2,553	546
Clarke	9,756	4,083	Greene	2,216	385
Clay	551	93	Gwinnett	31,562	23,474
Clayton	21,216	12,317	Habersham	3,183	1,143
Clinch	609	116	Hall	10,597	4,717
Cobb	49,282	34,438	Hancock	1,263	170
Coffee	3,112	709	Haralson	3,027	1,287
Colquitt	3,982	1,231	Harris	2,242	909
Columbia	7,680	2,939	Hart	2,347	671
Cook	1,690	349	Heard	1,236	475

County	Democrat Joe Frank Harris	Republican Guy Davis	County	Democrat Joe Frank Harris	Republican Guy Davis
Henry	6,766	3,854	Rabun	1,780	551
Houston	11,567	3,366	Randolph	1,599	338
Irwin	1,183	256	Richmond	27,257	7,203
Jackson	3,765	1,120	Rockdale	6,876	4,402
Jasper	1,274	447	Schley	528	146
Jeff Davis	1,351	246	Screven	1,904	355
Jefferson	2,621	425	Seminole	972	443
Jenkins	967	214	Spalding	5,985	3,375
Johnson	1,340	240	Stephens	2,618	848
Jones	2,905	777	Stewart	986	172
Lamar	1,853	659	Sumter	3,723	945
Lanier	688	121	Talbot	1,025	251
Laurens	5,282	1,364	Taliaferro	510	71
Lee	1,830	755	Tattnall	1,936	493
Liberty	3,503	559	Taylor	1,674	280
Lincoln	1,444	288	Telfair	1,894	368
Long	642	137	Terrell	1,484	419
Lowndes	7,298	2,221	Thomas	4,379	1,248
Lumpkin	1,615	583	Tift	3,185	1,043
Macon	2,174	318	Toombs	2,431	865
Madison	2,596	852	Towns	1,045	668
Marion	949	278	Treutlen	990	129
McDuffie	2,576	529	Troup	7,432	2,039
McIntosh	1,695	284	Turner	1,782	334
Meriwether	3,078	1,042	Twiggs	1,782	232
Miller	613	206	Union	2,150	891
Mitchell	3,063	625	Upson	3,996	1,032
Monroe	2,561	673	Walker	6,438	2,116
Montgomery	1,051	238	Walton	3,777	1,644
Morgan	2,044	638	Ware	5,096	820
Murray	1,743	520	Warren	1,135	185
Muscogee	24,937	7,261	Washington	2,573	463
Newton	5,151	2,049	Wayne	2,817	680
Oconee	2,428	998	Webster	461	127
Oglethorpe	1,552	461	Wheeler	616	101
Paulding	4,191	1,727	White	1,846	873
Peach	3,021	646	Whitfield	7,224	2,694
Pickens	1,650	662	Wilcox	1,321	265
Pierce	1,695	225	Wilkes	2,032	497
Pike	1,679	693	Wilkinson	1,993	305
Polk	3,517	2,358	Worth	2,330	804
Pulaski	1,414	335	Total	828,465	346,512
Putnam	1,649	520			
Quitman	388	56	Total Votes Cast	1,174,977	

Senatorial Election Results: 1986

County	Democrat Wyche Fowler, Jr.	Republican Mack Mattingly	County	Democrat Wyche Fowler, Jr.	Republican Mack Mattingly
Appling	1,250	1,258	Baker	873	790
Atkinson	707	524	Baldwin	2,989	3,370
Bacon	724	625	Banks	1,126	792

County	Democrat Wyche Fowler, Jr.	Republican Mack Mattingly	County	Democrat Wyche Fowler, Jr.	Republican Mack Mattingly
Barrow	2,791	2,552	Glascock	364	360
Bartow	5,023	4,107	Glynn	5,530	8,805
Ben Hill	1,614	1,057	Gordon	2,707	2,818
Berrien	1,234	886	Grady	1,710	1,530
			Greene	1,740	855
Bibb	19,318	14,117	Gwinnett	19,796	35,845
Bleckley	1,168	1,204	Habersham	2,310	2,351
Brantley	954	720	Hall	8,363	7,726
Brooks	1,094	1,169	Hancock	1,263	394
Bryan	983	1,446			
Bulloch	3,110	4,179	Haralson	2,351	2,022
Burke	1,954	1,574	Harris	1,662	1,792
Butts	1,832	1,376	Hart	1,679	1,352
Calhoun	778	438	Heard	970	800
Camden	989	1,074	Henry	4,911	5,768
			Houston	8,287	7,854
Candler	739	728	Irwin	835	718
Carroll	6,011	6,514	Jackson	2,650	2,267
Catoosa	3,531	5,545	Jasper	1,036	814
Charlton	392	473	Jeff Davis	1,123	708
Chatham	21,187	24,418			
Chattahoochee	245	193	Jefferson	1,860	1,480
Chattooga	2,479	2,098	Jenkins	712	652
Cherokee	4,324	6,001	Johnson	956	742
Clarke	8,131	6,892	Jones	2,151	2,075
Clay	454	196	Lamar	1,453	1,142
			Lanier	475	381
Clayton	14,956	18,743	Laurens	4,155	3,498
Clinch	388	346	Lee	1,012	1,607
Cobb	31,163	53,417	Liberty	2,432	2,143
Coffee	2,380	2,050	Lincoln	893	849
Colquitt	2,649	3,502			
Columbia	3,343	7,302	Long	497	394
Cook	1,231	819	Lowndes	4,783	5,096
Coweta	3,929	5,071	Lumpkin	1,239	999
Crawford	965	618	Macon	1,829	952
Crisp	1,392	1,674	Madison	1,521	2,014
			Marion	725	523
Dade	608	1,056	McDuffie	1,698	1,792
Dawson	756	803	McIntosh	1,191	959
Decatur	1,689	2,271	Meriwether	2,497	1,601
DeKalb	70,012	57,725	Miller	374	488
Dodge	1,881	1,292			
Dooly	1,468	1,091	Mitchell	2,320	1,409
Dougherty	10,711	11,540	Monroe	1,911	1,289
Douglas	5,169	7,042	Montgomery	766	600
Early	1,335	1,233	Morgan	1,637	1,185
Echols	153	151	Murray	1,142	1,215
			Muscogee	18,220	14,834
Effingham	1,476	2,118	Newton	3,857	3,434
Elbert	2,073	1,438	Oconee	1,500	2,028
Emanuel	1,578	1,641	Oglethorpe	980	1,055
Evans	764	797	Paulding	2,758	3,215
Fannin	1,683	1,842			
Fayette	4,200	8,106	Peach	2,527	1,639
Floyd	9,019	8,084	Pickens	1,276	1,178
Forsyth	3,160	3,779	Pierce	1,149	913
Franklin	1,426	1,102	Pike	1,085	1,236
Fulton	103,155	52,262	Polk	3,160	2,971
Gilmer	1,350	1,607	Pulaski	1,162	716

County	Democrat Wyche Fowler, Jr.	Republican Mack Mattingly	County	Democrat Wyche Fowler, Jr.	Republican Mack Mattingly
Putnam	1,145	1,160	Treutlen	701	437
Quitman	291	171	Troup	4,851	4,829
Rabun	1,297	1,169	Turner	1,308	902
Randolph	1,199	808	Twiggs	1,448	631
Richmond	16,901	18,057	Union	1,629	1,460
Rockdale	4,461	6,899	Upson	2,899	2,312
Schley	366	376	Walker	3,711	5,048
Screven	1,126	1,369	Walton	2,962	2,871
Seminole	862	701	Ware	3,641	2,724
Spalding	4,877	4,984	Warren	860	515
Stephens	1,891	1,758	Washington	2,201	1,394
Stewart	810	424	Wayne	1,916	1,680
Sumter	2,733	2,466	Webster	339	235
Talbot	889	480	Wheeler	439	326
Taliaferro	412	176	White	1,358	1,377
Tattnall	1,308	1,509	Whitfield	4,117	6,091
Taylor	1,233	783	Wilcox	1,067	679
Telfair	1,889	977	Wilkes	1,654	1,038
Terrell	1,203	885	Wilkinson	1,598	910
Thomas	2,566	3,432	Worth	1,627	1,584
Tift	2,248	2,498	Total	623,707	601,241
Toombs	1,496	2,282	Total Votes Cast	1,224,948	
Towns	922	913			

Congressional Election Results, 1986

First Congressional District

County	Lindsay Thomas (D)	County	Lindsay Thomas (D)
Brantley	1,243	Jenkins	956
Bryan	1,516	Liberty	2,816
Bulloch	5,469	Long	624
Burke	2,355	McIntosh	1,463
Camden	1,391	Montgomery	1,027
Candler	929	Screven	1,686
Chatham	24,800	Tattnall	1,741
Effingham	2,462	Toombs	2,218
Emanuel	1,971	Wayne	2,660
Evans	1,088	Total	69,440
Glynn	11,025		

Second Congressional District

County	Charles Hatcher (D)	County	Charles Hatcher (D)
Baker	905	Calhoun	997
Ben Hill	2,187	Clay	522
Berrien	1,641	Colquitt	3,820
Brooks	1,592	Cook	1,746

151

Second Congressional District

County	Charles Hatcher (D)	County	Charles Hatcher (D)
Crisp	1,973	Quitman	308
Decatur	2,624	Randolph	1,510
Dougherty	17,486	Seminole	1,217
Early	2,136	Stewart	829
Echols	241	Terrell	1,393
Grady	2,521	Thomas	3,967
Irwin	1,128	Tift	3,174
Lanier	658	Turner	1,724
Lee	1,909	Webster	369
Lowndes	7,854	Worth	2,436
Miller	617	Total	72,482
Mitchell	2,998		

Third Congressional District

County	Richard Ray (D)	County	Richard Ray (D)
Bleckley	1,497	Peach	2,877
Butts	2,430	Pike	1,541
Chattahoochee	315	Pulaski	1,315
Crawford	1,034	Schley	523
Dooly	1,354	Sumter	3,320
Harris	2,098	Talbot	946
Houston	10,002	Taylor	1,697
Lamar	1,785	Troup	7,479
Macon	1,788	Upson	3,919
Marion	850	Total	75,850
Meriwether	3,640		
Muscogee	25,440		

Fourth Congressional District

County	Ben Jones (D)	Pat Swindall (R)
DeKalb (in part)	54,832	58,046
Fulton (in part)	12,374	18,196
Newton	4,004	3,360
Rockdale	4,682	6,764
Total	75,892	86,366
Grand Total	162,258	

Fifth Congressional District

County	John Lewis (D)	Portia A. Scott (R)
DeKalb (in part)	11,544	1,485
Fulton (in part)	81,685	29,077
Total	93,229	30,562
Grand Total	123,791	

Sixth Congressional District

County	Crandle Bray (D)	Newt Gingrich (R)	County	Crandle Bray (D)	Newt Gingrich (R)
Carroll	5,230	7,250	Henry	4,366	6,312
Clayton	13,553	20,248	Paulding	2,579	3,246
Coweta	3,212	5,782	Polk	2,847	2,866
Douglas	3,785	7,990	Spalding	3,868	5,436
Fayette	3,300	8,954	Total	51,352	75,583
Fulton (in part)	5,564	4,589	Grand Total	126,935	
Haralson	2,206	2,072			
Heard	842	838			

Seventh Congressional District

County	George (Buddy) Darden (D)	Joe Morecraft (R)	County	George (Buddy) Darden (D)	Joe Morecraft (R)
Bartow	6,893	1,624	Floyd	12,927	3,833
Catoosa	6,142	2,743	Walker	5,715	3,052
Chattooga	3,590	829	Total	88,636	44,891
Cobb	52,294	32,220	Grand Total	133,527	
Dade	1.075	590			

Eighth Congressional District

County	J. Roy Rowland (D)	Eddie McDowell (R)	County	J. Roy Rowland (D)	Eddie McDowell (R)
Appling	1,629	334	Laurens	6,214	698
Atkinson	839	182	Monroe	2,677	481
Bacon	1,000	168	Pierce	1,615	192
Baldwin	4,540	1,092	Putnam	1,719	358
Bibb	25,523	4,174	Taliaferro	480	41
Charlton	595	171	Telfair	1,859	201
Clinch	552	108	Treutlen	953	79
Coffee	2,990	587	Twiggs	1,577	192
Dodge	2,495	299	Ware	4,894	806
Glascock	512	124	Washington	2,587	306
Greene	2,189	319	Wheeler	615	66
Hancock	1,167	88	Wilcox	1,372	178
Jasper	1,288	336	Wilkinson	1,977	222
Jeff Davis	1,349	177	Total	82,254	12,952
Jefferson	2,492	338	Grand Total	95,206	
Johnson	1,389	138			
Jones	3,166	497			

Ninth Congressional District

County	Ed Jenkins (D)	County	Ed Jenkins (D)
Banks	1,494	Jackson	3,979
Cherokee	6,154	Lumpkin	1,705
Dawson	1,047	Murray	1,663
Fannin	1,916	Pickens	1,683
Forsyth	5,372	Rabun	1,819
Franklin	2,031	Stephens	2,677
Gilmer	1,707	Towns	1,068
Gordon	3,409	Union	2,206
Gwinnett (in part)	18,939	White	2,078
Habersham	3,225	Whitfield	6,573
Hall	11,338	Total	84,303
Hart	2,220		

Tenth Congressional District

County	Doug Barnard, Jr. (D)	Jim Hill (R)	County	Doug Barnard, Jr. (D)	Jim Hill (R)
Barrow	3,548	1,171	Oconee	2,347	1,020
Clarke	9,972	3,407	Oglethorpe	1,452	465
Columbia	6,665	3,962	Richmond	26,130	8,373
Elbert	2,803	547	Walton	3,734	1,370
Gwinnett (in part)	11,789	15,542	Warren	976	175
Lincoln	1,367	286	Wilkes	1,972	412
Madison	2,395	815	Total	79,548	38,714
McDuffie	2,425	615	Grand Total	118,262	
Morgan	1,973	554			

ELECTORAL VOTE

The state of Georgia has 12 electoral votes.

ELEVATIONS, LATITUDES, AND LONGITUDES

The average elevation in Georgia is 600 feet. Brasstown Bald is the highest point in the state with an altitude of 4,784 feet. The Atlantic Ocean is the lowest point at one foot. Georgia lies between 30° and 35° north latitude and from 81° to 85° 30' west longitude. Similar values for selected locales in the state follow.

City	Altitude	Latitude	Longitude
Albany	180	31°32'N	84°08'W
Atlanta	1,010	33°39'N	84°26'W
Augusta	148	33°22'N	81°58'W
Columbus	385	32°31'N	84°56'W
Macon	354	32°42'N	83°39'W
Savannah	46	32°06'N	81°12'W

EMPLOYMENT

County	Revised Unemployment Rate 1986	Rate 1987	Employment	Estimates April 1988 Unemployment Number	Rate
Appling	7.8	8.7	7,353	772	9.5
Atkinson	7.4	5.7	3,463	168	4.6
Bacon	8.3	6.9	4,386	393	8.2
Baker	8.7	10.3	1,499	166	10.0
Baldwin	5.2	6.2	15,783	729	4.4
Banks	4.5	4.1	5,106	276	5.1
Barrow	7.0	5.9	13,012	764	5.5
Bartow	8.7	7.4	19,600	1,656	7.8
Ben Hill	8.2	7.6	6,692	483	6.7
Berrien	5.4	4.7	7,364	389	5.0
Bibb	6.4	5.5	68,864	3,840	5.3
Bleckley	4.8	3.6	6,105	353	5.5
Brantley	9.3	9.1	3,757	368	8.9
Brooks	5.3	4.9	6,124	325	5.0
Bryan	6.9	6.2	5,219	395	7.0
Bulloch	5.3	4.5	16,574	804	4.6
Burke	7.4	10.4	10,675	1,038	8.9
Butts	8.3	7.9	6,680	408	5.8
Calhoun	11.0	9.6	1,844	189	9.3
Camden	5.2	4.8	10,377	631	5.7
Candler	6.1	4.4	3,061	176	5.4
Carroll	6.4	5.7	28,591	1,869	6.1
Catoosa	4.9	4.0	19,609	906	4.4
Charlton	7.5	6.4	2,678	200	6.9
Chatham	6.5	5.9	94,643	7,104	7.0
Chattahoochee	11.6	11.1	1,485	242	14.0
Chattooga	8.9	6.5	8,227	772	8.6
Cherokee	3.4	3.9	37,996	2,115	5.3
Clarke	5.0	4.1	38,396	1,655	4.1
Clay	8.1	6.9	972	77	7.3
Clayton	4.4	4.7	93,629	5,204	5.3
Clinch	7.1	7.2	2,566	378	12.8
Cobb	3.3	3.4	230,419	10,012	4.2
Coffee	8.3	6.7	11,956	1,044	8.0
Colquitt	7.9	7.8	15,847	1,001	5.9
Columbia	3.7	4.3	24,603	1,230	4.8
Cook	6.6	6.7	6,007	383	6.0
Coweta	5.1	4.8	22,345	1,574	6.6
Crawford	6.8	6.1	3,282	245	6.9
Crisp	10.2	7.6	8,567	619	6.7
Dade	6.5	6.0	5,171	393	7.1
Dawson	7.7	6.6	2,441	153	5.9
Decatur	6.5	5.9	10,632	668	5.9
DeKalb	4.4	4.4	310,258	15,756	4.8

County	Revised Unemployment Rate 1986	Rate 1987	Employment	Estimates April 1988 Unemployment Number	Rate
Dodge	10.2	7.8	5,248	485	8.5
Dooly	9.5	6.8	3,947	268	6.4
Dougherty	11.4	9.6	44,097	4,630	9.5
Douglas	3.9	4.4	34,441	1,790	4.9
Early	9.6	7.7	4,678	338	6.7
Echols	5.5	5.8	1,037	57	5.2
Effingham	5.6	5.9	8,997	745	7.6
Elbert	8.9	7.5	8,070	600	6.9
Emanuel	9.8	7.2	8,104	568	6.5
Evans	7.5	5.9	3,346	172	4.9
Fannin	7.5	7.5	5,830	774	11.7
Fayette	2.6	2.9	25,206	792	3.0
Floyd	6.7	6.1	37,564	2,479	6.2
Forsyth	3.7	4.0	19,484	1,040	5.1
Franklin	7.5	5.6	8,337	383	4.4
Fulton	6.5	6.2	311,757	21,362	6.4
Gilmer	7.0	5.9	5,105	429	7.8
Glascock	6.8	5.1	1,214	60	4.7
Glynn	5.4	5.0	28,425	1,758	5.8
Gordon	7.0	5.6	18,592	1,125	5.7
Grady	6.5	6.6	9,039	610	6.3
Greene	7.9	7.5	5,552	395	6.6
Gwinnett	3.2	3.7	158,941	6,261	3.8
Habersham	6.1	4.2	11,575	593	4.9
Hall	5.7	4.9	42,388	2,218	5.0
Hancock	8.5	9.1	3,416	217	6.0
Haralson	7.9	6.6	8,090	704	8.0
Harris	5.7	5.0	8,305	395	4.5
Hart	5.8	4.5	9,236	495	5.1
Heard	7.6	6.4	3,049	193	6.0
Henry	4.2	4.3	23,900	1,069	4.3
Houston	4.8	4.5	36,446	2,469	6.3
Irwin	6.8	5.4	3,834	236	5.8
Jackson	5.7	5.5	13,691	642	4.5
Jasper	7.2	6.3	2,875	164	5.4
Jeff Davis	5.8	5.5	5,423	455	7.7
Jefferson	9.7	7.4	2,916	234	7.4
Jenkins	12.3	8.6	6,854	538	7.3
Johnson	7.7	6.0	3,596	187	4.9
Jones	5.6	4.9	8,363	351	4.0
Lamar	7.2	6.1	4,691	415	8.1
Lanier	5.4	4.9	2,882	136	4.5
Laurens	8.2	7.6	15,346	1,184	7.2
Lee	7.4	6.9	6,782	496	6.8
Liberty	5.8	5.5	11,214	925	7.6
Lincoln	9.2	6.8	3,065	291	8.7

County	Revised Unemployment Rate 1986	Rate 1987	Employment	Estimates April 1988 Unemployment Number	Rate
Long	9.8	6.5	1,425	130	8.4
Lowndes	5.8	5.6	32,041	1,897	5.6
Lumpkin	4.4	3.9	5,839	232	3.8
Macon	14.1	13.2	3,893	597	13.3
Madison	5.7	5.1	9,277	440	4.5
Marion	6.8	5.7	2,934	196	6.3
McDuffie	7.5	7.0	8,679	611	6.6
McIntosh	8.8	8.2	3,394	421	11.0
Meriwether	10.3	8.4	8,117	593	6.8
Miller	5.9	6.3	2,689	168	5.9
Mitchell	9.6	9.1	8,279	963	10.4
Monroe	7.1	6.0	7,257	406	5.3
Montgomery	7.7	7.0	2,813	219	7.2
Morgan	7.3	6.8	5,795	534	8.4
Murray	6.7	5.5	11,412	795	6.5
Muscogee	6.7	6.0	71,428	5,172	6.8
Newton	6.8	5.7	19,540	1,476	7.0
Oconee	3.5	2.8	7,864	320	3.9
Oglethorpe	7.8	7.3	3,776	247	6.1
Paulding	4.5	5.2	15,207	1,118	6.8
Peach	6.7	5.7	8,137	403	4.7
Pickens	6.3	4.4	5,522	529	8.7
Pierce	10.1	9.7	4,895	470	8.8
Pike	5.2	4.6	4,778	247	4.9
Polk	8.9	7.1	12,547	1,142	8.3
Pulaski	9.9	5.3	3,215	257	7.4
Putnam	6.7	12.3	4,693	614	11.6
Quitman	10.5	9.2	647	123	16.0
Rabun	8.3	4.7	5,509	289	5.0
Randolph	8.5	6.9	3,256	287	8.1
Richmond	6.7	6.7	78,748	5,717	6.8
Rockdale	4.1	4.0	24,331	1,348	5.2
Schley	7.1	7.4	1,473	134	8.3
Screven	8.3	9.2	4,911	425	8.0
Seminole	6.0	6.0	3,468	253	6.8
Spalding	6.3	5.6	25,469	1,908	7.0
Stephens	10.2	6.3	9,939	593	5.6
Stewart	14.3	9.8	1,780	196	9.9
Sumter	8.7	7.6	13,204	1,001	7.0
Talbot	9.7	9.4	2,426	164	6.3
Taliaferro	11.0	9.0	635	62	8.9
Tattnall	5.6	4.4	6,897	410	5.6
Taylor	8.7	7.4	2,672	245	8.4
Telfair	10.1	7.8	4,468	304	6.4
Terrell	9.1	9.0	4,362	425	8.9
Thomas	7.2	7.3	17,225	1,233	6.7
Tift	6.4	5.8	15,370	882	5.4

County	Revised Unemployment Rate 1986	Revised Unemployment Rate 1987	Employment	Estimates April 1988 Unemployment Number	Estimates April 1988 Unemployment Rate
Toombs	8.7	7.9	9,332	755	7.5
Towns	5.1	4.1	3,318	104	3.0
Treutlen	8.2	7.6	2,361	162	6.4
Troup	7.8	7.4	25,495	1,795	6.6
Turner	12.2	9.3	3,035	287	8.6
Twiggs	7.4	6.4	3,443	317	8.4
Union	6.3	4.6	4,974	219	4.2
Upson	8.4	5.6	10,667	706	6.2
Walker	7.1	5.7	25,270	1,637	6.1
Walton	6.1	5.6	16,109	972	5.7
Ware	9.5	9.1	14,824	1,242	7.7
Warren	6.8	7.4	2,760	279	9.2
Washington	6.4	5.4	7,631	498	6.1
Wayne	9.4	8.0	7,798	642	7.6
Webster	11.3	10.2	642	85	11.7
Wheeler	6.0	5.5	2,572	174	6.3
White	6.4	4.5	6,056	225	3.6
Whitfield	5.9	4.6	40,330	2,179	5.1
Wilcox	9.1	5.6	2,853	117	3.9
Wilkes	8.5	5.1	4,693	406	8.0
Wilkinson	5.5	5.1	4,237	262	5.8
Worth	12.5	10.2	6,278	659	9.5
Total	5.9	5.5	2,905,724	179,572	5.8

ENDANGERED SPECIES

The following are the federally listed endangered and threatened species. The status code is: E-endangered; T-threatened; CH–with critical habitat designated; (S/A)–due to similarity of appearance to a listed species (affects mostly trade); E,T–different status in different parts of range.

Common Name	Scientific Name	Status
Birds		
Curlew, Eskimo	*Numenius borealis*	E
Eagle, bald	*Haliaeetus leucocephalus*	E,T
Falcon, American peregrine	*Falco peregrinus anatum*	ECH
Falcon, Arctic peregrine	*Falco peregrinus tundrius*	T
Falcon, peregrine	*Falco peregrinus*	E(S/A)
Plover, piping	*Charadrius melodus*	E,T
Stork, wood	*Mycteria americana*	E
Warbler (wood), Bachman's	*Vermivora bachmanii*	E
Woodpecker, ivory-billed	*Campephilus principalis*	E
Woodpecker, red-cockaded	*Picoides borealis*	E
Fishes		
Chub, spotfin	*Hybopsis monacha*	T
Darter, amber	*Percina antesella*	ECH
Darter, snail	*Percina tanasi*	T
Logperch, Conassauga	*Percina jenkinsi*	ECH
Madtom, yellowfin	*Noturus flavipinnis*	T
Sturgeon, short nose	*Acipenser brevirostrum*	E
Mammals		
Bat, gray	*Myotis grisescens*	E
Bat, Indiana	*Myotis sodalis*	ECH
Manatee, West Indian (Florida)	*Trichechus manatus*	ECH
Panther, Florida	*Felis concolor coryi*	E
Wolf, red	*Canis rufus*	E
Plants		
Rattleweed, hairy	*Baptisia arachnifera*	E
Dropwort, canby's	*Oxypolis canbyi*	E
Pitcher plant, green	*Sarracenia oreophila*	E
Pondberry	*Lindera melissifolia*	E
Skullcap, large-flowered	*Scutellaria montana*	E
Torreya, Florida	*Torreya taxifolia*	E
Trillium, persistent	*Trillium, persistens*	E
Reptiles		
Alligator, American	*Alligator mississippiensis*	T(S/A)
Snake, eastern indigo	*Drymarchon corais couperi*	T
Turtle, green sea	*Chelonia mydas*	T
Turtle, hawksbill sea (-carey)	*Eretmochelys imbricata*	ECH
Turtle, Kemp's (Atlantic) Ridley sea	*Lepidochelys kempii*	E
Turtle, leatherback sea	*Dermochelys coriacea*	ECH
Turtle, loggerhead sea	*Caretta caretta*	T

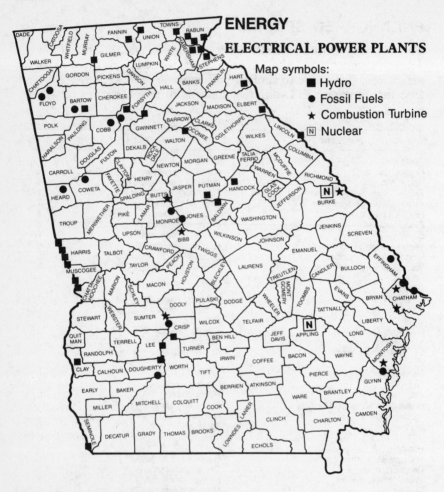

ENERGY

ELECTRICAL POWER PLANTS

Map symbols:
- ■ Hydro
- ● Fossil Fuels
- ★ Combustion Turbine
- Ⓝ Nuclear

FAMOUS GEORGIANS

The following list is merely representative of the many hundreds of Georgians—native born or "transplated"—who have made their mark on the development of Georgia and the United States.

Aaron, Henry Louis "Hank" (1934–   ). Born in Mobile, Alabama. Baseball player, holder of 21 Major League records, including Most Home Runs. Member of the Baseball Hall of Fame. Corporate vice president of the *Atlanta Braves*.

Aiken, Conrad Potter (1889–1973). Born in Savannah. Poet, novelist, short story writer and critic. Educated at Harvard University. Works include *Selected Poems*, for which he won the Pulitzer Prize in 1930, *Blue Voyage, The Short Stories of Conrad Aiken,* and his autobiography, *Ushant.*

Alexander, Edward P. (1835–1910). Born in Washington, Georgia; died in Savannah. Before the war, this Confederate general, while in the U.S. Army, co-developed the semaphore communications system.

Anderson, George T. (1824–1901). Born in Covington; died in Anniston, Alabama. Confederate general who served as Atlanta's chief of police after the war.

Anderson, James William "Bill" (1937–   ). Born in Columbia, South Carolina, grew up in Griffin and Decatur. Country music performer, songwriter, restaurant and music publishing entrepreneur. He holds 50 BMI awards and was elected to the Country Music Songwriters Hall of Fame before the age of forty.

Anderson, Robert H. (1835–1888). Born in Savannah; died in Savannah. Confederate general who served as Savannah's chief of police after the war.

Arnall, Ellis Gibbs. See section on Governors (1943–1947).

Arp, Bill (1826–1903). Born in Lawrenceville. Pseudonym for Charles Henry Smith. Attorney and humorist. Author of several books including *Bill Arp's Peace Papers.*

Atkinson, William Yates. See section on Governors (1894–1898).

Bainbridge, William (1774–1833). Naval officer, commanded the *U.S. Constitution.* Decatur County town named in his honor.

Baldwin, Abraham (1754–1807). Born in North Guilford, Connecticut; one of Georgia's signers of the United States Constitution in 1787. Played a key role in the establishment of the University of Georgia. U.S. representative and senator.

Bartram, William (1739–1823). Born in Philadelphia, died in Kingsessing, Pennsylvania. Early naturalist who roamed much of the state of Georgia.

Battle, Cullen A. (1829–1905). Born in Powelton (Hancock County), Georgia; died in Greensboro, North Carolina. Confederate general who, without formal military training, excelled on the battlefield. After the war, he became the editor of a New Bern, North Carolina newspaper.

Bell, Griffin B. (1918–   ). U.S. attorney general, cabinet member of Jimmy Carter.

Benning, Henry Lewis (1814–1875). Born in Columbia County; died in Columbus. Educated at the University of Georgia. Confederate general. Fort Benning named in his honor.

Berrien, John McPherson (1781–1856). Graduate of Princeton, 4 times U.S. senator, attorney general in Andrew Jackson's cabinet.

Berry, Martha (1866–1942). Born near Rome, Georgia; died in Atlanta. Educator. Became Georgia's first female member of the Board of Regents. Founder of the Berry Schools.

Bethune, Thomas Green (1849–1908). A slave on the Bethune plantation near Columbus, "Blind Tom" became an internationally famous blind pianist and composer.

Birney, Alice McClellan (1858–1907). Born in Marietta. Founder of the National Congress of Mothers, which later became the National Parent-Teacher Association.

Blackburn, Joyce (–). Author of prize-winning fiction and historical biographies, including fiction for children such as *Suki and the Invisible Peacock*, *Suki and the Old Umbrella*, and biographies of Martha Berry, John Adams, James Edward Oglethorpe and others.

Boggs, William R. (1829–1911). Born in Augusta; died in Winston-Salem, North Carolina. Confederate general who served as the chief engineer of the state of Georgia.

Boudinot, Elias (circa 1803–1839). Born in Georgia, murdered in Georgia. Editor of the *Cherokee Phoenix*, an Indian newspaper. Was killed for his role in the 1835 treaty with the United States.

Bowen, John S. (1830–1863). Born in Savannah; died in Mississippi. Confederate general who died of dysentery less than two months after his commission.

Boynton, James S. See section on Governors (1883).

Brown, Joseph Emerson. See section on Governors (1857–1865).

Brown, Joseph Mackey. See section on Governors (1909–1911; 1912–1913).

Brownson, Nathan. See section on Governors (1781–1782).

Brumby, Thomas M. (–). Spanish-American War hero from Marietta who served as Admiral Dewey's flag officer at the Battle of Manila.

Bryan, Goode (1811–1885). Born in Hancock County; died in Augusta. Confederate general who was a veteran of the Mexican War and a delegate to the Georgia Secession Convention.

Bulloch, Archibald. See section on Governors (1776–1777).

Bulloch, James D. (1823–1901). Born near Savannah; died in Liverpool, England. Confederate naval figure who was responsible for the purchase of the *C.S.S. Shenandoah*. Was as uncle of President Theodore Roosevelt.

Bullock, Rufus B. See section on Governors (1868–1871).

Busbee, George Dekle. See section on Governors (1975–1983).

Butler, Selena Sloan (1872–1964). Born in Thomasville; died in Los Angeles, Ca. Educator. Founder of the Georgia Colored Parent-Teacher Association and the National Congress of Colored Parents. She fought against racial discrimination.

Caldwell, Erskine Preston (1903–   ). Born in White Oak. Noted novelist. Best known for his stories about hard times in the American South. Author of *Tobacco Road* and *God's Little Acre*.

Callaway, Cason J. (1894–1961). Textile magnate who created Callaway Gardens, the resort with botanical and vegetable gardens.

Campbell, John A. (1811–1889). Born in Washington, Georgia; died in New Orleans, Louisiana. Was Assistant Confederate Secretary of War. Later, practiced law in New Orleans.

Candler, Allen Daniel. See section on Governors (1898–1902).

Carter, James Earl, Jr., "Jimmy" (1924–   ). Born in Plains. Nuclear physicist, naval officer, peanut farmer, school board member, state senator, governor, 39th president of the United States. Also see section on Governors (1971–1975).

Carter, John C. (1837–1964). Born in Waynesboro; died in Tennessee. Confederate general who was killed during the Battle of Franklin.

Carter, Rosalynn Smith (1927–   ). Born in Georgia. Wife of President Jimmy Carter.

Charles, Ezzard (1922–   ). Born in Georgia. Professional boxer. Held the World Heavyweight Boxing Championship from 1949, following Joe Louis's retirement, to 1951.

Charles, Ray (1932–   ). Born in Albany. Noted blind pianist and singer. His recordings have been on the charts in country, rhythm and blues, and popular categories.

Chivers, Thomas Holley (1809–1858). Born in Washington; died in Decatur. Was a noted poet and good friend of Edgar Allan Poe. Works include *The Path of Sorrow* (1832), *The Lost Pleiad* (1845), and *Conrad and Eudora* (1834).

Clanton, James H. (1827–1871). Born in Columbia County; died in Knoxville, Tennessee. Confederate general who first served in the Mexican War. Was killed in a quarrel in Knoxville.

Clark, Edward (1815–1880). Born in Wilkes County; died in Marshall,

Texas. Replaced Sam Houston as general of Texas when Houston refused to take the Confederate oath of allegiance.

Clarke, Elijah (1733–1799). Born in Edgecombe County, North Carolina; died in Richmond County, Georgia. Active in the Revolution. Land speculator, involved in the Yazoo Land Frauds. Clarke County is named in his honor.

Clarke, John. See section on Governors (1819–1823).

Clay, Lucius DuBignon (1879–1978). Born in Marietta. U.S. Army general, author of *Decision in Germany* (1950). Retired in 1949, then served as ambassador in West Berlin during President Kennedy's administration.

Clayton, Henry D. (1827–1889). Born in Pulaski County, died in Tuscaloosa, Alabama. Confederate general who became president of the University of Alabama after the war.

Cobb, Howell. See section on Governors (1851–1853).

Cobb, Thomas Reade Rootes (1823–1862). Born in Jefferson County; died in Virginia. Graduate of University of Georgia, author of the Confederate State Constitution, and co-founder of the first law school in Georgia. Confederate general who died of wounds inflicted during the Battle of Fredericksburg.

Cobb, Tyrus Raymond "Ty" (1886–1961). Born in Banks County. Baseball player from 1905 to 1928. Until Pete Rose recently broke his record, Cobb had more hits (4,191) than any player in history. Member of the Baseball Hall of Fame.

Coburn, Charles (1877–1961). Born in Macon. Popular character in movies of the 1930s and 1940s.

Colquitt, Alfred Holt. See section on Governors (1877–1882).

Conley, Benjamin F. See section on Governors (1871–1872).

Cook, Philip (1817–1894). Born in Twiggs County; died in Atlanta. Confederate general who, after the war, served in the U.S. Congress and as Georgia's secretary of state.

Cooper, Mark Anthony (1800–1885). Member of U.S. House of Representatives, pioneer iron industrialist.

Coulter, Ellis Merton (1890–1981). Born in Hickory, North Carolina; died in Atlanta. Educator and author. Taught history at the University of Georgia. His works include *The Civil War and Readjustment in Kentucky* (1926), *Georgia, A Short History* (1933), and in *The History of the South* series: *The South During Reconstruction, 1865–1877* and *The Confederate States of America, 1861–1865* (1950).

Crawford, George Walker. See section on Governors (1843–1847).

Crawford, William Harris (1772–1834). Born in Amherst County, Va.; died in Georgia. One of Georgia's most successful national politicians. U.S. senator, president pro tempore of the Senate, U.S. minister to France, secretary of War, secretary of the Treasury, and presidential hopeful.

Cumming, Alfred (1829–1910). Born in Augusta; died in Rome. Confederate general who, after the war, served with the American military commission to Korea.

Curry, Jabez L. M. (1825–1903). Born in Lincoln County; died near Asheville, North Carolina. Served in the First Confederate Congress. After the war, served as U.S. minister to Spain.

Davies, Myrick. See section on Governors (1781).

Dawson, William Crosby (1798–1856). Born in Greene County. Lawyer, legislator, captain of volunteers in the Indian War of 1836 in Florida, judge of the Ocmulgee judicial circuit, congressman, senator. Two cities and one county in Georgia are named for him.

Dill, Benjamin F. (1814–1866). Born in Augusta; died in Memphis, Tennessee. Editor of the Memphis *Appeal* during the War Between the States.

Dodd, Lamar (1909–   ). Born in Fairburn. Artist and art educator, lecturer, official artist for the National Aeronautics and Space Administration.

Dodd, Robert Lee "Bobby" (1908–1988). Born in Galax, VA; died in Atlanta. All-American quarterback for University of Tennessee, 1930. Head coach of Georgia Tech for 22 seasons.

Doles, George P. (1830–1864). Born in Milledgeville; died in Virginia. Confederate general, killed in Cold Harbor.

Dorsey, Hugh Manson. See section on Governors (1917–1921).

Douglas, Melvyn (1901–1981). Born in Macon; died in New York City. Noted movie actor. Won two Academy Awards for his performances in *Hud* in 1963 and *Being There* in 1979.

Early, Peter. See section on Governors (1813–1815).

Ector, Matthew D. (1822–1879). Born in Putnam County; died in Marshall, Texas. Confederate general who served as presiding judge of the Texas court of appeals after the war.

Edwards, Harry Stillwell (1855–1938). Born in Appling County. Author and columnist for the *Macon Telegraph*. Among his works are his most famous short story, "AEneas Africanus," and a tribute to his friend Sidney Lanier.

Elbert, Samuel. See section on Governors (1785–1786).

Ellis, Henry. See section on Governors (1757–1760).

Emanuel, David. See section on Governors (1801).

Evans, Clement A. (1833–1911). Born in Stewart County; died in Atlanta. Confederate general who edited the 12 volume *Confederate Military History* in 1899.

Felton, Rebecca Latimer (1835–1930). Born near Decatur; died in Atlanta. Was a writer and a leader for political and social reform. At the age of 87, she became the nation's first female U.S. senator.

Few, William (1748–1828). Born in Maryland; died in New York. One of Georgia's two signers of the U.S. Constitution. U.S. senator and judge. Moved to New York in 1799 where he became president of the City Bank.

Forsyth, John. See section on Governors (1827–1829).

Frémont, John Charles (1813–1890). Born in Savannah; died in New York City. Was a Union Army officer, celebrated explorer of the American West, senator and civil governor of California. Was the Republican Party's first presidential nominee.

Gardner, William M. (1824–1901). Born in Augusta; died in Memphis, Tennessee. Confederate general and commandant of military prisons east of the Mississippi River.

Gartrell, Lucius J. (1821–1891). Born in Wilkes County; died in Atlanta. Confederate general whose Georgia Reserves tried to halt Sherman's advance up the Georgia Coast.

George, Walter Franklin (1878–1957). Born in Webster County, Georgia. Served in the U.S. Senate for 34 years. Ambassador to NATO and special advisor to President Eisenhower. Law school at Mercer University named in his honor.

Gilmer, George Rockingham. See section on Governors (1829–1831; 1837–1839).

Gordon, John Brown. See section on Governors (1886–1890).

Gordon, William Washington (1796–1842). Educated at West Point. First President of the Central of Georgia Railroad. Third lieutenant, aide to General Gaines. Gordon County named for him.

Goulding, Dr. Frances Robert (1810–1881). Inventor of the sewing machine, wrote juvenile books *Young Marooners*, 1852, and *Marooners' Island*, 1862.

Grady, Henry Woodfin (1850–1889). Born in Athens; died in Boston, Ma. Newspaperman, editor and part owner of the *Atlanta Constitution* in the 1880s.

Graham, Patrick. See section on Governors (1752–1754).

Greene, Nathanael (1742–1786). Born in Potowomut, Rhode Island. While in command of the southern Revolutionary army, Greene conducted a notably successful campaign against the British in Georgia, forcing the enemy to retreat. Georgia honored him with the gift of Mulberry Grove, an estate on the Savannah River, where he retired after the war was won.

Griffin, Samuel Marvin. See section on Governors (1955–1959).

Gwinnett, Button. See section on Governors (1777).

Habersham, James (1713–1775). Born in England, died in Brunswick, New Jersey. Secretary and acting governor of the colony of Georgia from 1771 to 1773. Established the first orphanage in the new world. Raised and exported the first cotton ever shipped from America. Father of Joseph Habersham.

Habersham, Joseph (1751–1815). Died in Savannah. Leader of the Liberty Boys; colonel in the Continental Army. Served in the Continental Congress, speaker of the Georgia House of Representatives, mayor of Savannah, first postmaster general of the United States.

Hadas, Moses (1900–1966). Born in Atlanta; died in Aspen, Co. Classical scholar, educated at Emory University. Edited and translated many Latin, Greek, Hebrew and German works into English. His works include *A History of Greek Literature* (1950) and *Humanism: The Greek Ideal and Its Survival* (1960).

Hall, Lyman. See section on Governors (1783–1784).

Handley, George. See section on Governors (1788–1789).

Hardee, William Joseph (1815–1873). Born in Savannah; died in Wytheville, Va. Educated at West Point. Taught at West Point, then took command of Confederate forces when Georgia seceded the Union in 1861. Attained the rank of general, and in 1864 he commanded the forces that defended Savannah against General Sherman's troops. Known for his classic book, *Rifle and Light Infantry Tactics*.

Hardman, Lamartine Griffin. See section on Governors (1927–1931).

Hardwick, Thomas William. See section on Governors (1921–1923).

Hardy, Oliver Norvell (1892–1957). Born in Harlem. Great comedian of Laurel and Hardy fame.

Harris, Joe Frank. See section on Governors (1983–   ).

Harris, Joel Chandler (1848–1908). Born in Eatonton. Assisted Henry W. Grady in running the *Atlanta Constitution*. Creator and author of the famous "Uncle Remus" stories. Founded the *Uncle Remus Magazine* in 1907, achieving a circulation of 200,000.

Harris, Nathaniel E. See section on Governors (1915–1917).

Hayes, Roland (1887–1976). Born in Curyville; died in Boston, Ma. International tenor. Son of a former slave, Hayes was the first black singer to get worldwide recognition in classical music.

Heard, Stephen. See section on Governors (1780–1781).

Herty, Charles (1867–1938). Born in Milledgeville. Taught Chemistry at the University of Georgia and the University of North Carolina. Concentrated on finding new industrial uses for Southern natural resources. Developed process for using pine in making wood pulp.

Hill, Benjamin Harvey (1823–1882). Born in Jasper County; died in Atlanta. Graduate of University of Georgia. Senator in the Confederate States of America. After the War Between the States, became a U.S. senator.

Hill, Joshua (1812–1891). Opponent of secession, Unionist during the war, U.S. senator (1871–1873).

Hill, Walter Barnard (1851–1905). Born in Talbot County. Lawyer and educator. Founded Georgia Bar Association. Chancellor of the University of Georgia, 1899–1905.

Hodges, Courtney (1887–1966). Born in Perry. American army officer, educated at the U.S. Military Academy at West Point. Participated in campaigns in France during World War I, served with the army of occupation in Germany in 1918. During World War II he was commanding general of the Tenth Army Corps from 1942 to 1943, and later commanded the Third Army and the First Army through many European campaigns.

Hogg, Joseph L. (1806–1862). Born in Morgan County; died in Mississippi. Mexican War veteran and Confederate general. Died at Corinth of dysentery on the eve of the Battle of Shiloh.

Holliday, John Henry "Doc" (1852–1887). Born in Georgia; died in Colorado. Training as a dentist, Holliday migrated to Texas as a young man for health reasons. Was a friend of lawman Wyatt Earp. Participated in the gunfight at the O.K. Corral.

Holloway, Sterling (1905–   ). Born in Cedartown. Actor, comedian and recording artist, appeared in numerous commercials and is best known for being the voice of Walt Disney's Winnie the Pooh and the narrator of *Jungle Book*.

Holtzclaw, James T. (1833–1893). Born in Henry County; died in Montgomery, Alabama. Confederate general who practiced law in Alabama before and after the war.

Hope, John (1868–1936). Born in Augusta; died in Atlanta. Educator and black leader. Educated at Brown University. Became the first black president of Morehouse College (1906–1929). Helped found and presided over Atlanta University. Helped organize the Commission of Interracial Cooperation.

Houstoun, John. See section on Governors (1778–1779; 1784–1785).

Howley, Richard. See section on Governors (1780).

Irwin, Jared. See section on Governors (1796–1798; 1806–1809).

Jackson, Henry Rootes (1820–1898). Born in Athens; died in Savannah. Minister to Austria, brigadier general in the Confederacy, and minister to Mexico. Helped organize the Army of Tennessee.

Jackson, James. See section on Governors (1798–1801).

James, Harry (1916–1983). Born in Albany; died in Las Vegas, Nevada. Famed band leader of the 1940s. Was married to Hollywood "pin-up" queen, Betty Grable.

Jenkins, Charles Jones. See section on Governors (1865–1868).

Johnson, Hershel Vespasian. See section on Governors (1853–1857).

Johnson, James. See section on Governors (1865).

Johnson, Nunnally (1897–1977). Born in Georgia; died in Los Angeles, Ca. Was a noted screenwriter, director, and producer. Was responsible for such films as *The Grapes of Wrath, The Man in the Gray Flannel Suit,* and *The Three Faces of Eve.*

Johnston, Joseph Eggleston (1807–1891). Born in Prince Edward County, Va.; died in Washington, D.C. Commander of the Confederate Army opposing Sherman on his March to Atlanta in 1864.

Jones, Charles Colcock (1831–1893). Born in Savannah; died in Augusta. Was an historian and prolific writer, among his books being *The Dead Towns of Georgia* (1878).

Jones, Joseph (1833–1896). Born in Liberty County; died in New Orleans. Was a physician, surgeon in the Confederate Army, and later, responsible for archaeological digs in Tennessee. Brother of Charles C. Jones.

Jones, Nobel Wimberly (circa 1724–1805). Born near London, England; died in Savannah. A physician in Savannah, member of the Continental Congress, and president of the Georgia Medical Society.

Jones, Robert Tyre, Jr., "Bobby" (1902–1971). Born in Atlanta. Noted golfer. Won the U.S. Amateur Championship in 1924, 1925, 1927, 1928, 1930; won the U.S. Open in 1923, 1926, and 1930.

Keach, Stacy (1941–   ). Born in Savannah. Movie actor, enjoyed great success in the television series, "Mike Hammer."

Kell, John M. (1823–1900). Born in Darien; died in Sunnyside, Georgia. Confederate naval figure who participated in Perry's expedition to Japan before the war.

Kemeys, Edward (1843–1907). Born in Georgia. Sculptor known for his animal sculptures, especially the bronze lions at the Art Institute of Chicago.

Kilpatrick, William Heard (1871–1965). Born in White Plains; died in New York City. Taught at Teachers College in Columbia University from 1909 to 1938. Among his works are *Fountains of Method*, 1925, and *Philosophy of Education*, 1951.

King, Coretta Scott (1927–   ). Born in Heiberger, Alabama. Educated at Antioch College in Ohio, and New England Conservatory of Music in Boston, Massachusetts. Met and married Martin Luther King, Jr. there. After his death, she continued to work with the Southern Christian Leadership Conference. President of the Martin Luther King, Jr. Center for Social Change.

King, Martin Luther, Jr. (1929–1968). Born in Atlanta; died in Memphis, Tennessee. Civil rights leader and organizer of the march on Washington in 1963. Assassinated in Memphis.

Knight, Gladys (1944–   ). Born in Atlanta. Pouplar singer and recording artist. Her group is known as "Gladys Knight and the Pips."

Lamar, Joseph Rucker (1857–1916). Born in Elbert County. Jurist. Was associate justice of the U.S. Supreme Court. Compiled *The Code of the State of Georgia* (2 vols. 1896).

Lamar, Lucius Q. C. (1825–1893). Born in Putnam County; died in Washington, D.C. U.S. congressman, Confederate envoy to Russia, U.S. senator, U.S. secretary of the Interior, and associate justice of the U.S. Supreme Court.

Lamar, Mirabeau Buonaparte (1798–1859). Born in Louisville. Served with Sam Houston at the Battle of San Jacinto in 1836. Was vice president of Texas in 1836 and president from 1838–1841.

Lanier, Sidney (1842–1881). Born in Macon; died in North Carolina. One of America's outstanding 19th century poets. Was a P.O.W. during the War Between the States. Was also a novelist, musician, lawyer, and university professor. Author of *The Marshes of Glynn*.

LeConte, Joseph (1823–1901). Born in Liberty County. Noted geologist. Was professor at the University of California at Berkeley from 1869–1896. Author of *Elements of Geology*.

Lee, Brenda (1944–   ). Born in Atlanta. Popular country singer and recording artist. Resides in Nashville, Tennessee.

Lincoln, Benjamin (1733–1810). Commander of the Department of the South in 1778. Leader of unsuccessful assault on the British in Savannah.

Long, Crawford Williamson (1815–1878). Born in Danielsville; died in Athens. Introduced the use of ether as a surgical anesthetic, an event that has been described as one of the "greatest events in the history of medicine."

Longstreet, Augustus Baldwin (1790–1870). Born in Augusta; died in Mississippi. Georgia's best known antebellum author. *Georgia Scenes* is recognized as a foremost example of American humor. President of the University of Mississippi. Was the uncle of General James Longstreet and the father-in-law of L. Q. C. Lamar.

Low, Juliette Gordon (1860–1927). Born in Savannah. Organized the first group of Girl Guides, later the Girl Scouts of America, in Savannah in 1912.

Lumpkin, Joseph Henry (1799–1867). Born in Oglethorpe County; died in Athens. Graduate of Princeton, first chief justice of the Supreme Court (1845–1867). Assisted in writing the state penal code, founder of Georgia's first law school, law teacher.

Lumpkin, Wilson. See section on Governors (1831–1835).

Maddox, Lester Garfield. See section on Governors (1967–1971).

Martin, John. See section on Governors (1782–1783).

Matthews, George. See section on Governors (1787–1788; 1793–1796).

McAdoo, William Gibbs (1863–1941). Born near Marietta. Attorney and railroad company executive. U.S. secretary of the treasury. Married Woodrow Wilson's daughter, Eleanor. Was U.S. senator from California.

McCullers, Carson Smith (1917–1967). Born in Columbus. Noted author and playwright. Wrote *Member of the Wedding* in 1946.

McDaniel, Henry D. See section on Governors (1883–1886).

McDonald, Charles James. See section on Governors (1839–1843).

McGill, Ralph Emerson (1898–1969). Publisher of the *Atlanta Constitution;* author of *The South and the Southerner* (1963).

McLaws, Lafayette (1821–1897). Born in Augusta; died in Savannah. Confederate general who served as postmaster of Savannah after the war.

McIntosh, Lachlan (1725–1806). Born in Scotland; died in Savannah. Brigadier in the revolution and duelist who killed Button Gwinnett. Appointed by the Continental Congress as commander of the military forces in Georgia.

Meigs, Montgomery C. (1816–1892). Born in Augusta; died in Washington, D.C. At the outbreak of the War Between the States, he was made quartermaster general of the U.S. Army upon the resignation of Joseph E. Johnston.

Melton, James (1904–1961). Born in Moultrie. Was lead tenor for the Metropolitan Opera Company. Starred on radio's "Texaco Star Theater" and the "Telephone Hour."

Mercer, Johnny (1909–1976). Born in Savannah. Popular music composer. Best known for such hit tunes as "Jeepers Creepers," "Old Black Magic," and "Moon River" (with Henry Mancini).

Milledge, John. See section on Governors (1802–1806).

Miller, Caroline (1903–   ). Noted writer. Won the Pulitzer Prize for fiction in 1934 for *Lamb in His Bosom.*

Miller, Zell (1932–   ). Educator, author, lieutenant governor of Georgia, he has been in office longer than any other person in the state's history. Author of *Great Georgians* and *They Heard Georgia Singing.*

Mitchell, David Brydie. See section on Governors (1809–1818; 1815–1817).

Mitchell, Margaret (1900–1949). Born in Atlanta; died in Atlanta. Author of *Gone With the Wind* in 1936. Over 1,000,000 copies were sold within the first six months of publication. Named Georgia's "most famous person" by legislative action in 1985. Also see section entitled *Gone With the Wind.*

Nelson, Allison (1822–1862). Born in Fulton County; died in Arkansas. Veteran of the Mexican War and the Cuban War of Independence, became a Confederate general before his death from the "fever."

Northern, William J. See section on Governors (1890–1894).

O'Conner, Mary Flannery (1925–1964). Born in Savannah. Noted novelist and short story writer. Wrote *Wise Blood* (1952), *A Good Man Is Hard to Find and Other Short Stories* (1955), and the acclaimed *The Violent Bear It Away* (1959).

Odum, Howard Washington (1884–1954). Born in Bethlehem, Georgia. Educator and writer. Was a pioneer in Southern sociological education. Author of *The Negro and His Songs.*

Oglethorpe, James. See section on Governors (1733–1743).

Parker, Henry. See section on Governors (1751–1752).

Parks, Bert (1914–   ). Born in Atlanta. Entertainer, master of ceremonies for the Miss America Pageant from 1956 to 1979.

Perry, William F. (1823–1901). Born in Jackson County; died in Bowling Green, Kentucky. Confederate general who taught English and philosophy at Ogden College after the war.

Price, Eugenia (–   ). Resides in Georgia. Internationally known author, whose works include the St. Simons Trilogy, *Lighthouse, New Moon Rising,* and *Beloved Invader,* and such best-sellers as *Savannah,* and *To See Your Face Again.* Her papers are collected by the Mugar Library at Boston University.

Pulaski, Count Casimir (1748–1779). Born in Podolia, Poland. Joined forces with General Benjamin Lincoln to drive the British out of Savannah and was mortally wounded during an attack on October 9, 1779. Fort Pulaski was named in his honor.

Rabun, William. See section on Governors (1817–1819).

Redding, Otis (1941–1967). Born in Dawson. Writer and singer of soul ballads, including "I've Been Loving You Too Long," "Respect," and "Sitting on the Dock of the Bay."

Reece, Byron Herbert (1917–1958). Born near Choestoe. Poet, winner of national awards, including the Georgia Distinguished Writers Award. Works include *Bow Down in Jericho,* a book of poetry, and a novel, *Better a Dinner of Herbs.*

Reed, Jerry (1937–   ). Born in Atlanta. Country music singer and guitarist. One of his more popular recordings was "When You're Hot You're Hot." Co-starred with Burt Reynolds in several movies.

Reynolds, Burt (1936–   ). Born in Waycross. Popular movie actor. One of his most popular appearances was in the movie *Smoky and the Bandit.*

Reynolds, John. See section on Governors (1754–1757).

Rivers, Eurith Dickinson. See section on Governors (1937–1941).

Robinson, Jackie (1919–1972). Born in Cairo, Georgia. First black to play major league baseball in the U.S. Most valuable player in the National League in 1949. Career spanned from 1947 to 1956. Member of the Baseball Hall of Fame.

Ross, John (1790–1866). Born near Lookout Mountain, Tennessee. Served with Andrew Jackson against the Creeks in 1812. Was president of the National Council of Cherokees and later, chief of the Cherokee nation.

Ruger, Thomas Howard. See section on Governors (1868).

Rusk, Dean (1909–   ). Born in Canton. Former president of the Rockefeller Foundation. U.S. secretary of state in the Kennedy and Johnson administrations.

Russell, Richard B. See section on Governors (1931–1933).

Ryan, Father Abram Joseph (1838–1886). Catholic priest and poet. Long-time Augusta resident whose works include such Southern Confederacy tributes as *The Conquered Banner* and *Sword of Lee.*

St. John, Isaac M. (1827–1880). Born in Augusta; died in White Sulphur Springs, West Virginia. Confederate general. A civil engineer of the Louisville, Cincinnati, and Lexington Railroad after the war.

Sanders, Carl E. See section on Governors (1963–1967).

Schley, William. See section on Governors (1835–1837).

Scott, Thomas M. (1829–1876). Born in Athens; died in New Orleans. Confederate general who was wounded at the Battle of Franklin. Ran a sugar plantation after the war.

Semmes, Paul J. (1815–1863). Born in Wilkes County; died in Pennsylvania. Confederate general killed at Gettysburg.

Simms, James P. (1837–1887). Born in Covington; died in Covington. Confederate general. Served in the state legislature after the war.

Slaton, John Marshall. See section on Governors (1913–1917).

Smith, Charles Henry (1826–1903). Humorist who wrote under the pseudonym Bill Arp.

Smith, Hoke. See section on Governors (1907–1909; 1911).

Smith, James Milton. See section on Governors (1872–1877).

Smith, Lillian (1897–1966). Born in Jasper, Florida; died in Atlanta. Author, civil rights activist. She co-founded *The North Georgia Review* in 1936. Novels include *Strange Fruit* (1944) and *Killers of the Dream* (1949) which condemned racism. Friend of Dr. Martin Luther King, Jr., she was also on the board of Congress of Racial Equality.

Smith, William D. (1825–1862). Born in Augusta; died in Charleston, South Carolina. Confederate general and Mexican War veteran who saw action at Vera Cruz, Cerro Gordo, and Contreras. Died of yellow fever in Charleston.

Sorrel, Gilbert M. (1838–1901). Born in Savannah; died near Roanoke, Virginia. Confederate general who wrote *Recollections of a Confederate Staff Officer.*

Spaulding, Thomas (1774–1851). Planter and banker. Born on St. Simons Island. State legislator, U.S. congressman. Agricultural experimenter, reformer and writer. Helped develop production of Sea Island cotton and sugar along Georgian coast.

Stallings, Laurence (1894–1968). Playwright, motion picture scenarist, critic, and novelist.

Stanton, Frank Lebby (1857–1927). Journalist who wrote for the *Atlanta Constitution*. Most popular poet of the 1890s, works include *Songs from Dixie Land* (1900), and a poem which was set to music, "Mighty Lak a Rose."

Stephens, Alexander Hamilton. See section on Governors (1882–1883).

Stephens, William. See section on Governors (1743–1751).

Stevens, Ray (1939–   ). Born in Clarksdale. Lives in Nashville, Tennessee. Popular country music recording star. His hit, "The Streak," sold over 5 million copies.

Stovall, Marcellus A. (1818–1895). Born in Sparta; died in Augusta. Confederate general who was conspicuous at Atlanta and in Hood's Tennessee campaign.

Talmadge, Eugene, See section on Governors (1933–1937; 1941–1943).

Talmadge, Herman Eugene. See section on Governors (1947; 1948–1955).

Tarkenton, Fran (1940–   ). Born in Richmond, Virginia. Moved to Athens, Georgia in 1951. Starred in football at Athens High School. Was All-American quarterback at the University of Georgia. Played professional football for the Minnesota Vikings and the New York Giants.

Tattnall, Josiah. See section on Governors (1801–1802).

Telfair, Edward. See section on Governors (1786–1787; 1789–1793).

Terrell, Joseph M. See section on Governors (1902–1907).

Thomas, Bryan M. (1836–1905). Born in Milledgeville; died in Dalton. Confederate general who later became superintendent of Dalton public schools.

Thomas, Edward L. (1825–1898). Born in Clarke County; died in Indian territory. Confederate general who, with little military training, excelled as a brigade commander in the Army of Northern Virginia.

Thompson, Melvin Ernest. See section on Governors (1947–1948).

Tomochichi (–   ). An old Creek chief who met General Oglethorpe when he landed in Georgia in 1733, and accompanied him to England in 1734. Travelled with Oglethorpe down the coast of Georgia in 1736.

Toombs, Robert Augustus (1810–1885). Born in Wilkes County; died in Washington, Georgia. U.S. congressman, U.S. senator. Secretary of state in the Confederate States of America. Participated in the Battles of Malvern Hill and Antietam. After the War Between the States, he never regained his U.S. citizenship.

Towns, George Washington Bonaparte. See section on Governors (1847–1851).

Tracy, Edward D. (1833–1863). Born in Macon; died in Mississippi. Confederate general who was killed in action at Port Gibson.

Treutlen, John Adam. See section on Governors (1777–1778).

Troup, George M. See section on Governors (1823–1827).

Twiggs, David E. (1790–1862). Born in Richmond County; died near Augusta. Confederate general who held U.S. command of the Department of Texas before the war. He was the senior U.S. officer to relinquish his command for the Confederacy.

Vandiver, Samuel Ernest. See section on Governors (1959–1963).

Vinson, Carl (–1981). Lawyer and congressman. Born near Milledgeville. Member, state House of Representatives, 1902–1912. Judge of county court of Baldwin County, 1912–1914. Congressman, 1914–1965.

Walker, Clifford Mitchell. See section on Governors (1923–1927).

Walker, William H. T. (1816–1864) born in Augusta; died in Atlanta. Confederate general killed at Atlanta. Previously had served with distinction in the Second Seminole War and the Mexican War.

Walton, George. See section on Governors (1779–1780; 1789–1790).

Watie, Stand (1806–1871). Born near Rome; died in Delaware County, Oklahoma. Was the highest ranking (brigadier general) officer in the Confederate Army. Was also the last Confederate general to surrender his command (one month after the war was over).

Watson, Thomas Edward (1856–1922). Born near Thomson. U.S. congressman, writer, and leader of Georgia's agrarian revolt in the late 19th century. Author of *The Story of France*. Also served in the U.S. Senate.

Wayne, Anthony (1745–1796). Commander of the American forces in Georgia when the British evacuated Savannah in 1782. Waynesboro and Wayne County were named for him.

Wayne, Henry C. (1815–1883). Born in Savannah; died in Savannah. Confederate general who, before the war, performed a study on the feasibility of using Egyptian camels in the American Southwest.

Wayne, James Moore (1790–1867). Born in Savannah. Graduate of Princeton. Was a U.S. congressman and associate justice of the U.S. Supreme Court.

Wereat, John. See section on Governors (1779).

Wesley, John (1703–1791). Born in England. Founder of Methodism, and minister of the Church of England in Georgia, 1735–1736.

Wheeler, Joseph (1836–1906). Born near Augusta; died in Brooklyn, N.Y. Confederate lieutenant general of Cavalry. U.S. congressman after the War Between the States. Also served in the Spanish-American War.

Whitefield, George (1714–1770). Born in Gloucester, England. Came to Georgia as a missionary in 1737. Founded Bethesda Orphans Home.

White, Walter Francis (1893–1955). Negro leader and author. A leader of the National Association for the Advancement of Colored People (NAACP).

Wilson, Claudius C. (1831–1863). Born in Effingham County; died near Chattanooga, Tennessee. Confederate general who died of "camp fever" only eleven days after his commission.

Wilson, Ellen Louise Axson (1860–1914). Born in Georgia. First wife of President Woodrow Wilson.

Wilson, Woodrow (1856–1924). Born in Virginia; grew up in Georgia during the War Between the States. Educator, scholar, writer, governor and president. Passed several bills including the Child Labor Legislation and the Nineteenth Amendment giving women the right to vote.

Wofford, William T. (1824–1884). Born in Habersham County; died near Cass Station. Confederate general who participated in the state constitutional convention of 1877.

Woods, William B. (1824–1887). Born in Newark, Ohio; died in Washington, D.C. Educated at Yale University. Brigadier general in the Union Army. Accompanied General Sherman on his march to the sea. Moved to Alabama to aid in reconstruction. U.S. Circuit Court judge for Georgia and neighboring states, 1869–1880, associate justice of U.S. Supreme Court, 1880.

Woodward, Joanne (1930–   ). Born in Thomasville. Noted film and television actress. Won the Academy Award in 1957 for her role in *The Three Faces of Eve*.

Wright, Ambrose R. (1826–1872). Born in Louisville, Georgia; died in Augusta. Confederate general who, after the war, died before he could take his seat in the U.S. House of Representatives.

Wright, Sir James. See section on Governors (1760–1782).

Yancey, William L. (1814–1863). Born in Warren County, died in Montgomery, Alabama. Author of the Alabama Ordinance of Secession and a senator in Confederate Senate.

Yerby, Frank (1916–   ). Born in Augusta. Noted novelist. Author of *The Foxes of Harrow, Goat Song, Judas, The Dahomean,* and many others.

Young, Andrew Jackson, Jr. (1932–   ). U.S. ambassador to the United Nations, civil rights leader and politician. Cabinet member of President Jimmy Carter.

FESTIVALS AND EVENTS

The following is a partial list of festivals and events with the general dates on which they usually take place. For more detailed list of events giving actual dates write: Calendar, P.O. Box 1776, Atlanta, Georgia 30301. If you desire more detailed information on a specific festival or event and no contact person is listed, consult the chamber of commerce in that area (see Chambers of Commerce chapter).

JANUARY
Fireside Arts/Crafts Show—Helen—White County, mid-January—mid-February. (Unicoi State Park, 404-878-2201)

Fasching Masquerade Karnival—Helen—White County, mid-January—mid-February. (Chamber of Commerce, 404-878-2181)

Rattlesnake Roundup—Whigham—Grady County, mid-January, Whigham High School. (Myron R. Prevatte, 912-762-4243)

FEBRUARY
Georgia Week—Savannah—Chatham County, early February, Savannah Historic District. (Marti Bowden, 912-233-7787)

Antiques at the Crossroads—Perry—Houston County, early February, National Guard Armory. (912-987-3119)

MARCH
Rattlesnake Roundup—Claxton—Evans County, mid-March. (Jimmy Waters, 912-739-3733)

St. Patrick's Festival—Dublin—Laurens County, mid-March. (Hal Ward, 912-275-0353)

St. Patrick's Day Festival—Savannah—Chatham County, March 17.

Peach Orchards in Bloom—Ft. Valley/Perry—Houston County, mid-March.

Hawkinsville Harness Festival—Hawkinsville—Pulaski County, mid- to late March.

Cherry Blossom Festival—Macon—Bibb County, mid- to late March. (Carolyn Crayton, 912-744-7429)

Historic Tour of Homes—Cuthbert—Randolph County, late March.

Great Golden Easter Egg Hunt—Jekyll Island—Glynn County, Easter.

Easter Sunrise Service—Pine Mountain—Harris County, Easter.

Tour of Homes and Gardens—St. Simons Island—Glynn County, late March.

Tour of Homes and Gardens—Savannah—Chatham County, late March.

APRIL
Master's Golf Tournament—Augusta—Richmond County, early April.

Livestock Festival—Sylvania—Screvens County, early April. (Norma K. Howard, 912-564-7878)

Westville's Spring Festival—Lumpkin, Westville—Stewart County, early April. (Jerald N. Baxter, 912-838-6310)

Atlanta Dogwood Festival—Atlanta—Fulton County, early April. (Clara L. Wells, 404-892-0539)

Georgia Steam and Gas Show—Tifton—Tift County, early April.

Berry Patch—Rome—Floyd County, mid-April.

Trout Festival—Dahlonega—Lumpkin County, mid-April.

Rose Festival—Thomasville—Thomas County, mid-April. (Ruth Willett, 912-226-9600)

Atlanta Steeplechase—Atlanta—Fulton County, early April.

Pine Tree Festival—Swainsboro—Emanuel County, late April—early May. (Ed Schwabe, 912-237-8846)

Crackerland Country Fair—Howard—Taylor County, late April. (Fred Brown, 912-862-5253)

Affair on the Square—LaGrange—Troup County, late April.

"Night in Old Savannah"—Savannah—Chatham County, Visitors' Center, late April. (Thomas E. Newsome, 912-355-2422)

Georgia Mountain Jubilee—Gainesville—Hall County, late April—early May.

MAY

Westville's May Day—Lumpkin, Westville—Stewart County, May 1. (Jerald Baxter, 912-838-6310)

Prater's Mill Country Fair—Dalton—Whitfield County, Prater's Mill, early May. (J. Alderman/J. Harrell, 404-259-3420)

Enterprise 80/81—Athens—Clarke County, early May.

Gum Swamp Festival—Cochran—Bleckley County, early May.

Salisbury Fair—Columbus—Muscogee County, Ironworks, early May. (Celia Page, 404-322-0756)

Cotton Pickin' Antique Arts/Crafts (Country) Fair—Gay—Meriwether County, Old Cotton Gin Complex, early May. (Joann Gay, 404-538-6 814)

Mayfest—Dahlonega—Lumpkin County, Pavilion, mid-May. (Chamber of Commerce, 404-878-2181)

Blessing of the Fleet—Darien—McIntosh County, May.

Brunswick Gold Isles Spring Fiesta/Blessing of the Fleet—Brunswick—Glynn County, mid-May.

Arts Festival of Atlanta—Atlanta—Fulton County, mid-May.

Ogeechee River Raft Race—Statesboro—Bulloch County, May.

Vidalia Onion Festival—Vidalia—Toombs County, mid-May. (Priscilla Oxley, 912-537-9838)

Memorial Day Festival—Jekyll Island—Glynn County, Memorial Day. (Morgan Rodgers, 912-635-2232)

Arts & Crafts Festival—Thomasville—Thomas County, Exchange Club Fairgrounds, late May. (Al Stone, 912-226-3108)

JUNE

Helen to the Atlantic Ocean Balloon Race—Helen—White County, early June. (Chamber of Commerce, 404-878-2181)

Savannah River Days Raft Race—Augusta—Richmond County, early June.

Marigold Festival—Winterville—Clarke County, early June.

Putnam County Dairy Festival—Eatonton—Putnam County, early June.

Currahee Arts/Crafts Festival—Toccoa—Stephens County, mid-June.

Spring Lake Bluegrass Festival/Old Time Fiddlers' Reunion—Rhine—Dodge County, mid-June.

Blueberry Festival—Alma—Bacon County, Recreation Park, late June. (Jerri L. Taylor, 912-632-5859)

Bluegrass Festival—Dahlonega—Lumpkin County, Music Park, late June. (Norman Adams, 404-864-7203)

JULY
Appalachian Wagon Train—Chatsworth—Murray County, Saddle Club Grounds, early July. (C. W. Bradley, 404-695-2361)

4th of July Celebration—Colbert—Madison County, July 4.

Peachtree Road Race—Atlanta—Fulton County, 4th of July.

Watermelon Festival—Cordele—Crisp County, early July.

Masters Water Ski Tournament—Pine Mountain—Harris County, mid-July.

Blessing of the Fleet—Thunderbolt—Chatham County, July.

AUGUST
Lake Trahlyta Arts & Crafts Fair—Blairsville—Union County, Vogel State Park, early August. (David Foote, 404-745-2628)

Clown Festival—Macon—Bibb County, Museum of Arts and Sciences, early August. (Ray Hooten, 912-788-0808)

Georgia Mountain Fair—Hiawassee—Towns County, early August.

Sea Island Festival—Sea Island—Glynn County, early August.

Artifacts Fair—Macon—Bibb County, Ocmulgee National Monument, mid-August. (912-742-0447)

Gold Leaf Festival—Pelham—Mitchell County, mid-August.

Old Time Fiddlin' Convention—Dalton—Whitfield County, mid-August.

Mountain Do Arts/Crafts Festival—Buford, Lake Lanier Islands—Gwinnett County, mid-to late August. (Kurt Sutton, 404-945-6701)

Chattahoochee Mountain Fair—Clarkesville—Habersham County, Fairgrounds, late August. (Les Smith, 404-778-8207)

Tybee Regatta—Tybee Island—Chatham County, August.

SEPTEMBER
County Fair of 1896—Tifton—Tift County, Georgia Agrirama, early September. (Geraldine Walters, 912-386-3344)

Yellow Daisy Festival—Stone Mountain—DeKalb County, Park, early September. (Kathi Hayes, 404-469-9831)

Powers Crossroads Country Fair/Arts Festival—Newnan—Coweta County, Labor Day Weekend. (Harriet Alexander, 404-253-2011)

Oktoberfest—Helen—White County, early September to mid-October. (Chamber of Commerce, 404-878-2181)

Hamburg Harvest Festival—Mitchell-Glascock County, Hamburg State Park, early September. (Julian Price, 912-552-2393)

Barnesville Buggy Days—Barnesville—Lamar County, mid-September. (Sue Bankston, 404-358-2732)

Festival of the Painted Rock—Roswell—Fulton County, Chattahoochee Nature Center, mid-September. (Dotty Ertis, 404-992-2055)

Chattahoochee Folk Festival—Columbus—Muscogee County, mid-September.

Ft. Mountain Village Crafts Fair—Chatsworth—Murray County, September.

Apple Festival—Tallulah Falls—Rabun County, Terrora Visitor Center, mid- to late September. (Wanda Phillips, 404-754-3276)

Pecan Festival—Albany—Dougherty County, late September to mid-October. (Sara Pearson, 912-883-6900)

Crackerland County Fair—Howard—Taylor County, late September. (Fred Brown, 912-862-5253)

OCTOBER

Praters' Mill County Fair—Dalton—Whitfield County, early October.

Sunbelt Expo—Moultrie—Colquitt County, early October.

Andersonville Historic Fair—Andersonville—Sumter County, early October.

Cotton Pickin' Antique Arts/Crafts Fair—Gay—Meriwether County, early October. (Bill Gay, 404-538-6814)

Autumn Leaf Festival—Maysville—Banks County, early October. (Elbert Maybry, 404-652-2536)

Great Pumpkin Festival—Cochran—Bleckley County, early October. (Mary Brown, 912-934-2965)

Crowe Springs Craftsmen's Fair—Cartersville—Bartow County, mid-October.

Fabric Creations from the Mountains—Helen—White County, Unicoi State Park, mid-October. (Bob Slack, 404-878-2201 ext. 282 or 283)

Heritage Holidays—Rome—Floyd County, mid-October.

Georgia Marble Festival—Jasper—Pickens County, early to mid-October. (Lawton Baggs, 404-692-6598)

Apple Festival—Ellijay—Gilmer County, mid-October. (Gene Wright, 404-635-7400)

Sorghum Festival—Blairsville—Union County, mid-October.

Gold Rush Days—Dahlonega—Lumpkin County, Gold Museum, mid-October. (Sharon Johnson, 404-864-2257)

Fall Country Music/Bluegrass Festival—Hiawassee—Towns County, mid-October.

Scottish Festival & Highland Games—Stone Mountain Park—DeKalb County, mid-October. (Kathi Hayes, 404-469-9831)

Golden Isles Art Festival—St. Simons Island—Glynn County, Neptune Park, mid-October. (Gordi Wood, 912-638-2425)

Brown's Crossing Craftsmen's Fair—Milledgeville—Baldwin County, mid-October.

Southern Open Golf Tournament—Columbus—Muscogee County, Green Island Country Club, early to mid-October. (John Patterson, 404-324-0411)

Cherokee Fall Festival—Calhoun—Gordon County, New Echota Historic Site, late October. (Ed Reed, 404-629-8151)

War of 1812 Fair—Midway—Liberty County, Sunbury Historic Site, late October. (Don McGhee, 912-884-5999)

Six County Fair—Swainsboro—Emanuel County, late October.

Long County Wild Life Festival—Ludowici—Long County, October.

Steam & Gas Fair—Tifton—Tift County, Georgia Agrirama, late October. (Geraldine Walters, 912-386-3344)

Corn Festival—Camilla—Mitchell County, late October.

Fair of 1850—Lumpkin—Stewart County, late October to early November. (Jerald Baxter, 912-838-6310)

NOVEMBER
Mule Day—Calvary—Grady County, early November. (Charles Butler, 912-872-3211)
Pioneer Skills Day Fair—Royston—Franklin County, Victoria Bryant State Park, early November. (Robert Emery, 404-245-6270)
Red Clay Hill Arts & Crafts Festival—Calhoun—Gordon County, Cherokee Capital Fairgrounds, early November. (Sharon Harrell, 404-629-7561)
Million Pines Arts & Crafts Festival—Soperton—Treutlen County, Iva Park, early November. (Jeanne McLendon, 912-529-6611)
Fair of 1850—Westville—Stewart County, early November.
Jasper County Deer Festival—Monticello—Jasper County, early November. (Gene Bailey, 404-468-8194)
Cane Grinding Fair—Tifton—Tift County, Georgia Agrirama, mid-November. (Geraldine Walters, 912-386-3344)
Holiday Marketplace—Gainesville—Hall County, Georgia Mountain Center, mid-November. (Holly Duggan, 404-534-6080)
Piddlers & Peddlers Fair—Perry—Houston County, National Guard Armory, late November. (Norma Wilson, 912-987-2079)

DECEMBER
Old Fashion Christmas—Dahlonega—Lumpkin County, early December.
Tour of Homes—Madison—Morgan County, early December.
Sugarplum Festival—Stone Mountain—DeKalb County, Village, early to mid-December. (Betty Fogel, 404-939-7351)
Yuletide Season—Lumpkin—Stewart County, mid- to late December.
Christmas Activities and Living Nativity Pageant—Stone Mountain—DeKalb County, mid- to late December.

FLORA AND FAUNA

In colonial times, Georgia was covered almost entirely with forests and the land is still heavily wooded. Much of the Appalachian and Blue Ridge mountain areas are covered with a mixture of deciduous and coniferous trees. Some of the species represented are ash *(Fraxinus)*, black walnut *(Juglans nigra)*, birch *(Betula)*, yellow poplar *(Liriodendron)*, beech *(Fagus)*, hemlock *(Tsuga)*, sweet gum *(Liquidambar styraciflua)*, red and white oak *(Quercus)*, hickory *(Carya)*, sycamore *(Platanus occidentalis)*, and loblolly pine *(Pinus taeda)*. On the Piedmont and the coastal plains, pines predominate, especially loblolly and long-leaf pines *(Pinus palustris)*. In the southern portion of the coastal plains the state tree, live oak *(Quercus virginiana)*, thrives. In sandy soil palmettos *(Sabal)* are common. Swampy and poorly drained areas are the natural habitat for tupelo gums *(Nyssa aquatica)*, bald cypresses *(Taxodium distichum* and *T. ascendens)*, and pond cypress *(T. ascendens)*. Black cherry *(Prunus serotina)*, dogwood *(Cornus)*, chestnut *(Castanea dentata)*, butternut *(Juglans cinerea)*, sweet bay *(Magno-*

lia virginiana), evergreen magnolia *(Magnolia grandiflora),* sassafras *(Sassafras albidum),* red maple *(Acer rubrum),* and cottonwood *(Populus deltoides)* are also indigenous to the state.

Known to the Indians as the Land of the Trembling Earth, Okefenokee Swamp is a very unusual wilderness of wild orchids, floating green lily pads *(Nymphaea odorata)* and bald cypresses with pendant tufts of Spanish moss *(Tillandsia usneoides).*

Georgia is blessed with a great profusion of flowering plants, including the state flower, Cherokee rose *(Rosa laevigata).* Other kinds include bellwort *(Uvularia),* bloodroot *(Sanguinaria canadensis),* columbine *(Aquilegia canadensis),* galax *(Galax aphylla),* hepatica *(Hepatica),* trillium *(Trillium),* mayapple *(Podophyllum peltatum)* and violet *(Viola).* Species of flame azalea *(Azalea calendulacea),* rhododendron, redbud *(Cercis canadensis),* mimosa, and laurel are some of the shrubs and small flowering trees which abound in Georgia.

Of the larger animals still found in the state, white-tailed deer are the most plentiful. In the Okefenokee Swamp and the northern mountains black bears *(Ursus americanus)* roam, and wildcats *(Lynx)* prowl in some rural areas. The wooded areas are profuse with muskrat *(Ondatra zibethica),* opossums *(Didelphis virginiana),* gray squirrels *(Sciurus carolinensis),* red squirrels *(Tamiasciurus hudsonius),* gray foxes *(Urocyon cinereoargenteus),* red foxes *(Vulpes vulpes),* and raccoon *(Procyon lotor).* Many swamps and rivers are inhabited by beaver *(Castor canadensis)* and otter *(Lutra canadensis).*

There are more than 300 species of birds east of the Mississippi, most of which can be viewed in Georgia. Of that number, approximately 160 are indigenous to the state; 120 of them breed below the Fall Line, which is an imaginary line between the Piedmont and the coastal plain marked by waterfalls and rapids, where rivers descend abruptly from an upland to a lowland. This line not only divides the species of birds but of trees and plants as well. Many of the birds that winter in Georgia migrate from Canada and the northern United States. Anhinga or snakebird, *(Anhinga anhinga),* clapper rail *(Rallus longirostris),* egrets *(Egretta),* wood duck *(Aix sponsa),* wood ibis *(Mycteria americana),* and many species of herons *(Ardeidae)* are common along the coast, in marshes, and inland swamps. In cultivated areas mourning doves *(Zenaidura macroura)* and bobwhites *(Colinus virginianus)* are plentiful and black vultures *(Coragyps atratus),* turkey buzzards *(Cathartes aura)* and hawks *(Accipitridae)* are visible throughout the state. From brushy thickets the distinctive calls of the brown thrasher, the state bird *(Toxostoma rufum),* mockingbird *(Mimus polyglottos),* and the catbird *(Dumetella carolinensis)* ring out. Ruby-throated hummingbird *(Archilochus colubris),* crow *(Corvus brachyrhynchos),* robin *(Turdus migratorius),* cardinal *(Richmondena cardinalis),* meadowlark *(Sturnella magna),* blue jay *(Cyanocitta cristata)* and the towhee *(Pipilo)* are familiar sights in the state. There are numerous species of sparrows *(Fringillidae),* wrens *(Troglodytes)*, vireas *(Vireo)* and warblers *(Parulidae)* also. In 1967 an ivory-billed woodpecker *(Campephilus principalis)*, which was thought to be extinct, was sighted in Georgia.

In the great Okenfenokee and coastal swamps the state's largest reptile, the alligator, is found. The poisonous snakes found in the state are copperhead *(Ancistrodon contortrix)*, cottonmouth *(Ancistrodom piscivorous)*, water moccasin *(Natrix)*, coral snake *(Micrurus fulvius)*, and pygmy diamondback rattlesnake in addition to many types of nonpoisonous snakes.

Channel bass *(Sciaenops ocellatus)*, spotted weakfish *(Cynoscion regalis)*, sailfish *(Istiophorus)*, and tarpon *(Tarpon atlanticus)* are the saltwater fish most commonly found. Along the coastal areas oysters *(Ostreidae)*, crabs *(Brachyura)*, and shrimps *(Crangon)* are available. Mountain trout, bream *(Lepomis)*, pike *(Esox)*, catfish *(Nematognathi)*, and black basses *(Micropterus)* are in the lakes and streams of northern and central Georgia. The rivers of the Coastal Plain have an abundant supply of bass, drum *(Sciaenidae)*, mackerel *(Scomber scombrus)*, mullet *(Mugilidae)* and redfish *(Sebastes marinus)*.

FORTS

Fort Allatoona. A Union-held fort saved from Confederate attack by General Sherman, with the first effective use of signals perfected by General Albert J. Myer.

Fort Augusta. Built around 1735 by Governor James E. Oglethorpe, after he designed the town of Augusta. He named the fort and the town for the mother of King George III. Both town and fort were taken by the Tories and the fort renamed Fort Cornwallis. In June, 1781, Colonel "Light Horse Harry" Lee took the fort and forced the British to surrender.

Fort Benning. Established during World War I, nine miles from Columbus. Named for Confederate General Henry L. Benning of Columbus.

Fort Cornwallis. Built around 1735 by Governor James E. Oglethorpe and orginally called Fort Augusta, the fort was taken by Tory Lieutenant Colonels Brown and Grierson and the name changed to Fort Cornwallis. The Colonials captured the fort, but the British retook it. In June, 1781, Colonel "Light Horse Harry" Lee forced the British to surrender.

Fort Edwards. Built in 1789 in Watkinsville. Established as a defense against Cherokee Indians.

Fort Fidius. Built in 1793 at Milledgeville, nine years before the town became the capital of Georgia. This fort had the largest garrison of Federal troops south of the Ohio River.

Fort Frederica. Built in 1736 by Governor James E. Oglethorpe. The fort and the town surrounding it were named in honor of Frederick, the only son of King George II of England. The fort, which commanded the channel between St. Simons Island and the mainland, was erected as a defense for the English colonists in Georgia against the Spanish in Florida. In 1742 a Spanish force dispatched from

Cuba threatened the English settlers, but the expedition was turned back a few miles south of the fort by General James E. Oglethorpe in the Battle of Bloody Marsh.

Fort Gaines. In Clay County, overlooking the Chattahoochee River. The fort was named for General Gaines. Today the town of Fort Gaines occupies the site.

Fort George. Built in 1761, the first fort on Cockspur Island. American patriots destroyed it in 1801.

Fort Greene. Built in 1794, a hurricane destroyed it in 1804. It was the second fort built on Cockspur Island.

Fort Grierson. Built near Fort Augusta by Tory Lieutenant Colonel Grierson. The fort was captured by the colonials and retaken by the British, but in June, 1781, Colonel "Light Horse Harry" Lee took the fort and the British surrendered.

Fort Hawkins. Built in 1806 on the Ocmulgee River, 35 miles from Milledgeville. The fort was named for Benjamin Hawkins, a Government Indian agent. Its main purpose was to protect the state against Indian insurrection, and served as a meeting place for Federal agents and Creek Indians. During the War of 1812 this fort was the assembling place for troops who were equipped and sent to the aid of General Andrew Jackson before the Battle of New Orleans.

Fort Hughes. Near the town of Bainbridge, not far from Fort Scott. Mainly an earthwork used by General Jackson's troops during the Seminole War.

Fort Jackson. Built during the War of 1812 on the Savannah River, 2 miles south of Savannah. Confederates seized it in March, 1861 and held it until Savannah was taken by the Union forces.

Fort King George. Built in 1721, near Darien at the mouth of the Altahama River. Named for King George of England, it was the first English settlement on Georgia land. The fort was built to protect the colonists from encroachments of the French and Spanish. In 1727, the fort was almost destroyed by fire. It was rebuilt but the garrision was moved to South Carolina.

Fort McAllister. Built by Confederate forces at the start of the War Between the States, on the Great Ogeechee River, 12 miles south of Savannah and opposite Genesis Point. One of the principal defenses of the city, the fort withstood attacks in 1862 and 1863. On December 13, 1864, the fort was captured, the final event of Sherman's march to the sea.

Fort McPherson. The fort was named for Union General James Birdseye McPherson, who was killed in the Battle of Atlanta. In 1883 Spelman College acquired the grounds and buildings of the fort, and the fort was moved to a location four miles south of Atlanta.

Fort Morris. Built in 1776 at Sunbury, south of Savannah. Defended by Continental troops in several attacks until 1779, when the fort was taken and destroyed by the British. The destruction of the fort brought about the end of Republican power in eastern Georgia.

Fort Mountain. Believed to have been built by De Soto in 1540 on a peak in the Cohutta Mountains, in the western portion of the state. Now a state park, the United States Forest Service has a lookout tower on the site.

Fort Oglethorpe. Near Dodge, a United States Military Post established in 1903. Named for James E. Oglethorpe, founder of Georgia.

Fort Pulaski. Built in 1829–47, the third fort on Cockspur Island. The fort was designed by Simon Bernard, Napoleon's Chief engineer, and named in honor of the Polish count Casimir Pulaski, hero of the Battle of Savannah during the American Revolution. Seized and garrisoned by the Confederates at the outbreak of the War Between the States, it was bombarded by the Federals for thirty hours on April 10–11, 1862, and was forced to surrender, due to the ineffectiveness of forts of brick and masonry against the artillery of the day. With the fall of Fort Pulaski, the Savannah River was closed to blockade runners, British merchant steam vessels who traded guns and ammunition for cotton and tobacco. The shells fired by the Federals during the siege are still embedded in its walls.

Fort St. Andrew. Built on Cumberland Island to protect the entrance to the St. Marys River.

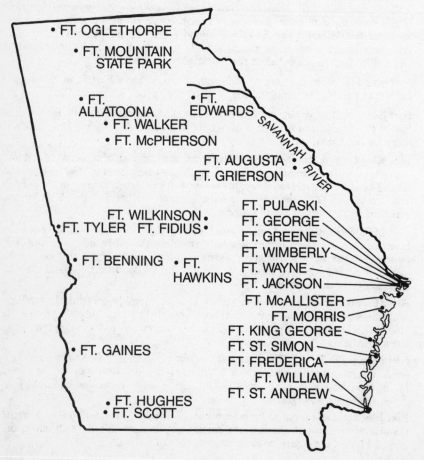

Fort St. Simon. Built about 1736 on the eastern tip of St. Simons Island. On July 5, 1742, Spanish vessels sailed into the harbor at St. Simons, and forced General James E. Oglethorpe to retreat. The Spanish swarmed over the island, and on July 7, Oglethorpe defeated the Spanish at Grenadier Marsh, which became known as Bloody Marsh.

Fort Scott. Built in 1816 on the bank of the Flint River, near the Georgia-Florida line. The fort was the headquarters for the first Seminole War.

Fort Tyler. Built on a hill at West Point to protect the city from the fire of Federal guns in the War Between the States. The fort was named for Confederate General Robert C. Tyler, who was killed in the battle at the fort on Easter, April 16, 1865.

Fort Walker. A War Between the States fort in Atlanta, used by a Confederate battery during the Battle of Atlanta in 1864. The fort was named in honor of William T. Walker, a Confederate General killed in the Battle of Atlanta.

Fort Wayne. Built in 1762. The fort was named for General "Mad Anthony" Wayne. The fort was captured and strengthened by the British in 1779, and Americans rebuilt it during the War of 1812.

Fort Wilkinson. Built in 1796, a few miles north of Fort Fidius. The fort was named for General James Wilkinson. In 1802 representatives of 32 Creek towns signed the Indian treaty of 1802 that ceded the lands of that area to the state of Georgia.

Fort William. Built in 1736, by Governor James E. Oglethorpe on Cumberland Island. The purpose of the fort was to command the entrance to the St. Marys River.

Fort Wimberly. Built in the early 1700s by Governor James E. Oglethorpe on the Isle of Hope, south of Savannah. The fort was built to guard the narrows of the Skiaway River. The original wooden structure was replaced in 1741 by a concrete one. During the War Between the States a Confederate Battalion stationed there prevented Federal ships from passing along the inland water route.

GEOGRAPHIC CENTER

The geographic center of Georgia is about about 17½ miles southeast of Macon or specifically 4¾ miles south-southeast of the junction of Turvin and Savage Creeks in Twiggs County.

GOLD

Gold was discovered in the mountains of northern Georgia in 1829. Almost immediately over 10,000 miners descended upon the region to try their hand at getting rich. A U.S. mint was established in nearby Dahlonega and before it became inactive, it processed millions of dollars worth of gold coins. A sad aspect of this, America's first major gold rush, was that the yellow metal's discovery sealed the fate of the Cherokee Indians who lived in the surrounding countryside. White settlers were already envious of the Cherokees' holdings; the finding of gold in the Indian lands merely brought about the inevitable sooner. The "Trail of Tears" happened shortly thereafter.

GONE WITH THE WIND

Gone With the Wind, the fiery novel set in Georgia, spanning the years before, during, and immediately after the War Between the States, was one of the best-selling books ever to be published in the United States. Likewise, the movie rendition of the same has become one of Hollywood's all-time money makers. The book, written by Atlanta's Margaret Mitchell, was an immediate success, upon its publication in 1936, selling over 700,000 copies in its first four months. *Gone With the Wind* won the 1937 Pulitzer Prize, and it was translated into 30 foreign languages.

Hollywood was quick to see its potential and film magnate David O. Selznick paid $50,000 Depression dollars for the film rights. The movie was no less spectacular than the book. Winner of 10 Academy Awards, it starred Clark Gable and Vivien Leigh.

Georgians in general and Atlanteans in particular are proud that one of their natives, Margaret Mitchell, contributed this outstanding piece of Southern literature to future generations of Americans.

GOVERNORS

UNDER THE TRUSTEES

Oglethorpe, James Edward, 1733—1743. Born in England on December 22, 1696. Served in House of Commons, 1722 to 1743. The death of a friend in one of England's debtor prisons caused Oglethorpe to want to do something about the prison situation. Early settlers left England November, 1732 and arrived in Savannah February, 1733. He was in charge of the government, 1733 to 1743; accepted Treaty of Frederica, 1736; defended Georgia in England, and secured regiment, 1737; fought Spanish, 1742; court-martialed, 1744. Died June 30, 1785.

THE THREE PRESIDENTS OF GEORGIA

There were three presidents that served as heads of the government in Georgia between the time Oglethorpe left and the coming of the three royal governors.

Stephens, William, 1743—1751 (President of Colony). Born in England, *c*. 1671. Served in Parliament, was a colleague of Oglethorpe. He went from England to Ireland and then to America. He was 66 years old when he came to Georgia in 1737. Oglethorpe had been too busy to keep the trustees in England informed, so Stephens was appointed secretary, and sent to help him. In 1741 the Trustees divided Georgia into two separate parishes; Stephens was made president of the one in Savannah. When Oglethorpe left Georgia, 1743, he recommended the trustees make Stephens president of all Georgia. Stephens presided over the first representative assembly, January 15, 1751. He retired April, 1751 and became the first Georgian to be pensioned. He died August, 1753.

Parker, Henry, 1751—1752. He served as an assistant to President Stephens. Was a constable, 1733; third bailiff, 1734; first bailiff, 1738 and first assistant under the new government. Became vice-president, March, 1750, and president April 8, 1751 when Stephens retired. He organized Georgia's first militia, June, 1751. He died while in office, 1752.

Graham, Patrick, 1752—1754. Was owner of a small plantation and a seller of medicines. In May, 1751, he was sent into Creek country to secure a grant of the reserved lands from the Indians to the colony of Georgia. He became president when President Parker died in 1752. Georgia became more prosperous while Graham was president. People who had moved away because of the trustees' harsh laws came back, and new settlers moved in, among them the Puritans in 1752. He was president until the first royal governor arrived in 1754.

THE THREE ROYAL GOVERNORS

By 1754, King George II and his ministers had come up with a plan to govern Georgia, since the Trustees had given up their charter. The plan was to have a royal governor, with a twelve-man advisory council named by the King, which would serve as the upper house of the Assembly. The lower house would be made up of delegates elected by the people.

Reynolds, John, 1754—1757. Born in England in 1700. Was a navy captain. Arrived in Savannah October 29, 1754 and the government was turned over to him. He did implement the royal plan of government, but was not a popular governor, and the people wanted him removed. He was summoned to England to answer charges. He was dismissed from office, and returned to the Navy, where he became an admiral. He died in 1776.

Ellis, Henry, 1757—1760. Born in England in 1721. He was a scientist and explorer. His father was wealthy but stern, and he ran away to sea when he was young. He was welcomed by the settlers, who were glad to be rid of Reynolds. He was a popular governor. There were eight parishes created during his administration, when the Church of England was the tax-supported church in Georgia. He had a good relationship with the

Indians. His failing health caused him to leave Georgia in November, 1760. He died in Naples, Italy, January 21, 1800.

Wright, Sir James, 1760—1782. Believed to have been born in England, Wright grew up in South Carolina, where his father was chief justice. He held various jobs in the courts, becoming acting attorney general in 1742; attorney general, 1747—1757. He went to London for three years as provincial agent for South Carolina. He was appointed royal governor May 13, 1760. He strengthened defenses and worked at keeping the Indians friendly. He was a well respected governor until the Stamp Act, when some of the Liberty Boys suggested he be hanged. It was another ten years before he was actually arrested. He left the colony in 1776, when the patriots took control, but returned in 1779 as governor of the part of Georgia then in British hands. He left office when Savannah was surrendered to the Americans, 1782.

GOVERNORS OF THE STATE

Bulloch, Archibald, 1776—1777. Born in Charleston, South Carolina in 1730. He moved to Georgia to set up his law practice, and lived in Savannah. Was president of Provincial Congress, and in charge of the Council of Safety. When Governor Wright was arrested, Georgians took over their government and elected Bulloch. He called the first constitutional convention, October, 1775. The first legislature under the new constitution was to meet in May, 1777, to elect the first constitutional governor. But Bulloch died in March, 1777.

Gwinnett, Button, 1777. Born in Gloucestershire, England in 1732. Came from England shortly before the Revolutionary War. He was a merchant, and settled in Savannah. Elected to the Assembly in 1769. Was a delegate from Georgia to the Second Continental Congress in Philadelphia and was one of the signers of the Declaration of Independence. When Bulloch died, Gwinnett was named acting president. He served two months until an election was held and he was defeated. He died of injuries sustained in a duel, May 19, 1777.

Treutlen, John Adam, 1777—1778. Born in Austria, brought to Georgia when he was six. Was a member of the Council of Safety and Georgia's Provincial Congress. Was elected governor May, 1777 and served until the following January. When his term was up, he took his family to visit relatives in South Carolina and he vanished without a trace.

Houstoun, John, 1778—1779; 1784—1785. Was the son of a British nobleman. After serving as Mayor of Savannah, was elected to Provincial Congress, 1775, Second Provincial Congress, 1775. He was one of four men to sign an advertisement that appeared in the Savannah *Gazette* which roused Georgians to be supportive of the Revolution. He was just ending his first term as governor, 1778—1779, when the British captured Savannah. According to the constitution, he could not remain in office, so for a while Georgia had no governor. He was elected to the office again 1784 to 1785, making him the first governor to serve a second term. During his second term, forty thousand acres of land was set aside to be sold to raise funds to charter the University of Georgia.

Wereat, John, 1779. Two factions of Georgia's Patriot or Whig government developed in Augusta. One elected John Wereat head of the government, and the other elected George Walton. But January 4, 1780 they settled their differences and elected Richard Howley.

Walton, George, 1779—1780; 1789—1790. Born in Prince Edward County, Virginia, near Farmville, 1741. Was a Continental Congress delegate, signed the Declaration of Independence, and served in the Revolutionary War. Was appointed governor the first time by a separate faction that was caused by the confusion of the Revolutionary War. He only served a few months. He was elected again by a joint ballot of the State Legislature. Peace was established with the Creek Indians, a new State Constitution was ratified, and Augusta was established as the capital during his administration. Walton County, Georgia was named in his honor. He died in Georgia, near Augusta, February 2, 1804.

Howley, Richard, 1780. After the two factions of the Patriot or Whig government settled their differences, they elected Howley. He was also elected to Continental Congress, and a few days after taking office, he left for Washington.

Heard, Stephen, 1780—1781 (Acting Governor). Born in Ireland. As Council president, he was made acting governor while Howley served as a delegate in Washington. Later he went to North Carolina.

Davies, Myrick, 1781 (Acting Governor). When Heard went to North Carolina, Davis was made acting head of the government. He was later murdered.

Brownson, Nathan, 1781—1782. Born in Connecticut. Graduated from Yale. A doctor who was head of the hospitals in the South during the war. A member of the Continental Congress, 1776 to 1778; one of the signers of the United States Constitution. He was sent to Augusta to take over as governor, 1781. He helped design the charter for the University of Georgia.

Martin, John, 1782—1783. Born in Rhode Island. Was a member of the first Provincial Congress, 1775. Served as lieutenant during the Revolutionary War. He was elected governor near the end of the war and carried the government back to Savannah.

Hall, Lyman, 1783—1784. Born in Connecticut April 12, 1734. A doctor who graduated from Yale. Went from New England to the Carolina

Colony, and then came to Georgia with the Puritans to be their doctor. Was delegate to the Continental Congress; delegate to Second Provincial Congress, 1775; a signer of the Declaration of Independence, 1776. Became governor 1783. He urged the people to set up seminaries of learning during his term, and he helped plan the University of Georgia. He died October 19, 1791.

Houstoun, John, 1784—1785 (Second Term).

Elbert, Samuel, 1785—1786. Born in South Carolina. Served on committee to arm state in readiness for war, 1776. Was general in Revolutionary War. After serving term as governor, 1785 to 1786, he served as sheriff in Chatham County.

Telfair, Edward, 1786—1787; 1789—1793. Born in Scotland, c. 1735, on the Telfair estate, "Town Head," emigrated c. 1758 to Virginia and later, in 1766, settled in Savannah, Georgia. Was a member of the Continental Congress and a signer of the Articles of Confederation. During his second term, from 1789—1793, there was conflict with the federal government regarding the Indian question defined in the Treaty of New York, which resulted in the passage of the Eleventh Amendment. Telfair County, Georgia, was named in his honor. He died September 17, 1807, in Savannah.

Mathews, George, 1787—1788; 1793—1796. Born in Augusta County, Georgia, September 10, 1739. Commanded a company of volunteers against the Indians, 1757; fought in the Battle of Point Pleasant, 1774; also the battles of Brandywine and Germantown, where he was wounded and captured. Was a delegate to the First Congress, 1789 to 1791. Was appointed governor, 1787 to 1788. Became governor for a second term, 1793 to 1796, defeating Edward Telfair by a joint ballot of the State Legislature. The major issue of his administration was the Yazoo Land Sale. The Virginia Yazoo Company, the South Carolina Land Company and the Tennessee Land Company purchased 2,500,000 acres of land for 200,000 dollars. The purchasers failed to comply with the terms and the agreement lapsed. Five other companies combined to purchase 35,000,000 acres for 500,000 dollars and the transaction was approved by the state legislature in spite of Governor Mathews' veto. Died in Augusta, August 30, 1812.

Handley, George, 1788—1789. Less is known about him than any other governor. He was a former soldier with a valiant record and a dependable civil officer.

GOVERNORS (Following the ratification of the State Constitution)

Telfair, Edward, 1789—1793 (Second Term).

Mathews, George, 1793—1796 (Second Term).

Irwin, Jared, 1796—1798, 1806—1809, Democratic-Republican. Born in Mecklenburg County, North Carolina in 1750. After moving to Georgia, he was active in the American Revolution; commanded a Georgia militia detachment against the Indians on the Georgia frontier. Was inaugurated as governor on January 15, 1796 after being elected by a joint ballot of the State Legislature. He signed a bill during his administration, rescinding the Yazoo Land Sale, which had caused so much controversy that the State Legislature ordered that the record of the sale be removed from official records. His first term ended January 12, 1798. He assumed the office again on September 23, 1806 when Governor John Milledge resigned and remained in that capacity until his own inauguration on November 6, 1807, since he had again been elected by a joint ballot of the State Legislature. He died in Union Hill, Washington County, Georgia on March 1, 1815. Irwin County was named in his honor.

Jackson, James, 1798—1801, Democratic-Republican. Born in Moreton-Hampstead, Devonshire, England on September 21, 1757. Emigrated in 1772 to Georgia, served in the Constitutional Army during the Revolutionary War, served from 1789 to 1791 in the First Congress, served in the U.S. Senate, 1793 to 1795. He was elected governor by a joint ballot of the State Legislature, inaugurated January 12, 1796. He resigned March 3, 1801. The next day, March 4, 1801, he began a term as U.S. Senator where he served until his death March 19, 1806, in Washington. Jackson County was named in his honor.

Emanuel, David, 1801, Democratic-Republican. Born in Georgia, c. 1744, served in the Georgia Militia during the Revolutionary War as a captain and then as colonel. He served as president of the Georgia Senate and as such, assumed the office of governor on March 3, 1801 when Governor James Jackson resigned and served until Josiah Tattnall was inaugurated November 7, 1801. Then he returned to the Senate to serve as president until he died February 19, 1808 at his Burke County plantation. Emanuel County was named in his honor.

Tattnall, Josiah, 1801—1802, Democratic-Republican. Born near Savannah in 1764; accompanied his father to England at the outbreak of the Revolutionary War; returned to Savannah and enlisted in 1782 under General Anthony Wayne. Was U.S. Senator, 1796—1799. Elected governor by joint ballot of State Legislature and was inaugurated November 7, 1801, resigned November 4, 1802 for health reasons, traveled to Nassau, New Providence and British West Indies, where he died June 6, 1803. Tattnall County was named in his honor.

Milledge, John, 1802—1806, Democratic-Republican. Born in 1757 in Savannah; served in the Revolutionary War army and unofficially as a "Liberty Boy." He and James Jackson (another future governor) were captured by the British; they escaped, only to be held by American soldiers as spies, and at the last minute were saved from the gallows. Served in the U.S. House, 1793 to 1799; 1801 to 1802; became governor 1802. During his term he dealt with matters concerning land cessions and the Creek Indians and a road was built from Tennessee to Augusta. Greatly interested in education, and served as a trustee of the University of Georgia. He resigned during his second term to accept the U.S. Senate seat vacated by the death of James Jackson. He was a loyal supporter of Thomas Jefferson and was made president pro tempore of the Senate, 1809. He died in Augusta in 1818.

Irwin, Jared, 1806—1809 (Second Term).

Mitchell, David Brydie, 1809—1813, 1815—1817, Democratic-Republican. Born in Scotland October 22, 1766. At seventeen he moved to Savannah. Served in state General Assembly, 1794—1796; Savannah's mayor, 1801 to 1802; U.S. Attorney General, 1803 to 1805. He served three two-year terms, with emphasis on internal improvements, improving highways and building new roads, establishing better banking facilities and strengthening the militia. An act prohibiting dueling was passed during his administration. He resigned in 1817 to become Federal Indian Agent to the Creek Indians. Died April 22, 1837.

Early, Peter, 1813—1815, Democratic-Republican. Born June 30, 1773 in Madison County, Virginia. Upon completion of law school in Philadelphia, he set up practice in Washington, Georgia. Served three terms in U.S. House of Representatives, 1801 to 1807. Was judge of the newly-created Superior Court of the Ocmulgee Circuit until he was elected governor in 1813. Unlike most of the previous governors, he cooperated fully with the federal government. He vetoed the reenactment of the so-called "Alleviating Law" (extending debtor's repayment time under certain conditions), but his veto was overriden, and he was defeated in the next election. He was promptly elected to the state Senate in 1816 by his home county, Greene. He died August 15, 1817. Early County was named in his honor.

Mitchell, David Brydie, 1815—1817 (Third Term).

Rabun, William, 1817—1819, Democratic-Republican. Born in Halifax, North Carolina on April 8, 1771. In 1775 he moved to Wilkes County, Georgia. Served six one-year terms in the state Senate starting in 1810; President of the Senate, 1812 to 1816. Was made *ex-officio* Governor March 1817 upon Governor David B. Mitchell's retirement and continued to serve one term. He served during a time of general prosperity, and due to his influence the legislature appropriated money for waterways, canals, roads and other internal improvements, and revised the penal code. The state Penitentiary was finished, and a steamboat company was chartered. He died October 25, 1819, while still in office. Rabun County was named in his honor.

Clark, John, 1819—1823, Democratic-Republican. Born in Edgecombe County, North Carolina, February 28, 1766, moved to Wilkes County, Georgia 1774. He had little formal education; joined the army at age fifteen as lieutenant. After running unsuccessfully in 1813 and 1817, he was elected governor in 1819. He served two terms, during which time a treaty was signed (1821) with the Creeks, giving the state the area between the Flint and Ocmulgee Rivers, which was divided into five new counties. On October 2, 1832 in St. Andrew's Bay, Florida, Clark died of yellow fever.

Troup, George Michael, 1823—1827, Democratic-Republican. Born on the Tombigbee River, Alabama, September 8, 1780. His family moved to Savannah when he was two. In 1797 he graduated from Princeton. Was U.S. representative three terms, 1807 to 1815; chairman of Military Affairs Committee during the War of 1812; U.S. Senator, 1816 to 1818. He was elected governor by the legislature by a slim margin of four votes. In 1825 he was reelected in the first gubernatorial race decided by popular vote. He was an ardent supporter of States' Rights and internal improvements. The removal of the Creek Indians from the state and the making of their land accessible to white settlers took place during his terms in office. Returned to the U.S. Senate 1829, but retired in 1833 because of poor health. He died in Montgomery County on April 26, 1856. Troup County was named in his honor.

Forsyth, John, 1827—1829, Democratic-Republican. Born in Fredericksburg, Virginia on October 22, 1780. Princeton graduate, 1799; served three terms in U.S. House of Representatives, 1813 to 1818; resigned to fill short term in the U.S. Senate, 1818 to 1819. Resigned to become minister to Spain until 1823; then three more terms as U.S. representative, 1823 to 1827. Inaugurated governor November 7, 1827 following election by popular vote. He was opposed to the 1828 "Tariff of Abominations" and was in favor of neutralizing it by state action. Returned to U.S. Senate, 1829 to 1834. Joined President Andrew Jackson's cabinet as secretary of state, was reappointed by President Martin Van Buren, 1834 to 1841. Died in Washington, D.C., October 21, 1841. Forsyth County was named in his honor.

Gilmer, George Rockingham, 1829—1831, 1837—1839, Democratic-Republican. Born near Lexington, Wilkes (now Oglethorpe) County on April 11, 1790. First Lieutenant, Forty-third Regiment, U.S. Infantry, 1813 to 1815 in the campaign against the Creek Indians. Served in U.S. House of Representatives, 1819 to 1823, 1827 to 1829 as a Democrat. Served as governor 1829 to 1831 as a Democratic-Republican. His second term, 1837 to 1839 he ran as States' Rights candidate. Gold was discovered in the Nacoochee Valley, in an area belonging to the Cherokee Indians. Gold seekers presence, in spite of a proclamation demanding their departure, created troubles with the Cherokees during his first term. His second term was marked by the Panic of 1837. Author of *Sketches of Some of the First Settlers of Upper Georgia*. Gilmer died in Lexington, Georgia on November 16, 1859. Gilmer County was named in his honor.

Lumpkin, Wilson, 1831—1835, Union Party. Born in Pittsylvania County, Virginia on January 14, 1783. Served in U.S. House of Representatives, 1815 to 1817. He was appointed as a commissioner to determine the boundaries of treaties made with the Creek Indians by President James Monroe in 1818 to 1819. U.S. House of Representatives as a Jacksonian Democrat, 1826 to 1831. He took the office of governor as a Union Party candidate. His primary interest as governor was the removal of the Cherokees from north Georgia. In his second term he worked for a revision of the state's tax laws, called for a system of teacher training and mass education, a railroad to join the Ohio Valley with Georgia's coast, and State Penitentiary improvements. He died December 1, 1870 and was buried in Athens. Lumpkin County was named in his honor.

Schley, William, 1835—1837, Union Party. Born in Frederick, Maryland, December 10, 1786. Served Ninth Regiment, Georgia militia as a private; studied law; admitted to Georgia Bar 1812. Served state legislature, 1830 to 1832; U.S. House of Representatives, 1832 to 1835 as a Democrat. Elected governor as a Union Party candidate. He died November 20, 1858 and was buried near Augusta. Schley County was named in his honor.

Gilmer, George Rockingham, 1837—1839 (Second Term).

McDonald, Charles James, 1839—1843, Union Party. Born in Charleston, South Carolina, July 9, 1793. In 1794, his family moved to Hancock County, Georgia. Served in the Georgia militia as brigadier general, 1823 to 1825. Served as Democratic representative in the Georgia Legislature, 1830; state senate 1834 to 1839. Elected governor as the Union Party candidate, 1839. His term had to deal with the problems created by the Panic of 1837, and a legislature dominated by Whigs. He sought to establish a state Supreme Court, and an adequate educational system. He concentrated on the state's economy during his second term, as well as supporting the programs he began in his first administration. He died December 16, 1860 in Marietta, Georgia.

Crawford, George Walker, 1843—1847, Whig. Born in Columbia County, Georgia, December 22, 1798. Served Georgia House of Representatives, 1837 to 1843. He served one month (February to March 1843) as U.S. Representative to finish term following the death of Richard Habersham. He was inaugurated governor November 7, 1843 and was the only Whig to ever hold that office. He served two terms and was a successful and popular administrator. Sound currency, liquidation of the state bank, payment of the state debt, railroad construction, establishment of a

State Supreme Court, and penal reform were some of his objectives. He served as Secretary of War in President Zachary Taylor's cabinet, 1848 to 1850. He died July 27, 1872.

Towns, George Washington Bonaparte, 1847—1851, Democrat. Born in Wilkes County, Georgia, May 4, 1801. Served as U.S. Representative 1835 to 1836, 1837 to 1839, 1846 to 1847. Served two terms as governor, 1847 to 1851 and favored the use of poll taxes, the revenue from the state railroad, and other sources of revenue to fund public education. He supported the Mexican War. He died in Macon on July 15, 1854. Towns County was named in his honor.

Cobb, Howell, 1851—1853, Constitutional Union. Born in Jefferson County, Georgia, September 7, 1815. Served as U.S. Representative, 1842 to 1851 and was Speaker of the House 1849 to 1851. Served one term as governor, 1851 to 1853. Annual legislative sessions, election of a state attorney general, Supreme Court sessions in the state capital, leasing of the state-owned Western and Atlantic Railroad, and financial aid for the State Library and education were some of his objectives. Returned to the U.S. House of Representatives in 1854. He joined President James Buchanan's cabinet as secretary of the treasury in 1857, resigned in 1860. He was President of the Provisional Congress of the Confederacy, as well as a delegate. He died while on a business trip to New York, October 9, 1868.

Johnson, Hershel Vespasian, 1853—1857, States' Rights Democratic. Born in Burke County, Georgia, September 18, 1812. Appointed to fill a vacancy in the U.S. Senate 1848 to 1849. Became governor in 1853 and served two terms. Favored public education and States' Rights. He ran unsuccessfully for vice president of the United States on the Douglas Democratic ticket in 1860. He served as judge of the Middle Circuit of Georgia from 1873 until his death, August 16, 1880.

Brown, Joseph Emerson, 1857—1865, Democrat. Born April 15, 1821 in Pickens District, South Carolina. Graduated in 1846 from Yale Law School, and began his practice in Canton, Georgia. Served in Georgia Senate, 1849—1855. Was the only Georgian to serve four successive terms as governor, 1857 to 1865. He was a strong pro-slavery states' rights leader who favored secession and made great efforts to prepare the state for war. He quarreled with President Jefferson Davis over various issues. His passion for state sovereignty weakened the Confederate war effort. At the end of the war he was jailed briefly and he resigned as governor June, 1865. He advocated Reconstruction. Served as U.S. senator, 1880 to 1891. Died November 30, 1894.

Johnson, James, 1865, Democrat (Provisional). Born February 12, 1811 in South Carolina. Graduated from University of Georgia in 1832 and was an attorney in Columbus. Served one term in Congress, 1851 to 1853. He opposed secession and was loyal to the Union throughout the war, unlike most Georgians. He was appointed Provisional Governor by President Andrew Johnson to help the state form a new government. During his brief tenure (June 17 to December 14, 1865) he called a state convention which ratified the 13th Amendment, disclaimed the Confederate debt, repealed the Ordinance of Secession, and wrote a new state constitution which called for the election of a governor and other state officials; then Johnson gave up his position. He later served as judge of the Superior Court. He died November 20, 1891.

Jenkins, Charles Jones, 1865—1868, Constitutional Union Party. Born in Beaufort, South Carolina, January 6, 1805; moved to Jefferson County, Georgia in 1816. A lawyer who served many terms in the state House of Representatives; four sessions as Speaker. In 1852 he was National Constitutional Union Party vice presidential candidate, and in 1853 the Constitutional Union Party candidate for governor but was twice defeated. He did assume the office as governor in 1865, however, and had the difficult problems of rebuilding the state treasury and state property that had been destroyed in the War Between the States. By the end of his term there was money in the treasury and the state railroad had been repaired. He died June 14, 1883. Jenkins County was named in his honor.

Ruger, Thomas Howard, 1868 (Military Governor). Born in Livingston County, New York. Graduated from West Point in 1854, served in U.S. Army Corps of Engineers; lieutenant colonel of the Third Wisconsin Regiment (June, 1861); colonel (August, 1861); brigadier general (November, 1862); brevetted to major general for gallantry at the Battle of Franklin, Tennessee, November 30, 1864. When Governor Jenkins was removed from office for refusing to pay for the State Convention out of state funds, General Ruger was named governor of Georgia (January 17, 1868) by Major General George W. Meade, commander of the Third Military District. He served until June 28, 1868. He then served as superintendent of the U.S. Military Academy at West Point, 1871 to 1876. He died June 3, 1907.

Bullock, Rufus Brown, 1868—1871, Republican. Born in Bethlehem, New York March 28, 1834. Was a telegraphic expert and became an official of a telegraph company in Augusta, Georgia. He served the Confederacy at the outbreak of the War Between the States, even though he was opposed to secession, establishing railroad and telegraph lines. Elected governor by popular vote and took office when Governor Ruger was removed. Numerous allegations were brought against him: bribing the press, selling pardons, allowing the state penitentiary to be plundered, and encouraging corruption in state government. He resigned office October 23, 1871 and left the state when a Democratic majority returned to the state legislature and he faced the possibility of criminal indictment. He was arrested and returned to Georgia in 1876, but was acquitted on charges of embezzlement of public funds due to lack of evidence. He remained in Atlanta to be president of the Chamber of Commerce, and officer of several businesses, including director of the Union Pacific Railroad. He died April 27, 1907.

Conley, Benjamin F., 1871—1872, Republican. Born March 1, 1815 in Newark, New Jersey. He moved to Augusta, Georgia at age fifteen, where he became a successful merchant. From 1857 to 1859, he was mayor of Augusta. He retired to a plantation in Alabama rather than take part in the War Between the States. After the war, he became active in politics and became president of the state Senate. He advanced to the office of governor when Governor Bullock abruptly resigned October 30, 1871. He held that office two months and twelve days and partisan battles raged. His honesty was praised by his opponents, in spite of the fact that his vetoes were usually overridden. His brief term marked the end of Republican control in the Reconstruction era. President Grant appointed him Postmaster of the city of Atlanta, 1875 to 1883 and he died there in 1885.

Smith, James Milton, 1872—1877, Democrat. Born October 24, 1823 in Twiggs County, Georgia. Attained rank of colonel in the Confederate Army and served a year in the Confederate Congress, 1864 to 1865. He was Speaker of the Georgia House of Representatives. His inauguration as governor (January 12, 1872) marked the end of five years of Republican rule. As governor, he faced serious economic problems in the aftermath of Reconstruction. The Georgia State College of Agriculture and Mechanical Arts (in Athens), the office of State Geologist and the Department of Agriculture were all created during his term in office. For six years he served the State Railroad Commission, before being appointed Judge of the Superior Court of the Chattahoochee Circuit in 1887. He died November 25, 1890.

Colquitt, Alfred Holt, 1877—1882, Democrat. Born April 20, 1824 in Walton County, Georgia. He began a long and successful career in politics after serving in the Mexican War. He served in Congress, the state legislature, and the Georgia Secession Convention before serving the Confederate Army first as a captain and later as major general. He was elected to a four-year term as governor in 1876, then reelected to a two-year term. He brought reductions in the floating and bonded debts and taxes, thus strengthening the state's financial structure. A new state Constitution was approved which served the state until 1945. Was elected to the U.S. Senate in 1883 and again in 1888. He died while serving in the Senate, March 26, 1894.

Stephens, Alexander Hamilton, 1882—1883, Democrat. Born February 11, 1812 in Wilkes County, Georgia. Served State House of Representatives, 1836 to 1841; state Senate, 1842 to 1843; and U.S. House of Representatives, 1843 to 1859. He was vice president of the Confederacy, a reluctant secessionist who believed in states' rights and constitutional law, and was involved in numerous conflicts with President Jefferson Davis over the conduct of the war. After being defeated for the Senate in 1872, he was elected U.S. Representative and served ten years. Became governor November 4, 1882 but the demands were too much in his weakened condition and he died four months later, March 4, 1883. Stephens County was named in his honor.

Boynton, James S., 1883, Democrat. Born May 7, 1833 in Henry County, Georgia. Served as colonel in Confederate Army; Mayor of Griffin, 1869 to 1872; Georgia Senate, 1880 to 1884 and was president of the Senate both terms. Became acting governor when Governor Stephens died and until May 10, 1883 when a replacement could be elected. He died December 22, 1902.

McDaniel, Henry D., 1883—1886, Democrat. Born September 4, 1836 in Monroe, Georgia. A lawyer who served in the Confederate Army, State House of Representatives and Senate before being elected governor. Strengthening the state's finances, taxing the railroads, supervising the building of a new state Capitol, and improving services for the blind, deaf and insane were some of his accomplishments. He died July 25, 1926.

Gordon, John B., 1886—1890, Democrat. Born in Upson County, Georgia February 6, 1832. Was regarded as one of the finest untrained soldiers of the Confederacy, being one of only three Georgians to attain rank of Lieutenant General. He was believed to be the head of the Ku Klux Klan in Georgia and was an adamant opponent of Radical Reconstruction. Elected to the U.S. Senate, 1871 to 1880; became successful businessman; then elected governor 1886 and again in 1888. The state's bonded indebtedness was reduced, and there was an increase in capital, factories, railroads and population, though few reforms were enacted in his term. He toured the country lecturing on the Confederacy in his last years, and published *Reminiscences of the Civil War* in 1903. He died January 9, 1904.

Northern, William J., 1890—1894, Democrat. Born July 9, 1835 in Jones County, Georgia. An educator and president of the State Agricultural Society who served two terms in the state House of Representatives and one term in the state Senate before being elected to two terms as governor. Progress was made in the field of education and he conducted the office in an efficient and frugal manner. He was involved in religious and scholarly pursuits after his terms in office, editing *Men of Mark in Georgia,* a seven-volume collection of biographical sketches published 1907 to 1912. He served briefly as state Historian. He died March 25, 1913.

Atkinson, William Yates, 1894—1898, Democrat. Born in Meriwether County, Georgia, November 11, 1854. Served four terms in Georgia Legislature; the last one as Speaker of the House. Was chairman of the Georgia Democratic Convention in 1890. Served two terms as governor. He sought educational, electoral, and penal reforms but failed in his efforts to establish the office of Lieutenant Governor and to eliminate lynching. He publicized the Atlanta Exposition of 1895 and stressed industrial expansion. He died August 8, 1899. Atkinson County was named in his honor.

Candler, Allen Daniel, 1898—1902, Democrat. Born November 4, 1834 in Lumpkin County, Georgia. An educator and businessman who served four terms in the U.S. Congress and four years as Georgia's secretary of state before being elected to two terms as governor. He was not known for any changes or reforms but rather for being honest and frugal. His greatest service to the state came from his serving as state Historian. Twenty-eight large volumes on Georgia's colonial, revolutionary and confederate history were published. He published with Clement Evans a three-volume encyclopedia of Georgia in 1906. He died October 26, 1910. Candler County was named in his honor.

Terrell, Joseph M., 1902—1907, Democrat. Born in Meriwether County, Georgia, June 6, 1861. A lawyer who served two terms in the state House of Representatives, 1884 to 1888; Georgia Senate, 1890; state Attorney General, 1892 to 1902; and two terms as governor, 1902 to 1907. In spite of opposition from his conservative legislature, many of his progressive reforms were enacted. His most important accomplishments were in the field of education, with the establishment of the College of Agriculture, and an agricultural and mechanical school for each Congressional district was authorized. He was appointed to the U.S. Senate in 1910, following the death of Senator Alexander Clay. He resigned July 14, 1911 to resume his law practice and died November 17, 1912 in Atlanta.

Smith, Hoke, 1907—1909, 1911, Democrat. Born in Newton, North Carolina, September 2, 1855. He was active in the state Democratic Party and an avid supporter of Grover Cleveland. Was Democratic State Convention Chairman, 1888 and Democratic National Convention delegate in 1892. Was secretary of interior, 1893 to 1896 and then was out of office ten years before being elected governor in 1906. The Railroad Commission was strengthened; the convict lease system abolished; juvenile courts and a parole system were established during his term. He was defeated in his bid for reelection in 1908 but won again in 1910. In 1911 the legislature named him U.S. Senator and he resigned his position as governor. He died on November 27, 1931.

Brown, Joseph Mackey, 1909—1911, 1912—1913, Democrat. Born in Canton, Georgia, December 28, 1851. Was employed with the Western and Atlantic Railroad, 1877; appointed to the Railroad Commission, 1904; became governor 1909. He sought economy in government, lower taxes, enforcement of Prohibition, and a reduction in the power of the Railroad

Commission. He was defeated in his bid for reelection by Hoke Smith but when Smith was appointed to the Senate, Brown easily won reelection. He wrote two books entitled *Mountain Campaigns in Georgia* and *Astanax* as well as numerous articles. He died March 3, 1932 at his home in Marietta.

Smith, Hoke, 1911 (Second Term).

Slaton, John Marshall, 1911—1912, 1913—1915, Democrat. Born December 25, 1866 in Meriwether County, Georgia. Graduated from the University of Georgia in 1866 and set up a law practice in Atlanta which lasted sixty-eight years. Served thirteen years in the Georgia House of Representatives, starting in 1896, and was Speaker of the House twice. He advanced to the Senate and was President of the Senate. He served two months as acting governor when Governor Smith gave up the office to become U.S. Senator (November 16, 1911 to January 10, 1912) and was later elected Governor 1913 to 1915. He was a conservative who stressed governmental frugality, tax equalization, and regulation of public utilities. Child labor legislation, the establishment of the Georgia Training School for Girls, and the creation of four new counties also took place during his term. He was unanimously elected president of the Georgia Bar Association in 1928. He died January 11, 1955.

Brown, Joseph Mackey, 1912—1913 (Second Term).

Slaton, John Marshall, 1913—1915 (Second Term).

Harris, Nathaniel E., 1915—1917, Democrat. Born in Jonesboro, Tennessee on January 21, 1846. Served in Confederate Army, graduated in 1870 from the University of Georgia and practiced law in Macon. Served four years in Georgia House of Representatives 1882 to 1886, and helped to establish the Georgia Institute of Technology. Elected to state Senate, 1894. As governor, 1915 to 1917, he struggled with dislocations caused by World War I, the renewed activity of the Ku Klux Klan, and the much divided issue of Prohibition. He was successful in securing pension increases for Confederate veterans, a compulsory education law and a fifty-year lease of the state-owned railroad. His main interest in his last years was service to Georgia Tech. He was the last Confederate veteran to serve as governor of Georgia. He died September 21, 1929.

Dorsey, Hugh Manson, 1917—1921, Democrat. Born in Fayetteville, Georgia, July 10, 1871. A member of the Georgia Bar Association; was solicitor general of the Atlanta Judicial Circuit, 1910 to 1916. During his terms as governor, he strongly objected to lynching and peonage, a system in which debtors or legal prisoners were forced to work for their creditors or those persons who leased their services from the state. He brought to public attention the unjust treatment of blacks in the state with his book *The Negro in Georgia*. He favored compulsory education for both races and conferences to discuss racial affairs. He returned to practicing law, was appointed Judge of the City Court of Atlanta, and finally Judge of the Atlanta Judicial Circuit until his death, June 11, 1948.

Hardwick, Thomas William, 1921—1923, Democrat. Born in Thomas County, Georgia, December 9, 1872. Served in state House of Representatives, 1890 to 1899, 1903 to 1914; U.S. Senate, 1914 to 1919. During his term as governor (1921 to 1923) there was a revival of the Ku Klux Klan, due to the "Red Scare" which developed after World War I. Hardwick demanded that its members unmask and end their violent activities and they retaliated by securing his defeat for reelection. He died in Sandersville, Georgia January 31, 1944.

Walker, Clifford Mitchell, 1923—1927, Democrat. Born in Monroe, Georgia, July 4, 1877. Mayor of Monroe, 1905 to 1907; served as Solicitor General of the Western Judicial Circuit of Georgia, 1909 to 1913; Attorney General of Georgia, 1914 to 1919. He served two terms as governor. Georgia received national criticism because of the state's cruel treatment of prisoners during his administration. When the use of the lash was abolished in prison camps, the Ku Klux Klan turned their wrath on him. He was in favor of the League of Nations. He died November 9, 1954.

Hardman, Lamartine Griffin, 1927—1931, Democrat. Born in Commerce, Georgia, April 14, 1856. After studying medicine and becoming a successful businessman he became a member of the Georgia House of Representatives, 1902 to 1907, and the state Senate, 1908 to 1910. He served two terms as governor, 1927 to 1931. He was an opponent to the repeal of Prohibition; cotton production declined greatly and manufacturing took on an increasing percentage of the labor force during his administration. He died in Atlanta, February 18, 1937.

Russell, Richard B., 1931—1933, Democrat. Born November 2, 1897 in Winder, Georgia. Served state House of Representatives, 1920 to 1930; Speaker of the House, 1926 to 1930. Became governor during the Great Depression, bringing about such austerity measures as the Reorganization Act of 1931 which reduced the number of state agencies from 102 to 18. Placing all state-supported colleges under one Board of Regents was his most resolute change. Elected to U.S. Senate in 1932 and continued to serve for the next thirty-eight years. He was one of only three men ever to be elected for seven consecutive terms in the Senate and the only man to have served more than half his life there. He advocated military preparedness and states' rights. He served as a respected advisor to six presidents; chairman of the Senate Appropriations Committee; was third-in-line for presidency; and at the time of his death, January 21, 1971, was president pro tempore of the Senate.

Talmadge, Eugene, 1933—1937, 1941—1943, Democrat. Born in Forsyth, Georgia on September 23, 1884. He farmed, practiced law and operated a saw mill before being elected Commissioner of Agriculture in 1926.

He served three terms before being elected governor. He was against public welfare and government debt, sought frugal government and low taxes. He often ruled by martial law and was a spokesman of the farmer. He lowered the cost of license tags, property taxes and utility rates, and used federal funds to build highways and other state services. Reelected in 1934 to a second term by an overwhelming margin. Won a third term in 1940 and a fourth in 1946, but died on December 21, 1946 before taking office.

Rivers, Eurith Dickinson, 1937—1941, Democrat. Born in Center Point, Arkansas on December 1, 1895. Was editor of a newspaper. Elected to Georgia legislature in 1924; Georgia Senate, 1926. Ran unsuccessfully for office of governor in 1928 and again in 1930. Elected to Georgia House of Representatives, 1932 and 1934; served as speaker both terms. After being elected governor in 1936, he gave complete support to Roosevelt's New Deal. State services were increased, especially welfare benefits, public health and housing, electricity expanded in rural areas, increased highway expansion, and more funds to public schools because of increased federal assistance. He was elected to a second term, but his administration was spoiled by charges of corruption and mismanagement. He died on June 11, 1967 in Atlanta.

Talmadge, Eugene, 1941—1943 (Third Term).

Arnall, Ellis Gibbs, 1943—1947, Democrat. Born in Newnan, Georgia on March 20, 1907. Elected to General Assembly, 1932; speaker pro tempore, 1933 and 1935 and attorney general of Georgia, 1939—1943. In 1943, he became governor. He sponsored numerous progressive changes that the legislature adopted; accreditation was restored to the state's colleges; elimination of the chain gang and other prison reforms; Georgia became the first state to lower the voting age to eighteen; the poll tax was abolished; without increasing taxes the state debt was paid and a new constitution was adopted. He lost a reelection bid in 1966 to Lester Maddox.

Thompson, Melvin Ernest, 1947—1948, Democrat. Born in Millen, Georgia on May 1, 1903. Was elected Georgia's first lieutenant governor in 1946. He became acting governor two days after his inauguration on January 18, 1947. Thompson succeeded to the office after Governor Ellis Arnall left office, since Governor-Elect Eugene Talmadge had died on December 21, 1946. (However, the office was controlled by Herman Talmadge, appointed by the legislature, until the state Supreme Court ruled that Thompson was the chief executive.) Thompson was more of a liberal, with emphasis on education, the passage of a sales tax, and the purchase of Jekyll Island. He died October 3, 1980.

Talmadge, Herman Eugene, 1947, 1948—1955, Democrat. Born in Telfair County, Georgia on August 9, 1913. His father, Eugene Talmadge, died before taking office to a fourth term as governor in 1947 and Talmadge was elected governor in 1947 by the Georgia Legislature. He served sixty-seven days before the state Supreme Court put him out of office. In 1948 and in 1950, he was elected a total of six years by popular vote. By introducing a three percent sales tax he was able to expand state services, especially education. Money for public schools nearly tripled and new schools were built, funded by the new State Building Authority. The State Forestry Commission was established, a network of hospitals and health facilities was constructed and the Highway Department was reorganized. He was first elected to the U.S. Senate in 1956 and served as chairman of Agriculture and Forestry. He was considered to be one of the most powerful members of the Senate.

Griffin, Samuel Marvin, 1955—1959, Democrat. Born in Bainbridge, Georgia on September 4, 1907. Elected to the General Assembly, 1934; executive secretary to Governor Rivers, 1940; U.S. Army, 1941 to 1944; adjutant general, 1944 to 1947; lieutenant governor, 1948 to 1952. Elected governor in 1954, he favored segregation and the county unit system, as did his predecessor, Governor Talmadge. Rural roads were paved through the sale of bonds; an atomic reactor was built at Georgia Tech; an eight-million-dollar science center was begun at the University of Georgia and funds were increased to public schools and the university system. When he left office he returned to Bainbridge to run the *Post-Searchlight*, the newspaper his father had edited before him and which he turned over to his son in 1963. He died June 13, 1982.

Vandiver, Samuel Ernest, 1959—1963, Democrat. Born July 31, 1918 in Franklin County, Georgia. He began to practice law in Winder, after serving in World War II as a pilot. Was mayor of Lavonia; aide to Governor Eugene Talmadge; Governor Herman Talmadge's campaign manager, 1948; state adjutant general 1948 to 1954; director of selective service, 1948 to 1954; and lieutenant governor, 1955 to 1959. Elected Governor in 1958 by an overwhelming majority. The problems he faced during his administration were of reapportionment and school integration. He was strongly in favor of segregation and states' rights and was hesistant to implement the rulings of the federal courts and allow the public schools to be integrated. The legislature eliminated the state's segregation laws and the county unit system which was used to nominate candidates for the Democratic primary during his term. He favored governmental efficiency, expanded tourism, the development of foreign trade, and increased funding for education. He suffered a heart attack in 1966, causing him to withdraw from his bid for reelection for governor. He served as adjutant general in 1971.

Sanders, Carl E., 1963—1967, Democrat. Born in Augusta, Georgia on May 15, 1925. Elected to state Senate, 1954; served as Senate Floor Leader, then as president pro tempore of the Senate. Elected governor 1962. Education, highway construction, hospitals and mental health facilities, recreational areas, and community airports received additional funding through his efforts. His greatest concern was education. The construction of 6,000 classrooms, the hiring of 10,000 additional teachers, and the Minimum Foundation Program (which established uniform standards for education) were his major accomplishments. When his term expired, he returned to his law practice. He ran again for governor in 1970, but was defeated by Jimmy Carter.

Maddox, Lester Garfield, 1967—1971, Democrat. Born in Atlanta, Georgia, September 30, 1915. Believing in segregation, he gained widespread attention in 1964 by closing the restaurant he had operated since 1947 rather than serve blacks. He became nationally known for his one-man campaign against the Supreme Court, President Johnson, Martin Luther King, Jr., the Atlanta newspapers, Communists and Socialists. He ran for governor in 1966 and since neither candidate had a majority (Bo Callaway—453,665; Maddox—450,626) the election was decided by the legislature which elected Maddox, 182 votes to 66. He carried out few reforms during his term, because of his political inexperience and the strange circumstances of his election. He expanded the Department of Industry and Trade, secured pay increases for teachers and state employees, released hundreds of prisoners before the expiration of their terms, and in fact appointed more blacks to office than any previous governor.

Carter, James Earl, 1971—1975, Democrat. Born in Plains, Georgia, October 1, 1924. He graduated in 1946 from United States Naval Academy at Annapolis; served on the nuclear submarine program with Admiral Hyman G. Rickover, under the auspices of the Atomic Energy Commission in 1951. He resigned from the Navy in 1953 and returned to Georgia to manage family business interests after death of his father. He served in the state Senate, 1963 to 1967; the Educational Matters Committee; and the Highways, Agriculture, and Appropriations Committees. Became governor in 1971; reorganized the state government; reinstated capital punishment for certain crimes; disclosure laws for political candidates; a "no fault" auto insurance plan; and the right by counties to vote to exempt themselves from the state's "blue laws." He was inaugurated President of the United States January 20, 1977.

Busbee, George Dekle, 1975—1983, Democrat. Born in Vienna, Georgia on August 7, 1927. During World War II, he served with the United States Naval Reserve. Served state House of Representatives, 1957 to 1974; assistant Administration Floor Leader, 1963 to 1965; Administration Floor Leader, 1966; and House Majority Leader, 1967 to 1974. The federal Equal Rights Amendment was defeated by the state legislature; new revenue sources were approved for local governments, including local sales taxes and hotel-motel taxes; and an investigation of some of Georgia's doctors for alleged overcharging was initiated by the governor.

Harris, Joe Frank, 1983—, Democrat. Born in Cartersville, Georgia on February 16, 1936. After receiving a B.A. degree from the University of Georgia, and serving in the Army, he became a businessman. Served 18 years in the state House of Representatives, the last eight of which he was chairman of the House Appropriations Committee. Education reform has been his priority in office, with $1.5 billion being appropriated without the aid of any new state taxes and he is also working to enhance economic development in the state. He has been involved in campaigns against drunk driving, child abuse, and drug trafficking.

HIGHER EDUCATION

Universities, Colleges, Vocational-Technical Schools

Abraham Baldwin Agricultural College, Tift County, Junior College (2 Yr.). A unit of the University System of Georgia, enrollment 1723, M-871, F-852. Tifton, GA 31793, Telephone 912-386-3236. Founded 1908.

Agnes Scott College, DeKalb County, Senior College (4 Yr.) Private, enrollment 549, M-O, F-549, Decatur, GA 30030, Telephone 404-373-2571. Founded 1889.

Albany Area Technical School, Dougherty County, Area Technical. Area school developed under State Department of Education policies, enrollment 2684, M-1114, F-1570. Albany, GA 31708, Telephone 912-888-1320.

Albany Junior College, Dougherty County, Junior College (2 Yr.). A unit of the University System of Georgia, enrollment 1760, M-616, F-1144. Albany, GA 31707, Telephone 912-888-8888. Founded 1963.

Albany State College, Dougherty County, Senior College (4 Yr.). A unit of the University System of Georgia, enrollment 2005, M-711, F-1294. Albany, GA 31705, Telephone 912-439-4600. Founded 1903.

American College for Applied Arts, Fulton County, Senior College (4 Yr.). Atlanta, GA 30342. Founded 1975.

Andrew College, Randolph County, Junior College (2 Yr.). Private, United Methodist, enrollment 320, M-168, F-152. Cuthbert, GA 31740, Telephone 912-732-2171. Founded 1854.

Armstrong State College, Chatham County, Senior College (4 Yr.). A unit of the University System of Georgia, enrollment 3051, M-1041, F-2010. Savannah, GA 31406, Telephone 912-927-5243. Founded 1935.

Athens Area Technical School, Clarke County, Area Technical. Area school developed under State Department of Education policies, enrollment 4021, M-1487, F-2534. Athens, GA 30601, Telephone 404-549-2360.

Atlanta Area Technical School, Fulton County, Area Technical. Area school developed under State Department of Education policies, enrollment 5748, M-2129, F-3619. Atlanta, GA 30310, Telephone 404-758-9451. Founded 1967.

Atlanta Christian College, Fulton County, Bible College (4 Yrs.). Private, Christian, enrollment 180, M-113, F-67 (1982). East Point, GA 30344, Telephone 404-761-8861. Founded 1937.

Atlanta College of Art, Fulton County, Art College (4 Yr.). Private, enrollment 270, M-126, F-144 (1982). Atlanta, GA 30309, Telephone 404-898-1164. Founded 1928.

Atlanta Junior College, Fulton County, Junior College (2 Yr.). A unit of the University System of Georgia, enrollment 1367, M-570, F-797. Atlanta, GA 30310, Telephone 404-656-6444. Founded 1974.

Atlanta University, Fulton County, Doctoral. Private, enrollment 1065, M-507, F-558. Atlanta, GA 30314, Telephone 404-681-0251. Founded 1867.

Augusta Area Technical School, Richmond County, Area Technical. Area school developed under State Department of Education policies, enrollment, 5684, M-2553, F-3131. Augusta, GA 30906, Telephone 404-796-6900. Founded 1961.

Augusta College, Richmond County, Senior College (4 Yr.). A unit of the University System of Georgia, enrollment 4461, M-1630, F-2831. Augusta, GA 30910, Telephone 404-828-2987. Founded 1925.

Bainbridge Junior College, Decatur County, Junior College (2 Yr.). A unit of the University System of Georgia, enrollment 814, M-345, F-496. Bainbridge, GA 31717, Telephone 912-246-7941. Founded 1973.

Ben Hill-Irwin Area Technical School. Ben Hill County, Area Technical. Area school developed under State Department of Education policies, enrollment 747, M-337, F-410, Fitzgerald, GA 31750, Telephone 912-468-7487.

Berry College, Floyd County, Senior College (4 Yr.). Private, enrollment 1403, M-560, F-836. Mount Berry, GA 30149, Telephone 404-232-5374. Founded 1902.

Brenau College, Hall County, Senior College (4 Yr.). Private, enrollment 1602, M-593, F-1009. Gainesville, GA 30501, Telephone 404-534-6109. Founded 1878.

Brewton-Parker College, Montgomery County, Junior College (2 Yr.). Private, Baptist, enrollment 1277, M-667, F-610, Mount Vernon, GA 30445, Telephone 912-583-2241. Founded 1904.

Brunswick Junior College, Glynn County, Junior College (2 Yr.). A unit of the University System of Georgia, enrollment 1297, M-468, F-829. Brunswick, GA 31520, Telephone 912-264-7235. Founded 1961.

Carroll County Area Technical School, Carroll County, Area Technical. Area school developed under State Department of Education policies, enrollment 1885, M-719, F-1166. Carrollton, GA 30117, Telephone 404-834-3391.

Carver Bible Institute and College, Fulton County, Senior College (4 Yr.) Atlanta, GA 30313. Founded 1943.

Chattahoochee Technical Institute, Cobb County, Area Technical. Area school developed under State Department of Education policies, enrollment 3606, M-1747, F-1859. Marietta, GA 30060, Telephone 404-422-1660.

Clark College, Fulton County, Senior College (4 Yr.). Private, United Methodist, enrollment 1936, M-692, F-1244. Atlanta, GA 30314, Telephone 404-681-3080. Founded 1869.

Clayton State College, Clayton County, Senior College (4 Yr.). A unit of the University System of Georgia, enrollment 3603, M-1487, F-2116. Morrow, GA 30260, Telephone 404-961-3400. Founded 1969.

Columbia Theological Seminary, DeKalb County, Doctoral. Private, Presbyterian, enrollment 502, M-408, F-94. Decatur, GA 30031, Telephone 404-378-8821. Founded 1828.

Columbus Area Technical School, Muscogee County, Area Technical. Area school developed under State Department of Education policies, enrollment 3233, M-1578, F-1655. Columbus, GA 31995, Telephone 404-571-1837.

Columbus College, Muscogee County, Senior College (4 Yr.). A unit of the University System of Georgia, enrollment 3626, M-1450, F-2176. Columbus, GA 31993, Telephone 404-568-2001. Founded 1958.

Coosa Valley Area Technical School, Floyd County, Area Technical. Area school developed under State Department of Education policies, enrollment 2133, M-831, F-1302. Rome, GA 30161, Telephone 404-235-1142.

Covenant College, Dade County, Senior College (4 Yr.). Private, enrollment 515, M-267, F-248. Lookout Mountain, TN 37350, Telephone 404-820-1560.

Dalton Junior College, Whitfield County, Junior College (2 Yr.). A unit of the University System of Georgia, enrollment 1693, M-726, F-967. Dalton, GA 30720, Telephone 404-278-3113. Founded 1963.

DeKalb Area Technical School, DeKalb County, Area Technical. Area school developed under State Department of Education policies, enrollment 7709, M-3650, F-4059. Clarkston, GA 30621, Telephone 404-297-9522.

DeKalb College, DeKalb County, Junior College (2 Yr.). A unit of the University System of Georgia, enrollment 9116, M-3976, F-5140. Decatur, GA 30089-0601, Telephone 404-299-4331.

DeKalb Community College, DeKalb County, Junior College (2 Yr.). A community junior college of the public education system of DeKalb County, enrollment 14,877 M-6908, F-7969. Clarkston, GA 30021, Telephone 404-299-4331. Founded 1964.

DeVry Institute of Technology, Fulton County, Senior College (4 Yr.). Atlanta, GA 30341. Founded 1969.

Draughon's Junior College, Chatham County, Junior College (2 Yr.). Savannah, GA 31406. Founded 1899.

Emanuel County Junior College, Emanuel County, Junior College (2 Yr.). A unit of the University System of Georgia, enrollment 513, M-193, F-320. Swainsboro, GA 30401, Telephone 404-237-7831. Founded 1973.

Emmanuel College, Franklin County, Junior College (2 Yr.). Private, Pentecostal Holiness, enrollment 352, M-150, F-202, Franklin Springs, GA 30639, Telephone 404-245-7226. Founded 1919.

Emory University, DeKalb County, Doctoral. Private, Methodist, enrollment 9168, M-4535, F-4633. Atlanta, GA 30322, Telephone 404-727-6123. Founded 1836.

Floyd Junior College, Floyd County, Junior College (2 Yr.). A unit of the University System of Georgia, enrollment 1204, M-431, F-773. Rome, GA 30161, Telephone 404-295-6339. Founded 1970.

Fort Valley State College, Peach County, Senior College (4 Yr.). A unit of the University System of Georgia, enrollment 1735, M-764, F-971. Fort Valley, GA 31030, Telephone 912-825-6211. Founded 1895.

Gainesville Junior College, Hall County, Junior College (2 Yr.). A unit of the University System of Georgia, enrollment 1905, M-899, F-1006. Gainesville, GA 30501, Telephone 404-535-6239. Founded 1964.

Georgia College, Baldwin County, Senior College (4 Yr.). A unit of the University System of Georgia, enrollment 4302, M-1687, F-2615. Milledgeville, GA 30161, Telephone 912-453-5187. Founded 1889.

Georgia Institute of Technology, Fulton County, Doctoral. A unit of the University System of Georgia, enrollment 11,771, M-9183, F-2588. Atlanta GA 30332, Telephone 404-894-2000. Founded 1885.

Georgia Military College, Baldwin County, Junior College (2 Yr.). Private, enrollment 1403, M-980, F-423. Milledgeville, GA 31061, Telephone 912-453-3481. Founded 1879.

Georgia Southern College, Bulloch County, Senior College (4 Yr.). A unit of the University System of Georgia, enrollment 8766, M-3946, F-4820. Statesboro, GA 30460, Telephone 912-681-5611. Founded 1906.

Georgia Southwestern College, Sumter County, Senior College (4 Yr.). A unit of the University System of Georgia, enrollment 2080, M-804, F-1276. Americus, GA 31709, Telephone 912-928-1279. Founded 1906.

Georgia State University, Fulton County, Doctoral. A unit of the University System of Georgia, enrollment 22,116, M-9475, F-12,641. Atlanta, GA 30303, Telephone 404-658-2000. Founded 1913.

Gordon Junior College, Lamar County, Junior College (2 Yr.). A unit of the University System of Georgia, enrollment 1290, M-514, F-776. Barnesville, GA 30204, Telephone 404-358-1700. Founded 1852.

Griffin-Spalding Area Technical School, Spalding County, Area Technical. Area school developed under State Department of Education policies, enrollment 1796, M-829, F-967. Griffin, GA 30223, Telephone 404-277-1322.

Gwinnett Area Vocational-Technical School, Gwinnett County, Area Technical. Area school developed under State Department of Education policies, enrollment 4584, M-2310, F-2274. Lawrenceville, GA 30246, Telephone 404-962-7580.

Heart of Georgia Vocational-Technical School, Laurens County, Area Technical. Area school developed under State Department of Education policies, enrollment 1394, M-602, F-792. Dublin, GA 31021, Telephone 912-275-0672.

Immanuel Baptist Schools, Fulton County, Senior College (4 Yr.). Atlanta, GA 30316. Founded 1952.

Interdenominational Theological Center, Fulton County, Doctoral. Private, enrollment 310, M-253, F-57. Atlanta, GA 30314, Telephone 404-522-1772. Founded 1958.

John Marshall Law School, Fulton County, Doctoral. Atlanta, GA 30316. Founded 1952.

Kennesaw College, Cobb County, Senior College (4 Yr.). A unit of the University System of Georgia, enrollment 7946, M-3176, F-4770. Marietta, GA 30061, Telephone 404-429-2700. Founded 1963.

LaGrange College, Troup County, Senior College (4 Yr.). Private, Methodist, enrollment 947, M-397, F-550. LaGrange, GA 30240, Telephone 404-882-2911. Founded 1831.

Lanier Area Technical School, Hall County, Area Technical. Area school developed under State Department of Education policies, enrollment 1939, M-901, F-1038. Oakwood, GA 30566, Telephone 404-532-7243.

Life Chiropractic College, Cobb County, Doctoral. Private, enrollment 1876, M-1446, F-430. Marietta, GA 30060, Telephone 404-424-0554. Founded 1974.

Macon Area Technical School, Bibb County, Area Technical. Area school developed under State Department of Education policies, enrollment 4704, M-1528, F-3176. Macon, GA 31206, Telephone 912-781-0551.

Macon Junior College, Bibb County, Junior College (2 Yr.). A unit of the University System of Georgia, enrollment 2948, M-1157, F-1791. Macon, GA 31297, Telephone 912-474-2700. Founded 1968.

Medical College of Georgia, Richmond County, Doctoral. A unit of the University System of Georgia, enrollment 2262, M-1165, F-1097. Augusta, GA 30912, Telephone 404-828-0211. Founded 1828.

Mercer University, Bibb County, Doctoral. Private, Baptist, enrollment 2880, M-1465, F-1415. Macon, GA 31207, Telephone 912-744-2700. Founded 1833.

Mercer University in Atlanta, DeKalb County, Senior College (4 Yr.). Private, Baptist, enrollment 1868, M-1001, F-867. Atlanta, GA 30341, Telephone 404-451-0331. Founded 1964.

Mercer University Southern School of Pharmacy, Fulton County, Doctoral. Private, Baptist, enrollment 316, M-191, F-125. Atlanta, GA 30312, Telephone 404-688-6291. Founded 1903.

Middle Georgia College, Bleckley County, Junior College (2 Yr.). A unit of the University System of Georgia, enrollment 1385, M-633, F-752. Cochran, GA 31014, Telephone 912-934-6221. Founded 1884.

Middle Georgia Technical Institute, Houston County, Vocational Center. Area school developed under State Department of Education policies, enrollment 2735, M-869, F-1866. Warner Robins, GA 31056, Telephone 912-929-9600.

Morehouse College, Fulton County, Senior College (4 Yr.). Private, enrollment 2056, M-2056, F-0. Atlanta, GA 30314, Telephone 404-681-2800. Founded 1867.

Morehouse School of Medicine, Fulton County, Doctoral. Private, enrollment 127, M-69, F-58. Atlanta, GA 30310, Telephone 404-752-1000.

Morris Brown College, Fulton County, Senior College (4 Yr.). Private, African Methodist Episcopal, enrollment 1268, M-549, F-719. Atlanta, GA 30314, Telephone 404-525-7831. Founded 1881.

Moultrie Area Technical School, Colquitt County, Area Technical. Area school developed under State Department of Education policies, enrollment 1315, M-556, F-759. Moultrie, GA 31768, Telephone 912-985-2297.

North Georgia College, Lumpkin County, Senior College (4 Yr.). A unit of the University System of Georgia, enrollment 2120, M-861, F-1259. Dahlonega, GA 30533, Telephone 404-864-3391. Founded 1873.

North Georgia Technical-Vocational School, Habersham County, Technical-Vocational. Area school developed under State Department of Education policies, enrollment 4316, M-1938, F-2378. Clarkesville, GA 30523, Telephone 404-754-2131. Founded 1943.

Oglethorpe University, DeKalb County, Senior College (4 Yr.). Private, enrollment 1029, M-422, F-607. Atlanta, GA 30319, Telephone 404-261-1441. Founded 1835.

Oxford College of Emory University, Newton County, Senior College (2 Yr.). Private, Methodist, enrollment 463, M-244, F-219 (1982). Oxford, GA 30267, Telephone 404-786-7051. Founded 1836.

Paine College, Richmond County, Senior College (4 Yr.). Private, Methodist, enrollment 752, M-240, F-512. Augusta, GA 30910, Telephone 404-722-4471. Founded 1882.

Pickens Area Technical School, Pickens County, Area Technical. Area school developed under State Department of Education policies, enrollment 1445, M-544, F-901. Jasper, GA 30143, Telephone 404-692-3411.

Piedmont College, Habersham County, Senior College (4 Yr.). Private, Congregational, enrollment 388, M-203, F-185. Demorest, GA 30535, Telephone 404-778-8033. Founded 1897.

Phillips College, Richmond County, Junior College (2 Yr.). Augusta, GA 30902. Founded 1948.

Phillips College, Muscogee County, Junior College (2 Yr.). Columbus, GA 31901. Founded 1951.

Reinhardt College, Cherokee County, Junior College (2 Yr.). Private, Methodist, enrollment 514, M-215, F-299. Waleska, GA 30183, Telephone 404-479-1454. Founded 1883.

Savannah Area Technical School, Chatham County, Area Technical. Area school developed under State Department of Education policies, enrollment 3797, M-1475, F-2322. Savannah, GA 31499, Telephone 912-352-1464.

Savannah College of Art and Design, Chatham County, Senior College (4 Yr.). Private, enrollment N/A. Savannah, GA 31401, Telephone 912-236-7458.

Savannah State College, Chatham County, Senior College (4 Yr.). A unit of the University System of Georgia, enrollment 1824, M-843, F-981. Savannah, GA 31401, Telephone 912-356-2186. Founded 1890.

Shorter College, Floyd County, Senior College (4 Yr.). Private, Baptist, enrollment 726, M-319, F-407. Rome, GA 30161, Telephone 404-291-2121.

Southern College of Technology, Cobb County, Senior College (4 Yr.). A unit of the University System of Georgia, enrollment 3769, M-3160, F-609. Marietta, GA 30060, Telephone 404-424-7272. Founded 1948.

South Georgia College, Coffee County, Junior College (2 Yr.). A unit of the University System of Georgia, enrollment 784, M-305, F-479. Douglas, GA 31533, Telephone 912-384-1100. Founded 1906.

South Georgia Technical and Vocational School, Sumter County, Technical-Vocational. Area school developed under State Department of Education policies, enrollment 2037, M-1085, F-952. Americus, GA 31709, Telephone 912-928-0283.

Spelman College. Fulton County, Senior College (4 Yr.). Private, enrollment 1642, M-0, F-1642. Atlanta, GA 30314, Telephone 404-681-3643. Founded 1881.

Swainsboro Area Technical School, Emanuel County, Area Technical. Area school developed under State Department of Education policies, enrollment 1577, M-549, F-1028. Swainsboro, GA 30401, Telephone 912-237-6465.

Thomas Technical Institute, Thomas County, Area Technical. Area school developed under State Department of Education policies, enrollment 1305, M-442, F-863. Thomasville, GA 31799, Telephone 912-228-6428.

Thomas College, Thomas County, Junior College (2 Yr.). Private, enrollment 391, M-136, F-255. Thomasville, GA 31792, Telephone 912-226-1621. Founded 1950.

Tift College, Monroe County, Senior College (4 Yr.). Private, Baptist enrollment 494, M-59, F-435. Forsyth, GA 31029, Telephone 912-994-2515. Founded 1847.

Toccoa Falls College, Stephens County, Senior College (4 Yr.). Private, enrollment 642, M-335, F-307. Toccoa Falls, GA 30598, Telephone 404-886-6831. Founded 1907.

Troup County Area Technical School, Troup County, Area Technical. Area school developed under State Department of Education policies, enrollment 1222, M-555, F-687. LaGrange, GA 30240, Telephone 404-882-0080.

Truett-McConnell College, White County, Junior College (2 Yr.). Private, Baptist, enrollment 902, M-412, F-490. Cleveland, GA 30528, Telephone 404-865-2135. Founded 1946.

University of Georgia, The. Clarke County, Doctoral. A unit of the University System of Georgia, enrollment 26,547, M-12,476, F-14,071. Athens, GA 30602, Telephone 404-542-3030. Founded 1785.

Upson County Area Technical School, Upson County, Area Technical. Area school developed under State Department of Education policies, enrollment 718, M-244, F-474. Thomaston, GA 30286, Telephone 404-647-9616.

Valdosta Area Technical School, Lowndes County, Area Technical. Area school developed under State Department of Education policies, enrollment 1915, M-782, F-1133. Valdosta, GA 31602, Telephone 912-333-2100.

Valdosta State College, Lowndes County, Senior College (4 Yr.). A unit of the University System of Georgia, enrollment 7056, M-2914, F-4142. Valdosta, GA 31698, Telephone 912-335-5800. Founded 1906.

Walker County Area Technical School, Walker County, Area Technical. Area school developed under State Department of Education policies, enrollment 2492, M-817, F-1675. Rock Springs, GA 30739, Telephone 404-764-1016.

Waycross-Ware Technical School, Ware County, Area Technical. Area school developed under State Department of Education policies, enrollment 1497, M-527, F-970. Waycross, GA 31501, Telephone 912-283-2002.

Waycross Junior College, Ware County, Junior College (2 Yr.). A unit of the University System of Georgia, enrollment 536, M-176, F-360. Waycross, GA 31501, Telephone 912-285-6135. Founded 1976.

Wesleyan College, Bibb County, Senior College (4 Yr.). Private, Methodist, enrollment 387, M-4, F-383. Macon, GA 31207, Telephone 912-477-1110. Founded 1836.

West Georgia College, Carroll County, Senior College (4 Yr.). A unit of the University System of Georgia, enrollment 6396, M-2476, F-3920. Carrollton, GA 30118, Telephone 404-834-1311. Founded 1933.

Woodrow Wilson College of Law, Fulton County, Doctoral. Atlanta, GA 30308. Founded 1932.

Young Harris College, Union County, Junior College (2 Yr.). Private, United Methodist, enrollment 382, M-169, F-213. Young Harris, GA 30582, Telephone 404-379-3112. Founded 1886.

HIGHWAYS

Georgia can boast an excellent network of Interstate, Federal, State, and County highways. According to the Department of Transportation records for 1987, the Georgia highway mileage is as follows: state routes, 17,821.55 miles; county roads, 76,655.35 miles; city streets, 11,842.29 miles; total paved, 67,720.21 miles; for a state total of 106,385.67. A chart showing a breakdown by county follows.

Highway Mileage: 1987

County	Total Road Mileage	Rank[1] of Total	State Routes	County Roads	City Streets	Total Paved
Appling	1,056.12	15	119.94	899.07	37.11	324.66
Atkinson	518.43	99	83.67	412.59	22.17	203.14
Bacon	606.05	75	58.68	517.28	30.09	216.11
Baker	382.30	140	78.08	298.77	5.45	175.01
Baldwin	513.83	102	87.35	359.80	66.59	399.49
Banks	435.28	125	111.26	306.37	17.65	255.52
Barrow	464.70	114	102.10	302.58	60.02	376.50
Bartow	1,001.82	19	168.63	751.56	81.63	861.69
Ben Hill	496.29	105	82.85	360.43	53.01	267.53
Berrien	832.55	37	117.68	664.67	50.20	302.81
Bibb	1,005.01	17	148.26	416.20	436.81	901.99
Bleckley	419.68	130	72.87	317.97	28.84	271.42
Brantley	602.23	76	96.83	484.85	20.55	196.80
Brooks	775.31	46	112.60	607.74	54.97	367.41
Bryan	391.57	138	117.65	253.59	20.33	222.61
Bulloch	1,417.24	6	180.92	1,140.61	95.71	589.13
Burke	1,106.17	14	194.79	864.04	47.34	524.26
Butts	406.73	133	60.96	313.21	32.56	250.35
Calhoun	354.16	143	96.40	233.44	24.32	216.58
Camden	481.03	109	126.53	290.77	62.40	295.78
Candler	487.69	108	81.99	376.10	29.60	222.55
Carroll	1,280.36	7	180.31	980.93	119.12	883.65
Catoosa	467.92	112	67.29	365.45	35.18	461.63
Charlton	398.51	136	119.63	255.27	23.61	217.67
Chatham	1,138.33	11	153.20	349.88	634.70	972.73
Chattahoochee	101.12	159	32.75	62.67	5.70	75.98
Chattooga	527.86	93	77.61	403.96	46.29	456.02
Cherokee	945.31	24	136.35	763.48	45.48	814.14
Clarke	519.72	96	50.25	303.09	165.39	493.74
Clay	250.54	153	52.84	185.28	12.42	144.86
Clayton	776.75	45	91.62	555.59	129.54	740.62
Clinch	614.62	72	151.17	438.18	25.27	264.77
Cobb	1,899.63	3	196.64	1,471.00	231.99	1,813.38
Coffee	1,133.20	12	184.55	848.07	100.58	504.94
Colquitt	1,130.93	13	139.96	866.76	124.21	611.61
Columbia	606.83	74	119.07	468.99	17.71	449.66
Cook	531.82	90	69.13	394.47	68.22	281.83
Coweta	934.92	26	146.50	701.64	86.76	846.61
Crawford	421.65	128	69.17	347.21	5.27	177.13
Crisp	696.04	54	91.31	528.12	76.61	390.97
Dade	324.91	148	90.98	214.23	19.49	265.28

County	Total Road Mileage	Rank[1] of Total	State Routes	County Roads	City Streets	Total Paved
Dawson	334.45	147	82.42	249.52	2.51	177.74
Decatur	988.68	21	223.20	662.90	102.58	540.87
DeKalb	2,039.85	2	187.43	1,624.87	223.15	1,926.24
Dodge	916.19	28	146.70	710.84	58.65	432.45
Dooly	797.52	41	131.85	625.77	39.90	319.55
Dougherty	753.38	49	106.11	277.52	369.25	632.56
Douglas	652.28	62	88.02	514.83	48.27	565.83
Early	732.79	52	148.98	544.57	39.24	358.26
Echols	272.20	151	93.12	174.68	4.40	147.89
Effingham	651.02	64	100.97	516.83	33.22	288.76
Elbert	676.57	57	93.23	544.97	37.00	404.41
Emanuel	1,210.70	9	219.80	897.44	93.46	516.40
Evans	361.75	142	61.41	273.07	27.27	196.43
Fannin	534.65	89	67.05	439.42	28.18	232.24
Fayette	521.37	95	83.02	347.88	90.47	389.90
Floyd	1,053.12	16	134.39	773.41	145.32	1,005.54
Forsyth	655.81	60	104.40	536.87	14.54	514.82
Franklin	651.85	63	169.65	438.25	43.95	417.09
Fulton	3,124.22	1	355.12	1,080.61	1,682.70	2,878.02
Gilmer	497.70	104	80.18	401.58	15.94	267.29
Glascock	231.69	156	40.28	188.61	2.80	133.08
Glynn	597.69	78	125.88	388.17	83.64	429.10
Gordon	733.57	51	142.70	547.33	43.25	634.00
Grady	802.00	40	108.94	615.33	77.73	490.03
Greene	569.88	85	98.72	431.86	39.30	286.91
Gwinnett	1,845.71	4	212.41	1,433.60	199.70	1,576.57
Habersham	628.99	67	111.94	450.65	66.40	412.88
Hall	1,235.15	8	234.69	903.59	94.54	981.28
Hancock	587.05	80	75.01	501.73	10.31	285.31
Haralson	642.26	65	86.37	491.14	64.67	398.18
Harris	641.26	66	181.45	429.18	30.63	445.73
Hart	666.47	58	92.73	638.02	35.72	437.03
Heard	441.69	122	67.12	366.03	6.52	191.93
Henry	856.50	35	117.21	696.80	42.49	572.39
Houston	820.25	38	142.34	401.45	250.02	686.80
Irwin	588.74	79	91.06	474.79	22.89	280.78
Jackson	771.74	48	189.90	534.71	47.13	518.50
Jasper	568.39	86	110.77	442.70	13.26	265.97
Jeff Davis	628.86	68	64.97	525.73	38.16	212.61
Jefferson	810.59	39	185.81	559.35	65.10	473.89
Jenkins	516.32	100	79.89	409.87	26.56	249.59
Johnson	530.51	91	85.62	421.01	23.88	253.66
Jones	519.23	97	85.84	420.78	12.61	241.05
Lamar	402.98	135	52.07	320.03	29.33	268.48
Lanier	337.13	146	90.97	223.97	22.19	157.86
Laurens	1,517.74	5	264.91	1,112.22	140.61	746.99
Lee	430.50	126	90.54	325.43	14.53	243.49
Liberty	405.62	134	129.59	198.31	77.72	256.69
Lincoln	353.07	144	76.73	267.40	8.94	213.31
Long	310.63	149	61.02	238.72	10.89	131.11
Lowndes	1,166.35	10	175.63	793.87	196.22	620.68
Lumpkin	437.33	124	79.78	336.58	20.97	228.89
Macon	619.68	70	128.04	447.66	43.98	318.13
Madison	691.10	55	107.85	563.03	20.22	338.49

217

County	Total Road Mileage	Rank[1] of Total	State Routes	County Roads	City Streets	Total Paved
Marion	451.36	118	130.07	312.26	9.03	269.35
McDuffie	490.48	107	92.85	357.40	40.23	322.25
McIntosh	290.22	150	92.49	181.47	16.26	163.78
Meriwether	850.83	36	169.94	617.65	63.24	536.89
Miller	476.77	110	65.97	393.06	17.74	218.86
Mitchell	906.48	29	177.87	659.72	68.89	496.07
Monroe	599.88	77	154.49	423.68	20.31	406.25
Montgomery	451.03	119	84.73	329.31	36.99	234.68
Morgan	570.29	84	88.26	451.27	30.76	423.69
Murray	526.80	94	100.38	400.18	26.17	364.13
Muscogee	859.32	34	84.31	99.33	672.21	835.03
Newton	733.84	50	128.14	527.04	78.66	534.53
Oconee	376.22	141	52.63	309.55	14.04	251.46
Oglethorpe	575.19	83	77.64	488.02	9.53	262.54
Paulding	619.16	71	105.51	494.26	19.39	384.72
Peach	341.79	145	64.87	223.36	53.56	240.62
Pickens	456.61	116	73.70	365.09	17.65	276.34
Pierce	657.10	59	75.05	541.32	40.73	245.31
Pike	417.26	131	67.25	340.81	9.20	215.86
Polk	683.22	56	74.29	535.24	73.69	583.64
Pulaski	391.77	137	105.73	261.74	24.30	235.37
Putnam	530.15	92	81.88	422.93	25.34	375.61
Quitman	168.88	158	39.19	122.00	7.69	102.75
Rabun	475.13	111	63.39	384.65	27.09	227.19
Randolph	513.95	101	83.92	391.23	38.80	296.93
Richmond	1,004.15	18	121.34	702.15	180.44	908.99
Rockdale	450.18	120	54.00	366.13	30.05	409.15
Schley	243.96	154	58.12	174.49	11.35	151.82
Screven	790.95	43	126.15	632.99	31.81	412.61
Seminole	462.79	115	90.98	343.63	26.46	280.81
Spalding	652.97	61	63.59	494.37	95.01	532.13
Stephens	491.23	106	70.25	371.22	49.76	353.22
Stewart	429.27	127	103.53	302.02	23.72	206.67
Sumter	781.63	44	177.58	518.93	85.12	545.39
Talbot	466.82	113	132.72	320.42	13.68	259.24
Taliaferro	234.72	155	58.33	173.21	3.18	131.33
Tattnall	929.34	27	145.06	724.59	59.69	390.71
Taylor	575.88	82	147.94	402.91	25.03	287.83
Telfair	609.07	73	150.47	393.35	65.25	306.18
Terrell	512.11	103	90.23	382.95	38.93	280.28
Thomas	943.24	25	163.20	621.93	158.11	604.04
Tift	707.07	53	91.43	524.15	91.49	419.81
Toombs	772.92	47	149.90	494.17	128.85	366.74
Towns	227.89	157	55.43	163.74	8.72	139.24
Treutlen	421.25	129	117.66	283.59	20.00	233.37
Troup	860.88	33	175.77	525.98	158.30	731.74
Turner	552.35	88	100.36	412.29	39.70	243.84
Twiggs	440.88	123	107.82	322.65	10.41	248.15
Union	455.58	117	90.60	359.30	5.68	191.85
Upson	586.26	81	75.95	458.81	51.50	500.83
Walker	886.82	31	166.76	638.77	81.29	814.36
Walton	793.36	42	101.35	621.52	70.49	610.73
Ware	965.04	22	132.14	703.50	129.40	405.61
Warren	443.97	121	94.56	329.15	20.26	246.37
Washington	957.90	23	153.75	751.79	52.36	474.55

County	Total Road Mileage	Rank[1] of Total	State Routes	County Roads	City Streets	Total Paved
Wayne	902.15	30	109.72	716.79	75.64	364.86
Webster	259.45	152	50.85	204.81	3.79	152.38
Wheeler	412.81	132	84.98	313.09	14.74	213.41
White	389.61	139	102.67	269.43	15.45	230.95
Whitfield	867.11	32	95.00	652.93	119.18	812.70
Wilcox	621.53	69	112.17	481.59	27.77	239.93
Wilkes	563.85	87	100.16	422.66	41.03	337.78
Wilkinson	518.91	98	123.35	350.61	44.95	293.28
Worth	998.11	20	154.93	784.78	58.40	417.24
Georgia	106.385.67		17,821.55	76,655.35	11,842.29	67,720.21

[1]Rank: 1 = highest (range, 1–159)
When counties share the same rank, the next lower rank is omitted. Because of rounded data, counties may have identical values shown, but different ranks.

HISTORICAL SOCIETIES

ALBANY
Thronateeska Heritage Foundation
100 Roosevelt Ave. (31701)
912-432-6955

ALMA
Historical Society of Alma-Bacon County
P.O. Box 2026 (31510)
912-632-8450

ALPHARETTA
Old Milton County Historical and Genealogical Society, Inc.
367 Karen Dr. (30201)

ATHENS
Athens-Clarke Heritage Foundation
Fire Hall 2, 489 Prince Ave. (30601)
404-353-1801

Southern Historical Association
Dept. of History, University of Georgia (30602)
404-542-8848

ATLANTA
Atlanta Historical Society, Inc.
3101 Andrews Dr., N.W. (30305)
404-261-1837

Georgia Trust for Historic Preservation, Inc.
1516 Peachtree St., N.W. (30309)
404-881-9980

Hart County, Georgia Historical Society
2073 McLendon Ave., N.W. (30307)
404-377-5612

Historic Preservation Section, Department of Natural Resources
270 Washington St., Room 704 (30334)
404-656-2840

AUGUSTA
Richmond County Historical Society
Reese Library, Augusta College, 2500 Walton Way (30910)
404-737-1745

BARNESVILLE
Barnesville-Lamar County Historical Society
888 Thomaston St. (30204)
404-358-1289

BAXLEY
Appling County Historical Society, Inc.
P.O. Box 1063 (31513)
912-367-2431

BLAKELEY
Early County Historical Society, Inc.
255 N. Main (31723)

BRUNSWICK
Coastal APDC Advisory Council on
  Historic Preservation
P.O. Box 1917 (31521)
912-264-7363

BUCHANAN
Haralson County Historical Society,
  Inc.
Courthouse Square (30113)

CALHOUN
Gordon County Historical Society,
  Inc.
P.O. Box 342 (30701)

CARROLLTON
Carroll County Historical Society,
  Inc.
%West Georgia Regional Library
P.O. Box 160 (30117)

CARTERSVILLE
Etowah Valley Historical Society
Rt. 2, Kingston (30145)

CEDARTOWN
Polk County Historical Society
P.O. Box 7 (30125)

CLEVELAND
White County Historical Society
Box 281 (30528)

CLINTON
Old Clinton Historical Society, Inc.
  (31032)
912-986-3384

COCHRAN
Bleckley County Historical Society
Middle Georgia College (31014)
912-934-6221

COLLEGE PARK
College Park Historical Society, Inc.
P.O. Box F (30337)

COLUMBUS
Historic Columbus Foundation, Inc.
P.O. Box 5312 (31906)
404-322-0756

Historic District Preservation
  Society, Inc.
P.O. Box 263 (31902)
404-571-2245

CONYERS
Rockdale County Historical Society
P.O. Box 351 (30207)

CRAWFORDVILLE
Taliaferro County Historical Society,
  Inc.
P.O. Box 32 (30631)
404-456-2140

CUTHBERT
Randolph Historical Society, Inc.
P.O. Box 456 (31740)

DALTON
Whitfield-Murray Historical Society,
  Inc.
715 Chattanooga Ave. (30720)
404-278-0217

DECATUR
DeKalb History Society
Old Courthouse on the Square
  (30030)
404-373-1088

DUBLIN
Laurens County Historical Society,
  Inc.
P.O. Box 1461 (31021)
912-272-9242

EAST POINT
East Point Historical Society, Inc.
City Hall Annex, 2847 Main St.
  (30344)
404-767-4656

EATONTON
Eatonton-Putnam County Historical
  Society, Inc.
P.O. Box 331 (31024)
404-485-7701

ELBERTON
Elbert County Historical Society, Inc.
P.O. Box 1033 (30635)

FAIRBURN
Old Campbell County Historical Society, Inc.
P.O. Box 153 (30213)

FAYETTEVILLE
Fayette County Historical Society, Inc.
P.O. Box 421 (30214)
404-461-7152

FOLKSTON
Charlton County Historical Society
Rt. 3, Box 142-C (31537)
912-496-7401

FORT GAINES
Ft. Gaines Historical Society, Inc.
P.O. Box 6 (31751)

GRIFFIN
Griffin Historical and Preservation Society
P.O. Box 196 (30224)

GUYTON
Guyton Historical Society
P.O. Box 15 (31312)
912-772-3344

HAWKINSVILLE
Pulaski Historical Commission, Inc.
P.O. Box 447 (31036)
912-738-1717

HINESVILLE
Liberty County Historical Society
P.O. Box 797 (31313)

JEFFERSON
Jackson County Historical Society
% President, Rt. 2, Box 222
Commerce (30529)

JONESBORO
Historical Jonesboro, Inc.
P.O. Box 922 (30236)

LAFAYETTE
Walker County Historical Society
P.O. Box 707 (30728)

LAGRANGE
Ockuskee Historical Society, Inc.
P.O. Box 1051 (30241)

Troup County Historical Society, Inc.—Archives
P.O. Box 1051 (30241)
404-884-1828

LAWRENCEVILLE
Gwinnett County Historical Society, Inc.
P.O. Box 261 (30246)
404-963-9584

LUMPKIN
Stewart County Historical Commission
P.O. Box 817 (31815)
912-838-4201

MACON
Georgia Baptist Historical Society
Mercer University Library,
Colman Ave. (31207)
912-745-6811

Macon Heritage Foundation, Inc.
P.O. Box 6092 (31208)
912-742-5084

Middle Georgia Historical Society, Inc.
935 High Street (31201)
912-743-3851

METTER
Candler County Historical Society
P.O. Box 235 (30439)
912-685-2771

MILLEDGEVILLE
Old Capital Historical Society
P.O. Box 4 (31061)

MONROE
Historical Society of Walton County, Inc.
238 N. Broad St. 30655

MONTICELLO
Jasper County Historical
  Foundation, Inc.
128 Robert Dr. (31064)
404-468-6637

MORROW
Clayton County Heritage
  Association
P.O. Box 305 (30260)
404-961-3460

MOULTRIE
Colquitt County Historical Society
Norman Park, Rt. 1 (31711)

NEWNAN
Newnan-Coweta Historical Society
P.O. Box 1001 (30264)
404-251-0207

OXFORD
Oxford Historical Shrine Society
P.O. Box 243 (30267)

PORTAL
Portal Heritage Society
% Denver Hollingsworth
301 College Blvd., Statesboro (30458)
912-764-3047

REIDSVILLE
Tattnall County Historic
  Preservation, Inc.
P.O. Box 392 (30453)
912-557-4802

ROME
Northwest Georgia Historical and
  Genealogical Society
P.O. Box 2484 (30161)

ROOPVILLE
Roopville Historical Society and
  Archives
124 Old Franklin St. (30171)
404-854-4170

ROSWELL
Roswell Historical Society
P.O. Box 274 (30075)
404-992-1665

ST. MARYS
Guale Historical Society, Inc.
P.O. Box 398 (31558)

St. Marys Historic Preservation
  Commission
414 Osborne St. (31558)
912-882-4667

ST. SIMONS ISLAND
Coastal Georgia Historical Society—
  Museum of Coastal History
P.O. Box 1136 (31522)
912-638-4666

Historical Society of the South
  Georgia Conference, United
  Methodist Church
P.O. Box 407 (31522)
912-638-4050

SAVANNAH
Coastal Heritage Society
1 Ft. Jackson Rd. (31402)
912-232-3945

Georgia Historical Society
501 Whitaker St. (31499)
912-944-2128

Historic Savannah Foundation, Inc.
P.O. Box 1733 (31402)

SOCIAL CIRCLE
Historic Preservation Society of
  Social Circle, Inc.
P.O. Box 832 (30279)
404-464-2345

SOPERTON
Treutlen County Historical Society
Treutlen County Courthouse (30457)
912-529-6711

SWAINSBORO
Emanuel Historic Preservation
  Society
P.O. Box 1101 (30401)

THOMASVILLE
Thomas County Historical Society,
  Inc.

P.O. Box 1922 (31799)
912-226-7664

VALDOSTA
Lowndes County Historical Society
P.O. Box 434 (31601)
912-247-4780

Southern Jewish Historical Society
P.O. Box 179 (31698)
912-333-5947

WASHINGTON
Washington-Wilkes Historical
  Foundation, Inc.
308 E. Robert Toombs Ave. (30673)
404-678-2105

WATKINSVILLE
Watkinsville Historical Society
Main Street (30177)

WAYNESBORO
Burke County Historical Association
% Mrs. Alden Dye
Quaker Rd. (30830)

WINDER
Barrow County Historical Society
409 Candler St. (30680)
404-867-9003

WRIGHTSVILLE
Johnson County Historical Society,
  Inc.
P.O. Box 86 (31096)

HISTORIC SITES

Historic Sites are features of extreme historical significance. These sites are maintained by the Georgia Department of Natural Resources. Listed below are the Historic Sites throughout the state and a brief description of each. Normal operating hours for all are: Tuesday through Saturday 9 to 5; Sunday 2 to 5:30; Closed Mondays, Thanksgiving and Christmas.

Alexander H. Stephens House and Confederate Museum. In Crawfordsville on Ga. 22. Was the antebellum home of the Vice President of the Confederacy.

Dahlonega Gold Museum. Town Square. Commemorates the country's first major gold rush near here in 1828. A branch of the U.S. Mint operated in the vicinity for 23 years.

Etowah Indian Mounds. 3 miles S.W. of Cartersville. Area was occupied between A.D. 1,000 and A.D. 1,500. Was the largest Indian town in the Etowah Valley.

Fort King George. Near Darien. Fort was the southernmost outpost of the British colonies in 1721. Formerly was an Indian village site and Spanish mission site.

Fort McAllister. Near Richmond, 10 miles E. on Ga. 144. Was the key to Savannah's fortifications during the War Between the States. Fell to Sherman in 1864.

Hofwyl-Broadfield Plantation. 7 mile S. of Darien. An antebellum rice plantation.

Jarrell Plantation. 8 miles S.E. of Juliette. A 7.5 acre working farm spanning the years from the 1840s to the 1940s, complete with animals, crops, mill, blacksmith shop, and syrup evaporators.

Kolomoki Indian Mounds. 9 miles N. of Blakely. Historic settlement dating to A.D. 800 includes seven burial and temple mounds.

Lapham-Patterson House. In Thomasville at 626 N. Dawson St. Victorian mansion built in 1884.

Midway Museum. On U.S. 17 next to Church. Raised cottage style. Furniture, documents, and artifacts date from the early 18th to the mid-19th centuries.

New Echota. Exit 131, I-75. Capital of the Cherokee Indian Nation from 1825 to 1838. Sequoyah, the inventor of the Cherokee alphabet, lived here for a time.

Sunbury. Near Midway, 8 miles E. of I-95. Marks the spot of Georgia's second largest colonial seaport. An important Revolutionary War and War of 1812 site.

Toombs House. In Washington on Augusta Road. Built in 1797, the present structure is the core of the home of Confederate General Robert Toombs.

Traveler's Rest. 6 miles W. of Toccoa on U.S. 123. Built between 1815 and 1830. Served as a plantation house, tavern, trading post, and post office. Authentic furnishings.

Vann House. U.S. 76, 3 miles W. of Chatsworth. House was built in 1804 and is a fine example of Cherokee Indian wealth and culture.

HISTORY

Georgia, the largest state east of the Mississippi River with 58,876 square miles and a 1970 population of 4,589,575 (estimated to be over 5 million in 1976), was first explored by the Spaniards, when Francisco Gordillo and Esteban Gómez traveled the island-fringed coast. Later the interior was penetrated by Hernando de Soto. The absence of gold and the failure of the earliest colonies nearby discouraged serious efforts to settle the area until 1566. In that year Pedro Menéndez de Avilés, founder of St. Augustine only one year before, arrived on Santa Catalina (St. Catherine's) Island and conferred with the local Indian chief Guale, by whose name the entire section ultimately came to be known. First the Jesuits and then later the Franciscans acted as missionaries to the natives. After the nearly disastrous Juanillo revolt of 1597, the Spanish reconstituted Guale so effectively that in 1606 Bishop Altamirano of Cuba made an official episcopal visitation and confirmed more than 1,000 natives in their Roman Catholic faith.

The half-century following Altamirano's visit is usually looked upon as the golden age of the Spanish in Georgia. During this period the priests at the missions, protected by Spanish troops, catechized the Indians and instructed them in settled agricultural ways. Periodic attempts were made to expand the mission system into the interior (Tama), but Guale remained throughout the Spanish period an exposed, lightly defended mission province that never, so far as is known, attracted "permanent" European settlers.

With the coming of the English to Charles Town (Charleston) in 1670, Guale was immediately threatened. The Carolina traders in the interior and the raids against the missions by English and French pirates signaled the end for the Spanish in Georgia. They had little choice but to fall back on St. Augustine, and by 1686 had retreated beyond the St. Mary's River (later part of Georgia's southern boundary). Old Guale became land disputed by Spain, England, and France.

English period. At first the English in Carolina had much their own way with the Indians, but the Yamassee War, which broke out in 1715, nearly destroyed Carolina and caused its influence to suffer. The Spanish reasserted their position on the Chattahoochee, and the French built Ft. Toulouse in the heart of the Alabama country in 1717.

There had been many English schemes to settle old Guale, including Sir Robert Montgomery's Azilia, but they had all come to naught. So the Carolinians cooperated with a group of philanthropists, members of Parliament, and merchants, who in the late 1720s and early 1730s seemed to have an excellent chance of bringing a new British colony to reality. The leaders of this movement were Sir John Perceval (earl of Egmont) and James Edward Oglethorpe. Initially Oglethorpe, who made a national name for himself as chairman of a parliamentary jails committee, thought of a new American colony as a refuge for released debtors, but as the movement gained momentum the debtor-province idea was pushed aside by other philanthropic, mercantile, and imperial motives. As finally constituted, Georgia was peopled not by debtors but by small merchants and shopkeepers, unemployed laborers, and a few gentlemen.

A royal charter for Georgia, named in honor of George II, was granted to 21 trustees on June 9, 1732. Georgia's chartered limits were defined as lying between the Savannah and Altamaha rivers and extending from their origins to the western sea. The power of the trust was restricted to 21 years, after which time governmental power reverted to the crown.

Oglethorpe volunteered to escort the first settlers to the colony. He moved to a high bluff on the south bank of the Savannah River, arriving there February 1, 1773. Here Oglethorpe formally received Tomochichi of the Yamassee and proceeded, through the good offices of trader John Musgrove and his half-breed wife Mary, to make an alliance of friendship. His initial success with the natives was followed by a treaty with the Creek in May. Later understandings were reached with the Cherokee, Chickasaw, and even the remote Choctaw. Oglethorpe's Indian diplomacy, based upon an acute awareness of the importance of friendly relations along the southern frontier, was climaxed by his trip to Coweta in the heart of Creek country just prior to the outbreak of the War of Jenkins' Ear in 1739.

One of Oglethorpe's most noted successes was his town plan for Savannah, with its wards and tithings focused upon squares placed at regular intervals. The basic design was used at various other settlements including Ebenezer, Darien, and later Brunswick, but nowhere has the original layout survived so well as in Savannah.

Georgia proved to be a haven for both British and continental political and religious refugees. The Salzburg Lutherans, who arrived in 1734, fled persecution at the hands of their Roman Catholic archbishop. They were industrious and frugal, and their settlement at Ebenezer was the most prosperous Georgia town during the trusteeship period. The Highland Scots first came in a group in 1735, and founded New Inverness

(Darien). In the same year the first Moravians to come to America arrived in Savannah. They soon opened a school for Indians at Irene, which, however, did not survive the Moravians' departure from the colony by 1740. According to the charter, "liberty of conscience" was permitted to all "in the worship of God," but Roman Catholics were specifically excluded from entering Georgia. In July, 1733, a group of Jewish immigrants was welcomed by Oglethorpe in spite of what he knew would be trustee disapproval. Jews were not singled out for exclusion, however, so he used this oversight as the basis upon which to permit them.

After escorting the first transport of Salzburgers (under John Martin Bolzius) to Ebenezer in 1734, Oglethorpe returned to England. From the trustees he secured passage of three acts that would give Georgia the distinctive character he wanted it to assume. The presence of Negroes or Negro slavery was forbidden, rum was outlawed, and a third act regulated the Indian trade in Georgia's chartered limits. It was clear from the start that the trustees' regulations would not be docilely accepted. The restriction on rum was impossible to enforce, and the act became a dead letter by 1742; the interdicts against the size and nature of land-holding were gradually withdrawn, and even the Indian Act was emasculated when the apprehensive South Carolinians resorted to legal action in Britain. The Negro Act was abandoned too in spite of support from the Salzburgers and the Highland Scots.

Oglethorpe originally was instructed by Robert Walpole to make no belligerent moves on the frontier, but the English and Spanish drifted into war by the fall of 1739. Oglethorpe had returned to America in 1738 with his own regiment and was anxious to seize Florida, but his 1740 expedition against St. Augustine failed and he fell back to his Ft. Frederica base. The Spaniards invaded Georgia in 1742 and captured part of St. Simon's Island but, after several sharp skirmishes on July 7, they beat a hasty retreat to Florida. Thus Spain's last serious effort to regain its old mission territory was repelled. In 1743 Oglethorpe made another unsuccessful effort to take St. Augustine, and shortly afterward he sailed to England for the last time.

By 1741 Georgia had grown so that it was

225

divided administratively into two counties, one centered at Frederica and the other at Savannah. Oglethorpe was entrusted with the southern district, and William Stephens the northern, but as long as Oglethorpe remained in the province he assumed overall control. After Oglethorpe's departure, Stephens was made president of a united colony and presided over a group of assistants until 1751. In that same year the trust called together Georgia's first elected assembly; although it had no power to legislate, it made sensible recommendations to London.

Religion and men of the cloth played a large role in the founding and forwarding of Georgia. The Church of England was expected to be prominent in the colony and an Anglican priest accompanied the first settlers, but this faith never prospered. Usually the ministers died, left the colony, or were found unsuited to their posts. Charles and John Wesley crossed with Oglethorpe in 1735–1736, but both became disillusioned and left Georgia; George Whitefield was more often out of the colony than in it, and he was more interested in his orphanage at Bethesda than in traditional pastoral cares. From the beginning the dissenters outnumbered the Anglicans. The Scottish Presbyterians and the Lutheran Salzburgers were the most homogeneous religious groups in trustee Georgia.

Efforts to secure competent schoolmasters for the colony proved unsatisfactory. Whitefield's school at the Bethesda orphanage was the most reliable during th period prior to the American Revolution, but his plans to see it develop into a colonial college never materialized. Georgians were too busy hacking a place in the wilderness to engage in *belles lettres*. However, there was much polemical literature written about Georgia, some of it by people who actually lived in the colony. One of the finest satires in eighteenth-century America was done by a group of Georgia "refugees" in Carolina. *A True and Historical Narrative of the Colony of Georgia*, first published in Charleston in 1741, was a general attack on trustee policy preceded by a witty mock dedication to Oglethorpe. William Stephens produced a lively and topical journal, and Francis Moore published one of the century's best travel accounts. The Wesleys' journals and diaries, similar to Whitefield's, reveal more about their authors than about Georgia.

These and other records of the period show that one of the striking failures of the trustees was their inability to establish a firm economic foundation for their colony. They did little to create a practical alternative to a staple crop economy. It was impossible to initiate a rum-sugar-molasses for staves-shingles-lumber trade with the West Indies, and Oglethorpe's idea of a province of subsistence farmers was not feasible on a warlike frontier. The economic situation seemed desperate during the Spanish war, but an upturn was apparent before the trust relinquished its charter.

The experiment with silk, upon which the trustees pinned so many hopes, seemed to be approaching success in the 1750s, but sericulture, which prospered only with subsidies, declined when those subsidies were withdrawn. The same held true for indigo. Some rice and cotton were grown for home use during the trusteeship, but the periods of significant production of both crops lay in the future. Various timber products were the most valuable Georgia exports during trustee years, and, although Savannah was hardly more than a crude village, by the 1740s it had begun to develop a distinctive life of its own. In response to its growth, merchants such as the Moravian John Brownfield, Francis Harris, and James Habersham engaged in a bustling trade that belied the comments of the province's critics that it was a wasteland. Although Georgia was largely undeveloped both politically and economically, the trustees surrendered a colony of about 3,500 people—perhaps as many as 1,000 of them black—to the king in 1752. After the surrender of the charter, Georgia, with the Negro and land restrictions removed, was free to develop as a colony reliant upon a staple crop economy supported by the institution of slavery.

With the coming of royal rule Georgia had for the first time a governor and a bicameral legislature comprised of an elected lower and an appointed upper house. The crown provided Georgia with effective courts, and a battery of royal officials saw to the running of government. The governor was a stronger official than in most of England's royal colonies. The salaries of Georgia's crown officials were provided by the British treasury, so they were less dependent upon the legislature than in other provinces.

Governor John Reynolds, who arrived in Savannah in 1754, had a highly unsatisfactory two-year term, during which he alienated virtually all political factions. He was succeeded by the clever and politic Henry Ellis, whose three years in office saw Georgia experience growth and prosperity as its internal affairs steadied. Ellis was followed by James Wright, who served from 1760 to 1776. His personal popularity, his obvious fondness for Georgia, and the respect in which he was held help explain why the colony was slow to join the Revolutionary movement.

Georgia was spared the hostilities associated with the French and Indian War (1754—1763), but profited enormously by its outcome. The southern boundary was extended to the St. Mary's River, and the Spanish and French were removed from Georgia's borders. Governor Wright, whose key words for the colony were expansion and defense, was able to secure an Indian cession in 1763 of all lands between the Ogeechee and Savannah to a point even north of Augusta. At the same time the natives gave up their claims to coastal lands south of the Altamaha River. Ten years later other significant cessions were made by the Creek and Cherokee, and settlers poured into these newly opened regions. Upper Georgia, in fact, was developing quite differently from the low country, where more organized settlement patterns still prevailed. In the later area a large and well-equipped group of Puritans moved into the Midway district and prospered so that their town of Sunbury was in 1761 designated an official port of entry; the Scotch-Irish located on the Ogeechee at Queensborough; more Germans came into Georgia and settled north of Savannah; a Quaker colony was created at Wrightsborough.

Revolution and early national period. By 1775 Georgia contained about 50,000 people, probably not quite half of them slaves. These blacks were concentrated in the lowcountry parishes, where rice and indigo were grown. Although there were some large slaveholders and landholders in Georgia, among them Wright, most people lived on small- to medium-sized farms. Augusta, with its strategic location on the Savannah, was the "metropolis" of the backcountry. Larger and more sedate Savannah prospered as the center of Georgia's administrative machinery. Its wharves hummed with activity, and its architecture reflected the prosperity of Oglethorpe's onetime modest creation. Georgia's first printer, James Johnston, arrived in Savannah in 1762 and began publication the following year of the *Georgia Gazette*. Dancing masters, booksellers, cobblers, peruke makers and teachers of all descriptions advertised in its pages, reflecting the vivid life of the town.

Politically all went smoothly for Wright until the Stamp Act Crisis. Although he weathered that storm, it had sharply divided the colony and made a complete return to the harmonious days before 1765 impossible. The lower house began to assert powers it had not claimed before. In 1771–1772 it engaged in a struggle over Wright's rejection of a Speaker for that body, and in 1773 a committee of correspondence was created. Georgia's reaction to the Intolerable Acts put the province more into the stream of the Revolutionary movement. Still Georgia failed to name delegates to the First Continental Congress (1774).

Wright used every legal means to keep Georgia out of the Revolution. He prorogued the assembly in January, 1775, to prevent it from appointing delegates to the Second Continental Congress, but this was his last effective step. Wright lingered on until January, 1776, but royal government was replaced during 1775 by a council of safety, a provincial congress, and organizations at the local level. Meeting in the summer of 1775, Georgia's second provincial congress named delegates to the Continental Congress. Lyman Hall, George Walton, and Button Gwinnett ultimately signed the Declaration of Independence.

By no means all Georgians thought that this action was a good thing. Royal officials, those recently arrived in America, numerous Anglicans, and many others counseled patience. Dissenters (in a large majority by 1775), small merchants and businessmen, much of the youth, and farmers in the backcountry seemed to favor the more redical party. It is likely that Georgia radicals outnumbered the Loyalists; however, the large undecided group might weight the scales in favor of either at a given time.

The radical camp drew up a constitution in 1776 and another in 1777, the later vesting a unicameral legislature with most authority. A judiciary and a weak executive were provided, the state was carved into eight counties, and the franchise was broadened. Religious freedom was granted to all, but non-Protestants could not sit in the assembly. Trial by jury as well as other customary privileges were assured in a bill of rights.

The hostilities threatened to destroy Georgia. In the backcountry there was civil warfare where quarter was neither asked nor given. On the coast unsuccessful forays were made against Florida, but Savannah itself was seized by British forces late in 1778. Augusta was captured also, but the English were disappointed when the up-country did not embrace George III. A Loyalist band was defeated by Elijah Clarke and others at Kettle Creek in 1779, but this was largely offset by an English victory at Brier Creek in March of the same year. The crowning blow for American hopes in Georgia came in the autumn at the bungled siege of Savannah. Liaison between the French commander Count d'Estaing and the Americans was sadly lacking; a final assault against the British on October 9, 1779, was a disaster. Among the numerous allied casualties were Sergeant William Jasper and Count Casimir Pulaski. Only a few upcountry partisan bands continued harrying tactics.

As the war raged, Georgia's Revolutionary government was riddled by factionalism, which weakened Georgia's war effort. At times the Revolutionary government was forced to roam through the backcountry, having been expelled even from its de facto capital of Augusta. So strong was the factional division that in 1779, in spite of the desperate situation, Georgia had two Revolutionary regimes that contended with one another almost as violently as they did the redcoats. The British on their part brought Governor Wright back and charged him with reconstituting Georgia. He worked astutely, but by late 1781, as the British position in the South crumbled, Wright was confined to governing a shrinking perimeter around Savannah. He evacuated in July, 1782.

The war had not been won without great personal suffering and privation. Commerce, agriculture, and the economy had suffered badly. Loyalist estates were confiscated, but often such property was returned if the person recanted or paid a fine. Although some large estates were broken up, there was no massive land redistribution. All told, Georgia lost in the neighborhood of 1,000 whites and perhaps as many as 4,000 slaves at the time of Savannah's evacuation, and probably a good many before that. The state ran up a large debt in financing the war. Ultimately these debts were either repudiated or only partially paid.

The Revolution had a dramatic effect on Georgia. In religion, the Church of England lost both membership and prestige. On the lusty frontier, where thousands moved even during the war, the new and more emotional faiths of the Baptists and Methodists came to predominate. These same new up-country settlers brought with them to northeast Georgia the culture of tobacco, a crop supplanted by cotton in the early 1800s. Politically, Augusta had been the seat of government and the center of resistance to the British in the war's last phases. It was made capital of the state of Georgia in 1785, and the backcountry became politically dominant over Savannah and the low country.

After the war the state was in a strongly nationalistic mood. Georgia promptly ratified the U.S. Constitution, which it was hoped would create a government to help with the Indians on the frontier. The Indians occupied lands Georgians wanted badly. In addition, the natives were being manipulated by the Spanish in Florida. Another indication of nationalistic fervor was the state constitution of 1789, which provided for a more centralized government and a stronger executive. The constitution of 1798 went even farther and was to last over 60 years.

Georgia earlier showed an awareness of the need for higher education by chartering the first state-supported university in 1785 and by encouraging an academy movement in each county. The academies did not prosper, but the University of Georgia, which opened its doors in 1801, achieved distinction even though it received only a handful of public funds during the first century of its life.

In the late eighteenth and early nineteenth centuries there were two dominant interrelated issues facing Georgians: physical expansion and the problem of Indian removal. White Georgians generally felt the Indians hampered progress. The state presumed that the federal government felt the same way, but often there were differences of policy. Such conflicts colored state-federal relations and local politics until after the final Cherokee removal in 1838. A large land cession was wrung from the Creeks at the Treaty of New York in 1790, but pressure on the frontier continued as Georgia's population virtually doubled between 1790 and 1800. Treaties in 1801 and 1804 pushed the western boundary to the Ocmulgee River, and a baker's dozen new counties were set up.

Land grants were often shot through with fraud and corruption during the 1790s, first on the local and finally on the state level. The Yazoo Land Frauds of 1796 stemmed from Georgia's continuing claim to the huge stretch of land from the Chattahoochee west to the Mississippi. Speculators convinced the legislature to grant more than 30 million of these acres to various land companies for about $500,000. The stench of corruption hung over the assembly, and the people of the state became enraged. The assembly of 1797, following the lead of the dynamic James Jackson, rescinded the grants. Before this action, however, some of the Yazoo property was sold to people who wanted to occupy their grants. The whole issue was ultimately decided by the U.S. Supreme Court in the case of Fletcher v. Peck (1810). By 1802 Georgia was chastened by the Yazoo experience and ceded its western claims to the central government with the understanding that Indian land titles east of the line of the Chattahoochee be extinguished as quickly as possible.

Early in the nineteenth century the state adopted a unique arrangement to replace the old head-right system. Lands were surveyed in advance in plots of varying size and were granted free (save for a slight fee) to citizens of Georgia on a lottery basis. Each person was to have an equal opportunity to receive land, but such elements in the population as war veterans, heads of families with one or more children, and widowed heads of families received additional chances. The system worked well, and, although it has been criticized for not bringing money to Georgia's treasury, it was at least as democratic and efficient as the systems used elsewhere. Under the lottery the state's lands were parceled out until there were no more to distribute.

In the political arena, the state became outspokenly Jeffersonian once party lines emerged, backing the Virginia Dynasty until 1828. James Jackson became Georgia's first popular political leader, and his party developed close ties with the Jeffersonians. After Jackson's death in 1806 William H. Crawford and George M. Troup assumed leadership of the faction. Crawford spent most of his time in various cabinet positions in Washington and was also ambassador to France; Troup, in addition to serving in Congress, became one of the strongest governors in the state's history.

Opposition to the Jackson-Troup faction was headed by John Clark. At first the Troupites triumphed, and then there was a period of general understanding that everyone should work to drive the Spanish from Florida. All raids into Florida during the War of 1812 aborted, but Georgians reveled in Andrew Jackson's sweeping victory over the Creeks at Horseshoe Bend. At the peace table the Indians surrendered claims to southern Georgia, thus isolating themselves from their former supply base in Pensacola. The Spanish realized their position was hopeless and ceded their colony to the United States in 1819. Georgia's southern boundary was set at the St. Mary's River.

Now that Georgia had reached the Chattahoochee in the southwest, pressure mounted to clear all remaining Creek Indian claims in the state. A voluntary cession to the Flint River in 1821 temporarily staved off the inevitable. In 1825 Governor Troup, who had berated federal officials for their delay, secured the surrender of the Lower Creeks' remaining land in Georgia. When the Upper Creeks (and the national government) questioned the legality of this Treaty of Indian Springs, Troup denounced Washington and threatened war. Feeble efforts by the national government to block implementation of the treaty were useless, and by the end of 1827 the Creeks had been forced from Georgia. The lands that had been ceded were fertile and ideal for cotton culture. Macon and Columbus were settled in 1823 and 1828

229

respectively, and both towns quickly became marketing and transportation centers first for river navigation and then for railways. In addition, the power of the Ocmulgee and the Chattahoochee rivers was harnessed to operate the mills built at these sites.

By the time the crisis with the Cherokee had developed, Georgia's factions had been replaced by Union and States' Rights parties brought on by the tariff and nullification fight. In general Clarkites were pro-Jackson Union party men, and Troupites were more attracted to the pro-Calhoun States' Rightists. John Forsyth followed Troup as governor, serving 1827 to 1829. He was no exception in his attitude toward the Indians, urging prompt Cherokee removal once the Creeks were gone.

The Cherokee would not give in to the whites without a fierce struggle. By 1830 they had their own written language, a constitution, and a capital at New Echota. As a sedentary people living under a government modeled upon that of the whites, the Cherokee claimed to be a nation. When it was apparent that Georgia would neither observe their border nor respect their lives and after the discovery of gold in the mountains seemed to seal their fate, the Indians appealed to the U.S. Supreme Court. In Cherokee Nation v. Georgia (1831) the Court refused to forbid Georgia from extending its laws over the Indians because the Cherokee were not a sovereign power. However, in 1832, in Worcester v. Georgia, the state's laws were declared inoperative on Cherokee land. So violent was Jackson's and Georgia's anger over this decision that the executive order enforcing it was not issued. In effect the Indians were left to fend for themselves. As a result of intimidation and a series of treaties of questionable validity, the Cherokee had been forcibly removed by the end of 1838.

Andrew Jackson's policy on Indian removal increased his popularity among Georgians, who had long been his admirers. They supported him particularly strongly after 1824, when it was clear that Crawford's chances for the White House were gone. Jackson's familiarity with frontier life and his apparent distaste for the second Bank of the United States also appealed to most Georgians. With John C. Calhoun's articulated philosophy of STATE'S RIGHTS many

Georgians could also agree, but his dour personality, political ambitions, and rivalry with Crawford turned some against him. So when the nullification conflict arose, Georgia was divided. Following a short, severe struggle, the Jacksonians emerged winners.

Inferences should not be drawn that Georgia was protariff. The state resented the imposts of 1828 and 1832, but leaders such as Forsyth felt a federal constitutional convention should be called before taking radical action. Nor did Georgians deplore all banking institutions. By 1837 Georgia had more than 20 commercial banks, some with branches, and the state's system of regulation had worked so well that the effects of the Panic of 1819 had been minimized. The state could not have experienced the enormous growth in people, size, and wealth that it had through the 1830s without properly extended commercial credit, agricultural loans, bank notes issued by state-chartered institutions, and activities of the state's own Central Bank of Georgia.

In a brawling, frontier state such as Georgia before 1838, it is unreasonable to expect a flowering of culture. Colleges were few, and enrollments were small; there were probably less than 40 academies in the state in 1820 (and not many more assorted private schools). Academies were weighted to Latin and Greek, and girls' schools emphasized the more "gentle" sciences. However, Georgia Female College (1836), later Wesleyan College, was a leader in higher education for women in the South. In the 1830s the state's main religious groups—the Baptists, Methodists, and Presbyterians—founded Mercer, Emory, and Oglethorpe colleges respectively, and in 1859 a law school was established at the University of Georgia. Georgia Medical College was set up in Augusta in 1828. For basic educational needs, tutoring at home was still important.

Newspapers had begun to flourish in Georgia by the 1820s, and most of the reading done by literate Georgians was from their pages. Theater was confined largely to the older settled areas, but traveling puppet shows, carnivals, and "circuses" made their way into the backcountry. One play, *The Mysterious Father* by William Bulloch Maxwell of Savannah, dates from 1807, and Hugh McCall's two-volumed *History of*

Georgia antedates 1820. A.B. Longstreet *(Georgia Scenes)* was probably the best of the Georgia humorists who used local color in their writings, but William T. Thompson was a capable writer. Richard Henry Wilde and Thomas Holley Chivers were Georgia's first poets of note. Some of the most competent writing was done by William B. Stevens in his *History of Georgia*, produced a generation after McCall's work. The Georgia Historical Society was formed in Savannah in 1839 and encouraged the interest of Georgians in their history, and library societies, debating groups, and literary organizations advanced knowledge throughout the state.

Georgia's homes began to take on more pretensions of the eastern segment of the state with the coming of William Jay to Savannah in 1817. In the Piedmont, Daniel Pratt built fine houses in the countryside and in Milledgeville, which became the capital of the state in 1806. Athens boasted its distinguished Old College, and handsome townhouses appeared in Savannah and Augusta. Still, the typical Georgia house throughout the antebellum period was rural and simple. By 1860 some of these early houses had additional rooms added and Greek Revival façades imposed.

During frontier days—and most of Georgia was hardly more than two generations from frontier by 1860—families often slept in a one- or two-room cabin, sharing common sleeping quarters and meals with their slaves. Although these rugged folk appeared to enjoy their religion immensely, it was for many an exercise in emotional release. The Baptist itinerant preacher and the Methodist circuit rider did what they could to bring God to the frontier, but the rest of organized religion in Georgia made little effort to conquer the back-country. By the time of the Civil War there was an increase in church membership, some of which may have been organization of southern branches of the Methodist and Baptist churches. All things considered, however, Georgians were not a religious people.

Antebellum Georgia. In 1793 Eli Whitney's cotton gin, invented at Mulberry Grove plantation on the Savannah River, made profitable the cultivation of the green seed, short-staple cotton throughout most of Georgia and the South. This coincided with the incorporation by Georgia of large chunks of Indian lands, and when Columbus was established in 1828 there was already an incipient "plantation belt" stretching across the state. Significant numbers of Negro slaves were introduced into the backcountry to cultivate and harvest the crop. The size of the average plantation, held down initially by the limited grants under the lottery system, soon tended to grow larger, especially in the lower Piedmont. In some instances small farmers were forced out, but even in the 1850s many white yeomen were found in the areas of large landholdings. In fact, throughout antebellum days the small farmer, usually working with little or no black labor, remained the typical Georgian. By 1860 about 60 percent of Georgia's farm families owned no slaves although plantation life remained the white ideal.

As cotton boomed, other crops were often neglected, and tobacco, once a staple in northeast Georgia, all but disappeared from that section. It did well in south Georgia, however, and by 1860 the state was producing approximately 1 million pounds annually. But it was cotton culture that took on an almost mystic quality, and by the mid-1820s Georgia was the world's largest cotton producer; in 1839 it grew 326,000 bales. Although trailing Alabama's total in 1850, the state's production stood at almost 500,000 bales; the 1860 crop was greater than 700,000. Corn and other grains were widely grown, largely for local consumption. Although crop diversification was more common than is usually thought, upland cotton along with rice in the low country and long-staple cotton on the Sea Islands provided Georgia's primary cash crops.

There is little question that planters dominated Georgia's politics in the antebellum period. Although frequently falling out among themselves, these men all agreed on the question of the right of an individual to own slaves. The state's economic and social system, in spite of flirtations with liberal eighteenth-century thought, became more closely entwined with the South's "peculiar institution" as the nineteenth century advanced. By the time of the Civil War, even the areas where slaveholding was not predominant were willing to follow the planters in secession.

Socially the state was overwhelmingly

middle class; most of the prosperous planters were self-made men. They had little time for leisure or refinements, and hence Georgia's antebellum cultural life appeared to be fairly restricted to Savannah, Augusta, and Athens. If Georgia had anything that might be called an aristocracy, it was made up of a few planters and merchants along the coast and up the river to Augusta.

Where adequate books were kept and sensible business practices followed, slavery was a profitable institution in Georgia. It is true that Georgia, in 1860, had more plantations of over 1,000 improved acres than any other state, but only one planter owned more than 500 slaves. Twenty-three men owned in excess of 200 Negroes, and 212 planters had 100 or more. Therefore only 236 men owned more than 100 slaves each. Most farms were below 100 improved acres in size, many of them employing no Negroes. All told there were about 50,000 farms in Georgia under 500 improved acres, and only 3,500 that were larger. It was on the smaller plots that the yeoman farmers lived. In the towns and cities the artisan and mechanic groups grew as did the numbers of lawyers, doctors, and ministers, all adding to Georgia's middle-class orientation.

Below the middle class were the poor whites, some of whom owned small farms, usually in marginal or abandoned areas. They hunted and fished and often hired themselves out as seasonal laborers to planters or yeomen farmers and performed menial tasks in the towns. Not to be confused with the poor whites were the "poor white trash," scorned by blacks as well as whites. These were the drifters, the diseased, the illiterate, living on the periphery of society. The state was saddled with a 20 percent illiteracy rate among the whites. The poor were particularly penalized by the fact that Georgia had no real system of public education prior to the Civil War.

There was also a number of free Negroes in Georgia, but they were feared and were discriminated against. They concentrated in the towns and cities, especially Savannah and Augusta. Although they were usually employed as unskilled labor, there are examples of intelligent and skilled free blacks in Georgia holding positions of respect and prominence within their communities.

By 1860 there were roughly 465,000 slaves in Georgia. This institution was given its rules by state and local codes, which prescribed the limits and fashion of Negro behavior. Although in theory the slaves were carefully regulated, in practice many of the strictures in the statute books were not enforced. The individual slave owner exercised wide latitude, for good or ill, among his chattels. There are examples in Georgia of extreme cruelty by the owner to his slave as well as acts of generosity. Most of Georgia's slaves lived in houses that were barely adequate, ate food of about the same degree, and were shabbily clothed and often unshod. The plantation system did provide the slave with a certain amount of "free time," and it was during these periods that the blacks refined their rich subsociety that contributed so much of value and spontaneity to the mainstream of American life. In the final analysis, slavery by 1860 appeared to be alive and well in Georgia. Although most of the planters had been wasteful with the soil, causing erosion and/or depletion, slavery seemed to thrive wherever the land was fertile and wisely used.

Even before Georgia reached its ultimate boundaries it was obvious that an effective system of transportation and communication was needed. Road building was slow and expensive, and upkeep was always a problem, so Georgia naturally turned to its rivers. Because of increasing traffic and cargo flow and the need for service to and from the backcountry, steamboats began to ply Georgia's major streams after 1820. These boats gave Columbus, Macon, and Milledgeville relatively quick and reliable contacts with the coast. (Augusta had enjoyed river traffic with Savannah since the 1730s.) The canal frenzy hardly touched Georgia, primarily because a state board of public works recommended other types of public expenditures, particularly for the construction of railroads. It was the railroad boom that knitted the state together by 1860.

The two largest private antebellum railways, the Georgia Railroad and the Central of Georgia, were both chartered in 1833 and immediately prospered. At about the same time a strong movement to build a line to connect the Chattahoochee and the Tennessee valleys caused the creation of the state-owned Western & Atlantic Railroad. Although construction on all roads was delayed by depression in the early 1840s, the W & A reached Chattanooga in 1851, completing its main line. The southern terminus of the W & A, at Zero Milepost, became Atlanta. When it was clear that the W & A would succeed, the rival Georgia and Central systems vied with one another to see which could reach Atlanta first, thereby linking up with the Mississippi-Ohio system. Augusta's Georgia Railroad won the race in 1845, but Savannah's Central of Georgia was only a year behind. The Atlanta & West Point reached out to tap the flow of northern Alabama railroads, and in south Georgia the Atlantic & Gulf system, connecting the Eastern Seaboard directly with south Georgia and Alabama, was virtually complete by 1861. From these main routes were built feeder lines and connectors, which gave Georgia in 1860 over 1,200 miles of track and a system that had no rival in the Deep South.

Georgia was slow in developing its industrial potential, due largely to the emphasis on agriculture. Although there were numerous earlier mills in the state, textile mill construction prospered in the 1830s, especially in the fall-line cities, and by 1860 Georgia was a leader in the southern textile field. Other industries included numerous tanneries, a few brickworks and iron foundries, nail factories, machine shops, and the like. Savannah was the state's main industrial city, with lumber interests being particularly important, but upstart Atlanta was in 1860 already producing about half the value of the older center. Atlanta's rolling mill and machine shops were to be crucial during the Civil War, as were Augusta's powder works and Columbus' foundries. Georgia produced industrial goods in 1860 valued at almost $17 million. Dahlonega had been a center of gold mining and the location of a branch U.S. mint since 1838. Iron and clays, coal and marble were all being taken from Georgia's hills. On the eve of the Civil War, however, the state's image was largely agricultural, but the economy was more diversified than is generally thought.

Georgia's political structure became even more complex during the years leading to secession. In the 1840s there were two well-organized and evenly balanced parties. Many of the Old Troupite-States' Rights faction became Whigs and carried the state for

William Henry Harrison in 1840. Most of the Clark-Unionist element gravitated to the Democratic pole. Each group evolved able leaders: the Whigs had John Mcpherson Berrien, Alexander H. Stephens, George W. Crawford, and Robert Toombs; the Democrats relied on Howell Cobb, Herschel V. Johnson, and Joseph E. Brown. The Whigs tended to be more cautious with state financing, but the parties agreed on many points. The Whig Crawford saw to the creation of a state supreme court during one of his terms as governor and also pushed construction of the W & A. Howell Cobb, in the 1850s, was an important railroad booster, but he also broadened the state's tax base, increased expenditures for schools, and expanded state services. Brown, a Democratic dark horse nominee in 1857, instituted needed reforms in the state railroad and advocated larger allocations of funds for public education. This popular man from the north Georgia hill country was reelected in 1859 and twice during the Civil War.

Many Georgia Whigs were thrown on the defensive by the issue of the annexation of Texas. Stephens, Berrien, and Toombs all opposed the Mexican War that followed, but found it difficult to stay in the same party with the now-strident antislavery northern Whigs who backed the Wilmot Proviso. Georgia Whigs opposed the proviso and were able to concentrate party strength to carry the state for popular war hero Zachary Taylor in 1848.

The Democrats were having troubles too. A schism developed between the Calhounites and the moderates. Cobb, elected Speaker of the U.S. House, took the lead in rallying the moderate Democrats to the cause of the Compromise of 1850. Stephens and Toombs, also in Congress, backed the compromise as well, and all three men worked hard to convince the Georgia electorate they had acted properly. Old political labels disappeared as these men and their allies appeared under the name Constitutional Union Party of Georgia; the radicals chose the Southern Rights party as their standard. The Unionists stumped the state counseling acceptance of the Georgia Platform, adopted by a state convention in December, 1850. This document called for Georgia voters' approval of the compromise but also issued a stern warning that if the

233

North failed to live up to its guarantees then the South would no longer feel bound. Georgia gave the platform and the Union a ringing endorsement at the polls; the state's position became a model for Union supporters in the rest of the South.

The furor over the compromise effectively destroyed the Whigs, and although Stephens and Toombs were deeply suspicious of Democrats, they had little choice but to cooperate with them, particularly after the formation of the Republican party. The close call James Buchanan had at the hands of the politically inexperienced Republican, John C. Frémont, a Savannah native, in the presidential election of 1856 demonstrated the danger ahead for the Democrats. John Brown's Harper's Ferry Raid convinced many Georgians that, should a Republican be elected in 1860, the state would be better off out of the Union than in it.

Georgia 1860—1900. At the Democrats' Charleston Convention in 1860, most of Georgia's delegation walked out when southern demands that slavery be protected in the territories were not met, a tactic repeated at the Baltimore Convention. Stephen A. Douglas was nominated for president by this second convention with loyalist Herschel V. Johnson of Georgia as his running mate. Most Georgia Democrats backed the candidacy of John C. Breckinridge of Kentucky, and many old Whigs and Know-Nothings supported John Bell of Tennessee, the Constitutional Union Party candidate. Abraham Lincoln had no open supporters in Georgia. If Bell's and Douglas' votes in Georgia had been combined, Breckinridge would have lost the state, but the moderate votes were split. Lincoln's election caused Governor Brown to call for a state convention to evaluate Georgia's ties with the Union. The vote for delegates to this convention was no clearcut mandate for seccession, but Brown, Cobb, Toombs, and others chose to interpret it as such. Stephens, Johnson, Benjamin H. Hill, and others fought the inflamed rhetoric of the secessionists. A key issue was rejected, 164 to 133, after which a secession ordinance was passed on January 20, 1861.

Because Georgia was the most populous and wealthy state of the Deep South, it seemed only appropriate for its role in the early days of the Confederacy to be a significant one. Howell Cobb's brother, the jurist T. R. R. Cobb, was one of the framers of the Confederate constitution; Howell was presiding officer of the Montgomery convention; Stephens was picked as Confederate vice-president; Toombs was chosen secretary of state.

Governor Brown clashed with the Confederate government on its use of Georgia troops, seizure of state goods and munitions, the right to use of the writ of habeas corpus, the appointment of militia officers, and especially conscription. His public postures may have encouraged desertions and a general lowering of morale in Georgia as well as in Confederate military and administrative circles. Still, well over 100,000 Georgians ultimately served in the army, and the state's rich farmlands helped supply Confederate commissaries. Many plantations became self-sufficient and grew more grains and foodstuffs (and less cotton) than previously. Wartime demand stimulated manufacturing and trade, but there was a shortage of skilled labor, and replacement parts for machinery were almost nonexistent. Georgia's railroads were used extensively, the rolling stock wore out, and no new track was laid during the war.

As the war progressed the state found it increasingly difficult to provision its troops. There were acute shortages of medical supplies, salt, and other necessities. The legislature levied new taxes, but as the Confederate cause waned coins disappeared from circulation and paper money became highly inflated. Sherman's March virtually wrecked Georgia's economy and left the state prostrated.

Life in Georgia, until the coming of William T. Sherman, did not alter radically from prewar days. Newspapers operated without censorship, but many were forced to close because of paper shortages. The black work force remained on the plantations and was even pressed into semimilitary service if the occasion demanded. When Union forces drew near, many slaves did leave the plantations, and black colonies were set up on the Union-occupied coastal islands early in the war. All men's colleges except Mercer closed, but the women's colleges stayed open. Schooling on the lower level continued as it had until near the end of the war.

With the exception of early action on the

coast (resulting in the surrender of Ft. Pulaski and the isolation of Savannah's port in April, 1862), there were no military encounters in Georgia between large numbers of troops until 1864. Efforts in 1862 and 1863 to cut the W & A Railroad were frustrated, but Sherman led an army of 100,000 men into Georgia in late spring, 1864, with intent to divide the Confederacy and cripple Georgia's war effort. He marched down the main line of the W & A toward Atlanta, consistently outflanking Joseph E. Johnston's smaller army. After a sharp encounter at Kennesaw Mountain Johnston fell back upon Atlanta's defenses. He was replaced by John B. Hood, whose efforts to break through federal lines were bloodily repulsed. All but surrounded, Hood withdrew from Atlanta on September 1. Sherman took the city, regrouped his forces, burned most of the town, and set off on his virtually unopposed and highly destructive march to the sea. Savannah fell by mid-December, 1864. The war, as far as Georgia was concerned, had ended.

In defeat Georgia suffered severe economic, political, and social dislocation. But the sheer necessities of survival dictated that by 1870 man and land had gotten together again to the point that cotton production approached the 500,000-bale mark. Various systems of landowner-tenant relationships were attempted, but the one that came to be used most frequently was sharecropping. Although the tenant was clearly the more oppressed by the system, few landowners actually profited from the arrangement. Both landlord and cropper were hit by periodic agricultural depressions, high interest charges, deflation, and other economic circumstances they could neither understand not alter. Much of the unrest in Georgia during the last decades of the nineteeth century is incomprehensible unless viewed in the light of these conditions.

The people of the state seemed willing to accept military defeat with some equanimity. Georgia did what was necessary to reenter the Union under President Andrew Johnson's plan, but the rise of the Radical Republicans in Congress doomed presidential efforts at Reconstruction. A military government was instituted in 1867, and a purged convention drew up a new state constitution. The document granted the franchise to the blacks, and although it provided for general public education, it was left to subsequent governments to develop the system. Altanta was made Georgia's capital, signifying its growing importance and the state's continued population swing north and west. Republican Rufus Bullock was inaugurated governor in 1868, but that autumn the state voted for Democrat Horatio Seymour and the house turned out its black members, thus bringing about a return of military rule. After additional Radical requirements were met, Georgia was again allowed to reenter the Union (1870) for the third time in four years.

By 1872 Georgia had returned to Democratic control and Bullock had left the state in temporary disgrace. His legacy was an administration that was careless with the W & A and with state bonds, but his sins were not so vile as the Democrats claimed. In fact his Reconstruction government broadened the scope of state activity and did worthwhile groundwork in education and allied fields. The Freedmen's Bureau was effective in helping the former slave adjust to his new status, and it took an active part in establishing Atlanta University in 1867. Perhaps the bureau's finest achievement was to bring into the state a number of dedicated teachers, who worked without hope of material reward to offer education to the blacks.

With the exception of the Union-repaired and state-owned W & A, the main Georgia railroads were bankrupt in 1865. And yet so swift was the state's economic recovery in this area that the biggest systems were soon making profits again. By 1873 almost 1,000 miles of new track had been put down, and a second railroad boom was in the making. Savannah once again exported vast amounts of cotton, although its leadership was threatened for a time by competition from the deepwater port of Brunswick.

By the end of the century Georgia was first in the country in naval stores, and its timber remained important. New industries had grown up to transform cottonseed into stock food and fertilizer. The textile mills along the fall line were rebuilt or retooled, and by 1890 this industry was turning out goods worth more than $12.5 million. The growth of Atlanta, however, eclipsed other economic developments. The city was the focal point of Georgia's surge, and Henry W.

235

Grady, editor of the Atlanta, *Constitution*, with his New South philosophy became the men of the hour. Atlanta's spirit of bustle and optimism was well illustrated by the successful expositions held there in 1887 and 1895. Still, in spite of the trumpetings of the heralds of the New South, Georgia industry in 1900 was not the sort that attracted or required skilled labor. In fact, important considerations for northern capital to move South were low taxes and even lower wage scales. At the turn of the century Georgia remained overwhelmingly agrarian and lagged behind most states in all economic indicators.

Culturally the Gilded Age in Georgia offered more dross than gold. Indicative of the times, the best prose authors were also journalists. Joel Chandler Harris got his early training on the *Countryman*, a magazine printed on Joseph Addison Turner's Putnam County plantation, but Harris' stories of Uncle Remus did not appear until 1879. At the same time another writer on the *Constitution*, Bill Arp (Charles H. Smith), spun tall tales in the rural Georgia tradition. Sidney Lanier was Georgia's most talented poet. Several of his best poems deal intimately with the state, notably "The Song of the Chattahoochee" and "The Marshes of Glynn." Charles C. Jones, Jr., was a prominent historian, although he wrote with a strong southern bias.

Church membership up to 1900 increased regularly. After the war the blacks formed their own churches, overwhelmingly Baptist or Methodist. Sectarian efforts at higher education were continued, but Oglethorpe College was a victim of the war. Emory at Oxford and Mercer increased in size; the University of Georgia reopened in 1866 and soon broadened its horizons and curriculum. An offshoot of the university was founded in Dahlonega in 1871, and an agricultural school was created in Athens. Along New South lines, the state chartered the Georgia Institute of Technology in 1885 to teach effective industrial practices in the state. Four years later a women's college was founded at Milledgeville to train young women in similar practical skills such as the teaching of "telegraphy, stenography, typewriting, photography, bookkeeping," and so on.

After Bullock left Georgia, many of the old Confederate leaders regained control, al-

though it took Joe Brown some time to convince the state that he was cleansed of his Reconstruction Republicanism. The postwar politicians were more interested in keeping themselves in power than in helping the Georgia farmer, so it was not long before independent Democrats were challenging "regular" Democratic candidates for Congress and seats in the legislature. William H. Felton was the advance guard of independency, being first elected to Congress in 1874; ane Emory Speer won election in 1878. The independents denounced the Atlanta-based politicians and pledged the farmer—Georgia's forgotten man—a fair hearing. In 1882 the independents nearly convinced Stephens to be their candidate for governor, but the regulars, sensing disaster, prevailed upon him to be their candidate instead. With the wind taken from their sails the independents declined. But they had set in motion an opposition movement that was to bear fruit in the 1890s.

In the meantime, the state drew up its "home rule constitution" in 1877. The document tried to ensure fiscal economy and by so doing wound itself in knots that had to be untied by generations of subsequent lawmakers. It was at last replaced in 1945. The work of 1877, however, is also important for what it did not do: it made no serious attempts to reverse the movement for public education, nor did it attack the right of the blacks at the polls.

With independency scotched the old line was once again in control. Brown, old war hero John B. Gordon, and Alfred H. Colquitt composed a threesome that dominated the governorship and the senatorial posts for almost 15 years. Government was best that governed least, but what "least" there was should be in the interests of the group in power. The convict lease, begun under Reconstruction, was abused during this period; Georgia's archaic tax laws were retained; the newly formed school system was inadequately funded; rural roads were a disgrace; and freight rates seemed pegged to discriminate against the little man.

Against such a background, heightened by agricultural depression, an organization called the Farmer's Alliance carried all before it. By 1890 the Georgia Alliance was so strong that it dominated the general assembly of that year. A torrent of legislation was pushed through, mainly aimed at state government taking a positive role in the lives of Georgia's citizens. Some leaders, such as Thomas E. Watson, elected to Congress in 1890, had misgivings about working within the Democratic party. Watson became a Populist, but most of the Alliance men were afraid to leave the Democrats lest the Republicans and blacks take advantage of the split in white ranks to assume control. Gradually the concept grew that if whites were to have open political disagreement, then the power of the blacks at the ballot box must be eliminated.

The Populist party never assumed control of Georgia; its high point came in 1896, and Watson, the party's candidate for the vice-presidency that year, became increasingly disillusioned. Embittered and frustrated, he retired to his home at Hickory Hill and from there issued a steady stream of magazines, books, and political propaganda. No single man, with the possible exception of Eugene Talmadge (who modeled himself on Watson), has ever so dominated Georgia politics.

Georgia, 1900–1945. The new century started calmly, but 1906 saw one of Georgia's most bitter gubernatorial primary battles. The main contestants were newspapermen: Hoke Smith, onetime owner of the Atlanta *Journal*, with Watson's support, and Clark Howell of the *Constitution*. The mood was such that a violent race riot claiming 17 lives broke out in Atlanta during the same year. Fear of the black man was never far below the surface of Georgia life, and Smith's promise to disfranchise the Negro appealed to Watson as well as to Georgia's white voters. Smith was overwhelmingly elected, but in addition to disfranchisement he pushed through the assembly a program of progressive legislation. The convict lease system was outlawed (although experiments with substitute solutions proved almost as offensive), and statewide prohibition was enacted. In addition, state controls over railroad and corporate activities were broadened.

With the help of disfranchisement the Democrats reinforced their hold on Georgia politics. The Democratic white primary became the de facto election in Georgia, and the county unit arrangement, which heavily favored the agricultural areas, was embraced as a rule of the party. In 1917 the county unit system was given legal status as a law of the state. In such an atmosphere it is no surprise that the dominance of personal factions within the party from 1900 to 1950 reinforced an early characteristic of Georgia's political life. This kind of elitist politics caused a decline of interest by the electorate, invitations to demagoguery, do-nothingism, and the occasional use of questionable administrative practices. At about the same time as the phenomena occurred elsewhere, nativism, anti-Semitism, and anti-Catholicism appeared in Georgia. The Ku Klux Klan was resurrected to capitalize on these feelings. Such sentiments were also indicated by the sensational Leo Frank murder trial in Atlanta.

In the 1920s Georgia slipped farther behind the rest of the nation in most categories, and even behind other states in the South. By 1920, the boll weevil raged uncontrolled in Georgia's fields; cotton production, which had reached almost 2 million bales in 1909, fell by more than 300,000 bales ten years later. In 1924 barely 1 million bales were raised in the state. Although tobacco enjoyed an enormous increase, the drop in the cotton dollar was a major one. In fact, a general agricultural depression caused thousands to go to the cities seeking employment, but many Georgians simply left the state. As one example of this migration, there were more blacks in Georgia in 1920 than there were in 1970. Political leadership from the governor's mansion was at its nadir; the state seemed powerless. During the 1920s Georgia, always a southern leader in population and manufacturing, saws its top position in the former usurped by North Carolina, and it fell even more dramatically in the latter category. The state lagged in highway construction, health care, and other state services; the state university, which opened the century with bright promise under Walter Hill, stagnated. Illiteracy was still high in Georgia's rural districts, and the state stood last in support of its public schools. By 1930 over 60 percent of all Georgia's farms were of the tenant variety, but some of the countryside was virtually abandoned. For the state's paralysis during the decade a lack-luster assembly must bear much of the blame.

Georgia began to come out of its lethargy

237

under the leadership of the young Richard B. Russell, who became governor in 1931 and presided over an effective program of reorganization. The number of state boards was reduced to 18, and businesslike practices were introduced. Probably Russell's finest act as governor was to take the various boards of trustees that ran the numerous state supported colleges and combine them under a single board of regents with final authority over the policies of the entire system. To show his disdain for the Klan, Russell appointed Hughes Spalding, Atlanta attorney and Roman Catholic, as the board's first chairman. Reorganization followed; weaker schools were eliminated or absorbed by stronger ones. The result was to create a university the state could understand and afford to support.

Russell was succeeded in the governor's office by Eugene Talmadge, a flamboyant figure whose postures and words conjured up images of days gone by. He detested Franklin Roosevelt and fought the various agencies and relief measures of the New Deal. The electorate loved the show he put on, but twice denied him the U.S. senatorship. In 1936 Russell defeated Talmadge handily, and in the same year Eurith D. Rivers, a strong New Dealer, was elected governor over Talmadge's handpicked choice. Rivers supported health services, old-age pensions, teacher pay raises, free texts, an extended school year, and other measures opposed by Talmadge, and his program was enacted. After reelection in 1938, Rivers had trouble financing his policies and ran afoul of the powerful highway department. Talmadge returned in 1940, but again he made a serious blunder. He tried to manipulate the board of regents and the university system in the same way he had intimidated other state officials. The university's accreditation was removed and Talmadge found himself confronted by an electorate incensed by his attacks. The result was a stunning victory for Ellis G. Arnall in the gubernatorial campaign of 1942. Prosperity, brought along by World War II, helped Arnall get a program that took the university system largely out of politics and that revamped state government. Arnall's fight to secure equal freight rates, his educational efforts, his prison reforms, and the new constitution in 1945 all gained national

attention. But no single act of his administration claimed the public imagination as much as granting the vote to qualified eighteen-year-olds. In this particular, Georgia was first in the nation.

Recent Georgia. The year 1946 saw Arnall, Georgia's first four-year-term governor, unable to succeed himself. Although for a second time Talmadge failed to secure a majority of the popular votes, he won the county unit votes in the Democratic primary. A constitutional crisis occurred when Talmadge died after the election but before his inauguration. (The Republicans had no candidate on the ballot in the general election.) Was the lieutenant governor elect Melvin Thompson to be the new governor, should Arnall remain as caretaker chief executive, or should the person with the next highest number of votes for governor in the general election be designated? The general assembly, reflecting the county unit system that had made Talmadge the Democratic candidate, decided on the last. It was no coincidence that the man who trailed Talmadge in the voting was his own son Herman Talmadge. The state supreme court decided that the assembly had gone too far, and Thompson, who had been sworn in as lieutenant governor, took possession of the governorship. Talmadge then narrowly defeated Thompson in a special election called in 1948 and again in 1950 for a full four-year term.

The basic issue, even more in 1948 and 1950 than in 1906, was one of race, with Talmadge vowing as strongly as Hoke Smith that Georgia would remain a white citadel. Also like that of Smith, Talmadge's record as governor was one of a relatively progressive nature. More money than ever before was put into public education—including a futile effort to build up the state's black schools to something resembling a "separate but equal" status with the whites'. In some ways Herman surprised his father's followers by expanding state services and by securing passage of a sales tax to help pay for new programs.

Progressive or conservative though the individuals concerned might be, the first half of the twentieth century demonstrated that Georgia politics, based upon personal followings within the Democratic party, had changed hardly at all. Gradually, however, even the Democratic party and the general assembly had to recognize that the practices of the past were gone. Industry and commerce boomed during the 1940s and 1950s, and tens of thousands of new people moved to the state. A better-educated electorate began to ask more questions and expect rational answers. Georgians were chagrined by the state's position in education and undertook to remedy it. A seven-month obligatory school term, authorized in 1935, was increased to nine months in 1952. Herman Talmadge's sales tax helped boost quality education in the state through the Minimum Foundation Association, and school consolidation made the system of public education more efficient. By the 1950s free textbooks were provided for public school children.

The boll weevil and the New Deal brought lasting change to rural Georgia. The Rural Electrification Administration ran electric lines to many areas not served before, bringing not only lighting and labor-saving machinery, but radio (and later television). The various agricultural and financial programs of the Roosevelt years helped tide the farmers over difficult times, and extension services and county agents spread the word of sensible use of Georgia's soil. Tractors and farm machinery, along with automobiles and trucks, made their appearances; roads were paved to connect market towns with outlying areas. Poultry, livestock, corn, tobacco, pecans, and peanuts all surpassed cotton in importance. Forest products, spurred by Charles Herty's experiments developing newsprint from pine, poured new money into the state. Soybeans, to become a dominant crop by the 1970s, began to be widely grown some two decades earlier, and in the 1950s Georgia led the nation in the production of broilers. Naval stores continued to be prominent, but old King Cotton declined to fewer than 500,000 bales annually in the 1950s, until by the 1970s each succeeding year showed a marked decrease in acreage planted. In 1975 only 210,000 of Georgia's acres were devoted to cotton, roughly half the size of the 1974 planting.

Industry expanded significantly after the 1930s. Textiles remained important, with the state holding fourth place nationally, but new plants and manufacturing interests challenged the old. Attracted to the urban center of Atlanta—with its key location, transportation facilities, favorable tax structure, and source of relatively inexpensive labor—automobile assembly plants, chemical firms, trucking lines, and other businesses made Georgia's capital their regional headquarters. The state's permissive attitude toward industry meant that pollution of the rivers and air for the first time came to be a problem.

Aiding and abetting the industrial-commercial emphases of the post-World War II years was the state's unquestioned position as a regional leader in transportation and communication. The railroads, which made Atlanta, helped move the city past other national urban centers in the 1940s and 1950s. When airline passenger and airfreight services developed fully, Atlanta led in these aspects of transportation. Construction of the interstate highway system triggered land speculation and real estate booms in Atlanta's metropolitan area. By the 1970s the four main interstate roads into the city, as well as the perimeter highway around it, were paralleled by light and heavy industry interspersed by apartment developments. The city remained a railway freight hub although track mileage in the state, due to various mergers, is less than it was 50 years ago. As for shipping, the state port and docks in Savannah have been successful and have helped boost the commercial life of Georgia's oldest city. State wharves have revived Brunswick somewhat as a port, but similar terminals elsewhere have fared less well. Augusta, Macon, and Columbus have grown enormously, as have the smaller cities of Albany, Rome, Athens, Valdosta, and others.

In the field of religion, Baptists and Methodists still dominate Georgia's religious spectrum, there being approximately twice as many of the former as of the latter. Presbyterians lagged far behind, but were well organized and influential. By mid-century Roman Catholics ranked fourth in number, being concentrated mainly in the urban centers of Atlanta, Savannah, and Augusta. Lutherans, many of them descendants of the early Salzburgers, are present in some strength, and there are significant Jewish elements in the state's cities.

Georgia writers have lent distinction to the state in the twentieth century. Byron

239

Herbert Reece used local mountain themes in his poetry and prose, and Lillian Smith shocked the state with *Strange Fruit*. In south Georgia, Caroline Miller's *Lamb in His Bosom* won the 1934 Pulitzer Prize. Erskine Caldwell in the 1930s wrote *Tobacco Road* and *God's Little Acre*. Combining social purpose, humor, and realism, Caldwell chronicled rural and textile mill Georgia and America. Conrad Aiken, from Savannah, was one of the best poets America produced in the twentieth century. With an Atlanta newspaper background similar to Harris' and Caldwell's, Margaret Mitchell wrote her best-seller *Gone with the Wind*. Ralph McGill of the *Constitution*, Pulitzer Prize winner, was an effective spokesman for southern liberals. In the study of history, Ulrich B. Phillips, whose field was the South and slavery, was a Georgia native, and Gainesville's Fletcher M. Green, of the University of North Carolina, trained more southern historians than any other man. Conversely the University of Georgia's distinguished and prolific historian, E. Merton Coulter, was born in North Carolina. Carson McCullers, from Columbus, wrote *The Heart Is a Lonely Hunter* and *Member of the Wedding*, and Calder Willingham was the author of *End as a Man*. Atlantan James Dickey's poetry has been well received as has his novel *Deliverance*, but no author in Georgia, and perhaps none in the nation, has recently equaled the talent of Milledgeville's Flannery O'Connor.

Atlanta became the cultural as well as the economic and sports center of the state. The Atlanta Symphony Orchestra rose to national eminence under Robert Shaw. The High Museum of Art is the largest in the state, but the University of Georgia Museum of Art is also distinguished. Museums in Savannah, Augusta, and Columbus possess important holdings. The University System of Georgia, which has roughly sextupled in size since the 1950s, has seen its budgetary allocations rise in proportion.

By and large the higher standards of living enjoyed by most Georgians are owing to the commitment by the state to education at all levels. Even so, Georgia still ranks forty-third in the nation in expenditures per pupil in its public schools. When it is realized that funds for education make up about one-half the total budget, this rating seems to indicate that Georgia needs to overhaul its tax structure to uncover newer sources of revenue.

World War II changed Georgia drastically. Society was more fluid, and certain industries, such as aircraft construction, became important in the state's economy for the first time. Thousands of people, many of them young blacks, left the state, a migration pattern that began in the 1920s and continued into the 1970s. The number of blacks in relation to the state's total population was about 33 percent in 1940 and dipped to approximately 25 percent in 1970. In some of Georgia's cities, however, the black population has found itself in the majority. Even in the midst of Mayor Ivan Allen's Forward Atlanta campaign in the 1960s, whites left the city for the suburbs while blacks poured in from the countryside. Faced by a lack of job opportunities, by discrimination, by exposure to drugs, and by deplorable living conditions, many blacks experienced disillusionment and anger and turned to violence in the late 1960s. The decline of Atlanta's inner city has continued since that time. Reflecting black voting power in Atlanta in the 1970s, Andrew Young represented the Fifth Congressional District in Washington and Maynard Jackson was elected the first black mayor of the city of 1974.

In one fashion or another, though, race was injected into almost every political contest form 1940 to the 1970s. Harry Truman's executive order to desegregate the armed forces had a minimum effect on most Georgians, but the passing of the white primary seemed serious indeed. There were clear warnings before 1954 that Plessy v. Ferguson would be overturned, so the actual shock of the Brown v. Board of Education decision was not overwhelming. Many Georgians construed "all deliberate speed" to mean "never," and Marvin Griffin, elected governor in 1954, pledged eternal loyalty to the county unit system and segregation, promises repeated by his successor Ernest Vandiver. Vandiver wrestled with the problems of keeping Georgia's colleges and schools open even though integrated and did not buckle under extremist pressure. Integration was accomplished, and the school systems survived. Desegregation of Atlanta's public schools began in 1961 and was carried out in an orderly fashion, a pattern followed by Athens, Brunswick, and other cities.

To lead the fight against local segregation, Martin Luther King, Jr., returned to Georgia and blanketed the state with demonstrations. Although Vandiver and the assembly assumed hard-line stances, municipal officials usually reached reasonable accords with integration leaders. By 1976 legal *de jure* segregation had disappeared in Georgia, but busing to achieve racial balance in the state's schools appeared to have had the opposite effect from that desired. Combined with the rising crime and violence rates in the public schools, busing accelerated the white flight to the suburbs and to private schools. In the rural counties, where school systems had been consolidated, many white students were placed in private academies. The effect has been to resegregate the public schools. In Atlanta the situation developed in roughly the same way, with blacks composing about 90 percent of the registered students in the 1975–1976 academic year.

That single-party politics helped hold Georgia in the grip of the past can scarcely be doubted by those who study the state's history since the Civil War. There was no chance the general assembly, which each year became less responsive to the majority will, would willingly alter the county unit rule, which gave the least populous counties control of the legislature and the primary. But in the spring of 1962 the county unit system was invalidated by the courts (Baker v. Carr), and the legislature was ordered to reapportion itself on a more representative basis. The effect of the decision was felt immediately, when Carl Sanders swept Georgia's urban areas and defeated Marvin Griffin in a popular vote primary. In Atlanta, Charles Longstreet Weltner, a liberal young lawyer who later voted in favor of the Civil Rights Act of 1964, turned out the incumbent congressman, who would have won if the county unit system had still been operative. Encouraged by the drift of opinion, by the disorganized opposition, and by the prosperous suburbs, the Georgia Republican party roused itself. Instead of presenting themselves as the party of Georgia moderation, the Republicans decided to "out rightwing" the Democrats. At first the strategy seemed successful, and in 1964 Georgia, which had never gone Republican in a presidential year, cast its electoral votes for Barry

Goldwater. The Democrats were in their usual disarray, and in the gubernatorial primary the favorite, Ellis Arnall, was forced into a runoff by Lester Maddox; Maddox defeated Arnall handily. The contested general election that followed was exceedingly close. Maddox, with his folksy style, captured the imagination of the nonurban voter, but Republican Howard ("Bo") Callaway did well in the cities. Thousands of Georgians rejected both men and wrote in Arnall's name on election day. The error of the Republicans in ignoring the disillusioned moderate voters proved fatal: neither Callaway nor Maddox received a majority of the votes cast, so the legislature was left to decide. And there Maddox was chosen.

While in office Maddox provided a minimum of executive leadership. He lacked political *savoir* and did not relish the details of office. He did, however, appoint blacks to state positions and by so doing helped soften some of his own strident race-baiting.

His successor was James E. Carter, who ran a strong third in 1966 and put together an unbeatable coalition of urban and rural voters to beat Carl Sanders in the 1970 primary. To some he seemed the heir to Maddox and a follower of George Wallace, who had carried Georgia in the presidential election of 1968, but Carter soon gave notice that he was his own man. As governor he presided over a tough state reorganization plan, developed cordial relations with Georgia's black leaders, attacked racial discrimination with energy and effectiveness, created the Heritage Trust program to purchase properties and sites essential for an understanding of Georgia's past, rammed through a campaign financial disclosure act, and encouraged state environmentalists by making difficult decisions on issues weaker men might have avoided. In addition, Carter commissioned the writing of a new history of the state. Carter's meteoric rise to national prominence was capped by his unexpected seizure of the Democratic nomination and his subsequent election to the presidency of the United States. It was a victory in which the entire state took pride. His triumph on the national level seemed to symbolize the final success of the principles of the New South.

George Busbee, who followed Carter, had the misfortune to be governor during a time of recession and declining state revenues. But in his primary runoff victory over Maddox in 1974, he showed agility and restraint. His landslide majorities in the cities were no surprise, but his breaking even with Maddox in rural Georgia may have indicated the ultimate decline of the brand of provincial politics once so dominant in the state.

In some ways the physical face of Georgia has changed little since the days of the Indian and the Spanish mission. Lumber and pulpwood companies own about one-half of the state, and approximately 70 percent of Georgia was covered by trees in the 1970s; the deer, the bear, the alligator, and other wild creatures have returned. However, resemblance to the past ends with the physical appearance. A population of 5 million in 1976 is concentrated in about ten metropolitan areas. The number of farms decreases yearly just as the average farm size increases; agriculture represents only 20 percent of the gross value produced by Georgia industry in a society that becomes more and more urban. Yet in some ways Georgia is still basically a rural state—almost pastoral, in fact. In this respect it is extraordinarily fortunate; because of its space, ample rains, and generous rivers the state has escaped having its environment ruined. For the future, how-

ever, the guidance of an enlightened electorate and a responsive government will have to guard against the philosophy of growth for its own sake. As Georgia's open spaces and unspoiled rivers, beaches, islands, and mountains attract thousands of new visitors, the question thoughtful citizens are inclined to ask themselves is whether the state can stand so much unplanned prosperity and at the same time retain its appeal and its individuality.

—B. PHINIZY SPALDING
University of Georgia

Reprinted by permission of Louisiana State University Press from *The Encyclopedia of Southern History* edited by David C. Roller and Robert W. Twyman. Copyright © 1979 by Louisiana State University Press.

Editor's Note

Since this article was written, Georgia has continued its unprecedented growth and prosperity. Joe Frank Harris, a Democrat, was elected governor in 1982 and again in 1986. Governor Harris's emphasis has been education reform, and $1.5 billion has been earmarked for this priority.

Chronology

The following chronology only scratches the surface of Georgia's history. For brevity's sake, some important events in the state's past have been omitted. Also, see the sections "War Between the States," "Women's Rights," "Forts," and "Famous Georgians" for information about these related topics.

1540—De Soto explores region today called Georgia.

1562—French explorer, Jean Ribaut, explores the St. Marys River.

1565—The Spanish King sent Pedro Menendez de Aviles to get rid of the French. But with the French and Indians against them, the Spanish soldiers were forced back to the islands along the coast.

1679—Spanish friars, led by Father Juan Ocon, visit the Cherokee town of Coweta.

1681—Franciscans pass through Coweta.

1696—James Oglethorpe is born in England on December 22.

1715—A South Carolinian, Thomas Nairne, was the first to suggest that England colonize the area which is now Georgia. The Indians, not liking his idea, burned him at the stake.

1732—King George II of England grants a royal charter for the establishment of Georgia.

—November 17, the *Queen Anne* with 114 settlers on board and led by General James Oglethorpe, sailed from England.

1733—On February 12 the *Queen Anne* landed at the site of Savannah with the settlers who were to establish Georgia.

1734—By March Oglethorpe's followers have built 91 log houses facing the Savannah River.

1736—Oglethorpe brings many more individuals to Georgia from England, among them John and Charles Wesley.

—John Wesley, founder of Methodism, came to Georgia as missionary for the Church of England. He began what is reported to be the world's first Protestant Sunday school.

1736—Fort Frederica is built on St. Simons Island.

—The first golf course in Georgia, and possibly in the United States, was constructed by once wealthy landowners from the Scottish Highlands who settled at the present site of Darien.

1737—John Wesley was so disliked that he was forced to return to England and was replaced by George Whitefield, who established Bethesda Orphanage. He also established the first English-speaking school in the state.

1739—Tomochichi, the Indian leader who helped get the Georgia colony on its feet, dies at the age of 97.

1742—The British defeat the Spanish in the Battle of Bloody Marsh. Spanish influence wanes.

1743—The first advocate of communism, Christian Priber, died in prison on St. Simons Island. He came to Georgia from Germany and taught of the advantages of communistic government. Then he encouraged the French traders to compete with the English, was accused of being a French spy, and was arrested and imprisoned.

1751—Henry Parker organizes Georgia's first militia.

1752—Forty-three families of Puritans, with their 536 slaves, arrive in Georgia.

1754—The first of three royal governors from England arrives in Georgia after the colony's original trustees relinquish their charter.

1765—John and William Bartram travel through Georgia.

1766—The Georgia penal institutions were so filled with debtors that a law was passed by the State Legislature requiring creditors to pay for food for the people that had been thrown into jail.

1773—Slave population swells to over 15,000.

243

1774—The first Continental Congress meets in Philadelphia, without representation from Georgia.

1775—Georgia holds its first Provincial Congress.

1776—British warships arrive in Savannah Harbor.

—Button Gwinnett, George Walton, and Lyman Hall sign Declaration of Independence at Philadelphia.

1777—The Georgia Legislature adopts the state's first constitution.

1778—Savannah falls to British forces.

1779—Americans defeat British at Kettle Creek near Washington, Georgia. British defeat Americans at Brier Creek.

1781—Americans, under the command of General "Light Horse Harry" Lee, recapture Augusta, which has been occupied by the British since 1779.

1782—British forces surrender at Savannah.

1785—The University of Georgia is chartered.

1786—General Nathanael Greene, who had taken command of the Southern theater late in the war, dies at Mulberry Grove after retiring there in 1785.

1788—Georgia becomes the fourth state of the new United States of America by unanimously ratifying the Federal Constitution.

1790—Georgia's population is 82,548.

—The first Georgia game law was passed by the State Assembly to conserve wildlife.

1793—Eli Whitney invents the cotton gin near Savannah.

1796—The slave market in Louisville is believed to have been built when the town was the state capital, but there are no documents to prove it.

1799—The Great Seal is authorized by the Legislature.

1801—Georgia's first divorce was granted. It was required by the State Constitution that the Superior Court authorize and both Houses of Legislature agree by two-thirds majority to grant a divorce.

1802—Jekyll Island was purchased by Poulain DuBignon and became a haven for French Royalists who were fleeing the Revolution in their homeland.

1819—The steamship, *Savannah,* becomes the first such ship to cross the Atlantic Ocean.

1820—Population of the state is 340,985.

1821—Creek Indians relinquish to Georgia the land between the Flint and the Ocmulgee Rivers.

1824—A hurricane destroyed Sunbury, the second largest city of Georgia. It was the home town of Dr. Lyman Hall and Button Gwinnett, who signed the Declaration of Independence; Richard Hawley and Nathan Brownson; two governors; and other famous Georgians. After it survived an attack from the British, a hurricane, and a malaria epidemic, another hurricane destroyed it completely.

1825—Creek Chief William McIntosh is murdered.

—General LaFayette visits Georgia.

1828—The nation's first gold rush took place at Dahlonega in Lumpkin County, north Georgia.

1829—Gold is discovered at Duke's Creek in today's White County.

—Augustine S. Clayton set up the first cotton mill near Athens, operated with waterpower from the Oconee River.

1830—State's population is 516,823.

1831—United States Supreme Court rejects Cherokee plea against federal removal law.

1832—Georgia charters its first railroad.

1834—Georgian Mirabeau Lamar migrates to Texas; he will become Texas's second president.

1835—Oglethorpe University founded in Atlanta.

1836—Emory University founded in Atlanta and Wesleyan College (the first woman's college with authority to confer degrees) chartered in Macon.

1838—Cherokees' "Trail of Tears" begins.

1839—The lot for the first residence in Atlanta is purchased.

1840—Georgia's population climbs to 691,392.

1842—Dr. Crawford Long, a Jefferson physician, becomes the first doctor to administer ether to kill pain during surgery.

—Sidney Lanier is born in Macon on February 3.

1846—Georgia Supreme Court meets for the first time.

1851—The Georgia Military Institute was founded at Marietta.

1860—Juliette Gordon Low, founder of the Girl Scouts, is born in Savannah.

1861—Georgia secedes from the Union on January 19.

—Governor Joseph Brown orders the State Militia to occupy Fort Pulaski.

1863—Nathan Bedford Forrest captures 1500 Union soldiers near Rome.

—Battle of Chickamauga is fought.

1864—The Battle of Atlanta begins. In November Sherman and his troops set fire to Atlanta.

1865—Georgia adopts the 13th Amendment, outlawing slavery.

1867—The first Rich's Department Store opens in Atlanta.

1868—Georgia is readmitted to the Union.

1874—On February 28 Georgia became the first state in the Union to establish a Department of Agriculture.

1875—Postwar population of Georgia is 1,184,068.

1877—Atlanta becomes permanent capital.

1878—Walter George is born near Preston on January 19.

1886—Ty Cobb is born in Banks County on December 18.

1888—The Atlanta Bar Association is organized.

—Georgia Tech begins classes.

1889— Capitol building is completed.

1892—The Coca-Cola company is granted its first charter by the Fulton Superior Court.

1895—A "moving picture show" at the Cotton States Exposition in Atlanta, believed to be the first before a paid audience.

1897—Richard Russell is born in Winder on November 2.

—February 17 the National Congress of Mothers was organized in Washington, D.C., an idea conceived by Mrs. Theodore Birney, a native of Marietta and Cobb County teacher. Later the name was changed to National Parent-Teacher Association.

1900—Margaret Mitchell is born in Atlanta on November 8.

1902—Bobby Jones is born in Atlanta on March 17.

1909—Dean Rusk is born in Cherokee County on February 9.

1912—Juliette Gordon Low organizes the first Girl Scout Troop in the United States in Savannah.

1914—Carl Vinson is sworn in as the nation's youngest member of Congress.

1915—"Nat" Harris becomes Georgia's last "Confederate Veteran" governor.

1922—Rebecca Felton becomes the nation's first female United States Senator.

1924—James Earl Carter is born in Plains.

1925—The holly bush was developed by Thomas W. Burford, botanist of Atlanta.

1928—The Cloisters opens.

1929—Martin Luther King, Jr. is born in Atlanta on January 15.

1930—Rebecca Latimer Felton dies in Atlanta on January 24.

—Population climbs to 2,908,521.

1935—The Brown Thrasher becomes Georgia's state bird.

1936—*Gone With the Wind* is published.

1937—Okefenokee Swamp becomes a National Wildlife Refuge.

1939—The movie, *Gone with the Wind,* premiers in Atlanta.

1943—Georgia becomes first state to allow 18-year-olds to vote.

1945—Franklin Roosevelt dies at Warm Springs.

1947—The state of Georgia purchases Jekyll Island for $650,000.

1961—Baseball great Ty Cobb dies on July 17.

1962—Members of the Atlanta Symphony are killed in a Paris plane crash.

1964—Georgia voters go Republican in the presidential election.

1973—Maynard Jackson, Jr. becomes Atlanta's first black mayor.

1974—Hank Aaron hits his 715th home run in Atlanta.

1976—James Earl Carter is elected President of the United States.

1977—Toccoa Dam bursts, causing much property damage.

1979—"Georgia on My Mind" is adopted as the state song.

1980—Population of the state is 5,463,105.

1981—University of Georgia wins the national football championship.

1982—Georgia experiences the second highest population growth rate (3.2 percent since 1980) in the South Atlantic region.

1984—Georgians give Ronald Reagan 60.1 percent of the vote in the presidential election.

1985—Robert Woodruff, empire-building president of Coca-Cola Company, dies at age 95 on March 7.

1986—Bob Horner of the *Atlanta Braves* ties a major league baseball record when he hits four home runs in a single game.

1987—Football coaching great, Pat Dye, is inducted into the Georgia Sports Hall of Fame.

1988—Second edition of *The Georgia Almanac and Book of Facts* is published.

HOLIDAYS AND DAYS OF SPECIAL OBSERVANCE

The following legal holidays are observed in Georgia.

New Year's Day .... January 1
Martin Luther King, Jr.'s Birthday .... January 15
   (will be observed the third Monday of January)
Robert E. Lee's Birthday .... January 19
   (will be observed the Friday following Thanksgiving)
Washington's Birthday .... February 22
   (will be observed December 24)
Confederate Memorial Day .... April 15
National Memorial Day .... May 25
Independence Day .... July 4
Labor Day .... First Monday in September
Columbus Day .... October 12
Veterans' Day .... November 11
Thanksgiving Day .... Fourth Thursday in November
Christmas Day .... December 25

HOUSING

There are approximately 2,012,640 occupied housing units in Georgia. About 60% of this amount are owner occupied units and 33% are occupied by renters.

County	Year-Round Housing Units	Owner-Occupied Housing Units	Renter-Occupied Housing Units	Mobile Homes	Housing Units Built Before 1939
Appling	5,768	3,818	1,299	1,105	953
Atkinson	2,313	1,413	596	399	437
Bacon	3,379	2,314	802	402	445
Baker	1,264	826	382	189	162
Baldwin	11,723	6,713	3,438	1,708	1,670
Banks	3,277	2,400	634	630	817
Barrow	7,768	5,228	2,086	1,153	1,452
Bartow	14,536	10,210	3,594	2,035	2,548
Ben Hill	6,184	3,828	1,842	734	1,762
Berrien	5,113	3,318	1,335	839	855
Bibb	55,561	31,131	21,449	1,295	10,053
Bleckley	3,920	2,587	965	396	821
Brantley	3,043	2,357	427	836	395
Brooks	5,362	3,378	1,612	750	1,698
Bryan	3,498	2,531	683	823	476
Bulloch	12,600	7,059	4,280	1,659	2,220
Burke	6,787	3,968	2,244	802	1,582
Butts	4,663	2,798	1,189	573	1,174
Calhoun	1,942	1,198	635	156	570
Camden	5,142	3,411	977	1,078	408
Candler	2,824	1,664	863	349	580
Carroll	20,276	13,297	5,705	2,626	3,835
Catoosa	13,389	10,069	2,579	1,733	1,268
Charlton	2,496	1,726	500	501	376
Chatham	76,718	42,368	28,955	3,827	13,542
Chattahoochee	3,200	473	2,539	286	486
Chattooga	8,245	5,876	1,857	781	2,133
Cherokee	17,666	13,842	3,006	2,462	2,217
Clarke	27,576	12,423	14,164	1,789	3,396
Clay	1,325	792	401	113	419
Clayton	52,989	32,458	17,991	1,568	1,057
Clinch	2,342	1,348	772	340	465
Cobb	113,271	70,759	35,836	3,252	4,526
Coffee	9,701	6,249	2,656	1,579	1,545
Colquitt	12,936	8,187	3,965	1,492	2,621
Columbia	14,010	10,326	2,508	2,056	749
Cook	4,849	3,278	1,198	587	779
Coweta	14,082	9,736	3,571	1,149	3,207
Crawford	2,546	1,816	541	527	392
Crisp	7,074	4,093	2,466	832	1,458
Dade	4,275	3,185	813	800	503
Dawson	1,818	1,405	258	341	299
Decatur	9,046	5,926	2,389	1,059	1,774
DeKalb	181,803	102,842	70,080	711	12,164
Dodge	6,394	4,379	1,488	655	1,346
Dooly	3,765	2,388	1,141	383	1,191

County	Year-Round Housing Units	Owner-Occupied Housing Units	Renter-Occupied Housing Units	Mobile Homes	Housing Units Built Before 1939
Dougherty	34,705	17,677	15,366	1,940	2,523
Douglas	17,746	14,067	2,844	2,254	1,223
Early	4,667	2,886	1,417	519	1,279
Echols	808	582	153	194	174
Effingham	6,265	4,754	1,033	1,421	1,013
Elbert	7,038	4,794	1,760	770	1,938
Emanuel	7,723	4,911	2,080	740	2,089
Evans	3,175	1,879	980	506	687
Fannin	6,061	4,547	975	832	1,071
Fayette	9,608	8,041	1,167	794	895
Floyd	30,173	19,182	9,295	1,989	6,618
Forsyth	10,321	7,807	1,588	2,179	1,013
Franklin	5,833	4,117	1,246	711	1,359
Fulton	246,352	104,679	120,629	964	39,273
Gilmer	4,391	3,044	893	821	657
Glascock	910	610	226	142	292
Glynn	21,894	12,800	7,026	1,855	2,732
Gordon	10,904	7,630	2,650	1,097	1,798
Grady	7,089	4,865	1,755	862	1,489
Greene	4,117	2,860	898	362	1,110
Gwinnett	58,015	43,115	12,112	3,581	2,994
Habersham	8,912	6,569	1,827	1,332	1,562
Hall	27,342	18,631	7,440	3,583	3,711
Hancock	3,095	1,988	803	319	971
Haralson	6,966	5,007	1,497	781	1,321
Harris	5,927	4,137	1,099	634	1,307
Hart	7,494	4,982	1,304	972	1,234
Heard	2,434	1,705	499	458	618
Henry	12,244	9,553	2,077	1,403	1,764
Houston	27,390	17,324	8,185	2,361	742
Irwin	3,326	2,121	892	354	1,104
Jackson	9,088	6,372	2,247	1,746	2,056
Jasper	2,802	1,843	710	292	869
Jeff Davis	4,042	2,784	987	602	597
Jefferson	6,503	3,966	1,980	656	1,572
Jenkins	3,282	1,945	961	380	953
Johnson	3,284	2,148	807	322	1,091
Jones	5,820	4,321	949	1,165	752
Lamar	4,297	2,840	1,170	407	1,109
Lanier	2,029	1,263	559	369	285
Laurens	13,442	8,580	3,867	1,614	2,370
Lee	3,870	2,678	964	864	265
Liberty	10,674	4,696	4,933	2,315	643
Lincoln	3,030	1,706	479	532	767
Long	1,733	1,050	486	488	272
Lowndes	24,279	13,785	8,824	2,514	3,149
Lumpkin	3,727	2,505	883	718	590
Macon	4,675	3,023	1,348	536	1,165
Madison	6,468	4,923	1,202	1,371	1,233
Marion	1,841	1,217	470	314	445
McDuffie	6,739	4,428	1,842	954	990
McIntosh	3,094	2,190	440	716	495

County	Year-Round Housing Units	Owner-Occupied Housing Units	Renter-Occupied Housing Units	Mobile Homes	Housing Units Built Before 1939
Meriwether	7,594	5,105	1,772	1,078	2,196
Miller	2,561	1,698	707	249	571
Mitchell	7,026	4,406	2,080	720	1,476
Monroe	4,908	3,350	1,317	621	1,212
Montgomery	2,533	1,617	597	376	789
Morgan	3,901	2,661	1,002	427	1,182
Murray	6,887	5,033	1,506	1,493	845
Muscogee	63,802	33,739	25,373	1,814	8,834
Newton	11,812	8,199	2,777	1,185	2,421
Oconee	4,488	3,194	1,043	517	811
Oglethorpe	3,131	2,347	600	550	839
Paulding	9,150	7,185	1,560	1,151	1,376
Peach	6,631	4,130	2,050	715	1,171
Pickens	4,443	3,231	930	683	963
Pierce	4,279	2,962	966	592	913
Pike	3,086	2,269	573	413	992
Polk	12,040	8,458	2,955	822	3,208
Pulaski	3,345	2,163	904	324	821
Putnam	3,659	2,541	857	491	615
Quitman	882	520	252	89	215
Rabun	4,673	3,022	869	649	754
Randolph	3,535	2,109	1,017	241	1,145
Richmond	64,763	35,211	24,290	3,243	8,944
Rockdale	12,144	9,564	2,028	1,029	938
Schley	1,235	832	293	166	418
Screven	5,501	3,278	1,491	922	1,193
Seminole	3,806	2,361	690	620	450
Spalding	17,023	10,337	5,840	1,225	3,380
Stephens	8,308	5,704	2,083	1,093	1,165
Stewart	2,086	1,258	633	221	758
Sumter	10,090	6,022	3,443	925	2,237
Talbot	2,362	1,571	515	283	693
Taliaferro	866	558	200	81	403
Tattnall	6,254	3,655	1,935	694	1,226
Taylor	2,862	1,951	702	358	723
Telfair	4,363	2,930	977	605	999
Terrell	4,138	2,329	1,510	281	1,522
Thomas	13,774	8,669	4,120	1,473	3,216
Tift	11,000	7,119	3,618	1,627	1,603
Toombs	8,345	4,884	2,788	876	1,169
Towns	3,184	1,733	291	814	326
Treutlen	2,331	1,395	678	158	492
Troup	18,316	11,266	6,189	1,054	5,141
Turner	3,208	2,006	1,072	335	761
Twiggs	3,137	2,203	609	430	498
Union	4,150	2,809	560	601	551
Upson	9,732	6,496	2,674	759	3,155
Walker	20,878	15,384	4,250	1,997	3,395
Walton	10,425	7,132	2,874	1,550	2,515
Ware	13,771	8,761	4,027	1,282	2,733
Warren	2,312	1,620	490	224	687
Washington	6,587	4,188	1,888	690	1,910

County	Year-Round Housing Units	Owner-Occupied Housing Units	Renter-Occupied Housing Units	Mobile Homes	Housing Units Built Before 1939
Wayne	7,586	4,932	1,947	951	1,095
Webster	828	532	224	123	246
Wheeler	1,906	1,311	422	282	471
White	4,042	2,861	638	571	613
Whitfield	23,780	15,452	7,014	2,821	2,603
Wilcox	2,773	1,972	624	284	766
Wilkes	4,165	2,899	981	392	1,139
Wilkinson	3,787	2,607	743	688	907
Worth	6,353	4,210	1,601	1,055	1,209
Georgia	2,012,640	1,216,459	655,193	152,948	296,662

Indian Lands in Georgia

INDIANS

It is difficult at this late date to attempt to determine the Indian population of North America at the beginning of European discovery and exploration. Even more difficult is to try to come up with figures for a small segment of the continent—a segment that one day would become a state of the United States. Various estimates, however, have placed the aboriginal population of the contiguous states at around one million individuals, divided among 2,000 tribes. Of these, probably less than 10,000 Indians lived in the region which became Georgia.

The accompanying map depicts the various tribes that made Georgia their home during the 17th century, a time which closely corresponds with the opening of the historic period in this part of the country. Most of the tribes shown, with the exception of the *Cherokees* in the northeast, were part of the powerful *Creek* Confederacy. Speaking languages belonging to the *Muskhogean* stock, all of these tribes maintained a similar life style, that indigenous to the southeastern part of North America. Mostly village dwellers, these Indians practiced agriculture, but still depended on hunting, fishing, and gathering for a sizable portion of their livelihood.

The Cherokees, who spoke an *Iroquoian* language, lived in the northeast and comprised the largest Indian tribe in the south. Consisting at one time of an estimated 22,000 individuals, the majority lived in Tennessee and North and South Carolina. In later years, Georgia attained a sizable number of Cherokees, before they were driven west by the U.S. Government in the 1830s.

Those Muskhogean, or Creek, tribes shown on the map are:

Apalachicola	Oconee
Chiaha	Osochi
Creek	Okmulgee
Guale	Tacatacuru
Hitchiti	Tamathli
Icafui	Yamasee
Kasihta	Yui

LABOR

Commuters, Travel Time, and Mode of Transportation: 1980.

County	Number Worked in County of Residence	Number Worked Outside County of Residence	Mean Travel Time (Minutes)	Car, Truck or Van — Percent Drive Alone	Percent Carpool	Percent Public Means
Appling	3,234	1,270	19	63.9	26.0	0.4
Atkinson	1,133	759	24	61.4	30.6	0.0
Bacon	2,490	451	14	66.8	20.5	0.8

| County | Number Worked in County of Residence | Number Worked Outside County of Residence | Mean Travel Time (Minutes) | Car, Truck or Van | | Percent Public Means |
				Percent Drive Alone	Percent Carpool	
Baker	593	564	25	55.9	34.7	0.3
Baldwin	11,353	1,427	17	73.2	21.4	1.2
Banks	1,105	2,423	23	58.3	28.9	1.9
Barrow	5,535	2,887	23	64.6	30.0	0.4
Bartow	12,609	3,862	21	66.2	28.4	0.7
Ben Hill	5,067	546	14	74.0	20.1	0.4
Berrien	3,760	1,246	16	69.0	23.1	0.3
Bibb	47,752	8,203	20	69.9	22.7	3.1
Bleckley	2,557	1,370	22	57.2	32.3	1.7
Brantley	1,038	1,969	29	57.9	32.6	1.0
Brooks	2,932	1,711	20	61.6	27.7	0.6
Bryan	1,279	2,325	29	62.0	31.4	0.5
Bulloch	11,794	1,688	17	65.4	24.3	0.3
Burke	4,828	1,323	20	55.2	35.2	0.8
Butts	2,786	1,944	26	61.3	32.8	1.2
Calhoun	1,072	577	20	57.7	34.6	0.2
Camden	3,927	780	20	62.1	29.0	1.6
Candler	1,916	643	16	66.6	22.2	0.4
Carroll	16,919	4,888	21	67.5	26.8	0.9
Catoosa	4,115	11,128	21	75.8	20.2	0.5
Charlton	1,343	912	25	52.7	38.6	1.1
Chatham	70,330	4,804	21	67.7	18.6	5.6
Chattahoochee	11,321	1,398	10	25.2	15.8	1.5
Chattooga	6,267	1,931	21	62.5	30.2	0.3
Cherokee	8,254	13,336	31	65.2	29.1	0.6
Clarke	27,649	2,899	16	66.7	20.0	3.2
Clay	627	216	17	53.5	34.7	0.5
Clayton	29,432	37,295	24	75.0	20.8	1.4
Clinch	2,208	245	17	64.5	28.1	0.5
Cobb	68,032	72,425	25	76.0	19.4	1.2
Coffee	8,304	846	16	67.4	22.6	0.8
Colquitt	9,408	1,969	19	68.3	23.3	0.6
Columbia	3,539	12,606	23	74.3	21.5	0.3
Cook	3,327	1,222	18	69.2	21.8	0.2
Coweta	10,504	4,369	23	68.4	27.0	0.3
Crawford	857	1,806	29	59.1	34.8	0.6
Crisp	4,824	805	16	67.7	23.2	0.8
Dade	1,758	2,646	26	59.4	29.5	0.5
Dawson	943	997	27	62.1	29.2	0.0
Decatur	6,355	1,107	19	66.7	25.6	0.7
DeKalb	112,887	112,110	25	69.3	17.5	9.4
Dodge	3,808	1,672	21	71.0	23.6	1.0
Dooly	2,444	771	18	61.3	27.5	0.4
Dougherty	33,615	2,088	17	73.2	19.3	1.7
Douglas	6,273	15,719	29	69.0	27.4	0.7
Early	3,540	620	16	65.0	26.8	0.5
Echols	246	472	26	64.8	29.2	0.1
Effingham	1,859	4,102	29	64.6	29.6	0.1
Elbert	6,030	1,335	18	69.7	24.5	0.2
Emanuel	6,092	917	18	64.3	28.3	0.0
Evans	2,291	596	17	61.1	25.6	0.4
Fannin	2,850	1,863	24	70.5	23.4	1.6

253

County	Number Worked in County of Residence	Number Worked Outside County of Residence	Mean Travel Time (Minutes)	Car, Truck or Van Percent Drive Alone	Percent Carpool	Percent Public Means
Fayette	4,337	7,991	27	74.0	21.8	0.9
Floyd	29,278	3,060	20	74.2	19.3	1.5
Forsyth	4,715	7,231	30	64.3	30.4	0.5
Franklin	3,443	2,322	22	63.3	28.9	0.0
Fulton	176,276	49,665	26	61.3	15.8	17.4
Gilmer	2,997	1,033	25	64.6	26.4	1.2
Glascock	363	405	22	60.1	30.8	0.0
Glynn	21,752	877	17	72.2	20.8	1.0
Gordon	9,980	2,637	18	71.3	23.2	0.3
Grady	5,107	1,655	18	62.7	27.3	0.9
Greene	3,188	740	21	55.0	36.2	1.3
Gwinnett	28,873	48,428	26	72.9	22.6	1.3
Habersham	8,281	1,541	18	68.0	24.1	1.1
Hall	28,041	4,506	20	72.0	21.5	0.8
Hancock	1,216	1,453	27	44.2	48.0	1.2
Haralson	5,050	2,202	21	66.8	27.3	0.5
Harris	2,253	3,662	25	66.8	27.2	0.8
Hart	4,525	2,294	18	66.2	27.4	0.3
Heard	1,040	1,276	27	61.7	32.3	1.0
Henry	4,615	10,103	29	72.0	23.6	1.0
Houston	27,035	5,210	17	69.0	24.8	0.7
Irwin	1,794	1,186	19	65.6	24.7	0.2
Jackson	5,548	4,456	21	65.7	27.9	0.5
Jasper	1,635	945	27	60.4	32.9	1.5
Jeff Davis	3,614	597	15	72.1	19.7	0.0
Jefferson	4,697	1,106	18	56.4	33.9	0.5
Jenkins	2,333	659	19	62.8	27.1	0.3
Johnson	1,683	1,097	23	55.0	38.3	0.4
Jones	1,334	4,618	25	71.1	24.9	0.8
Lamar	2,497	1,870	22	62.7	30.0	0.6
Lanier	868	873	20	66.9	27.4	0.3
Laurens	11,943	1,428	18	69.0	23.8	1.3
Lee	1,120	3,631	23	71.1	23.3	0.5
Liberty	10,320	1,755	14	43.8	24.9	1.0
Lincoln	1,416	973	26	58.9	34.4	1.4
Long	392	1,175	23	58.5	35.1	0.1
Lowndes	24,675	1,919	16	71.7	19.0	0.8
Lumpkin	2,172	1,761	23	63.1	24.9	0.6
Macon	3,186	931	18	57.3	30.6	1.3
Madison	2,089	4,448	23	64.3	28.7	0.2
Marion	929	661	25	59.0	33.4	0.7
McDuffie	4,561	1,970	19	67.4	26.6	0.3
McIntosh	1,465	912	26	61.5	28.1	2.7
Meriwether	5,108	2,253	22	62.3	31.3	1.1
Miller	1,693	941	20	67.0	21.0	1.1
Mitchell	5,131	1,634	19	61.9	29.9	0.6
Monroe	3,586	1,781	23	59.9	33.5	0.5
Montgomery	1,251	1,064	19	58.9	32.2	1.0
Morgan	3,084	1,068	21	62.4	28.9	1.4
Murray	5,251	2,983	19	72.4	23.5	0.2
Muscogee	49,092	17,365	18	70.4	17.0	2.5
Newton	7,111	6,202	24	66.2	28.5	0.4
Oconee	1,425	3,948	20	71.7	22.6	0.2

County	Number Worked in County of Residence	Number Worked Outside County of Residence	Mean Travel Time (Minutes)	Car, Truck or Van		Percent Public Means
				Percent Drive Alone	Percent Carpool	
Oglethorpe	1,258	2,227	26	59.4	34.9	0.8
Paulding	2,962	6,586	33	62.9	32.8	0.6
Peach	4,099	2,624	19	62.4	28.6	0.7
Pickens	3,020	1,262	26	63.8	31.6	0.2
Pierce	2,626	1,553	22	67.3	27.1	0.2
Pike	1,083	2,443	26	61.2	30.4	0.4
Polk	8,459	3,262	21	68.1	27.4	0.7
Pulaski	2,347	892	19	59.0	29.5	2.3
Putnam	2,810	824	18	61.5	29.8	0.0
Quitman	144	413	25	57.6	37.2	0.8
Rabun	3,635	426	18	64.9	28.7	0.2
Randolph	2,297	468	16	61.7	28.5	0.2
Richmond	64,289	7,404	18	62.4	19.8	3.1
Rockdale	5,888	9,199	28	70.3	24.5	1.0
Schley	717	501	17	65.6	27.0	0.8
Screven	3,966	925	18	65.5	28.8	0.3
Seminole	2,209	896	20	64.6	26.9	0.1
Spalding	14,157	4,708	21	66.0	26.7	2.2
Stephens	7,662	1,012	16	71.0	22.6	0.2
Stewart	993	368	22	52.6	32.4	1.7
Sumter	9,308	1,149	16	65.1	26.8	1.1
Talbot	738	1,574	29	51.0	43.6	0.7
Taliaferro	262	378	25	56.2	32.6	1.0
Tattnall	3,953	1,599	19	65.6	26.0	0.2
Taylor	1,777	766	22	52.0	38.8	1.4
Telfair	2,724	1,272	19	63.8	26.9	1.0
Terrell	2,643	668	15	61.3	26.8	2.3
Thomas	12,209	975	16	68.8	22.1	0.8
Tift	10,174	863	14	71.4	19.1	0.8
Toombs	6,126	1,668	19	68.1	23.1	1.6
Towns	1,233	611	19	62.5	27.2	0.3
Treutlen	1,160	755	22	64.3	28.8	0.0
Troup	16,661	2,253	17	68.6	22.8	3.2
Turner	2,656	469	15	70.3	23.6	0.2
Twiggs	1,103	1,832	28	62.4	33.2	0.4
Union	2,414	655	22	62.7	24.3	1.0
Upson	9,328	1,161	16	63.3	29.6	0.9
Walker	9,081	11,786	23	73.1	22.7	0.3
Walton	7,086	4,780	25	61.7	32.7	0.4
Ware	11,208	1,164	16	76.8	16.6	0.9
Warren	1,135	660	21	59.7	33.5	1.1
Washington	5,846	803	18	63.0	29.7	0.4
Wayne	6,062	721	17	71.9	20.4	0.4
Webster	171	370	24	57.2	31.6	2.9
Wheeler	809	836	21	60.8	31.1	0.4
White	2,247	1,727	23	68.2	24.7	0.0
Whitfield	27,729	2,271	17	72.7	22.0	0.5
Wilcox	1,389	783	22	62.5	26.8	2.4
Wilkes	3,513	546	17	65.3	26.0	0.3
Wilkinson	2,195	1,467	21	58.2	36.6	1.1
Worth	3,449	2,379	22	61.8	29.8	0.8
Georgia	1,453,389	693,518	22	67.5	22.1	3.9

LAND AREA

Georgia, from a land area standpoint, is the largest state east of the Mississippi River. It contains 58,909.6 square miles and ranks 21st in size in the country. The state's extreme North-South length is 315 miles; extreme East-West breadth is 250 miles. The chart below gives the individual counties in Georgia, along with their areas in square miles.

County	Area in Square Miles: 1980 Total	Land	Water	County	Area in Square Miles: 1980 Total	Land	Water
Appling	512.3	510.0	2.3	Dougherty	334.1	329.5	4.6
Atkinson	344.3	343.8	0.5	Douglas	202.7	202.7	0.0
Bacon	285.8	285.7	0.2	Early	517.7	516.1	1.6
Baker	347.9	347.1	0.8	Echols	420.6	420.6	0.0
Baldwin	267.8	257.4	10.4	Effingham	482.1	481.9	0.2
Banks	233.9	233.8	0.1	Elbert	374.2	366.7	7.5
Barrow	163.1	162.6	0.5	Emanuel	689.6	688.3	1.3
Bartow	470.7	456.1	14.6	Evans	187.0	186.5	0.5
Ben Hill	253.9	253.8	0.1	Fannin	390.3	384.2	6.1
Berrien	457.8	455.7	2.1	Fayette	199.5	199.0	0.5
Bibb	255.7	253.0	2.7	Floyd	520.2	518.7	1.5
Bleckley	219.0	219.0	0.0	Forsyth	246.9	226.2	20.6
Brantley	444.5	444.5	0.0	Franklin	266.7	263.8	2.9
Brooks	497.6	491.1	6.5	Fulton	534.9	533.9	1.0
Bryan	453.1	441.3	11.8	Gilmer	431.7	427.4	4.3
Bulloch	688.7	677.9	10.8	Glascock	144.3	144.3	0.0
Burke	834.1	832.8	1.3	Glynn	457.5	412.4	45.1
Butts	189.7	186.9	2.8	Gordon	355.2	355.0	0.2
Calhoun	284.0	283.8	0.2	Grady	459.9	459.0	0.9
Camden	689.0	649.5	39.6	Greene	406.2	389.5	16.7
Candler	248.8	248.2	0.7	Gwinnett	436.5	435.1	1.4
Carroll	503.2	501.3	1.9	Habersham	279.0	278.3	0.7
Catoosa	162.4	162.4	0.0	Hall	427.7	379.2	48.5
Charlton	782.4	779.5	2.9	Hancock	478.8	469.7	9.1
Chatham	498.4	443.4	55.0	Haralson	283.1	282.6	0.5
Chattahoochee	251.2	250.1	1.1	Harris	472.8	464.4	8.3
Chattooga	313.4	313.4	0.0	Hart	257.2	230.0	27.2
Cherokee	434.4	424.0	10.5	Heard	301.2	291.8	9.4
Clarke	121.9	121.9	0.0	Henry	321.1	320.6	0.5
Clay	216.8	196.4	20.4	Houston	380.4	379.8	0.6
Clayton	148.8	147.9	0.9	Irwin	362.6	362.2	0.4
Clinch	824.0	821.4	2.6	Jackson	342.1	342.1	0.0
Cobb	344.9	343.3	1.6	Jasper	373.7	371.3	2.4
Coffee	602.9	601.9	1.0	Jeff Davis	335.6	335.1	0.5
Colquitt	556.8	556.5	0.3	Jefferson	531.2	529.2	2.0
Columbia	307.8	290.2	17.6	Jenkins	352.7	352.6	0.1
Cook	232.8	232.6	0.2	Johnson	306.8	306.4	0.4
Coweta	445.2	444.5	0.7	Jones	394.4	394.3	0.1
Crawford	327.8	327.8	0.0	Lamar	186.0	185.6	0.4
Crisp	280.7	275.0	5.7	Lanier	199.5	193.7	5.8
Dade	175.7	175.7	0.0	Laurens	817.0	815.7	1.3
Dawson	214.1	210.0	4.1	Lee	361.9	358.4	3.5
Decatur	623.5	585.8	37.7	Liberty	541.9	516.7	25.2
DeKalb	270.5	270.0	0.6	Lincoln	258.2	195.7	62.5
Dodge	505.5	503.9	1.6	Long	403.2	402.1	1.1
Dooly	397.3	396.8	0.5	Lowndes	511.3	506.8	4.5

256

County	Area in Square Miles: 1980			County	Area in Square Miles: 1980		
	Total	Land	Water		Total	Land	Water
Lumpkin	287.6	287.1	0.5	Stewart	463.3	452.3	11.0
Macon	404.3	403.8	0.5	Sumter	492.1	488.5	3.6
Madison	285.6	285.2	0.5	Talbot	395.0	394.5	0.5
Marion	366.2	366.2	0.0	Taliaferro	195.9	195.9	0.0
McDuffie	266.2	256.0	10.2	Tattnall	487.1	483.9	3.2
McIntosh	478.3	425.0	53.3	Taylor	381.9	381.7	0.3
Meriwether	506.2	505.7	0.5	Telfair	444.2	443.9	0.3
Miller	283.6	283.6	0.0	Terrell	337.5	337.0	0.5
Mitchell	513.9	512.4	1.5	Thomas	552.7	550.6	2.1
Monroe	397.4	396.8	0.6	Tift	268.8	268.4	0.3
Montgomery	244.7	244.2	0.5	Toombs	372.3	371.0	1.3
Morgan	354.5	348.9	5.6	Towns	171.2	164.9	6.3
Murray	347.0	344.7	2.3	Treutlen	202.5	202.1	0.5
Muscogee	220.9	217.8	3.1	Troup	445.6	414.5	31.1
Newton	279.0	277.3	1.7	Turner	289.5	289.1	0.4
Oconee	186.5	186.4	0.1	Twiggs	362.5	361.7	0.8
Oglethorpe	441.7	441.6	0.1	Union	330.0	319.9	10.1
Paulding	312.7	312.3	0.4	Upson	325.9	325.7	0.2
Peach	151.5	151.5	0.0	Walker	446.4	446.0	0.4
Pickens	232.4	232.1	0.3	Walton	330.2	330.2	0.0
Pierce	343.9	343.9	0.0	Ware	907.3	907.1	0.2
Pike	219.3	219.3	0.0	Warren	286.0	285.5	0.5
Polk	311.5	311.4	0.1	Washington	684.4	683.5	0.8
Pulaski	249.9	249.2	0.7	Wayne	648.3	646.9	1.4
Putnam	361.0	343.5	17.5	Webster	210.0	209.9	0.1
Quitman	161.1	146.0	15.1	Wheeler	299.3	299.1	0.2
Rabun	377.1	370.4	6.7	White	242.2	242.0	0.2
Randolph	431.0	430.5	0.5	Whitfield	290.9	290.8	0.1
Richmond	328.6	325.9	2.7	Wilcox	383.4	381.9	1.5
Rockdale	132.0	132.0	0.1	Wilkes	473.8	470.1	3.7
Schley	169.0	169.0	0.0	Wilkinson	452.2	451.5	0.8
Screven	655.1	654.8	0.4	Worth	576.1	575.0	1.1
Seminole	256.7	225.3	31.4	Georgia	58,909.6	58.055.8	853.8
Spalding	199.7	199.2	0.5				
Stephens	183.8	177.1	6.7				

LEGISLATURE

President of Senate
Zell Miller
State Capitol, 3rd Floor
Atlanta 30334
404-656-5040

Members of Senate by Districts

District 1
Portion of Chatham
J. Tom Coleman, Jr. (D)
P.O. Box 22398
Savannah 31403
912-964-7308

District 2
Portion of Chatham
Al Scott (D)
P.O. Box 1704
Savannah 31402
912-234-6420

District 3
*Liberty, McIntosh; Portion
of Bryan, Chatham,
Glynn*
Glenn E. Bryant (D)
P.O. Box 585

257

Senatorial Districts

Hinesville 31313
912-368-3300

Atlanta 30345
404-938-2730

Nashville 31639
912-686-7454

District 4
Bulloch, Candler,
Effingham, Evans, Long,
Tattnall; Portion of Bryan
Joseph E. Kennedy (D)
P.O. Box 246
Claxton 30417
912-739-1163

District 6
Bacon, Brantley, Camden,
Charlton, Pierce, Wayne;
Portion of Appling, Glynn
Earl Nichols, Jr. (D)
P.O. Box 352
Patterson 31557
912-647-2217

District 8
Brooks, Cook, Echols,
Lowndes
Loyce W. Turner (D)
608 Howellbrook Drive
Valdosta 31602
912-242-5725

District 5
Portion of DeKalb
Joe Burton (R)
2598 Woodwardin Road,
NE

District 7
Atkinson, Berrien, Clinch,
Lanier, Tift, Ware
Ed Perry (D)
P.O. Box 925

District 9
Portion of Gwinnett
Tom Phillips (R)
1703 Pounds Road
Stone Mountain 30087
404-469-4735

Representative Districts

District 10
Decatur, Grady, Thomas;
Portion of Colquitt
Harold J. Ragan (D)
1269 Crine Blvd., NW
Cairo 31728
912-377-2593

District 11
Baker, Calhoun, Clay,
Early, Miller, Mitchell,
Quitman, Randolph,
Seminole, Stewart,
Webster; Portion of
Chattahoochee
Jimmy Hodge Timmons

(D)
132 Woodlawn Street
Blakely 31723
912-725-4891

District 12
Dougherty
Mark Taylor (D)
P.O. Box 1156
Albany 31703
912-883-5200

District 13
Ben Hill, Crisp, Dooly,
Irwin, Turner, Worth;
Portion of Colquitt
Rooney L. Bowen (D)

P.O. Box 1238
Cordele 31015
912-273-4531

District 14
Lee, Macon, Peach, Schley,
Sumter, Taylor, Terrell
Bud McKenzie (D)
P.O. Box 565
Montezuma 31063
912-472-8111

District 15
Portion of Chattahoochee,
Muscogee
Floyd Hudgins (D)
P.O. Box 12127

259

Columbus 31907
404-327-5135

District 16
Marion, Talbot; Portion of Muscogee
Ted J. Land (R)
1069 Standing Boy Court
Columbus 31904
404-322-1683

District 17
Butts, Henry; Portion of Clayton
Alex Crumbley (D)
P.O. Box 775
McDonough 30253
404-957-1815

District 18
Houston, Twiggs; Portion of Bibb
Ed Barker (D)
P.O. Box 5036
Warner Robins 31099
912-922-8238

District 19
Bleckley, Coffee, Dodge, Jeff Davis, Pulaski, Telfair, Wilcox
Walter S. Ray (D)
Box 295
Douglas 31533
912-384-0200

District 20
Johnson, Laurens, Montgomery, Toombs, Treutlen, Wheeler; Portion of Appling, Washington
Hugh Gillis, Sr. (D)
P.O. Box 148
Soperton 30457
912-529-3212

District 21
Burke, Emanuel, Glascock, Jefferson, Jenkins, Screven; Portion of Washington
Bill English (D)
214 Golf Drive
Swainsboro 30401
912-237-6954

District 22
Portion of Richmond

Thomas F. Allgood (D)
615 Telfair Bldg.
Augusta 30903
404-724-6526

District 23
Portion of Columbia, Richmond
1432 Reynolds St.
Augusta 30902
404-736-2876

District 24
Greene, Lincoln, McDuffie, Oglethorpe, Taliaferro, Warren, Wilkes; Portion of Columbia
Sam McGill (D)
P.O. Box 520
Washington 30673
404-678-2161

District 25
Baldwin, Hancock, Jasper, Jones, Morgan, Putnam, Wilkinson
Culver Kidd (D)
P.O. Box 370
Milledgeville 31061
912-452-1420

District 26
Portion of Bibb
Tommy C. Olmstead (D)
P.O. Box 5128
Macon 31298
912-742-2126

District 27
Crawford, Lamar, Monroe, Upson; Portion of Bibb
W. F. (Billy) Harris (D)
1261 Willingham Springs Road
Thomaston 30286
404-648-2851

District 28
Coweta, Pike, Spalding
Arthur B. "Skin" Edge, IV (R)
15 Jefferson St.
Newnan 30263
404-253-9885

District 29
Harris, Heard, Meriwether, Troup; Portion of Carroll

A. Quillian Baldwin, Jr. (D)
P.O. Box 1364
LaGrange 30241
404-882-8122

District 30
Portion of Carroll, Douglas
Wayne Garner (D)
109 Stonewall Dr.
Carrollton 30117
404-834-7038

District 31
Haralson, Paulding, Polk; Portion of Bartow
Nathan Dean (D)
340 Wingfoot Street
Rockmart 30153
404-684-7851

District 32
Portion of Cobb
Hugh A. Ragan (R)
4010 W. Cooper Lake Dr.
Smyrna 30080
404-438-8816

District 33
Portion of Cobb
Roy E. Barnes (D)
4841 Brookwood Drive
Mableton 30059
404-424-1500

District 34
Fayette; Portion of Douglas, Fulton
Bev Engram (D)
P.O. Box 908
Fairburn 30213
404-964-3391

District 35
Portion of Fulton
Arthur Langford, Jr. (D)
1544 Niskey Lake Tr. SW
Atlanta 30331
404-656-5039

District 36
Portion of Fulton
David Scott (D)
190 Wendell Drive, SE
Atlanta 30315
404-523-5317

District 37
Portion of Cherokee, Cobb

Carl Harrison (R)
P.O. Box 1374
Marietta 30061
404-427-7371

District 38
Portion of Fulton
Horace Edward Tate (D)
621 Lilla Drive, SW
Atlanta 30310
404-522-7512

District 39
Portion of Fulton
Hildred W. Shumake (D)
1103 Fair St.
Atlanta 30314
404-758-1815

District 40
Portion of Fulton
Paul D. Coverdell (R)
2622 Piedmont Rd. NE
Atlanta 30324
404-262-9100

District 41
Portion of DeKalb
James W. (Jim) Tysinger
(R)
3781 Watkins Place, NE
Atlanta 30319
404-457-2375

District 42
Portion of DeKalb
Pierce Howard (D)
592 Fidelity National Bank
Building
Decatur 30030
404-870-6310

District 43
Portion of DeKalb
Eugene P. (Gene) Walker
(D)
2231 Chevy Chase Lane
Decatur 30032
404-299-4212

District 44
Portion of Clayton

Terrell Starr (D)
4766 Tanglewood Lane
Forest Park 30050
404-366-5311

District 45
Newton, Rockdale, Walton
Harrill L. Dawkins (D)
1445-A Old McDonough
Road
Conyers 30207
404-483-0500

District 46
*Clarke, Oconee; Portion of
Jackson*
Paul Broun (D)
165 Pulaski Street
Athens 30610
404-546-6700

District 47
*Banks, Elbert, Franklin,
Hart, Madison; Portion of
Jackson*
C. Donald Johnson, Jr. (D)
P.O. Box 27
Royston 30662
404-245-9293

District 48
Barrow; Portion of Gwinnett
Donn M. Peevy (D)
P.O. Box 862
Lawrenceville 30246
404-963-0858

District 49
Hall; Portion of Forsyth
Nathan Deal (D)
P.O. Box 2522
Gainesville 30503
404-532-9978

District 50
*Dawson, Habersham,
Lumpkin, Rabun,
Stephens, Towns, Union,
White*
John C. Foster (D)
P.O. Box 100

Cornelia 30531
404-778-2919

District 51
*Fannin, Gilmer, Gordon,
Pickens; Portion of
Cherokee, Whitfield*
Max Brannon (D)
P.O. Box 1027
Calhoun 30701
404-629-4508

District 52
Floyd; Portion of Bartow
Ed Hine (D)
P.O. Box 5511
Rome 30161
404-291-2531

District 53
*Chattooga, Dade, Walker;
Portion of Catoosa*
Waymond (Sonny) Huggins
(D)
P.O. Box 284
LaFayette 30728
404-638-1409

District 54
*Murray; Portion of Catoosa,
Whitfield*
W. W. (Bill) Fincher, Jr.
(D)
P.O. Drawer 400
Chatsworth 30705
404-695-2334

District 55
Portion of DeKalb
Lawrence (Bud)
Stumbaugh (D)
1071 Yemassee Trail
Stone Mountain 30083
404-656-6030

District 56
*Portion of Cobb, Forsyth,
Fulton*
Sallie Newbill (R)
7205 Riverside Dr.
Atlanta 30328
404-394-5676

Members of Senate Alphabetically Listed

Albert, Frank A. (R)
District 23

Allgood, Thomas F. (D)
District 22

Baldwin, Quillian (D)
District 29

Barker, Ed (D)
District 18

Barnes, Roy E. (D)
District 33

Bowen, Rooney L. (D)
District 13

Brannon, Max (D)
District 51

Broun, Paul (D)
District 46

Bryant, Glenn E. (D)
District 3

Burton, Joe (R)
District 5

Coleman, J. Tom (D)
District 1

Coverdell, Paul D. (R)
District 40

Crumbley, Alex (D)
District 17

Dawkins, Harrill L. (D)
District 45

Deal, Nathan (D)
District 49

Dean, Nathan (D)
District 31

Edge, Arthur B. "Skin",
IV (R)
District 28

English, Bill (D)
District 21

Engram, Bev (D)
District 34

Fincher, W. W. (Bill) (D)
District 54

Foster, John C. (D)
District 50

Garner, Wayne (D)
District 30

Gillis, Hugh, Sr. (D)
District 20

Harris, W. F. (Billy) (D)
District 27

Harrison, Carl (R)
District 37

Hine, Ed (D)
District 52

Howard, Pierre (D)
District 42

Hudgins, Floyd (D)
District 15

Huggins, Waymond
(Sonny) (D)
District 53

Johnson, C. Donald, Jr.
(D)
District 47

Kennedy, Joesph E. (D)
District 4

Kidd, Culver (D)
District 25

Land, Ted J. (R)
District 16

Langford, Arthur, Jr. (D)
District 35

McGill, Sam (D)
District 24

McKenzie, Bud (D)
District 14

Newbill, Sallie (R)
District 56

Nichols, Earl, Jr. (D)
District 6

Olmstead, Tommy C. (D)
District 26

Peevy, Donn M. (D)
District 48

Perry, Ed (D)
District 7

Phillips, Tom (R)
District 9

Ragan, Harold J. (D)
District 10

Ragan, Hugh A. (R)
District 32

Ray, Walter S. (D)
District 19

Scott, Al (D)
District 2

Scott, David (D)
District 36

Shumake, Hildred W. (D)
District 39

Starr, Terrell (D)
District 44

Stumbaugh, Lawrence
(Bud) (D)
District 55

Tate, Horace Edward (D)
District 38

Taylor, Mark (D)
District 12

Timmons, Jimmy Hodge
(D)
District 11

Turner, Loyce W. (D)
District 8

Tysinger, James W. (Jim)
(R)
District 41

Walker, Eugene (D)
District 43

262

**Speaker of the House of
Representatives**
Thomas B. Murphy
State Capitol, 3rd Floor
Atlanta 30334
404-656-5020

Members of the House of Representatives by Districts

District 1—Post 1
Portion of Dade, Walker
Mike Snow (D)
Route 2, Box 1595
Chickamauga 30707
404-375-4238

District 1—Post 2
Portion of Dade, Walker
Robert H. (Bob) McCoy
(D)
181 S. Mission Ridge Dr.
Rossville 30741
404-856-5005

District 2
Portion of Catoosa
Robert G. Peters (D)
P.O. Box 550
Ringgold 30736
404-935-2111

District 3
*Murray; Portion of Catoosa,
Whitfield*
Tom Ramsey (D)
P.O. Box 1130
Chatsworth 30705
404-695-6642

District 4—Post 1
*Fannin, Gilmer, Lumpkin,
Rabun, Towns, Union*
Carlton H. Colwell (D)
P.O. Box 850
Blairsville 30512
404-745-6239

District 4—Post 2
*Fannin, Gilmer, Lumpkin,
Rabun, Towns, Union*
Ralph Twiggs (D)
P.O. Box 432
Hiawassee 30546
404-896-2574

District 5
*Chattooga; Portion of Dade,
Walker*
John G. Crawford (D)
P.O. Box 308
Lyerly 30730
404-895-4410

District 6—Post 1
Portion of Whitfield
Jim Tyson Griffin (D)
526 Varnell Rd.
Tunnel Hill 30755
404-673-2334

District 6—Post 2
Portion of Whitfield
Phil Foster (D)
4425 Airport Rd. SE
Dalton 30721
404-226-3249

District 7
Gordon
James Beverly Langford
(D)
P.O. Box 277
Calhoun 30701
404-629-2300

District 8—Post 1
Pickens; Portion of Cherokee
Allyn Pritchard (D)
Rt. 8, Stover Rd.
Canton 30114
404-345-5040

District 8—Post 2
Pickens; Portion of Cherokee
W. G. (Bill) Hasty, Sr. (D)
Route 9, Hilton Way
Canton 30114
404-479-8528

District 9—Post 1
*Dawson, Hall; Portion of
Gwinnett*
Joe T. Wood (D)
P.O. Drawer 1058
Gainesville 30503
404-536-0161

District 9—Post 2
*Dawson, Hall; Portion of
Gwinnett*
Bobby Lawon (D)
P.O. Box 53
Gainesville 30503
404-536-2304

District 9—Post 3
*Dawson, Hall; Portion of
Gwinnett*
Jerry D. Jackson (D)
P.O. Box 7275
Chestnut Mountain 30502
404-967-3466

District 10
Forsyth; Portion of Cherokee
Bill H. Barnett (D)
P.O. Box 755
Commings 30130
404-887-6582

District 11—Post 1
*Habersham, Stephens,
White; Portion of Banks*
Bill Dover (D)
Route 2, "Timbrook"
Clarksville 30523
404-754-6396

District 11—Post 2
*Habersham, Stephens,
White; Portion of Banks*
Jeanette Jamieson (D)
P.O. Box 852
Toccoa 30577
404-886-6889

District 12
Jackson; Portion of Banks
Lauren (Bubba)
  McDonald, Jr. (D)
Route 5, Dogwood Trail
Commerce 30529
404-335-7575

District 13—Post 1
*Franklin, Hart; Portion of
  Clarke, Madison*
Louie Clark (D)
RFD 2
Danielsville 30633
404-789-2236

District 13—Post 2
*Franklin, Hart; Portion of
  Clarke, Madison*
Billy Milford (D)
P.O. Box 3446
Hartwell 30643
404-376-4427

District 14
*Elbert, Oglethorpe; Portion
  of Madison*
Charles W. Yeargin (D)
P.O. Box 584
Elberton 30635
404-283-4376

District 15—Post 1
Portion of Bartow, Floyd
E. M. (Buddy) Childers
  (D)
28 Surrey Trail
Rome 30161
404-291-8203

District 15—Post 2
Portion of Bartow, Floyd
Forrest L. McKelvey (D)
1118 Old Rockmart Rd. SE
Silver Creek 30173
404-234-2067

District 16
Portion of Floyd
Paul E. Smith (D)
P.O. Box 486
Rome 30162
404-232-1997

District 17
Portion of Polk

Bill Cummings (D)
735 Morgan Valley Rd.
Rockmart 30153
404-684-3747

District 18
*Haralson; Portion of
  Paulding, Polk*
Thomas B. Murphy (D)
P.O. Drawer 1140
Bremen 30110
404-537-5201

District 19
Portion of Bartow
Boyd Pettit (D)
P.O. Box 1256
Cartersville 30120
404-382-9592

District 20—Post 1
Portion of Cobb
Joe Mack Wilson (D)
217 Northcutt St.
Marietta 30064
404-428-6581

District 20—Post 2
Portion of Cobb
Sam P. Hensley (D)
876 Old Mountain Rd.
Marietta 30064
404-429-0520

District 20—Post 3
Portion of Cobb
Herman Clark (R)
3708 Summit Dr.
Acworth 30101
404-974-5062

District 20—Post 4
Portion of Cobb
Steve Thompson (D)
4265 Bradley Drive
Austell 30001
404-941-3324

District 20—Post 5
Portion of Cobb
Terry Lawler (D)
P.O. Box 189
Clarkdale 30020
404-426-9229

District 21—Post 1
Portion of Cobb
Fred Aiken (R)
4020 Pineview Drive, SE
Smyrna 30080
404-432-1883

District 21—Post 2
Portion of Cobb
Johnny Isakson (R)
5074 Hampton Farms
  Drive
Marietta 30068
404-973-0303

District 21—Post 3
Portion of Cobb
Bill Atkins (R)
4719 Windsor Drive
Smyrna 30080
404-435-0490

District 21—Post 4
Portion of Cobb
Johnny Gresham (R)
1010 Richmond Hill Dr.
Marietta 30067
404-973-7686

District 21—Post 5
Portion of Cobb
Tom Wilder (R)
4195 Parish Dr.
Marietta 30066
404-924-7304

District 22
Portion of Fulton
Mrs. Dorothy Felton (R)
465 Tanacrest Drive, NW
Atlanta 30328
404-252-4172

District 23
Portion of Fulton
Luther S. Colbert (R)
495 Houze Way
Roswell 30076
404-993-4786

District 24
Portion of Fulton
Kil Townsend (R)
56 West Paces Drive, NW
Atlanta 30327
404-261-2682

District 25
Portion of Fulton
John M. Lupton (R)
594 Westover Drive
Atlanta 30305
404-874-3222

District 26
Portion of Fulton
Jim Martin (D)
Suite 504, 44 Broad St.
Atlanta 30303
404-522-0400

District 27
Portion of Fulton
Dick Lane (R)
2704 Humphries Street
East Point 30344
404-767-4451

District 28
Portion of Fulton
Bob Holmes (D)
P.O. Box 110009
Atlanta 30311-0009
404-755-9528

District 29
Portion of Fulton
Grace W. Davis (D)
670 Fair St. SW
Atlanta 30312
404-577-7113

District 30
Portion of Fulton
Nan Orrock (D)
1070 Delaware Ave. SE
Atlanta 30316
404-622-6687

District 31
Portion of Fulton
Mable Thomas (D)
P.O. Box 573
Atlanta 30301
404-525-7251

District 32
Portion of Fulton
Mrs. Helen Selman (D)
Jones Ferry Road, Box 315

Palmetto 30268
404-463-3374

District 33
Portion of Fulton
Lanett Stanley (D)
712 Gary Rd. NW
Atlanta 30318
404-794-8357

District 34
Portion of Fulton
Tyrone Brooks (D)
Station A—P.O. Box 11185
Atlanta 30310-0185
404-524-5531

District 35
Portion of Fulton
J. E. (Billy) McKinney (D)
765 Shorter Terrace, NW
Atlanta 30318
404-691-8810

District 36
Portion of Fulton
G. D. Adams (D)
3417 Northside Drive
Hapeville 30354
404-761-3397

District 37
Portion of Fulton
Georganna Sinkfield (D)
179 Tonawanda Drive, SE
Atlanta 30315
404-622-1515

District 38
Portion of Fulton
Lorenzo Benn (D)
579 Fielding Lane, SW
Atlanta 30311
404-349-4325

District 39
Portion of Fulton
John W. Greer (D)
Suite 605, 133 Carnegie
    Way, NW
Atlanta 30303
404-524-4223

District 40
Portion of Fulton

Barbara H. Couch (D)
18 Capitol Sq., Suite 609
Atlanta 30334
404-656-0305

District 41
Portion of Douglas, Paulding
Charlie Watts (D)
505 Hardee Street
Dallas 30132
404-445-2708

District 42
Portion of Douglas
Thomas (Mac) Kilgore (D)
1992 Tara Circle
Douglasville 30135
404-859-1912

District 43
Fayette
Paul W. Heard, Jr. (R)
102 Camp Creek Court
Peachtree City 30269
404-762-9573

District 44
Portion of DeKalb
John Linder (R)
5039 Winding Branch
    Drive
Dunwoody 30338
404-642-1663

District 45
Portion of DeKalb
Max Davis (R)
1177 W. Nancy Creek
    Drive, NE
Atlanta 30319
404-373-3316

District 46
Portion of DeKalb
Cathey W. Steinberg (D)
1732 Dunwoody Place, NE
Atlanta 30324
404-262-2244

District 47
Portion of DeKalb
Chesley Morton (R)
3580 Coldwater Canyon
    Court
Tucker 30084
404-496-0416

265

District 48
Portion of DeKalb
Betty Jo Williams (R)
2024 Castleway Drive, NE
Atlanta 30345
404-325-9051

District 49
Portion of DeKalb
Tom Lawrence (R)
2283 Stratmor Drive
Stone Mountain 30087
404-894-7885

District 50
Portion of DeKalb
Frank Redding (D)
P.O. Box 117
Decatur 30030
404-377-1458

District 51
Portion of DeKalb
Ken Workman (D)
200 Kenridge Pkwy.
Decatur 30032
404-981-0218

District 52
Portion of DeKalb
Eleanor L. Richardson (D)
755 Park Lane
Decatur 30033
404-636-5892

District 53
Portion of DeKalb
Mary Margaret Oliver (D)
150 E. Ponce de Leon Ave.
Decatur 30030
404-377-9254

District 54
Portion of DeKalb
Juanita T. Williams (D)
8 East Lake Drive, NE
Atlanta 30317
404-522-7254

District 55
Portion of DeKalb
Betty J. Clark (D)
P.O. Box 17852
Atlanta 30316
404-241-4033

District 56
Portion of DeKalb
Betty Aaron (D)
18 Capitol Sq., Suite 607
Atlanta 30334
404-656-0287

District 57—Post 1
*Rockdale; Portion of
DeKalb*
Troy Athon (D)
1161 Valley Drive, NE
Conyers 30207
404-922-1922

District 57—Post 2
*Rockdale; Portion of
DeKalb*
Wm. C. (Bill) Mangum, Jr.
(D)
4320 Pleasant Forest Drive
Decatur 30034
404-522-0185

District 57—Post 3
*Rockdale; Portion of
DeKalb*
Dean Alford (D)
20 Willowick Drive
Lithonia 30058
404-633-9099

District 58
Portion of DeKalb
Tommy Tolbert (R)
1138 Otello Ave.
Clarkston 30021
404-330-4195

District 59
Portion of Gwinnett
Mike Barnett (R)
4779 St. Moritz Dr.
Lilburn 30247
404-972-1575

District 60
Portion of Gwinnett
Ronald W. Pittman (R)
3636 Tinsley Pl.
Duluth 30136
404-476-1139

District 61
Portion of Gwinnett

Vinson Wall (D)
164 E. Oak Street
Lawrenceville 30245
404-963-9558

District 62
Portion of Gwinnett
Charles E. Bannister (R)
312 Emily Drive
Lilburn 30247
404-921-0884

District 63
Portion of Gwinnett
Bill Goodwin (R)
3823 Club Forest Drive
Norcross 30092
404-446-2889

District 64
Barrow; Portion of Gwinnett
John O. Mobley, Jr. (D)
102 Brandywine Dr.
Winder 30680
404-867-6887

District 65
Walton
Tyrone Carrell (D)
P.O. Box 561
Monroe 30655
404-267-7561

District 66
*Morgan, Oconee; Portion of
Newton*
Frank E. Stancil (D)
P.O. Box 694
Watkinsville 30677
404-548-6228

District 67
Portion of Clarke
Michael L. Thurmond (D)
1127 W. Hancock Ave.
Athens 30306
404-543-5513

District 68
Portion of Clarke
Lawton E. Stephens (D)
P.O. Box 8064
Athens 30603
404-546-0648

District 69
Portion of Carroll
Charles Thomas (D)
P.O. Box 686
Temple 30179
404-562-3028

District 70
Portion of Carroll, Douglas
John Simpson (D)
302-A Newnan St.
Carrollton 30117
404-834-0202

District 71
Portion of Carroll, Coweta
Neal Shepard (R)
94 Boy Scout Rd.
Newnan 30263
404-251-2909

District 72—Post 1
Clayton
William J. (Bill) Lee (D)
5325 Hillside Drive
Forest Park 30050
404-761-6522

District 72—Post 2
Clayton
Jimmy Benefield (D)
6656 Morning Dove Place
Jonesboro 30236
404-471-8825

District 72—Post 3
Clayton
Charles E. Holcomb (D)
P.O. Box 122
Jonesboro 30237
404-478-4383

District 72—Post 4
Clayton
Rudolph Johnson (D)
5604 Reynolds Road
Lake City 30260
404-961-5089

District 72—Post 5
Clayton
Frank I. Bailey, Jr. (D)
P.O. Box 777
Riverdale 30274
404-584-4608

District 73
Portion of Henry
Wesley Dunn (D)
P.O. Box 353
McDonough 30253
404-997-5600

District 74
Portion of Newton
Denny M. Dobbs (D)
329 Harold Dobbs Rd.
Covington 30209
404-593-3803

District 75
*Portion of Coweta, Pike,
Spalding*
John L. Mostiler (D)
150 Meadovista Drive
Griffin 30223
404-228-1172

District 76
Portion of Spalding
Suzi Johnson-Herbert (D)
110 Partridge Path
Griffin 30223
404-228-2017

District 77
*Heard; Portion of Coweta,
Troup*
J. Crawford Ware (D)
P.O. Box 305
Hogansville 30230
404-637-8655

District 78
*Butts, Lamar; Portion of
Henry*
Larry Smith (D)
P.O. Box 4155
Jackson 30233
404-775-5377

District 79
Upson; Portion of Pike
Marvin Adams (D)
709 Greenwood Road
Thomaston 30286
404-647-4632

District 80
*Jasper, Monroe; Portion of
Crawford, Jones*
Kenneth Waldrep (D)
87 N. Lee Street
Forsyth 31029
912-994-5171

District 81
Portion of Troup
Wade Milam (D)
P.O. Box 1361
LaGrange 30241
404-882-1182

District 82
*Glascock, Lincoln,
Taliaferro, Warren,
Wilkes; Portion of
Jefferson*
Edward D. Ricketson, Jr.
(D)
P.O. Drawer 732
Warrenton 30828
404-465-3313

District 83
Portion of Columbia
William S. (Bill) Jackson
(D)
3907 Washington Rd.
Martinez 30907
404-863-5819

District 84
*McDuffie; Portion of
Columbia*
Bobby Harris (D)
Rt. 5, Box 593
Thomson 30824
404-595-1327

District 85
Portion of Richmond
Charles W. Walker (D)
1402 Twelfth Street
Augusta 30901
404-722-4222

District 86
Portion of Richmond
Mike Padgett (D)
1140 Bennock Mill Rd.
Augusta 30906
404-793-9180

District 87
Portion of Richmond
Jack Connell (D)
328 10th St.
Augusta 30903
404-823-6212

District 88
Portion of Richmond
George Brown (D)
P.O. Box 1114
Augusta 30903
404-724-0953

District 89
Portion of Richmond
Don E. Cheeks (D)
3047 Walton Way
Augusta 30909
404-736-1397

District 90
Portion of Richmond
Dick Ransom (R)
445 Waverly Dr.
Augusta 30909
404-736-2166

District 91
*Meriwether, Talbot; Portion
of Coweta*
Leonard R. (Nookie)
Meadows (D)
P.O. Box 317
Manchester 31816
404-846-3181

District 92
Portion of Muscogee
Calvin Smyre (D)
P.O. Box 181
Columbus 31902
404-742-2387

District 93
Harris; Portion of Muscogee
Roy D. Moultrie (D)
P.O. Box 119
Hamilton 31811
404-628-5361

District 94
Portion of Muscogee
Sanford D. Bishop, Jr. (D)
P.O. Box 709

Columbus 31902
404-324-3531

District 95
Portion of Muscogee
Thomas B. Buck, III (D)
P.O. Box 196
Columbus 31902
404-323-5646

District 96
Portion of Muscogee
Pete Robinson (D)
3334 Coweta Dr.
Columbus 31907
404-324-3711

District 97
Portion of Muscogee
Mary Jane Galer (D)
7236 Lullwater Road
Columbus 31904
404-324-2931

District 98
*Peach; Portion of Crawford,
Macon*
Robert Ray (D)
Route 1, Box 2126
Fort Valley 31030
912-825-7202

District 99
Portion of Bibb
Denmark Groover, Jr. (D)
P.O. Box 755
Macon 31202
912-745-4712

District 100
Portion of Bibb
Frank C. Pinkston (D)
P.O. Box 4872
Macon 31208
912-741-1000

District 101
Portion of Bibb
William C. (Billy) Randall
(D)
P.O. Box 121
Macon 31202
912-743-6389

District 102
Portion of Bibb

David E. Lucas (D)
448 Woolfolk Street
Macon 31201
912-742-8486

District 103
Portion of Bibb
Floyd M. Buford, Jr. (D)
P.O. Box 13183
Macon 31208-3183
912-742-3605

District 104
*Twiggs, Wilkinson; Portion
of Jones*
Kenneth (Ken) W.
Birdsong (D)
Route One
Gordon 31031
912-746-3934

District 105
Portion of Baldwin
Bobby Eugene Parham (D)
P.O. Box 606
Milledgeville 31061
912-452-5152

District 106
Greene, Hancock, Putnam
George F. Green (D)
Rt. 1, Box 46F
White Plains 30678
404-444-6521

District 107
*Washington; Portion of
Baldwin, Johnson*
Jimmy Lord (D)
P.O. Box 254
Sandersville 31082
912-552-2515

District 108
Portion of Burke, Jefferson
Emory E. Bargeron (D)
P.O. Box 447
Louisville 30434
912-625-7285

District 109
*Candler, Emanuel; Portion
of Johnson*
Larry (Butch) Parrish (D)

224 W. Main Street
Swainsboro 30401
912-237-7032

District 110
Jenkins; Portion of Bulloch,
Burke, Screven
John Godbee (D)
401 Lane Street
Brooklet 30415
912-764-5208

District 111
Portion of Bulloch, Screven
Robert Lane (D)
205 Aldred Avenue
Statesboro 30458
912-764-6813

District 112
Marion, Schley, Taylor;
Portion of Chattahoochee
Ward Edwards (D)
P.O. Box 146
Butler 31006
912-862-5536

District 113
Portion of Houston
Ted W. Waddle (R)
113 Tanglewood Drive
Warner Robins 31093
912-923-7424

District 114
Portion of Houston
Roy H. (Sonny) Watson, Jr.
(D)
P.O. Box 1905
Warner Robins 31099
912-923-0044

District 115
Portion of Houston, Macon
Larry Walker (D)
P.O. Box 1234
Perry 31069
912-987-1415

District 116
Sumter
George Hooks (D)
P.O. Box 928
Americus 31709
912-924-2924

District 117
Bleckley, Pulaski, Wilcox;
Portion of Turner
W. N. (Newt) Hudson (D)
Route 1, Box 29 A
Rochelle 31079
912-365-2387

District 118
Dodge; Portion of Laurens,
Telfair
Terry L. Coleman (D)
P.O. Box 157
Eastman 31023
912-374-5594

District 119
Portion of Laurens
DuBose Porter (D)
P.O. Drawer B, CSS
Dublin 31040
912-272-5522

District 120
Montgomery, Treutlen,
Wheeler; Portion of
Toombs
Mrs. Pete (Mary Ida)
Phillips (D)
P.O. Box 166
Soperton 30457
912-529-4447

District 121
Evans, Long, Tattnall
Clinton Oliver (D)
P.O. Box 237
Glennville 30427
912-654-2660

District 122
Portion of Chatham
Jim Pannell (D)
P.O. Box 10186
Savannah 31412
912-236-3311

District 123
Portion of Chatham
Diane Harvey Johnson (D)
P.O. Box 5544
Savannah 31414
912-232-3695

District 124
Portion of Chatham
DeWayne Hamilton (D)
P.O. Box 14562
Savannah 31406
912-234-6199

District 125
Portion of Chatham
Jack Kingston (R)
30 Wylly Avenue
Savannah 31406
912-234-6621

District 126
Portion of Bryan, Chatham
Anne Mueller (R)
13013 Hermitage Road
Savannah 31419
912-925-2291

District 127
Portion of Chatham
Roy L. Allen (D)
1406 Law Drive
Savannah 31401
912-233-4914

District 128
Portion of Chatham
Tom Triplett (D)
P.O. Box 9586
Savannah 31402
912-944-3200

District 129
Effingham; Portion of
Bryan, Liberty
George Change (D)
P.O. Box 373
Springfield 31329
912-754-9262

District 130
Quitman, Randolph,
Stewart, Webster; Portion
of Chattahoochee
Gerald E. Greene (D)
Route 3, Box 119
Cuthbert 31740
912-732-2750

District 131
Calhoun, Clay, Terrell;
Portion of Lee
Bob Hanner (D)

269

P.O. Box 310
Dawson 31742
912-995-6627

District 132
Portion of Dougherty
John White (D)
P.O. Box 3506
Albany 31706
912-435-6330

District 133
Portion of Dougherty
Tommy Chambless (D)
P.O. Box 2008
Albany 31703-2001
912-436-1545

District 134
Portion of Dougherty
Mary Young Cummings
307 Whitney Ave.
Albany 31701
912-435-2679

District 135
Crisp, Dooly
Howard H. Rainey (D)
913 Third Avenue, E
Cordele 31015
912-273-3062

District 136
*Worth; Portion of Lee,
Turner*
Earleen Sizemore (D)
Route 3, 47D
Sylvester 31791
912-776-6943

District 137
*Ben Hill, Irwin; Portion of
Telfair*
Paul S. Branch, Jr. (D)
Route 4, Box 499-A
Fitzgerald 31750
912-423-4410

District 138
Portion of Tift
Henry Bostick (D)
P.O. Box 94
Tifton 31793
912-382-4828

District 139
Coffee; Portion of Atkinson
James C. Moore (D)
Route Two
West Green 31567
912-384-3637

District 140
*Baker, Early, Miller; Portion
of Dougherty*
Ralph J. Balkcom (D)
Route One
Blakely 31723
912-723-5074

District 141
Seminole; Portion of Decatur
Walter E. Cox (D)
202 West Street
Bainbridge 31717
912-246-4411

District 142
*Grady; Portion of Decatur,
Thomas*
Bobby Long (D)
1466 Sixth Street, NW
Cairo 31728
912-377-1723

District 143
Portion of Thomas
R. Allen Sherrod (D)
Route 1
Coolidge 31738
912-226-5272

District 144
*Mitchell; Portion of Colquitt,
Thomas*
A. Richard Royal (D)
20 N. Scott Street
Camilla 31730
912-336-7974

District 145
Portion of Colquitt
C. J. Powell (D)
Box 2534
Moultrie 31776-2534
912-985-1483

District 146
*Berrien, Cook; Portion of
Tift*

Hanson Carter (D)
808 River Road
Nashville 31639
912-686-2515

District 147
*Brooks, Echols; Portion of
Lowndes*
Henry L. Reaves (D)
Route 2, Box 83
Quitman 31643
912-263-4051

District 148
Portion of Lowndes
James M. Beck (D)
2427 Westwood Drive
Valdosta 31602
912-244-1106

District 149
Lanier; Portion of Lowndes
Robert Patten (D)
Route 1, Box 180
Lakeland 31635
912-482-3131

District 150
*Clinch; Portion of Atkinson,
Charlton, Ware*
Tom Crosby, Jr. (D)
705 Wacona Drive
Waycross 31501
912-283-1744

District 151
*Portion of Camden,
Charlton, Ware*
Harry Dixon (D)
1303 Coral Road
Waycross 31501
912-283-6527

District 152
*Bacon, Pierce; Portion of
Brantley, Camden*
Tommy Smith (D)
Route One
Alma 31510
912-632-0000

District 153—Post 1
*Appling, Jeff Davis, Wayne;
Portion of Brantley,
Toombs*

Lundsford Moody (D)
Rt. 1, Box 205
Baxley 31513
912-367-4169

District 153—Post 2
Appling, Jeff Davis, Wayne;
Portion of Brantley,
Toombs
Roger C. Byrd (D)
P.O. Box 756
Hazlehurst 31539

912-375-2571

District 154
Portion of Liberty
James M. Floyd (D)
Rt. 1, Box 23
Hinesville 31313
912-368-3332

District 155
Portion of Glynn
Virginia Ramsey (R)

393 Lake Circle Drive
Brunswick 31520
912-265-6103

District 156
McIntosh; Portion of Glynn
Willou Smith (R)
10 St. Andrews Court
Riverfront Plaza
Brunswick 31520
912-265-7766

Members of House Alphabetically Listed

Aaron, Betty (D)
District 56

Adams, G. D. (D)
District 36

Adams, Marvin (D)
District 79

Aiken, Fred (R)
District 21—Post 1

Alford, Dean (D)
District 57—Post 3

Allen, Roy L. (D)
District 127

Athon, Troy (D)
District 57—Post 1

Atkins, Bill (R)
District 21—Post 3

Bailey, Frank I., Jr. (D)
District 72—Post 5

Balkcom, Ralph J. (D)
District 140

Bannister, Charles E. (R)
District 62

Bargeron, Emory E. (D)
District 108

Barnett, Bill H. (D)
District 10

Barnett, Mike (R)
District 59

Beck, James M. (D)
District 148

Benefield, Jimmy (D)
District 72—Post 2

Benn, Lorenzo (D)
District 38

Birdsong, Kenneth (Ken)
W. (D)
District 104

Bishop, Sanford D., Jr. (D)
District 94

Bostick, Henry (D)
District 138

Branch, Paul S., Jr. (D)
District 137

Brooks, Tyrone (D)
District 34

Brown, George (D)
District 88

Buck, Thomas B., III (D)
District 95

Buford, Floyd M., Jr. (D)
District 103

Byrd, Roger C. (D)
District 153—Post 2

Carrell, Tyrone (D)
District 65

Carter, Hanson (D)
District 146

Chambless, Tommy (D)
District 133

Chance, George (D)
District 129

Cheeks, Don E. (D)
District 89

Childers, E. M.
(Buddy) (D)
District 15—Post 1

Clark, Betty J. (D)
District 55

Clark, Herman (R)
District 20—Post 3

Clark, Louie (D)
District 13—Post 1

Colbert, Luther S. (R)
District 23

Coleman, Terry L. (D)
District 118

Colwell, Carlton H. (D)
District 4—Post 1

Connell, Jack (D)
District 87

Couch, Barbara H. (D)
District 40

Cox, Walter E. (D)
District 141

Crawford, John G. (D)
District 5

Crosby, Tom, Jr. (D)
District 150

Cummings, Bill (D)
District 17

Cummings, Mary Young
 (D)
District 134

Davis, Grace W. (D)
District 29

Davis, Max (R)
District 45

Dixon, Harry (D)
District 151

Dobbs, Denny M. (D)
District 74

Dover, Bill (D)
District 11—Post 1

Dunn, Wesley (D)
District 73

Edwards, Ward (D)
District 112

Felton, Mrs. Dorothy (R)
District 22

Floyd, James M. (D)
District 154

Foster, Phil (D)
District 6—Post 2

Galer, Mary Jane (D)
District 97

Godbee, John (D)
District 110

Goodwin, Bill (R)
District 63

Greene, Gerald E. (D)
District 130

Green, George F. (D)
District 106

Greer, John W. (D)
District 39

Gresham, Johnny (R)
District 21—Post 4

Griffin, Jim Tyson (D)
District 6—Post 1

Groover, Denmark, Jr. (D)
District 99

Hamilton, DeWayne (D)
District 124

Hanner, Bob (D)
District 131

Harris, Bobby (D)
District 84

Hasty, W. G. (Bill), Sr. (D)
District 8—Post 2

Heard, Paul W., Jr. (R)
District 43

Hensley, Sam P. (D)
District 20—Post 2

Holcomb, Charles E. (D)
District 72—Post 3

Holmes, Bob (D)
District 28

Hooks, George (D)
District 116

Hudson, W. N. (Newt) (D)
District 117

Isakson, Johnny (R)
District 21—Post 2

Jackson, Jerry D. (D)
District 9—Post 3

Jackson, William S.
 (Bill) (D)
District 83

Jamieson, Jeanette (D)
District II—Post 2

Johnson, Diane Harvey (D)
District 123

Johnson, Rudolph (D)
District 72—Post 4

Johnson–Herbert, Suzi (D)
District 76

Kilgore, Thomas (Mac) (D)
District 42

Kingston, Jack (R)
District 125

Lane, Dick (R)
District 27

Lane, Robert (D)
District 111

Langford, James Beverly
 (D)
District 7

Lawler, Terry (D)
District 20—Post 5

Lawrence, Tom (R)
District 49

Lawson, Bobby (D)
District 9—Post 2

Lee, William J. (Bill) (D)
District 72—Post 1

Linder, John (R)
District 44

Long, Bobby (D)
District 142

Lord, Jimmy (D)
District 107

Lucas, David E. (D)
District 107

Lupton, John M. (R)
District 25

Mangum, Wm. C.
(Bill) (D)
District 57—Post 2

Martin, Jim (D)
District 26

McCoy, Robert H.
(Bob) (D)
District 1—Post 2

McDonald, Lauren
(Bubba), Jr. (D)
District 12

McKelvey, Forrest L. (D)
District 15—Post 2

McKinney, J. E. (Billy) (D)
District 35

Meadows, Leonard R.
(Nookie) (D)
District 91

Milam, Wade (D)
District 81

Milford, Billy (D)
District 13—Post 2

Mobley, John O., Jr. (D)
District 64

Moody, Lundsford (D)
District 153—Post 1

Moore, James C. (D)
District 139

Morton, Chesley (R)
District 47

Mostiler, John L. (D)
District 75

Moultrie, Roy D. (D)
District 93

Mueller, Anne (R)
District 126

Murphy, Thomas B. (D)
District 18

Oliver, Clinton (D)
District 121

Oliver, Mary Margaret (D)
District 53

Orrock, Nan (D)
District 30

Padgett, Mike (D)
District 86

Pannell, Jim (D)
District 122

Parham, Bobby Eugene (D)
District 105

Parrish, Larry (Butch) (D)
District 109

Patten, Robert (D)
District 149

Peters, Robert G. (D)
District 2

Pettit, Boyd (D)
District 19

Phillips, Mrs. Pete (Mary
Ida) (D)
District 120

Pinkston, Frank C. (D)
District 100

Pittman, Ronald W. (R)
District 60

Porter, DuBose (D)
District 119

Powell, C. J. (D)
District 145

Pritchard, Allyn (D)
District 8—Post 1

Rainey, Howard H. (D)
District 135

Ramsey, Tom (D)
District 3

Ramsey, Virginia (R)
District 155

Randall, William C.
(Billy) (D)
District 101

Ransom, Dick (R)
District 90

Ray, Robert (D)
District 98

Reaves, Henry L. (D)
District 147

Redding, Frank (D)
District 50

Richardson, Eleanor L. (D)
District 52

Ricketson, Edward D., Jr.
(D)
District 82

Robinson, Pete (D)
District 96

Royal, A. Richard (D)
District 144

Selman, Mrs. Helen (D)
District 32

Shepard, Neal (R)
District 71

Sherrod, R. Allen (D)
District 143

Simpson, John (D)
District 70

Sinkfield, Georganna (D)
District 37

Sizemore, Earleen (D)
District 136

Smith, Larry (D)
District 78

273

Smith, Paul E. (D)
District 16

Smith, Tommy (D)
District 152

Smith, Willou (R)
District 156

Smyre, Calvin (D)
District 92

Snow, Mike (D)
District 1—Post 1

Stancil, Frank E. (D)
District 66

Stanley, Lanett (D)
District 33

Steinberg, Cathey W. (D)
District 46

Stephens, Lawton E. (D)
District 68

Thomas, Charles (D)
District 69

Thomas, Mable (D)
District 31

Thompson, Steve (D)
District 20—Post 4

Thurmond, Michael L. (D)
District 67

Tolbert, Tommy (D)
District 58

Townsend, Kil (R)
District 24

Triplett, Tom (D)
District 128

Twiggs, Ralph (D)
District 4—Post 2

Waddle, Ted W. (R)
District 113

Waldrep, Kenneth (D)
District 80

Walker, Charles W. (D)
District 85

Walker, Larry (D)
District 115

Wall, Vinson (D)
District 61

Ware, J. Crawford (D)
District 77

Watson, Roy H. (Sonny),
Jr. (D)
District 114

Watts, Charlie (D)
District 41

White, John (D)
District 132

Wilder, Tom (R)
District 21—Post 5

Williams, Betty Jo (R)
District 48

Williams, Juanita T. (D)
District 54

Wilson, Joe Mack (D)
District 20—Post 1

Wood, Joe T. (D)
District 9—Post 1

Workman, Ken (D)
District 51

Yeargin, Charles W. (D)
District 14

LIBRARIES

Georgia has an extensive public and county library system, supplemented by excellent university libraries. The state's first library was established at Savannah in 1736.

The largest public libraries are in Atlanta, Columbus, Macon, and Savannah. The University of Georgia has special collections on Southern and Georgian history. The Asa Griggs Candler Library of Emory University houses collections relating to the Confederacy and to Methodist Church history. The Georgia Historical Society has extensive materials relating to Georgia's earliest days.

The following chart includes the name of the public library system in each county, the total number of books and media, and the total funds.

The accompanying map shows the county and regional library systems.

The number in parentheses following the name of the library system in each county helps pinpoint its location on the accompanying map.

Public Library Facilities: 1987

County	Library System (Region)	Number[1] of Libraries	Total Books & Media	Total Funds
Appling	Okefenokee (49)	6	211,459	406,783
Atkinson	Satilla (39)	6	95,690	252,600
Bacon	Okefenokee (49)	6	211,459	406,783
Baker	DeSoto Trail (43)	7	134,896	307,177
Baldwin	Middle Georgia (25)	15	446,726	2,619,454
Banks	Piedmont (12)	9	133,490	266,054
Barrow	Piedmont (12)	9	133,490	266,054
Bartow	Bartow County (8)	3	48,964	268,087
Ben Hill	Fitzgerald-Ben Hill (38)	1	48,525	171,657
Berrien	Coastal Plain (40)	6	305,804	620,422
Bibb	Middle Georgia (25)	15	446,726	2,619,454
Bleckley	Ocmulgee (30)	5	181,071	432,307
Brantley	Brunswick-Glynn (50)	8	321,361	791,912
Brooks	Brooks County (47)	2	29,254	54,215
Bryan	Statesboro (36)	6	128,583	581,715
Bulloch	Statesboro (36)	6	128,583	581,715
Burke	East Central Georgia (28)	12	464,824	2,104,627
Butts	Flint River (21)	13	282,503	1,108,928
Calhoun	Kinchafoonee (42)	8	154,118	445,145
Camden	Brunswick-Glynn (50)	8	321,361	791,912
Candler	Statesboro (36)	6	128,583	581,715
Carroll	West Georgia (14)	9	334,544	600,648
Catoosa	Dalton (2)	5	292,998	561,987
Charlton	Brunswick-Glynn (50)	8	321,361	791,912
Chatham	Chatham-Effingham-Liberty (37)	18	489,143	2,566,610
Chattahoochee	Chattahoochee Valley (34)	9	500,070	1,529,526
Chattooga	Chattooga County (6)	2	57,121	100,823
Cherokee	Sequoyah (5)	4	104,251	380,357
Clarke	Athens (13)	9	265,595	933,758
Clay	Kinchafoonee (42)	8	154,118	445,145
Clayton	Clayton (22)	4	193,241	944,379
Clinch	Okefenokee (49)	6	211,459	406,783
Cobb	Cobb County (15)	14	409,708	3,055,056
Coffee	Satilla (39)	6	95,690	252,600
Colquitt	Colquitt-Thomas (44)	7	220,420	567,072
Columbia	East Central Georgia (28)	12	464,824	2,104,627
Cook	Coastal Plain (40)	6	305,804	620,422
Coweta	Troup-Harris-Coweta (23)	6	176,465	680,753
Crawford	Middle Georgia (25)	15	446,726	2,619,454
Crisp	Lake Blackshear (33)	6	259,007	451,347
Dade	Cherokee (1)	4	155,991	366,460
Dawson	Lake Lanier (9)	9	305,455	2,400,313
Decatur	Southwest Georgia (45)	3	119,162	391,992
DeKalb	DeKalb/Rockdale/Newton (18)	18	638,551	4,528,615
Dodge	Ocmulgee (30)	5	181,071	432,307
Dooly	Lake Blackshear (33)	6	259,007	451,347
Dougherty	Dougherty County (41)	5	203,828	1,285,279
Douglas	West Georgia (14)	9	334,544	600,648
Early	DeSoto Trail (43)	7	134,896	307,177
Echols	South Georgia (48)	5	181,355	476,605
Effingham	Chatham-Effingham-Liberty (37)	18	489,143	2,566,610
Elbert	Elbert County (16)	2	46,326	92,090
Emanuel	Statesboro (36)	6	128,583	581,715

275

County	Library System (Region)	Number[1] of Libraries	Total Books & Media	Total Funds
Evans	Statesboro (36)	6	128,583	581,715
Fannin	Mountain Regional (3)	4	62,182	179,636
Fayette	Flint River (21)	13	282,503	1,108,928
Floyd	Sara Hightower (7)	4	351,207	1,111,066
Forsyth	Lake Lanier (9)	9	305,455	2,400,313
Franklin	Athens (13)	9	265,595	933,758
Fulton	Atlanta-Fulton (17)	26	1,746,792	11,743,912
Gilmer	Sequoyah (5)	4	104,251	328,357
Glascock	East Central Georgia (28)	12	464,824	2,104,627
Glynn	Brunswick-Glynn (50)	8	321,361	791,912
Gordon	Dalton (2)	5	292,998	561,987
Grady	Roddenberry Memorial (46)	2	161,322	332,592
Greene	Bartram Trail (20)	4	101,741	292,913
Gwinnett	Lake Lanier (9)	9	305,455	2,400,313
Habersham	Northeast Georgia (4)	6	176,861	543,611
Hall	Chestatee (10)	4	103,492	627,600
Hancock	Uncle Remus (19)	7	142,005	460,808
Haralson	West Georgia (14)	9	334,544	600,648
Harris	Troup-Harris-Coweta (23)	6	176,465	680,753
Hart	Hart County (11)	1	45,974	146,403
Heard	West Georgia (14)	9	334,544	600,648
Henry	Flint River (21)	13	282,503	1,108,928
Houston	Houston County (31)	3	140,242	454,493
Irwin	Coastal Plain (40)	6	305,804	620,422
Jackson	Piedmont (12)	9	133,490	266,054
Jasper	Uncle Remus (19)	7	142,005	460,808
Jeff Davis	Satilla (39)	6	95,690	252,600
Jefferson	Jefferson County (27)	3	74,128	115,506
Jenkins	Screven-Jenkins (29)	2	100,788	147,597
Johnson	Oconee (26)	6	224,473	651,832
Jones	Middle Georgia (25)	15	446,726	2,619,454
Lamar	Flint River (21)	13	282,503	1,108,928
Lanier	South Georgia (48)	5	181,355	476,605
Laurens	Oconee (26)	6	224,473	651,832
Lee	Kinchafoonee (42)	8	154,118	445,145
Liberty	Chatham-Effingham-Liberty (37)	18	489,143	2,566,610
Lincoln	East Central Georgia (28)	12	464,824	2,104,627
Long	Brunswick-Glynn (50)	8	321,361	791,912
Lowndes	South Georgia (48)	5	181,355	476,605
Lumpkin	Chestatee (10)	4	103,492	627,600
Macon	Middle Georgia (25)	15	446,726	2,619,454
Madison	Athens (13)	9	265,595	933,758
Marion	Chattahoochee Valley (34)	9	500,070	1,529,526
McDuffie	Bartram Trail (20)	4	101,741	292,913
McIntosh	Brunswick-Glynn (50)	8	321,361	791,912
Meriwether	Pine Mountain (24)	6	120,498	331,286
Miller	Southwest Georgia (45)	3	119,162	391,992
Mitchell	DeSoto Trail (43)	7	134,896	307,177
Monroe	Flint River (21)	13	282,503	1,108,928
Montgomery	Ohoopee (35)	6	125,128	319,571
Morgan	Uncle Remus (19)	7	142,005	460,808
Murray	Dalton (2)	5	292,998	561,987
Muscogee	Chattahoochee Valley (34)	9	500,070	1,529,526
Newton	DeKalb/Rockdale/Newton (18)	18	638,551	4,528,615
Oconee	Athens (13)	9	265,595	933,758

County and Regional Library Systems

County	Library System (Region)	Number[1] of Libraries	Total Books & Media	Total Funds
Oglethorpe	Athens (13)	9	265,595	933,758
Paulding	West Georgia (14)	9	334,544	600,648
Peach	Peach Public	2	47,149	156,707
Pickens	Sequoyah (5)	4	104,251	380,357
Pierce	Okefenokee (49)	6	211,459	406,783
Pike	Flint River (21)	13	282,503	1,108,928
Polk	Sara Hightower (7)	4	351,207	1,111,066
Pulaski	Ocmulgee (30)	5	181,071	432,307
Putnam	Uncle Remus (19)	7	142,005	460,808

County	Library System (Region)	Number[1] of Libraries	Total Books & Media	Total Funds
Quitman	Chattahoochee Valley (34)	9	500,070	1,529,526
Rabun	Northeast Georgia (4)	6	176,861	543,611
Randolph	Kinchafoonee (42)	8	154,118	445,145
Richmond	East Central Georgia (28)	12	464,824	2,104,627
Rockdale	DeKalb/Rockdale/Newton (18)	18	638,551	4,528,615
Schley	Lake Blackshear (33)	6	259,007	451,347
Screven	Screven-Jenkins (29)	2	100,788	147,597
Seminole	Southwest Georgia (45)	3	119,162	391,992
Spalding	Flint River (21)	13	282,503	1,108,928
Stephens	Northeast Georgia (4)	6	176,861	543,611
Stewart	Chattahoochee Valley (34)	9	500,070	1,529,526
Sumter	Lake Blackshear (33)	6	259,007	451,347
Talbot	Pine Mountain (24)	6	120,498	331,286
Taliaferro	Bartram Trail (20)	4	101,741	292,913
Tattnall	Ohoopee (35)	6	125,128	319,571
Taylor	Pine Mountain (24)	6	120,498	331,286
Telfair	Ocmulgee (30)	5	181,071	432,307
Terrell	Kinchafoonee (42)	8	154,118	445,145
Thomas	Colquitt-Thomas (44)	7	220,420	567,072
Tift	Coastal Plain (40)	6	305,804	620,422
Toombs	Ohoopee (35)	6	125,128	319,571
Towns	Mountain Regional (3)	4	62,182	179,636
Treutlen	Oconee (26)	6	224,473	651,832
Troup	Troup-Harris-Coweta (23)	6	176,465	680,753
Turner	Coastal Plain (40)	6	305,804	620,422
Twiggs	Middle Georgia (25)	15	446,726	2,619,454
Union	Mountain Regional (3)	4	62,182	179,636
Upson	Pine Mountain (24)	6	120,498	331,286
Walker	Cherokee (1)	4	155,991	366,460
Walton	Uncle Remus (12)	7	142,005	460,808
Ware	Okefenokee (49)	6	211,459	406,783
Warren	East Central Georgia (28)	12	464,824	2,104,627
Washington	Oconee (26)	6	224,473	651,832
Wayne	Brunswick-Glynn (50)	8	321,361	791,912
Webster	Kinchafoonee (42)	8	154,118	445,145
Wheeler	Oconee (26)	6	224,473	651,832
White	Northeast Georgia (4)	6	176,861	543,611
Whitfield	Dalton (2)	5	292,998	561,987
Wilcox	Ocmulgee (30)	5	181,071	432,307
Wilkes	Bartram Trail (20)	4	101,741	292,913
Wilkinson	Middle Georgia (25)	15	446,726	2,619,454
Worth	DeSoto Trail (43)	7	134,896	307,177
Georgia		333	11,664,481	49,960,286

[1]Number of libraries in system open for public service

LICENSE PLATE IDENTIFICATION

Georgia presently issues passenger vehicle license plates which carry three alphabetic (AAA through SZZ) and three numeric characters. The character structure is non-meaningful, but the county of origin is displayed at the bottom of the plate. Only one plate per vehicle is issued.

LITTLE WHITE HOUSE

Franklin D. Roosevelt, four-time president of the United States, lived in many sumptuous residences, including the ancestral home at Hyde Park and the White House in Washington; but in building for himself the kind of home he wanted, he built a very modest place. The Little White House, located on a beautiful site on the slopes of Pine Mountain, tells much of the nature of the man who played such an important role in the history of this country and of the world. It is an impressive home, but is small, with comfort and utility stressed. The Little White House, with three bedrooms, has only an entry, a combination living and dining room, a kitchen, and a spacious sun deck.

During his entire time in office, Mr. Roosevelt used the Little White House frequently. He came to Warm Springs first in 1924 hoping to recover from infantile paralysis which struck him in 1921. Believing exercise in the warm buoyant water beneficial, he became interested in developing the resort for others similarly afflicted. The Georgia Warm Springs Foundation and subsequent development of health facilities resulted from his efforts. The site on which the Little White House stands was personally selected by Mr. Roosevelt during his early stays at Warm Springs, and even before he built his house there, he used it for picnics. It is in a natural setting and Mr. Roosevelt permitted only essential landscaping.

The Little White House is retained substantially as it was when President Roosevelt died there on April 12, 1945. Keys to his personality are many: his collection of ship models denotes his great love of the sea; Fala, his dog, is remembered by a chain still hanging in the closet; a riding quirt denotes Mr. Roosevelt's enthusiasm for horseback riding. Mementos which he cherished more because of the giver than for the workmanship are on the walls. Visitors can see the famous unfinished portrait which was being painted when he suffered a stroke; the President's 1938 Ford convertible, fitted with hand controls which enabled him to drive it alone; the unusual Bump Gate; his 1940 Willys Roadster, the guest house where many notables were entertained; the servant's quarters; the Memorial Fountain; and the Walk of States with flags and stones leading to the Franklin D. Roosevelt Museum which depicts the President's life and displays rare items of memorabilia. A 12-minute movie, "FDR in Georgia" is shown here.

Visitors can see the springs and pools where Roosevelt and other polio victims exercised and played in the naturally warm spring water.

Warm Springs, 31830. 404-655-3511. Open daily 9–5, except Thanksgiving and Christmas.

MANUFACTURING

Manufacturing is one of the largest and most profitable industries in Georgia. Georgia is the nation's leader in the production of processed chicken, tufted textile products, paper and board. Transportation equipment, metal goods, chemicals, food products, and apparel are important components to the state economy.

Following are two charts. The first lists the state's 50 largest manufacturing plants by employment. The second chart shows the major manufactured products by county, the number of manufacturing plants, and the number of employees.

Georgia's 50 Largest Manufacturing Plants by Employment

Plant & Location	Total Employment
Lockheed Aeronautical Systems Co. (Marietta)	18,921
General Motors Corp. (Doraville)	9,274
Shaw Industries, Inc.* (Dalton)	7,665
National Service Industries* (Atlanta)	6,341
Oxford Industries* (Chamblee)	5,687
Gulfstream Aerospace Corp. (Savannah)	4,600
Amoco Corp. (Savannah)	4,525
Union Camp Corp. (Savannah)	3,975
Milliken & Co. (Alma)	3,853
The Bibb Co.* (Columbus)	3,781
Southwire Co.* (Carrollton)	3,651
Cagle's Inc.* (Atlanta)	3,450
J. P. Stevens & Co., Inc. (Dublin)	3,436
A T & T Technologies, Inc. (Norcross)	3,317
West-Point Pepperell, Inc.* (Dalton)	3,156
World Carpets, Inc.* (Dalton)	3,148
Cluett Peabody & Co., Inc. (Atlanta)	3,088
Scientific-Atlanta, Inc.* (Atlanta)	3,072
Fieldale Corp.* (Cornelia)	3,000
Great Dane Trailers, Inc. (Savannah)	2,979
Dundee Mills* (Griffin)	2,895
Ford Motor Co. (Atlanta)	2,842
Armstrong World Industries, Inc. (Macon)	2,823
The Mead Corp. (Atlanta)	2,730
Gold Kist, Inc.* (Atlanta)	2,670
Coats Viyella PLC (Acworth)	2,643
The William Carter Co. (Barnesville)	2,527
Georgia Pacific Corp.* (Atlanta)	2,464
Procter & Gamble Co. (Albany)	2,447
Fieldcrest Cannon, Inc. (Columbus)	2,441

Plant & Location	Total Employment
Brown and Williamson Tobacco Corp. (Macon)	2,369
Galaxy Carpet Mills (Chatsworth)	2,257
C B S Records (Carrollton)	2,248
Englehard Corp. (Attapulgus)	2,229
Burlington Industries, Inc. (Shannon)	2,219
Great Northern Nekoosa Corp. (Valdosta)	2,198
Riegel Textile Div., Mt. Vernon Mills (Trion)	2,177
Thomaston Mills, Inc.* (Thomaston)	2,165
ITT Corp. (Jesup)	2,120
Roper Corp. (Augusta)	2,050
Hercules, Incorporated (Savannah)	1,997
Salem Carpet Mills, Inc. (Ringgold)	1,898
Blue Circle, Inc. (Atlanta)	1,820
Coordinated Apparel, Inc. (Swainsboro)	1,812
Rockwell International Corp. (Duluth)	1,800
Queen Carpet Co.* (Dalton)	1,707
Bigelow-Sanford, Inc. (Lyerly)	1,634
Blue Bird Body Co.* (Fort Valley)	1,591
Gilman Paper Co. (St. Marys)	1,574
Coronet Carpets Div., Coronet Ind. (Dalton)	1,508

*Georgia based

Major Manufacturing Plants and Products

County	Number of Mfg. Plants	Number of Employees	Major Manufactured Products
Appling	22	1,024	apparel, lumber, chemicals, fabricated metal, mobile homes
Atkinson	11	704	lumber, apparel, mobile homes
Bacon	12	1,235	apparel, food, textiles
Baker	1	165	apparel
Baldwin	16	2,934	textiles, apparel, machinery, trans. equipment, pharmaceuticals
Banks	9	1,213	textiles, apparel
Barrow	31	4,514	textiles, apparel, fiberglass, chemicals, trans. equipment, mobile homes, food
Bartow	66	7,397	textiles, apparel, chemicals, primary metals, rubber/plastics, trans. equipment, concrete
Ben Hill	31	2,770	food, textiles, apparel, lumber, machinery, batteries, mobile homes
Berrien	18	2,516	textiles, apparel, lumber

County	Number of Mfg. Plants	Number of Employees	Major Manufactured Products
Bibb	138	13,563	food, tobacco, textiles, apparel, furniture, paper, printing, rubber/plastics, stone/clay/glass/concrete, fabricated metals, machinery, trans. equipment, insulation
Bleckley	5	1,311	apparel, fixtures
Brantley	6	191	apparel, lumber
Brooks	8	1,221	apparel, textile
Bryan	7	344	lumber, machinery
Bulloch	36	2,448	food, apparel, lumber, primary metals, fabricated metals, electric equipment
Burke	18	1,504	apparel, lumber, fabricated metals, machinery, textiles
Butts	12	1,175	textiles, apparel, cabinets, potting soil
Calhoun	6	557	apparel, furniture
Camden	9	1,393	paper, chemicals
Candler	12	516	apparel, printing
Carroll	67	12,727	food, textiles, apparel, lumber, furniture, rubber/plastics, primary & fabricated metal, printing, electric equipment, transportation equipment
Catoosa	44	3,760	textiles, furniture
Charlton	5	458	lumber, apparel
Chatham	140	18,409	food, apparel, lumber, paper, printing, chemicals, primary & fabricated metals, trans. equipment, stone/clay/glass/concrete, fiberglass, toiletries
Chattahoochee	0	0	—
Chattooga	17	5,140	food, textiles, apparel
Cherokee	39	2,014	food, apparel, rubber/plastics, lumber
Clarke	82	12,674	food, textiles, apparel, lumber, printing, fiberglass, fabricated metals, machinery, instruments, concrete
Clay	3	191	stone/clay/glass/concrete
Clayton	77	4,171	food, furniture, paper, chemicals, rubber/plastics, stone/clay/glass/concrete, fabricated metals, machinery, printing, trans. equipment, paint
Clinch	5	850	apparel, metal containers
Cobb	233	28,684	food, textiles, apparel, lumber, furniture, paper, printing, chemicals, primary & fabricated metals, machinery, trans. equipment, instruments, concrete, rubber/plastics, industrial supplies
Coffee	55	3,858	food, textiles, apparel, fabricated

County	Number of Mfg. Plants	Number of Employees	Major Manufactured Products
			metals, trans. equipment, paper, mobile homes
Colquitt	43	4,162	textiles, apparel, lumber, primary & fabricated metals, mobile homes
Columbia	22	2,639	food, apparel, machinery, printing, trans. equipment
Cook	18	1,906	apparel, lumber, fabricated metals, paper
Coweta	42	5,764	textiles, apparel, paper, rubber/plastics, primary & fabricated metals, machinery, instruments
Crawford	2	130	lumber
Crisp	37	2,542	apparel, machinery, trans. equipment, food, lumber, chemicals, textiles, mobile homes, fiberglass
Dade	8	852	primary metals, textiles, trans. equipment, lumber
Dawson	3	147	apparel, rubber/plastics
Decatur	30	3,806	textiles, apparel, rubber/plastics, chemicals, fabricated metals, machinery, petroleum refining, mobile homes, paper
DeKalb	383	28,720	food, apparel, paper, printing, chemicals, rubber/plastics, stone/clay/glass/concrete, fabricated metals, machinery, trans. equipment, lumber, petroleum, tobacco, electronic equipment
Dodge	12	974	food, apparel, rubber/plastics
Dooly	7	665	apparel, lumber, chemicals
Dougherty	69	8,022	food, textiles, paper, printing, chemicals, rubber/plastics, fabricated metals, machinery, lumber, stone/clay/glass/concrete, transportation equipment
Douglas	31	1,066	textiles, stone/clay/glass/concrete, transportation equipment, fabricated metals, asphalt refining
Early	26	2,320	food, apparel, lumber, paper
Echols	0	0	—
Effingham	6	198	apparel
Elbert	69	2,353	apparel, stone, transportation equipment
Emanuel	35	2,942	apparel, lumber, furniture, fabricated metals, machinery, food
Evans	16	1,109	food, apparel, lumber

283

County	Number of Mfg. Plants	Number of Employees	Major Manufactured Products
Fannin	6	604	apparel
Fayette	34	2,538	food, textiles, paper, rubber/plastics, concrete, fabricated metals, electronic equipment
Floyd	90	11,429	food, textiles, apparel, lumber, paper, furniture, printing, stone/clay/glass/ concrete, primary & fabricated metals, machinery, instruments, electronic equipment
Forsyth	34	2,315	food, apparel, machinery, rubber plastics
Franklin	20	1,332	textiles, apparel, concrete, toiletries, electronic equipment
Fulton	568	46,189	food, textiles, apparel, lumber, furniture, paper, printing, chemicals, rubber/plastics, stone/clay/glass/ concrete, primary & fabricated metals, machinery, trans. equipment, instruments, paint, electronic equipment
Gilmer	17	1,506	food, textiles, lumber, instruments, marble
Glascock	4	219	apparel
Glynn	50	5,135	food, paper, chemicals, clay/concrete, lumber, fabricated metals, paint
Gordon	79	6,933	textiles, clay, food, rubber/plastics, machinery
Grady	23	1,986	food, apparel, machinery
Greene	13	1,566	textiles, apparel, lumber, figerglass
Gwinnett	229	21,303	apparel, furniture, paper, printing, rubber/plastics, primary & fabricated metals, lenses, machinery, instruments, leather, electronic equipment, transportation equipment
Habersham	34	6,135	textiles, apparel, lumber, instruments, furniture, plastic, transportation equipment
Hall	110	11,560	food, textiles, apparel, furniture, paper, printing, rubber/plastics, fabricated metals, machinery, trans. equipment, stone/clay/glass/concrete, mobile homes
Hancock	7	438	apparel, lumber
Haralson	25	3,997	apparel, printing, rubber/plastics, fabricated metals
Harris	9	824	food, textiles
Hart	24	2,980	textiles, apparel, trans. equipment, fabricated metals, recreation equipment

County	Number of Mfg. Plants	Number of Employees	Major Manufactured Products
Heard	7	679	apparel, primary and fabricated metals
Henry	28	2,230	apparel, paper, glass, machinery, electronic equipment
Houston	26	2,307	food, apparel, lumber, glass, concrete, textiles, plastic
Irwin	5	435	apparel, mobile homes
Jackson	19	3,397	food, textiles, apparel, machinery
Jasper	8	881	apparel, lumber
Jeff Davis	18	2,840	apparel, lumber, textiles, machinery
Jefferson	27	2,707	textiles, apparel, clay, machinery, lumber, transportation equipment
Jenkins	6	798	apparel, fabricated metals, mobile homes
Johnson	9	1,248	apparel
Jones	5	89	stone/clay/glass/concrete, machinery
Lamar	9	1,687	textiles, apparel, lumber, rubber
Lanier	1	2	food
Laurens	40	4,302	textiles, apparel, lumber, furniture, paper, electronic equipment
Lee	3	357	apparel, machinery
Liberty	11	771	apparel, paper
Lincoln	4	337	textiles, apparel
Long	0	0	—
Lowndes	62	6,222	food, lumber, paper, chemicals, fabricated metals, machinery, trans. equipment, apparel, printing
Lumpkin	6	797	textiles, machinery, transportation equipment
Macon	11	1,685	food, apparel
Madison	14	419	apparel
Marion	3	499	food, furniture
McDuffie	24	2,118	textiles, apparel, lumber, asphalt, prefab homes, transportation equipment
McIntosh	6	421	food, apparel
Meriwether	22	1,476	food, apparel, lumber, printing, plastic
Miller	7	110	food, apparel, chemicals
Mitchell	25	2,182	food, textiles, apparel, lumber, trans. equipment
Monroe	15	1,929	textiles, apparel, lumber
Montgomery	5	624	apparel, lumber
Morgan	15	1,813	food, textiles, apparel, lumber, furniture, rubber/plastics
Murray	47	5,510	textiles, electronic equipment

County	Number of Mfg. Plants	Number of Employees	Major Manufactured Products
Muscogee	138	17,997	food, textiles, printing, chemicals, rubber/plastics, primary & fabricated metals, machinery, trans. equipment, apparel, lumber, stone/clay/glass/ concrete, instruments
Newton	22	3,638	textiles, apparel, lumber, printing, rubber/plastics, hospital goods, transportation equipment
Oconee	17	504	textiles, elec. wire & cable, trans. equipment
Oglethorpe	5	68	apparel
Paulding	16	591	textiles, apparel
Peach	18	2,664	chemicals, trans. equipment, textiles, office supply
Pickens	14	1,447	apparel, rubber/plastics, stone/marble
Pierce	13	558	apparel, lumber
Pike	4	552	apparel, textiles
Polk	30	3,989	food, textiles, apparel, furniture, paper, chemicals, rubber/plastics, fabricated metals, machinery, ceramic
Pulaski	5	557	textiles, electronic equipment
Putnam	13	1,148	textiles, apparel, lumber, fabricated metals, mobile homes
Quitman	0	0	—
Rabun	14	1,409	textiles, apparel, instruments
Randolph	10	743	lumber, textiles
Richmond	133	13,821	food, textiles, apparel, paper, chemicals, clay, printing, trans. equipment, instruments, hospital supply, plastic
Rockdale	49	5,196	food, apparel, lumber, furniture, rubber/plastics, fabricated metals, machinery, chemicals, fixtures, electronic equipment
Schley	11	871	lumber, mobile homes
Screven	20	1,807	textiles, apparel, machinery
Seminole	9	393	apparel
Spalding	42	6,579	textiles, apparel, rubber/plastics, machinery
Stephens	33	4,804	textiles, apparel, furniture, printing, fabricated metals, machinery, transportation equipment
Stewart	8	173	mobile homes
Sumter	36	3,429	food, apparel, furniture, chemicals, rubber/plastics, lumber, trans. equipment, fixtures, mobile homes

County	Number of Mfg. Plants	Number of Employees	Major Manufactured Products
Talbot	2	71	furniture
Taliaferro	1	2	food
Tattnall	15	604	apparel, machinery
Taylor	9	334	apparel
Telfair	14	1,978	food, textiles, apparel, lumber, machinery
Terrell	12	1,317	food, apparel, rubber/plastics
Thomas	72	4,885	food, textiles, apparel, lumber, furniture, chemicals, rubber/plastics, fabricated metals, machinery, mobile homes, transportation equipment
Tift	41	3,425	textiles, apparel, paper, machinery, trans. equipment, mobile homes
Toombs	39	2,825	apparel, machinery, fabricated metals
Towns	6	202	apparel
Treutlen	4	524	textiles, apparel
Troup	62	9,372	textiles, apparel, paper, printing, rubber/plastics, fabricated metals, machinery, stone, glass, concrete, food, batteries, transportation equipment
Turner	12	636	textiles, apparel, mobile homes
Twiggs	5	909	clay
Union	6	608	apparel, leather, food
Upson	16	4,103	textiles, apparel, paper, electronic equipment
Walker	38	5,838	food, textiles, paper, rubber/plastics, fabricated metals, apparel, machinery
Walton	32	3,513	food, textiles, apparel, rubber/plastics, clay, china, mobile homes, furniture
Ware	44	2,326	food, tobacco, apparel, lumber, rubber/plastics, concrete, trans. equipment, marble, mobile homes, paper
Warren	10	1,312	apparel, lumber, furniture, rubber/plastics
Washington	22	2,712	textiles, apparel, clay, adhesive, electronic equipment
Wayne	25	2,004	textiles, apparel, furniture, chemicals
Webster	1	10	lumber
Wheeler	2	344	apparel
White	10	348	textiles, apparel
Whitfield	227	28,374	food, textiles, apparel, printing, chemicals, rubber/plastics, leather, stone, concrete, lumber, electronic equipment
Wilcox	3	58	apparel, clay

County	Number of Mfg. Plants	Number of Employees	Major Manufactured Products
Wilkes	29	1,868	textiles, apparel, lumber, rubber/plastics, food
Wilkinson	11	1,889	apparel, clay
Worth	19	1,169	food, textiles, apparel, mobile homes
Georgia	5,410	548,017	.

MEDICAL RESOURCES

Physicians, Hospitals[1], Nursing Homes: 1985

County	Active Physicians Total	General Hospitals		Nursing Homes	
		Number of Facilities	Bed Cap.	Number of Facilities	Bed Cap.
Appling	7	1	41	2	101
Atkinson	1	0	—	0	—
Bacon	7	1	47	1	88
Baker	—	0	—	0	—
Baldwin	110	1	160	4	444
Banks	0	0	—	0	—
Barrow	12	1	60	1	156
Bartow	27	1	80	1	118
Ben Hill	10	1	75	2	245
Berrien	7	1	71	1	54
Bibb	349	4	1,034	10	1,275
Bleckley	5	1	64	1	75
Brantley	—	0	—	0	—
Brooks	5	1	45	1	186
Bryan	3	0	—	0	—
Bulloch	34	1	158	4	309
Burke	11	1	57	2	156
Butts	10	1	28	1	197
Calhoun	2	1	40	1	60
Camden	15	1	39	1	69
Candler	4	1	60	3	298
Carroll	70	3	287	4	350
Catoosa	23	1	237	2	145
Charlton	4	1	50	1	92
Chatham	418	3	1,105	11	1,224
Chattahoochee	5	0	—	0	—
Chattooga	5	1	31	1	90
Cherokee	32	2	85	3	234
Clarke	159	2	471	4	444
Clay	3	1	35	1	49
Clayton	163	1	367	3	386
Clinch	3	1	49	1	92
Cobb	503	4	1,096	9	1,008
Coffee	30	1	145	2	148
Colquitt	32	1	155	4	277
Columbia	95	0	—	1	120

County	Active Physicians Total	General Hospitals		Nursing Homes	
		Number of Facilities	Bed Cap.	Number of Facilities	Bed Cap.
Cook	10	1	60	1	80
Coweta	47	2	244	2	174
Crawford	1	0	—	1	100
Crisp	16	1	70	2	243
Dade	4	1	39	1	65
Dawson	2	0	—	0	—
Decatur	16	1	82	2	207
DeKalb	840	6	1,855	16	2,012
Dodge	11	1	113	2	200
Dooly	8	1	47	1	102
Dougherty	146	2	673	2	418
Douglas	54	2	456	1	246
Early	5	1	49	1	127
Echols	—	0	—	0	—
Effingham	6	1	45	1	56
Elbert	11	1	64	3	187
Emanuel	8	1	72	3	260
Evans	7	1	73	1	87
Fannin	6	1	51	1	101
Fayette	31	0	—	0	—
Floyd	170	2	515	7	661
Forsyth	16	1	36	2	203
Franklin	10	1	95	1	144
Fulton	2,651	18	4,945	24	3,242
Gilmer	3	1	51	1	50
Glascock	—	0	—	1	104
Glynn	109	1	340	4	370
Gordon	22	1	65	2	218
Grady	10	1	60	1	108
Greene	7	1	68	1	71
Gwinnett	191	5	475	4	518
Habersham	12	1	59	2	196
Hall	138	2	462	6	502
Hancock	2	1	52	2	152
Haralson	10	1	85	3	242
Harris	5	0	—	1	100
Hart	7	1	98	2	209
Heard	2	1	29	1	78
Henry	17	1	104	1	180
Houston	64	2	295	5	402
Irwin	1	1	34	2	113
Jackson	10	1	90	2	122
Jasper	2	1	28	1	44
Jeff Davis	6	1	56	1	74
Jefferson	8	1	65	2	244
Jenkins	4	1	40	1	99
Johnson	1	0	—	2	153
Jones	5	0	—	2	162
Lamar	5	0	—	1	117
Lanier	2	1	40	1	62
Laurens	54	1	190	3	387
Lee	1	0	—	0	—
Liberty	15	1	50	1	169

289

MEDICAL RESOURCES

County	Active Physicians Total	General Hospitals		Nursing Homes	
		Number of Facilities	Bed Cap.	Number of Facilities	Bed Cap.
Lincoln	2	0	—	0	—
Long	—	0	—	0	—
Lowndes	101	2	359	4	367
Lumpkin	9	1	52	1	102
Macon	3	1	50	3	248
Madison	4	0	—	1	100
Marion	3	1	30	1	50
McDuffie	11	1	47	1	150
McIntosh	0	0	—	0	—
Meriwether	8	1	38	2	171
Miller	3	1	38	1	83
Mitchell	8	1	54	2	143
Monroe	5	1	40	3	276
Montgomery	2	0	—	0	—
Morgan	6	1	26	1	67
Murray	6	1	42	1	120
Muscogee	293	3	961	6	1,066
Newton	22	1	90	2	199
Oconee	10	0	—	1	100
Oglethorpe	1	0	—	0	—
Paulding	7	1	83	1	136
Peach	14	1	76	1	75
Pickens	5	1	40	3	149
Pierce	4	1	36	1	29
Pike	3	0	—	1	50
Polk	14	2	108	3	289
Pulaski	8	1	56	1	102
Putnam	6	1	50	1	92
Quitman	—	0	—	0	—
Rabun	8	2	88	1	117
Randolph	2	1	40	1	80
Richmond	850	4	2,077	10	1,180
Rockdale	34	1	100	1	164
Schley	—	0	—	0	—
Screven	7	1	76	1	128
Seminole	4	1	66	1	62
Spalding	53	1	222	3	350
Stephens	32	1	99	1	181
Stewart	1	1	32	0	—
Sumter	30	1	188	3	423
Talbot	—	0	—	0	—
Taliaferro	—	0	—	0	—
Tattnall	10	1	40	2	252
Taylor	3	0	—	0	—
Telfair	7	1	52	2	219
Terrell	6	1	34	1	74
Thomas	74	1	246	4	267
Tift	47	1	168	2	278
Toombs	17	1	124	2	317
Towns	6	1	42	1	30
Treutlen	3	0	—	1	50
Troup	67	1	280	4	416
Turner	2	1	40	1	76

290

County	Active Physicians Total	General Hospitals Number of Facilities	Bed Cap.	Nursing Homes Number of Facilities	Bed Cap.
Twiggs	1	0	—	1	132
Union	9	1	45	1	96
Upson	29	1	119	3	302
Walker	17	0	—	3	306
Walton	25	1	101	3	235
Ware	50	1	257	3	442
Warren	—	0	—	1	110
Washington	11	1	56	4	214
Wayne	18	1	138	3	224
Webster	—	0	—	0	—
Wheeler	2	1	40	1	62
White	6	0	—	2	149
Whitfield	85	1	297	3	330
Wilcox	1	0	—	2	203
Wilkes	8	1	66	1	47
Wilkinson	3	0	—	0	—
Worth	6	1	50	1	59
Georgia	9,045	173	26,051	330	34,390

—No Data
[1]Data does not include federal, state operated, private psychiatric, or special hospitals.

MILITARY POSTS

There are ten military bases in Georgia. These installations, the branch of service which is domiciled on each, and the nearest large town follow.

Base	Branch of Service	Town
Dobbins Air Force Base	Air Force	Marietta
Fort Benning	Army	Columbus
Fort Gillem	Army	Atlanta
Fort Gordon	Army	Augusta
Fort McPherson	Army	Atlanta
Fort Stewart	Army	Savannah
Hunter Army Air Field	Army	Savannah
Kings Bay Submarine Support Base	Navy	Savannah
Moody Air Force Base	Air Force	Valdosta
Robins Air Force Base	Air Force	Macon

MILEAGE CHART

Mileages are approximated	ALBANY	ATHENS	ATLANTA	AUGUSTA	BAINBRIDGE	BRUNSWICK	COLUMBUS	CORDELE	DALTON	DUBLIN	GAINESVILLE	LaGRANGE	MACON	MILLEDGEVILLE	ROME	SAVANNAH	TIFTON	VALDOSTA	WAYCROSS
ALBANY	0	200	174	210	57	172	86	40	260	112	227	129	107	138	223	216	42	80	113
AMERICUS	38	164	134	194	95	203	61	32	222	95	187	104	72	103	188	206	73	118	143
ATHENS	200	0	66	101	257	256	167	159	132	119	39	131	92	72	129	214	202	247	230
ATLANTA	174	66	0	157	231	274	109	144	88	139	53	68	84	93	68	256	183	234	240
AUGUSTA	210	101	157	0	267	189	217	170	245	98	140	222	124	93	225	133	197	216	177
BAINBRIDGE	57	257	231	267	0	198	124	97	305	168	282	167	164	195	261	245	84	80	141
BRUNSWICK	172	256	274	189	198	0	255	170	362	147	298	268	189	194	340	78	129	118	57
CARROLLTON	170	115	49	206	209	303	85	163	96	170	102	41	115	131	53	288	204	251	265
CARTERSVILLE	212	101	41	197	259	313	134	185	48	179	71	91	125	134	28	296	224	275	281
COLUMBUS	86	167	109	217	124	255	0	93	181	141	162	44	93	124	138	252	128	166	198
CORDELE	40	159	144	170	97	170	93	0	232	72	187	136	67	98	208	174	41	88	113
DAHLONEGA	245	60	71	161	303	319	180	208	73	175	21	139	141	128	91	313	254	301	325
DALTON	260	132	88	245	305	362	181	232	0	227	93	137	172	181	43	344	271	322	328
DUBLIN	112	119	139	98	168	147	141	72	227	0	158	149	55	47	208	124	101	137	111
ELBERTON	233	36	102	79	285	249	206	188	162	134	69	167	121	96	165	196	227	263	224
FITZGERALD	68	187	174	173	110	126	139	43	262	75	208	169	93	115	239	157	26	62	68
GAINESVILLE	227	39	53	140	282	298	162	187	93	158	0	121	120	107	99	252	228	275	265
GRIFFIN	133	89	40	153	189	244	78	110	128	110	93	60	55	70	108	227	151	198	208
JESUP	149	223	243	151	184	40	213	128	331	112	262	253	159	159	311	65	107	99	38
LaGRANGE	129	131	68	213	167	268	44	136	137	149	121	0	93	124	94	266	170	209	239
MACON	107	92	84	124	164	189	93	67	172	55	120	93	0	31	152	172	108	148	155
MILLEDGEVILLE	138	72	93	93	195	194	124	98	181	47	107	124	31	0	160	171	139	177	160
MOULTRIE	38	215	202	224	57	148	124	56	290	128	243	168	123	154	261	197	27	42	91
NEWNAN	152	163	37	194	200	274	76	141	119	149	90	33	94	109	74	266	176	223	247
ROME	223	129	68	225	261	340	138	208	43	208	99	94	152	160	0	324	250	297	308
SAVANNAH	216	214	256	133	249	78	252	174	344	124	252	266	172	171	324	0	176	167	104
STATESBORO	180	160	211	81	233	110	213	140	299	72	199	221	167	108	279	53	149	163	102
THOMASTON	106	113	68	169	163	225	57	86	156	100	121	49	45	75	129	217	127	174	191
THOMASVILLE	62	244	230	248	39	163	148	85	318	155	270	188	150	181	281	212	56	43	106
TIFTON	42	202	183	197	84	129	128	41	271	101	228	170	108	139	250	176	0	49	71
TOCCOA	253	50	98	125	307	295	207	211	128	169	45	166	144	122	138	242	252	295	275
VALDOSTA	80	247	234	216	84	118	166	88	322	137	275	209	148	177	297	167	47	0	61
WAYCROSS	113	230	240	177	145	57	198	113	328	111	265	239	155	160	308	104	71	61	0

MISS GEORGIA

Each year a "Miss Georgia" is selected in competition at Columbus. The winner represents the state in the annual "Miss America" contest. Since the contest's inception in 1945, the following "Miss Georgias" have been selected.

1945 Doris Coker
1946 Mary Lou Henderson
1947 Robbie Sauls
1948 Gwen West
1949 Dorothy Johnson
1950 Louise Thomas
1951 Carol Taylor

1952 Neva Jane Langley
1953 Lucia Hutchinson
1954 Mary Jane Doar
1955 Jeanine Parris
1956 Jane Morris
1957 Jody Shattuck
1958 Jeanette Ardell

1959 Kayanne Shoeffner	1973 Gail Bullock
1960 Sandra Talley	1974 Gail Nelson
1961 Glenda Brunson	1975 Seva Day
1962 Eugenia "Jeanie" Cross	1976 Sandy Adamson
1963 Nancy Middleton	1977 Pam Souders
1964 Vivian Davis (deceased)	1978 Deborah Mosely
1965 Mary Jane Yates	1979 Sandra Eakes
1966 Maudie Walker	1980 Kristl Anne Evans
1967 Sandra McRee	1982 Bobbie Eakes
1968 Burma Davis	1983 Tammy Fulwider
1969 Marilyn Olley	1984 Camille Bentley
1970 Nancy Carr	1985 Samantha Mohr
1971 Cynthia Cook	1986 Marlesa Ball
1972 Lisa Lawalin	1987 Kelly Jerles

MUSEUMS

ALBANY
Albany Museum of Art, 311 Meadowlark Dr., Albany 31707. 912-435-0977. Small permanent collection of purchase awards from our annual arts festivals; African art collection. *Hours & Admission Prices:* Tues.-Fri. 11–5; Sat.-Sun. 2–5. No charge. Closed New Year's; Memorial Day; July 4; Labor Day; Thanksgiving Day; Christmas.

Thronateeska Heritage Foundation, Inc., 100 Roosevelt Ave., Albany 31701. 912-432-6955. History Museum featuring costumes; pioneer tools; rocks; minerals; shells; historic artifacts; Indian artifacts; Nelson Tift furnishings; antique carriages; 1880's Hearse; Confederate War Items; local artifacts of the history of Southwest Georgia area; railroad cars with model train exhibit; 1911 steam locomotive. Historic Buildings: 1913, Union Station; 1857, depot; 1854, Kendall-Jarrard House; 1919, Railway Express Bldg.; manuscripts. *Hours & Admission Prices:* Tues.-Sun. 2–5; Train: Wed., Sat.-Sun. 2–5; Planetarium: Wed. 4:00; Fri. 7:30; Sat. 2:30 & 4:00; Sun. 3:00. Museum: no charge; Planetarium: adults $1; children & senior citizens 50¢. Closed New Year's; Thanksgiving; Christmas.

ANDERSONVILLE
Andersonville National Historic Site, Andersonville 31711. 912-924-0343. Civil War P.O.W. camp featuring items related to the Andersonville Prison located in War Museum; limited number of items related to P.O.W. camps; Civil War & later conflicts. Historic House Museum: 1872, Cemetery Sexton's residence; 1908, Cemetery Chapel. *Hours & Admission Prices:* Daily 8:30–5. No charge. Visitor Center closed Christmas.

ATHENS
Athens-Clarke Heritage Foundation, Fire Hall #2, Prince Ave., Athens 30601. 404-353-1801. Museum housed in 1901 Victorian Fire Hall featuring photographs; period furnishings; period herb garden; c. 1820 Brumby House. *Hours & Admission Prices:* Mon.-Fri. 10–4; other times by appointment. No charge. Closed Legal Holidays.

The Garden Club of Georgia, Inc., 325 S. Lumpkin St., Athens 30602. 404-542-3631. Historic House Museum in 1857, brick house, state headquarters for The Garden Club of Georgia Inc., located on the campus of the University of Georgia featuring 18th & 19th century furniture and rugs; Founders Memorial Garden; old smoke house contains memorabilia, pictures relating to the first garden club in America, c. 1891. *Hours & Admission Prices:* Mon.-Fri. 9–4; $1 per person.

Georgia Museum of Art, the University of Georgia, Jackson St., North Campus, Athens 30602. 404-542-3253. American paintings and sculpture; American and Japanese graphics; Kress Study Collection. *Hours & Admission Prices:* Mon.-Sat. 9–5; Sun. 1–5. No charge. Closed Legal Holidays.

Lyndon House Art Center, 293 Hoyt St., Athens 30601. 404-549-3838. Activities include, guided tours; lectures; gallery talks; arts festivals; meeting & workshops for local art organizations; formally organized education/awareness programs for children, adults, specialized groups & general public; art courses in painting, printmaking, weaving & youth art; stained glass, internships for students at the University of Georgia. *Hours & Admission Prices:* scheduled exhibitions Mon.-Fri. 1:30–5. No charge; donations accepted. Closed City of Athens Legal Holidays.

Navy Supply Corps Museum, Navy Supply Corps School, Athens 30606. 404-354-7348. Nautical history museum; artifacts relating to logistics; Supply Corps functions; housed in 1907 Carnegie Library. *Hours & Admission Prices:* Mon.-Fri. 9–4:30. No charge.

The State Botanical Garden of Georgia, 2450 S. Milledge Ave., Athens 30605. 404-542-1244. Collections: Woody plant collections; native flora; native & adapted trees & shrubs including shade & ornamental trees. *Hours & Admission Prices:* Grounds: Oct.-April Daily 8–5; May-Sept. Daily 8–8; Callaway Building: Mon.-Fri. 8–5; Sat. & Sun. 2–4:30. No charge.

Taylor-Grady House, 634 Prince Ave., Athens 30601. 404-549-8688. 1838 antebellum home belonging to Henry W. Grady, called the spokesman of the New South. *Hours & Admission Prices:* Mon., Wed., Fri. 10–12; adults $1; children under 12 50¢. Closed Thanksgiving; Christmas; last week in December.

University of Georgia Museum of Natural History, Biological Science Bldg., University of Georgia, Athens 30602. 404-542-1663. Anthropology, botany, entomology, geology, mycology, zoology of Georgia & the Southeast. *Hours & Admission Prices:* Mon.-Fri. 8–5; tours by appointment. No charge. Closed Holidays.

ATLANTA

Atlanta Botanical Garden, P.O. Box 77246, Atlanta 30357. 404-876-5858. 300-vol. library of botany, horticulture, taxonomy books available for research for members & visitors on premises; botanical gardens; visitors center; auditorium; classroom. Gifts relating to horticulture, books & containers for sale. *Hours & Admission Prices:* April-Oct. Daily 9-dusk; Nov.-March Mon.-Sat. 9–4; Sun. 12–4; no charge; scheduled tours adults $1; students 25¢. Closed New Year's; July 4; Thanksgiving; Christmas.

The Atlanta College of Art, 1280 Peachtree St., N.E., Atlanta 30309. 404-898-1164. Art Gallery, 13,000-vol. library of bin arts books available for inter-library loan during regular library hours; classrooms. Art supplies for sale. *Hours & Admission Prices:* Tues.-Fri. 10–5; Sat. 11–3. No charge. Closed Holidays.

The Atlanta Cyclorama, 800 Cherokee Ave., S.E., Atlanta 30315. 404-658-7625. Historic Structure: c. 1885, cyclorama 42-ft. high x 356 ft. in circumference depicting 1864, Battle of Atlanta. *Hours & Admission Prices:* Daily 9:30–4:30; adults $3; senior citizen $2.50; children 6–12 $1.50; group rates available.

Atlanta Historical Society, 3101 Andrews Drive, N.W., Atlanta 30305. 404-261-1837. Manuscripts; 50,000 photographs; maps, books; architectural drawings; Atlanta newspapers; Margaret Mitchell memorabilia; early 19th century furniture and tools; extensive costume collection; folklife collection; Civil War artifacts; decorative arts. Historic Houses: 1840, Tullie Smith House; 1890, Victorian Playhouse; 1928, Swan House; Palladian style mansion. *Hours & Admission Prices:* Mon.-Sat. 9–5:30; Sun. 12–5; Library: Mon.-Sat. 9–5; adults $5; children 6–12 $2; family & senior citizens, rates avaliable. Closed New Year's; Christmas.

Atlanta Museum, 537–39 Peachtree St., N.E., Atlanta 30308. 404-872-8233. Housed in 1900, R. M. Rose Mansion, last Victorian mansion standing on Peachtree St. in downtown area & home of distiller of Four Roses Liquor; confederate money; collections of George Washington, Thomas Jefferson, Robert E. Lee, Jefferson Davis, John Tyler, John C. Calhoun, Napoleon, Gen. Robert Toombs, F. D. Roosevelt, Hitler; Georgian and Confederate history; Margaret Mitchell personal items; Coca Cola items; early captured Japanese Zero plane; early Chinese items; early glass, porcelains, bronzes, furniture; original Eli Whitney cotton gin; Eli Whitney gun collection; paintings; sculpture; decorative arts; Indian artifacts. *Hours & Admission Prices:* Mon.-Fri. 10–5; adults $2; children $1; special group rates. Closed New Year's; July 4; Labor Day; Thanksgiving; Christmas.

Atlanta Zoological Park, 800 Cherokee Ave., Atlanta 30315. 404-658-7060. *Hours & Admission Prices:* Daily 10–5:30; adults $2.50; children $1.25; group rates available; tours no charge.

Callanwolde Fine Arts Center, 980 Briarcliff Rd., N.E., Atlanta 30306. 404-872-5338. Performing Arts Center; housed in 1917–1920, Callanwolde, home of Charles Howard Candler, son of Asa Candler of Coca Cola fame, exhibit space; classrooms; gallery; rental gallery. Paintings, prints, sculpture, woven items, pottery, jewelry for sale. *Hours & Admission Prices:* Mon.-Thurs. 9–9; Fri. 9–4; Sat. 10–4. No charge. Closed Legal Holidays.

Emory University Museum of Art and Archaeology, Carlos Hall, 571 Kilgo Circle, Atlanta 30322. 404-727-4282. Archaeology; ethnology; prints; drawings; photography; painting; sculpture. *Hours & Admission Prices:* Tues.-Sat. 11–4:30, no charge.

Fernbank Science Center, 156 Heaton Park Dr., N.E., Atlanta 30307. 404-378-4311. Skins; hides; entomology; ornithology; herbarium; geology; skeletal; gems; minerals; birds; mammals; insects. Classes in nature art, molding, casting, taxidermy; guided tours; lectures; films. *Hours & Admission Prices:* Mon. 8:30–5; Tues.-Fri. 8:30 a.m.-10 p.m.; Sat. 10–10; Sun. 1–8. No charge for museum. Planetarium: adults $1.50; students 75¢. Closed National Holidays.

Georgia State Museum of Science and Industry, Room 431, Georgia State Capitol, Atlanta 30334. 404-656-2846. Rocks; minerals; dioramas of industry; reptiles; Indian artifacts; mounted birds, animals and fish. *Hours & Admission Prices:* Mon.-Fri. 8–5:30; Sat. 10–2; Sun. 1–3. No charge. Closed Legal Holidays.

Georgia State University Art Gallery, Georgia State University, University Plaza, Atlanta 30303. 404-658-2257. American contemporary paintings, prints, photographs & crafts. *Hours & Admission Prices:* Mon.-Fri. 8–8. No charge. Closed New Year's; July 4; Labor Day; Thanksgiving; Friday after Thanksgiving; Last Week in December.

The High Museum of Art, 1280 Peachtree St., N.E., Atlanta 30309. 404-892-3600. Western art from early Renaissance to present; decorative arts with emphasis on 18th, 19th & early 20th century American objects; 18th century European ceramics; graphics; sculpture; objects representing most sub-Saharan & African styles; 19th and 20th century photography. *Hours & Admission Prices:* Tues., Thurs.-Sat. 10–5; Wed. 10–9; Sun. 12–5. adults $3; students and senior citizens $1; children under 18 and members no charge; no charge Thurs. 1–5. Closed New Year's; July 4; Labor Day; Thanksgiving; Christmas.

Martin Luther King, Jr. Center for Nonviolent Social Change, 449 Auburn Ave., N.E. Atlanta 30312. 404-524-1956. History Museum, Educational Center & Archive located on the grounds of the Martin Luther King, Jr. National Historic Site. Furnishings of the King family; personal effects of Dr. King; artwork; memorabilia donated by the public; works of art executed by artists in memory of Dr. King. Historic House: 1895, birth home of Dr. Martin Luther King, Jr. Historic Site: Tomb of Dr. King. *Hours & Admission Prices:* Center: Mon.-Sat. 9–5; Sun. 2–5, No charge. Various fees & tours; call for verification & reservations. Closed Legal Holidays.

Martin Luther King, Jr., National Historic Site and Preservation District, 522 Auburn Ave., N.W., Atlanta 30312. 404-221-5190. Neighborhood where Dr. Martin Luther King, Jr. grew up, includes birthplace, boyhood home, church & gravesite. Historic photos; local history; oral history.

Photographic Investments Gallery, 468 Armour Dr., Atlanta 30324. 404-876-7260. 19th century photography representing all processes & images worldwide. *Hours & Admission Prices:* Mon.-Fri. 10–4; Sat.-Sun. by appointment. No charge. Closed Legal Holidays.

Wren's Nest, 1050 Gordon St., S.W., Atlanta 404-753-8535. Historic House, 1881, home of Joel Chandler Harris, author of the Uncle Remus Stories. Original furnishings belonging to the Harris family; personal artifacts of Mr. Harris including his typewriter, hat & umbrella and rolltop desk which he used while employed at the Atlanta Constitution and where the Uncle Remus stories were introduced; photographs and other memorabilia related to Harris, his family and the Uncle Remus stories. *Hours & Admission Prices:* Mon.-Sat. 9:30–5; Sun. 2–5; adults $2.50; Senior Citizen $2; teens $1.25; children under 12 75¢; group rates available. Closed New Year's Eve; New Year's; Easter; July 4; Labor Day; Thanksgiving; Christmas Eve; Christmas Day.

AUGUSTA
Augusta Richmond County Museum, 540 Telfair St., Augusta 30901. 404-722-8454. Local and military history; regional archaeology; natural science; geology; costumes; early American artifacts. Historic House: 1850, Brahe House at 456 Telfair St. *Hours & Admission Prices:* Tues.-Sat. 10–5; Sun. 2–5. No charge. Closed National Holidays.

Ezekiel Harris House, 1840 Broad St., Augusta 30904. 404-733-6768. Furnishings, late 18th century artifacts. *Hours & Admission Prices:* conducted tours: by appointment; call Historic Augusta 404-733-6768; adults $2; children 50¢.

Gertrude Herbert Memorial Institute of Art, 506 Telfair St., Augusta 30901. 404-722-5495. Paintings; graphics; monthly changing exhibitions. Historic House: 1818, Ware's Folly. *Hours & Admission Prices:* Tues.-Fri. 10–5; Sat.-Sun. 2–5. No charge. Closed New Year's; Easter; May 30; July 4; August; Thanksgiving; Christmas.

Laney-Walker Museum, Inc., 821 Laney-Walker Blvd., Augusta 30901. 404-724-5614. African art; Afro-American arts; local artists. *Hours & Admission Prices:* Call for hours. No charge.

Meadow Garden, 1320 Nelson St., Augusta 30904. 404-724-4174. Historic House: Meadow Garden, 1791–1804 residence of George Walton, signer of the Declaration of Independence. *Hours & Admission Prices:* Tues.-Sat. 10–4; adults $2; children 50¢.

BLAIRSVILLE
Brasstown Bald Visitor Center, Hwy. 19 & 129 S. Blairsville 30512. 404-745-6928. Park Museum, located within the Chattahoochee National Forest. Natural history; exhibits pertaining to "Man and the Mountain." *Hours & Admission Prices:* Memorial Day-Oct. Daily 10–6; mid April-Memorial Day Sat.-Sun. 10–5:30. No charge.

BLAKELY
Kolomoki Mounds Museum, Rt. 1, Blakely 31723. 912-723-5296. 13th Century Indian Burial Mound and village site. Archaeology; Indian artifacts; excavated mound. *Hours & Admission Prices:* Tues.-Sat., Holiday Mondays 9–5; Sun. 2–5:30; 17 & over $1; 6–17 50¢; children under 6 no charge. Closed Thanksgiving; Christmas.

BRUNSWICK
Hofwyl-Broadfield Plantation, Rt. 2, Box 83, Brunswick 31520. 912-264-9263. Dairy equipment; rice tools; furnishings from the period 1830–1972. *Hours & Admission Prices:* Tues.-Sat. 9–5; Sun. 2–5:30; adults $1; youth 50¢; groups of 15 or more 25¢; children, no charge. Closed Mondays except Holiday Mondays; Thanksgiving; Christmas.

BUFORD
Bowman-Pirkle House, 2601 Buford Dam Rd., Buford 30518. 404-945-3543. 1818 plantation homestead belonging to one of the first white settlers in the area. Pioneer furniture & furnishings; utensils; barn & corn crib; blacksmith shop; smokehouse; covered wagon; tannery; syrup mill. *Hours & Admission Prices:* Tues.-Fri. 8:30–4; Sun. 2–5:30; No charge.

Lanier Museum of Natural History, 2601 Buford Dam Rd., Buford 30518. 404-945-3543. Located in Lanier Water Park. Birds; mammals; fish; butterflies & insects; rocks; minerals; fossils; shells; Indian artifacts; snakes; old & rare books; photographs; paintings; large collection of "touch" items. *Hours & Admission Prices:* Tues.-Fri. 10–4:30; Sun. 2–5:30. No charge.

CALHOUN
New Echota, Rt. 3, Calhoun 30701. 404-629-8151. 1825 Capital town of Cherokee Nation. Historic Buildings, 1828 Rev. Samuel Worcester's Mission, Vann Tavern, replica of Cherokee Phoenix Print Shop, Courthouse. *Hours & Admission Prices:* Tours: Tues.-Sat. 9:30, 11, 1:30, 3, adults $1; children 6–11 50¢; children 5 & under, no charge; organized groups of 15 or more 25¢. Closed Thanksgiving; Christmas.

CARTERSVILLE
Etowah Indian Mounds Historical Site, Rt. 2, Cartersville 30120. 404-382-2704. Archaeological excavations of prehistoric Indian center. *Hours & Admission Prices:* Tues.-Sat., Holiday Mondays 9–5; Sun. 2–5:30; adults $1; children 12–17 50¢; 12 & under no charge; groups of 15 or more 25¢. Closed New Year's, Thanksgiving, Christmas.

Roselawn Museum, 224 West Cherokee Ave., Cartersville 30120. 404-386-0300. 1880, Victorian mansion, former home of evangelist Samuel Porter Jones. Furniture; documents; clothing & costumes; silver; memorabilia belonging to Samuel Porter Jones; documents & memorabilia belonging to Rebecca Latimer Felton, first woman U.S. Senator. *Hours & Admission Prices:* Mon.-Fri. 9–5; other times by appointment; adults $1; children 50¢. Closed All Holidays.

CEDARTOWN
The Polk County Historical Society, College St., Cedartown 30125. 404-748-5906. Museum housed in 1921, former Hawke's Childrens' Library. *Hours & Admission Prices:* 4th Sun. of each month 12–6. No charge; donations accepted.

CHATSWORTH
Fort Mountain State Park, Rt. 7, Box 1K, Chatsworth 30705. 404-695-2621. Pre-historic stone wall. Woodland period; ceremonial sites; fault zone geology. *Hours & Admission Prices:* Daily 7–10. No charge.

Vann House, Rt. #7, Box 235, Chatsworth 30705. 404-695-2598. 1804, Vann House with furniture; personal items. *Hours & Admission Prices:* Winter: Tues.-Sat., Holiday Mondays 9–5; Sun. 2–5; Summer: Tues.-Sat., Holiday Mondays 9–5:30; Sun. 2–5:30; adults 18 & over $1; children 12–17 50¢; children under 12 no charge; groups of 15 or more, 25¢. Closed Thanksgiving; Christmas.

CLEVELAND
White County Historical Society, Rt. 3, Box 4, Cleveland 30528. 404-865-3225. Historic Building: 1859–60, Courthouse, old newspapers; Civil War documents; diaries and letters. *Hours & Admission Prices:* call for hours. No charge.

COCHRAN
Middle Georgia College Museum, Cochran 31014. 912-934-6221. Housed in 1860s Pace House, home of Paleman J. King, 1st president of college, & 1890 Ebenezer Hall, home of presidents of original college. Period furniture; historical documents. *Hours & Admission Prices:* Mon.-Fri. 10–4; other times by appointment; adults $1. Closed School Holidays.

COLUMBUS

Columbus Museum of Arts and Sciences, Inc., 1251 Wynnton Rd., Columbus 31906. 404-323-3617. Paintings; sculpture; graphics; archaeology; general natural history; decorative arts; paleontology; southern history; ethnology; costumes. *Hours & Admission Prices:* Mon.-Sat. 10–5; Sun. 2–5. No charge. Closed New Year's; July 4; Thanksgiving; Christmas.

Confederate Naval Museum, 202 4th St., Columbus 31902. 404-327-9798. Confederate naval gunboats; CSS Muscogee and CSS Chattahoochee, on display; other exhibits pertaining to Confederate Navy and Marine Corps. *Hours & Admission Prices:* Tues.-Sat. 10–5; Sun. 2–5. No charge. Closed Thanksgiving; Christmas.

Historic Columbus Foundation, Inc., 700 Broadway, Columbus 31901. 404-322-0756. Historic Houses: 1850, The Rankin House, houses an authenticated Victorian furniture collection; 1828, The Walker-Peters-Langdon House, houses 1828–1835 furnishings; 1870, 700 Broadway House, houses late Victorian furnishings; 1840, Pemberton House, houses mid-Victorian furnishings & authenticated Coca-Cola collectibles & memorabilia. *Hours & Admission Prices:* Museum: Mon.-Fri. 9–5. No charge; donations accepted. Heritage Tour: Wed. & Sat. 10–12; adults $5; children $2.50.

CORDELE

Georgia Veterans Memorial Museum, Rt. 3, Box 385, Cordele 31015. 912-273-2190. Historic aircraft; fighting vehicles; uniforms; weapons; accoutrements. *Hours & Admission Prices:* Tues.-Sat., Holiday Mondays 9–5; Sun. 2–5:30. No charge. Closed New Year's; Thanksgiving; Christmas.

CRAWFORDVILLE

Confederate Museum, Alexander St., Crawfordville 30631. 404-456-2221. Arms & memorabilia of Civil War. Historic House: 1875, Liberty Hall, home of Alexander H. Stephens; furnishings; slave quarters & outbuildings. *Hours & Admission Prices:* Tues.- Sat., Holiday Mondays 9–5; Sun. 2–5:30; adults $1; youth 12–17 50¢; children 11 and under no charge; special group rate 15 or more 25¢ per person. Closed Thanksgiving; Christmas.

DAHLONEGA

Dahlonega Courthouse Gold Museum, 1-A Public Square, Dahlonega 30533. 404-864-2257. Native Georgian gold & Dahlonega Mint coins; mining equipment; photographs. *Hours & Admission Prices:* Tues.-Sat., Holiday Mondays 9–5; Sun. 2–5:30; adults $1; children 12–17 50¢; children under 12, no charge; organized groups of 15 or more 25¢ per person. Closed Thanksgiving; Christmas.

DALTON

Creative Arts Guild, 520 West Waugh St., Dalton 30720. 404-278-0168. Various types of art media; guided tours; lectures; concerts; dance recitals; arts festivals; drama; rental Gallery; docent programs; permanent, temporary, and traveling exhibitions. *Hours & Admission Prices:* Mon.-Fri. 9–5; Sat. 11–2. Closed New Year's; Memorial Day; July 4; Thanksgiving; Christmas.

Crown Gardens and Archives, 715 Chattanooga Ave., Dalton 30720. 404-278-0217. Handmade tufted bedspreads; machines for making spreads, material; textiles; artifacts pertaining to the Black community; Sims Collection of hand-carved wooden objects; c. 1890, furniture from the Loveman home; records of Mills; 1860, Whitfield Co. Census Index; 1860, Murray Co. Census Index. *Hours & Admission Prices:* Tues.-Sat. 9–5. No charge. Closed New Year's; July 4; Thanksgiving; Christmas.

DARIEN

Fort King George Historic Site, P.O. Box 711, Darien 31305. 912-437-4770. Aboriginal & Spanish artifacts; reproductions of uniforms, weapons and accoutrements of British garrison.

Hours & Admission Prices: Tues.-Sat., Monday Holidays 9–5; Sun. 2–5:30; adults $1; youth 50¢; groups of 15 or more 25¢; children 5 and under no charge. Closed Thanksgiving; Christmas.

DECATUR

Dalton Galleries, Agnes Scott College, College & Candler, Decatur 30030. 404-373-2571. Art gallery featuring Harry L. Dalton collection; Steffen Thomas collection; Ferdinand Warren collection; Clifford Clarke collection. *Hours & Admission Prices:* Mon.-Fri. 9 a.m.-10:30 p.m.; Sat. 9–5; Sun. 2–5. No charge.

DeKalb Historical Society Museum, Old Courthouse on the Square, Decatur 30030. 404-373-1088 & 3076. Museum housed in the Old Courthouse on Decatur Square; three exhibit rooms containing memorabilia of the first hundred years, 1822–1922, of DeKalb; Civil War memorabilia; manuscripts. Historic Buildings: 1830–40, Benjamin Swanton House; 1825, Thomas-Barber Cabin; 1822, John Biffle Cabin. *Hours & Admission Prices:* Museum: Mon.-Fri. 8:30–4:30. No charge. Swanton House & Biffle Cabin: open by appointment; adults $2; children 50¢. Closed National Holidays.

DUBLIN

Dublin-Laurens Museum, Academy & Bellevue Aves., Dublin 31021. 912-272-9242. Housed in 1904, restored Carnegie Library; textiles; photographs; farm tools & implements; art memorabilia. *Hours & Admission Prices:* Tues., Thurs., Sat. 1–4:30; other times by appointment. No charge.

DULUTH

Southeastern Railway and Museum, 3966 Buford Hwy., Duluth 30136. 404-476-2013. Railroad & transportation equipment; locomotives; rolling stock; business records; blueprints; maps; books; magazines; trade journals & house organs; newspaper articles. *Hours & Admission Prices:* Sat. 9–5. No charge; donations accepted. Closed July 4, Christmas, New Year's.

DUNWOODY

Chattahoochee River National Recreation Area, 1900 Northridge Rd., Dunwoody 30338. 404-394-8324. Herbarium; biological specimens of the area. Historic Structures: 1840, Allenbrook; 1850, ruins of Akers Mill-Marietta Paper Mill; 1840 Ivy (Laurel) Mill Ruins; prehistoric village sites, rock shelters and fish weirs; historic Indian village sites and Civil War remains. Recreational and educational opportunities; guided walks; lectures; canoe/kayak/raft rentals; shuttle service; skill instructional clinics. *Hours & Admission Prices:* Daily call for hours. 404-394-8335. No charge.

EATONTON

Uncle Remus Museum, 360 Oak St., Eatonton 31024. 404-485-6856. Slave cabin, c. 1820, furniture; artifacts; books of Joel Chandler Harris, author of the Uncle Remus stories. *Hours & Admission Prices:* June-Aug. Mon.-Sat. 10–12 & 1–5; Sun. 2–5; Sept.-May Mon., Wed.-Sat. 10–12 & 1–5; adults 50¢; students 25¢. Closed New Year's; Christmas.

ELBERTON

Elberton Granite Museum & Exhibit, 1 Granite Plaza, Elberton 30635. 404-283-2551. Historical exhibits; artifacts; educational displays; granite monuments. *Hours & Admission Prices:* mid Jan.-mid Nov. Daily 2–5; other times on limited schedule. No charge. Closed Holidays.

FARGO

Stephen C. Foster State Park, Fargo 31631. 912-637-5274. Natural history of Okefenokee Swamp; lumbering; turpentining. *Hours & Admission Prices:* Daily 7–7. No charge. Boat tours: $3 adults; children $1.50; children under 8, no charge.

FORT BENNING
National Infantry Museum, U.S. Army Infantry Center, Fort Benning 31905. 404-544-4762. Militaria; weapons; military art; local Indian and early military archeological materials; archives of photographs; collection of firearms including experimental U.S. items; presidential collection; 1896, Sutler's store. *Hours & Admission Prices:* Tues.-Fri. 10–4:30; Sat.-Sun. 12:30–4:30. No charge. Closed New Year's; Thanksgiving; Christmas.

FORT OGLETHORPE
Chickamauga-Chattanooga National Military Park, Fort Oglethorpe 30742. 404-866-9241. Civil War relics; Fuller gun collection of American military shoulder arms. Historic Houses: 1866, Cravens House; 1850, Brotherton, Snodgrass and Kelley Cabins. *Hours & Admission Prices:* May-Oct. Daily 8–5:45; Nov.-April Daily 8–4:45. No charge. Closed Christmas.

FORT STEWART
24th Infantry Division and Fort Stewart Museum, Wilson Ave. & Utility St., Fort Stewart 31314. 912-767-7885. Artifacts, uniforms, arms, equipment & photographs from the Civil War through the Vietnam War; towed & self propelled artillery pieces; tanks; anti-aircraft equipment. *Hours & Admission Prices:* Tues.-Fri. 12–4; Sat.-Sun. 1–5; other times by appointment. No charge. Closed Federal Holidays.

FORT VALLEY
American Camellia Society, Rural Rt. 3 Box 155, Fort Valley 31030. 912-967-2358. Rare books; original paintings & prints; gallery of Boehm Porcelains; 10 acre gardens; greenhouse of plants. *Hours & Admission Prices:* Mon.-Fri. 8:30–4. No charge; donations accepted. Closed National Holidays.

INDIAN SPRINGS
Indian Museum, Indian Springs State Park, Indian Springs 30231. 404-775-7241. Pottery; items that reflect stages of Indian civilization. *Hours & Admission Prices:* Memorial Day-Labor Day Tues.-Sat. 9–5; Sun. 2–5.

JEFFERSON
Crawford W. Long Medical Museum, U.S. Highway 129, Jefferson 30549. 404-367-5307. Located on site of the first operation using ether, performed by Dr. Crawford W. Long. History of the discovery of anaesthetic. *Hours & Admission Prices:* Tues.-Sat. 10–5; Sun. 2–5. No charge; donations accepted. Closed New Year's; July 4; Labor Day; Memorial Day; Thanksgiving; Christmas.

JEKYLL ISLAND
Jekyll Island Museum, Old Village Rd., Jekyll Island 31520. 912-635-2236. Furnishings; documents; photographs; clothing & memorabilia; Tiffany stained-glass window. Historic Houses: 1896, Moss Cottage, former home of Struther-Macy; 1903, Goodyear cottage, former F. H. Goodyear home; 1892, Indian Mound, former McKay-W. Rockefeller home; 1898, Sans Souci Apartments, former J. P. Morgan apartments; 1887, Jekyll Island Club House; 1917, Crane Cottage, former R. T. Crane, Jr. home; 1893, Hollybourne Cottage, former C. S. Maurice home; 1927, Villa Ospo, former W. Jennings home; 1928, Villa Marianna, former F. M. Gould home; 1905, Cherokee Cottage, former Shrady-James home; 1904, Faith chapel; 1914, service facilities including Club Dock; 1927, J. P. Morgan, Jr. indoor tennis court; 1891, infirmary; Baker-Crane Stable; Boat engineer's house and servants quarters; 1742, tabby ruins of Major Horton House; 1880, DuBignon Cottage; 1901, Misletoe Cottage, former Portor-Claflin home. *Hours & Admission Prices:* Memorial Day-Labor Day Daily 9–6; Labor Day-Memorial Day Daily 10–5; tours at 10 & 2; adults $6; students 6–18 $4; 12 group rates available, children $1.

JULIETTE

Jarrell Plantation Georgia State Historic Site, Jarrell Plantation Rd., Juliette 31046. 912-986-5172. Tools; furnishings; clothing; implements; grist mill; cotton gin; planing mill; boiler and steam engines; syrup evaporators; cane mill; saw mill; blacksmith forge. *Hours & Admission Prices:* Tues.-Sat. 9–5; Sun. 2–5:30; adults $1; children 12–17 50¢; groups of 15 or more 25¢; children 12 & under no charge. Closed Thanksgiving; Christmas.

KENNESAW

Big Shanty Museum, 2829 Cherokee St., Kennesaw 30144. 404-427-2117. Industrial Museum located on the site where the Great Locomotive chase began. Civil war locomotive; general and related memorabilia. Historic Structure: c. 1875, railroad depot. *Hours & Admission Prices:* March-Nov. Mon.-Sat. 9:30-5:30; Sun. 12–5:30; Dec.-Feb. Fri.-Sun. 12–5:30; adults $2; children 9–15, 50¢; 8 and under with adult no charge.

LAGRANGE

Chattahoochee Valley Art Association, 112 Hines St., LaGrange 30240. 404-882-3267. Contemporary American works of art housed in 1892 Victorian structure, originally a county jail. Guided tours; lectures; gallery talks; workshops; formally organized education programs for children & adults; temporary exhibitions. Museum Sponsors: annual Affair on the Square, art festival; LaGrange National. *Hours & Admission Prices:* Tues.-Fri. 9–5; Sat. 9–4; Sun. 1–5. No charge. Closed New Year's; July 4; Thanksgiving; Christmas.

LAWRENCEVILLE

Gwinnett Historical Society, 221 N. Clayton St., Lawrenceville 30245. 404-962-1450. Museum with post cards; scrapbooks; county newspapers 1872–1907; 1853 ca-sword U.S. Navy & scabbard; family history files; Cemetery card file; 120-vol. official Records of the War of the Rebellion; 1880 Soundex cards for state of Georgia; manuscript collections; photo albums. *Hours & Admission Prices:* Mon.-Fri. 9:30–12:30. No charge; donations accepted.

LINCOLNTON

Elijah Clark State Park Museum, Rt. 4, Lincolnton 30817. 404-359-3458. Archives; uniforms; history artifacts of 1770's; reconstructed log house and outbuildings. *Hours & Admission Prices:* Memorial Day-Labor Day Tues.-Sat. by appointment. No charge.

LITHIA SPRINGS

Sweetwater Creek State Park, Rt. 1, Mount Vernon Rd., Lithia Springs 30057. 404-944-1700. Located at the site of the ruins of an 1842 textile mill burned in Gen. Sherman's Atlanta Campaign. Boating; canoeing; hiking; picnicking. *Hours & Admission Prices:* April 15-Sept. 14; Sept. 15-April 14. No charge.

LUMPKIN

Bedingfield Inn, Cotton St., Lumpkin 31815. 912-838-4201. Historic Building Museum, 1836 Stagecoach Inn; decorative arts. *Hours & Admission Prices:* Tues.-Sun. 1–5; adults $1; students 50¢. Closed New Year's; Thanksgiving; Christmas.

Providence Canyon State Park, Rt. 2, Box 54A, Lumpkin 31815. 912-838-6202. Natural history museum; self-guided tours; wildflower audio-visual program. *Hours & Admission Prices:* Tues.-Sat. 9–5; Sun. 2–5:30. No charge. Closed Mondays except Holidays; Thanksgiving; Christmas.

Westville Village Museum, Troutman Rd., Lumpkin 31815. 912-838-6310. Early 19th century decorative arts; 1825–1860 appropriate Georgia landscaping & gardens. 34 Historic Houses & Structures dating from 1800–1864: 1850, Randle-Morton Store; 1832, Stewart County Academy; 1842, Grimes-Feagin House; 1843, McDonald House; 1836, Cabinet Shop; 1838, Shoemakers Shop; 1838, Singer House; 1845, Doctor's Office; 1854, Chattahoochee County Courthouse; 1851, Climax Presbyterian Church; 1831, Bryan-Worthington House; 1840, Bagley Gin House; Log Cabins; Patterson-Marrett Farmhouse; Mule Barn; 1827, Wells House; 1850, Blacksmith Shop; c. 1850, Carriage Shelter; Adam's Store; 1836, Lawson House; 1840, Yellow Creek Camp Meeting Tabernacle; 1840, Moye Whitehouse; Pottery Pug Mill; Damascus Methodist Church. *Hours & Admission Prices:* Mon.-Sat. 10–5; Sun. 1–5; adults $3.50; senior citizens & college students $2.50; children $1.50; group rates available. Closed New Year's; Thanksgiving; Christmas.

MACON

Hay House Museum, 934 Georgia Ave., Macon 31201. 912-742-8155. 1855–60 Italianate Mansion; period furnishings; ceramics; pictures; decorative arts relative to house & region. *Hours & Admission Prices:* Tues.-Sat. 10:30–4:30; Sun. 2–4; adults $3; students $1.50; children $1; group rates available; members no charge. Closed All Legal Holidays.

Middle Georgia Historic Society, Inc., 935 High St., Macon 31201. 912-743-3851. Housed in 1840 birthplace of poet Sidney Lanier, documents and photographs; archives of Middle Georgia; memorabilia of Sidney Lanier. *Hours & Admission Prices:* Lanier Cottage: Mon.-Fri. 9–1 & 2–4; Sat. 9:30–12:30; adults $2; senior citizens $1.50; students $1; children 5–12 50¢. Closed New Year's; July 4; Labor Day; Thanksgiving; Christmas.

Museum of Arts and Science, 4182 Forsyth Rd., Macon 31210. 912-477-3232. Archaeological artifacts; exotic moths and butterflies; zyghoriza fossil; rocks & minerals; local, wildlife specimens; toys; paintings; drawings; prints and sculpture by Georgian, American and European artists. Historic House: c. 1928, The Kingfisher Cabin. *Hours & Admission Prices:* Mon.-Thurs. 9–5; Fri. 9–9; Sat. 9–5; Sun. 1–5. Museum: adults & children 50¢; members no charge; no charge on Mon., Thurs., Sat. Planetarium programs: Fri. 7:30 p.m.; Sat. 2 p.m.; Sun. 3 p.m.; adults $1.50; children $1; members no charge. Closed New Years; July 4; Labor Day; Thanksgiving; Christmas.

Ocmulgee National Monument, 1207 Emery Hwy., Macon 31201. 912-742-0447. Museum: Indian artifacts; archaeology representing six culture levels covering 10,000 years; anthropology; history; ethnology; British Colonial Trading Post; Lamar Type Site. Historic Building: A.D. 1016, Earthlodge. *Hours & Admission Prices:* Mon.-Sat. 9–7. No charge. Closed New Years; Christmas.

MADISON

Madison-Morgan Cultural Center, 434 S. Main St., Madison 30650. 404-342-4743. Artifacts, photographs, papers pertaining to the history of Madison, Morgan County & the Piedmont region of Georgia; decorative arts; costumes; architectural fragments; tools; household utensils; Civil War materials; school related artifacts & furnishings, housed in the 1895 Madison Graded School, in Madison Historic District. *Hours & Admission Prices:* Mon.-Fri. 10–4:30; Sat.-Sun. 2–5; adults $2; tour group $1.50; students $1; members & children under 6 no charge; Wednesday no charge except to tour groups. Closed Holidays.

MARIETTA

Cobb County Youth Museum, 649 Cheatham Hill Dr., Marietta 30064. 404-427-2563. Jet trainer; a caboose; street car stop; changing exhibits of living history. *Hours & Admission Prices:* scheduled school and group tours Mon.-Fri. 9:30–1:30; children $3; puppet show 1st Sunday of Oct., Nov., March & June 2–4. No charge on Sundays.

Kennesaw Mountain National Battlefield Park, Jct. Stilesboro Rd. and Old Hwy. 41, Marietta 30060. 404-427-4686. Museum: located on the site of a Civil War battlefield. Dress and weapons of Civil War soldiers. Historic House: 1836 Kolb Farm. *Hours & Admission Prices:* Oct.-Apr. Daily 8:30–5; May-Sept. Mon.-Fri. 8:30–5; Sat.-Sun. 8:30–6. No charge. Closed New Year's; Christmas.

MIDWAY

Midway Museum, Inc., U.S. Hwy. 17, Midway 31320. 912-884-5837. Permanent exhibitions; 1700's–1800's furnishings; museum related items for sale. *Hours & Admission Prices:* Tues.-Sat. 10–4; Sun. 2– 4; adults $1; children 6–18 50¢; children under 6 no charge. Closed Holidays.

Sunbury Historic Site, Rt. 1, Midway 31320. 912-884-5999. Military Museum; 1814 earthwork. *Hours & Admission Prices:* Tues.-Sat., Holidays 9–5; Sun. 2–5:30; adults $1; children 12–17 50¢; groups over 15 25¢. Closed Thanksgiving; Christmas.

MILLEDGEVILLE
Museum & Archives of Georgia Education, 131 Clark St., Milledgeville 31061. 912-453-4391. Memorabilia & artifacts relating to education; books; school furniture; housed in c. 1900, Victorian building; 3,000-vol. library of textbooks prior to 1950; records of school systems; biographical information on computers of state's retired teachers available for research by special request; reading room; exhibit space. *Hours & Admission Prices:* Mon.-Fri. 12–5; Sat. 10–12; Sun. 4–5:30. No charge.

MITCHELL
Hamburg State Park Museum, Mitchell 30820. 912-552-2393. Industrial Museum: housed in 1920, water turbine powered gin and milling complex; farm tools; ginning equipment; milling machinery. Corn meal for sale. *Hours & Admission Prices:* Tues.-Sat. 9–5; Sun. 2–5:30. No charge. Closed Thanksgiving; Christmas.

PINE MOUNTAIN
Callaway Gardens, Pine Mountain 31822. 404-663-2281. Southeastern U.S. native plants. Historic House: 1799, Log Cabin; guided tours; lectures; films; concerts; art festivals; formally organized educational programs for children, adults, undergraduate & graduate college students; summer intern program for students in horticulture & natural history; slide lending library. *Hours & Admission Prices:* Nov., Feb. Daily 7–5; March-May, Oct. Daily 7–6; June-Aug. Daily 7–7; Dec.-Jan. Daily 8–5; adults $3.50; children 6–11 $1; annual pass $20.00.

RICHMOND HILL
Fort McAllister, P.O. Box 198, Richmond Hill 31324. 912-727-2339. 1861 Confederate Fort; restored earthworks; military; summer living history demonstrations. *Hours & Admission Prices:* Tues.-Sat., Holiday Mondays 9–5:30; Sun. 2–5:30; adults $1.; children 50¢ children under 11 no charge; 25¢ per person for prearranged group. Closed Thanksgiving; Christmas.

RINCON
Georgia Salzburger Society Museum, Rt. 1, Box 478, Rincon 31326. 912-754-6333. Tools; furniture; letters; books; Bibles; deeds; maps; records of early settlers or their descendants before or just after the Civil War; Historic Church: 1769, Jerusalem Lutheran Church. *Hours & Admission Prices:* Wed., Sat.-Sun. 3–5. No charge; donations accepted.

ROME
Chieftains Museum, 80 Chatillon Rd., Rome 30161. 404-291-9494. Local history artifacts; items from Archaic Indian occupation to present time; trading post artifacts from archaeological dig; antique furniture; costumes; relics of Sherman's March through Rome; photographs; housed in 1794 log cabin, expanded into a plantation house, 1820, & belonging to Cherokee leader Major Ridge. *Hours & Admission Prices:* Tues.-Fri. 11–3; Sun. 1–5. No charge. Closed Christmas thru second week in January; National Holidays.

ROSSVILLE
The Chief John Ross House, P.O. Box 32, Rossville 30741. 404-861-0342. Cherokee alphabet; arrowheads; pictures; letters; furniture; rugs & linens; guided tours; arts festivals; permanent exhibitions. *Hours & Admission Prices:* May-Sept. Mon.-Tues., Thurs.-Sun. 1–5. No charge.

ROSWELL

Bulloch Hall, 180 Bulloch Ave., Roswell 30075. 404-992-1731 & 587-1840. Historic House: c. 1839, Antebellum Greek Revival House and Cottage, childhood home of Mittie Bulloch, mother of Theodore Roosevelt. Period furnishings; family photos; costumes; manuscripts. *Hours & Admission Prices:* Wed. 10–3; $2 per person. Closed Christmas; New Year's.

ST. MARYS

Cumberland Island National Seashore, P.O. Box 806, St. Marys 31558. 912-882-4335. National Park & Historic District: human occupation on island since 200 B.C. Historic site: c. 1800–1900, Indian Village Site & Dungeness Ruins. Historic Houses: c. 1880–1910, Plum Orchard Mansion; 1800, Tabby House; Ice House Museum; outbuildings. *Hours & Admission Prices:* Office: Daily 8:30–4:30. Ferry: May-Oct. Daily; Oct.-May Thurs.-Mon.; leaves from St. Marys at 9:15 & 1:45; adults $7.80; children $4; call office for reservations.

ST. SIMONS ISLAND

Coastal Center for the Arts, 2012 Demere Rd., St. Simons Island 31522. 912-638-8770. Gallery. Yesterday's Gold Isles series, early primitive paintings of the area; guided tours; lectures; films; gallery talks; concerts; dance recitals; arts festivals; drama; study clubs; TV programs; formally organized education programs for children & adults; docent program; traveling exhibitions. *Hours & Admission Prices:* Mon.-Sat. 11–5. No charge; fees charged for special events. Closed New Year's; July 4; Labor Day; Thanksgiving; Christmas.

Fort Frederica National Monument, Frederica Rd., St. Simons Island 31522. 912-638-3639. Park Museum. Historic sites: 1736–1746, ruins of 18th century English barracks, fort and house foundations; study collection of artifacts found at Fort Frederica and town of Frederica. *Hours & Admission Prices:* Daily 8–5. No charge. Closed Christmas.

The Methodist Museum, Box 407, St. Simons Island 31522. 912-638-4050. On site of Oglethorpe & John & Charles Wesley's activities in 1736. John & Charles Wesley memorabilia, letters, land grants. *Hours & Admission Prices:* Mon. 1–4; Tues.-Fri. 9–12 & 1–4; Sat. 9–12. No charge. Closed New Year's; July 4; Thanksgiving; Christmas.

Museum of Coastal History, 610 Beachview Dr., St. Simons Island 31522. 912-638-4666. Located on the site of Colonial Fort St. Simons. Artifacts, books, journals, manuscripts, photographs, slides, graphic arts, audio-visual material of the coastal Georgia area from 1788–present. Historical Structures: c. 1872, Lighthouse; 1890, Oil House. *Hours & Admission Prices:* Winter, Spring & Fall: Tues.-Sat. 1–4; Sun. 1:30–4; June-Labor Day. Tues.-Sat. 10–5, Sun. 1:30–5; adults $1.50; children under 12 $1; children under 6 no charge; tour group rates available. Closed New Year's; Thanksgiving; Christmas Eve; Christmas; Easter.

SAVANNAH

Archives Museum, Temple Mickve Israel, 20 E. Gordon St., Savannah 31401. 912-233-1547. Housed in c. 1876, Gothic style, Congregation Mickve Israel Synagogue, oldest congregation in the South & third oldest in the Nation. 18th–20th century artifacts of Jewish life. 20,000-vol. library pertaining to Jewish studies available for research by special permission. Ceremonial objects, books & jewelry for sale. *Hours & Admission Prices:* Mon., Tues. & Thurs. 10–12. When tour guide available. No charge. Closed Holidays.

Bethesda Museum-Cunningham Historic Center, 9520 Ferguson Ave., Savannah 31406. 912-355-0905. Lady Huntington memorabilia; George Whitefield memorabilia; historic figure dolls; model of first Bethesda buildings; The Union Society through the years; photographs; copy of American papers collection in Cambridge; ship models and artifacts; documents & portraits; exhibits relating to the 13th colony and the Bethesda Home for Boys. *Hours & Admission Prices:* Mon.-Fri. 8:30–5. No charge.

Davenport House Museum, 119 Habersham St., Savannah 31401. 912-236-8097. Chippendale, Hepplewhite and Sheraton furniture; Davenport china. *Hours & Admission Prices:*

Mon.-Sat. 10–4:30; Sun. 1:30–4:30; adults $2.50; students 10–17 $1.25; children under 10 no charge. Closed Holidays.

Georgia Historical Society, 501 Whitaker St., Savannah 31499. 912-944-2128. Housed in 1874–1875, building designed by Detlef Lienau. Books, manuscripts, maps, photographs, prints, newspapers, paintings, portraits, artifacts, relating to the history of Georgia and Savannah; manuscripts. *Hours & Admission Prices:* Mon.-Fri. 10–6; Sat. 9:30–1. No charge. Closed National Holidays.

Historic Savannah Foundation, Inc., William Scarbrough House, 41 W. Broad St., Savannah 31401. 912-233-7787. Furniture & furnishings of the period. Historic House: 1820, Davenport House. *Hours & Admission Prices:* Scarbrough House: Mon.-Fri. 10–4; adults $1.50; students 75¢. Davenport House: Mon.-Sat. 10–4:30; Sun. 1:30–4:30; adults $2; students 75¢. Closed Major Holidays.

Juliette Gordon Low Girl Scout National Center, 142 Bull St., Savannah 31401. 912-233-4501. Historic House Museum: 1818–1821, Wayne-Gordon House; memorabilia, art and furniture of Juliette Gordon Low and the Gordon family; Girl Scouts of the USA. *Hours & Admission Prices:* Mon.-Tues., Thurs.-Sat. 10–4; Sun. 11–4:30; Girl Scout adults $2; Girl Scouts under 18 $1.25; non-Girl Scout adults $2.25; under 18 $1.50; under 6 no charge. Closed New Year's; Thanksgiving; Christmas Eve; Christmas; Sundays in Dec. & Jan.

Kiah Museum—A Museum for the Masses, 505 W. 36 St., Savannah 31401. 912-236-8544. Howard J. Morrison, Jr. Zoology Exhibit; Harmon Foundation Collection of African Art; personal items of Marie Dressler, movie actress; 18th & 19th century furniture, china, silver, glass; art works from the 15th century; contemporary art; photography of William Anderson; Indian artifacts and crafts from Hilton Head Island; pre-Civil War and Civil War artifacts; items of Ulysses Davis, a Savannah folk artist; 15,000,000 year old fossil from Chesapeake Bay-Maryland area; Windsor chair, c. 1790. *Hours & Admission Prices:* Sept.-June first & third weeks of the month Tues.- Thurs. 11–5; other days by appointment. No charge.

Museum of Antique Dolls, 505 President St., East, Savannah 31401. 912-233-5296. Antique dolls; doll houses; doll furniture; paper dolls; china, glass, silver, linens for dolls; toys; banks; Victorian clothing; fashion prints; children's books; other artifacts relating to childhood. *Hours & Admission Prices:* Tues.-Sat. 10–5; $1.50 per person. Closed September; Major Holidays.

Oatland Island Education Center, 711 Sandtown Rd., Savannah 31410. 912-897-3773. Wild animals indigenous to state of Georgia; Phillips barn; Martin Cane mill. Historic Houses: 1835, Delk-Sawson House; 1835, Wayne County Cabin. *Hours & Admission Prices:* Mon.-Fri. 8:30–5 by calling in advance or writing to the director; other times by appointment. Call for admission fees. Closed Easter; July 4; Labor Day; Thanksgiving; Christmas.

Old Fort Jackson, 1 Ft. Jackson Rd., Savannah 31404. 912-232-3945. Military Museum; objects relating to Fort Jackson and Savannah's history. *Hours & Admission Prices:* Summer: Daily 9–5; Winter: Tues.-Sun. 9–5; adults $1.75; students, retired persons & military personnel $1.25. Closed New Year's; Thanksgiving; Christmas.

Owens-Thomas House, 124 Abercorn, Savannah 31401. 912-233-9743. Historic Building: 1816–1819, originally designed as home of Richard Richardson and later owned by Owens-Thomas families. Period rooms housing 18th and 19th century decorative arts; European and Chinese export porcelains; American Silver; English and American furniture before 1830; Oriental and European carpets. *Hours & Admission Prices:* Oct.-Aug. Sun.-Mon. 2–5; Tues.-Sat. 10–5; adults $2.50; students $1; special groups of 10 or more $1; children under 6 no charge. Closed Major Holidays.

Savannah Science Museum, Inc., 4405 Paulsen St., Savannah 31405. 912-355-6705. Reptile and amphibian programs and exhibits; planetarium presentations; laser shows; educational puppet shows; classes in the natural, physical, health, and technological sciences. *Hours &*

Admission Prices : Tues.-Sat. 10–5; Sun. 2–5; non-member adults $1; children & senior citizens 50¢; second Sundays no charge; members no charge. Closed New Year's; July 4; Labor Day; Thanksgiving; Christmas.

Ships of the Sea Maritime Museum, 503 E. River St., Savannah 31401. 912-232-1511. Ship models; ships in bottles; figureheads; scrimshaw; marine oil paintings; ships chandlery; 19th century English tavern signs; macrame; historical artifacts; housed in an old restored cotton warehouse located on Savannah's historic riverfront. *Hours & Admission Prices:* Daily 10–5; adults $2; senior citizens & active military $ 1; children 75¢; special group rates available.

Telfair Academy of Arts and Science, Inc., 121 Barnard St., Savannah 31401. 912-232-1177. Art Museum & Historic House: housed in 1818, Regency mansion, designed by architect William Jay; 1883, wing added by architect Detlef Lienau. Many Telfair family objects from late 18th and early 19th century, including pieces commissioned from Duncan Phyfe; Savannah-made silver; portraits. Art museum wing contains 18th, 19th & 20th century American & European paintings; prints; drawings; porcelain; costumes; collection of works by Kahlil Gibran. *Hours & Admission Prices:* Tues.-Sat. 1–5; Sun. 2–5; adults $2; students & children 12 & over $1; senior citizens & children under 12 50¢; children under 6 no charge. Closed Holidays.

William Scarbrough House, 41 West Broad St., Savannah 31402. 912-233-7787. Museum: housed in restored 1819 Regency style mansion; various exhibits; local history; decorative arts; architecture; five exhibition rooms. *Hours & Admission Prices:* Mon.-Fri. 10–4; adults $1.50; students 10–17 75¢; children under 10 no charge. Closed National Holidays.

Wormsloe Historic Site, P.O. Box 13852, Savannah 31406. 912-352-2548. Ruins of 1739, fortified house; archaeological artifacts from period c. 1733–1850. *Hours & Admission Prices:* Tues.-Sat. 9–5; Sun. 2–5:30; adults $1; children 12–17 50¢; group rate of 15 or more 25¢ each; children under 11 no charge. Closed Mondays except Holiday Mondays; Thanksgiving; Christmas.

STATESBORO
Georgia Southern Museum, Box 8061, Rosenwald Bldg., Statesboro 30460. 912-681-5444. Exhibits emphasizing natural, cultural, & geological history; fossil skeletons; 29-foot Mosasaur; 20-foot Middle-eocene whale; Southeastern Indians; timber raftsmen; fossil oysters; fish; invertabrates. *Hours & Admission Prices:* Tues.-Fri. 9–4; Sat. & Sun. 2–5. No charge. Closed New Year's; July 4; Labor Day; Thanksgiving; Christmas.

STOCKBRIDGE
Panola Mountain State Park, 2600 Hwy. 155, Stockbridge 30281. 404-474-2914. Granite monadnock; ecology; butterflies; moths; skippers. Visitor center; trails; scenic vistas; picnic area. *Hours & Admission Prices:* mid April-mid Sept. 7–9; mid Sept.-mid April 7–6. No charge.

STONE MOUNTAIN
Georgia's Stone Mountain Park, Box 778, Stone Mountain 30086. 404-469-9831. General Museum. Indian artifacts; Civil War; preservation projects; Revolutionary War, Colonial; early automobiles; musical instruments; 19th century band organs; c. 1830, Georgia-made furniture; 18th and 19th century English and American furniture. Historic Houses: 1790, Thornton House; 1845, Kingston House; 1845, Dickey House; 1845, Clayton House; 1869, Grist Mill; 1892, Covered Bridge. *Hours & Admission Prices:* Park: Daily 6 a.m.-12 midnight; Museums: Summer Daily 10–9; Winter Daily 10–5:30; Plantation: adults $2.50; children $1.50; Auto Museum: adults $2.50; children $1.50; Heritage Museum: adults 50¢; children no charge. Closed Christmas.

THOMASVILLE
Lapham-Patterson House, 626 N. Dawson St., Thomasville 31792. 912-266-0405. Historic

House: c. 1884, Lapham-Patterson House, Victorian home; furnishings; period rooms. *Hours & Admission Prices:* Tues.-Sat., Holiday Mondays 9–5; Sun. 2–5:30; adults $1; children 50¢; group rates 25¢ each; tour 75¢ each. Closed Thanksgiving; Christmas.

TIFTON
Georgia Agrirama—The State Museum of Agriculture, Interstate 75 Exit 20 at 8th St., Tifton 31793. 912-386-3344. Agriculture equipment; printing and typesetting equipment; furniture and furnishings of the period; naval stores implements. Historic Buildings: 1896, farmhouse; 1882, log cabin; 1879, grist mill; 1888, printing office; 1899, railroad depot; 1887, doctor's office; 1882, church; 1879, commissary. *Hours & Admission Prices:* Winter: Mon.-Sat. 9–5; Sun. 12:30–5. Summer: Daily 9–6; Family $8.50; adults $3; children 6–16 $1.50; children under 5 no charge; groups of 20 or more, discount rates available. Closed New Year's; Thanksgiving; December 22, 23 & 24; Christmas.

TOCCOA
Historic Traveler's Rest, Rt. 3, Toccoa 30577. 404-886-2256. Museum: 1825 former stagecoach inn; furnishings; guided tours; permanent exhibitions. *Hours & Admission Prices:* Tues.-Sat. 9–5; Sun. 2–5:30; adults $1; children 12–17 50¢. Closed Thanksgiving; Christmas.

TYBEE ISLAND
Fort Pulaski National Monument, Box 98, Tybee Island 31328. 912-786-5787. History Museum and Park located on land purchased for Ft. Pulaski. Civil War cannon and projectiles; uniform accessories; personal effects of soldiers; bottle collection; c. 1862 antique and replica room furnishings; c. 1890 battery Horace Hambright. *Hours & Admission Prices:* Memorial Day-Labor Day Daily 8:30–6:45; Labor Day-Memorial Day Daily 8:30–5:15; $1 per car. Closed New Year's; Christmas.

Tybee Museum, Tybee Island 31328. 912-786-4077. Housed in old Spanish-American War Coastal Defense Battery. Guns and pistols; antique dolls. *Hours & Admission Prices:* April-Sept. Daily 10–6; Oct.-March Daily 1–5; adults $1; children under 13 accompanied by adult no charge; special rates for school and scout groups.

VALDOSTA
The Crescent, Valdosta Garden Center, 900 N. Patterson St., Valdosta 31601. 912-244-4632. Nature Center & Historic House: 1898, antebellum mansion, home of former U.S. Sen. William S. West; completely furnished with antique pieces; Day Lily & Azalea gardens. *Hours & Admission Prices:* Fri. 2–5; other times by appointment. No charge; donations accepted.

Valdosta State College Art Gallery, Valdosta 31698. 912-333-5832. Library; planetarium; reading room; exhibit space; auditorium; theater; classrooms. *Hours & Admission Prices:* Mon.-Fri. 10–4. No charge. Closed School Holidays.

WARM SPRINGS
Little White House Historic Site, Little White House Historic Site, Warm Springs 31830. 404-655-3511. 1932 Georgia home of Pres. Roosevelt, where he died April 12, 1945; c. 1900 Georgia M. Wilkins Home which houses the museum. Personal items; gifts to Pres. Roosevelt from individuals, states and foreign countries; personal & official correspondence. *Hours & Admission Prices:* Daily 9–5; adults $3; children 6–12 $2; group rate $2. Closed Thanksgiving; Christmas.

WASHINGTON
Robert Toombs House, 216 E. Robert Toombs Ave., Washington 30673. 404-678-2226. Historic house; outbuildings; orchard; furniture and furnishings from the period c. 1840–1900. *Hours & Admission Prices:* Summer: Tues.-Sat. 9–5; Sun. 2–5; adults $1; children 2–17 50¢. Closed Thanksgiving; Christmas.

Washington—Wilkes Historical Museum, 308 E. Robert Toombs Ave., Washington 30673. 404-678-2105. 1836, Barnett-Slaton House, built by Albert Gallatin Semmes. Confederate history. Guided tours; permanent exhibitions. *Hours & Admission Prices:* Tues.-Sat. 10–5; Sun. 2–5; adults $1; children 6–12 50¢; group rates available. Closed New Year's; Thanksgiving; Christmas Eve; Christmas.

WATKINSVILLE
Eagle Tavern Welcome Center, U.S. Highway 441, Watkinsville 30677. 404-769-5197. Historic Building: stage coach stop, c. 1700's, furnishings. *Hours & Admission Prices:* Mon.-Fri. 9–5; other times by appointment. No charge.

WAYCROSS
Okefenokee Heritage Center, North Augusta Ave., Waycross 31501. 912-285-4260. Museum. History of Okefenokee Swamp and areas surrounding the swamp; renovated 1912 train, including steam engine and tender, 1 baggage car, 1 baggage/postal car, passenger car and caboose. Historic Buildings: 1900's Depot; c. 1832, General Thomas Hilliard House; late 1800's, print shop; Power House exhibit of antique vehicles; Nature Trails. *Hours & Admission Prices:* Tues.-Sat. 10–5; Sun. 2–4; adults $2; children 5–18 $1; 25% group rate discount. Closed National Holidays.

Southern Forest World, North Augusta Ave., Waycross 31501. 912-285-4056. Artifacts & specimens relating to the history & development of forestry in the South, including a 38″ tall model of a Loblolly Pine; a cross-section of the nation's largest Slash Pine; 1905, steam powered logging locomotive; naval stores tools & cups; giant Cypress; working scale model of a turpentine still; 22″ fire tower. *Hours & Admission Prices:* Tues.-Sat. 10–5; Sun. 2–4; adults $2; youth 5–18 $1; children under 5 no charge; tour groups 25% discount when prearranged. Closed Major Holidays.

WINDER
Fort Yargo State Park, Georgia Hwy. 81, Winder 30680. 404-867-3489. Historic Building: restored 1790 Timber Blockhouse used during the Creek Indian Wars. *Hours & Admission Prices:* by reservation only for conducted tours.

WINTERVILLE
Carter-Coile Country Doctors Museum, Bolton Drive, Winterville 30683. 404-742-8600. Housed in 1874 frame building used as an office by Dr. Warren Carter and Dr. Frank Coile. Medical equipment, furnishings, instruments, books, & special anatomy exhibits received from medical and other health personnel chiefly used in Clarke, Ga. and adjacent counties in the late 1800's and early 1900's and from Loree Florence, first woman graduate, 1926, of University of Georgia Medical School. *Hours & Admission Prices:* Call 404-742-5891 or 742-8284 for appointment. No charge; donations accepted.

NATIONAL FORESTS

Two National Forests, administered by the Department of Agriculture, U.S. Forest Service, lie within Georgia's borders. Both forests are located in the northern section of the state.

Oconee National Forest, containing 260,855 acres, is divided into two sections. The largest and southern-most division lies immediately north of Macon between Interstate Highways 75 and 20. The other smaller segment is situated in Greene County, north of Interstate Highway 20.

Chattahoochee National Forest, a huge expanse of land stretching along the Tennessee border, consists of 1,571,790 acres. It is divided into three sections, the largest of which lies east of U.S. Highway 411 and running to the South Carolina border. The other two areas are situated immediately east and west of Interstate Highway 75.

NATIONAL HISTORIC LANDMARKS

National Historic Landmarks are buildings, structures, sites, and objects of *National* significance that commemorate and illustrate the history and culture of the United States. Listed are the National Historic Landmarks in Georgia.

ATHENS
Henry W. Grady House. 634 Prince Avenue. Built circa 1845. Home (1863–72) of a major proponent of national reconciliation in the era following the War Between the States, who delivered his famous "New South" speech in 1886 in New York City.

ATLANTA
Dixie Coca-Cola Bottling Company Plant. 125 Edgewood Avenue. Built in 1891. This small brick building served in 1900–01 as the headquarters of what has become the Coca-Cola Bottling Company.

Fox Theatre. 660 Peachtree Street. Built in 1929. Known as "The Fabulous Fox," designed in a Neo-Mideastern Eclectic style, and one of the largest movie palaces at the time of its opening in 1929.

Joel Chandler Harris House. 1050 Gordon Street, SW. Built pre-1881. Harris, author of the "Uncle Remus" tales, lived here from 1881 until his death in 1908. The house contains many original furnishings.

Martin Luther King, Jr. Historic District. Includes the environs in which Martin Luther King, Jr. grew up. His birth home, grave, and the church which he served as assistant pastor are within the district.

State Capitol. Capitol Square. Built in 1889. This monumental domed and columned structure prefigures the American Renaissance style. Its neoclassicism reflects Georgians' hopes for national unity after the War Between the States, and the spirit of the New South.

Stone Hall (Fairchild Hall), Atlanta University. Morris-Brown College. Built in 1882. Stone Hall is closely associated with the history of the university, founded in 1866 by the American Missionary Association to provide education for freed blacks.

Sweet Auburn Historic District. Built in the early 20th century. The center of Black economic, social, and cultural activities in Atlanta from the 1890s to the 1930s. The Sweet Auburn District reflects an important element in the life of the Afro-American community in a segregated South.

AUGUSTA

College Hill (Walton-Harper House). 2216 Wrightsboro Road. Built in 1795. Property once owned by George Walton, a signer of the Declaration of Independence. He served as Georgia's Governor, Chief Justice of the State Supreme Court, and U.S. Senator.

Stephen Vincent Benét House (Commandant's House). 2500 Walton Way. Built in the 19th–20th centuries. Stephen Vincent Benét, known for his poetry and short stories, began his writing career in this 2-story Federal-style house after moving here in 1911.

Historic Augusta Canal and Industrial District. West bank of the Savannah River. Built in 1845–80s. Intact canal system and mills representative of industrial aspects of the New South. The best surviving example of an engineering system singularly important to the southeastern United States.

Stallings Island. 8 miles northwest of Augusta in the Savannah River. Built before 2000 B.C. One of the most important shell mound sites in the Southeast, giving information on Archaic Indians who lived in the Savannah River drainage area.

George Walton House (Meadow Garden). 1230 Nelson Street. The home of George Walton from 1791 to 1804. Appointed to the Continental Congress in 1776, at 26 he became the youngest signer of the Declaration of Independence. After the war he served as Georgia's Governor and as a United States Senator. Now owned by the Daughters of the American Revolution.

BLAKELY

Kolomoki Mounds. Built circa 1400–1600. Excavations have revealed details of burial practices at this type site for the Kolomoki culture. Contains one of the largest mound groups on the Southeastern coastal plain. Now a state park.

CARTERSVILLE

Etowah Mounds. 3 miles south of Cartersville. Built circa 1350. Important as an expression of the eastern expansion of Mississippian culture.

COLUMBUS

Columbus Historic Riverfront Industrial District. East bank of the Chattahoochee River, 8th-38th Streets North. Built in the 19th century. The area exemplifies use of hydrotechnology and its contributions to the growth of an important Southern textile center.

Octagon House. 527 1st Avenue. Built in 1829–30. Among the few fully realized double octagon houses in the United States. Exemplifies a fad that climaxed following publication of Squire Fowler's *A Home for All* on octagon design.

Springer Opera House. 105 10th Street. Built in 1871. This opera house hosted celebrated entertainers in the late 19th and early 20th centuries. It was converted to a movie house after the Depression of the 1930s sapped the traditions of the circuit of live theatrical "road show."

CRAWFORDVILLE
Liberty Hall. Built in 1858–59, ell; circa 1875 main house. Alexander Stephens, the Vice-President of the Confederate States of America, who also enjoyed a remarkable political career before and after the War Between the States, lived at his Liberty Hall estate from 1834 until his death in 1883.

DAHLONEGA
Calhoun Mine. Associated with the discovery of gold in Georgia and the subsequent gold rush, which drove the Cherokees from their land.

GORDON
New Echota. Built in 1825. First national capital of the Cherokees, established in 1825. Contains first Cherokee newspaper shop.

JEKYLL ISLAND
Jekyll Island. Riverview Drive and Old Village Boulevard. Built in 1880s-1930. A millionaires' village established in the 1880s provided a setting for fashionable architecture. The complex is administered by the Georgia State Parks Authority.

LAGRANGE
Belleview (Benjamin Harvey Hill House). 204 Ben Hill Street. Built in 1853-55. Georgia statesman's home. A significant example of the "domesticated temple" form of the Greek Revival style, with noteworthy plaster cornices.

MACON
Carmichael House. 1183 Georgia Avenue. Built in the last 1840s. Exemplifies the variety and individuality possible within the Greek Revival style, in its use of classical detail in combination with a modified Greek cross plan and spiral staircase in a central tower.

Hay House. 934 Georgia Avenue. Built in 1855–60. An Italian Renaissance villa that offers a striking contrast to Georgia's Neoclassical antebellum mansions. Among interior features are curved marble stairs and a 50-foot ballroom.

MILLEDGEVILLE

Governor's Mansion. 120 S. Clark Street. Built in the 1840s. A Palladian facade with prostyle portico and a plan with round and octagonal rooms distinguish this, the home of Georgia governors when Milledgeville was State capital from 1804 to 1868.

ROME

Chieftains (Major Ridge House). 80 Chatillon Road. Built circa 1792. The hand-hewn log cabin built by Major Ridge, a Cherokee leader, is incorporated into the present larger house. Ridge operated a ferry and trading post and was the speaker of the Cherokee National Council.

ROSSVILLE

John Ross House. Lake Avenue and Spring Streets. Two-story square-timbered log house, home of the Cherokees' most prominent leader, a hero of the 1812 Creek War and senior Cherokee leader during the War Between the States.

SAVANNAH

Central of Georgia Railroad Shops and Terminal (Depot and Trainshed). W. Broad Street at Liberty. Built in 1860–66. Early attempt to build a comprehensive railroad terminal and shop complex. The trainshed is the oldest remaining example of early iron roof construction, the first step in the evolution of modern steel building methods.

Green-Meldrim House. Bull and Harvis Streets. Built in 1850–54. This Gothic Revival house, built for the Green family, was General William T. Sherman's headquarters in 1864–65.

Juliette Gordon Low Birthplace. 10 Oglethorpe Avenue. Built in 1818–21. Low established the Girl Scout movement in the United States, holding the first meeting in her carriage house. She became the first president of the Girl Scouts after their incorporation in 1915.

Owens-Thomas House. 125 Abercorn Street. Built in 1816–19. English Regency style residence with such unique features as indirect lighting, curved walls and doors, and an elegant central stairway.

Savannah Historic District. Built in 1732. The district retains much of James Oglethorpe's original city plan and includes many buildings of architectural merit.

William Scarbrough House. 41 W. Broad Street. Built in 1818–19. Marks the height of neo-classical townhouse design in the United States. Reception hall and mezzanine have been called one of the grandest spatial compositions in United States architecture.

Telfair Academy of Arts and Sciences. 121 Barnard Street. Built in 1818–20. Among the oldest museums in the southeast, opened as a free art museum in 1886. Includes an 1818 townhouse with later additions and renovations in the 1880s, retaining masterful classical elements. Houses an important collection of paintings, including colonial and Federal portraits.

ST. CATHERINE'S ISLAND
St. Catherine's Island. 10 miles off the Georgia coast, S. Newport vicinity. Built in 16th–20th centuries. Important Spanish mission center (1566–1684). Button Gwinnett, delegate to the Continental Congress and signer of the Declaration of Independence, purchased the island in 1765 and lived here.

THOMASVILLE
Lapham-Patterson House. 626 N. Dawson Street. Built in the 1880s. Built as a resort home for a Chicago businessman, this 3-story Victorian mansion represents the eclectic, picturesque, and romantic resort cottage of the High Victorian 1880s. Its design and detailing are both exuberant and individualistic.

THOMPSON
Thomas E. Watson House. 310 Lumpkin Street. Built circa 1875. Watson was a principal founder of the Populist Party and first to urge a united front between white and black farmers. Embitterment, after defeat at the polls in 1892 and 1896, led to an extreme reversal of his attitudes and gave him a considerable following among Southern rural whites.

TOCCOA
Traveler's Rest. 6 miles east of Toccoa. Built in 1764. Erected by Major Jesse Walton, soldier in the Revolution and in conflicts with Native Americans. Example of an early tavern and inn in a rural frontier environment.

WARM SPRINGS
Warm Springs Historic District. Built in 1924–45. The district includes two vacation homes (1928–32 and 1932–45) of Franklin D. Roosevelt, who found relief from his polio in the "warm springs" that gave this town its name, and the Warm Springs Hospital, founded by Roosevelt to aid fellow victims of the ravaging disease. Roosevelt's efforts led to the "March of Dimes." He died at his "Little White House" in Warm Springs (April 12, 1945).

WASHINGTON
Robert Toombs House. E. Robert Toombs Avenue. Built in 1797, en-

larged circa 1835, 1840, 1870. Toombs served in the United States Congress and became Secretary of State of the Confederacy and a general in the Confederate Army. House enlarged by original owners and by Toombs.

Tupper-Barnett House. 101 W. Robert Toombs Avenue. Built circa 1832–60. Among the finest examples of 19th century conversions of Federal period homes into Neoclassical mansions by addition of colonnades. Symbolic of the wealth brought to the South by the cotton trade, this house has a finely detailed Doric peristyle colonnade skillfully joined to an existing structure.

NATIONAL PARKS

Georgia contains eight units of the National Park Service. These units, along with their acreages and the nearest large town follow.

Andersonville National Historic Site commemorates the largest Confederate military prison. This was built in 1864 after Confederate leaders decided to move a large number of Federal prisoners from Richmond to a place of greater security and more abundant food. The information program at the site tells how they miscalculated and of the tragedy that ensued. Located near Albany; 476 acres.

Chickamauga and Chattanooga National Military Park is located on one of the most important battlefields of the War Between the States. Exhibits and an audio-visual program at the Visitor Center explain the battle and its place in Civil War history. Situated in Chattanooga, TN; 8,095 acres.

Cumberland Island National Seashore is one of the finest remaining natural preserves on the east coast. There are over 28,000 acres of forest, marsh, dunes, and spacious, unspoiled beach. Reached only by boat from St. Marys. Near Savannah; 36,978 acres.

Fort Frederica National Monument on St. Simons Island was established by Georgia's founder, General James Edward Oglethorpe, in 1736. It played a vital role in the English-Spanish struggle (1739-1748) for control of what is now the southeastern United States. Ruins of the fort and town may be seen by taking a self-guided walk through the historic area. Near Savannah; 214 acres.

Fort Pulaski National Monument in Savannah is an early 19th century fort whose bombardment by Federal rifled canon in 1862 first demonstrated the ineffectiveness of old-style masonry fortification. Most of the fort is in the original condition. It contains 5,623 acres.

Kennesaw Mountain National Battlefield Park in Marietta marks the locale of skirmish that led to the fall of Atlanta in 1864. Living history demonstrations are staged here during summer months. Contains 2,884 acres.

Ocmulgee National Monument preserves remnants of important Indian mounds and villages of the Macon area. These represent 10,000 years of cultural evolution in the Indian mound-building civilizations of the South. Contains 683 acres.

Martin Luther King, Jr. National Historic Site in Atlanta is a district of 23 acres surrounding the birthplace, boyhood home, church and memorial gravesite of the famed Civil Rights leader. Tours and other interpretive programs are slated to focus on the continuing memorial to Dr. King through the Center for Social Change which is located here.

For more information write Tour Georgia, Georgia Department of Industry and Trade, P.O. Box 1776, Atlanta 30301.

NATIONAL WILDLIFE REFUGES

The U.S. Department of Interior, Fish and Wildlife Service, maintains eight National Wildlife Refuges in Georgia. These units, their mailing addresses, and the facilities available are described below. Always check with the refuge manager (regarding activities, fees, schedules, etc.) before making a trip to a refuge.

Blackbeard Island, Georgia Coastal Complex, Box 8487, Savannah 31402. Facilities: foot trails, environmental study area, hunting, fishing, and a refuge leaflet.

Harris Neck, Georgia Coastal Complex, Box 8487, Savannah 31402. Facilities: foot trails, auto tour, environmental study area, hunting, fishing, a refuge leaflet, and food and lodging nearby.

Okefenokee, Box 117, Waycross 31501. Facilities: visitor center, contact station, foot trails, auto tour, bicycling, non-motorized boating, environmental study area, hunting, fishing, camping, picnicking, refuge leaflet, species list, and food and lodging nearby.

Located in southeastern Georgia and extending slightly into northern Florida, this is the largest national wildlife refuge in the eastern U.S. The refuge contains approximately 396,000 acres of the 438,000-acre Okefenokee Swamp. The threatened American alligator, red cockaded woodpecker, Florida sandhill crane, round-tailed water rats, and osprey may be observed in the refuge.

315

Piedmont, Round Oak 31038. Facilities: visitor center, contact station, foot trails, auto tour, environmental study area, hunting, fishing, refuge leaflet, species list, and food and lodging nearby.

Savannah, Georgia Coastal Complex, Box 8487, Savannah 31402. Facilities: foot trails, auto tour, environmental study area, hunting, fishing, refuge leaflet, species list, and food and lodging nearby.

Tybee, Georgia Coastal Complex, Box 8487, Savannah 31402. Facilities: environmental study area and refuge leaflet.

Wassaw, Georgia Coastal Complex, Box 8487, Savannah 31402. Facilities: foot trails, environmental study area, hunting, and refuge leaflet.

Wolf Island, Georgia Coastal Complex, Box 8487, Savannah 31402. Facilities: environmental study area, and refuge leaflet.

NATURAL RESOURCES

A wide variety of productive mineral deposits are found in the state of Georgia. These include asbestos, cement rock, coal, raw clay, granite, limestone, graphite, manganese, mica, talc, silver, and gold. Georgia is a leader in the production of barite, bauxite, and marble and about 75% of the kaolin produced in the United States, as well as being one of the leading states in the production of fuller's earth. In various parts of northern and central Georgia, minor deposits of such precious stones as amethysts, diamonds, and rubies may be found. Some of the most common minerals are listed in the chart that follows.

Mineral Production:

County	Number of Active Surface Mines	Number of Acres Permitted	Minerals Produced
Baldwin	3	228	Sand, Kaolin, Fill Material
Banks	1	11	Crushed Stone
Barrow	5	34	Crushed Stone, Sand
Bartow	10	495	Limestone, Barite, Ochre, Umber, Sand, Gravel, Shale
Bibb	8	608	Clay, Fill Material, Sand
Brantley	1	54	Sand
Burke	1	5	Fill Material
Carroll	3	76	Crushed Stone, Sand, Gravel, Granite
Charlton	1	8	Sand
Chatham	22	335	Fill Material, Sand

County	Number of Active Surface Mines	Number of Acres Permitted	Minerals Produced
Chattooga	1	5	Fill Material
Cherokee	8	45	Sand, Limestone, Beryl
Clarke	1	78	Granite
Clay	1		Clay
Clayton	2	147	Granite, Sand
Cobb	4	171	Sand, Gravel, Granite
Columbia	2	49	Clay, Shale, Crushed Stone
Cook	3	247	Sand, Peat
Coweta	1	77	Granite
Crawford	4	84	Sand, Fill Material
Decatur	8	1,099	Fill Material, Sand, Fuller's Earth
DeKalb	9	597	Sand, Gravel, Granite
Dougherty	3	89	Sand, Gravel, Fill Material
Douglas	7	314	Sand, Gravel, Clay, Granite
Echols	1		Sand
Effingham	4	110	Sand, Gravel, Fill Material
Elbert	12	35	Granite, Sand
Evans	2	20	Sand
Fannin	2	—	Stone
Fayette	2	317	Granite
Floyd	7	437	Shale, Limestone, Clay, Crushed Stone
Forsyth	5	579	Sand, Granite, Quartzite
Franklin	1		Granite
Fulton	13	497	Sand, Schist, Fill Material, Granite
Gilmer	6	70	Granite, Crushed Stone
Glascock	1	80	Kaolin
Glynn	6	33	Fill Material
Gordon	2	286	Limestone, Fill Material
Grady	3	105	Fuller's Earth, Sand, Fill Material
Greene	4	138	Sand, Gravel, Feldspar, Amethyst, Granite
Gwinnett	4	489	Sand, Granite
Habersham	1	63	Granite
Hall	3	264	Granite, Limestone, Crushed Marble
Hancock	1	27	Kaolin
Hart	2	153	Mica
Heard	1	15	Granite
Henry	1	178	Granite
Houston	7	605	Limestone, Fill Material, Kaolin, Fuller's Earth
Jackson	6	12	Sand
Jasper	2	10	Feldspar, Sand

County	Number of Active Surface Mines	Number of Acres Permitted	Minerals Produced
Jefferson	4	198	Kaolin, Fuller's Earth
Jones	2	350	Granite
Laurens	2	6	Fill Material, Sand
Lee	2	232	Sand, Limestone
Lincoln	1	188	Kyanite, Pyrite
Long	2	16	Sand, Peat
Lowndes	4	148	Fill Material, Sand
Lumpkin	6	21	Sand, Gravel, Gold
Macon	3	96	Bauxite, Kaolin
Madison	2		Granite
Marion	1	65	Sand
McDuffie	3	53	Sand, Kaolin
Miller	1	4	Peat
Mitchell	1		Limestone
Monroe	1	190	Granite
Montgomery	1	50	Sand
Murray	3	50	Limestone, Slate, Talc
Muscogee	5	348	Clay, Sand, Granite
Newton	1	28	Granite
Oconee	1		Sand
Oglethorpe	20		Granite
Paulding	2	24	Granite, Crushed Stone
Peach	1	47	Fill Material
Pickens	12		Flagstone, Crushed Marble
Pierce	4	40	Fill Material, Sand
Pike	1	51	Sand
Polk	2	112	Slate, Sericite
Rabun	1	93	Granite
Richmond	18	1,364	Kaolin, Fill Material, Sand, Granite
Spalding	1	97	Granite
Stephens	2	42	Granite
Sumter	3	134	Bauxite, Kaolin, Fill Material
Talbot	2	63	Sand
Tattnall	2	5	Sand, Fill Material
Taylor	2	66	Sand
Thomas	11	460	Fuller's Earth, Sand, Fill Material
Toombs	1	10	Sand
Towns	1	6	Granite
Troup	1	87	Granite
Turner	1	20	Sand
Twiggs	36	3,797	Kaolin, Sand

County	Number of Active Surface Mines	Number of Acres Permitted	Minerals Produced
Union	1	68	Granite
Walker	3	125	Limestone, Shale
Ware	5	25	Sand, Fill Material
Warren	8	867	Kaolin, Granite
Washington	37	5,136	Kaolin
Wheeler	1	28	Sand
White	9	7	Fill Material, Gold, Sand
Whitfield	1	284	Limestone
Wilkes	3		Feldspar, Granite
Wilkinson	33	5,630	Kaolin
Georgia	479	30,217	

NEWSPAPERS

Daily and Sunday Newspapers

ALBANY (Dougherty County)
The Albany Herald
P.O. Box 48, 31703
912-888-9300
Circulation:
Daily 38,070
Sunday 44,730
Pub. Days: Daily

AMERICUS (Sumter County)
Americus Times-Recorder
P.O. Box 1247, 31709
912-924-2751
Circulation: 7,317
Pub. Days: Daily
ex. Sunday

ATHENS (Clarke County)
Athens Banner-Herald
P.O. Box 912, 30613
404-549-0123
Circulation:
Daily 12,546
Sunday 27,548
Pub. Days: Daily

Athens Daily News
P.O. Box 912, 30613
404-549-0123

Circulation:
Daily 10,315
Sunday 27,548
Pub. Days: Daily

ATLANTA (Fulton County)
The Atlanta Constitution
P.O. Box 4689, 30302
404-526-5193
Circulation:
Daily 264,812
Sunday 645,916
Pub. Days: Daily

The Atlanta Journal
P.O. Box 4689, 30302
404-526-5193
Circulation:
Daily 188,617
Sunday 645,916
Pub. Days: Daily

Fulton County Daily Report
190 Pryor St., SW, 30303
404-521-1227
Circulation: 2,105
Pub. Days: Mon.-Fri.

AUGUSTA (Richmond County)

The Augusta Chronicle
P.O. Box 1928, 30913
404-724-0851
Circulation:
Daily 63,081
Sunday 85,553
Pub. Days: Daily

The Augusta Herald
P.O. Box 1928, 30913
404-724-0851
Circulation:
Daily 17,577
Sunday 85,553
Pub. Days: Daily

BRUNSWICK (Glynn County)
The Brunswick News
P.O. Box 1557, 31521
912-265-8320
Circulation: 15,588
Pub. Days: Daily
ex. Sunday

CARROLLTON (Carroll County)
The Daily Times-Georgian
P.O. Box 460, 30117
404-834-6631

● Weeklies 129
■ Dailies 30
Total 159

Circulation: 10,538
Pub. Days: Tues.-Sun.

CARTERSVILLE (Bartow
County)
The Daily Tribune News
P.O. Box 70, 30120
404-382-4545
Circulation: 8,102
Pub. Days: Mon.-Fri.

COLUMBUS (Muscogee
County)
**The Columbus Ledger-
Enquirer**
P.O. Box 711, 31994

404-884-7311
Circulation:
  Daily 60,451
  Sunday 68,507
Pub. Days: Daily

CONYERS (Rockdale
County)
The Rockdale Citizen
P.O. Box 136, 30207
404-483-7108
Circulation: 8,902
Pub. Days: Mon.-Fri.

CORDELE (Crisp County)
The Cordele Dispatch

P.O. Box 1058, 31015
912-273-2277
Circulation: 5,932
Pub. Days: Mon.-Fri.

DALTON (Whitfield
County)
The Daily Citizen-News
P.O. Box 1167, 30720
404-278-1011
Circulation: 12,008
Pub. Days: Daily

DUBLIN (Laurens
County)
The Courier Herald

Drawer B, Court Square
Station 31040
912-272-5522
Circulation: 10,166
Pub. Days: Daily
ex. Sunday

GAINESVILLE (Hall
County)
The Times
P.O. Box 838, 30503
404-532-1234
Circulation:
Daily 21,121
Sunday 22,242
Pub. Days: Daily
ex. Saturday

GRIFFIN (Spalding
County)
Griffin Daily News
P.O. Drawer M, 30224
404-227-3276
Circulation: 12,387
Pub. Days: Daily
ex. Sunday

JONESBORO (Clayton
County)
Clayton News/Daily
P.O. Box 368, 30237
404-478-5753
Circulation: 7,922
Pub. Days: Mon.-Fri.

LAGRANGE (Troup
County)
LaGrange Daily News
P.O. Box 929, 30241
404-884-7311
Circulation: 15,073
Pub. Days: Daily
ex. Sunday

LAWRENCEVILLE
(Gwinnett County)
Gwinnett Daily News
P.O. Box 1,000, 30246
404-963-0311
Circulation:
Daily 28,114
Wed. & Sat. 31,609
Pub. Days: Daily

MACON (Bibb County)
**The Macon Telegraph
and News**
P.O. Box 4167, 31213

912-744-4200
Circulation:
Daily 71,687
Sunday 95,724
Pub. Days: Daily

MARIETTA (Cobb
County)
**The Marietta Daily
Journal**
P.O. Box 449, 30061
404-428-9411
Circulation:
Daily 22,996
Sunday 24,333
Pub. Days: Daily

MILLEDGEVILLE
(Baldwin County)
The Union Recorder
P.O. Box 520, 31061
912-452-0567
Circulation: 7,357
Pub. Days: Tues.-Sat.

MOULTRIE (Colquitt
County)
The Moultrie Observer
P.O. Box 889, 31768
912-985-4545
Circulation: 7,444
Pub. Days: Daily
ex. Sunday

ROME (Floyd County)
The Rome News-Tribune
P.O. Drawer F, 30161
404-291-6397
Circulation:
Daily 22,479
Pub. Days: Daily
ex. Saturday

SAVANNAH (Chatham
County)
Savannah Morning News
P.O. Box 1088, 31402
912-236-9511
Circulation:
Daily 55,797
Sunday 74,810
Pub. Days: Daily

Savannah Evening Press
P.O. Box 1088, 31402
912-236-9511
Circulation:
Daily 20,220

Sunday 74,810
Pub. Days: Daily

STATESBORO (Bulloch
County)
The Statesboro Herald
P.O. Box 888, 30458
912-764-9031
Circulation: 7,132
Pub. Days: Daily

THOMASVILLE
(Thomas County)
**Thomasville Times-
Enterprise**
P.O. Box 650, 31792
912-226-2400
Circulation: 11,377
Pub. Days: Daily
ex. Sunday

TIFTON (Tift County)
The Tifton Gazette
P.O. Box 708, 31793
912-382-4321
Circulation: 9,494
Pub. Days: Mon.-Sat.

VALDOSTA (Lowndes
County)
The Valdosta Daily Times
P.O. Box 968, 31603
912-244-1880
Circulation: 18,470
Pub. Days: Daily

WARNER ROBINS
(Houston County)
The Daily/Sunday Sun
P.O. Box 2768, 31099
912-923-6432
Circulation:
Daily 10,176
Sunday 11,411
Pub. Day: Daily
ex. Saturday

WAYCROSS (Ware
County)
Waycross Journal-Herald
P.O. Box 219, 31502
912-283-2244
Circulation: 13,547
Pub. Day: Daily
ex. Sunday

321

Weekly Newspapers

ADAIRSVILLE (Bartow County)
The North Bartow News
P.O. Box 374, 30103
404-773-3754
Circulation: 955
Pub. Day: Thurs.

ADEL (Cook County)
The Adel News-Tribune
131 S. Hutchinson Ave.,
31620
912-896-2233
Circulation: 3,381
Pub. Day: Wed.

ALAMO (Wheeler County)
The Wheeler County Eagle
P.O. Box 409, 30411
912-537-2076
Circulation: 1,686
Pub. Day: Wed.

ALMA (Bacon County)
The Alma Times-Statesman
P.O. Box 428, 31510
912-632-7201
Circulation: 2,968
Pub. Day: Thurs.

ASHBURN (Turner County)
The Wiregrass Farmer
109 N. Gordon St., 31714
912-567-3655
Circulation: 2,817
Pub. Day: Thurs.

ATHENS (Clarke County)
The Athens Observer
P.O. Box 112, 30613
404-548-6346
Circulation: 6,616
Pub. Day: Thurs.

ATLANTA (Fulton County)
Atlanta Business Chronicle
1800 Water Pl., NW
St. 100, 30339
404-952-6397
Circulation: 30,941
Pub. Day: Mon.

Atlanta Jewish Times
P.O. Box 250287, 30325
404-355-6139
Circulation: 8,111
Pub. Day: Fri.

BAINBRIDGE (Decatur County)
The Post-Searchlight
301 N. Crawford St.,
31717
912-246-2827
Circulation: 5,805
Pub. Days: Wed. & Sat.

BARNESVILLE (Lamar County)
The Herald-Gazette
P.O. Box 220, 30204
404-358-0754
Circulation: 4,045
Pub. Day: Tues.

BAXLEY (Appling County)
The Baxley News-Banner
P.O. Box 409, 31513
912-367-2468
Circulation: 4,241
Pub. Day: Thurs.

BLACKSHEAR (Pierce County)
The Blackshear Times
P.O. Box 410, 31516
912-449-0693
Circulation: 2,628
Pub. Day: Thurs.

BLAIRSVILLE (Union County)
North Georgia News
P.O. Box 748, 30512
404-745-6343
Circulation: 8,000
Pub. Day: Thurs.

BLAKELY (Early County)
Early County News
209 S. Main St., 31723
912-723-4376
Circulation: 3,559
Pub. Day: Thurs.

BLUE RIDGE (Fannin County)

The Blue Ridge Summit-Post
P.O. Box 989, 30513
404-632-2019
Circulation: 389
Pub. Day: Fri.

BOWDON (Carroll County)
The Bowdon Bulletin
109 Shirley St., 30108
404-258-2146
Circulation: 2,320
Pub. Day: Thurs.

BREMEN (Haralson County)
The Haralson Gateway-Beacon
222 Tallapoosa St., 30110
404-537-2434
Circulation: 5,181
Pub. Day: Thurs.

BUTLER (Taylor County)
Taylor County News
P.O. Box 1979, 31006
912-862-5101
Circulation: 2,315
Pub. Day: Thurs.

CALHOUN (Gordon County)
The Calhoun Times
P.O. Box 8, 30701
404-629-2231
Circulation: 9,249
Pub. Days: Wed. & Sat.

CAMILLA (Mitchell County)
The Camilla Enterprise
13 S. Scott St., 31730
912-336-5265
Circulation: 3,264
Pub. Days: Wed. & Fri.

CANTON (Cherokee County)
The Cherokee Tribune
64 Academy St., 30114
404-479-1441
Circulation: 7,159
Pub. Days: Sun. & Wed.

CARTERSVILLE (Bartow County)

The Herald Tribune
P.O. Box 70, 30120
404-382-4545
Circulation: 960
Pub. Day: Thurs.

CEDARTOWN (Polk
County)
The Cedartown Standard
P.O. Box 308, 30125
404-748-1520
Circulation: 3,214
Pub. Days: Tues. & Thurs.

CHATSWORTH (Murray
County)
The Chatsworth Times
P.O. Box 130, 30705
404-695-4646
Circulation: 4,944
Pub. Day: Wed.

CLARKESVILLE
(Habersham County)
Tri-County Advertiser
P.O. Box 256, 30523
404-754-4139
Circulation: 5,595
Pub. Day: Thurs.

CLAXTON (Evans
County)
The Claxton Enterprise
24 S. Newton St., 30417
912-739-2132
Circulation: 3,550
Pub. Day: Thurs.

CLAYTON (Rabun
County)
The Clayton Tribune
P.O. Box 435, 30525
404-782-3312
Circulation: 5,125
Pub. Day: Thurs.

CLEVELAND (White
County)
White County News
Box 456, 30528
404-865-4718
Circulation: 2,835
Pub. Day: Thurs.

COCHRAN (Bleckley
County)
The Cochran Journal
106 Cherry St., 31014

912-934-6303
Circulation: 2,779
Pub. Day: Wed.

COLQUITT (Miller
County)
Miller County Liberal
P.O. Box 37, 31737
912-758-5549
Circulation: 2,539
Pub. Day: Thurs.

COMER (Madison
County)
The Comer News
422 Main St., 30629
404-783-2553
Circulation: 1,457
Pub. Day: Thurs.

COMMERCE (Jackson
County)
The Commerce News
35 S. Broad St., 30529
404-335-5121
Circulation: 3,773
Pub. Day: Wed.

CORNELIA (Habersham
County)
The Northeast Georgian
P.O. Box 190, 30531
404-778-4215
Circulation: 6,545
Pub. Day: Tues.

COVINGTON (Newton
County)
The Covington News, Inc.
P.O. Box 1278, 30209
404-786-3401
Circulation: 6,560
Pub. Day: Thurs.

CRAWFORDVILLE
(Taliaferro County)
The Advocate-Democrat
P.O. Box 149, Greensboro
30642
404-453-7988
Circulation: 671
Pub. Day: Fri.

CUMMING (Forsyth
County)
The Forsyth County News
P.O. Box 210, 30130
404-887-3126

Circulation: 4,104
Pub. Days: Wed. & Sun .

CUTHBERT (Randolph
County)
**Cuthbert Times & News
Record**
208 W. Dawson St. 31740
912-732-2731
Circulation: 2,019
Pub. Day: Thurs.

DAHLONEGA (Lumpkin
County)
The Dahlonega Nugget
P.O. Box 476, 30533
404-864-3613
Circulation: 3,770
Pub. Day: Thurs.

DALLAS (Paulding
County)
Dallas New Era
P.O. Box 246, 30132
404-445-3379
Circulation: 5,615
Pub. Day: Wed.

DANIELSVILLE
(Madison County)
The Danielsville Monitor
P.O. Box 9, 30633
404-795-3102
Circulation: 1,612
Pub. Day: Fri.

DARIEN (McIntosh
County)
The Darien News
106 Broad St., 31305
912-437-4251
Circulation: 2,592
Pub. Day: Thurs.

DAWSON (Terrell County)
The Dawson News
139 W. Lee St., 31742
912-995-2175
Circulation: 2,745
Pub. Day: Thurs.

DAWSONVILLE (Dawson
County)
**Dawson County
Advertiser**
P.O. Box 225, 30534
404-265-2345
Circulation: 2,060

Pub. Day: Thurs.

DECATUR (DeKalb County)
Decatur-DeKalb News Era
739 DeKalb Ind. Way, 30033
404-292-3536
Circulation: 9,490
Pub. Day: Thurs.

DONALSONVILLE (Seminole County)
Donalsonville News
P.O. Box 338, 31745
912-524-2343
Circulation: 3,111
Pub. Day: Thurs.

DOUGLAS (Coffee County)
The Douglas Enterprise
P.O. Box 551, 31533
912-384-2323
Circulation: 6,325
Pub. Day: Wed.

DOUGLASVILLE (Douglas County)
Douglas County Sentinel
P.O. Box 1586, 30133
404-942-6571
Circulation: 7,544
Pub. Days: Tues. & Thurs.

EASTMAN (Dodge County)
Times Journal-Spotlight
277 College Ave., 31023
912-374-5562
Circulation: 4,453
Pub. Day: Thurs.

EATONTON (Putnam County)
The Eatonton Messenger
P.O. Box 402, 31024
404-485-3501
Circulation: 3,470
Pub. Day: Thurs.

ELBERTON (Elbert County)
The Elberton Star
P.O. Box 280, 30635
404-283-3100
Circulation: 5,363
Pub. Days: Tues. & Thurs.

ELLIJAY (Gilmer County)
Times-Courier
13 River St., 30540
404-635-4313
Circulation: 5,152
Pub. Day: Thurs.

FAYETTEVILLE (Fayette County)
Fayette County News
P.O. Box 96, 30214
404-461-6317
Circulation: 3,997
Pub. Day: Wed. & Sat.

FITZGERALD (Ben Hill County)
The Herald-Leader
P.O. Box 40, 31750
912-423-9331
Circulation: 5,315
Pub. Day: Wed.

FOLKSTON (Charlton County)
Charlton County Herald
P.O. Box 68, 31537
912-496-7304
Circulation: 2,534
Pub. Day: Wed.

FORSYTH (Monroe County)
The Monroe County Reporter
P.O. Box 795, 31029
912-994-2538
Circulation: 3,803
Pub. Day: Wed.

FORT VALLEY (Peach County)
Leader-Tribune
205 Main St., 31030
912-825-2432
Circulation: 3,456
Pub. Day: Wed.

FRANKLIN (Heard County)
The News and Banner
P.O. Box 97, 30217
404-675-3374
Circulation: 1,075
Pub. Day: Wed.

GLENNVILLE (Tattnall County)

The Glennville Sentinel
P.O. Box 218, 30427
912-654-2515
Circulation: 3,113
Pub. Day: Thurs.

GRAY (Jones County)
The Jones County News
P.O. Box 637, 31023
912-986-3929
Circulation: 2,025
Pub. Day: Thurs.

GREENSBORO (Greene County)
The Herald-Journal
P.O. Box 149, 30642
404-453-7988
Circulation: 4,120
Pub. Day: Fri.

GREENVILLE (Meriwether County)
The Meriwether Vindicator
P.O. Box A, 30222
404-846-3188
Circulation: 2,361
Pub. Day: Fri.

HAMILTON (Harris County)
Harris County Journal
P.O. Box 75, 31811
404-846-3188
Circulation: 1,776
Pub. Day: Thurs.

HARTWELL (Hart County)
The Hartwell Sun
P.O. Box 700, 30643
404-376-8025
Circulation: 5,289
Pub. Day: Thurs.

HAWKINSVILLE (Pulaski County)
Hawkinsville Dispatch & News
329 Commerce St., 30136
912-783-1291
Circulation: 2,780
Pub. Day: Wed.

HAZELHURST (Jeff Davis County)
The Jeff Davis County Ledger

102 Railroad St., 31539
912-375-4225
Circulation: 3,201
Pub. Day: Wed.

HIAWASSEE (Towns County)
Towns County Herald
P.O. Box 375, 30546
404-745-6343
Circulation: 2,621
Pub. Day: Thurs.

The Mountain News
P.O. Box 417, 30546
404-896-4244
Circulation: 2,389
Pub. Day: Wed.

HINESVILLE (Liberty County)
The Coastal Courier
P.O. Box 498, 31313
912-876-0156
Circulation: 4,166
Pub. Days: Wed. & Fri.

HOMERVILLE (Clinch County)
The Clinch County News
210 E. Dame Ave., 31634
912-487-5337
Circulation: 1,710
Pub. Day: Thurs.

IRWINTON (Wilkinson County)
Wilkinson County News
P.O. Box 205, 31042
912-946-2218
Circulation: 2,112
Pub. Day: Thurs

JACKSON (Butts County)
Jackson Progress-Argus
P.O. Box 249, 30233
404-775-3107
Circulation: 4,520
Pub. Day: Wed.

JASPER (Pickens County)
Pickens County Progress
P.O. Box 67, 30143
404-692-2457
Circulation: 4,824
Pub. Day: Thurs.

JEFFERSON (Jackson County)

The Jackson Herald
P.O. Box 908, 30549
404-367-5233
Circulation: 6,365
Pub. Day: Wed.

JEFFERSONVILLE (Twiggs County)
Twiggs Co. New Era
P.O. Box 292, 31044
912-945-3566
Circulation: 1,540
Pub. Day: Wed.

JESUP (Wayne County)
The Press-Sentinel
P.O. Box 607, 31545
912-427-3757
Circulation: 7,072
Pub. Days: Tues. & Thurs.

KINGSLAND (Camden County)
The Southeast Georgian
P.O. Box 1059, 31548
912-729-5231
Circulation: 4,010
Pub. Day: Thurs.

LAFAYETTE (Walker County)
Walker County Messenger
P.O. Box 766, 30728
404-638-1859
Circulation: 4,500
Pub. Days: Wed. & Fri.

LAKELAND (Lanier County)
Lanier County News
P.O. Box 278, 31635
912-482-3367
Circulation: 1,438
Pub. Day: Thurs.

LAVONIA (Franklin County)
Franklin County Citizen
P.O. Box 148, 30553
404-356-8557
Circulation: 4,247
Pub. Day: Thurs.

LAWRENCEVILLE (Gwinnett County)
The Home Weekly
P.O. Box 603, 30246
404-963-9205

Circulation: 8,725
Pub. Day: Wed.

LEESBURG (Lee County)
The Lee County Ledger
P.O. Box 715, 31763
912-759-2413
Circulation: 1,633
Pub. Day: Thurs.

LEXINGTON (Oglethorpe County)
The Oglethorpe Echo
P.O. Box 260, 30648
404-743-5510
Circulation: 2,767
Pub. Day: Thurs.

LOUISVILLE (Jefferson County)
The News and Farmer
P.O. Box 487, 30434
912-625-7722
Circulation: 2,938
Pub. Day: Thurs.

LUDOWICI (Long County)
The Ludowici News
P.O. Box 218, 31316
912-545-2103
Circulation: 1,105
Pub. Day: Thurs.

LYONS (Toombs County)
The Lyons Progress
P.O. Box 312, 30436
912-526-3516
Circulation: 2,985
Pub. Day: Thurs.

MADISON (Morgan County)
The Madisonian
Drawer 191, 30650
404-342-2424
Circulation: 4,222
Pub. Day: Thurs.

MANCHESTER (Meriwether County)
Manchester Star-Mercury
P.O. Box 426, 31816
404-846-3188
Circulation: 4,270
Pub. Day: Wed.

McDONOUGH (Henry County)

The Henry Herald
P.O. Box 233, 30253
404-957-9161
Circulation: 6,297
Pub. Day: Wed.

McRAE (Telfair County)
The Telfair Enterprise
P.O. Box 269, 31055
912-868-6015
Circulation: 3,042
Pub. Day: Wed.

Telfair Times
P.O. Box 429, 31055
912-868-5776
Circulation: 2,117
Pub. Day: Wed.

METTER (Candler County)
Metter News and Advertiser
P.O. Box 8
912-685-6566
Circulation: 2,896
Pub. Day: Wed.

MILLEN (Jenkins County)
The Millen News
P.O. Box 909, 30442
912-982-5460
Circulation: 2,125
Pub. Day: Thurs.

MONROE (Walton County)
The Walton Tribune
P.O. Box 808, 30655
404-267-8371
Circulation: 6,021
Pub. Days: Wed. & Fri.

MONTEZUMA (Macon County)
Citizen & Georgian
P.O. Box 387, 31063
912-472-7755
Circulation: 2,663
Pub. Day: Wed.

MONTICELLO (Jasper County)
The Monticello News
P.O. Box 30, 31064
404-468-6511
Circulation: 2,188
Pub. Day: Thurs.

NASHVILLE (Berrien County)
The Berrien Press
P.O. Box 455, 31639
912-686-3523
Circulation: 3,864
Pub. Day: Wed.

NEWNAN (Coweta County)
The Newnan Times-Herald
P.O. Box 1052, 30263
404-253-1576
Circulation: 11,980
Pub. Days: Tues. & Thurs.

OCILLA (Irwin County)
The Ocilla Star
P.O. Box 25, 31774
912-468-5433
Circulation: 2,431
Pub. Day: Thurs.

PEACHTREE CITY (Fayette County)
This Week in Peachtree City
P.O. Box 2468, 30269
404-487-7729
Circulation: 3,815
Pub. Day: Wed. & Sat.

PELHAM (Mitchell County)
The Pelham Journal
P.O. Box 472, 31779
912-294-3661
Circulation: 3,381
Pub. Day: Thurs.

PEMBROKE (Bryan County)
Bryan County Times
P.O. Box 798, 31321
912-653-4570
Circulation: 1,440
Pub. Day: Wed.

PERRY (Houston County)
The Houston Home Journal
P.O. Box M, 31069
912-987-1823
Circulation: 1,732
Pub. Day: Wed. & Sat.

QUITMAN (Brooks County)

The Quitman Free Press
P.O. Box 72, 31643
912-263-4615
Circulation: 3,030
Pub. Day: Thurs.

REIDSVILLE (Tattnall County)
The Tattnall Journal
P.O. Box 278, 30453
912-557-6761
Circulation: 3,735
Pub. Day: Thurs.

RINGGOLD (Catoosa County)
The Catoosa County News
P.O. Box 40, 30736
404-935-2621
Circulation: 4,615
Pub. Day: Wed.

ROBERTA (Crawford County)
The Georgia Post
P.O. Box 860, 31078
912-836-3195
Circulation: 750
Pub. Day: Thurs.

ROCKMART (Polk County)
The Rockmart Journal
P.O. Box 609, 30153
404-684-7811
Circulation: 3,091
Pub. Day: Wed.

ROYSTON (Franklin County)
The News Leader
P.O. Box 26, 30662
404-245-7351
Circulation: 2,580
Pub. Day: Thurs.

ST. MARYS (Camden County)
Camden County Tribune
P.O. Box 470, 31558
912-882-4927
Circulation: 3,366
Pub. Day: Thurs.

ST. SIMONS ISLAND (Glynn County)
The Islander

P.O. Box 539, 31522
912-264-6751
Circulation: 2,325
Pub. Day: Mon.

SANDERSVILLE
(Washington County)
The Sandersville Progress
P.O. Box 431, 31082
912-552-3032
Circulation: 4,738
Pub. Day: Thurs.

SOPERTON (Treutlen
County)
The Soperton News
P.O. Box 537, 30457
912-529-6624
Circulation: 2,802
Pub. Day: Wed.

SPRINGFIELD
(Effingham County)
The Herald
P.O. Box 799, 31326
912-826-5012
Circulation: 4,515
Pub. Day: Wed.

STATESBORO (Bulloch
County)
Southern Beacon
P.O. Box 888, 30458
912-764-9031
Circulation: 2,000
Pub. Day: Wed.

SWAINSBORO (Emanuel
County)
The Blade
P.O. Box 938, 30401
912-237-9971
Circulation: 5,503
Pub. Day: Wed.

SYLVANIA (Screven
County)
The Sylvania Telephone
P.O. Box 10, 30467
912-564-2045
Circulation: 3,800
Pub. Day: Thurs.

SYLVESTER (Worth
County)
The Sylvester Local News
P.O. Box 397, 31791
912-776-3991
Circulation: 3,685
Pub. Day: Thurs.

THOMASTON (Upson
County)
The Thomaston Times
P.O. Box 430, 30286
404-647-5414
Circulation: 6,272
Pub. Days: Mon. & Wed.

THOMSON (McDuffie
County)
The McDuffie Progress
P.O. Box 1090, 30824
404-595-1601
Circulation: 3,770
Pub. Day: Wed.

TRENTON (Dade
County)
Dade County Sentinel
P.O. Box 277, 30752
404-657-6182
Circulation: 2,923
Pub. Day: Wed.

VIDALIA (Toombs
County)
The Advance
P.O. Box 669, 30474
912-537-3131
Circulation: 4,772
Pub. Day: Thurs.

VIENNA (Dooly County)
Vienna News-Observer
P.O. Box 186, 31092
912-268-2096
Circulation: 2,098
Pub. Day: Thurs.

WASHINGTON (Wilkes
County)
The News-Reporter
P.O. Box 340, 30673
404-678-2636

Circulation: 4,660
Pub. Day: Thurs.

WATKINSVILLE (Oconee
County)
The Oconee Enterprise
P.O. Box 535, 30677
404-769-5175
Circulation: 2,497
Pub. Day: Wed.

WAYNESBORO (Burke
County)
The True Citizen
P.O. Box 948, 30830
404-554-2111
Circulation: 3,890
Pub. Days: Thurs.

WINDER (Barrow County)
The Winder News
P.O. Drawer C, 30680
404-867-7557
Circulation: 6,048
Pub. Day: Wed.

WRENS (Jefferson
County)
The Jefferson Reporter
P.O. Box 277, 30833
404-547-6629
Circulation: 1,661
Pub. Days: Wed. & Mon.

WRIGHTSVILLE
(Johnson County)
**The Wrightsville
Headlight**
P.O. Box 290, 31096
912-864-3528
Circulation: 1,632
Pub. Day: Thurs.

ZEBULON (Pike County)
**Pike County Journal &
Reporter**
P.O. Box 789, 30295
404-567-3446
Circulation: 2,300
Pub. Day: Wed.

OCCUPATIONS

	Executive, Admin'tive, Managerial	Professional Specialties	Technicians & Related Support	Sales	Clerical	Farming, Fishing, Forestry	Precision Production, Craft/Repair	Machine Operators, Assemblers, Inspectors	Trans. and Mat'l Moving	Handlers, Equipment, Cleaners, Helpers, Laborers	Household Occupations	Protective Services	Other Service Occupations
Appling	288	438	113	406	494	737	1,009	1,092	382	402	55	63	441
Atkinson	72	136	8	105	207	407	249	379	184	191	11	18	115
Bacon	238	250	64	253	436	451	591	569	214	174	35	36	340
Baker	52	89	44	54	154	429	125	240	39	66	19	4	142
Baldwin	1,036	2,095	801	1,226	1,651	161	1,687	1,144	506	408	130	471	2,287
Banks	244	261	61	245	410	390	506	970	270	280	8	60	212
Barrow	579	541	175	755	1,055	226	1,450	2,359	615	610	64	94	731
Bartow	1,158	1,098	303	1,299	2,420	462	2,797	4,385	1,278	1,108	113	172	1,456
Ben Hill	311	507	122	663	669	354	736	1,184	457	318	89	70	465
Berrien	345	412	87	532	648	652	704	1,206	353	307	55	43	377
Bibb	6,591	7,237	1,834	7,369	10,668	478	7,920	4,552	2,688	3,714	932	1,226	6,441
Bleckley	296	349	155	314	719	379	551	702	220	112	84	37	389
Brantley	158	217	29	307	362	247	650	532	263	260	3	25	222
Brooks	306	436	78	476	534	850	625	719	267	319	54	64	690
Bryan	299	232	44	320	500	135	692	401	329	286	20	49	388
Bulloch	1,382	1,927	314	1,481	2,008	1,134	1,854	1,319	621	714	177	169	1,719
Burke	331	699	126	509	801	744	829	1,274	305	580	116	144	651
Butts	260	379	103	361	671	144	814	1,221	213	291	122	120	458
Calhoun	128	169	41	84	180	353	194	375	149	173	63	43	141
Camden	444	382	83	472	651	110	716	732	375	353	20	102	621
Candler	224	283	88	364	231	365	365	371	118	142	34	28	276
Carroll	1,816	2,509	591	2,130	3,530	449	3,637	4,162	1,192	1,314	210	234	2,155
Catoosa	1,404	1,282	454	1,834	2,933	131	2,580	2,572	1,264	762	22	159	1,128
Charlton	155	195	66	151	303	130	325	334	256	179	38	66	352
Chatham	8,061	10,034	2,315	8,969	12,790	704	11,008	4,716	4,847	4,605	1,259	1,557	8,985
Chattahoochee	101	157	27	202	288	18	100	112	90	96	9	19	216
Chattooga	345	606	168	579	797	164	1,263	3,035	518	676	52	49	750
Cherokee	2,016	1,889	654	2,246	3,738	729	4,455	3,022	1,208	1,197	47	397	1,737
Clarke	3,036	6,831	1,914	3,238	5,082	568	2,735	2,792	1,054	1,215	396	446	3,639
Clay	54	126	39	54	119	175	85	150	62	108	19	6	141
Clayton	7,132	5,148	2,104	7,675	17,130	281	11,728	4,335	4,681	4,379	173	1,523	6,101
Clinch	160	267	21	155	275	161	217	635	308	232	51	49	178
Cobb	23,950	17,965	5,306	20,912	31,596	982	19,807	8,085	4,781	5,312	458	1,895	12,195
Coffee	865	859	146	969	1,351	1,399	1,166	1,132	644	682	76	155	780
Colquitt	1,023	1,206	286	1,635	1,853	1,500	1,827	2,325	621	913	151	227	1,125

County													
Cook	377	381	110	308	640	545	679	919	347	390	49	66	578
Coweta	1,217	1,611	508	1,187	2,210	269	2,655	2,897	954	1,156	324	317	1,270
Crawford	189	236	83	230	409	161	527	611	174	147	42	30	199
Crisp	619	623	267	627	978	570	834	1,055	404	460	185	81	912
Dade	216	432	82	260	590	130	787	1,050	400	276	29	8	588
Dawson	137	134	3	133	197	191	381	486	99	129	0	38	182
Decatur	832	927	326	702	1,155	836	1,229	1,718	654	538	96	134	960
DeKalb	37,521	36,793	9,028	31,336	53,990	1,446	21,846	12,664	7,765	8,793	1,612	2,817	22,593
Dodge	398	630	142	487	840	411	791	1,163	250	357	52	72	479
Dooly	213	374	67	217	373	624	363	678	184	294	115	54	478
Dougherty	4,141	4,629	1,268	4,567	6,634	677	5,223	4,001	1,939	2,175	510	664	4,212
Douglas	2,492	1,781	670	2,217	4,604	213	4,390	2,303	1,551	1,368	76	468	2,023
Early	369	433	71	411	523	727	559	576	295	305	135	47	461
Echols	47	54	4	33	87	107	124	156	65	76	4	9	56
Effingham	248	476	162	516	817	316	1,581	888	717	462	43	96	479
Elbert	566	643	153	618	1,020	220	1,301	1,691	491	582	94	86	610
Emanuel	449	601	154	698	818	666	997	1,726	469	419	50	57	596
Evans	279	228	66	320	358	345	402	509	230	207	64	44	371
Fannin	355	441	99	370	479	184	883	944	400	384	8	48	409
Fayette	1,712	1,483	701	1,501	2,854	155	2,059	711	633	621	65	145	919
Floyd	2,783	3,510	982	3,555	5,217	407	4,759	5,710	1,662	1,810	318	547	3,808
Forsyth	1,062	936	278	1,220	1,984	524	2,290	1,602	1,005	708	55	123	919
Franklin	390	515	92	425	575	395	1,007	1,603	365	376	31	59	431
Fulton	33,022	35,455	7,871	29,778	50,745	1,885	21,028	15,852	10,197	12,982	3,793	3,907	32,396
Gilmer	254	359	70	366	409	275	687	978	325	280	8	45	307
Glascock	59	42	22	42	101	101	116	220	56	91	10	9	73
Glynn	2,430	2,648	658	2,875	3,463	581	3,388	1,891	1,100	1,094	310	541	3,640
Gordon	876	855	254	1,086	1,755	433	1,562	3,637	836	734	52	248	904
Grady	466	553	237	636	791	1,253	1,111	1,227	397	742	85	93	581
Greene	225	256	17	167	406	387	568	1,075	286	426	90	35	396
Gwinnett	12,861	8,900	2,812	10,713	17,942	609	11,353	6,727	2,765	2,678	305	1,028	5,281
Habersham	691	907	169	749	1,167	491	1,614	2,340	487	854	28	122	839
Hall	3,213	3,182	776	3,449	4,554	1,268	5,148	5,834	1,749	2,487	148	495	2,857
Hancock	86	331	108	146	278	176	356	640	189	229	59	72	558
Haralson	469	494	225	625	941	125	1,222	1,953	455	449	63	111	637
Harris	659	513	107	624	804	345	951	871	380	425	78	141	666
Hart	462	585	128	573	672	258	1,182	2,385	262	419	104	63	589
Heard	97	234	60	179	245	127	440	599	199	144	7	44	206
Henry	1,474	1,113	457	1,594	3,238	115	2,958	1,673	983	977	203	244	1,244
Houston	3,187	3,418	1,229	3,044	5,317	590	4,920	2,226	952	1,607	225	511	3,107
Irwin	198	220	67	255	327	687	408	505	201	186	44	24	310
Jackson	778	828	135	741	1,449	710	1,664	2,273	533	705	61	166	1,128
Jasper	263	276	80	184	278	170	369	553	151	259	47	36	266

	Executive, Admin'tive, Managerial	Professional Specialties	Technicians & Related Support	Sales	Clerical	Farming, Fishing, Forestry	Precision Production, Craft/Repair	Machine Operators, Assemblers, Inspectors	Trans. and Mat'l Moving	Handlers, Equipment, Cleaners, Helpers, Laborers	Household Occupations	Protective Services	Other Service Occupations
Jeff Davis	381	357	112	323	537	422	654	1,033	204	267	42	35	431
Jefferson	339	510	85	425	712	619	768	1,605	389	419	161	42	660
Jenkins	166	179	54	281	263	422	430	696	239	189	60	34	190
Johnson	121	177	88	195	295	196	585	966	205	196	53	38	261
Jones	593	677	171	708	1,133	164	1,019	790	416	437	42	166	562
Lamar	372	363	176	231	590	145	699	1,110	262	301	99	81	440
Lanier	119	145	75	125	240	203	304	308	82	147	21	21	143
Laurens	1,188	1,406	311	1,350	1,884	667	2,003	2,719	703	695	178	129	1,469
Lee	494	430	101	544	856	383	790	609	152	287	40	78	391
Liberty	612	766	144	935	1,087	205	1,001	592	404	384	99	135	1,115
Lincoln	141	253	46	156	257	171	420	734	212	186	33	12	190
Long	90	157	44	90	205	130	260	152	109	112	5	35	214
Lowndes	2,575	2,890	614	3,308	3,846	885	3,144	3,035	1,231	1,490	279	491	3,402
Lumpkin	247	350	69	169	435	409	677	696	256	272	6	41	575
Macon	317	411	80	232	603	518	564	780	299	389	113	88	530
Madison	506	458	164	548	1,072	329	1,356	1,486	519	416	43	95	651
Marion	115	105	17	98	183	243	213	310	108	188	28	15	252
McDuffie	540	634	136	739	940	251	1,191	1,252	463	450	89	105	688
McIntosh	235	210	39	205	242	260	360	410	230	217	21	55	301
Meriwether	468	622	160	464	901	275	1,065	1,996	608	716	108	60	802
Miller	150	206	75	230	318	595	325	466	108	89	48	36	255
Mitchell	498	488	195	510	921	1,059	1,059	1,648	342	599	125	54	709
Monroe	472	544	82	510	809	299	823	1,201	347	385	160	136	629
Montgomery	155	208	44	188	291	279	269	471	198	148	36	41	219
Morgan	272	374	73	399	536	443	445	878	365	259	120	43	534
Murray	573	482	85	502	1,184	243	1,284	2,868	668	369	0	69	403
Muscogee	6,832	7,170	1,803	7,565	10,235	386	7,105	6,218	2,609	2,900	926	1,349	7,205
Newton	843	1,038	273	1,339	2,125	207	2,251	3,004	1,000	1,010	143	184	1,248
Oconee	538	760	267	661	1,044	305	652	744	259	226	37	70	405
Oglethorpe	263	273	100	166	411	236	688	924	218	193	67	30	246
Paulding	677	688	281	849	1,651	185	2,185	1,825	608	553	20	232	944
Peach	492	992	211	462	999	482	974	1,002	308	466	87	86	710
Pickens	285	335	100	364	426	118	844	1,113	329	373	16	58	449
Pierce	274	288	85	406	501	533	839	602	282	227	52	48	425
Pike	251	273	184	196	491	288	476	848	165	300	30	62	252
Polk	804	876	280	988	1,435	176	1,826	3,264	929	894	141	278	1,065
Pulaski	228	335	117	232	421	333	490	589	118	184	32	42	337
Putnam	253	387	109	321	478	316	545	1,033	206	265	67	146	301

County													
Quitman	43	52	13	58	65	103	85	131	42	81	9	11	75
Rabun	326	363	108	373	469	133	652	1,047	219	236	28	46	465
Randolph	187	273	15	249	330	521	316	494	170	220	149	56	351
Richmond	5,805	9,510	2,899	6,715	10,794	595	8,013	6,030	2,834	3,963	845	1,284	9,831
Rockdale	1,893	1,453	453	1,857	3,073	106	2,955	1,584	968	794	41	304	1,137
Schley	55	76	37	105	163	106	188	193	84	67	27	22	147
Screven	266	432	145	403	634	557	717	1,210	281	231	100	25	438
Seminole	262	265	96	358	392	435	370	447	156	266	45	83	348
Spalding	1,445	1,635	527	1,981	2,941	335	2,761	3,935	951	1,353	299	347	1,666
Stephens	597	808	249	667	1,156	134	1,441	2,196	410	515	46	117	788
Stewart	135	154	29	115	184	237	170	310	80	183	89	32	182
Sumter	1,093	1,498	299	855	1,807	821	1,541	1,569	559	598	247	133	1,187
Talbot	103	232	44	125	232	195	308	622	239	224	54	14	193
Taliaferro	42	57	8	44	63	46	72	205	49	52	7	1	61
Tattnall	324	530	133	415	754	801	630	805	294	307	45	318	534
Taylor	190	215	50	165	308	336	428	458	199	296	84	24	222
Telfair	276	418	91	320	422	458	534	789	284	239	35	73	357
Terrell	238	389	24	377	476	445	501	685	351	327	130	55	374
Thomas	1,457	1,652	452	1,233	1,963	1,127	1,893	1,859	781	1,028	275	199	1,611
Tift	1,086	1,355	505	1,235	1,900	1,043	1,704	1,681	683	788	209	100	1,372
Toombs	623	824	203	839	1,190	535	1,139	1,284	689	420	77	200	718
Towns	160	233	41	124	162	65	401	287	149	108	0	27	235
Treutlen	115	122	25	118	261	182	306	452	123	115	23	16	189
Troup	1,868	1,774	506	1,765	2,253		2,861	4,661	921	1,284	413	325	1,866
Turner	317	261	65	306	437	388	514	673	264	115	73	50	375
Twiggs	140	171	121	179	457	317	653	418	349	365	47	35	240
Union	173	310	56	211	306	89	536	546	202	245	19	42	341
Upson	797	853	255	717	1,198	368	1,560	3,123	387	705	155	180	1,115
Walker	1,574	1,385	462	2,238	2,914	231	3,702	4,808	1,556	1,485	85	387	1,756
Walton	823	709	243	1,004	1,613	374	2,519	2,849	757	910	122	159	963
Ware	1,293	1,432	299	1,559	1,824	506	2,227	1,232	965	765	160	217	1,285
Warren	104	162	28	118	196	192	302	479	143	167	52	12	196
Washington	455	695	262	440	638	450	1,033	1,323	468	433	162	50	671
Wayne	492	628	237	584	855	406	1,244	1,062	531	540	79	153	831
Webster	54	35	9	34	88	150	98	142	84	54	28	8	63
Wheeler	103	174	49	96	188	296	186	414	139	84	16	22	164
White	245	389	112	404	517	317	704	675	251	261	20	76	361
Whitfield	3,081	2,104	556	2,656	4,868	444	3,909	7,600	2,058	1,461	133	447	2,517
Wilcox	105	283	52	243	262	432	404	424	160	144	52	17	210
Wilkes	323	371	101	432	436	310	492	904	279	296	73	70	422
Wilkinson	251	348	267	227	355	104	726	588	367	265	61	17	459
Worth	471	562	103	532	907	836	972	1,033	433	448	114	75	501
Georgia	237,945	250,429	67,417	239,377	382,738	66,750	297,604	274,920	112,669	122,618	23,331	34,559	225,478

331

PEANUTS

Peanuts represent Georgia's number one agricultural product. The 1984 crop was a bin-buster, with a record setting production of 2.16 billion pounds, with a record value of $521 million. Peanuts alone accounted for one-third of the total value of all crops in 1984. Georgia remains unchallenged as the nation's leading peanut producing state.

Below are a few tantalizing recipes using peanuts or peanut butter in them. Try them today and get set for a pleasant, tasty surprise.

Cream of Peanut Butter Soup

½ cup butter or margarine
1 tablespoon onion, minced
1 tablespoon all-purpose flour

1 cup peanut butter
1 quart chicken stock
Salt and pepper to taste
1 cup cream

Melt butter or margarine, add onion and simmer until tender, but not brown. Add flour and peanut butter and stir to a smooth paste. Add stock gradually, season and cook 20 minutes in a double boiler, stirring constantly until thickened. Strain and add cream.

Makes 8 to 10 servings.

Waldorf Salad

2 cups diced apple
½ cup raisins
½ cup diced celery
½ cup chopped salted peanuts

Toss ingredients together. Serve on a bed of lettuce with dressing.

Makes 4 servings.

DRESSING:
¼ cup creamy peanut butter
¼ cup honey
½ cup mayonnaise

Blend ingredients. Serve over Waldorf Salad.

Strawberry Dips

½ cup creamy peanut butter
2 ounces milk chocolate, melted
2 tablespoons prepared, whipped topping

14 large, fresh strawberries
3 ounces semi-sweet chocolate, melted

In a medium bowl, combine peanut butter, milk chocolate and whipped topping; mix well. Slice strawberries in half lengthwise. Spread peanut butter mixture on half of sliced strawberries. Top with remaining strawberry halves. Refrigerate until filling is set. Dip each filled strawberry into melted semi-sweet chocolate coating only half the berry. Refrigerate until ready to serve.

Makes 14 filled strawberries.

Peanut-Banana Shake

1 medium banana
½ cup creamy peanut butter
1 cup skim milk

2 tablespoons honey
½ teaspoon cinnamon
1 cup club soda

Cut the banana into thin slices and freeze. When banana slices are frozen, place bananas in blender container and add peanut butter, milk, honey and cinnamon. Blend on medium speed until well mixed. Before serving, blend in club soda.

Makes 3 (8-ounce each) servings.

Orange Peanutwich

½ orange
1 English muffin, split
⅓ cup crunchy peanut butter

1 teaspoon honey
¼ teaspoon grated orange rind

Cut peel and all white membrane from orange half. Cut into two slices. Toast English muffin. Spread peanut butter on each English muffin half. Top with an orange slice. In a small saucepan, heat honey and orange rind. Drizzle over orange slices on muffins.

Makes 2 servings.

Oriental Chicken

2 chicken breasts, boned and skinned
½ cup orange juice
1 tablespoon soy sauce
1 tablespoon sherry
1 tablespoon cornstarch

¼ teaspoon red pepper flakes
2 tablespoons peanut oil
1 cup scallions, cut into 2-inch pieces
½ cup salted peanuts
Hot cooked rice

Cut chicken into 1-inch pieces. In a medium bowl, combine orange juice, soy sauce, sherry, cornstarch, pepper flakes and ginger; mix well. Add chicken; let stand 30 minutes. Heat oil in skillet. Add chicken with marinade and stir-fry over high heat 2-3 minutes. Remove chicken. Add scallions and peanuts; stir-fry 1 minute. Return chicken to skillet; cook 1 minute. Serve over hot cooked rice.

Makes 4 servings.

Peanut Pie

3 eggs
½ cup sugar
1½ cups dark corn syrup
¼ cup butter, melted

¼ teaspoon salt
½ teaspoon vanilla
1½ cup chopped, roasted peanuts
9″ unbaked pie shell

Beat eggs until foamy. Add sugar, syrup, butter, salt and vanilla. Continue to beat until thoroughly blended. Stir in peanuts. Pour into unbaked pie shell. Bake in preheated 375°F. oven for 45 minutes. Delicious served warm or cold; may be garnished with whipped cream or ice cream.

Makes a 9″ pie.

Chili Nuts

1 tablespoon peanut oil
1 egg white
2 teaspoons chili powder
1 teaspoon ground cumin

1 teaspoon garlic salt
⅛ teaspoon Tabasco sauce
1 pound unsalted dry roasted peanuts

Grease bottom of a 15½x10½-inch jelly roll pan or baking sheet with peanut oil. In medium bowl, beat egg white until foamy. Fold in chili powder, cumin, garlic salt and Tabasco sauce. Add peanuts; stir to coat evenly. Spread peanuts in pan. Bake in a 325°F oven for 20 minutes. Remove from oven; break up pieces if necessary. Store in airtight container.

Makes 1 pound.

Nuts and Bolts Mix

2 packages (6 ounces each) dried
   apricots, chopped
½ cup vacuum packed wheat germ

2 cups salted peanuts
1 cup raisins
1 cup toasted flaked coconut

In a medium bowl, combine apricots and wheat germ; toss well. Stir in peanuts, raisins and coconut. Store in airtight container. Eat as a snack, pack in small plastic bags for toting, spoon into plain yogurt, or add to cereal and milk for breakfast.

Makes 6 cups.

POPULATION

The following charts provide information on population estimates and projections from 1980 to 2000; population by age groups; comparison of Georgia cities with others in the Southeast; and Georgia population figures every ten years since 1790.

Population Estimates and Projections: 1980-2000

County	1980[1]	Estimated 1985	Projected 1990	Projected 1995	Projected 2000
Appling	15,565	16,300	18,061	18,967	19,878
Atkinson	6,141	6,400	7,137	7,349	7,561
Bacon	9,379	9,400	10,289	10,766	11,250
Baker	3,808	3,700	3,930	4,090	4,259
Baldwin	34,686	38,000	42,745	47,004	51,270
Banks	8,702	9,900	9,737	10,197	10,661
Barrow	21,354	24,900	26,475	28,370	30,268
Bartow	40,760	45,500	51,266	53,794	56,325
Ben Hill	16,000	17,300	18,544	19,974	21,409
Berrien	13,525	13,900	14,911	15,430	15,950
Bibb	150,256	156,400	166,271	171,888	177,506
Bleckley	10,767	10,700	11,003	11,091	11,174
Brantley	8,701	9,700	10,341	11,573	12,810
Brooks	15,255	15,200	16,651	17,496	18,341

County	1980[1]	Estimated 1985	Projected 1990	Projected 1995	Projected 2000
Bryan	10,175	12,200	12,733	15,062	17,387
Bulloch	35,785	37,500	40,200	41,103	42,008
Burke	19,349	20,800	22,358	23,746	25,142
Butts	13,665	15,100	16,539	17,880	19,218
Calhoun	5,717	5,500	5,891	5,928	5,967
Camden	13,371	18,100	37,453	38,121	38,784
Candler	7,518	7,700	7,736	7,981	8,225
Carroll	56,346	63,300	68,880	73,189	77,495
Catoosa	36,991	39,500	43,074	44,996	46,911
Charlton	7,343	7,600	8,449	9,166	9,885
Chatham	202,226	214,700	228,166	238,736	249,312
Chattahoochee	21,732	21,000	27,693	29,404	31,117
Chattooga	21,856	21,500	22,749	22,590	22,436
Cherokee	51,699	68,600	74,849	88,314	101,778
Clarke	74,498	77,400	84,521	87,520	90,522
Clay	3,553	3,400	3,825	4,099	4,375
Clayton	150,357	167,000	188,548	201,046	213,545
Clinch	6,660	6,800	7,411	7,523	7,639
Cobb	297,718	375,000	436,972	459,380	481,786
Coffee	26,894	28,900	31,476	32,949	34,421
Colquitt	35,376	36,400	39,294	40,356	41,425
Columbia	40,118	53,200	57,254	68,955	80,656
Cook	13,490	13,900	14,821	15,251	15,682
Coweta	39,268	44,800	47,358	50,340	53,323
Crawford	7,684	7,400	8,812	10,341	11,872
Crisp	19,489	20,400	20,493	21,411	22,325
Dade	12,318	11,700	13,369	13,808	14,248
Dawson	4,774	6,300	6,286	6,725	7,162
Decatur	25,495	26,800	28,643	30,191	31,736
DeKalb	483,024	516,300	569,383	583,139	596,899
Dodge	16,955	17,100	19,120	19,520	19,925
Dooly	10,826	10,500	11,773	12,292	12,818
Dougherty	100,718	104,300	116,139	125,262	134,383
Douglas	54,573	65,500	69,360	82,687	96,013
Early	13,158	13,200	14,506	15,152	15,797
Echols	2,297	2,400	2,615	2,787	2,967
Effingham	18,327	21,300	22,543	24,773	27,004
Elbert	18,758	19,000	20,165	20,698	21,236
Emanuel	20,795	21,500	23,194	24,344	25,494
Evans	8,428	8,500	9,384	9,769	10,156
Fannin	14,748	15,400	15,764	15,848	15,932
Fayette	29,043	42,900	46,831	68,013	89,193
Floyd	79,800	78,700	84,318	84,878	85,431
Forsyth	27,958	35,600	36,518	41,723	46,936
Franklin	15,185	15,600	17,081	17,537	17,992
Fulton	589,904	620,100	682,239	708,648	735,060
Gilmer	11,110	12,200	12,719	13,276	13,834
Glascock	2,382	2,400	2,421	2,483	2,542
Glynn	54,981	58,800	63,660	65,555	67,454
Gordon	30,070	32,900	36,207	38,013	39,821
Grady	19,845	21,200	21,685	22,571	23,453
Greene	11,391	12,000	13,117	14,010	14,902
Gwinnett	166,903	253,000	289,786	360,014	430,246
Habersham	25,020	26,900	28,951	29,930	30,910
Hall	75,649	84,000	92,442	96,960	101,476

POPULATION

County	1980[1]	Estimated 1985	Projected 1990	Projected 1995	Projected 2000
Hancock	9,466	9,400	9,930	10,575	11,226
Haralson	18,422	20,000	21,516	21,899	22,285
Harris	15,464	17,000	18,378	20,645	22,912
Hart	18,585	19,400	20,633	21,071	21,513
Heard	6,520	6,900	7,305	7,895	8,481
Henry	36,309	44,700	47,875	57,756	67,640
Houston	77,605	85,800	93,463	100,332	107,200
Irwin	8,988	8,800	9,659	10,057	10,455
Jackson	25,343	27,600	28,766	29,982	31,205
Jasper	7,553	7,700	8,994	10,102	11,207
Jeff Davis	11,473	11,700	13,105	13,812	14,513
Jefferson	18,403	18,500	19,657	20,345	21,040
Jenkins	8,841	8,400	9,473	9,926	10,379
Johnson	8,660	8,800	9,042	9,355	9,654
Jones	16,579	18,300	20,825	23,193	25,560
Lamar	12,215	12,300	13,167	13,719	14,268
Lanier	5,654	5,800	6,085	6,307	6,524
Laurens	36,990	38,400	41,003	43,017	45,029
Lee	11,684	14,000	17,058	21,684	26,303
Liberty	37,583	41,900	52,244	63,956	75,670
Lincoln	6,716	7,000	7,689	8,091	8,492
Long	4,524	5,700	6,020	6,821	7,621
Lowndes	67,972	72,900	82,224	87,251	92,276
Lumpkin	10,762	12,000	12,976	13,630	14,286
Macon	14,003	14,000	15,124	15,938	16,747
Madison	17,747	19,200	21,275	22,900	24,520
Marion	5,297	5,400	5,837	6,001	6,158
McDuffie	18,546	19,600	20,938	22,173	23,407
McIntosh	8,046	8,100	8,891	9,226	9,561
Meriwether	21,229	20,700	21,892	22,753	23,609
Miller	7,038	6,900	7,755	8,102	8,450
Mitchell	21,114	21,700	24,022	25,401	26,781
Monroe	14,610	15,400	16,457	18,051	19,652
Montgomery	7,011	7,000	8,441	8,653	8,867
Morgan	11,572	12,400	14,132	15,063	15,992
Murray	19,685	21,700	23,684	26,564	29,446
Muscogee	170,108	178,500	206,754	214,699	222,639
Newton	34,489	39,000	42,653	46,060	49,466
Oconee	12,427	14,600	17,305	20,555	23,807
Oglethorpe	8,929	9,400	10,078	10,619	11,163
Paulding	26,110	30,600	32,872	36,989	41,106
Peach	19,151	19,600	22,047	23,668	25,287
Pickens	11,652	13,300	14,477	14,967	15,457
Pierce	11,897	12,900	13,354	14,350	15,344
Pike	8,937	9,000	9,845	11,103	12,364
Polk	32,386	33,500	35,715	36,265	36,805
Pulaski	8,950	8,800	9,529	9,922	10,309
Putnam	10,295	11,700	12,399	13,389	14,382
Quitman	2,357	2,300	2,368	2,441	2,517
Rabun	10,466	10,800	11,774	12,140	12,506
Randolph	9,599	9,100	9,642	10,364	11,087
Richmond	181,629	191,600	203,530	218,211	232,888
Rockdale	36,747	44,100	45,896	56,544	67,190
Schley	3,433	3,400	3,730	3,968	4,204
Screven	14,043	14,600	15,257	16,181	17,102

336

County	1980[1]	Estimated 1985	Projected 1990	Projected 1995	Projected 2000
Seminole	9,057	8,700	9,195	9,867	10,540
Spalding	47,899	51,500	55,611	58,328	61,049
Stephens	21,763	22,400	23,911	24,034	24,158
Stewart	5,896	5,600	6,285	6,314	6,342
Sumter	29,360	30,200	34,333	35,880	37,424
Talbot	6,536	6,700	6,787	6,998	7,203
Taliaferro	2,032	2,100	2,020	2,001	1,976
Tattnall	18,134	17,900	17,981	18,978	19,976
Taylor	7,902	8,000	8,229	8,373	8,523
Telfair	11,445	11,200	12,066	12,224	12,383
Terrell	12,017	11,600	13,494	14,216	14,938
Thomas	38,098	38,300	44,371	46,373	48,374
Tift	32,862	34,000	36,889	39,160	41,435
Toombs	22,592	23,600	25,357	26,679	27,992
Towns	5,638	6,200	6,102	6,278	6,458
Treutlen	6,087	6,000	6,650	6,848	7,040
Troup	50,003	53,700	56,949	59,195	61,439
Turner	9,510	9,600	10,498	10,967	11,435
Twiggs	9,354	9,900	11,204	11,897	12,597
Union	9,390	10,500	10,662	11,432	12,194
Upson	25,998	26,100	26,587	26,839	27,090
Walker	56,470	56,300	60,980	61,427	61,866
Walton	31,211	33,000	37,665	41,649	45,638
Ware	37,180	37,100	39,732	41,006	42,281
Warren	6,583	6,500	6,905	7,115	7,326
Washington	18,842	19,200	20,951	21,966	22,978
Wayne	20,750	22,100	24,015	25,066	26,119
Webster	2,341	2,200	2,440	2,536	2,634
Wheeler	5,155	5,100	5,022	5,262	5,506
White	10,120	11,400	11,701	12,275	12,851
Whitfield	65,789	68,400	77,147	79,449	81,752
Wilcox	7,682	7,600	7,760	8,062	8,375
Wilkes	10,951	11,300	12,252	12,747	13,238
Wilkinson	10,368	10,800	11,819	12,487	13,159
Worth	18,064	18,300	20,592	22,072	23,551
Georgia	5,463,105	5,976,100	6,584,057	7,034,663	7,485,310

[1]1980 census figures included for comparative purposes.

Farm, Rural, Urban Population: 1980

County	Urban[1]	Rural Nonfarm	Rural[2] Farm	Total Population
Appling	3,586	10,001	1,978	15,565
Atkinson	0	5,208	933	6,141
Bacon	3,819	3,821	1,739	9,379
Baker	0	3,109	699	3,808
Baldwin	21,153	13,171	362	34,686
Banks	0	7,929	773	8,702
Barrow	6,705	13,927	722	21,354
Bartow	9,508	30,386	866	40,760
Ben Hill	10,187	5,313	500	16,000
Berrien	4,808	7,045	1,672	13,525

POPULATION

County	Urban[1]	Rural Nonfarm	Rural[2] Farm	Total Population
Bibb	127,792	22,129	335	150,256
Bleckley	5,121	4,926	720	10,767
Brantley	0	7,818	883	8,701
Brooks	5,188	8,590	1,477	15,255
Bryan	0	10,034	141	10,175
Bulloch	14,866	18,707	2,212	35,785
Burke	5,760	12,234	1,355	19,349
Butts	4,133	9,129	403	13,665
Calhoun	0	5,343	374	5,717
Camden	3,596	9,651	124	13,371
Candler	3,520	3,194	804	7,518
Carroll	17,492	37,724	1,130	56,346
Catoosa	18,433	18,027	531	36,991
Charlton	0	7,043	300	7,343
Chatham	189,373	12,792	61	202,226
Chattahoochee	15,074	6,645	13	21,732
Chattooga	4,843	16,395	618	21,856
Cherokee	15,166	35,204	1,329	51,699
Clarke	62,397	12,012	89	74,498
Clay	0	3,333	220	3,553
Clayton	141,291	8,934	132	150,357
Clinch	3,104	3,378	178	6,660
Cobb	271,109	26,478	131	297,718
Coffee	10,980	12,795	3,119	26,894
Colquitt	15,703	16,776	2,897	35,376
Columbia	23,712	16,045	361	40,118
Cook	5,592	6,723	1,175	13,490
Coweta	11,499	27,088	681	39,268
Crawford	0	7,190	494	7,684
Crisp	10,914	7,534	1,041	19,489
Dade	0	11,966	352	12,318
Dawson	0	4,623	151	4,774
Decatur	10,532	13,087	1,876	25,495
DeKalb	470,862	12,076	86	483,024
Dodge	5,330	10,200	1,425	16,955
Dooly	2,785	7,114	927	10,826
Dougherty	87,181	13,143	394	100,718
Douglas	37,420	16,996	157	54,573
Early	5,855	5,956	1,347	13,158
Echols	0	2,027	270	2,297
Effingham	0	17,810	517	18,327
Elbert	5,686	12,449	623	18,758
Emanuel	7,552	11,482	1,761	20,795
Evans	2,702	5,163	563	8,428
Fannin	0	14,463	285	14,748
Fayette	10,297	18,458	288	29,043
Floyd	51,216	27,879	705	79,800
Forsyth	0	26,556	1,402	27,958
Franklin	0	13,797	1,388	15,185
Fulton	565,341	24,325	238	589,904
Gilmer	0	10,421	689	11,110
Glascock	0	2,133	249	2,382
Glynn	30,360	24,564	57	54,981
Gordon	5,563	23,411	1,096	30,070
Grady	8,752	8,713	2,380	19,845

County	Urban[1]	Rural Nonfarm	Rural[2] Farm	Total Population
Greene	2,878	8,037	476	11,391
Gwinnett	116,611	49,464	828	166,903
Habersham	3,203	21,148	669	25,020
Hall	18,058	55,761	1,830	75,649
Hancock	0	9,279	187	9,466
Haralson	6,589	11,406	427	18,422
Harris	924	14,200	340	15,464
Hart	4,855	12,815	915	18,585
Heard	0	6,242	278	6,520
Henry	6,034	29,745	530	36,309
Houston	64,118	12,810	677	77,605
Irwin	3,436	3,932	1,620	8,988
Jackson	4,092	19,832	1,419	25,343
Jasper	0	6,962	591	7,553
Jeff Davis	4,249	6,142	1,082	11,473
Jefferson	2,823	14,497	1,083	18,403
Jenkins	3,988	3,868	985	8,841
Johnson	2,526	5,288	846	8,660
Jones	3,018	13,125	436	16,579
Lamar	4,887	6,904	424	12,215
Lanier	2,647	2,492	515	5,654
Laurens	19,000	15,838	2,152	36,990
Lee	1,554	9,524	606	11,684
Liberty	26,326	11,179	78	37,583
Lincoln	0	6,337	379	6,716
Long	0	4,277	247	4,524
Lowndes	37,533	29,276	1,163	67,972
Lumpkin	2,844	7,362	556	10,762
Macon	4,830	8,424	749	14,003
Madison	0	16,402	1,345	17,747
Marion	0	4,778	519	5,297
McDuffie	7,001	11,174	371	18,546
McIntosh	0	8,016	30	8,046
Meriwether	4,626	16,010	593	21,229
Miller	0	5,760	1,278	7,038
Mitchell	9,739	9,759	1,616	21,114
Monroe	4,624	9,591	395	14,610
Montgomery	0	6,244	767	7,011
Morgan	2,907	7,437	1,228	11,572
Murray	0	19,040	645	19,685
Muscogee	167,507	2,538	63	170,108
Newton	10,586	23,433	470	34,489
Oconee	418	11,382	627	12,427
Oglethorpe	0	8,079	850	8,929
Paulding	2,508	23,171	431	26,110
Peach	9,000	9,759	392	19,151
Pickens	0	11,335	317	11,652
Pierce	3,222	7,308	1,367	11,897
Pike	0	8,233	704	8,937
Polk	12,244	19,620	522	32,386
Pulaski	4,357	3,836	757	8,950
Putnam	4,833	4,988	474	10,295
Quitman	0	2,242	115	2,357
Rabun	0	10,324	142	10,466
Randolph	4,340	4,518	741	9,599

POPULATION

County	Urban[1]	Rural Nonfarm	Rural[2] Farm	Total Population
Richmond	165,974	15,451	204	181,629
Rockdale	11,284	25,303	160	36,747
Schley	0	3,086	347	3,433
Screven	3,352	9,293	1,398	14,043
Seminole	3,320	4,797	940	9,057
Spalding	24,459	23,045	395	47,899
Stephens	9,104	12,372	287	21,763
Stewart	0	5,720	176	5,896
Sumter	16,120	11,945	1,295	29,360
Talbot	165	6,074	297	6,536
Taliaferro	0	1,870	162	2,032
Tattnall	4,144	11,890	2,100	18,134
Taylor	0	7,454	448	7,902
Telfair	3,388	6,804	1,253	11,445
Terrell	5,647	5,374	996	12,017
Thomas	18,463	17,955	1,680	38,098
Tift	13,749	17,451	1,662	32,862
Toombs	14,591	6,513	1,488	22,592
Towns	0	5,526	112	5,638
Treutlen	2,981	2,710	396	6,087
Troup	30,837	18,816	350	50,003
Turner	4,766	3,728	1,016	9,510
Twiggs	0	9,084	270	9,354
Union	0	8,857	533	9,390
Upson	12,298	13,350	350	25,998
Walker	30,815	25,015	640	56,470
Walton	11,445	18,703	1,063	31,211
Ware	22,910	13,369	901	37,180
Warren	0	6,111	472	6,583
Washington	6,068	11,962	812	18,842
Wayne	9,365	10,402	983	20,750
Webster	0	1,862	479	2,341
Wheeler	0	4,555	600	5,155
White	0	9,586	534	10,120
Whitfield	20,939	44,122	728	65,789
Wilcox	0	6,876	806	7,682
Wilkes	4,662	5,680	609	10,951
Wilkinson	2,768	7,446	154	10,368
Worth	5,860	9,856	2,348	18,064
Georgia	3,408,267	1,933,749	121,089	5,463,105

[1]Urban areas are places with 2500 or more inhabitants.

[2]A farm is a place with $1000 or more in sales of crops, livestock, or other farm products during the preceding calendar year.

Population by Age: 1986

County	0–4 Years	5–19 Years	20–34 Years	35–49 Years	50–64 Years	65 Years & Over
Appling	1,483	4,959	3,963	2,672	2,232	1,757
Atkinson	586	1,983	1,438	1,066	906	763
Bacon	910	2,741	2,180	1,518	1,438	1,135

County	0–4 Years	5–19 Years	20–34 Years	35–49 Years	50–64 Years	65 Years & Over
Baker	348	1,092	836	532	531	532
Baldwin	2,725	10,632	10,509	6,196	5,428	4,030
Banks	694	2,385	2,217	1,589	1,336	1,096
Barrow	1,872	6,509	5,701	4,049	3,394	2,899
Bartow	3,488	12,930	11,043	8,170	6,657	4,774
Ben Hill	1,505	4,385	3,999	2,538	2,637	2,463
Berrien	1,075	3,789	3,212	2,353	2,078	1,852
Bibb	11,744	40,970	40,282	24,829	23,942	18,095
Bleckley	732	3,150	2,344	1,767	1,533	1,368
Brantley	803	2,878	2,278	1,627	1,159	942
Brooks	1,336	4,608	3,212	2,203	2,290	2,443
Bryan	1,129	3,396	2,877	1,892	1,498	918
Bulloch	2,679	10,941	10,946	5,398	4,420	4,047
Burke	2,003	6,247	4,826	2,835	2,844	2,401
Butts	1,162	4,085	4,007	2,402	2,023	1,708
Calhoun	475	1,666	1,206	764	865	844
Camden	1,430	4,882	4,188	2,812	2,159	1,328
Candler	522	1,951	1,557	1,074	1,179	1,373
Carroll	4,631	17,636	16,095	10,467	8,034	7,007
Catoosa	3,009	10,636	9,926	7,654	5,374	4,044
Charlton	704	2,477	1,686	1,296	965	878
Chatham	17,640	54,824	56,709	32,515	31,436	24,665
Chattahoochee	2,113	8,771	11,374	2,436	434	179
Chattooga	1,579	5,548	4,846	3,647	3,680	3,091
Cherokee	5,442	18,039	18,174	11,638	7,250	5,039
Clarke	4,998	19,155	30,920	10,206	8,109	7,124
Clay	293	1,002	740	463	614	606
Clayton	14,159	48,367	51,044	32,849	18,038	8,814
Clinch	594	2,122	1,620	1,090	940	748
Cobb	26,777	95,875	114,463	76,910	44,639	22,608
Coffee	2,577	8,363	7,110	4,435	4,015	3,142
Colquitt	3,037	10,085	8,071	5,727	5,591	5,216
Columbia	4,414	14,132	13,767	9,553	5,526	3,006
Cook	1,141	4,073	3,009	2,165	2,037	1,862
Coweta	3,453	11,803	10,120	7,600	6,182	4,962
Crawford	657	2,459	1,943	1,444	1,013	844
Crisp	1,746	5,563	4,514	2,781	2,894	2,592
Dade	996	3,530	3,294	2,237	1,686	1,199
Dawson	422	1,446	1,338	936	822	712
Decatur	2,375	7,606	6,177	3,840	3,867	3,521
DeKalb	34,188	133,603	156,982	98,463	69,717	41,885
Dodge	1,351	5,023	3,841	2,805	2,783	2,448
Dooly	1,069	3,268	2,369	1,572	1,616	1,499
Dougherty	9,870	31,821	29,431	16,780	13,205	8,862
Douglas	5,453	18,217	16,718	11,848	6,685	4,523
Early	1,190	4,090	2,798	2,052	1,905	1,930
Echols	240	725	595	430	265	234
Effingham	1,826	6,089	4,962	3,690	2,691	1,600
Elbert	1,463	4,973	4,344	3,096	2,958	2,766
Emanuel	2,012	5,987	4,846	3,323	3,232	2,838
Evans	755	2,531	1,944	1,337	1,214	1,221
Fannin	931	3,452	3,104	2,532	2,735	2,605
Fayette	2,767	11,496	8,985	9,042	4,614	2,809
Floyd	5,344	20,466	19,282	13,939	12,585	10,898
Forsyth	2,512	8,881	8,233	6,031	4,281	3,155
Franklin	1,052	4,136	3,490	2,747	2,589	2,306

POPULATION

County	0–4 Years	5–19 Years	20–34 Years	35–49 Years	50–64 Years	65 Years & Over
Fulton	44,382	155,609	189,217	106,490	86,033	63,569
Gilmer	842	2,921	2,690	2,122	1,829	1,671
Glascock	162	565	476	367	407	428
Glynn	4,355	15,317	14,443	9,924	8,865	7,286
Gordon	2,484	9,188	7,861	5,980	4,687	3,551
Grady	1,683	5,846	4,462	3,120	2,941	2,894
Greene	1,140	3,359	2,672	1,773	1,784	1,695
Gwinnett	20,042	64,483	71,509	48,662	23,494	12,442
Habersham	1,844	7,123	6,701	4,444	3,933	3,332
Hall	6,269	21,986	20,949	15,345	12,124	9,057
Hancock	805	2,986	2,063	1,288	1,270	1,330
Haralson	1,349	5,373	4,326	3,552	3,066	2,612
Harris	1,187	4,369	3,777	2,843	3,017	2,022
Hart	1,395	5,118	4,264	3,080	3,021	2,936
Heard	499	1,901	1,499	1,132	1,058	898
Henry	3,364	11,355	10,518	7,774	5,968	4,297
Houston	7,094	24,260	22,907	16,428	10,854	5,579
Irwin	718	2,543	1,854	1,426	1,441	1,410
Jackson	2,008	7,179	6,448	4,723	3,814	3,228
Jasper	694	2,138	1,975	1,313	1,166	1,131
Jeff Davis	995	3,504	2,938	1,965	1,702	1,346
Jefferson	1,603	5,467	4,195	2,518	2,699	2,673
Jenkins	740	2,560	2,053	1,302	1,393	1,173
Johnson	768	2,297	1,868	1,283	1,377	1,300
Jones	1,507	5,215	4,731	3,368	2,524	1,780
Lamar	936	3,522	2,851	2,020	1,897	1,557
Lanier	538	1,720	1,313	921	755	668
Laurens	3,159	10,205	8,634	6,152	5,757	5,494
Lee	1,293	4,383	4,116	2,461	1,714	944
Liberty	5,477	13,212	17,465	5,634	3,065	1,526
Lincoln	549	1,942	1,599	1,132	1,171	907
Long	562	1,522	1,504	749	689	392
Lowndes	6,449	21,197	21,318	11,802	9,093	6,665
Lumpkin	789	3,417	3,119	1,977	1,514	1,274
Macon	1,297	4,145	3,369	2,000	1,984	1,887
Madison	1,510	5,314	4,884	3,465	2,685	2,003
Marion	405	1,719	1,201	894	756	650
McDuffie	1,609	5,415	4,605	3,218	2,836	2,299
McIntosh	639	2,599	1,923	1,305	1,120	965
Meriwether	1,784	5,933	4,823	3,197	3,088	2,802
Miller	606	2,038	1,549	1,132	1,105	1,041
Mitchell	2,052	6,905	4,988	3,268	3,042	2,603
Monroe	1,079	4,204	3,765	2,625	2,188	1,857
Montgomery	621	2,155	2,056	1,166	1,007	865
Morgan	1,018	3,694	2,905	1,996	1,643	1,849
Murray	1,804	6,349	5,557	4,023	2,512	1,836
Muscogee	15,277	50,269	51,795	29,823	27,373	17,558
Newton	3,075	11,378	8,989	6,691	5,175	4,076
Oconee	1,164	4,048	4,318	2,793	1,704	1,326
Oglethorpe	678	2,681	2,104	1,653	1,283	1,217
Paulding	2,428	8,332	7,680	5,304	3,705	2,714
Peach	1,688	6,017	5,220	3,384	2,621	1,962
Pickens	923	3,323	2,995	2,325	1,951	1,831
Pierce	1,067	3,564	2,910	2,062	1,737	1,434
Pike	739	2,492	2,011	1,649	1,357	1,233

County	0–4 Years	5–19 Years	20–34 Years	35–49 Years	50–64 Years	65 Years & Over
Polk	2,354	8,880	7,290	5,657	5,332	4,868
Pulaski	696	2,478	1,941	1,502	1,378	1,304
Putnam	809	3,033	2,647	1,795	1,824	1,446
Quitman	169	643	460	288	413	385
Rabun	636	2,573	2,402	1,846	1,885	1,905
Randolph	818	2,675	1,974	1,215	1,415	1,537
Richmond	14,946	51,504	56,124	29,246	24,922	18,027
Rockdale	3,267	12,002	10,004	8,559	5,164	3,239
Schley	291	1,099	757	548	458	460
Screven	1,267	3,833	3,397	2,057	2,214	2,005
Seminole	711	2,499	1,886	1,331	1,427	1,286
Spalding	4,117	14,125	12,179	8,915	7,404	5,791
Stephens	1,599	5,595	5,326	3,576	3,591	3,363
Stewart	449	1,815	1,210	828	951	874
Sumter	2,550	9,208	8,087	4,472	4,152	3,874
Talbot	505	1,842	1,501	989	903	953
Taliaferro	144	485	381	258	338	419
Tattnall	1,323	4,179	4,760	2,853	2,463	2,463
Taylor	547	2,286	1,676	1,279	1,175	1,136
Telfair	979	3,005	2,497	1,679	1,811	1,843
Terrell	1,160	3,679	2,860	1,769	1,791	1,643
Thomas	3,265	11,555	9,334	6,516	6,119	5,075
Tift	2,976	10,089	8,630	5,344	4,489	3,750
Toombs	2,037	6,682	5,333	3,919	3,374	2,913
Towns	259	1,424	1,056	801	1,022	1,353
Treutlen	518	1,801	1,398	926	934	844
Troup	4,150	13,650	13,041	7,916	8,241	7,176
Turner	945	2,868	2,149	1,474	1,392	1,272
Twiggs	936	3,020	2,330	1,555	1,452	1,174
Union	602	2,441	2,120	1,609	1,563	1,817
Upson	1,803	6,485	5,496	4,169	4,290	4,109
Walker	4,445	14,584	13,351	10,154	8,944	7,697
Walton	2,788	9,925	7,858	5,974	4,664	3,872
Ware	3,087	10,151	8,776	5,910	5,785	5,004
Warren	523	1,887	1,386	922	1,007	1,053
Washington	1,647	5,683	4,603	2,886	2,763	2,523
Wayne	1,845	6,110	5,325	3,645	3,278	2,503
Webster	189	667	538	332	375	304
Wheeler	447	1,378	1,009	693	750	803
White	724	2,727	2,414	1,897	1,623	1,682
Whitfield	5,706	19,398	18,388	13,247	9,359	6,508
Wilcox	585	1,966	1,605	1,103	1,247	1,225
Wilkes	860	2,918	2,515	1,837	1,875	1,730
Wilkinson	942	3,234	2,583	1,735	1,508	1,235
Worth	1,524	5,690	4,434	3,064	2,612	2,256
Georgia	464,765	1,614,576	1,614,678	1,027,164	803,441	599,980

Population Comparison—Large Cities in the Southeast

City	July 1, 1982 Population	Rank in United States	Rank in Southeast	April 1, 1980 Population	Rank in United States	Rank in Southeast
Memphis, TN	645,760	16	1	646,170	15	1
New Orleans, LA	564,561	20	2	557,927	22	2
Jacksonville, FL	556,370	23	3	540,920	23	3
Nashville-Davidson, TN	455,252	26	4	455,651	26	4
ATLANTA, GA	428,153	30	5	425,022	30	5
Miami, FL	382,726	34	6	346,865	41	6
Baton Rouge, LA	361,572	41	7	346,029	42	7
Charlotte, NC	323,972	48	8	315,474	49	8
Louisville, KY	293,531	50	9	298,694	50	9
Birmingham, AL	283,239	53	10	286,799	51	10
Virginia Beach, VA	282,588	54	11	262,199	57	13
Tampa, FL	276,413	55	12	271,599	54	11
Norfolk, VA	266,874	57	13	266,979	56	12
St. Petersburg, FL	241,214	61	14	238,647	59	14
Richmond, VA	218,237	66	15	219,214	65	15
Shreveport, LA	210,881	68	16	205,820	67	16
Lexington-Fayette, KY	207,668	69	17	204,165	68	17
Mobile, AL	204,586	70	18	200,452	71	19
Jackson, MS	204,195	71	19	202,895	70	18
Montgomery, AL	182,406	79	20	177,857	76	20
Knoxville, TN	175,298	84	21	175,045	77	21
COLUMBUS, GA	174,348	85	22	169,441	88	23
Chattanooga, TN	168,016	90	23	169,728	87	22
Little Rock, AR	167,974	91	24	167,602	89	24
Greensboro, NC	157,337	99	25	155,642	100	25
Hialeah, FL	154,713	103	26	145,254	108	28
Raleigh, NC	154,211	104	27	150,255	105	27
Fort Lauderdale, FL	153,755	106	28	153,279	101	26
Newport News, VA	151,240	108	29	144,903	109	29
SAVANNAH, GA	145,699	111	30	141,655	112	31
Huntsville, AL	145,421	112	31	142,513	111	30
Winston-Salem, NC	140,846	115	32	138,584	116	32
Orlando, FL	134,255	121	33	128,291	124	33
Hampton, VA	124,966	127	34	122,617	128	34
Hollywood, FL	122,051	131	35	121,323	129	35
Chesapeake, VA	119,749	135	36	114,486	137	37
MACON, GA	118,730	136	37	116,896	135	36
Portsmouth, VA	105,807	153	38	104,577	154	38
Alexandria, VA	104,276	159	39	103,217	160	39
Tallahassee, FL	102,579	166	40	101,482	166	40
Columbia, SC	101,457	169	41	101,202	168	41
Durham, NC	101,242	171	42	100,538	170	42
Roanoke, VA	100,187	175	43	100,220	171	43

Population, Past

The following figures give the population of Georgia at each decade since 1790. Also given are figures showing the percentage increase in population for each decade and the population of Georgia as a percentage of the entire nation's population.

Year	Population	% Increase	% of U.S.
1790	82,548		2.1
1800	162,686	97.1	3.1
1810	252,433	55.2	3.5
1820	340,989	35.1	3.5
1830	516,823	51.6	4.0
1840	691,392	33.8	4.1
1850	906,185	31.1	3.9
1860	1,057,286	16.7	3.4
1870	1,184,109	12.0	3.1
1880	1,542,180	30.2	3.1
1890	1,837,353	19.1	2.9
1900	2,216,331	20.6	2.9
1910	2,609,121	17.7	2.8
1920	2,895,832	11.0	2.7
1930	2,908,506	0.4	2.4
1940	3,123,723	7.4	2.4
1950	3,444,578	10.3	2.3
1960	3,943,116	14.5	2.2
1970	4,589,575	16.4	2.3
1980	5,463,087	19.0	2.3

PUBLIC ASSISTANCE

Medicaid Recipients, Households Participating in the Food Stamp Program, 1985.

County	Medicaid Recipients	Households Participating in the Food Stamp Program	Aid to Families With Dependent Children	Persons Under Age 18 Receiving Aid to Families With Dependent Children
Appling	1,656	746	273	544
Atkinson	893	325	124	223
Bacon	1,365	601	212	405
Baker	498	227	76	155
Baldwin	3,684	1,111	562	1,131
Banks	494	245	55	96
Barrow	1,706	633	187	388
Bartow	2,589	1,124	375	648
Ben Hill	2,276	939	353	734
Berrien	1,259	511	179	369
Bibb	16,837	7,164	3,183	6,189
Bleckley	1,240	450	194	357

County	Medicaid Recipients	Households Participating in the Food Stamp Program	Aid to Families With Dependent Children	Persons Under Age 18 Receiving Aid to Families With Dependent Children
Brantley	722	400	96	191
Brooks	2,492	1,031	370	807
Bryan	1,174	541	184	365
Bulloch	3,679	1,439	700	1,314
Burke	3,724	1,383	697	1,448
Butts	1,600	515	228	443
Calhoun	970	311	108	243
Camden	1,155	636	238	436
Candler	1,301	450	122	274
Carroll	4,233	1,684	598	1,171
Catoosa	1,738	948	288	509
Charlton	803	441	166	304
Chatham	20,998	8,455	4,428	9,061
Chattahoochee	288	212	64	106
Chattooga	1,986	1,046	312	577
Cherokee	1,834	606	185	322
Clarke	5,625	2,178	951	1,931
Clay	836	358	176	310
Clayton	5,296	1,975	860	1,599
Clinch	955	381	156	306
Cobb	6,571	2,476	820	1,465
Coffee	3,338	1,399	493	927
Colquitt	4,316	1,962	763	1,581
Columbia	2,021	707	344	646
Cook	1,373	489	170	369
Coweta	3,818	1,725	704	1,397
Crawford	812	347	144	250
Crisp	3,593	1,561	639	1,392
Dade	868	437	109	186
Dawson	405	188	25	42
Decatur	4,019	1,487	625	1,293
DeKalb	19,577	5,906	3,414	6,519
Dodge	2,451	1,145	353	675
Dooly	1,961	649	301	610
Dougherty	13,583	5,250	2,916	6,185
Douglas	2,146	772	249	492
Early	2,786	1,049	459	953
Echols	241	102	34	64
Effingham	1,417	601	290	555
Elbert	2,210	1,104	398	735
Emanuel	3,512	1,366	481	1,039
Evans	1,247	516	198	369
Fannin	1,267	604	154	271
Fayette	540	205	58	101
Floyd	6,133	2,520	1,032	2,071
Forsyth	1,340	479	118	207
Franklin	1,908	522	168	309
Fulton	66,246	28,225	14,859	29,834
Gilmer	1,412	578	101	188
Glascock	261	99	25	41
Glynn	4,217	2,169	794	1,497
Gordon	1,581	749	187	341
Grady	1,979	966	287	566

County	Medicaid Recipients	Households Participating in the Food Stamp Program	Aid to Families With Dependent Children	Persons Under Age 18 Receiving Aid to Families With Dependent Children
Greene	1,274	542	179	452
Gwinnett	3,181	893	281	498
Habersham	1,592	499	102	179
Hall	4,471	1,721	541	1,008
Hancock	1,762	686	275	532
Haralson	1,667	936	231	400
Harris	1,047	451	150	269
Hart	1,580	732	193	372
Heard	545	282	81	154
Henry	2,278	791	361	681
Houston	4,807	1,807	915	1,693
Irwin	1,157	474	158	341
Jackson	1,620	567	177	311
Jasper	708	437	122	225
Jeff Davis	993	452	135	230
Jefferson	3,469	1,102	570	1,149
Jenkins	1,526	561	203	379
Johnson	1,035	550	154	332
Jones	1,245	450	219	377
Lamar	952	452	178	335
Lanier	823	395	130	262
Laurens	4,952	2,218	803	1,687
Lee	932	384	182	361
Liberty	2,553	1,392	588	1,066
Lincoln	753	327	127	253
Long	461	228	95	174
Lowndes	6,836	2,973	1,257	2,634
Lumpkin	754	329	63	107
Macon	2,622	1,246	468	890
Madison	1,557	594	157	304
Marion	788	419	113	204
McDuffie	2,542	795	423	791
McIntosh	1,051	514	164	304
Meriwether	2,642	913	387	781
Miller	754	358	114	231
Mitchell	3,443	1,413	573	1,286
Monroe	1,344	369	170	304
Montgomery	917	395	105	200
Morgan	1,472	550	195	360
Murray	878	320	85	151
Muscogee	15,533	7,339	3,322	6,381
Newton	3,104	1,309	545	1,102
Oconee	436	176	60	100
Oglethorpe	882	423	157	302
Paulding	1,602	754	193	341
Peach	2,749	1,262	535	1,056
Pickens	724	314	61	105
Pierce	1,096	540	135	243
Pike	706	237	87	169
Polk	3,233	1,239	400	771
Pulaski	1,285	626	211	413
Putnam	1,090	492	208	364
Quitman	431	230	77	142

County	Medicaid Recipients	Households Participating in the Food Stamp Program	Aid to Families With Dependent Children	Persons Under Age 18 Receiving Aid to Families With Dependent Children
Rabun	805	416	64	99
Randolph	1,540	748	253	635
Richmond	18,668	7,168	4,079	8,007
Rockdale	1,370	559	174	342
Schley	424	219	89	155
Screven	2,151	965	382	725
Seminole	1,244	526	217	437
Spalding	4,368	1,701	818	1,534
Stephens	1,728	866	236	450
Stewart	1,124	513	217	404
Sumter	4,216	1,731	811	1,625
Talbot	834	382	148	275
Taliaferro	424	180	62	114
Tattnall	2,579	1,073	386	766
Taylor	1,389	578	274	495
Telfair	1,861	756	267	531
Terrell	1,781	800	303	594
Thomas	4,105	1,631	708	1,386
Tift	3,616	1,536	554	1,148
Toombs	3,645	1,382	491	984
Towns	415	159	20	38
Treutlen	983	440	126	273
Troup	4,686	1,549	692	1,439
Turner	1,510	514	272	631
Twiggs	1,244	488	272	484
Union	838	350	64	109
Upson	2,707	934	515	912
Walker	3,069	1,392	400	718
Walton	2,350	696	302	621
Ware	4,353	1,921	677	1,408
Warren	983	383	181	341
Washington	2,668	1,021	447	824
Wayne	2,725	1,110	414	797
Webster	251	172	56	102
Wheeler	917	369	120	244
White	705	197	24	41
Whitfield	2,863	1,332	309	517
Wilcox	1,185	438	149	305
Wilkes	1,108	512	254	466
Wilkinson	1,034	495	227	440
Worth	2,326	1,158	477	971
Georgia	470,000	192,238	82,358	162,169

RADIO STATIONS

Commercial Radio Stations

Adel
WBIT-TV
Box 508, 31620

WDDQ-FM
P.O. Box 508, 31620
912-896-4571

Albany
WALG-AM
P.O. Box W, 31702
912-436-7233

WGPC-AM/Stereo FM
2011 Gillionville Rd.,
31707
912-883-6500

WJAZ-AM
P.O. Box 505, 31702
912-432-9181

WJIZ-FM
P.O. Box 545, 31702
912-432-7447

WKAK-FM
P.O. Box W, 31702
912-436-9929

WQDE-AM
P.O. Box 1624, 31702
912-436-0544

Alma
WULF-AM
P.O. Box 1987, 31510
912-632-4411

Americus
WADZ-FM
605 McGarrah St., 31709
912-924-1290

WDEC-AM
P.O. Box 1307, 31709
912-924-1290

WISK-AM
P.O. Box 727, 31709
912-924-6500

WPUR-FM
P.O. Box 727, 31709
912-924-6500

Ashburn
WMES-AM
Box 848, 31714
912-567-3355

Athens
WAGQ-Stereo FM
2500 W. Broad St.,
Executive Office Park,
Suite 205, 30606
404-546-7350

WGAU-AM
850 Bobbin Mill Rd.,
30606
404-549-1340

WNGC-FM
850 Bobbin Mill Rd.,
30606
404-549-1340

WRFC-AM
255 S. Milledge Ave.,
30605
404-549-6222

Atlanta
WAEC-AM
1665 Peachtree St., NW,
30309
404-875-7777

WAOK-AM
401 W. Peachtree St.,
NE, Suite 1947, 30365
404-659-1380

WCNN-AM
3954 Peachtree Rd.,
NE, 30319
404-261-6800

WFOX-FM
2000 Riveredge Pkwy.,
Suite 797, 30328
404-953-9369

WGKA-AM
P.O. Box 52128, 30305
404-231-1190

WGST-AM
550 Pharr Rd., 30363
404-231-0920

WIGO-AM
1422 W. Peachtree St.,
NW, 30309
404-892-8000

WKHX-FM
360 Interstate N, Suite
101, 30339
404-955-0101

WKLS-AM/Stereo FM
1800 Century Blvd.,
NE, Suite 1200, 30345
404-325-0960

WPCH-Stereo FM
550 Pharr Rd., NE,
30363
404-261-9500

WPLO-AM
120 Ralph McGill Blvd.,

Suite 1000, 30365
404-898-8900

WQXI-AM/Stereo FM
3340 Peachtree Rd.,
Suite 240, 30026
404-261-2970

WRMM-FM
1459 Peachtree St., 30309
404-892-7766

WSB-AM/Stereo FM
1601 W. Peachtree St.,
NE, 30309
404-897-7000

WTJH-AM
P.O. Box 967, 30364
404-344-2233

WVEE-Stereo FM
120 Ralph McGill Blvd.,
Suite 1000, 30365
404-898-8900

WXLL-AM
P. O. Box 49485, 30359
404-321-1830

WYZE-AM
1111 Broadway, SE,
30312
404-622-4444

WZGC-FM
P.O. Box 54577, 30308
404-881-0093

Augusta
WBBQ-AM
P.O. Box 2066-13, 30913
803-279-6610

WBIA-AM
P.O. Box 1230, 30903
404-724-2421

WGAC-AM
P.O. Box 1131, 30903
404-863-5800

WGUS-AM
P.O. Box 1475, 30903
803-279-1380

WHGI-AM
P.O. Box 669, 30903
404-722-6077

WKZK-AM
2 Milledge Rd., 30904
404-738-9191

349

WRDW-AM
P.O. Box 1405, 30903
404-724-1480

WTHB-AM
P.O. Box 1584, 30903
803-279-2330

WYMX-FM
P.O. Box 669, 30903
404-722-1302

WZZW-FM
P.O. Box 1584, 30903
404-279-2300

Austell
WCKZ-AM
P.O. Box 746, 30001
404-941-0016

Bainbridge
WJAD-FM
P.O. Box 706, 31717
912-246-1650

WMGR-AM
P.O. Box 706, 31717
912-246-1650

WYSE-AM
1317 E. Carter St.,
31717
912-246-9973

Barnesville
WBAF-AM
Rte. 2, Box A, 30204
404-358-1090

Baxley
WUFE-AM
Highway 341 West,
31513
912-367-3000

Blackshear
WBSG-AM
Box 400, 31516

WKUB-FM
P.O. Box 112, 31516
912-449-3391

Blakely
WBBK-AM/FM
P.O. Box 568, 31723
912-723-4311

Blue Ridge
WPPL-FM
Box 938, Highland St.,
30513
404-632-2803

Bremen
WSLE-AM
P.O. Box 397, 30110
404-537-3275

Brunswick
WBGA-AM
801 Mansfield St., 31520
912-265-3870

WGIG-FM
801 Mansfield St., 31520
912-265-3870

WMOG-AM
F. J. Torras Causeway,
31520
912-265-5980

WPIQ-FM
Hwy. 303, Rte. 6, 31520
912-264-3820

WYNR-AM
Hwy. 303, Rte. 6, 31520
912-264-3820

Buford
WDYX-AM
Box 609, 30518
404-945-9953

WGCO-FM
Box 609, 30518
404-945-9953

Cairo
WGRA-AM
U.S. 84 W, 31728
912-377-4392

Calhoun
WEBS-AM
427 S. Wall St., 30701
404-629-2238

WJTH-AM
102 Memorial Rd.,
30701
404-629-6397

Camilla
WCLB-AM
Drawer 113, 31730
912-336-5614

WOFF-FM
P.O. Box 434, 31730
912-336-8767

Canton
WCHK-AM
P.O. Box 231, 30114
404-479-2101

WCHK-FM
P.O. Box 1290, 30114
404-479-2101

Carrollton
WBTR-FM
Bremen Rd., 30117
404-836-0092

WLBB-AM
Bremen Rd., 30117
404-832-7041

WPPI-AM
808 Newman Rd., 30117
404-834-1058

Cartersville
WBHF-AM
West Avenue, 30120
404-382-3000

WYXC-AM
Route 6, N. Tennessee
Rd., 30120
404-382-1270

Cedartown
WGAA-AM
413 Lake View Dr., 30125
404-748-1340

Chatsworth
WQMT-FM
P.O. Box 738, 30705
404-695-6777

Clarkesville
WIAF-AM
109 Washington St., 30523
404-754-6272

350

Claxton
WCLA-AM/FM
316 N. River St., 30417
912-739-3055

Clayton
WGHC-AM
P.O. Box 1149, 30525
404-782-4251

Cleveland
WRWH-AM
Box 181, 30528
404-865-3181

Cochran
WVMG-AM
Industrial Park, 31014
912-934-4548

WVMG-Stereo FM
P.O. Box 570, Industrial
Park, 31014
912-934-4548

Columbus
WCGQ-FM
Box 1537, 31994
404-324-0338

WCLS-AM
P.O. Box 229, 31902
205-298-1580

WDAK-AM
1846 Buena Vista Rd.,
31902
404-322-5447

WEIZ-Stereo FM
P.O. Box 2744, 31902
205-298-1001

WFXE-FM
Box 1998, 31902
404-324-0261

WHYD-AM
1825 Buena Vista Rd.,
31906
404-323-3603

WOKS-AM
P.O. Box 1998, 31902
404-324-0261

WPNX-AM
P.O. Box 687, 31902
404-322-2270

WRCG-AM
P.O. Box 1537, 31902
404-324-0338

WVOC-Stereo FM
P.O. Box 5387, 31906
404-324-2441

Commerce
WJJC-AM
220 Little St., 30529
404-335-3155

Conyers
WCGA-AM
954 S. Main St., 30207
404-483-1000

Cordele
WFAV-FM
P.O. Box 340, 31015

WMJM-AM
20th Ave., E, 31015
912-273-1404

Cornelia
WCON-AM/FM
1 Burrell St., 30531
404-778-2241

Covington
WGFS-AM
P.O. Box 869, 30209
404-786-1430

Cumming
WHNE-AM
Box 609, 30130
404-887-3136

Cuthbert
WCUG-AM
P.O. Box 348, 31740
912-732-3725

Dahlonega
WDGR-AM
P.O. Box 292, 30533
404-864-4477

Dallas
WKRP-AM
362 W. Memorial Dr.,
30132
404-445-1500

Dalton
WBLJ-AM
P.O. Box 809, 30720
404-278-3300

WRCD-AM
P.O. Box 1284, 30720
404-278-5511

WTTI-AM
118 N. Hamilton
St., Dalton Federal
Bldg., 30720
404-226-2700

Dawson
WAZE-FM
Box 390, 31742
912-995-5846

WHIA-AM
110 N. Main St., 31742
912-995-5846

Decatur
WAVO-AM
P.O. Box 111, 30031
404-292-3800

WGUN-AM
215 Church St., 30031
404-373-2521

Donalsonville
WGMK-FM
P.O. Box 236, 31745
912-524-5124

WSEM-AM
Box 87, 31745
912-524-5123

Douglas
WDMG-AM/FM
620 E. Ward St., 31533
912-384-3250

WOKA-AM/FM
Rocky Pond Rd., 31533
912-384-8153

Douglasville
WDGL-AM
8470 Hospital Dr., 30134
404-942-5186

Dublin
WKKZ-FM
Glenwood Ave., 31021
912-272-9270

WMLT-AM
807 Belleview, 31021
912-272-4422

WQZY-FM
P.O. Box 130, 31021
912-272-4422

WXLI-AM
Glenwood Ave., 31021
912-272-9270

Eastman
WUFF-AM
731 College, Box 626,
31023

WUFF-FM
721 College St., 31023
912-374-3437

Eatonton
WXPQ-AM
202A Jefferson St., 31024
404-485-8055

Elberton
WSGC-AM
Jones St., 30635
404-283-1400

WWRK-FM
Jones St., 30635
404-283-1400

Ellijay
WLEJ-AM
P.O. Box 635, 30540
404-276-2016

Fitzgerald
WBHB-AM
601 W. Roanoke Dr., 31750
912-423-2077

Forsyth
WFNE-FM
P.O. Box 693, 31029
912-994-9494

Fort Valley
WXKO-AM
P.O. Box 1150, 31030
912-825-5547

Gainesville
WDUN-AM
1102 Thompson Bridge
Rd., NW, 30501
404-532-9921

WGGA-AM
P.O. Box 1318, 30501
404-532-6211

WLBA-AM
303 Washington St., 30501
404-532-6331

WWID-Stereo FM
1102 Thompson Bridge
Rd., NW, 30501
404-532-9921

Glennville
WKIG-AM/FM
226 E. Bolton St., 30427
912-654-3580

Greensboro
WGRG-FM
P.O. Box 376, 30642
404-453-4140

Greenville
WGRI-AM
P.O. Box 156, 30224

Griffin
WHIE-AM
P.O. Drawer G, 30223

WKEU-AM/FM
1000 Memorial Dr., 30223
404-227-5507

Hartwell
WKLY-AM
Box 666, 30643
404-376-2233

Hawkinsville
WCEH-AM/FM
P.O. Box 489, 31036
912-892-9061

Hazlehurst
WVOH-AM/FM
P.O. Box 757, 31539
912-375-4511

Hinesville
WGML-AM
P.O. Box 15, 31313
912-876-3599

Homerville
WBTY-FM
303 Court St., 31634
912-487-5350

Jackson
WJGA-Stereo FM
P.O. Box 3878, 30233
404-775-3151

Jasper
WYYZ-AM
Hood Rd., 30143
404-692-6446

Jesup
WIFO-Stereo FM
P.O. Box 647, 31545
912-427-3711

WLOP-AM
P.O. Box 647, 31545
912-427-3711

WSOJ-Stereo FM
P.O. Box 251-B, 31545
912-427-2003

LaGrange
WJYA-FM
304 Broome St., 30240
404-883-6420

WLAG-AM
304 Broome St., 30241
404-882-3505

WTRP-AM
806 Franklin Rd., 30241
404-884-8611

WWCG-Stereo FM
P.O. Box 1429, 30241
404-882-3505

LaFayette
WLFA-AM
P.O. Box 746, 30728
404-638-3276

Lawrenceville
WLAW-AM
P.O. Box 33, 30246
404-963-2222

Louisville
WPEH-AM/FM
Box 425, 30434

Lyons
WBBT-AM
389 N. Victory Dr., 30436
912-526-8122

Macon
WAYS-FM
P.O. Box 5008, 31208
912-741-9494

WBML-AM
P.O. Box 6298, 31208
912-743-5453

WDDO-AM
544 Mulberry St., 31202
912-745-3375

WDEN-Stereo FM
173 First St., 31202
912-745-3383

WIBB-AM
P.O. Box 6517, 31213
912-742-2505

WMAZ-AM
P.O. Box 5008, 31213
912-741-9494

WNEX-AM
P.O. Box 6318, 31208
912-745-3301

WPEZ-FM
Box 900, 31202
912-746-6286

WPTC-AM
173 First St., 31202
912-745-3383

WQXM-AM/FM
P.O. Box 356, 31208
912-628-2000

Madison
WYTH-AM
U.S. 441 South, 30650
404-342-1250

Manchester
WUFJ-AM
Main St., 31816

WVFJ-FM
Main St., 31816
404-846-3115

Marietta
WFOM-AM
835 S. Cobb Drive, 30060
404-428-3396

WJYA-AM
P.O. Box 1080, 30061
404-424-1080

McDonough
WZAL-AM
12 N. Cedar St., 30253
407-957-1549

McRae
WDAX-AM/FM
P.O. Box 247, 31055
912-868-5611

Metter
WHCG-FM
S. Broad St., 30439
912-685-2136

WMAC-AM
P.O. Box 238, 30439
912-685-2136

Milledgeville
WKGQ-AM
P.O. Box 832, 31061
912-452-7291

WKZR-FM
1250 W. Charlton St.,
  31061
912-452-0586

WMVG-AM
1250 W. Charlton St.,
  31061
912-452-0586

Millen
WGSR-AM
P.O. Box 869, 30442
912-982-4142

Monroe
WKUN-AM
702 East Spring St., 30655
404-267-6558

Montezuma
WMNZ-AM
Box 511, 31063

Morrow
WSSA-AM
P.O. Box 831, 30260
404-361-8843

Moultrie
WMGA-AM
Box 1380, 31768
912-985-1130

WMTM-AM/Stereo FM
Hwy. 33 SE, 31768
912-985-1300

Nashville
WNGA-AM
Box 645, 31639

Newnan
WNEA-AM
8 Madison St., 30264
404-253-4711

WCOH-AM
154 Boone Dr., 30263
404-253-4636

Ocilla
WSIZ-AM
Hwy. 129 N, 31774
912-468-7429

Perry
WPGA-AM/FM
P.O. Drawer 980, 31069
912-987-2980

Quitman
WSFB-AM
P.O. Box 632, 31643
912-263-4373

Reidsville
WTNL-AM
P.O. Drawer 820, 30453
912-557-6731

Rockmart
WPLK-AM
W. Elm St., 30153
404-684-7848

WZOT-FM
W. Elm St., Box 192,
  30153
404-684-7848

Rome
WIYN-AM
P.O. Box 5226, 30161
404-291-9496

WKCX-FM
710 Turner-McCall Blvd.,
30161
404-291-9705

WLAQ-AM
Box 228, 30161
404-232-7767

WQTU-FM
E. 6th Ave., 30161
404-295-1023

WRGA-AM
E. 6th Ave., 30161
404-291-9742

WROM-AM
710 Turner-McCall Blvd.,
30161
404-291-9766

Rossville
WRIP-AM
203 Alice Rd., 30741
615-867-9898

Royston
WBLW-AM
431 Radio Ranch, 30662
404-245-6101

Sandersville
WSNT-AM/FM
312 Morningside Dr.,
31082
912-552-5182

Savannah
WAEV-FM
P.O. Box 9705, 31412
912-232-0097

WCHY-FM
P.O. Box 1247, 31402
912-964-7794

WEAS-Stereo FM
Box 737, 31404
912-234-7264

WJCL-FM
P.O. Box 13646, 31406
912-925-0022

WKBX-AM
P.O. Box 876, 31402
912-897-1529

WNMT-AM
P.O. Box 7042, 31408
912-964-8124

WSGA-AM
P.O. Box 8247, 31401
912-233-8807

WSGF-FM
Box 876, 31402
912-897-1529

WSOK-AM
24 W. Henry St., 31402
912-232-3322

WWAM Radio
P.O. Box 2026, 31402
912-236-4444

WWJD-AM
P.O. Box 5860, 31414
912-238-0059

WWSA-AM
P.O. Box 1247, 31402
912-964-7794

WZAT-Stereo FM
P.O. Box 8247, 31412
912-233-8807

Smyrna
WYNX-AM
2460-A Atlanta St., SE,
30080
404-436-6171

Soperton
WMPZ-AM/FM
1003 Main St., 30457
912-529-3311

Springfield
WGEC-FM
P.O. Box C, 31329
912-754-6486

Statesboro
WMCD-FM
P.O. Box 958, 30458
912-764-5446

WPTB-AM
Williams Rd., 30458
912-764-6621

WWNS-AM
561 E. Oliff St., 30458
912-764-5446

Summerville
WGTA-AM
State Highway 100, 30747
404-857-2466

Swainsboro
WJAT-AM/Stereo FM
P.O. Box 289, 30401
912-237-2011

WXRS-AM/FM
P.O. Box 1590, 30401
912-237-1590

Sylvania
WSYL-AM
P.O. Box 519, 30467
912-564-7461

Sylvester
WRSG-AM
102 N. Isabella St., 31791
912-776-3421

Tallapoosa
WKNG-AM
P.O. Box 606, 30176
404-574-7655

Thomaston
WSFT-AM
Box 689, 30286
404-647-5421

WTGA-AM/FM
P.O. Box 550, 30286
404-647-7121

Thomasville
WLOR-AM
Tallahassee Hwy., 31792
912-226-7911

WPAX-AM
P.O. Box 129, 31792
912-226-1240

WTUF-FM
Tallahassee Hwy., 31792
912-226-7911

Thomson
WTHO-FM
1530 Hickory Hill Dr.,
30824
404-595-5122

WTWA-AM
1530 Hickory Hill Dr.,
30824
404-595-1561

Tifton
WCUP-FM
P.O. Box 1466, 31794
912-382-1100

WTIF-AM
P.O. Box 968, 31794
912-382-1340

WWGS-AM
1434 N. Tift Ave., 31794
912-382-1234

Toccoa
WLET-AM/FM
423 Prather Bridge Rd.,
30577
404-886-2191

WNEG-AM
100 Boulevard, 30577
404-886-3131

Valdosta
WAFT-FM
94 W. Morven Rd., 31603
912-244-5180

WGAF-AM
P.O. Box 100, 31601
912-242-5520

WGOV-AM
P.O. Box 1207, 31601
912-242-4513

WJEM-AM
P.O. Box 368, 31603
912-242-1565

WLGA-FM
P.O. Box 1327, 31603
912-244-8642

WVLD-AM
P.O. Box 1529, 31601
912-242-4821

Vidalia
WTCQ-Stereo FM
Hwy. 280 W, 30474
912-537-9202

WVOP-AM
Hwy. 280 W, 30474
912-537-9202

Vienna
WWWN-AM
Hwy. 41 N, 31092
912-273-1550

Warner Robins
WCOP-AM
P.O. Box 916, 31093
912-929-0523

WRBN-AM/FM
707 Elberta Dr., 31093
912-922-2222

Washington
WLOV-AM/FM
P.O. Box 400, 30673
404-678-2125

Waycross
WACL-AM/FM
Memorial Dr., 31502
912-283-4660

WAYX-AM
P.O. Box 1989, 31501

WQCW-FM
1600 Carswell Ave., 31501
912-283-1230

Waynesboro
WBRO-AM
McBean Rd., 30830
404-554-2139

WWGA-FM
P.O. Box 815, 30830
404-554-3942

West Point
WCJM-FM
705 W. 4th Ave., 31833
404-645-1310

WZZZ-AM
705 W. 4th Ave., 31833
404-645-1310

Winder
WIMO-AM
Old Monroe Hwy., 30680
404-867-9158

Wrens
WRNZ-FM
Drawer 869, 30833
404-547-2596

Public/Educational Radio Stations

Athens
WUOG-Stereo FM
P.O. Box 2065, 30602
404-542-7100

Atlanta
WABE-FM
740 Bismark Rd., NE,
30324
404-873-4477

WCLK-FM
111 James P. Brawley Dr.,
SW, 30314
404-522-8776

WRAS-FM
Georgia State University
Plaza, 30303
404-658-2240

WREK-Stereo FM
P.O. Box 32743, 30332
404-894-2468

WRFG-FM
P.O. Box 5332, 30307
404-523-3471

Augusta
WACG-FM

355

Augusta College, 30910
404-737-1661

WLPE-FM
3213 Huxley Dr., 30909
404-736-9568

Carrollton
WWGC-FM
P.O. Box 10014, 30118
404-834-1355

Cartersville
WCCV-FM
P.O. Box 921, 30120
404-382-8333

Cochran
WDCO-FM
1540 Stewart Ave., SW,
30310
404-656-5961

Columbus
WFRC-FM
1010 7th Place, Phenix
City, Ala., 36867
205-291-0399

WTJB-FM
University Lane, Troy,
Ala., 36082
205-566-5814

Cumming
WWEV-FM
P.O. Box 1511, 30130
404-889-0095

Fort Valley
WHGW-FM
2711 Chelsea Terrace,
Baltimore, Maryland
21217

Gainesville
WBCX-FM
Brenau College, 30501
404-534-6187

La Grange
WOAK-FM
1291 Hamilton Rd., 30241
404-884-2950

Marietta
WGHR-FM
1112 Clay St., 30060
404-424-7354

McDonough
WMVV-FM
19 Griffin St., 30253
404-957-2211

Milledgeville
WXGC-FM
P.O. Box 3146, 31061
912-453-4101

Savannah
WHCJ-FM
P.O. Box 20484, 31404
912-356-2399

WSVH-FM
409 E. Liberty St., 31401
912-238-0911

WYFS-FM
1300 Battlefield Blvd.,
Chesapeake, VA, 23320

Statesboro
WVGS-FM
P.O. Box 11619, 30460
912-681-5507

Tifton
WABR-FM
Abraham Baldwin
Agriculture College,
31794
912-386-2005

Toccoa Falls
WRAF-FM
P.O. Box 800128, Toccoa
Falls College, 30598
404-886-1912

Valdosta
WVVS-FM
P.O. Box 142, 31698
912-333-5661

Warm Springs
WJSP-FM
1540 Stewart Ave., SW,
30310
404-656-5961

Waycross
WXGA-FM
1540 Stewart Ave., SW,
Atlanta, 30310
404-656-7483

RAILROADS

Listed below are the railroads which operate within the State of Georgia.
The three-letter abbreviation after some lines indicates the name of the
larger system of which that line is a part.

Alabama Great Southern Railroad Company
    (SOU)
AMTRAK service
Atlanta and West Point Rail Road Company
    (SBD)
Central of Georgia Railroad Company (SOU)

356

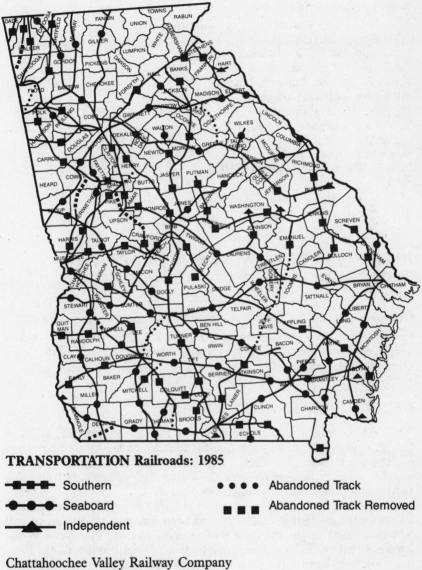

TRANSPORTATION Railroads: 1985

▪▪▪▪ Southern

●●●● Seaboard

▲ Independent

●●●● Abandoned Track

▪ ▪ ▪ Abandoned Track Removed

Chattahoochee Valley Railway Company
Chattahoochee Industrial Railroad
Colonel's Island Railroad Company
Gainesville Midland Railroad Company (SBD)
Georgia Northern Railway Company (SOU)
Georgia Southern and Florida Railway Company
  (SOU)

Hartwell Railway Company
Live Oak, Perry and South Georgia Railway
   Company (SOU)
Louisville and Wadley Railway Company
Sandersville Railroad Company
Seaboard System Railroad, Inc.
St. Marys Railroad Company
Southern Railway Company
Tennessee, Alabama & Georgia Railway
   Company (SOU)
Valdosta Southern Railroad
Western Railway of Alabama (SBD)

SOU = Southern Railway Company
SBD = Seaboard System Railroad, Inc.

RELIGIOUS BODIES WITH HEADQUARTERS IN GEORGIA

The following religious denominations maintain their headquarters in Georgia. Number of churches and membership figures are as follows:

Presbyterian: Presbyterian Church in America. Organized 1973; *address* 1852 Century Place, Atlanta 30345; 404-320-3366; churches, 951; missions, 91; membership, 197,575.

REVOLUTIONARY WAR

The first battle of the Revolutionary War took place April 19, 1775, in Concord, Massachusetts, but the difficulties which led up to the war began ten years earlier. The French and Indian Wars had created such massive debts that Parliament imposed the Stamp Act as a means of recovering some of the funds, but the colonists objected.

Georgia was the last to join the other colonies in protest for several reasons. A substantial sum of money had been invested by Parliament and private citizens to get the colony of Georgia started. The fact that the governor Parliament had appointed, Sir James Wright, was well-liked, capable and very loyal to the King was another factor. The strong family ties of Georgians with the mother country were of great influence also.

The Stamp Act, which was passed by Parliament March 22, 1765, met with much opposition. William Pitt, Earl of Chatham and Edmund Burke (for whom Chatham and Burke counties were named), spoke out in Parliament on behalf of the colonists. Benjamin Franklin, hired by Georgia in 1768 to act as its agent in England, also spoke out against the British taxes.

The Liberty Boys, as the local organization of the Sons of Liberty were called, were determined that no stamps would be sold in Georgia. Their behavior made Governor Wright very nervous.

The Liberty Boys made their feelings known in October of 1765 when the celebration of the King's birthday usually took place by hanging in effigy dummies of the governor and the stampseller, who had not yet arrived. They paraded about Savannah shouting, "Liberty, Property, and NO STAMPS!"

Only seventy stamps were sold in all of Georgia, and they were for clearance papers for a ship with perishable cargo. Some South Carolina citizens became so angry that the stamps were bought that they threatened to burn the ship.

Georgia's first, and for a long time only, newspaper, the *Georgia Gazette*, was forced to suspend its publication in May, 1765, after publishing for just two years. The editor, James Johnston, cited the Stamp Act as the reason because it had made publication too expensive.

The paper was again published in May, 1766, when it was reported that the Stamp Act would be repealed. This event took place July 16, 1766, when Parliament voted to repeal it by a vote of 275 to 176.

In 1767 taxes were again imposed by Parliament for paint, lead, glass, paper and tea. The colonists rebelled by boycotting British exports, until finally all taxes were repealed except tea (three cents per pound).

The Boston Tea Party, which took place as a result of the tea tax, brought the war nearer. The British closed the port at Boston, and said it would remain closed until the tea was paid for; but the tax was never paid. As a result, food supplies from England were not permitted shipment to the colonies.

When the First Continental Congress was held in September, 1774, the Tories, loyal to the King, were influential enough to prevent Georgia from sending any delegates to it. But when the call for a Second Continental Congress was sounded, Georgia held its first Provincial Congress in January, 1775, and elected three delegates to go to Philadelphia. These delegates refused to attend because they were convinced that all of Georgia was not fairly represented.

The Puritans in Georgia were concerned because their kinsmen in Boston were hungry; so they sent their own delegate, Dr. Lyman Hall. He carried food and money on the journey, and sat in on the deliberations of the Second Continental Congress, but did not attempt to vote.

George Washington was named commander-in-chief of America's raw troops by Congress. In the colonies there were about 282,000 men capable of serving in the troops, but at any one time he never had more than 25,000 of them on active duty.

Fourteen months after the Boston Tea Party, April 19, 1775, the first shooting war took place at Lexington, about sixteen miles outside Boston. Georgia organized a Council of Safety, June 22, 1775, two months after the war started in Lexington. The Council called for a meeting of the Second Provincial Congress.

The Second Provincial Congress met in July, 1775, and at this meeting Georgia seceded from England. Also, five delegates were chosen to attend the Second Continental Congress: Archibald Bulloch, Lyman Hall, John Houstoun, Noble Wymberly Jones, and Reverend Joachim Zubly. In February, 1776, the delegates to the Continental Congress were Bulloch, Hall, and Houstoun, and George Walton and Button Gwinnett, who replaced Jones and Zubly. Hall, Walton, and Gwinnett were the representatives from Georgia who signed the Declaration of Independence.

The war took place in the north for the first three and a half years. In November, 1778, the British failed in their effort to move the war south. Savannah was captured, however, in December, 1778, and held by the British for three and one-half years.

In January, 1779, Sunbury and Fort Morris were captured and in February Augusta fell under siege. The Americans were successful in defeating the British near Kettle Creek, about eight miles from Washington, Georgia, in February, 1779; but the British overcame the Americans at Brier Creek a month later.

The British held the colony of Georgia during the year of 1780. Ogeechee Ferry was the site of the last Revolutionary battle fought on Georgian soil.

Parliament negotiated for peace in February, 1782; and in July, 1782, the British surrendered Savannah. The Treaty of Paris, signed in November, 1782, ended the war. England, France, and America ratified a more detailed treaty, and it was signed September, 1783.

In 1786, a group representing several states met in Annapolis, which suggested that the Continental Congress should meet to work out problems and strengthen the Articles of the Confederation. When the men did meet, they drew up what is probably the most powerful political document in the world, the Constitution of the United States of America.

RIVERS

A —**Conasauga River** rises in Fannin County. About 60 miles long, it merges with Coosawattee and Oostanaula rivers.

B —**Coosawattee River** flows from Carters Lake to Oostanaula River. About 25 miles long.

C —**Ellijay River** rises in Gilmer County, empties into Carters Lake. About 20 miles long.

D —**Tallulah River** rises in Rabun County near the Georgia-North Carolina boundary line. About 20 miles long, it junctions with the Chattooga River to form the Tugaloo River.

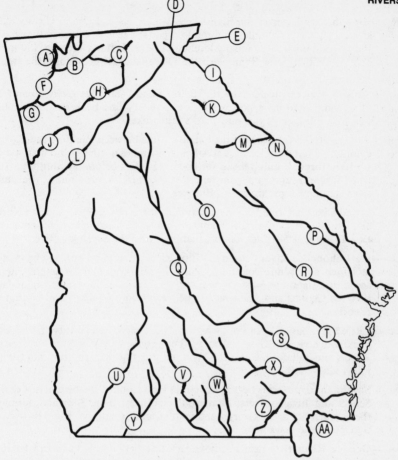

E —**Chattooga River** rises near the state boundary line between Georgia and North and South Carolina, and empties into the Tugaloo River. About 25 miles long, it forms the uppermost portion of the boundary line between Georgia and South Carolina and is one of the headwaters of the Savannah River.

F —**Oostanaula River** rises in the Blue Ridge Mountains in Gordon County, zig zags southwesterly for 47 miles to junction with the Etowah River at Rome, Floyd County, to form the Coosa River.

G —**Coosa River** is formed at Rome by the junction of the Etowah and Oostanaula rivers, flows westward about 30 miles through a wide valley between high ridges before it reaches the Alabama line. Junctions with the Tallapoosa River in Elmore County, Alabama, for a total length of about 250 miles.

H —**Etowah River** rises in the Blue Ridge Mountains in Lumpin County, falls steeply for about 60 miles in a random pattern that is south southeast and then west southwest, gradually leveling in slope. It flows a total of 150 miles before junctioning at Rome with the Oostanaula River to form the Coosa River.

I —**Tugaloo River** is formed by the Tallulah and Chattooga rivers. About 25 miles long, it forms a portion of the boundary line between Georgia and South Carolina. Empties into Clarks Hill Lake.

J —**Tallapoosa River** rises near the boundary line between Paulding and Carroll counties (about 40 miles west of Atlanta). It arches northerly and then southwesterly through hilly terrain for about 45 miles before crossing into Alabama where it junctions with the Coosa River in Elmore County, Alabama, after traveling approximately 210 miles.

K —**Broad River** is formed by the junction of the Hudson River and the North and Middle Forks, near the boundary line of Franklin and Madison counties. It is about 50 miles long and empties into the Savannah River.

L —**Chattahoochee River** rises in the Blue Ridge Mountains near the boundary of Union and White counties, about 410 miles long, flows southwesterly across the state into West Point Lake, then southerly, forming a boundary between Georgia and Alabama and between Georgia and a small portion of Florida.

M —**Little River** has a North Fork which rises in Oglethorpe County and a South Fork which rises in Greene County. They converge at the boundary line of Wilkes and Taliaferro counties. About 40 miles long, it empties into Clarks Hill Lake.

N —**Savannah River** forms near Hartwell, in Hart County, by the junction of the Seneca and Tugaloo rivers. Flows south southeast about 300 miles, forming the boundary between Georgia and South Carolina, emptying into the Atlantic Ocean near Savannah.

O —**Oconee River** rises near the boundary line between Jackson and Barrow counties, flows southeasterly about 150 miles. It joins the Ocmulgee River to form the Altamaha River near Hazlehurst.

P —**Ogeechee River** rises in Greene County with North and South Forks that converge in Taliaferro County. About 245 miles long, it empties into Ossabaw Sound 15 miles south of Savannah.

Q —**Ocmulgee River** begins within Jackson Lake where the South, Yellow, and Alcovy rivers join together. It flows steeply over rocky shoals through a generally narrow valley until it reaches Macon, then has a more gentle slope the remainder of its 150 (approximate) miles. It joins the Oconee River near Hazlehurst to form the Altamaha River. The confluence is known locally as The Forks.

R —**Canoochee River** originates in Emanuel County. About 85 miles long, it flows somewhat parallel to the Ogeechee River until it joins the Ogeechee about 35 miles above its mouth.

S —**Big Satilla River** rises in Jeff Davis County, flows southeasterly for about 60 miles until it joins the Satilla River in Brantley County.

T —**Altamaha River** is formed by the Ocmulgee and Oconee rivers, near Hazlehurst, flows southeasterly about 90 miles, empties into Altamaha Sound.

U —**Flint River** rises in Clayton on the southeastern edge of Atlanta, flows in a wide arc that bends southeastward and then southwestward for 349 miles to its junction with the Chattahoochee River.

V —**Withlacoochee River** rises near Tifton, in Tift County, flows southeasterly about 86 miles to join the Suwannee River at Ellaville, Florida.

W —**Alapaha River** forms near the boundary line between Turner and Irwin counties, flows south southeast about 134 miles to its confluence with the Suwannee River in Florida.

X —**Satilla River** rises near the boundary line of Ben Hill and Irwin counties, twists and turns for 260 miles through southeastern Georgia before emptying into the Atlantic Ocean through St. Andrews Sound.

Y —**Ochlockonee River** rises in the southeastern portion of Worth County, is about 190 miles long, flows south southeasterly into Florida and empties into the Gulf of Mexico.

Z —**Suwannee River** forms near Fargo from numerous channels at the Okefenokee Swamp. It is 240 miles long, flows southerly 46 miles, then loops westward and joins its principal tributaries, the Alapaha, Withlacoochee, and Santa Fe rivers, continues southward across Florida and empties into the Gulf of Mexico. It is the river of Stephen Foster's famous song, "The Old Folks at Home."

AA—**St. Mary's River** rises in the Okefenokee Swamp in Charlton and Ware counties, twists and winds around the southernmost tip of Georgia forming part of the boundary line between Georgia and Florida. About 125 miles long, it empties into the Atlantic Ocean through Cumberland Sound.

SENATORS, UNITED STATES

Wyche Fowler, Jr. (D)
Washington, D.C. 20510
Telephone 202-224-3643

Sam Nunn (D)
Washington, D.C. 20510
Telephone: 202-224-3521

SHERMAN'S MARCH

General William Tecumseh Sherman's march, which ravaged the countryside, is shown on this map. Sherman's troops—63,000 men—left Atlanta on November 16, 1864, after setting fire to it, and headed to the sea, following the rail line. They traveled over a swath of 30 miles on either side of the rail line, pilfering the land. Their aim was to destroy General Lee's food supply and to break the will of the poeple. They took food, livestock, vehicles of various kinds, and other objects from plantations and small farms along the way. Among the cities and towns they passed through were Milledgeville, Sandersville, Louisville, and Millen. They reached Savannah, their destination, on December 21.

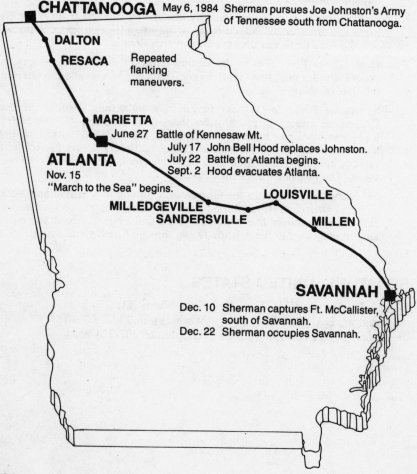

CHATTANOOGA   May 6, 1984   Sherman pursues Joe Johnston's Army
of Tennessee south from Chattanooga.

DALTON

RESACA   Repeated
flanking
maneuvers.

MARIETTA
June 27   Battle of Kennesaw Mt.
July 17   John Bell Hood replaces Johnston.
ATLANTA   July 22   Battle for Atlanta begins.
Nov. 15   Sept. 2   Hood evacuates Atlanta.
"March to the Sea" begins.
LOUISVILLE
MILLEDGEVILLE
SANDERSVILLE   MILLEN

SAVANNAH
Dec. 10   Sherman captures Ft. McCallister,
south of Savannah.
Dec. 22   Sherman occupies Savannah.

SPORTS

Georgia Sports Hall of Fame

The Georgia Prep Sports Hall of Fame was established in 1956. In 1963 it was reorganized and merged with the State of Georgia Athletic Hall of Fame to encompass the prep, college, professional and amateur fields. This organization was the result of significant efforts on the part of Coach Dwight Keith, Dean George Griffin and many others dedicated to honoring those individuals and teams which through their athletic endeavors have brought honor and fame to the state of Georgia.

The 1978 Georgia Legislature, through a bill sponsored by House Speaker Tom Murphy and supported by Lt. Governor Zell Miller, created the Georgia Sports Hall of Fame. The bill was later signed into law by Governor George Busbee. One of the first official acts of the Board of the newly created Georgia Sports Hall of Fame was to pass a resolution declaring that all previous inductees of the above Halls of Fame would be members of the Georgia Sports Hall of Fame.

The stated purpose of the Georgia Sports Hall of Fame is as follows:

To honor those who, by their outstanding achievement of service, have made lasting contributions to the cause of sports in Georgia, the nation, and the entire world.

To preserve records of teams and individuals who deserve to be included in Georgia's sports history.

To maintain and improve the high ideals and traditions of sports as a positive influence on the youth of our state as a potent factor in our American way of life.

To emphasize and encourage sports participation on a broad basis and and on a high plane of sportsmanship, under competent leadership and in a wholesome environment.

To inspire our Georgia youth to be physically fit and to strive for the greatest achievement within the bounds of their physical and mental endowment—and, in their athletic and community activities, reflect credit on sports and on the State of Georgia as good citizens.

To serve sports at the "grass roots" level where the groundwork of our great American sports program is laid—and here build the foundation of strong character, good citizenship and a brave, strong Georgia.

1956
Selby H. Buck
Clint Castleberry
Joe H. Jenkins
Vernon "Catfish" Smith
Claude T. "Gabe"
  Tolbert
John Varnedoe

1957
John R. Carson
R. L. "Shorty" Doyal
Harold E. McNabb
Eric P. Staples
John G. "Stumpy"
  Thomason

1958
Joseph W. Bean
W. O. Cheney
Quinton Lumpkin
George M. Phillips
Jack Roberts
Sidney Scarborough

1959
Ray Beck
Sam Burke
H. D. Butler
George Mathews
Mark Smith
A. Drane Watson

1960
Wright Bazemore
Dwight Keith, Sr.
Henry I. Langston
Julian H. "Joe" Pittard
James Skipworth, Jr.
Thomas J. Slate

1961
George Gardner
Thomas E. Greene
Oliver Hunnicutt
Thomas H. Paris
Alfred W. Scott
Kimsey R. Stewart

1962
D. B. Carroll
Vassa "Gus" Cate
Sam Glassman, Sr.
William Henderson
Jim Nolan
George H. O'Kelly

1964
William A. Alexander
Lucius "Luke" Appling
Tyrus Raymond Cobb
Robert G. Hooks
Robert T. Jones, Jr.
Robert McWhorter
Albert H. Staton
Bobby Walthour, Sr.

1965
Robert L. "Bobby"
  Dodd
Bryan M. "Bitsy" Grant
William L. "Young"
  Stribling
Charley Trippi

1966
Frank B. Anderson, Sr.
Wallace "Wally" Butts
Ivy M. "Chick" Shiver
Louise Suggs

1967
John Heisman
Charles Morgan
Nap Rucker
Frank Sinkwich
Forrest "Spec" Towns

1969
Jim Cavan
Spurgeon Chandler
Allen Ralph "Buck"
  Flowers
Joseph T. "Phoney"
  Smith

1971
Frank Broyles
Earl Mann

Harry Mehre
Herman J. Stegeman

1972
Joel H. Eaves
Joe Guyon
Carlton Lewis
Tom Nash, Jr.
Alline Banks Sprouse

1973
Weems O. Baskin
Wayman O. Creel
Howell T. Hollis
John R. Mize

1974
Paul Anderson
James "Doc" Harper
Dorothy Kirby
Martin W. "Marty"
  Marion
Jim Parker
Everett Strupper

1975
Henry L. "Hank"
  Aaron
William F. "Bill"
  Fincher
Fred Missildine
Larry Morris
Doug Sanders
Cecil H. Travis

1976
James P. "Buck" Cheves
Theo "Tiger" Flowers
Dan Magill
Virlyn Moore, Jr.
Wyomia Tyus
Perrin Walker
Whitlow Wyatt
Charles Yates

1977
David "Red" Barron
Sterling A. Dupree
Sam J. "Sambo" Elliott

Elmer B. Morrow
Henry R. "Peter" Pund
Francis A. Tarkenton
Rudolph P. "Rudy"
   York

1978
Vince Dooley
J. Timothy "Tim" Flock
Alexa Stirling Fraser
James E. "Jimmy" Orr
Nolen Richardson
Harold Sargent
Doug Wycott

1979
Arnold Blum
Alice Coachman Davis
Charles Grisham
Frank "Hop" Owens
William A. "Billy"
   Paschal
Johnny Rauch
B. L. "Crook" Smith
George "Tweedy"
   Stallings
Sidney "Beau Jack"
   Walker

1980
Tommy Aaron
Maxie Baughan
Edmund R. "Zeke"
   Bratkowski
Edith McGuire Duvall
John "Whack" Hyder
H. Boyd McWhorter
Ralph Metcalfe
Garland Pinholster
Sherrod Smith

1981
Thomas William Barnes
Marion Campbell
William C. Hartman, Jr.
Leonard Moore Hauss
Herbert Maffett
George A. Morris, Jr.

1982
James C. Bagby, Sr.
Lew Cordell
Edward B. Hamm
Milton Leathers
George Poschner

1983
Robert T. "Bobby"
   Davis
Mary Louise Fowler
James T. "Jim" Hearn
Tommy Nobis
Reid Patterson
James B. "J. B."
   Scearce
Mildred McDaniel
   Singleton

1984
Joseph J. Bennett
Jimmy Carnes
George C. Griffin
Roger Kaiser
Oscar Bane Keeler
Melvyn Pender, Jr.
Williams Thomas
   Stanfill

1985
John Donaldson
Leonidas Epps

William L. Goodloe, Jr.
Watts Gunn
J. C. "Jakes" Hines
Fred W. Hooper
Phil Niekro
William L. Shaw

1986
Morris M. Bryan, Jr.
Bobby Lee Bryant
Walter Frazier, Jr.
Joe Gerson
Billy Lothridge
Anthony "Zippy"
   Morocco
Martha Hudson
   Pennyman
Jacob E. "Jake" Scott,
   III

1987
Harley Bowers
Patrick F. Dye
Joseph A. "Cy" Grant
Isabelle D. Holston
Thomas L. Lyons
Johnny Moon
Hugh Royer, Jr.
Erskine Russell

1988
Edgar Chandler
Douglas L. "Buddy"
   Fowlkes
Leon Hardeman
Graham Hixon
Jim Luck
Amater Z. Traylor
LeRoy T. Walker
Rayfield Wright

Baseball

Atlanta is the only city in Georgia with a major league baseball team, the *Atlanta Braves*. The Braves play their home games in Atlanta Stadium, which has a capacity of 52,934 people. The fence distances at Atlanta Stadium are: left, 330 feet; center, 402 feet; and right, 330 feet.

The Atlanta Braves finished the 1987 season in 5th place in the Western

Division of the National League, with 69 wins and 92 losses for an average of .429.

Bob Horner of the Braves tied a major league record in 1986 when he hit four home runs in a single game.

Dale Murphy, a Brave, led the National League in runs, with 118, and in home runs, with 37, in 1985.

On April 8, 1974, Hank Aaron, of the Braves, broke Babe Ruth's career home run record by hitting his 715th homer over the left-center field fence at Atlanta.

For ticket or game information pertaining to the Atlanta Braves, call 404-577-9100.

Two other cities in Georgia have AA baseball clubs, associated with the Southern Association: *Savannah Braves*, affiliated with the Atlanta Braves; and *Columbus Astros*, affiliated with *Houston Astros*.

Columbus had a 1987 record of 67 wins and 76 losses for an average of .469.

Savannah had a 1987 record of 69 wins and 69 losses for an average of .500.

The Columbus Astros made baseball history in 1981 when its game with the Nashville Sounds became the first AA performance ever broadcast over nationwide television.

Basketball

There is one professional basketball team in Georgia, the *Atlanta Hawks*. The Hawks are in the Central Division of the Eastern Conference of the National Basketball Association (NBA).

The Hawks finished the 1987–1988 season in 2nd place in their division with 50 wins, 32 loses, and a .610 winning percentage.

For ticket or game information on the Atlanta Hawks, call 404-681-3600.

In Southeastern Conference (SEC) competition among college teams, the University of Georgia finished its 1987-1988 season with an average of .559, with 19 wins and 15 losses for all the games played in the season. In conference play their average was .444 with 8 wins and 10 losses.

Georgia Tech plays in the Atlantic Coast Conference (ACC). They finished the 1987-1988 season with an average of .700, 21 wins, and 9 losses for all games played. Their conference average was .571 with 8 wins and 6 losses.

Football

Atlanta is the only city in Georgia with a professional football team. The *Atlanta Falcons* Club is a member of the National Football League (NFL).

368

The Falcons' record in 1987 was 3 wins, 12 losses, for a percentage of 200. For ticket or game information about the Falcons, call 404-588-1111.

In Southeastern Conference (SEC) competition among college teams, the University of Georgia traditionally ranks high. The Bulldogs' 1987 season resulted in 4 wins and 2 losses within the SEC and 8 wins and 3 losses overall. The University of Georgia defeated Arkansas 20–17 in the Liberty Bowl. Georgia Tech is a member of the Atlantic Coast Conference (ACC). For the 1987 regular season, they had 0 wins, 6 losses, for a percentage of .000 in conference games. For all their games they won 2, lost 9, for a percentage of .182.

Georgia Football's Major Bowl Games

Rose Bowl—Pasadena, California
1929 Georgia Tech 8, California 7
1943 Georgia 9, UCLA 0

Orange Bowl—Miami, Florida
1940 Georgia Tech 21, Missouri 7
1942 Georgia 40, Texas Christian 26
1945 Tulsa 26, Georgia Tech 12
1948 Georgia Tech 20, Kansas 14
1949 Texas 41, Georgia 28
1952 Georgia Tech 17, Baylor 14
1960 Georgia 14, Missouri 0
1967 Florida 27, Georgia Tech 12

Sugar Bowl—New Orleans, Louisiana
1944 Georgia Tech 20, Tulsa 18
1947 Georgia 20, North Carolina 10
1953 Georgia Tech 24, Mississippi 7
1954 Georgia Tech 42, West Virginia 19
1956 Georgia Tech 7, Pittsburgh, 0
1969 Arkansas 16, Georgia Tech 2
1977 Pittsburgh 27, Georgia 3
1981 Georgia 17, Notre Dame 10
1982 Pittsburgh 24, Georgia 20
1983 Penn State 27, Georgia 23

Cotton Bowl—Dallas, Texas
1943 Texas 14, Georgia Tech 7
1955 Georgia Tech 14, Arkansas 6
1967 Georgia 24, Southern Methodist 9
1976 Arkansas 31, Georgia 10
1984 Georgia 10, Texas 9

Sun Bowl—Tempe, Arizona
1965 Georgia 7, Texas Tech 0
1970 Nebraska 45, Georgia 6
1971 Georgia Tech 17, Texas Tech 9

Gator Bowl—Jacksonville, Florida
1947 Maryland 20, Georgia 20
1956 Georgia Tech 21, Pittsburgh 14
1959 Arkansas 14, Georgia Tech 7
1961 Penn State 30, Georgia Tech 15
1965 Georgia Tech 31, Texas Tech 21
1971 Georgia 7, North Carolina 3

Astro-Bluebonnet Bowl—Houston, Texas
1962 Missouri 14, Georgia Tech 10
1978 Stanford 25, Georgia 22

Liberty Bowl—Memphis, Tennessee
1967 N.C. State 14, Georgia 7
1972 Georgia Tech 31, Iowa State 30
1987 Georgia 20, Arkansas 17

Peach Bowl—Atlanta, Georgia
1971 Mississippi 41, Georgia Tech 18
1973 Georgia 17, Maryland 16
1978 Purdue 41, Georgia Tech 21

All-American Bowl—Birmingham, Alabama
1985 Georgia Tech 17, Michigan State 14

Interesting Football Facts

The University of Georgia football team was the National Champion in 1980.

Georgia was SEC champion in 1942, tied with Tennessee in 1946, 1948, 1959, tied with Alabama in 1966, 1968, 1976, 1980, 1981, and 1982.

Georgia Tech was SEC champion in 1939 (tied with Tennessee), 1943–1944, tied with Tennessee in 1951, and 1952.

The University of Georgia team was undefeated during regular season play in 1980 and 1982.

Georgia Tech has had three undefeated seasons: 1917, 1928, and 1952.

The University of Georgia has furnished two Heisman Trophy winners: Frank Sinkwich in 1942 and Herschel Walker in 1982.

Georgia Tech holds the all-time scoring record for a single game against Cumberland College in 1916: 222-0.

The University of Georgia's stadium is named Sanford Stadium. It holds 82,122 people and is located in Athens.

Georgia Tech plays its home games at Grant Field in Atlanta; capacity 58,121.

Georgia Tech is the only school to have 3 of its former coaches inducted into the Georgia Hall of Fame after winning 100 games each: William A. Alexander, Robert L. "Bobby" Dodd, and John Heisman.

Public Golf Courses

There are over 110 public golf courses in Georgia. These courses and their locations, along with the number of holes and par of each, are given in the table below:

Albany
Metro Golf Course; Ga. 91 N.; 9 holes; par 35.
Turner Field Golf Course; Turner Field Rd.; 9 holes; par 36.

Americus
Brickyard Plantation Golf Course; 7 mi. East on U.S. 280; 9 holes; par 35.

Ashburn
Wanne Lake Country Club; Ga. 112; 9 holes; par 36.

Athens
Creekwood Country Club; Kathwood Dr.; 9 holes; par 34.
University Golf Course; Milledge Extension; 18 holes; par 73.

Atlanta
Adams Park Golf Course (City Course); 2300 Wilson Dr., SW; 18 holes; par 72.
Bobby Jones Golf Course; 384 Woodward Way, NW; 18 holes; par 71.
Brown's Mill Golf Course; 430 Cleveland Ave., SE; 18 holes; par 72.
Candler Park Golf Course (City); 585 Candler Park Dr., NE; 9 holes; par 32.
North·Fulton Golf Course; 216 W. Wieuca Rd., NE; 18 holes; par 71.
Piedmont Park Golf Course; Piedmont Park/10th St., NE; 9 holes; par 33.
Sugar Creek Golf Course; 2706 Bouldercrest Rd., SE; 18 holes; par 72.

Augusta
Augusta Golf Club; Highland Ave.; 18 holes; par 71.
Forest Hill Golf Club; Comfort Rd.; 18 holes; par 72.

Austell
Dogwood Golf and Country Club; 4207 Flint Hills Rd.; 18 holes; par 72.
Lithia Springs Golf Course; West Bankhead Hwy.; 9 holes; par 34.

Avondale
Avondale Golf Club; 30 Covington Rd.; 9 holes; par 35.

Avondale Estates
Forest Hills Golf Club; 205 Clarendon Ave.; 9 holes; par 34.

Bainbridge
Industrial Park Golf; U.S. 27 N./Ind. Air Park; 9 holes; par 35.

Barnesville
Barnesville Golf Course; College Dr.; 9 holes; par 36.

Baxley
Appling County Country Club; U.S. 1 South; 9 holes; par 36.

Blairsville
Butternut Creek Golf Course; U.S. 19; 9 holes; par 32.

Bremen
East Maple Lakes Golf Course; Cashtown Rd.; 9 holes; par 36.

Brunswick
Glynco Golf Course; Ga. 303, off U.S. 17 N.; 9 holes; par 36.

Buena Vista
Cedar Creek Golf and Country Club; Just off Ga. 137 N.; 9 holes; par 36.

Buford
Pine Isle Golf Course; Lake Lanier Islands; 18 holes; par 72.

Carrolton
Goldmine Golf Club; R. 3 off Bonner Goldmine Rd.; 9 holes; par 36.

Cartersville
Green Valley Greens; Exit 125 off I-75, Rudy York Rd.; 9 holes; par 36.
Royal Oaks; Exit 124 off I-75, Dallas Hwy.; 9 holes; par 36.

Cedartown
Cedar Valley Country Club; U.S. 27 South; 9 holes; par 36.

Clarksville
Heritage Golf Course; Stonepile Rd. off Ga. 197; 9 holes; par 36.

Clayton
Rabun County Country Club; Old U.S. 441; 9 holes; par 36.

Cleveland
Skitt Mountain Golf Course; Ga. 254; 18 holes; par 72.

College Park
Gordon Morris Memorial Golf Course; 3711 Fairway Dr.; 9 holes; par 36.

Columbus
Bull Creek Municipal Golf Course; 7333 Lynch Rd.; 18 holes; par 72.
Victory Drive Golf Course; 603 Lumpkin Rd.; 9 holes; par 27.

Commerce
Commerce Golf and Country Club; Hwy. 15; 9 holes; par 36.

Conyers
Fieldstone Golf and Country Club; 2720 Salem Rd.; 18 holes; par 72.
Highland Golf Club; 2271 Flat Shoals Rd.; 18 holes; par 72.
Honey Creek Golf and Country Club; 635 Clubhouse Dr.; 18 holes; par 72.

Covington
Newton Country Golf Course; Brown Bridge Rd.; 18 holes; par 72.

Dallas
Dallas Country Club Estates; Hwy. 92 South to Nebo Rd.; 9 holes; par 36.

Dalton
Tunnel Hill; Exit 137 off I-75, Hwy. 41 North; 9 holes; par 36.

Decatur
Clifton Springs Par 3 Golf Course; 2340 Clifton Springs Rd.; 9 holes; par 27.

Demorest
Piedmont College Golf Course; Demorest/Mt. Airy Rd.; 9 holes; par 36.

Douglas
South Georgia College Golf Course; South Georgia College Campus; 9 holes; par 35.

Dublin
Riverview Park; Off Ga. 19 S.; inside Dublin city limits; 18 holes; par 72.

Folkston
Folkston Golf and Country Club; Okefenokee Dr., North; 9 holes; par 35.

Forsyth
Forsyth Golf Club; Country Club Dr.; 9 holes; par 36.

Gainesville
Chattahoochee Golf Club; Tommy Aaron Dr.; 18 holes; par 72.

Griffin
Griffin Municipal Golf Course; Country Club Dr.; 18 holes; par 72.

Gay
Beaver Lake Golf and Country Club; Old Ga. 85 (5 mi. N. of Gay); 18 holes; par 72.

Haddock
Jonesco Golf Course; Hwy. 22. 4 mi. E. of Gray; 9 holes; par 36.

Hartwell
Hartwell Golf Course; U.S. 29 South; 18 holes; par 72.

Jackson
Deer Trail Golf Course, Biles Rd.; 9 holes; par 36.

Jakin
Green Valley Golf and Recreation Center, U.S. 84 (6 mi. W. of Donalsonville); 9 holes; par 36.

Jasper
Bent Creek; East of Jasper; 18 holes; par 72.
Arrowhead; Ga. 5; 9 holes; par 36.

Jekyll
Jekyll Island Golf Courses:
Indian Mound; 322 Capt. Wylly Rd.; 18 holes; par 72.
Oceanside; Beachview Dr.; 9 holes; par 36.
Oleander; 322 Capt. Wylly Rd.; 18 holes; par 72.
Pine Lakes; 322 Capt. Wylly Rd.; 18 holes; par 72.

Jonesboro
Country Greens Golf Course; 9350 Thomas Rd.; 18 holes; par 71.
Flint Acres Golf Course; 360 Hewell Rd.; 27 holes; par 35/35/36.

LaFayette
Municipal Golf Course; 638 S. Main Street; 9

holes; par 36.

LaGrange
American Legion; 9 holes; par 35.
Highland Country Club; 18 holes; par 72.

Lake Park
Francis Lake Golf Course; Exit 2, I-75 N.; 18 holes; par 72.

Lawrenceville
Windy Hills Country Club; Camp Perrin Rd.; 9 holes; par 36.

Lindale
Lin Valley Country Club; Eden Valley Rd.; 9 holes; par 36.

Lithonia
Idlewood Golf Course; 6465 Browns Mill Rd.; 9 holes; par 72.
Mystery Valley Golf Course; 694 Shadow Rock Dr.; 18 holes; par 72.

Lula/Homer
Pine Hills Golf Course; Lula/Homer Rd.-Ga. 51; 9 holes; par 72.

Loganville
Overlook Golf Club; Sharon Rd.; 18 holes; par 72.

Macon
Bowden; Hwy. 49 at Miller Field Rd., N. of Macon; 18 holes; par 70.

Manchester
Pebblebrook Golf Club; State Rd. 85; 9 holes; par 36.

Marietta
Par 56 Golf Course; 1471 Cobb Pkwy.; 18 holes; par 56.
Westwood Golf Club; 2250 Callaway Rd., SW; 18 holes; par 71.

McRae
Little Ocmulgee State Park; 441, 2 mi. N. of McRae; 18 holes; par 72.

Milledgeville
Little Fishing Creek; Hwy. 22 West; 18 holes; par 72.

Millen
Magnolia Country Club; Waynesboro Rd.; 9 holes; par 36.

Monroe
Monroe Golf and Country Club; Jersey Rd.; 18 holes; par 72.

Pine Mountain
Garden View (Callaway Gardens); U.S. 27; 18 holes; par 70.
Lake View (Callaway Gardens); U.S. 27; 18 holes; par 72.
Mountain View (Callaway Gardens); U.S. 27; 18 holes; par 72.

Skyview (Callaway Gardens); U.S. 27; 9 holes; par 31.

Rockmart
Goodyear Golf Course; Goodyear Ave.; 9 holes; par 36.
Prospect Valley Golf Course; Prospect Rd.; 9 holes; par 36.

Royston
Victoria Bryant State Park; 9 holes; par 36.

Rutledge
Hard Labor Creek State Park; Hwy. 24; 18 holes; par 72.

St. Marys
St. Marys Country Club; St. Marys Rd. off I-95; 9 holes; par 36.

Savannah
Bacon Park Golf Course; Skidaway; 18 holes; par 71.
Mary Calder Golf Course; St. Marys Rd. off I-95; 9 holes; par 35.

Senoia
Brown Bell Golf Course; Hwy. 16 between Newnan and Senoia; 9 holes; par 36.

Stone Mountain
Stone Mountain Park Golf Course; Stone Mountain Park; 18 holes; par 72.

Swainsboro
Swainsboro Golf and Country Club; Gum Log St.; 9 holes; par 36.

Sylvania
Brier Creek Country Club; Hwy. 301 N.; 9 holes; par 36.

Tallapoosa
Talley Mountain Golf Course; Hwy. 78; 9 holes; par 36.

Thomasville
Glen Arven Country Club; Old U.S. 19; 18 holes; par 72.
Country Oaks Golf Course; Ga. 122 E.; 9 holes; par 35.

Thunderbolt
Bonaventure Golf Club; 295 Bonaventure Rd.; 9 holes; par three course.

Toccoa
Toccoa Golf Club, Inc.; Black Mountain Rd.; 9 holes; par 72.

Trenton
Big Sandy Golf Course; Hwy. 136 West to 301 South; 9 holes; par 36.

Union Point
Greene County Country Club; U.S. 278; 9 holes; par 36.

Valdosta
Valdosta Country Club; Country Club Dr.; 36 holes.

Varnell
Nob North; Exit 135 off I-75; or Ga. 71; 18 holes; par 72.

Washington
Washington-Wilkes Country Club; U.S. 78; 9 holes; par 36.

Winder
Crossed Arrows; Hwy. 29; 18 holes; par 72.

Wrens
Four Seasons Country Club; Hwy. 80; 9 holes; par 36.

STATE FORESTS

There are only two state forests which are owned and managed by the Georgia Forestry Commission.

- **Dixon Memorial State Forest**—35,789 acres located in Ware and Brantley Counties.
- **Baldwin State Forest**—2,702 acres located in Baldwin and Wilkinson Counties.

Two other forests, the **Paulding Forest** and the **Dawson Forest** are owned by the city of Atlanta, but managed by the GFC. There is also the **B. F. Grant Memorial Forest, Hardeman Forest,** and **Whitehall Forest** that are owned and managed by the University of Georgia. The **Rock Eagle Forest** is operated by the Extension Service.

STATE GOVERNMENT

State Officers

Governor
Joe Frank Harris

Lieutenant Governor
Zell Miller

Secretary of State
Max Cleland

Attorney General
Michael J. Bowers

Commissioner of Agriculture
Tommy Irvin

Commissioner of Insurance
Warren D. Evans

State School Superintendent
Dr. Werner Rogers

Commissioner of Labor
Joe D. Tanner

Addresses and telephone numbers listed under **STATE DEPARTMENTS.**

State Departments

Administrative Services, Department of
Suite 1520, West Tower
200 Piedmont Avenue, Atlanta 30334
404-656-5514
Commissioner of Administrative Services, Larry L. Clark

Agriculture, State Department of
Agriculture Building
404-656-3600
Commissioner, Thomas T. Irvin, Room 204

Audits, State Department of
270 Washington Street, Room 214
404-656-2174
State Auditor, G. W. Hogan

Banking and Finance, Department of
2990 Brandywine Road, Suite 200
Atlanta, 30341-5565
404-393-7330
Commissioner, Edward D. Dunn

Building Authority, Georgia
1 Martin Luther King Dr., SW
404-656-3253
Director of Administration, Steve Polk

Community Affairs, State Department of
1200 Equitable Bldg., 100 Peachtree St.
404-656-3836
Commissioner, Jim Higdon

Commissioner of Insurance, Office of
Seventh Floor, West Tower, Floyd Bldg.
2 Martin Luther King Dr., SE
404-656-2056
Commissioner, Warren D. Evans

Corrections, Department of
Floyd Veterans Memorial Bldg.
East Tower, Room 756
2 Martin Luther King Dr., SE
Atlanta 30334
404-656-4593
Commissioner, David C. Evans

Courts, Administrative Office of the
Suite 550, 244 Washington Street
Atlanta, 30334
404-656-5171
Director, Robert L. Doss, Jr.

Court of Appeals of Georgia, Office of
Judicial Building, 4th Floor
Telephone: 404-656-3450

Chief Judge A. W. Birdsong, Jr.
Legal Assistant Henry R. Thomas
(For list of other judges see **COURTS**.)

Criminal Justice Coordinating Council, Office of the Governor
Balcony Level—East Tower
205 Butler St. SE
Atlanta 30334
404-656-1721
Director, William D. Kelley, Jr.

Defense, Department of
P.O. Box 17965, Atlanta, 30316
404-624-6000
The Adjutant General & Director, Georgia Emergency Management Agency, Maj. Gen. Joseph W. Griffin

Education, State Department of
Twin Towers East, Suite 2066
404-656-2800
State Superintendent of Schools, Dr. Werner Rogers

Employees' Retirement System of Georgia
Two Northside 75, Atlanta, 30318
404-352-6400
Board of Trustees, Joe Edwards, Ph.D., William E. Strickland, Robert T. Willis

Ethics Commission, State
2082 East Exchange Pl., Suite 235
Tucker 30084
404-493-5795
Chairman, J. Thomas Vance

Forestry Commission, State
Central Office: P.O. Box 819
Macon, 31298-4599
912-744-3211
Director and Executive Secretary,
John W. Mixon

General Assembly, Offices of
State Capitol, 3rd Floor
Senate:
404-656-5030
President, Zell Miller

House of Representatives:
404-656-5020
Speaker, Thomas B. Murphy

Legislative Counsel:
404-656-5000
Sewell R. Brumby

Legislative Fiscal Officer (Acting):
404-656-5054
Paul Lynch

Legislative Budget Analyst:
404-656-5050
John N. (Pete) Hackney

Governor, Office of
State Capitol, Rooms 201–203
404-656-1776
Governor, Joe Frank Harris

Human Resources, Department of
47 Trinity Ave., SW
404-656-5680
Commissioner, James G. Ledbetter,
Ph.D.

Industry and Trade, Department of
230 Peachtree Street, NW
Atlanta, 30303
404-656-3545
Commissioner, George Berry

Investigation, Georgia Bureau of
3121 Panthersville Road,
Decatur, 30034
404-244-2535
Director, J. R. Hamrick

Judicial Administration

District 1: 912-651-2040
Administrative Judge

James E. Findley, Reidsville
District Court Administrator
Daniel E. DeLoach, Jr., Savannah

District 2: 912-333-5266
Administrative Judge
A. Wallace Cato, Bainbridge
District Court Administrator
John Cowart, Valdosta

District 3: 912-751-6207
Administrative Judge
Walker P. Johnson, Jr., Macon
District Court Administrator
David L. Ratley, Macon

District 4: 404-371-4901
Administrative Judge
Curtis V. Tillman, Decatur
District Court Administrator
Richard F. Jugar, Decatur

District 5: 404-656-5358
Administrative Judge
Joel J. Fryer, Atlanta
District Court Administrator
John T. Shope, Atlanta

District 6: 404-228-7430
Administrative Judge
Andrew J. Whalen, Jr., Griffin
District Court Administrator
Fred Roney, Griffin

District 7: 404-382-5374
Administrative Judge
Arthur W. Fudger, Buchanan
District Court Administrator
William Martin, Cartersville

District 8: 912-526-6116
Administrative Judge
Hugh Lawson, Hawkinsville
District Court Administrator
Jack L. Bean, Lyons

District 9: 404-535-5730
Administrative Judge
Frank C. Mills, III, Canton
District Court Adminstrator
Art O'Neill, Gainesville

District 10: 404-721-3256
Administrative Judge
William M. Fleming, Jr., Augusta

District Court Administrator
Tom Gunnels, Augusta

Juvenile Court Judges, Council of
244 Washington St., Suite 550,
Atlanta, 30334
404-656-6411
Executive Director, J. Chris Perrin

Labor, State Department of
148 International Blvd.
Atlanta 30354
404-656-3011
Commissioner, Joe D. Tanner

Law, Department of
Judicial Building, Room 132
404-656-3300
Attorney General, Michael J. Bowers

Library, State
Judicial Building, Room 301
404-656-3468
State Librarian, Mrs. Carroll T.
Parker

Lieutenant Governor, Office of
State Capitol, Room 240
404-656-5030
Lieutenant Governor, Zell Miller

Medical Assistance, Department of
Floyd Veterans Memorial Building
West Tower, 2 Martin Luther King,
Jr., Drive, SE Atlanta, 30334
404-656-4479
Commissioner, Aaron J. Johnson

**Merit System of Personnel
Administration, State**
200 Piedmont Avenue, West Tower
404-656-2705
Commissioner, Charles E. Storm

Natural Resources, Department of
205 Butler St., East Tower
404-656-3500
Commissioner J. Leonard Ledbetter

Pardons & Paroles, State Board of
Floyd Veterans Memorial Building
Fifth Floor, East
2 Martin Luther King, Jr., Drive, SE
Atlanta, 30334
404-656-5651

Chairman, Wayne Snow, Jr.

Planning and Budget, Office of
Trinity-Washington Building,
6th Floor
270 Washington St., SW
Atlanta 30334
404-656-3820
Director, Clark T. Stevens

**Prosecuting Attorneys' Council of
Georgia**
3951 Snapfinger Pkwy.,
Decatur, 30035
404-289-6278
Director, Joseph L. Chambers

Public Safety, Department of
959 E. Confederate Ave., SE
(P.O. Box 1456), Atlanta, 30371
404-624-7710
Commissioner, State Patrol,
Col. Curtis D. Earp, Jr.

**Public Service Commission, Office
of**
244 Washington St., Room 162
404-656-4501
Chairman, Gary B. Andrews

Regents, Board of
244 Washington St., SW, Room 468
404-656-2200
Chancellor, H. Dean Propst

Revenue, State Department of
270 Washington St., SW, Room 410
404-656-4015
Commissioner, Marcus E. Collins, Sr.

Secretary of State, Office of
State Capitol, Room 214
404-656-2881
Secretary of State, Max Cleland

**Soil and Water Conservation
Committee, Georgia**
624 South Milledge Avenue
Athens, 30603
404-542-3065
Executive Director, F. Graham
Liles, Jr.

Student Finance Committee
2082 East Exchange Place, Suite 200

377

Tucker 30084
404-493-5402
Executive Director, Stephen H. Dougherty

Supreme Court of Georgia, Office of
244 Washington Street, SW
404-656-3470
Chief Justice Thomas O. Marshall
(For a complete list of justices, see
COURTS.)

Teachers' Retirement System of Georgia
Two Northside 75, Suite 400
Atlanta, 30381
404-352-6500
Executive Secretary-Treasurer, Gerald S. Gilbert

Transportation, Department of
2 Capitol Square
404-656-5206
Commissioner, Hal Rives

Veterans Service, State Department of
Floyd Veterans Memorial Building, Suite E-970, Atlanta, 30334
404-656-2300
Commissioner, Pete Wheeler

Workers' Compensation, State Board of
Suite 1000, South Tower, One CNN Center
Atlanta, 30303-2705
404-656-3875
Chairman, James W. Oxendine

STATE PARKS AND HISTORIC SITES

Map Key	County	Park or Site	Address, Zip	Telephone	Activities, Facilities and Rentals[1]
1	Barrow	Fort Yargo, Will-A-Way,	Winder 30680 Winder 30680 (reserved for handicapped)	404-867-3489 404-867-5313	TT,DS,S,B,E,C C,S,B,E,M,TT,DS
2	Bartow	Red Top Mountain	Cartersville 30120	404-974-5182	TT,DS,C,S,B, E,CS
3	Bartow	Etowah Mounds	Route 2, Cartersville 30120	404-382-2704	M
4	Bryan	Ft. McAllister Historic Site	Rt. 2, Box 394-A, Richmond Hill 31324	912-727-2339	M,TT,DS,B,F
5	Butts	Indian Springs	Indian Springs 30231	404-775-7241	TT,DS,C,S,B,E,M
6	Camden	Crooked River	St. Mary's 31558	912-882-5256	TT,DS,C,S,B,F
7	Emanuel	George L. Smith, II	P.O. Box 57, Twin City 30471	912-763-2759	E,TT,DS,B
8	Carroll	John Tanner	354 Tanners Bch. Rd., Carrollton 30117	404-832-7545	TT,DS,C,B, E,CS
9	Charlton	Stephen C. Foster	Fargo 31631	912-637-5274	TT,DS,C,B,E,CS
10	Chatham	Skidaway Island	Savannah 31406	912-356-2523	TT,DS,S,F
11	Chatham	Wormsloe	7501 Skidaway Road, Savannah 31406	912-352-2548	M
12	Chattooga	James H. Floyd	Route 1, Summerville 30747	404-857-5211	TT,DS,B,F
13	Clay	George T. Bagby	Rt. 661, Fort Gaines 31751	912-768-2660	TT,DS,C,B
14	Coffee	General Coffee	Route 2, Box 83, Nicholls 31554	912-384-7082	TT,DS,S,F
15	Columbia	Mistletoe	Route 1, Appling 30802	404-541-0321	TT,DS,C,S,B,F
16	Colquitt	Reed Bingham	Rt. 2, Box 394B-1, Adel 31620	912-896-3551	TT,DS,S,B,F
16	Cook	Reed Bingham	Rt. 2, Box 394B-1, Adel 31620	912-896-3551	TT,DS,S,B,F

Map Key	County	Park or Site	Address, Zip	Telephone	Activities, Facilities and Rentals[1]
17	Crisp	Georgia Veterans	Route 3, Cordele 31015	912-273-2190	TT,DS,C,S,B,F,M
18	Dade	Cloudland Canyon	Rising Fawn 30738	404-657-4050	TT,DS,C,S,CS
19	Dawson	Amicalola Falls	Star Route, Dawsonville 30534	404-265-2885	TT,DS,C,F
20	Douglas	Sweetwater Creek Conservation Park	P.O. Box 816, Lithia Springs 30057	404-944-1700	B,F,CS
21	Early	Kolomoki Mounds	Route 1, Blakely 31723	912-723-5296	TT,DS,S,B,F,M
22	Elbert	Bobby Brown	Route 4, Box 232, Elberton 30635	404-283-3313	TT,DS,S,B,F
23	Franklin	Victoria Bryant	Route 1, Box 257, Royston 30662	404-245-6270	TT,DS,S,F
24	Franklin	Tugaloo	Route 1, Lavonia 30553	404-356-4362	TT,DS,C,S,B,F
25	Glynn	Hofwyl Plantation Historic Site	Route 2, Box 83, Brunswick 31520	912-264-9263	M
26	Gordon	New Echota	Route 3, Calhoun 30701	404-629-8151	M
27	Harris	F. D. Roosevelt	Box 749, Pine Mountain 31822	404-663-4858	TT,DS,C,S,B, F
28	Hart	Hart	1515 Hart Park Road, Hartwell 30643	404-376-8756	TT,DS,C,S,B, F,CS
29	Henry	Panola Mountain Conservation Park	2600 Highway 155 Southwest, Stockbridge 30281	404-474-2914	M
30	Jenkins	Magnolia Springs	Route 5, Box 488, Millen 30442	912-982-1660	TT,DS,C,S,F,B
31	Jones	Jarrell Plantation	Route 1, Juliette 31046	912-986-5172	M
32	Liberty	Sunbury	Route 1, Box 236, Midway 31320	912-856-2256	M
33	Lincoln	Elijah Clark	Route 4, Box 293, Lincolnton 30817	404-359-3458	TT,DS,C,S,B, M,F
34	Lumpkin	Dahlonega Gold Museum	Public Square, Box 2042, Dahlonega 30533	404-864-2257	M
35	Madison	Watson Mill Bridge	Rt. 1, Box 190, Comer 30629	404-783-5349	TT,DS,F,B
36	McIntosh	Ft. King George	P.O. Box 711, Darien 31305	912-437-4770	M
37	Meriwether	FDR Little White House Historic Site	P.O. Drawer 68, Warm Springs 31830	404-655-3511	M
38	Monroe	High Falls	Route 5, Box 108, Jackson 30233	912-994-5080	TT,DS,S,B,F
39	Morgan	Hard Labor Creek	Rutledge 30663	404-557-2863	TT,DS,C,S,F, CS,B
40	Murray	Fort Mountain	Route 7, Box 1-K, Chatsworth 30705	404-695-2621	TT,DS,C,S,F,B
41	Murray	Vann House	Route 7, Box 235, Chatsworth 30705	404-695-2598	M
42	Oglethorpe	Watson Mill Bridge	Route 1, Box 190, Comer 30629	404-783-5349	TT,DS,F,B
43	Rabun	Black Rock Mountain	Mountain City 30562	404-746-2141	TT,DS,C, CS,F
44	Rabun	Moccasin Creek	Route 1, Lake Burton 30523	404-947-3194	TT,DS,B,F

379

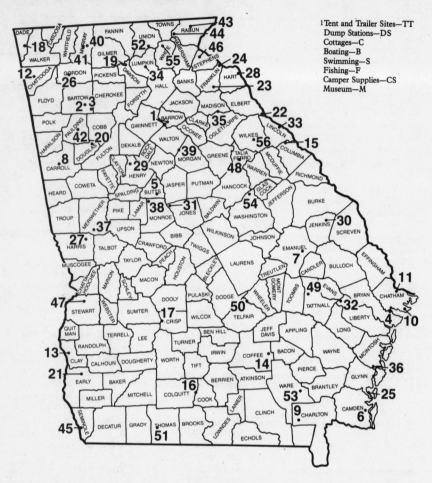

1 Tent and Trailer Sites—TT
Dump Stations—DS
Cottages—C
Boating—B
Swimming—S
Fishing—F
Camper Supplies—CS
Museum—M

Map Key	County	Park or Site	Address, Zip	Telephone	Activities, Facilities and Rentals[1]
45	Seminole	Seminole	Route 2, Donalsonville 31745	912-861-3137	TT,DS,C,S, B,F
46	Stephens	Traveler's Rest	Route 3, Toccoa 30577	404-886-2256	M
42	Stewart	Florence Marina	Rt. 1, Box 36, Omaha 31821	912-838-4244	TT,DS,C,S,B, F,CS
47	Stewart	Providence Canyon	Route 1, Box 158, Lumpkin 31815	912-838-6202	M
48	Taliaferro	A. H. Stephens Memorial	Box 235, Crawfordsville 30631	404-456-2221	M
		A. H. Stephens State Park	Box 235, Crawfordville 30631		TT,S,F,CS,M
49	Tattnall	Gordonia-Altamaha	P.O. Box 1047, Reidsville 30453	912-557-6444	TT,S,B,F

Map Key	County	Park or Site	Address, Zip	Telephone	Activities, Facilities and Rentals[1]
50	Telfair	Little Ocmulgee	Box 97, McRae 31055	912-868-2832	TT,DS,C,S,B,F
51	Thomas	Lapham-Patterson House	626 N. Dawson Street, Thomasville 31792	912-226-0405	M
52	Union	Vogel	Route 1, Box 1230, Blairsville 30512	404-745-2628	TT,DS,C,S,F,CS
39	Walton	Hard Labor Creek	Rutledge 30663	404-557-2863	TT,DS,C,S,B,F,CS
53	Ware	Laura S. Walker	Route 6, Box 205, Waycross 31501	912-283-4424	TT,DS,S,B,F
54	Washington	Hamburg	Route 1, Box 233, Mitchell 30820	912-552-2393	TT,DS,B,F,CS,M
50	Wheeler	Little Ocmulgee	McRae 31055	912-868-2832	TT,DS,C,S,B,F
55	White	Unicoi Unicoi Lodge/Conference Center	P.O. Box 849, Helen 30545	404-878-2201	TT,DS,C,S,F,CS
56	Wilkes	Robert Toombs House	P.O. Box 605, Washington 30673	404-678-2226	M

STATE PATROL PHONE NUMBERS

City	County	Phone Number	City	County	Phone Number
Albany	Dougherty	404-430-4248	LaFayette	Walker	404-638-1400
Americus	Sumter	912-928-1200	LaGrange	Troup	404-882-8104
Athens	Clarke	404-542-8660	Lawrenceville	Gwinnett	404-995-5710
Atlanta	Fulton/DeKalb	404-656-3514	Madison	Morgan	404-342-1515
Blue Ridge	Fannin	404-632-2215	Manchester	Meriwether	404-846-3106
Brunswick	Glynn	912-265-6050	Marietta	Cobb	404-429-0045
Calhoun	Gordon	404-629-8694	Milledgeville	Baldwin	912-453-4717
Canton	Cherokee	404-479-2155	Newnan	Coweta	404-253-3212
Cartersville	Bartow	404-382-3232	Perry	Houston	912-987-1100
Cedartown	Polk	404-748-3334	Reidsville	Tattnall	912-557-4378
Conyers	Rockdale	404-922-4634	Rome	Floyd	404-295-6002
Cordele	Crisp	912-273-3131	Savannah	Chatham	912-232-6414
Cuthbert	Randolph	912-732-2167	Statesboro	Bulloch	912-764-5654
Dalton	Whitfield	404-272-2200	Swainsboro	Emanuel	912-237-7818
Donalsonville	Seminole	912-524-2177	Sylvania	Screven	912-564-2018
Douglas	Coffee	912-384-1600	Thomaston	Upson	404-647-7153
Dublin	Laurens	912-272-2300	Thomasville	Thomas	912-228-2300
Forsyth	Monroe	912-994-5159	Thomson	McDuffie	404-595-2622
Gainesville	Hall	404-535-5428	Tifton	Tift	912-386-3333
Griffin	Spalding	404-227-2121	Toccoa	Stephens	404-886-4949
Hapeville	Fulton	404-363-7670	Valdosta	Lowndes	912-333-5215
Helena	Telfair	912-868-6441	Villa Rica	Carroll	404-459-3661
Hinesville	Liberty	912-876-2141	Washington	Wilkes	404-678-3232
Jekyll Island	Glynn	912-635-2303	Waycross	Ware	912-283-6622

To inquire about Georgia road conditions, call:
Weekdays 8:15 to 4:45   404-656-5882
Nights and Weekends   404-656-5267

STATE SYMBOLS

The following list and illustrations present the state symbols, nickname, seal and flag.

State Flower
Cherokee Rose

State Bird
Brown Thrasher

State Tree
Live Oak

State Fish
Largemouth Bass

State Song
"Georgia on My Mind"

State Motto
"Wisdom, Justice, and Moderation"

State Nickname
"The Empire State of the South"

State Seal

State Flag

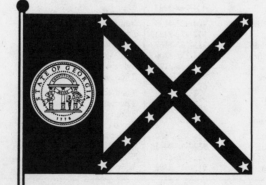

TAXES

Sales Tax

Georgia has a three percent state sales tax. The maximum conbined state and local rate is five percent.

There is a 1% local transit tax (M) in two counties that started April 1, 1972. The local option 1% sales tax (L) that originated on April 1, 1976 is in effect in 145 counties. A Special 1% tax (S) was started on July 1, 1985 and now has 75 counties participating. The tax applies in certain cities only.

The first two local taxes are permanent and would take a public majority vote to remove. The new special 1% sales tax is voted in to finance specified capital projects and has automatic "sun-set" provisions that remove this tax in a period of five years or less.

County	% Rate on 4-1-86	County	% Rate on 4-1-86	County	% Rate on 4-1-86
Appling (L)	4	Columbia (L)	4	Haralson (L)	4
Atkinson (LS)	5	Cook (L)	4	Harris (L)	4
Bacon (L)	4	Coweta (LS)	5	Hart (S)	4
Baker (L)	4	Crawford (LS)	5	Heard (LS)	5
Baldwin (L)	4	Crisp (LS)	5	Henry (L)	4
Banks (LS)	5			Houston (L)	4
Barrow (LS)	5	Dade (LS)	5	Irwin (LS)	5
Bartow (L)	4	Dawson (LS)	5	Jackson (LS)	5
Ben Hill (L)	4	Decatur (L)	4	Jasper (L)	4
Berrien (LS)	5	DeKalb (M)	4	Jeff Davis (LS)	5
		Dodge (LS)	5		
Bibb (L)	4	Dooley (LS)	5	Jefferson (LS)	5
Bleckley (L)	4	Dougherty (LS)	5	Jenkins (L)	4
Brantley (L)	4	Douglas (LS)	5	Johnson (L)	4
Brooks (LS)	5	Early (L)	4	Jones (L)	4
Bryan (LS)	5	Echols	3	Lamar (L)	4
Bulloch (LS)	5			Lanier (LS)	5
Burke (L)	4	Effingham (L)	4	Laurens (L)	4
Butts (LS)	5	Elbert (L)	4	Lee (L)	4
Calhoun (L)	4	Emanuel (LS)	5	Liberty (L)	4
Camden (LS)	5	Evans (LS)	5	Lincoln (L)	4
		Fannin (L)	4		
Candler (L)	4	Fayette (L)	4	Long	3
Carroll (LS)	5	Floyd (L)	4	Lowndes (LS)	5
Catoosa (L)	4	Forsyth (LS)	5	Lumpkin (L)	4
Charlton (L)	4	Franklin (L)	4	Macon (LS)	5
Chatham (LS)	5	Fulton (LM)	5	Madison (LS)	5
Chattahoochee (L)	4			Marion (L)	4
Chattooga (LS)	5	Gilmer (L)	4	McDuffie (LS)	5
Cherokee (S)	4	Glascock (L)	4	McIntosh (LS)	5
Clarke (LS)	5	Glynn (LS)	5	Meriwether (L)	4
Clay (LS)	5	Gordon (LS)	5	Miller (L)	4
		Grady (L)	4		
Clayton	3	Greene (LS)	5	Mitchell (LS)	5
Clinch (L)	4	Gwinnett (S)	4	Monroe (L)	4
Cobb (S)	4	Habersham (L)	4	Montgomery (L)	4
Coffee (LS)	5	Hall (L)	4	Morgan (LS)	5
Colquitt (LS)	5	Hancock (LS)	5	Murray (L)	4

County	% Rate on 4-1-86	County	% Rate on 4-1-86	County	% Rate on 4-1-86
Muscogee (L)	4	Screven (LS)	5	Turner (LS)	5
Newton (LS)	5	Seminole (L)	4	Twiggs (LS)	5
Oconee (LS)	5	Spalding (L)	4	Union (LS)	5
Oglethorpe (S)	4	Stephens (LS)	5	Upson (L)	4
Paulding (LS)	5	Stewart (L)	4	Walker (LS)	5
		Sumter (L)	4	Walton (LS)	5
Peach (LS)	5	Talbot (L)	4	Ware (LS)	5
Pickens (L)	4			Warren (LS)	5
Pierce (L)	4	Taliaferro (S)	4	Washington (L)	4
Pike (L)	4	Tattnall (LS)	5		
Polk (L)	4	Taylor (LS)	5	Wayne (L)	4
Pulaski (L)	4	Telfair (L)	4	Webster	3
Putnam (L)	4	Terrell (L)	4	Wheeler (L)	4
Quitman (L)	4	Thomas (S)	4	White (L)	4
Rabun (L)	4	Tift (L)	4	Whitfield (L)	4
Randolph (L)	4	Toombs (L)	4	Wilcox (LS)	5
		Towns (LS)	5	Wilkes (S)	4
Richmond (LS)	5	Treutlen (L)	4	Wilkinson (LS)	5
Rockdale (S)	4			Worth (LS)	5
Schley (LS)	5	Troup (L)	4		

Georgia Personal Income Tax: 1984—1985

	Adjusted Gross Income Less Deficit		Net Taxable Income	Amount of Tax Liability	
County	Total	Average Per Return		Total	Average Per Return
Appling	85,850,604	17,146	54,054,815	2,522,743	510
Atkinson	27,593,357	14,078	16,226,139	722,147	368
Bacon	47,033,307	15,767	28,714,669	1,307,866	438
Baker	14,989,512	14,638	8,972,893	408,179	399
Baldwin	252,657,742	20,480	167,626,449	8,338,966	676
Banks	43,591,835	16,506	27,162,535	1,243,966	471
Barrow	181,281,686	18,768	117,357,167	6,074,788	629
Bartow	352,046,502	19,552	232,113,024	11,428,795	635
Ben Hill	99,864,885	17,936	64,948,858	3,186,624	572
Berrien	73,518,229	16,987	47,259,745	2,217,184	512
Bibb	1,268,250,976	22,351	854,405,274	43,812,057	772
Bleckley	67,890,175	18,339	43,861,938	2,135,923	577
Brantley	46,024,230	16,496	28,909,939	1,335,722	479
Brooks	53,697,097	14,274	32,306,088	1,460,633	388
Bryan	75,752,503	19,862	49,682,911	2,419,387	634
Bulloch	204,047,555	18,876	130,120,393	6,263,480	579
Burke	113,266,728	17,936	74,624,830	3,538,138	560
Butts	87,373,818	17,846	55,407,827	2,629,951	537
Calhoun	27,473,957	15,038	16,976,848	786,263	430
Camden	103,599,725	19,150	70,430,752	3,356,525	620
Candler	36,125,077	16,309	22,254,943	1,023,532	462
Carroll	456,788,916	19,194	295,359,237	14,416,988	606
Catoosa	223,688,301	20,573	149,116,290	7,215,891	664

County	Adjusted Gross Income Less Deficit		Net Taxable Income	Amount of Tax Liability	
	Total	Average Per Return		Total	Average Per Return
Charlton	34,299,651	17,635	21,670,986	1,017,690	523
Chatham	1,606,432,419	22,239	1,089,851,580	55,414,595	767
Chattahoochee	13,092,595	12,625	8,765,563	386,609	373
Chattooga	127,079,764	16,741	83,543,890	3,752,639	494
Cherokee	584,685,255	24,384	398,399,564	19,978,524	833
Clarke	549,205,776	19,923	360,913,058	18,742,726	680
Clay	12,667,908	15,894	8,289,785	396,087	497
Clayton	1,485,029,257	23,345	998,564,019	51,083,077	803
Clinch	32,782,528	17,364	20,293,925	962,928	510
Cobb	4,436,809,023	27,787	3,113,855,690	166,202,406	1,041
Coffee	149,452,129	16,738	95,323,185	4,439,075	497
Colquitt	199,369,042	17,556	128,053,332	6,097,285	537
Columbia	440,823,252	24,493	305,938,009	15,428,530	857
Cook	68,725,434	15,763	42,486,348	2,016,338	462
Coweta	375,803,769	22,076	250,296,395	12,566,801	738
Crawford	39,507,794	18,410	25,602,372	1,228,793	573
Crisp	106,857,993	16,307	66,539,514	3,168,759	484
Dade	53,165,743	18,773	34,920,573	1,619,186	572
Dawson	52,230,762	19,606	34,432,118	1,715,554	644
Decatur	128,458,578	18,037	81,518,494	3,849,889	541
DeKalb	5,171,237,013	25,429	3,515,619,800	188,937,521	929
Dodge	86,593,596	15,959	54,565,241	2,540,239	468
Dooly	50,890,786	16,718	32,808,652	1,554,050	511
Dougherty	731,924,587	21,575	490,662,671	25,142,349	741
Douglas	559,980,253	23,603	373,393,443	18,722,860	789
Early	64,368,056	18,523	43,180,424	2,155,490	620
Echols	7,727,222	17,058	4,798,257	231,919	512
Effingham	139,577,179	21,580	94,544,123	4,809,495	744
Elbert	112,230,463	16,193	69,620,812	3,307,299	477
Emanuel	102,816,659	15,692	62,125,239	2,848,424	435
Evans	47,319,432	17,114	29,908,098	1,435,786	519
Fannin	75,578,753	15,664	48,491,061	2,192,434	454
Fayette	532,419,084	31,699	370,409,772	20,180,815	1,202
Floyd	610,304,266	20,440	404,233,768	20,071,719	672
Forsyth	303,760,754	24,927	208,107,902	10,608,523	871
Franklin	102,220,592	16,835	65,356,451	3,037,814	500
Fulton	7,005,915,079	26,012	4,784,547,325	273,315,992	1,015
Gilmer	74,594,688	17,050	47,350,407	2,365,132	541
Glascock	13,386,784	17,053	8,656,590	410,257	523
Glynn	470,892,526	21,578	313,969,232	15,931,845	730
Gordon	241,333,559	19,137	158,633,418	8,303,408	658
Grady	94,526,977	15,534	57,951,907	2,624,502	431
Greene	63,336,127	15,755	39,038,152	1,766,528	439
Gwinnett	2,936,008,420	28,471	2,044,585,380	108,702,532	1,054
Habersham	181,132,835	18,408	117,927,947	5,639,068	573
Hall	740,948,529	21,477	493,970,036	24,917,746	722
Hancock	38,461,660	13,605	22,827,775	975,058	345
Haralson	130,917,564	18,201	84,467,174	4,018,592	559
Harris	108,539,126	19,613	71,613,514	3,438,174	621
Hart	108,974,915	17,719	71,012,191	3,912,764	636
Heard	38,223,390	16,846	23,417,575	1,118,473	493

385

County	Adjusted Gross Income Less Deficit		Net Taxable Income	Amount of Tax Liability	
	Total	Average Per Return		Total	Average Per Return
Henry	411,989,577	23,836	275,066,515	14,289,793	827
Houston	662,927,851	22,246	451,724,224	22,871,768	768
Irwin	42,377,527	16,451	26,923,371	1,272,010	494
Jackson	175,121,500	17,204	111,000,833	5,143,908	505
Jasper	46,053,382	17,726	30,461,847	1,469,431	566
Jeff Davis	70,496,878	16,785	44,986,053	2,154,074	513
Jefferson	96,716,429	16,130	60,334,143	2,836,900	473
Jenkins	40,354,137	16,007	24,850,337	1,150,603	456
Johnson	41,130,065	14,731	25,024,286	1,135,239	407
Jones	118,979,800	21,609	78,738,173	3,997,105	726
Lamar	75,546,374	17,479	47,266,126	2,288,540	530
Lanier	23,357,097	15,356	14,681,718	638,917	420
Laurens	240,767,223	17,925	153,672,178	7,284,951	542
Lee	92,917,055	21,041	62,099,599	2,953,581	669
Liberty	117,559,811	16,197	75,533,077	3,558,968	490
Lincoln	37,773,758	15,700	22,732,597	1,056,112	439
Long	19,990,490	16,841	12,197,596	570,994	481
Lowndes	432,314,415	19,112	282,008,256	14,012,176	619
Lumpkin	70,264,384	18,346	45,497,574	2,213,488	578
Macon	62,705,613	16,029	38,898,266	1,834,549	469
Madison	122,931,416	17,826	79,077,404	3,686,301	535
Marion	24,815,891	15,766	14,997,131	708,647	450
McDuffie	119,887,612	17,302	75,664,135	3,586,965	518
McIntosh	39,310,616	14,773	23,707,391	1,084,140	407
Meriwether	115,932,629	16,301	71,732,101	3,515,486	494
Miller	33,475,113	16,907	21,223, 203	995,407	503
Mitchell	103,341,072	15,436	63,071,485	2,910,292	435
Monroe	100,728,525	19,223	65,953,465	3,193,969	610
Montgomery	31,594,057	14,924	19,530,899	897,555	424
Morgan	79,655,934	17,852	50,409,157	2,444,022	548
Murray	149,485,054	18,547	97,234,307	4,748,283	589
Muscogee	1,138,287,835	20,108	750,510,561	37,377,428	660
Newton	296,839,024	20,351	193,213,165	9,559,592	655
Oconee	117,471,765	22,431	77,659,736	3,869,158	739
Oglethorpe	50,273,117	16,814	32,058,610	1,480,280	495
Paulding	233,975,742	22,334	157,172,633	7,770,588	742
Peach	131,433,285	20,482	87,424,823	4,503,923	702
Pickens	87,306,593	18,655	56,752,552	2,761,869	590
Pierce	65,888,513	16,305	41,706,989	1,929,113	477
Pike	59,509,982	18,934	37,824,581	1,820,834	579
Polk	218,682,435	18,248	142,106,633	6,774,171	565
Pulaski	50,111,067	19,309	32,321,412	1,548,865	566
Putnam	81,290,239	19,443	53,794,350	2,628,740	629
Quitman	6,452,620	15,400	4,121,917	183,494	438
Rabun	63,067,707	15,890	38,564,372	1,791,127	451
Randolph	34,813,790	14,621	21,800,543	1,011,517	425
Richmond	1,309,512,903	20,752	884,223,781	45,021,377	713
Rockdale	432,143,345	25,577	294,364,090	15,099,640	894
Schley	17,416,216	16,666	11,182,168	534,898	512
Screven	76,531,709	16,857	47,977,885	2,245,748	495
Seminole	45,847,757	16,445	29,776,793	1,354,977	486
Spalding	371,010,046	19,755	238,533,122	11,777,009	627

County	Adjusted Gross Income Less Deficit			Net Taxable Income	Amount of Tax Liability	
	Total	Average Per Return			Total	Average Per Return
Stephens	151,368,532	17,160		95,722,312	4,441,996	504
Stewart	22,922,712	14,827		13,959,071	636,766	412
Sumter	182,004,867	18,923		118,139,651	6,110,715	635
Talbot	30,319,645	15,040		18,519,829	842,775	418
Taliaferro	9,127,646	14,988		5,788,975	269,823	443
Tattnall	81,141,060	15,710		50,196,556	2,369,282	459
Taylor	42,029,085	16,872		26,628,936	1,253,816	503
Telfair	57,145,787	15,023		35,424,410	1,570,106	413
Terrell	54,665,757	16,260		35,232,550	1,636,860	487
Thomas	247,264,908	18,513		158,086,798	7,714,721	578
Tift	215,313,709	19,194		140,944,367	6,817,174	608
Toombs	141,582,476	18,133		92,565,690	4,507,630	577
Towns	29,235,531	14,168		17,810,937	808,340	404
Treutlen	26,048,500	14,391		15,852,206	720,088	398
Troup	386,474,128	19,501		253,118,408	12,359,959	624
Turner	46,383,444	15,288		28,681,376	1,350,782	445
Twiggs	45,452,340	17,902		29,189,189	1,228,272	547
Union	48,665,416	14,685		29,090,856	1,288,311	389
Upson	160,515,739	16,970		103,094,708	4,799,111	507
Walker	345,020,580	18,926		224,371,273	10,792,810	592
Walton	240,287,877	19,801		155,919,682	7,927,381	653
Wake	228,065,579	18,483		147,596,159	7,217,193	585
Warren	30,526,890	14,783		18,520,174	835,598	405
Washington	110,214,841	17,944		70,906,843	3,675,852	598
Wayne	129,507,129	19,158		84,821,317	4,044,440	598
Webster	9,819,498	15,154		6,404,457	340,244	525
Wheeler	20,929,192	14,444		12,629,282	575,233	397
White	73,928,198	17,133		47,241,068	2,419,670	561
Whitfield	598,950,760	21,200		400,533,642	20,436,230	723
Wilcox	33,298,296	14,905		20,721,713	948,936	425
Wilkes	64,075,478	15,995		39,926,013	1,841,789	460
Wilkinson	68,934,628	19,707		45,255,769	2,231,134	638
Worth	100,754,269	17,896		65,041,084	3,151,600	560
Other	922,672,494			1,490,749,353	69,438,694	465
Georgia	49,028,039,229	21,224		35,445,198,884	1,741,511,900	754

TELEVISION STATIONS

Commercial TV Stations

Albany

WALB-TV (Channel 10)
NBC
Gray Communications
Systems, Inc.
P.O. Box 3130, 31708
912-883-0154

WTSG (Channel 13)
Gordon Communications, Inc.
Box 450, 31706
912-453-3100

Atlanta

WAGA-TV (Channel 5)
CBS
Storer Communications, Inc.
P.O. Box 4207, 30302
404-875-5551

WATL-TV (Channel 36)
WATL-TV
575 Ponce de Leon
Ave., 30308
404-892-3636

WGNX-TV (Channel 46)
Tribune Broadcasting
Co.
P.O. Box 98097, 30359
404-325-4646

WSB-TV (Channel 2)
NBC
Cox Broadcasting Corp.
1601 W. Peachtree St.,
NE, 30309
404-897-7000

WTBS (Channel 17)
Superstation, Inc.
1050 Techwood Dr.,
NW, 30318
404-892-1717

WVEU (Channel 69)
Broadcasting Corp. of
Georgia
2700 NE Expressway,
Bldg. A
Phoenix Business Park,
30345
404-325-6929

WXIA-TV (Channel 11)
ABC
Pacific & Southern
Broadcasting Co.,
Inc.
1611 W. Peachtree St.,
NE, 30309
404-892-1611

Augusta

WAGT-TV (Channel 26) NBC
P.O. Box 1526, 30903
404-722-0026

WJBF (Channel 6)
ABC, NBC
Fuqua Television, Inc.
Box 1404, 30903
803-722-6664

WRDW-TV (Channel 12)
Television Station
Partners
Drawer 1212, 30903
803-278-1212

Columbus

WLTZ (Channel 38)
NBC
Columbus TV, Inc.
Box 12289, 31995
404-561-3838

WRBL-TV (Channel 3)
CBS
Columbus Broadcasting
Co., Inc.

1350 13th Ave., 31902
404-322-0601

WTVM (Channel 9)
ABC
SFN Communications
of Columbus, Inc.
1909 Wynnton Rd.,
31906
404-324-6471

WXTX (Channel 54)
Columbus Family TV,
Inc.
Box 12188, 31907
404-561-5400

Macon

WGXA (Channel 24)
ABC
Russell Rowe
Communications
Box 340, 31297
912-745-2424

WMAZ-TV (Channel 13) CBS
Multimedia
Broadcasting Co.
Box 5008, 31213
912-746-1313

WMGT (Channel 41)
NBC
Morris Network, Inc.
Box 4328, 31208
912-745-4141

Savannah

WJCL (Channel 22)
ABC
Lewis Broadcasting
Corp.
10001 Abercorn St.,
Extension, 31406
912-925-0022

388

WSAV (Channel 3)
NBC
P.O. Box 2429, 31402
912-236-0303

WTOC (Channel 11)
CBS
American Savannah
Broadcasting Co.
516 Abercorn St., 31401
912-234-1111

Thomasville-Tallahassee (Fla.)
WCTV (Channel 6)
CBS
John H. Phipps
P.O. Box 3048,
Tallahassee, FL 32315
904-893-6666

Toccoa
WNEG-TV (Channel 32)

Stephens County
Broadcasting Co.
Box 970, 30577
404-886-0032

Valdosta
WVGA (Channel 44)
ABC
Hi-Ho Broadcasting,
Inc.
Box 1588, 31601
912-242-4444

Public/Educational TV Stations

Athens
WGTV (Channel 8)
GA Public TV Network
1540 Stewart Ave., SW,
Atlanta, 30310
404-656-5979

Atlanta
WPBA-TV (Channel 30)
Atlanta Board of
Education
740 Bismark Rd., NE,
30324
404-873-4471

Chatsworth
WCLP-TV (Channel 18)
GA Public
Telecommunications
Commission
Rt. 7, Box 1H, 30705
404-695-2422

Cochran
WDCO-TV (Channel 15)
GA Public
Telecommunications
Commission
P.O. Box 269,
31014–0269
912-934-2220

Columbus
WJSP-TV (Channel 28)
GA Public
Telecommunications
Commission
Rt. 1, Box 17, Warm
Springs, 31830
404-655-2145

Dawson
WACS-TV (Channel 25)
GA Public
Telecommunications
Commission
Rt. 1, Box 75A, Parrott,
31777
912-623-4883

Pelham
WABW-TV
(Channel 14)
GA Public
Telecommunications
Commission
P.O. Box 249, 31779
912-294-8313

Pembroke
WVAN-TV (Channel 9)
GA Public
Telecommunications
Commission

P.O. Box 367,
31321–0367
912-653-4996

Valdosta
WTKV (Channel 33)
Coastal Plains Area
Arts, Inc.
601 N. Lee St., 31601
912-247-3333

Waycross
WXGA-TV (Channel 8)
GA Public
Telecommunications
Commission
P.O. Box 842, 31501
912-283-4838

Wrens
WCES-TV (Channel 20)
GA Public
Telecommunications
Commission
P.O. Box 525, 30833
404-547-2107

TIME ZONE

The State of Georgia lies entirely within the Eastern Time Zone.

TOURIST ATTRACTIONS

ALBANY

Chehaw Wild Animal Park, Ga. 99, off US 19 bypass. 100 acre wildlife preserve. Animals roam free in natural habitat. Visitors protected by trails and elevated walkways.

Heritage Plaza, 100 Roosevelt. Thronateeska Heritage Museum (see "Museums"), 1857 train depot, Jarrad House—oldest frame in the city c. mid-1800s and the Hilsman Kitchen c. late 1800s.

Little Theatre, 514 Pine Ave. Restored antebellum home. Annually, a major season of five comedies, musicals, and dramas, summer musical, children's theatre productions, and theatre classes for young people. 912-439-7141.

Sand Hill, Radium Springs Rd., US 82. Fossil sand dunes.

ALVATON

White Oak Creek Bridge, 3 mi. SE of city, c. 1880. Long truss design. 80 feet long.

AMERICUS

Carter Library, Ga. Southwestern College. Memorabilia associated with US President Jimmy Carter who grew up in the area. Photos, slide and video tape presentation. M–F 8–5, Sa 11–4, Su 2–10.

Historic District. Victorian, antebellum. Greek Revival structures c. 1800 to present. Driving tour information at chamber office.

Lindbergh Memorial, Souther Airfield. Commemorates Charles A. Lindbergh's visit, purchase and solo flight of the single engine "Jenny" in 1923, four years prior to his historic solo flight over the Atlantic Ocean.

ANDERSONVILLE

Andersonville National Historic Site, Ga. 49. Confederate prison constructed in 1864 and in operation for 14 months. Over 12,900 Union prisoners died here. National Cemetery, Confederate prison, museum, State

monuments and special programs throughout the year. Prisoner of War Museum chronicles all American Wars from the Revolution to Viet Nam. Daily 8:30–5, Memorial Day 8:30–7.

Confederate Village, across from prison. Restored Village includes Museum, log church, prison officials' quarters, living farm, craft and antique stores, picnic areas, open air theatre and camping. Special programs periodically feature encampments with skirmishes between Confederate and Union troops.

Trail. 75 mi. driving tour. Includes Camellia Gardens, river ferry. Americus Historic District, Veterans Memorial State Park, Lake Blackshear, Plains, in addition to Andersonville sites.

APPLING

Old Kiokee Baptist Church, Augusta/ Washington Hwy., 3 mi. N. of city. Oldest Baptist Church in Georgia. Est. 1771.

ASHBURN

Peanut Monument. Visible along I-75. Largest in the world. Commemorates peanut processing industry. Tours of the world's largest peanut shelling plant. By appointment: 912-567-2541.

ATHENS

Athens of Old Tours. Begin at 280 E. Dougherty St., a Federal style house built in 1820 which serves as the Athens Welcome Center. Known as the Church-Waddel-Brumby House, the city's oldest surviving residence. Information on easy-to-follow-do-it-yourself tours of over 50 local historic sites, including the University of Georgia Campus, first state chartered university in the country. M–Sa 9–5, Su 2–5.

Double Barreled Cannon, Cannon Park, downtown. Only one of its kind in the world. Invented 1863. Failed to fulfill its mission of simultaneously firing two balls connected by a chain.

Fire Station Number Two, 489 Prince Ave. Built 1901. Victorian, two-story brick firehouse in the shape of a truncated triangle. Gallery and headquarters of the Athens-Clarke Heritage Foundation.

Founders Memorial Garden, 325 S. Lumpkin St. Built 1857. Filled with 18th and 19th century antiques. State headquarters of the Garden Club of Georgia. M–F 9–12, 1–4.

Joseph Henry Lumpkin House, 248 Prince Ave. Home of Georgia's first Chief Justice. Built 1843. Restoration under way.

Taylor Grady House, 634 Prince Ave. Built 1840. Former Atlanta Constitution Editor and nationally known orator Henry W. Grady lived there while attending the University and it was later bought by his father and kept in the family until 1872. Greek Revival architecture. M & F, 10–12, W 10–12, 2–5.

Tree That Owns Itself, Finley and Dearing St. Deeded the land that extends from the tree 8 feet on all sides by an early University professor who enjoyed its shade.

University Botanical Gardens, US 441 S. from city to S. Milledge Ave. Follow signs. Rose garden, annual/perennial garden, plant collections and five miles of nature/hiking trails. DA 8–5 October through April; 8–8 May through September.

University President's Home, 507 Prince Ave. Built 1856. Greek Revival. Corinthian columns on three sides. Doric columns at rear face a formal five-acre garden. Open special occasions.

ATLANTA

Atlanta International Raceway, I-75 S. at Hampton. 1½ mi. paved oval track. 2 Grand National race events annually. NASCAR, FIA sanctioned, plus Indy car races, motorcross and other motor sports.

Atlanta Stadium, 521 Capitol Ave. Home of the Braves Baseball team 404-577-9100, Falcons Football team 404-588-5425.

Archives, 330 Capitol Ave., SE. Houses the history of the state of Georgia. Research, displays, exhibits. M–F 8:00–4:30, Sa 9:30–3:30.

Capitol, downtown, Capitol Sq. Dome sheeted in gold brought from Dahlonega. Houses State Museum of Science and Industry, Hall of Flags, Georgia Hall of Fame. M–F 8–5.

City Hall, 68 Mitchell St., SE. Built 1929. M–F 8–5.

Fort Peachtree, 2630 Ridgewood Rd., NW. Site of first settlement in city, later a trading post. Log cabin, Indian pottery, arrowheads, artifacts. M–F 10–6.

Fox Theatre, 660 Peachtree St. MARTA'S North-South rail line to North Avenue Station. Opulently detailed 1929 movie palace. 4,000 seat theatre and three grand ballrooms for parties, conventions, performances. National Historic Landmark. Guided tour, Fox Theatre District, M at 1:00 p.m. and Sa at 11:00. It begins in front of the Fox Theatre on Peachtree St.

Governor's Mansion, 391 W. Paces Ferry Rd., NW. Greek Revival. Federal period furnishings. T–Th 10–11:45.

Herndon Mansion, 587 University Place, NW., c. 1910. Home of Alonzo F. Herndon, founder of black-owned and managed Atlanta Mutual Aid Society, now Atlanta Life Insurance Co. Tu–F 1–4.

Historical Society Complex, 3099 Andrews Dr., NW. 3 major structures—McElreath Hall houses an extensive collection of Atlanta historical data, Swan House is a 1928 Palladian style mansion and the Tullie Smith House is an 1840s farmhouse museum. Tu–Sa 10:30–4:30. MARTA Routes 4 Ridgewood or 23 Oglethorpe.

Martin Luther King Jr. National Historic Site. Begin at Information Center, 413 Auburn Ave., NE. MARTA's East-West rail line to King Memorial Station then take Route 99 Georgia Tech or take Route 3 Auburn Avenue. Includes tomb, birthplace, Ebenezer Church where he pastored. Tour hours: 404-221-3919.

Oakland Cemetery, 248 Oakland Ave. Est. 1850. Author Margaret Mitchell and golfer Bobby Jones are among the famous buried here.

Omni Sports Arena, Techwood Viaduct. Home of the Hawks Basketball Team 404-681-3600.

Peachtree Center and Omni Complex, downtown. MARTA'S East-West rail line to Omni Station; North-South rail line to Peachtree Center. Ultra modern hotels, restaurants, shopping. Omni also has cinemas, sports arena. Open DA, shop hours vary.

Rhodes Hall, 1516 Peachtree St. Built 1903. Victorian Romanesque Revival. M–F 8–4:30.

Six Flags Over Georgia, I-20 W., 12 mi. W. of downtown. MARTA'S East-West rail line to Hightower Station then take Route 201 Six Flags. 331-acre family entertainment center. Over 100 rides, shows, attractions. Spring: Weekends March 17–May 28, extended hours April 16–20. Summer: Su–F 10–10, Sa 10–12. 404-948-9290.

State Farmers' Market, 10 mi. S. of city off I-75, Forest Parkway Exit. Fresh fruits, vegetables, henhouse eggs, smokehouse meats, plants, shrubs, cafeteria. DA 24 hours.

Stone Mountain. From Atlanta, take I-20 E. to I-285 N. From I-75 or I-85 N. or S., take I-285 E., exit I-285, Stone Mountain/Athens Exit. MARTA'S East-West rail line to Avondale Station then take Route 120 Stone Mountain. 3,200-acre family recreation park surrounding world's largest granite monolith, world's largest work of sculptural art salutes the Confederacy, antebellum plantation, scenic railroad, riverboats, skylift, camping, motel, historic trails, fishing, boating. Summer: 10–9, DA otherwise 10–5:30 except Dec. 24, 25.

Sweet Auburn Historic District, Auburn Ave. Called "richest Negro street in the world" at one time, hub of Black enterprise 1890–1930.

Wren's Nest, 1050 Gordon St., SW. Home of Joel Chandler Harris who created Uncle Remus. M–Sa 9:30–4, Su 2–5 National Historic Landmark

Zero Mile Post. Underground. Erected 1850. Marks the birthplace of Atlanta.

AUGUSTA

Appleby House, 2260 Walton Way. Built 1830. Branch library. Summer garden concerts.

Augusta College Administration Building, 2500 Walton Way. Served as Augusta Arsenal. Est. 1793 by order of General George Washington, the Arsenal has been on this site since the 1820s.

Confederate Monument, 7th and 8th at Broad. 76-foot marble shaft containing life-size figures of Confederate heroes.

Confederate Powder Works, 1717 Goodrich St. An obelisk chimney 176 feet high is all that remains of the facility which once manufactured more than two million pounds of gunpowder. The chimney stands in front of the Sibley Mill built in 1880 and beside the Augusta Canal, built 1845.

Cotton Exchange, 775 Reynolds St. Built 1887. At one time, Augusta was the largest inland cotton market in the world.

First Christian Church/Parsonage, 629 Greene St. Built 1876 with an endowment from Augusta philanthropist Emily Tubman who also built the adjoining church. Parsonage houses Augusta Heritage Trust and Historic Augusta, Inc. M–F 9–4:30.

First Presbyterian, 7th and Telfair St. Built 1808. Woodrow Wilson's father pastored here during the former president's childhood.

Garden Center, 598 Telfair St. Built 1835. Chartered 1828, the first medical college in Georgia.

Harris Home, 1822 Broad St. Built 1797. 18th century furnishings. By appointment: 404-724-2324.

Meadow Garden, 1320 Nelson St. The part-time residence of George Walton, one of the Georgia signers of the Declaration of Independence. DA except Su & M 10–4.

Old Slave Market Column, 5th at Broad. Legend says a traveling minister, once refused permission to preach in the Lower Market, went into a rage and declared that the Market Place be destroyed. In 1878 a cyclone destroyed the building, except for this one pillar. Some say the curse persists.

St. Paul's Episcopal, 605 Reynolds St. Site of founding of Augusta, 1735. Celtic cross marks the location of Fort Augusta, known during the Revolution as Fort Cornwallis.

Signer's Monument, Green St. at Monument St. 50-foot obelisk of Stone Mountain granite honoring Georgia's signers of the

Declaration of Independence. Two of the three, Lyman Hall and George Walton, are buried here.

Springfield Baptist, 114 Twelfth St. Built 1801 by the Methodists. Sold to the Springfield Congregation in 1884. One of the oldest Black Baptist churches in the country.

Ware's Folly, 506 Telfair St. Built 1818. Federal style. Called "Ware's Folly" because the construction price of $40,000 seemed exorbitant at the time. Now houses Gertrude Herbert Memorial Institute of Art. Tu–F 11–5, Sa & Su 2–5. Closed M, July 4, Thanksgiving and Christmas.

Woodrow Wilson Boyhood Home, 419 7th St. Tu–Sa 9–5.

Yerby Home, 1112 8th St. Black author Frank Yerby grew up and lived here until his graduation from Paine College.

BAINBRIDGE
Willis Park, downtown. Restored Victorian gazebo. Focal point for driving tour of restored antebellum and Victorian homes in city.

BLAIRSVILLE
Blood Mountain Archeological Area, 15 mi. S. of city off US 19 & 129 via Appalachian Trail. Site of Cherokee and Creek Indian battle before the arrival of the white man.

Brasstown Bald Mountain, S. of city via US 19 & 129, via Ga. 180, then Ga. 66. Highest point in Georgia: 4,784 feet. 360° panoramic view of three states. Visitors center: May 23–Sept. 30: W–Su. Oct. 1–Oct. 31: DA.

Richard Russell Scenic Hwy., S. of city via 19 & 129. E. on Ga. 180. Designated Ga. 348. 14.1 mi. mountain drive. Elevations range from 1,600–3,000 feet.

Track Rock Archeological Area, 3 mi. S. of city, E. on county road 95 (town Creek Rd. for 5 mi.). A 52-acre preserved petroglyph of ancient Indian origin. Carvings resemble animal and bird tracks, crosses, circles and human footprints.

BLAKELY
Confederate Flag Pole, Courthouse Sq. Erected 1861. Last remaining.

Kolomoki Indian Mounds, 9 mi. N. of city. Historic settlement dating to A.D. 800, includes seven burial, temple and game mounds as well as ceremonial plaza. Museum depicts Indian cultures of the area. Historic Site.

Peanut Monument, Courthouse Sq. Salutes local peanut production.

BRUNSWICK
Coastal Exhibit Room, US 17 S. Marine exhibits, aquariums representing marine communities and a "petting" aquarium of spidercrabs, fiddler crabs, etc., for children. M–F 8–5. Operated by the Georgia Department of Natural Resources.

Coffin Park, US 17 & US 25. Tennis, baseball, football, auditorium.

Courthouse, downtown. Built 1907. Surrounded by moss-draped live oaks, tung and Chinese pistachio trees.

Lanier's Oak, US 17. The poet, Sidney Lanier, sat here to write many of his works, including "Marshes of Glynn."

Lover's Oak, Albany St. near Prince St. Over 900 years old.

Marshes of Glynn Overlook, US 17. Landscaped garden, picnicking. Unobstructed view of the largest salt marshes on the US east coast.

Oglethorpe Monument, Queen's Square. Honors James Edward Oglethorpe, founder of the Colony of Georgia.

Old Towne, downtown. Victorian architecture abounds. English street names such as Gloucester and Norwich have remained since before the American Revolution (many other American cities changed such names following the war). Driving tour map can be purchased at Old City Hall on Newcastle. National Register of Historic Places.

CAIRO
Hartsfield Farms. The Old Store. Ga. 112, 3 mi. N. of city. Early 1900s. Potbellied stove, phonograph, other antiques. Locally made crafts, Tu–Sa 11–7.

Roddenbery Memorial Library, 320 N. Broad St., History exhibits, wildlife, Art exhibits. M, Tu, W, F, 9–6; Th 9–8 Sa 9–12.

CALHOUN

Calhoun Musicland. Red Bud Rd., off I-75. Country/Western music, entertainment.

Confederate Cemetery, Hwy. 41, exit off I-75 at Resaca.

New Echota, exit 131, I-75. Capital of the Cherokee Indian Nation, 1825—1838. Inventor of the Cherokee alphabet, Sequoyah, lived here. See where and how the alphabet was used to print the only Indian newspaper in North America. Historic site.

Etowah Indian Mounds, 3 mi. SW of city. Occupied between A.D. 1000 and A.D. 1500. Largest Indian settlement in the Etowah Valley. Climb mounds, visit museum. Historic site.

Lowery Covered Bridge, also known as Euharlee Creek Bridge, 6 mi. W. of city, via Ga. 113, 2 mi. No. on county road to Euharlee. Built 1886. One span wide, 116-feet long. Town lattice design. Numbers still legible on timbers indicate the bridge was assembled elsewhere to assure perfect fit, then rebuilt over the stream.

Weinman Mineral Center, I-75 S., Exit 126, Culver Rd. Simulated limestone cave to explore, adjoining 20-linear foot waterfall. "Touch and Feel" exhibits. Precious gems, including rare amethyst collection. Tu–Sa 10–5, Su 2–5.

CARNESVILLE

Cromer's Mill Covered Bridge (or Nail's Creek Bridge), 8 mi. S. of city via Ga. 106, E. on county road. Built 1906. One span wide, 132 feet long. Town lattice design.

CLARKSVILLE

Mark of the Potter, Soque River, Ga. 197. Watch a potter at work and see the pet mountain trout from a porch built over the river. M–Sa 10–6, Su 1–6.

CHATSWORTH

Vann House, US 76, 3 mi. W. of city. Built 1804. Example of Cherokee Indian wealth and culture. Historic site.

Fort Mountain Crafts Village, top of Fort Mountain. Shops featuring handcrafted items unique to Georgia. Miniature golf. 404-695-9371.

CHICKAMAUGA

Chickamauga and Chattanooga Battlefield, US 27. Nation's oldest and largest military park. 5,000 acres. Visitor center houses slide program, bookstore and a 355-weapon collection of military shoulder arms. 50 miles of hiking trails slope Lookout Mountain. Open year round. Center closed Christmas. Operated by the National Parks Service.

Historic Chickamauga, downtown. Frontier and Victorian buildings. Many have National Register of Historic Places nominations. Visitor center, 30 min. slide show. Free 12-passenger limousine tour by appointment: 404-375-2650. Center M–Sa 8:30–6.

Gordon Lee Home, Chickamauga Battlefield. Built 1847. Served as Union Army headquarters and then as a hospital during the two bloodiest days of the War Between the States. Open May 29–Labor Day: Tu–Sa 12–5, Su 2–5.

CLAYTON

Bartram Trail. First blazed by Quaker naturalist William Bartram over 200 years ago. Mid-point of the trail is 3 mi. E. of city in Warwoman Dell on Warwoman Rd. Continues appx. 40 mi., marked with yellow and black signs.

CLEVELAND

Old White County Courthouse, downtown. Built 1857—1859. Used until 1965. Houses county historic society.

CLINTON

Historic District. Only Clinton, of Georgia's early 19th-century county seats, has survived sufficiently free of modern development to give an idea of the layout and appearance of an early town. Twelve houses built between 1808—1830 and the Methodist Church, built 1921, still stand. Self-guided driving tours.

COCHRAN

Pace House, 406 Beech St. Built 1870s. Said to be the oldest house in the city. Two-story, white frame, plantation plain style.

COLUMBUS

Bartlett's Ferry, N. of city on the Chattahoochee River. Also known as Lake Harding. 5,850 acres.

Columbus College Fine Arts Auditorium, Algonquin Dr. Quarterly productions by Dept. of Speech and Theatre. Musical presentations on a continuing schedule.

Fountain City. A designation inspired by the numerous fountains throughout the city.

Golden Park, Lumpkin Blvd. Home of the Columbus Astro's baseball team. Season begins in April.

Heritage. Originates Ga. Visitor Center, Hwy. 27. Two hours. Guided bus. Interiors include 4 house museums and Springer Opera House. W & Sa 10.

Historic Columbus Foundation, 700 Broadway. Two-story Italian villa style townhouse c. 1870. M–F 9:30–4, Sa & W Heritage Tour 10.

Historic District, part of the original city. Includes Chattahoochee Promenade, a riverwalk outdoor museum, amphitheatre. Historic Columbus Foundation headquarters, Columbus Ironworks, Steamboat Wharf, house museums, restaurants, antique stores and working artisan studios as well as a growing number of residential renovations.

Illges, 1428 2nd Ave. Built 1850. Embellished 1870. Greek Revival. Corinthian columns, flying balcony, wrought iron trim.

Ironworks Convention and Trade Center, 801 Front Ave. 19th-century structure that produced farm implements and munitions and weapons during the War Between the States. Renovation preserved massive timbers, exposed beams, old brick walls. Serves as a convention and meeting facility boasting 70,000 sq. ft. of exhibit space, 16 meeting rooms, outdoor amphitheatre and in-house catering services. National Register of Historic Places.

Jubilee Riverboat. Steamboat Wharf. Authentic split-sternwheel riverboat. Excursions available.

Patterson Planetarium, 2900 Woodruff Farm Rd. Daily shows 9:30, 10:45 and 12:45 by appointment.

Pemberton, 11 7th St. Home of Dr. John Styth Pemberton from 1855 to 1860, when he originated the Coca-Cola formula. Adjoining kitchen-apothecary.

Rankin, 1440 2nd Ave. Restored French Empire. Double walnut staircase. By appointment: 404-322-0756.

Springer Opera House, 103 Tenth St. State Theatre of Georgia. Restored Victorian theatre where Edwin Booth and FDR appeared. Museum sections house memorabilia of artists who have performed at the Springer and papers of Abe Feder. Tours Tu 11:00, or by appointment. National Register of Historic Places.

Three Arts Theatre, 1020 Talbotton Rd. Home of the Columbus Symphony.

Walkers-Peters-Langdon, 716 Broadway. Built 1828. Federal cottage style. Restored furnishings. M–F 9:30–4:30, Sa & W Heritage Tour 10.

CONYERS

Monastery of the Holy Ghost, 8 mi. SW of city via Ga. 138 & 212. Founded 1944 by a group of monks who practice self-sufficiency, cultivating their food. Men may visit inside 10–noon, year round. Afternoons-winter: 2:30–4:30, summer: 3:30–5:30. Women may attend services in church and visit grounds, which include a greenhouse and gift shop. Greenhouse: Th, F, Sa 2:30–4:30.

CORNELIA

Big Red Apple Monument, downtown. Honors the area's apple-growing industry.

COVINGTON

Historic Homes. Predate War Between the States and can be viewed on driving tour.

CRAWFORDSVILLE

Alexander H. Stephens Home and Confederate Museum, Ga. 22. Antebellum home of the Vice President of the Confederacy. Historic site.

CULLODEN

Historic Buildings. Pre-Civil War village. Built 1802, the Methodist Church has the oldest brick of any Methodist Church in the state. The Courthouse, c. 1894, features old furnishings and pressed metal ceiling.

DAHLONEGA
Crisson's Gold Mine, 3 mi. N. of city on Wimpy Rd. Gold panning, picnicking. April 12–Nov. 7.

DALLAS
New Hope Church Monument. Marks the spot of a crucial battle in the War Between the States where General John B. Hood's Confederate Corps met General Joseph Hooker's Army Corps of the Union Army.

DALTON
Creative Arts Guild, old firehouse, 520 W. Waugh St. Community Center for visual and performing arts M–F 9–5, Sa–Su 2–4.

Crown Gardens and Archives, 715 Chattanooga Ave. Built 1884. Former office of Crown Cotton Mills. A center for local history, meetings, exhibits, genealogy material, bedspread material. Tu–Sa 9–5, Su & M: Closed.

Prater's Mill Country Fair, Ga. 2, right on Ga. 2, 10 mi. NE of city. Exit I-75 at Hwy. 201 (Tunnel Hill). Travel N. 4.5 mi. to Ga. 2, right on Ga. 2, continue 2.6 mi. Built 1859. Site of country fairs twice a year: Mother's Day and Columbus Day weekends.

DARIEN
Butler Island, Altamaha River Delta. US 17 S. Owned by Pierce Butler. Was one of the richest rice plantations in the world. His wife, actress Fannie Kemble, wrote a book about her life on the island.

Fort King George. The southernmost out post of the British Colonies in 1721. Former Indian village and Spanish mission site. Historic site.

Hofwyl-Broadfield Plantation, 7 mi. S. of city, US 17. Antebellum rice plantation. Visitors center explains rice culture. House open to visitors. Historic site.

DILLARD
Hambidge Center. Est. 1934. See handweaving, pottery at this community center for the arts. Programs also feature dance, music, nature, creative writing, photography, painting and art history.

DUBLIN
Chappell's Mill, 13 mi. N. of city. US 441.

Built 1811. Still in operation. Uses original dam which brings 75 acres under water. M–F 8–5, Sa 8–12.

Fish Trap Cut, Oconee River, Ga. 19. Believed built 1000 B.C. to A.D. 1500 a large rectangular mound, a smaller round mound and a canal that may have been used as an aboriginal fish trap. National Register of Historic Places.

Historic Buildings. Greek Revival and Victorian homes can be seen driving along Bellevue Ave. Carnegie Library, built 1904, restored 1972 at Bellevue, Church St. and Academy Ave. intersection, houses Laurens County Historical Society and historic exhibits. Tu–Th Sa 1–5.

EATONTON
Rock Eagle Center, US 129 & 441. Named for a huge rock mound on the site believed to be made by the Indians nearly 4,000 years ago. Measures 101 feet head to tail, 120 feet across wing span. Can be seen year round.

Thompkins Inn, US 441, 6 mi. N. of city. Built 1811. One of 19 early 19th century buildings in the area featured on a driving tour map available at the chamber of commerce.

Uncle Remus Museum and Statue, downtown. Statue, courthouse lawn. Museum recalls slave cabin setting of Joel Chandler Harris' stories about Uncle Remus and his famous "critters" about which Harris began writing while living in the area. Summer: DA 10–12 & 1–5, Su 2–5, Sept.—May: Closed–Tu.

ELLIJAY
Apple Capitol of Georgia and home of Carter's Lake.

FAYETTEVILLE
Fayette County Court house, downtown. Built 1825. Oldest continually used courthouse in Georgia. M, Tu, Th, F 8–4:30, W & Sa 8–12.

Fife House, 140 Lanier St. Only unaltered antebellum home in county. Housed faculty, students of the Fayetteville Academy (1855–57), which was attended by the fictional Scarlett O'Hara in Margaret Mitchell's *Gone With the Wind.* Fayetteville

Methodist Church steeple bell is from the original academy.

Margaret Mitchell Library, between Ga. 85 and Lee St. Begun by Margaret Mitchell. One of the most complete War Between the States reference libraries.

FORSYTH

Commercial Historic District. Courthouse Square and surrounding eight blocks has 40 structures of mostly mid-1800s construction.

FORT GAINES

Driving Tour. Frontier homes, hotels, apothecary of the 1890s. Globe Tavern, cemetery, The Dill House dates to 1800s.

Frontier Village. Authentic log cabins brought from outlying areas.

Outpost Replica, S. Ga. 39, right on Commerce St., then 3 blocks on left. Reconstructed fort, one-third of original (c. 1816–1830) used to protect settlers from Creek, Seminole Indian attacks.

FORT VALLEY

Peaches. This is the heart of Georgia's peach production area. Blossoms peak mid-March. Fruit available June–August. Travel US 341 for best views.

GAINESVILLE

Green Street Station, downtown. Mark Trail of comic strip fame is alive here in a collection left by Ed Dodd. Also featured is a historical exhibit of Northeast Georgia, a collection of North Georgia Arts and Crafts, the Elachee Creative Museum and Nature Science Center and crafts. M–Sa 10–4, Su 2–5.

Poultry Park, Broad St. at Grove. Gardens and statuary salute the local poultry industry and the city's status as "Broiler Capital of the World."

Road Atlanta, 40 mi. N. of city, US 29. Premier road racing circuit with a 2.52 mi. asphalt track for cars, motorcycles, go karts. Home of Sports Car Club of America National Championship Race. Racing and sports car museum. M–F 9–5.

Quinlan Arts Center, US 129 and Ga. 60.

Traveling exhibits of regional, state and national artists. M–F 10–12 & 1–4, Su 2–4.

GREENSBORO

Courthouse, downtown. Antebellum, Greek Revival.

Old Greene County "Gaol," downtown. Built 1807. Rock jail patterned after bastilles of the 19th century.

HARTWELL

Train Rides. All aboard the Red Carpet Line for a 2-hour excursion aboard an authentic steam engine pulled train. March 15–Memorial Day weekend: Weekends, June–Oct: DA except W., Nov.—Dec. 15: Weekends. For hourly departures: 404-376-4901.

HAWKINSVILLE

Harness Training Tracks. Hwy. 129. Horses arrive in Nov. and train until early March for the series of races held every year in late March or early April.

Opera House, Broad and Lumpkin St. Built 1907. Restoration underway. Houses Chamber of Commerce. One of the oldest steam pumpers for fire fighting in the world, built 1883, is restored and on display on the side lawn. National Register of Historic Places.

Taylor Hall, Kibbee St. Built 1824. Restored. National Register of Historic Places.

HELEN

Bavarian Alpine Architecture is throughout Helen. Stone streets, unique shops, specialty foods. Oktoberfest in the Fall, Fasching Karnival in the winter and a variety of Spring events, such as a Balloon Race, make this a year-round resort. Shop and restaurant hours vary.

Old Sautee Store, Ga. 17 & 255. Unusual collection of old store merchandise from the early days when the General Store serviced every need of the pioneer. M–Sa 9:30–5:30, Su 1–6.

Stovall Covered Bridge, 3 mi. N. of city on Ga. 255. Georgia's smallest covered bridge. Built 1895. Kingpost design. One span wide, 33 feet long. Featured in the movie, *I'd Climb the Highest Mountain.*

HINESVILLE
Liberty County Jail, 301 Main St. At the completion of this jail, 1882, it was described by the press as "a handsome structure with all the modern conveniences"—running water, inside plumbing, fireplaces, 12″ brick walls and 36″ concrete floors. In use until 1972. Houses Chamber of Commerce office/visitor center.

JEKYLL ISLAND
Faith Chapel. Built 1904. English Gothic stained glass window designed, installed and signed by Louis Comfort Tiffany. Tours DA 10, 12, 2. Extend to 4 p.m. from Easter to Labor Day weekend.

Goodyear Cottage. Center for the Cultural Arts. Tu–Su 12–4 p.m.

Horton House. Remains of a two-story tabby house dating to 1742 when Major William Horton, one of General Edward Oglethorpe's (founder of Georgia) officers established an outpost here. Nearby, Georgia's first brewery ruins and the cemetery of the DuBignon family, first owners of Jekyll.

Millionaires' Village. From the beginning of the Jekyll Island Club in 1886 until the beginning of World War II, Jekyll was the remote winter retreat of Rockefellers, Morgans, Vanderbilts, Goodyears, Goulds and Pulitzers. Tour restored cottages DA. Details, group tour information: 912-635-2727.

JULIETTE
Jarrell Plantation, 8 mi. SE of city. 7.5 acre working farm complex spanning 1840s–1940s, complete with animals, crops, steam powered mill, blacksmith shop, can syrup evaporators. Self-guided tour and scheduled special activities. Historic site.

Juliette Grist Mill. Built 1927. Once was world's largest waterpowered grist mill. Great picnic spot.

KENNESAW
Big Shanty Museum, 293 N. Houses *The General,* one of two vintage locomotives used in the Great Locomotive Chase. Artifacts, War Between the States. DA 9:30–6.

The Doll Gallery, Rt. 4, 2000 Old US 41 Hwy. KOA Atlanta-North Campgrounds.

Antique and Modern Doll Museum. A fantasy land of over 1500 dolls; old, bisque, new, character, wax. Unique displays of the world. M–Sa 7 p.m.–10 p.m., Su 1–5 p.m.

LAGRANGE
Bellevue, 204 Ben Hill St. Built 1853. Greek Revival. Recently restored. Open Tu–Su. National Register of Historic Places.

Callaway Memorial Tower, Truitt & 4th Ave. Built 1929. Salutes Fuller E. Callaway, Sr., textile magnate of the area. Patterned after Campanile of St. Mark's Square in Venice, Italy.

Chattahoochee Valley Art Association, downtown. Built as a jail in the early 1800s. Recently restored.

LaFayette Fountain, LaFayette Square. Salutes Marquis de LaFayette for whose French estate La Grange was named. Replica of the LaFayette statue in LePuy, France.

LEESBURG
Chehaw Indian Monument, 3 mi. N. of city, Ga. 195. Marks site of Indian town home of the Chehaws, a friendly agricultural people of the Creek tribe.

LOUISVILLE
Old Time Capital of Georgia, 1796–1805. **Old Market,** downtown Louisville. Built 1758. Bell cast in France in 1772.

Pre-Revolutionary Cemetery, Ga. Hwy. 4, S. Thirty gravesites.

LUMPKIN
Bedingfield Inn and Drug Store Museum, town square. Restored 1836 stagecoach inn and family residence, with period furnishings. Museum fully equipped in turn-of-the-century fashion. Tu–Su 1–5.

Stagecoach Trail. Driving tour of 30 pre-1850 houses marked with stagecoach signs. Brochure available at Bedingfield Inn.

Westville, ½ mi. S. of city square. Re-created village of 1850. Authentic buildings were moved here, restored and furnished. Craftsmen demonstrate skills, such as basketweaving, blacksmithing. M–Sa 10–5, Su 1–5.

MACON

Cannonball House, 856 Mulberry St. Built 1853. Struck by cannonball during Federal attack, 1864. Restored. Houses Confederate museum. Tu–F 10:30–1 & 2:30–5, Sa & Su 1:30–4:30.

City Auditorium, Cherry & First St. Built 1925. Restored 1978. South's largest pipe organ, world's largest copper dome. Painting depicted the leading characters in the area's history across the proscenium which measures 10 feet wide, 60 feet long.

Fort Benjamin Hawkins, US 80 E. Reconstructed blockhouse of the style built when the federal government established the first modern settlement here in 1806. By appointment: 912-742-2627.

Grand Opera House, 651 Mulberry St. Built 1853. Restored 1970. One of the largest stages in the US. By appointment: 912-745-7925.

Hay House, 934 Georgia Ave. Built 1855–1861. Italian Renaissance, 24 rooms, priceless furnishings, secret room and 18 handcarved marble mantels and exquisite plaster cornices. Tu–Sa 10: 30–4:30, Su 2–4. Closed holidays.

Kingfisher Cabin, 4182 Forsyth Rd. (grounds Museum of Arts and Sciences). Dwelling and workshop of author Harry Stillwell Edwards.

Ocmulgee Indian Mounds, US largest archaeological restoration of ancient Indian civilization in the East. Visitor center, earthlodge, mounds and lodges detail the lifestyle of six groups of Indians that occupied the area 8,000 B.C. to A.D. 1717. Ceremonial earthlodge believed to be one of the oldest public buildings in the US. DA 9–5. Closed Christmas and New Year's Day.

Rose Hill Cemetery, Riverside Dr. DA 8–4, National Register of Historic Places.

Sidney Lanier Cottage, 935 High St. Birthplace of Sidney Lanier, Georgia poet for whom Lake Lanier Islands are named. By appointment: 912-743-3851. National Register of Historic Places.

US Federal Building/Post Office, College St. Murals by George Beattie depict the history of the area.

MADISON

Historic Homes. Referred to as "town Sherman refused to burn," Madison has a large collection of privately owned antebellum homes, over half of which are shown during home tours in May and December.

Presbyterian Church, S. Main St. Built 1800s. Old English style. Tiffany windows and a silver communion service which was stolen during the War Between the States and later returned by federal orders. Still used today.

MARIETTA

Kennesaw Battlefield, Old US 41 & Stilesboro Rd. Commemorates one of the most decisive battles of the War Between the States. Museum, slide presentation, exhibits. 18 mi. hiking trail. Picnicking. DA 8:30–5. Extended hours in summer. Closed Christmas Day and New Year's Day.

MARSHALLVILLE

Camellia Gardens, at Massee Lane Farms. From I-75 S., exit Byron onto Ga. 49. Headquarters American Camellia Society. Camellia gardens, library, Boehm porcelains. Blossoms peak Jan. 15–Mar. 15. Gardens open daylight hours, year round.

MERIDIAN

Sapelo Island. Home of the Sapelo Island National Estuarine Sanctuary. Formerly the home of millionaire R. J. Reynolds, currently operated by the Georgia Department of Natural Resources and the University of Georgia Marine Institute. Tours are available year round on W & Sa & F during summer months. All day tours are available to the first twenty-eight who make reservations: 912-264-7330.

METTER

Commissary, I-16, Exit Metter 23. Fully restored 1930 lumber mill commissary. Houses visitor center. M–F 8–12, 1–5.

Guido Gardens, Hwy. 121 S. Fountain, gazebo.

"The Sower" Studios, adjacent Guido Gardens. Radio, film center for religious broadcaster Michael A. Guido. Tours M–F 8–12, 1–5.

399

MIDWAY

Church, US 17. Built 1729. Congregation produced two signers of the Declaration of Independence, two Revolutionary generals and a US senator. Old slave gallery and high pulpit remain unchanged. Cemetery across US 17 dates to early days of Colonial Georgia.

Sunbury, 8 mi. E. of I-95. Marks the spot of Georgia's second largest Colonial seaport, an important site of the Revolutionary War and War of 1812. Visitor center displays history of the earthen Fort Morris and the "last" town of Sunbury. Historic Site.

MILLEDGEVILLE

Capital of Georgia, 1806–1867.
Marlor Home, 200 N. Wayne St. Built 1830. Headquarters Allied Arts. For exhibit information: 912-452-3950.

Museum and Archives of Georgia Education, 131 S. Clark St. across from Old Governor's Mansion. Built 1900. Photographs and memorabilia of the Georgia education systems. M–F 12–5.

Old Governor's Mansion, 120 S. Clark St. Home of ten Georgia governors. Built 1838. Greek Revival. Restored 1967. Tu–Sa 9–5, Su 2–5. Closed M. Thanksgiving, Christmas, New Year's.

Old State Capitol, 201 E. Green St. Milledgeville was laid out in 1803 as the state capital and today retains its original plan of parallel streets. This structure, used as the State Capitol from 1807–1867, has been rebuilt and is a part of the Georgia Military College.

Stetson-Sanford House. W. Hancock. Built 1812. Received nationwide acclaim for architectural design and beauty of worksmanship.

Trolley Tours, Historic District. Originate at Milledgeville Chamber of Commerce, 130 S. Jefferson. Tu & F 10 a.m. By appointment: 912-452-4687.

MONTICELLO

Town Square. Incorporated 1808. All buildings 1889—1906.

MONTROSE

Sanders Hill. Plantation House. National Register of Historic Places.

MILLEN

National Fish Hatchery, Hwy. 25, 5 mi. from city. 26-tank aquarium displays fish raised by the hatchery. DA 8–4 April–September, M–F 8–4 October–March.

MONROE

Davis Edwards House. Built 1845. Restored 1981. Mystery room featured in the children's book, *Uncle Robert's Secret,* by Wylly Folk St. John.

Kilgore's Mill Covered Bridge, N. of city on Walton-Barrow County lines. Built 1892. 100-foot span of Apalachee River. No supports in the river. Lattice type truss design.

McDaniel/Walker Homes, McDaniel St. Homes of two former Georgia governors face each other. Confederate Major Henry Dickerson McDaniel, Governor 1883–86 and Clifford M. Walker, 1923–27, occupied these brick residences built in 1887 and 1916.

Selman-Pollack-Williams Home, McDaniel St. Built 1832.

Social Circle, National Historic District. Est. 1980. More than 50 homes built before 1900.

MONTEZUMA

Flint River Ferry, 8 mi. N. of city, Ga. 127 at Flint River. 50-foot flat steel barge. Drawn by cable. Daily. Honk horn for ferryman.

Tours. Historic driving tour of Oglethorpe. Montezuma and Marshallville. Guide brochure available at the Macon County Chamber office and Andersonville National Historic Site.

NEWNAN

Historic Homes of the antebellum style are privately owned, but can be seen on a driving tour.

OXFORD

Historic District includes antebellum homes, Oxford College, Confederate cemetery and Methodist Church c. 1841, recently restored. National Register of Historic Places.

PERRY

Cranshaw's One Horse Farm & Day Lily Gardens, Sandefur Rd. 6 mi. N. of city. 400

varieties of lily on 25 acres. Pet peacocks. Picnic facilities. Lilies in bloom May and June.

Heileman Brewery, US 341 S. to Ga. 247 S., 5 mi. from city. Tour hours: 9, 10, 11 and 1, 2, 3, 4 M–F.

Peach Blossom Trail, US 341 N. Pink and white blossoms line the road between Perry and points north from mid- to late-March.

Peach Picking, US 41 N. of city. Orchards along this highway allow visitors to pick their own peaches and/or buy fresh from roadside stands from mid-May to mid-August.

PLAINS
Carter Hometown, US President Jimmy Carter grew up and reared his children here. See his home, birthplace, campaign headquarters, peanut warehouses.

RICHMOND
Fort McAllister, 10 mi. E. of I-95, Ga. 144. Earthwork. Key to Savannah's fortifications during War Between the States. Held under Naval assaults. Fell to Sherman, December, 1864. State Park Campground adjacent, picnic facilities, boat ramp, etc. Historic Site.

ROME
Capitoline Statue, Municipal Building. "Romulus & Remus" presented to the city by the Governor of Rome, Italy, 1929.

ROSSVILLE
John Ross House. A 1797 two-story log cabin. Home of John Ross, Cherokee Indian Nation Chief. Open Spring and Fall: Sa & Su 2–6. Summer: DA 2–6.

Lake Winnepesaukah Amusement Park, 1 mi. off US 27. Carousel, paddleboats, roller coaster, other rides. Picnicking. Entertainment weekends. May–Labor Day: Th–Su 12 noon—11 p.m. April & early Sept: Sa & Su 12 noon—11 p.m.

ROSWELL
Chattahoochee Nature Center, 9135 Willeo Rd. Natural Science Education Center offering animal rehabilitation program; nature trails and scenic boardwalk; on the banks of the Chattahoochee River. M–Sa 9–5; Su 1–5.

Crabapple Community, N. US 19, left 5 mi. Ga. 372. Originated as a cotton producing community. Cotton mill, mercantile stores (one c. 1849) have been restored and house antiques. M–Sa 10:30–5:00, Su 1–6. Antique Fair held third Saturday in May and October.

Historic Homes. Founded 1838 by a group of affluent families from the Georgia coast led by Roswell King, the city today features 15 structures which survived the War Between the States. The Roswell Historical Society, 98 Bulloch Ave., recommends a walking or driving tour. Stop by M–F 10–4. Write: Box 274, Roswell 30077 or call 404-992-1665.

ST. MARYS
Oak Grove Cemetery. Dates 1788. Graves from each American war. Tombstones with French inscriptions indicate a move by Acadian settlers from Nova Scotia, Canada in 1755.

Orange Hall, Osborne St. Antebellum style. Houses Chamber of Commerce office. Tour information Th–M 1–4:30.

Toonerville Trolley, Osborne St. Featured in 1930s Wash Tubbs cartoon.

ST. SIMONS
Bloody Marsh Battle Site, Frederica Rd. 1742 battle was a turning point in the Spanish invasion of Georgia.

Christ Church, Frederica Rd. Founded by John and Charles Wesley, 1736. Present structure built 1884 by Anson Green Phelps Dodge, Jr., as a memorial to his wife. M–F: winter—1–4, summer—2–5, Su services 8, 9, & 11.

Epworth-By-The-Sea. Methodist center on the site of the former Hamilton Plantation. Museum and former slave cabins open to the public.

Fort Frederica, Frederica Rd. Built by Oglethorpe 1736. Most expensive British fortification in country. Visitor center: DA 9–5. Film every hour, 10–4. DA park hours vary with season.

Retreat Plantation. Famous long staple, sea island cotton first raised here. Tabby ruins of slave hospital and plantation home still stand. Now part of the Sea Island Golf Club.

St. Simons Sojourns Tours. The islands' landmarks, lore and legends woven into an absorbing narrative. Available daily from the Pier Village, 223½ Mallory St. 912-638-1585.

SANDERSVILLE
Old Wooden Jail, N. of city. Built 1783. Site of Aaron Burr's incarceration in 1807 while en route to Virginia to stand trial for treason.

SAVANNAH
Site of founding of Georgia, 1733. Georgia Colonial Capital until 1782.
Barbra Negra, River St. Former whaling vessel. When in port, tours DA.

Bethesda Home for Boys, Ferguson Ave. 500 acre campus. 239 years old. Oldest continuously operating home for boys in country. Cunningham Historical Center houses items associated with home since 1700. M–F, 9–4.

Bonaventure Cemetery, Bonaventure Rd., edging Wilmington River. Once a lavish plantation. Moss-hung oaks, camellias, azaleas, dogwoods.

Cathedral of St. John the Baptist, 222 E. Harris St. Oldest Roman Catholic Church in Georgia, home of the Diocese of Savannah.

Christ Episcopal, 28 Bull St. First church in Georgia. Present structure replaced two others and was erected in 1840. John Wesley founded what is believed to be the world's first Sunday school here.

Colonial Park Cemetery, Abercorn and Oglethorpe St. Second burial ground for the early Colonists. 1750–1853.

Davenport, 324 E. State St. Built 19th century. Federal style. M–Sa 10–4:30, Su 1:30–4:30.

Factor's Walk, Bay St. Center of commerce during the years when cotton was king. World cotton prices were set here. Ornate iron bridgeways connect buildings which once were cotton factors' (merchants') offices. Other landmarks nearby include the City Exchange Bell, Old Cotton Exchange, Washington Guns, Old Harbor Light, fountain commemorating three famous ships named for Savannah and Oglethorpe Bench which marks the site of the landing of General Oglethorpe February 12, 1733 and founding of the colony that was to become the State of Georgia.

First African Baptist, 403 W. Bryan. Organized 1788. First Black church in USA. Present structure built 1859.

Fort Jackson, 3 mi. from city on the Savannah River. Oldest remaining brickwork fort in city. Built 1809–49. Displays, artifacts depicting the history of city and the coast. Tu–Sa 9–5.

Fort Pulaski, US 80 E. of city. Built 1829–42. Robert E. Lee's first engineering assignment. DA: winter—8:30–5:15, summer—8:30–6:45.

Fort Wayne, Bay at E. Broad St. Built mid-1800s. Named after General "Mad Anthony" Wayne.

Girl Scout Center, Bull & Oglethorpe, birthplace Juliette Gordon Low, founder of the Girl Scouts in Savannah in 1912. Restored to the period of her childhood. M, Tu, Th, Sa 10–4, Su 2–4:30, except Dec. & Jan.

Independent Presbyterian, 25 W. Oglethorpe Ave. Founded 1755. Woodrow Wilson married Ellen Axson, granddaughter of the pastor, here in 1885.

Isle of Hope. Community of privately owned antebellum homes overlooking Skidaway River.

Low Home, 329 Abercorn St. Built 1848 by Andrew Low, a cotton merchant whose son married Juliette Gordon. M–S 10:30–4:30.

Lutheran Church of the Ascension, Bull & State St. Organized 1741 by Salzburgers. Present church constructed 1878–79. Stained glass Ascension window.

Mickve Israel Temple, 20 W. Gordon. Oldest congregation in US practicing Reform Judaism. Founded 1733.

National Historic Landmark. Largest registered urban landmark district in the nation (2½ square mi.). More than 1100 restored buildings.

Olde Pink House, 23 Abercorn St. Built 1771. Georgia's first bank (1812). Headquarters Union General York 1864–65.

Owens Thomas, 124 Abercorn St. General LaFayette was a guest here in 1825. Tu–Sa 10–5, Su & M 2–5. Closed Sept.

402

Riverfront Plaza, River St. 9-block concourse dotted with fountains, benches, plantings, museums, pubs, restaurants, artist galleries, studios and boutiques housed in restored cotton warehouses. Waving girl statue, along the concourse, salutes Florence Martus, said to have greeted every ship that entered the Port of Savannah 1887–1931.

St. Johns Church and Parish House, 14 W. Macon St. Built 1852. Chimes, stained glass windows show Gothic influence. Parish House is former Green-Meldrim House, headquarters of Sherman after his 1864 march.

Scarborough, 41 W. Broad St. Built 1818. Houses Historic Savannah Foundation offices. M–Sa 10–4, Su 2–4, closed Th.

Squares, 21 half-acre parks in historic district. Laid out by State's founder, James Edward Oglethorpe. Each has a story behind its name and a central monument, fountain, etc. Some not to be missed are: *Columbia,* Habersham, York & State St., eastern limit when Savannah was walled city, 1757–1790. *Emmett Park,* Bay and E. Broad St., named for Irish Patriot Robert Emmett. Contains the old Harbor Light, erected 1852 and fountain. *Forsyth Park,* Gaston & Park Ave., fountain dates 1858, fragrance garden for the blind. *Johnson Square,* Bull, Bryan & Congress, monument and grave of Nathanael Greene, surrounded by sites of first inn, public oven, mill and general store in Georgia. *Madison Square,* Bull, Harris & Charlton St., honors President James Madison and Sgt. William Jasper who fell in the Siege of Savannah 1779.

Thunderbolt, off US 80. Shrimping village along intercoastal waterway.

Tours, *Black Heritage.* Three walking and/or driving routes highlight sites significant in Black History from early slave times. By appointment, 24 hours in advance: 912-233-2027. *Carriage.* Historic district by day, evening service to restaurants in restored horsedrawn carriages. By appointment: 912-236-6756. *Capt. Sam's Riverboat Tours:* 912-234-7248. *Harbor.* Paddlewheel sightseeing, area excursions and charters. River St. at the foot of Bull St. *Trolley Tours* by appointment: 912-233-0083. *Victory Drive,* US 80. Do-it-yourself driving along

route of early 1900 mansions. *Visitor Center,* 301 W. Broad St. Restored 1860 railroad station in historic district. Information, orientation, complimentary slide show, trained tour advisors, parking. M–F 8:30–5. Weekends, holidays 9–5. Closed Christmas.

Trustees Garden, E. Broad near Bay St. America's first public experimental garden. Herb Shop and Pirate's House where it is believed Blackbeard died.

Victorian Historic District. One square mi. adjacent to landmark district. Restorations under way.

Wesley Monumental Methodist, 429 Abercorn St. Commemorates the memory of John Wesley, founder of Methodism.

Wormsloe. Country estate established 1736 by Noble Jones one of the first Colonists, 500 acres. After over two centuries of single family ownership, estate (minus house, library and 65.5 acres) was bought by the State. Visitors center, exhibits, audio visual program, ruins of a tabby fortification and Fort Wimberly earthworks. Tu–Sa 9–5, Su 2–5:30.

SOPERTON

Troup's Tomb, 5 mi. SW of city via Ga. 46. Tomb of Georgia Governor George M. Troup located on his plantation. Ornate iron gate leads to elaborate granite tomb.

Visitor Center, Ga. 29 at I-16. Renovated log cabin built 1845. DA 9–5.

SPARTA

Historic Landmarks. Beautiful old homes, courthouse on square. Hotel Lafayette, across from Courthouse. Known as Edwards House and Drummers Home. Haven for refugees of the War Between the States.

STARR'S MILL

Scenic Stop, I-85 & Ga. 74. Mill believed to be over 200 years old.

SYLVANIA

Brier Creek Battle Site, 10 mi. E. of city, Brannen Bridge Rd. Revolutionary Battle Site. Breastworks visible.

TALLULAH FALLS

Gorge, US 441. Believed to be the oldest natural gorge in North America. 1½ mi.

long, 2,000 feet deep. Stop by Terrora Park Center for specifics.

Traveler's Rest, 6 mi. W. of Toccoa US 123. Built 1815–1830. Served as a plantation house, tavern, trading post and post office. Authentic furnishings. Historic Site.

THOMASTON
Auchumpkee Covered Bridge, 12 mi. S. of city, Allen Rd. Built 1898.

Pettigrew-White-Stamps House, S. Church & Andrews Dr. Built early 1800s. By appointment: 404-647-7838. Holds annual Christmas Open House.

THOMASVILLE
Confederate Prison, Wolf St. 5 acres bounded by a 6 feet to 8 feet deep ditch, 10 feet to 12 feet wide. Temporary when Andersonville officials feared a raid by Sherman. Now a park. Part of the original ditches visible.

Lapham-Patterson House, 626 N. Dawson St. Built 1884. Victorian. Historic Site.

Paradise Park, S. Broad St. 26-acre forest. Heart of the city. A natural wonder.

Pebble Hill Plantation, US 319 S. Site of an antebellum plantation, a winter resort home representative of the shooting plantations in the Thomasville area frequented by wealthy northern industrialists. Great number of out buildings house exhibits and artifacts including a carriage and automobile collection. Grounds open to the public Tu–Su 10–5. Guided house tours available for adults (over 12 yrs.) Tu–Su 10–5.

Thomasville Oak, E. Monroe & E. Crawford St. Nearly 300 years old. Limb spread of 155 feet, 65 feet high, 22 feet wide.

Tours: *Historic District.* Information, brochure at chamber office 401 S. Broad St. *Plantation.* M–Sa. Original chamber office.

Test Gardens, 1 mi. E. of city, US 84 (1840 Smith Ave.). Over 2000 plants on 2 acres. Varieties labeled for easy identification. Devoted to testing new and unnamed varieties for All American Rose Selections (one of 25 locations in the USA). Mid–April to mid–Nov.: Daylight hours.

THOMSON
Old Rock House, c. 1885. 4 mi. NW of city. Ga. 150 to 223 W. Stone residence, post Revolutionary, considered one of oldest dwellings in the State. By appointment: 404-595-5584.

Wrightsboro. Begun in 1768 by Quakers. Church built 1810. By appointment: 404-595-5584.

TIFTON
Agrirama, I-75 & 8th St. Exit 20. Living history village of rural Georgia prior to 1900. Over 35 authentic restorations. Gristmill, cotton gin, turpentine still, logging train, rural village. Summer: DA 9–6, Labor Day–May 31: M–Sa 9–5, Su 12:30–5.

Wiregrass Opry. Saturday nights, April–Oct. Outdoor performances include blue-grass, gospel, country music and clogging.

Fulwood Park, Tift Ave. & 12th St. 35 acres Virgin pines, azaleas, cookout, picnic facilities.

TOOMBSBORO
Swampland Opera House, intersection Ga. 57 & 112. Country, gospel, bluegrass music every Sa 4–12 except Christmas week.

TYBEE ISLAND
Fort Screven, near museum. Built 1875. Manned during Spanish-American War and WWI & II. Winter: DA except Tu 1–5, summer: DA 10–6.

Lighthouse, N. end of beach. One of the first public structures in Georgia. Marks the mouth of the Savannah River. Sa–Su 2–5.

UNADILLA
Southeastern Arena, S. Railroad St. One of the largest indoor horse arenas in the Southeast. Activities include horse and cattle shows, rodeo performances, circus and musical concerts. Open year round.

VALDOSTA
Barber House and Valdosta-Lowndes Co. Chamber of Commerce. Built 1915 for E. R. Barber, world's second bottler of Coca-Cola. Known for its outstanding examples of architectural design and craftsmanship. Walking or guided tours available M–F 9–5.

404

Crescent House, 904 N. Patterson St., US 221, 41 & 75. Built 1898. Third floor ballroom seats 300. F 2–5.

Lowndes County Historical Society, 305 W. Central Ave. Records, old photographs, exhibits of the naval and sea island cotton industries and local historical displays representative of Valdosta, once known as the smallest American city with a street car system. Su 3–6.

Converse-Dalton House, 305 N. Patterson St. 1902 Colonial home is the Jr. Service League's speech and hearing clinic. Tours available to the public M–F 9–5.

VIENNA
Tours: Historic driving, brochures available at City Hall.

VININGS VILLAGE
Antique shopping, West Paces Ferry Rd. Antique, gift shops, ski slope, teahouse.

WARM SPRINGS/PINE MOUNTAIN
Roosevelt's Little White House & Museum, Ga. 85 W. & US 27 A. Built 1932 by President Franklin Delano Roosevelt so that he could be close to Warm Springs for therapy for polio. House is exactly the way it was the day he died there in 1945. Every day of the year: 9:30–4:30.

WASHINGTON
Callaway Plantation, 5 mi. W. of city, US 78. Early American buildings furnished to illustrate life in the various periods of the history of the area. April 15–Dec. 10: DA 10–5:30, Su 1–5:30.

Kettle Creek Battlefield, 8 mi. SW of city off Ga. 44. Site of a decisive battle during Revolutionary War.

Toombs House, Augusta Rd. Core of home of Confederate General Robert Toombs, built 1797. Historic Site.

Mary Willis Library, Liberty and Jefferson St. Built 1888. High Victorian style. Tiffany windows.

Washington-Wilkes Historical Museum, 308 E. Robert Toombs St. Built 1835. Confederate gun collection. Indian artifacts. Tu–Sa 9–1, 2–5, Su 2–5:30.

WATKINSVILLE
Eagle Tavern, downtown. Early Georgia stage stop and store. Late 1700s furnishings. M–F 9–5, Weekends by appointment: 404-769-5197.

WAYCROSS
Okefenokee Entrance, 8 mi. S. of city, US 1. Guided boat trips, serpentarium show, observation tower, wildlife exhibits, ecology and swamp life exhibits, interpretive displays, 2-hour guided trip and all day excursions by appointment: 912-283-0583. DA hours seasonal.

Okefenokee Heritage Center/Southern Forest World, N. Augusta Ave. between US 1 & 82. 1912 steam locomotive, train, and depot; late 1800s print shop; the exhibit building houses antique arts, vehicles, nature trails info, an 1840s farmhouse and other exhibits of arts, sciences, and local history. Experience the fascinating story of the development of forestry in the South. Climb a fire tower and walk up inside a 38-foot-tall model of a Loblolly pine. Tu–Sa 10–5, Su 2–4, Closed M. 912-285-4260 or 4056.

WAYNESBORO
Dell-Goodall House, 6 mi. N. of US 301. 18th-century dwelling said to have been spared when an evangelist asked God to destroy the town of Jacksonborough.

Shell Bluff, off Ga. 80, 13 mi. NE of city. A 150′ x 140-foot bluff composed of giant fossilized oyster shells deposited over 60 million years ago.

WILLACOOCHEE
McCranie's Turpentine Still, just west of city limits on US 82, is a preserved wood burning turpentine still; operated from 1936–42, 19th century design.

WINDER
Old Railroad Station. Built 1912. Late American Queen Anne style. A polychromed, serpentine clay tile roof, smoothcut limestone lintels and window sills. Restored. Houses Chamber of Commerce.

WOODBURY
Big Red Oak Creek Bridge, 4 mi. N. of city. c. 1840s. Town lattice design. 116 feet long.

TOURIST INFORMATION

Visitor Centers

The State of Georgia maintains the following Visitor Centers where tourist, driving, and accommodations information can be obtained.

I-75 South/Ringgold (Tennessee Line) 404-937-4211
I-75 North/Valdosta (Florida Line) 912-559-5828
I-85 South/Lavonia (South Carolina Line) 404-356-4019
I-85 South/West Point (Alabama Line) 404-645-3353
I-20 West/Augusta (South Carolina Line) 404-737-1446
I-20 East/Tallapoosa (Alabama Line) 404-574-2621
        or GIST 337-1446
I-95 South/Savannah (South Carolina Line) 912-964-5094
I-95 North/Kingsland (Florida Line) 912-729-3253
US 301/Sylvania (South Carolina Line) 912-829-3331
US 280/Columbus (Alabama Line) 404-571-7455
        or GIST 259-7455
US 280/Plains 912-824-7477
Atlanta Airport (Baggage Claim Escalator) 404-767-3231

Welcome Centers

There are twenty-two Local Welcome Centers in the state. Some are located in historic sites and some have local arts and crafts. They work with the Georgia Department of Industry and Trade, area Chambers of Commerce and Convention and Visitors Bureaus. For more information, call Georgia Tourist Division, 404-656-3595 or write Georgia Local Welcome Centers, P.O. Box 1776, Atlanta 30301.

Albany Local Welcome Center
501 North Slappey Drive
Albany 31702 (Dougherty County)
912-883-6900

Andersonville Visitors Center
Old Railroad Depot
Andersonville 31711 (Sumter County)
912-924-2558

Athens Local Welcome Center
280 East Dougherty Street
Athens 30603 (Clarke County)
404-549-6800

Atlanta Local Welcome Center
3393 Peachtree Road, NE

Lenox Square Mall
Atlanta 30326 (Fulton County)
404-233-6767

Atlanta Local Welcome Center
233 Peachtree Street, NE
Peachtree Center
Atlanta 30303 (Fulton County)
404-523-6517

Brunswick-Golden Isles Welcome Center
I-95 between exits 8 and 9
Brunswick 31520 (Glynn County)
912-264-0202

**Brunswick-Golden Isles Local
   Welcome Center**
Glynn Avenue on U.S. 17
Brunswick 31520 (Glynn County)
912-264-5337

Claxton Welcome Center
4 North Duval Street
Claxton 30417 (Evans County)
912-739-2281

**Clayton County Local Welcome
   Center**
8712 Tara Blvd.
Jonesboro 30236 (Clayton County)
404-478-6549

Dalton Local Welcome Center
524 Holiday Avenue
Dalton 30720 (Whitfield County)
404-278-7373

Eagle Tavern Welcome Center
U.S. Hwy. 441—Main Street
Watkinsville 30677 (Oconee County)
404-769-5197

Gainesville Local Welcome Center
230 Sycamore Street
Gainesville 30501 (Hall County)
404-532-6206

Helen Welcome Center
Main Street
Helen 30545 (White County)
404-878-2521

Metter Welcome Center
I-16
Metter 30439 (Candler County)
912-685-6151

Million Pines Visitors Center
I-16 at Soperton Exit
Soperton 30457 (Treutlen County)
912-529-6263

**Rabun County Local Welcome
   Center**
Hwy. 441
Clayton 30525 (Rabun County)
404-782-5113

Rome Local Welcome Center
Civic Center Hill
Rome 30161 (Floyd County)
404-295-5576

**Savannah Visitors Center
   (Downtown)**
301 West Broad Street
Savannah 31401 (Chatham County)
912-233-6651

**Thomasville-Thomas County Local
   Welcome Center**
401 Broad Street
Thomasville 31792 (Thomas County)
912-226-1131

**Toccoa-Stephens County Local
   Welcome Center**
907 East Currahee Street
Toccoa 30571 (Stephens County)
404-886-2132

VEHICLE REGISTRATION

Motor Vehicle Registration (Estimated): 1986

County	Passenger Cars	Trucks	Trailers	Motor-cycles	Buses	1986 Total
Appling	7,787	5,383	1,497	164	20	14,851
Atkinson	2,758	1,829	366	55	4	5,012
Bacon	4,549	2,905	741	69	7	8,271
Baker	2,091	1,064	198	30	1	3,384
Baldwin	16,859	6,617	1,826	396	25	25,723
Banks	6,458	3,986	1,172	180	21	11,817
Barrow	16,114	8,175	2,441	515	57	27,302

VEHICLE REGISTRATION

County	Passenger Cars	Trucks	Trailers	Motor-cycles	Buses	1986 Total
Bartow	29,362	14,672	4,100	1,089	65	49,288
Ben Hill	7,611	3,717	1,184	188	14	12,714
Berrien	6,925	4,514	1,136	180	13	12,768
Bibb	83,103	24,083	8,319	1,747	144	117,396
Bleckley	5,229	2,829	1,001	142	5	9,206
Brantley	4,515	3,309	1,180	73	5	9,082
Brooks	6,878	3,889	895	104	31	11,797
Bryan	6,148	3,478	1,244	195	7	11,072
Bulloch	18,540	8,775	2,195	457	34	30,001
Burke	10,095	4,975	1,361	240	19	16,690
Butts	7,515	3,507	1,115	214	12	12,363
Calhoun	2,340	1,247	331	39	20	3,977
Camden	9,401	4,432	1,428	287	6	15,554
Candler	3,780	2,070	546	85	0	6,481
Carroll	34,498	15,792	4,358	944	65	55,657
Catoosa	24,453	10,481	2,247	709	26	37,916
Charlton	3,717	2,240	709	55	5	6,726
Chatham	117,875	30,873	13,787	2,476	218	165,229
Chattahoochee	2,977	1,088	227	188	6	4,406
Chattooga	11,581	5,503	1,184	272	28	18,568
Cherokee	43,685	22,467	6,259	1,574	78	74,063
Clarke	40,142	10,359	3,107	918	77	54,603
Clay	1,562	823	277	33	3	2,698
Clayton	119,669	39,257	12,108	3,272	267	174,573
Clinch	2,513	2,088	671	45	7	5,324
Cobb	265,458	68,898	24,785	7,041	332	366,514
Coffee	13,199	7,854	2,068	329	16	23,466
Colquitt	17,426	9,083	2,720	371	36	29,636
Columbia	31,770	11,633	4,606	781	79	48,869
Cook	6,043	3,277	1,046	108	9	10,483
Coweta	28,647	12,258	3,853	783	33	45,574
Crawford	4,385	2,465	727	119	13	7,709
Crisp	9,230	4,790	1,605	244	16	15,885
Dade	6,634	3,529	490	135	9	10,797
Dawson	5,926	3,352	948	186	14	10,426
Decatur	12,031	5,974	2,110	218	26	20,359
DeKalb	324,702	60,879	18,212	6,171	710	410,674
Dodge	8,152	4,340	1,086	171	26	13,775
Dooly	4,568	2,831	801	91	3	8,294
Dougherty	48,305	16,310	6,883	1,147	95	72,740
Douglas	38,916	18,273	5,353	1,252	110	64,904
Early	5,356	2,855	860	140	15	9,226
Echols	1,031	843	224	20	3	2,121
Effingham	11,063	6,488	2,582	303	11	20,447
Elbert	10,785	5,565	1,595	168	35	18,148
Emanuel	9,406	4,815	1,017	194	18	15,450
Evans	4,487	2,464	604	69	11	7,635
Fannin	8,857	5,182	1,024	347	23	15,433
Fayette	33,950	13,686	4,777	1,122	61	53,596
Floyd	46,072	18,154	5,024	1,356	97	70,703
Forsyth	23,745	13,658	4,697	865	37	43,002
Franklin	10,728	6,313	2,016	270	31	19,358
Fulton	332,624	63,343	21,658	5,456	526	423,607
Gilmer	7,609	4,833	1,005	210	18	13,675
Glascock	1,216	762	198	32	3	2,211

County	Passenger Cars	Trucks	Trailers	Motor-cycles	Buses	1986 Total
Glynn	34,262	11,184	4,671	852	55	51,024
Gordon	18,593	9,874	2,855	569	37	31,928
Grady	9,508	5,091	1,605	205	15	16,424
Greene	5,213	2,575	718	96	7	8,609
Gwinnett	178,610	58,222	19,556	5,043	243	261,674
Habersham	14,439	7,814	2,173	293	28	24,747
Hall	52,182	22,935	7,316	1,582	128	84,143
Hancock	3,703	1,358	256	48	5	5,370
Haralson	11,942	6,266	1,652	345	21	20,266
Harris	10,094	4,935	1,375	277	18	16,699
Hart	11,004	5,345	1,498	213	21	18,081
Heard	3,891	2,344	597	118	10	6,960
Henry	28,829	14,606	4,753	956	70	49,214
Houston	49,205	16,596	6,182	1,910	125	74,018
Irwin	3,930	2,689	604	67	1	7,291
Jackson	15,773	8,231	2,110	441	36	26,591
Jasper	4,276	2,307	766	124	9	7,482
Jeff Davis	5,702	3,613	1,805	120	14	11,254
Jefferson	8,161	3,939	1,142	156	18	13,416
Jenkins	3,660	1,987	487	55	5	6,194
Johnson	4,392	2,303	487	53	5	7,240
Jones	11,726	5,772	1,901	433	22	19,854
Lamar	7,210	3,047	898	183	15	11,353
Lanier	2,437	1,604	437	50	5	4,533
Laurens	20,040	9,377	2,582	385	48	32,432
Lee	7,095	3,776	1,486	251	13	12,621
Liberty	18,753	5,475	1,501	848	27	26,604
Lincoln	3,616	1,936	726	73	12	6,363
Long	2,531	2,008	903	72	6	5,520
Lowndes	38,225	14,868	5,080	1,139	89	59,401
Lumpkin	7,051	4,208	1,026	309	8	12,602
Macon	6,409	2,835	960	154	27	10,385
Madison	11,112	6,300	1,966	291	37	19,706
Marion	2,761	1,567	342	45	7	4,722
McDuffie	10,246	5,040	1,797	185	12	17,280
McIntosh	4,044	1,805	609	76	9	6,543
Meriwether	10,727	4,658	1,184	273	37	16,879
Miller	3,049	1,862	504	51	7	5,473
Mitchell	9,035	4,648	1,502	143	14	15,342
Monroe	8,970	4,142	1,296	282	23	14,713
Montgomery	3,387	2,131	790	76	7	6,391
Morgan	6,877	3,658	1,033	178	21	11,767
Murray	12,031	7,370	1,961	524	49	21,935
Muscogee	97,106	25,253	6,979	2,865	152	132,355
Newton	22,673	9,982	3,055	581	41	36,332
Oconee	9,318	4,538	1,489	287	29	15,661
Oglethorpe	5,315	3,152	935	143	8	9,553
Paulding	19,988	12,050	3,084	684	54	35,860
Peach	9,577	3,735	1,423	240	28	15,003
Pickens	8,012	5,204	1,123	235	22	14,596
Pierce	6,077	3,945	1,258	125	5	11,410
Pike	5,689	3,271	967	208	17	10,152
Polk	18,548	8,554	1,986	479	43	29,610
Pulaski	4,359	2,072	656	116	8	7,211
Putnam	6,151	3,464	1,380	150	12	11,157

County	Passenger Cars	Trucks	Trailers	Motor-cycles	Buses	1986 Total
Quitman	826	397	150	4	2	1,379
Rabun	7,010	4,132	989	173	25	12,329
Randolph	3,470	1,842	453	59	5	5,829
Richmond	104,065	27,370	8,507	2,134	255	142,331
Rockdale	30,677	12,540	4,016	894	41	48,168
Schley	1,638	1,053	227	48	4	2,970
Screven	6,740	3,828	826	133	9	11,536
Seminole	4,206	2,315	882	64	10	7,477
Spalding	28,975	10,806	3,220	660	67	43,728
Stephens	13,790	5,828	2,048	260	39	22,065
Stewart	2,490	1,341	300	32	7	4,170
Sumter	14,365	6,619	2,340	425	33	23,782
Talbot	3,652	1,673	330	74	11	5,740
Taliaferro	1,085	485	123	21	0	1,714
Tattnall	7,320	4,542	1,329	130	33	13,354
Taylor	3,570	2,137	512	71	6	6,296
Telfair	5,282	2,999	837	70	6	9,194
Terrell	5,076	2,231	706	94	10	8,117
Thomas	20,211	8,712	2,858	367	46	32,194
Tift	16,463	8,593	2,809	498	77	28,440
Toombs	11,622	6,073	1,919	226	61	19,901
Towns	4,216	2,631	862	134	8	7,851
Treutlen	3,099	1,661	378	46	6	5,190
Troup	28,053	10,895	2,963	626	61	42,598
Turner	3,796	2,429	518	72	10	6,825
Twiggs	4,941	2,603	656	124	15	8,349
Union	6,100	4,182	1.090	217	19	11,708
Upson	14,222	6,010	1,514	290	22	22,058
Walker	28,457	12,130	2,202	708	46	43,543
Walton	20,025	10,247	3,007	515	45	33,839
Ware	17,339	8,068	3,039	420	43	28,909
Warren	3,102	1,379	342	58	3	4,884
Washington	8,254	4,718	1,335	134	38	14,479
Wayne	10,034	5,837	2,190	196	19	18,276
Webster	1,010	702	118	11	4	1,845
Wheeler	2,422	1,485	439	36	3	4,385
White	7,475	4,571	1,088	187	15	13,346
Whitfield	39,837	19,284	9,034	1,188	110	69,453
Wilcox	3,080	2,018	444	74	2	5,618
Wilkes	5,945	3,206	1,003	130	16	10,299
Wilkinson	5,030	3,046	781	135	16	9,008
Worth	9,660	5,716	1,578	294	16	17,264
Georgia	3,410,198	1,246,913	391,173	84,542	6,755	5,140,487#

Total includes 913 registrations sold at State Window.

VOTERS, REGISTERED

In order to become a registered voter in the state of Georgia, you must be 18 years old or older; a resident of the state for 1 year; and in the county 6 months.

Registered Voters: 1984–1986

County	Total Registered 1984	Total Registered 1986	Percent Change 1984–86	Voters, 1986 White Total	Voters, 1986 Black Total
Appling	8,114	7,351	−9.4	6,015	1,333
Atkinson	3,549	3,237	−8.8	2,449	788
Bacon	5,331	4,891	−8.3	4,249	637
Baker	2,422	2,378	−1.8	1,295	1,082
Baldwin	14,334	14,396	0.4	9,945	4,451
Banks	4,459	4,238	−5.0	4,126	111
Barrow	9,558	9,461	−1.0	8,482	960
Bartow	18,157	19,357	6.6	17,360	1,925
Ben Hill	8,222	6,869	−16.5	5,081	1,788
Berrien	7,014	6,133	−12.6	5,493	639
Bibb	72,581	69,701	−4.0	46,756	22,945
Bleckley	5,647	5,470	−3.1	4,680	707
Brantley	5,391	5,329	−1.2	4,997	332
Brooks	6,016	6,392	6.3	4,120	2,272
Bryan	6,046	5,840	−3.4	4,631	1,206
Bulloch	17,339	15,047	−13.2	120,019	3,027
Burke	9,462	9,235	−2.4	5,076	4,155
Butts	6,344	6,266	−1.2	4,387	1,879
Calhoun	3,372	2,935	−13.0	1,402	1,489
Camden	7,369	7,493	1.7	5,186	2,275
Candler	4,107	3,878	−5.6	2,939	936
Carroll	24,865	24,371	−2.0	21,488	2,803
Catoosa	18,379	16,792	−8.6	16,613	157
Charlton	4,051	3,853	−4.9	2,779	1,071
Chatham	94,606	92,929	−1.8	62,376	30,522
Chattahoochee	1,488	1,310	−12.0	848	462
Chattooga	10,054	9,421	−6.3	8,666	755
Cherokee	23,877	22,815	−4.4	21,588	1,029
Clarke	33,428	31,376	−6.1	24,831	6,364
Clay	1,925	1,743	−9.5	813	929
Clayton	61,518	58,958	−4.2	55,056	3,533
Clinch	3,209	2,588	−19.4	1,994	594
Cobb	178,191	168,031	−5.7	160,006	4,808
Coffee	11,817	11,968	1.3	9,238	2,608
Colquitt	13,833	14,506	4.9	12,226	2,276
Columbia	22,608	22,118	−2.2	19,627	2,331
Cook	5,662	5,289	−6.6	3,956	1,333
Coweta	17,445	16,793	−3.7	14,111	2,682
Crawford	4,207	4,024	−4.3	2,667	1,357
Crisp	8,057	7,659	−4.9	5,631	2,021
Dade	6,700	5,911	−11.8	5,864	45
Dawson	3,143	3,184	1.3	3,178	0
Decatur	10,386	10,046	−3.3	6,872	3,174
DeKalb	263,675	234,937	−10.9	182,526	52,238
Dodge	11,203	9,318	−16.8	7,126	2,192
Dooly	5,132	4,650	−9.4	2,885	1,765
Dougherty	44,156	40,182	−9.0	25,190	14,959
Douglas	23,706	23,174	−2.2	21,883	1,226
Early	5,832	5,380	−7.8	3,603	1,774
Echols	1,365	1,319	−3.4	1,174	144

VOTERS, REGISTERED

County	Total Registered 1984	Total Registered 1986	Percent Change 1984–86	Voters, 1986 White Total	Voters, 1986 Black Total
Effingham	9,997	10,181	1.8	8,522	1,637
Elbert	9,179	8,664	−5.6	6,599	2,060
Emanuel	10,277	9,990	−2.8	7,417	2,504
Evans	4,110	4,019	−2.2	2,758	1,261
Fannin	11,517	11,188	−2.9	11,182	6
Fayette	20,461	20,952	2.4	19,809	380
Floyd	34,522	31,914	−7.6	28,750	3,105
Forsyth	13,679	13,734	0.4	13,730	0
Franklin	8,227	7,279	−11.5	6,903	371
Fulton	350,942	316,849	−9.7	169,840	145,922
Gilmer	6,818	6,155	−9.7	6,155	0
Glascock	1,575	1,392	−11.6	1,249	142
Glynn	27,838	28,517	2.4	22,033	6,334
Gordon	17,500	17,817	1.8	17,079	710
Grady	8,461	8,151	−3.7	6,285	1,866
Greene	6,110	5,819	−4.8	3,135	2,682
Gwinnett	106,856	107,346	0.5	104,742	1,577
Habersham	10,166	9,804	−3.6	9,595	204
Hall	33,159	32,530	−1.9	30,150	2,320
Hancock	7,059	6,750	−4.4	1,624	5,120
Haralson	10,555	10,049	−4.8	9,443	606
Harris	8,297	7,805	−5.9	5,847	1,946
Hart	9,305	8,171	−12.2	7,075	1,091
Heard	3,763	3,608	−4.1	3,142	461
Henry	19,674	18,885	−4.0	16,626	2,222
Houston	35,130	33,396	−4.9	27,641	5,621
Irwin	3,752	3,583	−4.5	2,770	813
Jackson	10,757	9,797	−8.9	8,932	728
Jasper	4,533	3,917	−13.6	2,606	1,311
Jeff Davis	6,286	5,929	−5.7	5,097	832
Jefferson	9,248	8,663	−6.3	4,650	4,011
Jenkins	4,200	4,304	2.5	2.814	1,490
Johnson	5,038	5,085	0.9	3,789	1,296
Jones	9,659	9,193	−4.8	6,603	2,569
Lamar	5,475	5,086	−7.1	3,784	1,300
Lanier	2,864	2,762	−3.6	2,071	687
Laurens	20,757	18,685	−10.0	13,432	5,208
Lee	6,102	5,725	−6.2	4,565	1,160
Liberty	8,830	8,903	0.8	5,274	3,538
Lincoln	4,095	3,944	−3.7	2,650	1,294
Long	3,030	2,883	−4.9	2,237	637
Lowndes	24,935	23,392	−6.2	17,474	5,918
Lumpkin	4,975	4,625	−7.0	4,527	95
Macon	6,233	6,169	−1.0	2,753	3,416
Madison	8,197	7,802	−4.8	7,146	644
Marion	3,088	2,926	−5.2	1,769	1,156
McDuffie	8,383	8,258	−1.5	5,792	2,460
McIntosh	5,080	4,678	−7.9	2,645	2,032
Meriwether	9,559	9,097	−4.8	5,948	3,149
Miller	3,511	3,352	−4.5	2,754	598
Mitchell	9,345	9,128	−2.3	5,823	3,236
Monroe	6,432	6,246	−2.9	4,358	1,888
Montgomery	4,342	4,371	0.7	3,159	1,199
Morgan	6,110	5,610	−8.2	3,854	1,756
Murray	9,158	8,588	−6.2	8,564	24
Muscogee	65.613	62,532	−4.7	44,373	18,159

County	Total Registered		Percent Change 1984–86	Voters, 1986	
	1984	1986		White Total	Black Total
Newton	13,506	12,275	−9.1	10,482	1,793
Oconee	6,971	6,498	−6.8	6,193	282
Oglethorpe	4,401	4,270	−3.0	3,331	939
Paulding	13,074	12,592	−3.7	12,114	447
Peach	9,435	8,464	−10.3	4,567	3,895
Pickens	7,257	7,175	−1.1	7,053	122
Pierce	6,000	5,970	−0.5	5,178	792
Pike	4,707	4,445	−5.6	3,381	1,057
Polk	13,530	12,543	−7.3	11,196	1,333
Pulaski	5,216	4,633	−11.2	3,403	1,230
Putnam	5,421	5,126	−5.4	3,558	1,560
Quitman	1,467	1,338	−8.8	643	695
Rabun	6,512	6,176	−5.2	6,155	21
Randolph	4,585	4,378	−4.5	2,269	2,107
Richmond	78,346	74,027	−5.5	48,938	24,705
Rockdale	19,314	19,482	0.9	18,360	1,075
Schley	1,661	1,417	−14.7	985	431
Screven	7,330	7,072	−3.5	4,012	3,068
Seminole	4,980	4,906	−1.5	3,481	1,419
Spalding	19,994	19,792	−1.0	15,812	3,926
Stephens	11,060	10,087	−8.8	9,212	875
Stewart	4,314	3,163	−26.7	1,475	1,685
Sumter	13,205	12,283	−7.0	8,087	4,194
Talbot	4,426	4,343	−1.9	1,716	2,533
Taliaferro	1,626	1,405	−13.6	642	763
Tattnall	9,238	8,880	−3.9	7,085	1,680
Taylor	4,446	3,904	−12.2	2,427	1,477
Telfair	6,742	6,412	−4.9	4,455	1,955
Terrell	5,729	5,779	0.9	2,637	3,140
Thomas	17,055	15,754	−7.6	10,757	4,773
Tift	13,307	10,957	−17.7	8,689	2,132
Toombs	11,634	10,661	−8.4	8,289	2,350
Towns	4,647	4,188	−9.9	4,188	0
Treutlen	3,553	3,626	2.1	2,615	1,011
Troup	22,164	20,016	−9.7	15,607	4,409
Turner	4,283	3,924	−8.4	2,730	1,194
Twiggs	4,913	4,575	−6.9	2,374	2,201
Union	6,783	7,152	5.4	7,151	0
Upson	12,472	12,340	−1.1	9,340	2,992
Walker	22,431	21,018	−6.3	20,136	869
Walton	11,701	11,627	−0.6	9,857	1,744
Ware	15,947	15,017	−5.8	12,169	2,837
Warren	3,707	3,460	−6.7	1,567	1,876
Washington	9,475	9,078	−4.2	4,976	4,094
Wayne	10,589	9,875	−6.7	8,325	1,545
Webster	1,501	1,370	−8.7	734	634
Wheeler	3,186	3,284	3.1	2,408	876
White	5,565	5,586	0.4	5,418	162
Whitfield	25,500	24,281	−4.8	23,195	1,033
Wilcox	4,605	4,519	−1.9	3,348	1,171
Wilkes	5,222	5,341	2.3	3,451	1,890
Wilkinson	5,421	4,925	−9.1	3,086	1,839
Worth	8,062	7,666	−4.9	5,785	1,875
Georgia	2,732,332	2,575,815	−5.7	1,990,088	575,567

WAR BETWEEN THE STATES

On January 3, 1861, Georgia state troops seized the mighty United States fortress, Fort Pulaski, near the mouth of the Savannah River. Then, on January 19, the State Legislature voted, 164 to 133, to take Georgia out of the Union. The next week, the State Militia occupied Fort Jackson, near Savannah, and the U.S. Federal Arsenal at Augusta.

Before the war was over, there had been 108 major engagements on Georgia soil, the least of any Confederate state with the exception of Alabama, Florida, and Texas. By far, Georgia's most active year in the war was 1864, when 92 of those 108 conflicts occurred. In addition to these, there were scores of lesser skirmishes.

The results of the various Georgia campaigns were mixed. At Chickamauga, in September of 1863, Confederate General Braxton Bragg scored a technical victory, but failed to follow up on his success. Consequently, the entire area around Chattanooga was lost. By May, 1864, Union General William T. Sherman and 112,000 soldiers were positioned near Chattanooga and began the long march to Atlanta. In front of them was Confederate General Joseph E. Johnston and 60,000 Southern troops. In mid-May, the two armies clashed at Resaca, and after holding the Federals for several days, Johnston was finally forced to retreat south. Sherman assaulted Johnston again in late June at Kennesaw Mountain. Johnston's valiant victory there did not deter his superiors from replacing him as commander of the Army of Tennessee, however.

By now, Sherman was at Atlanta's doorstep, and the impetuous John Bell Hood, Johnston's replacement, was eager for a contest. Within two days, in July, 1864, Hood lost over 11,000 troops in two ill-planned attacks against Sherman. The Union Army was then free to encircle Atlanta and the Confederate Army. Over a month of waiting ensued. Finally, with Confederate supply lines cut and overwhelmingly outnumbered, the Confederates evacuated Atlanta on September 1.

General Hood started to return to Tennessee and was subsequently overpowered at Franklin and Nashville. In the meantime, General Sherman headed for Savannah with 60,000 troops. In a path of destruction over 50 miles wide, Sherman destroyed everything in sight. By his own estimate, the General suggested that $100,000,000 worth of damage was done to property along the way. When he reached Savannah in December, he made President Lincoln a "Christmas-gift" of the city. The fall of Atlanta and Sherman's "march to the sea" all but obliterated further resistance in the Deep South.

In June, 1868, Georgia was readmitted to the Union, along with several other Southern states. The proud residents began the long, hard road to recovery amidst a shattered economy and a ruined land. As the title of perhaps the most famous book ever written by a Georgian indicates, the good years prior to the war were, indeed, "Gone With the Wind."

Today, there are several military parks which commemorate the War Between the States in Georgia, among them Chickamauga and Chattanooga National Military Park, Andersonville National Historic Site, Kennesaw Mountain National Battlefield Park, and Fort Pulaski National Monument. See the section on "National Parks" for more details of these and other interesting sites from the War Between the States.

WATERFALLS

Anna Ruby Falls—Fishing, hiking, and picnicking allowed. Location: ½ mile north of Unicoi State Park near Helen.

Helton Creek Falls—Beautiful triple falls in a deep hardwood forest located within US Forest Service lands. Location: 13 miles south of Blairsville on the first road past Vogel State Park.

Henderson Falls Park—Beautiful waterfall within 25-acre park of scenic attractions, active play areas, amphitheatre, tennis courts, and picnic pavilions. Location: adjacent to downtown Toccoa.

The Rocks—Waterfalls, trails, bluffs, caves, and geological formations, plus a primitive camping area. Location: off GA 107, 17 miles north of Douglas.

Toccoa Falls—Spectacular lacy mist cascades over a 186-foot precipice, 20 feet higher than Niagara Falls. Location: Toccoa Falls College campus, Hwy 17, about 1 mile north of downtown Toccoa.

WILDLIFE MANAGEMENT AREAS

The Wildlife Management Area (WMA) program began in Georgia in 1938 as a series of refuges that sought to restore the white-tailed deer herd. The WMAs are intensively managed for wildlife, with plantings, select cuttings, controlled burning, and stocking used to enhance the areas, overseen by a manager who lives in the area or nearby. Though the areas were established for hunting bears, deer, grouse, quail, squirrels, and turkey, there is also an abundance of nongame wildlife, rare plants, wildflowers and song birds.

There is a total of 65 WMAs in Georgia ranging in size from 235 acres to 120,000 acres, with a total acreage of over 1,149,000. Scattered throughout the state, these areas are managed through the Game Management Section of the Georgia Department of Natural Resources. The state owns about 5 percent of these lands. The remainder are leased from private individuals, private timber industries, and the Federal government.

Though camping, fishing, hiking, Wildlife Education tours, and research occur on WMAs, their primary purpose is sporthunting. In order to hunt on a WMA, an individual is required to purchase a WMA stamp that allows access to hunting on all 65 WMA areas. The monies received from the sale of these stamps is allocated for purchasing or leasing additional WMA lands. Where camping may occur, what types of vehicles are allowed, and when an area may be used are governed by WMA regulations.

Following is a list of all 65 areas and the counties in which they are located.

Area	County
Albany Nursery Area	Dougherty
Allatoona Area	Cherokee
	Bartow
Altamaha Area	McIntosh
	Glynn
Atkinson Tract	Glynn
Bacon Area	Bacon
Baldwin State Forest Area	Baldwin
Beaver Dam Area	Wilkinson
	Laurens
Berry College Area	Floyd
Big Lazer Creek Area	Talbot
Blanton Creek Area	Harris
Blue Ridge Area	Lumpkin
Broad River Area	Elbert
Cedar Creek Area	Jasper
Central Georgia Branch State Area	Jasper
	Morgan
	Putnam
Chattahoochee Area	White
Chestatee Area	Lumpkin
Chickasawhatchee Area	Calhoun
	Dougherty
Clark Hill Area	Wilkes
Cohutta Area	Murray
	Fannin
Coleman River Area	Towns
	Rabun
Cooper's Creek Area	Union
Coosawattee/Talking Rock Area	Murray
Dawson Forest Area	Dawson
	Forsyth
Dixon Memorial Forest Area	Ware
Fishing Creek Area	Wilkes
	Lincoln
Germany Creek Area	McDuffie
Grand Bay Area	Lowndes
Harrington Tract	Brantley
	Glynn
Hart County	Hart
Hazzards Neck Area	Camden

Area	County
Horse Creek Area	Telfair
Johns Mountain Area	Gordon
Keg Creek Area	Columbia
King Tract Area	Ware
Lake Burton Area	Rabun
	Habersham
Lake Russell Area	Stephens
	Habersham
Lake Seminole Area	Seminole
	Decatur
Lake Walter F. George Area	Clay
	Quitman
Little River Area	Cherokee
Little Satilla Area	Wayne
	Pierce
Midway Area	Clinch
Muskhogean Area	Telfair
Oaky Woods Area	Houston
Ocmulgee Area	Twiggs
	Bleckley
Oconee Area	Greene
	Hancock
Ogeechee Area	Hancock
	Warren
Ossabaw Island	Bryan
Paulding County Forest Area	Paulding
Crockford—Pigeon Mountain Area	Walker
Pine Log Area	Bartow
Rayonier Area	Wayne
	Brantley
Redlands Area	Greene
	Oglethorpe
	Oconee
Rich Mountain Area	Gilmer
Richmond Hill Area	Chatham
Rum Creek Area	Monroe
Sansavilla Tract	Glynn
Sapelo Island	McIntosh
Soap Area	Lincoln
Swallow Creek Area	Towns
Three Rivers Area	Wheeler
Tyler Tract	Wayne
Warwoman Area	Rabun
West Point Area	Heard
Whitehead Creek Area	Jeff Davis
	Bacon

WOMEN'S RIGHTS

Georgia has been an outstanding leader in matters having to do with women and women's rights. Among the more important of these issues and their associated dates are:

1802—Sarah Porter Hillhouse becomes the first woman in the U.S. to own and edit a newspaper *(The Washington Gazette).*

1819—The first women's foreign missionary society is formed.

1836—Wesleyan College at Macon becomes the first college in the world chartered to confer degrees to women.

1866—Georgia becomes the first state to pass legislation allowing women to have full property rights.

1912—Juliette Gordon Low of Savannah organizes the Girl Scouts of America.

1922—Georgia elects Rebecca Felton as the first woman U.S. senator.

ZIP CODES

Post Office and County	ZIP Code	Post Office and County	ZIP Code	Post Office and County	ZIP Code
Abac, Tifton	31794	Ambrose, Coffee	31512	Capitol Hill	30334
Abbeville, Wilcox	31001	Americus, Sumter	31709	Cascade Heights	30311
Acworth, Cobb	30101	Georgia Southwestern		Central City	30302
Oak Grove	30101	College	31709	Chamblee (DeKalb	
Adairsville, Bartow	30103	Andersonville, Sumter	31711	Co.)	30341
Adel, Cook	31620	Appling, Columbia	30802	Civic Center	30308
Adrian, Emanuel	31002	Arabi, Crisp	31712	College Park	30337
Agnes Scott College,		Aragon, Polk	30104	Cumberland (Cobb	
S Decatur	30030	Argyle, Clinch	31623	Co.)	30339
Ailey, Montgomery	30410	Arlington, Calhoun	31713	Doraville (DeKalb	
Airport Mall Facility,		Armuchee, Floyd	30105	Co.)	30340
Atlanta	30320	Arnoldsville,		Downtown	30301
Alamo, Wheeler	30411	Olgethorpe	30619	Druid Hills (DeKalb	
Alapaha, Berrien	31622	Ashburn, Turner	31714	Co.)	30333
Albany, Bridgeboro		Athens, Clarke	30603	Dunwoody (DeKalb	
(Doughtery Co.)	31705	Alps Road	30604	Co.)	30350
Federal Station	31702	Campus	30605	East Atlanta (DeKalb	
Four Points	31705	Gaines Community	30605	Co.)	30316
Marine Corps		Georgia University	30612	East Point	30344
Logistics Base	31704	Navy Supply Corps		Eastwood (DeKalb	
Alexander, Sardis	30456	School	30606	Co.)	30317
Allenhurst, Liberty	31301	Atlanta, Fulton	30301	Embry Hills B	
Allentown, Wilkinson	31003	Airport Mail Facility	30320	(DeKalb Co.)	30341
Alma, Bacon	31510	Ben Hill	30331	Emory University	
Alpharetta, Fulton	30201	Bolton	30318	(DeKalb Co.)	30322
Alps Road, Athens	30604	Briarcliff (DeKalb		Executive Park	
Alston, Montgomery	30412	Co.)	30329	(DeKalb Co.)	30347
Alto, Habersham	30510	Briarwood	30344	Federal Reserve	30308

Post Office and County	ZIP Code	Post Office and County	ZIP Code	Post Office and County	ZIP Code
Fort McPherson	30330	Berryton, Summerville	30748	Campus, Athens	30605
Gate City	30312	Bethlehem, Barrow	30620	Canon, Franklin	30520
Greenbriar	30331	Bibb City, Columbus	31904	Canoochee, Twin City	30471
Hapeville	30354	Big Canoe, Jasper	30143	Canton, Cherokee	30114
Industrial	30336	Bingville, Savannah	31403	Canton Plaza, Marietta	30066
Lakewood	30315	Bishop, Oconee	30621	Capitol Hill, Atlanta	30334
Lenox Square	30326	Blackshear, Pierce	31516	Carl, Auburn	30203
Martech	30377	Blairsville, Union	30512	Carlton, Madison	30627
Morris Brown	30314	Blakely, Early	31723	Carnesville, Franklin	30521
North Atlanta (DeKalb Co.)	30319	Bloomingdale, Chatham	31302	Carrollton, Carroll	30117
Northlake (DeKalb Co.)	30345	Blue Ridge, Fannin	30513	West Georgia College	30117
North Side	30355	Bluffton, Clay	31724	Carters, Chatsworth	30705
Old National	30349	Blythe, Richmond	30805	Cartersville, Bartow	30120
Peachtree Center	30343	Bogart, Clarke	30622	Cascade Heights, Atlanta	30311
Sandy Springs	30328	Bolingbroke, Monroe	31004	Cassville, Bartow	30123
Six Flags Over Georgia (Cobb Co.)	30336	Bolton, Atlanta	30318	Castle Park, Valdosta	31601
Toco Hills (DeKalb Co.)	30329	Bonaire, Houston	31005	Castle Park Sta Boxes, Valdosta	31604
Tuxedo	30342	Boneville, McDuffie	30806	Cataula, Harris	31804
West End	30310	Boston, Thomas	31626	Cave Spring, Floyd	30124
Attapulgus, Decatur	31715	Bostwick, Morgan	30623	Cecil, Cook	31627
Auburn, Barrow,	30203	Bowdon, Carroll	30108	Cedar Springs, Early	31732
Carl	30203	Bowdon Junction, Carroll	30109	Cedartown, Polk	30125
Augusta, Richmond	30903	Bowersville, Hart	30516	Centerville, Warner Robins	31028
Fort Gordon	30905	Bowman, Elbert	30624	Central City, Atlanta	30302
Martinez (Columbia Co.)	30907	Box Springs, Talbot	31801	Chamblee, Atlanta	30341
Medical Ctr. Eisenhower Hosp	30905	Juniper (Marion Co.)	31801	Chatsworth, Murray	30705
Peach Orchard	30906	Braselton, Jackson	30517	Carters	30705
The Hill	30904	Bremen, Haralson	30110	Chauncey, Dodge	31011
Austell, Cobb	30001	Briarcliff, Atlanta	30329	Cherrylog, Gilmer	30522
Avera, Jefferson	30803	Briarwood, Atlanta	30344	Chester, Dodge	31012
Avondale Estates, DeKalb	30002	Bridgeboro, Albany	31705	Chestnut Mountain, Gainesville	30502
Axson, Atkinson	31624	Brinson, Decatur	31725	Chickamauga, Walker	30707
Baconton, Mitchell	31716	Bristol, Pierce	31518	Chula, Tift	31733
Bainbridge, Decatur	31717	Bronwood, Terrell	31726	Cisco, Murray	30708
West Bainbridge	31717	Brookfield, Tift	31727	Civic Center, Atlanta	30308
Baker Village, Columbus	31903	Brooklet, Bulloch	30415	Clarkdale, Cobb	30020
Baldwin, Banks	30511	Brooks, Fayette	30205	Clarksville, Habersham	30523
Ball Ground, Cherokee	30107	Broxton, Coffee	31519	Hollywood	30523
Barnesville, Lamar	30204	Brunswick, Glynn	31521	Clarkston, DeKalb	30021
Barney, Brooks	31625	Main Office Boxes	31521	Claxton, Evans	30417
Bartow, Jefferson	30413	Glynco	31520	Bellville	30414
Barwick, Brooks	31720	Jekyll Island	31520	Manassas	30438
Baxley, Appling	31513	Saint Simons Island	31522	Clayton, Rabun	30525
Beallwood, Columbus	31905	Sea Island	31561	Clermont, Hall	30527
Bellville, Claxton	30414	Buchanan, Haralson	30113	Cleveland, White	30528
Belvedere, Decatur	30032	Buckhead, Morgan	30625	Climax, Decatur	31734
Bemiss, Valdosta	31602	Buena Vista, Marion	31803	Clinchfield, Houston	31013
Benevolence, Randolph	31740	Buford, Gwinnett	30518	Cloudland, Menlo	30731
Ben Hill, Atlanta	30331	Butler, Taylor	31006	Clyattville, Valdosta	31601
Berlin, Colquitt	31722	Byromville, Dooly	31007	Clyo, Effingham	31303
		Byron, Peach	31008	Cobb, Sumter	31735
		Cadwell, Laurens	31009	Cobb County Center, Smyrna	30080
		Cairo, Grady	31728	Cobbtown, Tattnall	30420
		Calhoun, Gordon	30701		
		Calvary, Grady	31729		
		Camak, Warren	30807		
		Camilla, Mitchell	31730		

Post Office and County	ZIP Code	Post Office and County	ZIP Code	Post Office and County	ZIP Code
Cochran, Bleckley	31014	Darien, McIntosh	31305	Eldorado, Tifton	31794
Empire (Dodge Co.)	31026	Davisboro, Washington	31018	Elko, Houston	31025
Cogdell, Homerville	31634	Dawson, Terrell	31742	Ellabell, Bryan	31308
Cohutta, Whitfield	30710	Dawsonville, Dawson	30534	Ellaville, Schley	31806
Colbert, Madison	30628	Juno	30534	Ellenton, Colquitt	31747
Coleman, Randolph	31736	Dearing, McDuffie	30808	Ellenwood, Clayton	30049
College, Fort Valley	31030	Decatur, DeKalb	30031	Ellerslie, Harris	31807
College Park, Atlanta	30337	Agnes Scott College	30030	Ellijay, Gilmer	30540
Collins, Tattnall	30421	Belvedere	30032	Elmodel, Newton	31748
Colquitt, Miller	31737	Dunaire	30032	Embry Hills, Atlanta	30341
Columbus, Muscogee	31902	North Decatur	30033	Emerson, Bartow	30137
Baker Village	31903	Snapfinger	30035	Emory University	
Beallwood	31904	South Decatur	30034	Atlanta	30322
Bibb City	31904	Vista Grove	30033	Empire, Cochran	31026
Custer Terrace	31905	Deepstep, Sandersville	31082	Enigma, Berrien	31749
Downtown	31902	Demorest, Habersham	30535	Epworth, Fannin	30541
Fort Benning	31905	Habersham	30544	Esom Hill, Polk	30138
Lindsay Creek	31907	Denton, Jeff Davis	31532	Eton, Murray	30724
Upatoi	31829	DeSoto, Sumter	31743	Evans, Columbia	30809
Windsor Park	31904	Devereux, Sparta	31087	Everett, Brunswick	31520
Wynnton	31906	Dewy Rose, Elbert	30634	Executive Park, Atlanta	30347
Comer, Madison	30629	Dexter, Laurens	31019	Experiment, Spalding	30212
Commerce, Jackson	30529	Dillard, Rabun	30537	Fairburn, Fulton	30213
Concord, Pike	30206	Dixie, Brooks	31629	Fairmount, Gordon	30139
Conley, Clayton	30027	Dobbins A F B,		Fair Oaks, Marietta	30060
Conyers, Rockdale	30207	Marietta	30060	Fargo, Clinch	31631
Coolidge, Thomas	31738	Doerun, Colquitt	31744	Farmington, Oconee	30638
Coosa, Floyd	30129	Donalsonville, Seminole	31745	Fayetteville, Fayette	30214
Cordele, Crisp	31015	Doraville, Atlanta	30340	Woolsey	30214
Cornelia, Habersham	30531	Douglas, Coffee	31533	Inman	30232
Cotton, Mitchell	31739	Douglasville, Douglas	30133	Peachtree City	30269
Court Square, Dublin	31021	Dover, Screven	30424	Federal Reserve,	
Covena, Emanuel	30422	Downtown, Atlanta	30301	Atlanta	30308
Covington, Newton	30209	Downtown, Columbus	31902	Federal Station, Albany	31702
Starrsville	30209	Druid Hills, Atlanta	30333	Felton, Haralson	30140
Crandall, Murray	30711	Dry Branch, Twiggs	31020	Fitzgerald, Irwin	31750
Crawford, Olgethorpe	30630	Dublin, Laurens	31040	Fleming, Liberty	31309
Crawfordville, Taliaferro	30631	Lollie	31021	Flintstone, Walker	30725
Crescent, McIntosh	31304	Court Square	31021	Flovilla, Butts	30216
Valona	31332	East Dublin	31021	Indian Springs	30231
Culloden, Monroe	31016	Scott (Johnson Co.)	31095	Flowery Branch, Hall	30542
Cumberland, Atlanta	30339	Dudley, Laurens	31022	Folkston, Charlton	31537
Cumming, Forsyth	30130	Duluth, Gwinnett	30136	Forest Park, Clayton	30050
Cusseta, Chattahoochee	31805	Dunaire, Decatur	30032	Main Office Boxes	30051
Custer Terrace,		Dunwoody, Atlanta	30350	Forsyth, Monroe	31029
Columbus	31905	DuPont, Clinch	31630	Fort Benning,	
Cuthbert, Randolph	31740	Eastanollee, Stephens	30538	Columbus	31905
Dacula, Gwinnett	30211	East Atlanta, Atlanta	30316	Fort Gaines, Clay	31751
Dahlonega, Lumpkin	30533	East Dublin, Dublin	31021	Fort Gordon, Augusta	30905
North Ga College	30597	East Ellijay, Gilmer	30539	Fort McPherson,	
Daisy, Evans	30423	Eastman, Dodge	31023	Atlanta	30330
Dallas, Paulding	30132	East Point, Atlanta	30344	Fort Oglethorpe,	
Dalton, Whitfield	30720	East Side, Dalton	30721	Rossville	30742
East Side	30721	Eastwood, Atlanta	30317	Fortson, Muscogee	31808
Damascus, Early	31741	Eatonton, Putnam	31024	Fort Stewart, Hinesville	31314
Danburg, Tignall	30668	Eden, Effingham	31307	Fort Valley, Peach	31030
Danielsville, Madison	30633	Edison, Calhoun	31746	College	31030
Danville, Twiggs	31017	Elberton, Elbert	30635	Four Points, Albany	31705

Post Office and County	ZIP Code	Post Office and County	ZIP Code	Post Office and County	ZIP Code
Fowlstown, Decatur	31752	Harrison, Washington	31035	June, Dawsonville	30534
Franklin, Heard	30217	Hartsfield, Colquitt	31756	Kathleen, Houston	31047
Franklin Springs,		Hartwell, Hart	30643	Kennesaw, Cobb	30144
Franklin	30639	Hawkinsville, Pulaski	31036	Keysville, Burke	30816
Funston, Colquitt	31753	Hazlehurst, Jeff Davis	31539	Gough	30811
Gaines Community,		Helen, White	30545	Kings Bay, Kingsland	31547
Athens	30605	Helena, Telfair	31037	Kingsland, Camden	31548
Gainesville, Hall	30503	Hephzibah, Richmond	30815	Kings Bay	31547
Chestnut Mountain	30502	Hiawassee, Towns	30546	Kingston, Bartow	30145
Westside	30501	High Shoals, Oconee	30645	Kite, Johnson	31049
Garden City, Savannah	31408	Hill City, Resaca	30735	Knoxville, Crawford	31050
Garfield, Emanuel	30425	Hillsboro, Jasper	31038	Lafayette, Walker	30728
Gate City, Atlanta	30312	Hilltonia, Sylvania	30467	LaGrange, Troup	30241
Gay, Meriwether	30202	Hinesville, Liberty	31313	Main Office Boxes	30261
Geneva, Talbot	31810	Fort Stewart	31314	Lakeland, Lanier	31635
Georgetown, Quitman	31754	Hiram, Paulding	30141	Lakemont, Rabun	30552
Georgia Southern,		Hoboken, Brantley	31542	Lake Park, Lowndes	31636
Statesboro	30458	Hogansville, Troup	30230	Lakewood, Atlanta	30315
Georgia Southwestern		Holcomb Bridge,		Lavonia, Franklin	30553
College, Americus	31709	Roswell	30076	Lawrenceville,	
Georgia University,		Holly Springs,		Gwinnett	30245
Athens	30612	Cherokee	30142	Shannon Oaks	30245
Gibson, Glascock	30810	Hollywood, Clarksville	30523	Leary, Calhoun	31762
Gillsville, Hall	30543	Homer, Banks	30547	Lebanon, Cherokee	30146
Girard, Burke	30426	Homerville, Clinch	31634	Leesburg, Lee	31763
Glenn, Heard	30219	Hortense, Brantley	31543	Lenox, Cook	31637
Glennville, Tattnall	30427	Hoschton, Jackson	30548	Lenox Square, Atlanta	30326
Glenwood, Wheeler	30428	Howard, Taylor	31039	Leslie, Sumter	31764
Glynco, Brunswick	31520	Huber, Macon	31201	Lexington, Oglethorpe	30648
Godfrey, Madison	30650	Hull, Madison	30646	Lilburn, Gwinnett	30247
Good Hope, Walton	30641	Hunter Army Airfield,		Main Office Boxes	30226
Gordon, Wilkinson	31031	Savannah	31409	Lilly, Dooly	31051
Stevens Pottery		Ideal, Macon	31041	Lincolnton, Lincoln	30817
(Baldwin Co.)	31031	Ila, Madison	30647	Lindale, Floyd	30147
Gough, Keysville	30811	Indian Springs, Flovilla	30231	Lindsay Creek,	
Gracewood, Richmond	30812	Industrial, Atlanta	30336	Columbus	31907
Grantwood, Coweta	30220	Inman, Fayetteville	30232	Lithia Springs, Douglas	30057
Graves, Dawson	31742	Iron City, Seminole	31759	Lithonia, DeKalb	30038
Gray, Jones	31032	Irwinton, Wilkinson	31042	Lizella, Bibb	31052
Grayson, Gwinnett	30221	Irwinville, Irwin	31760	Locust Grove, Henry	30248
Graysville, Catoosa	30726	Jackson, Butts	30233	Loganville, Walton	30249
Greenbriar, Atlanta	30331	Jacksonville, Telfair	31544	Lollie, Dublin	31021
Greensboro, Greene	30642	Jakin, Early	31761	Louisville, Jefferson	30434
Greenville, Meriwether	30222	Jasper, Pickens	30143	Louvale, Stewart	31814
Griffin, Spalding	30223	Big Canoe	30143	Lovejoy, Clayton	30250
Main Office Boxes	30224	Jefferson, Jackson	30549	Ludowici, Long	31316
Grovetown, Columbia	30813	Jeffersonville, Twiggs	31044	Lula, Hall	30554
Guyton, Effingham	31312	Jekyll Island,		Lumber City, Telfair	31549
Habersham, Demorest	30544	Brunswick	31520	Lumpkin, Stewart	31815
Haddock, Jones	31033	Jenkinsburg, Butts	30234	Luthersville,	
Hagan, Evans	30429	Jersey, Walton	30235	Meriwether	30251
Haldra, Lowndes	31632	Jesup, Wayne	31545	Lyerly, Chattooga	30730
Hamilton, Harris	31811	Jewell, Warren	31045	Lyons, Toombs	30436
Hampton, Henry	30228	Jonesboro, Clayton	30236	Mableton, Cobb	30059
Hapeville, Atlanta	30354	Main Office Boxes	30237	Macon, Bibb	31208
Haralson, Coweta	30229	Juliette, Monroe	31046	Huber P (Twiggs Co.)	31201
Hardwick, Baldwin	31034	Junction City, Talbot	31812	Macon Mall	31212
Harlem, Columbia	30814	Juniper, Box Springs	31801	Mercer University	31207

ZIP CODES

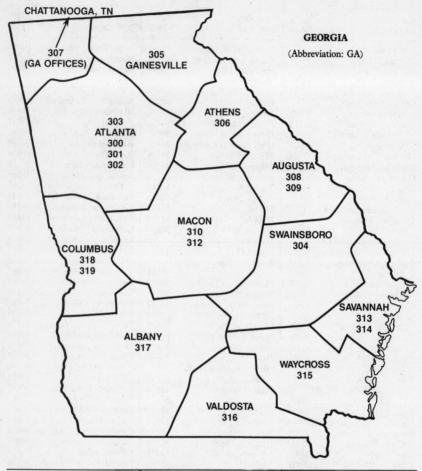

CHATTANOOGA, TN

GEORGIA
(Abbreviation: GA)

307
(GA OFFICES)

305
GAINESVILLE

ATHENS
306

303
ATLANTA
300
301
302

AUGUSTA
308
309

MACON
310
312

SWAINSBORO
304

COLUMBUS
318
319

SAVANNAH
313
314

ALBANY
317

WAYCROSS
315

VALDOSTA
316

Post Office and County	ZIP Code	Post Office and County	ZIP Code	Post Office and County	ZIP Code
Mulberry Street	31201	Forest Park	30051	Valdosta	31603
Pio Nono	31204	**Main Office Boxes,**		**Main Office Boxes,**	
Riverside	31209	Griffin	30224	Warner Robins	31099
Shurlington	31211	**Main Office Boxes,**		**Manassas,** Claxton	30438
South Macon	31205	Jonesboro	30237	**Manchester,**	
Wesleyan College	31297	**Main Office Boxes,**		Meriwether	31816
Wilson Airport	31206	LaGrange	30241	**Manor,** Ware	31550
Macon Mall, Macon	31212	**Main Office Boxes,**		**Mansfield,** Newton	30255
Madison, Morgan	30650	Lawrenceville	30246	**Marble Hill,** Pickens	30148
Godfrey	30650	**Main Office Boxes,**		**Marietta,** Cobb	30061
Madras, Coweta	30254	Rome	30162	Bellemeade	30064
Main Office Boxes,		**Main Office Boxes,**		Canton Plaza	30066
Brunswick	31521	Smyrna	30081	Dobbins A F B	30060
Main Office Boxes,		**Main Office Boxes,**		Fair Oaks	30060

Post Office and County	ZIP Code	Post Office and County	ZIP Code	Post Office and County	ZIP Code
Southern Tech	30060	Mount Berry, Rome	30149	Palmetto, Fulton	30268
Marine Corps		Mount Vernon,		Parrott, Terrell	31777
Logistics Base 3,		Montgomery	30445	Patterson, Pierce	31557
Albany	31704	Mountville, Troup	30261	Pavo, Thomas	31778
Marshallville, Macon	31057	Mount Zion, Carroll	30150	Peach Orchard,	
Martech, Atlanta	30377	Mulberry Street,		Augusta	30906
Martin, Stephens	30557	Macon	31201	Peachtree Center,	
Martinez, Augusta	30907	Murrayville, Hall	30564	Atlanta	30343
Matthews, Wrens	30818	Musella, Crawford	31066	Peachtree City,	
Mauk, Taylor	31058	Mystic, Irwin	31769	Fayetteville	30269
Maxeys, Union Point	30671	Nahunta, Brantley	31553	Pearson, Atkinson	31642
Mayfield, Sparta	31087	Nashville, Berrien	31639	Pelham, Mitchell	31779
Maysville, Banks	30558	Navy Supply Corps		Pembroke, Bryan	31321
McCaysville, Fannin	30555	School, Athens	30606	Pendergrass, Jackson	30567
McDonough, Henry	30253	Naylor, Lowndes	31641	Penfield, Union Point	30658
McIntyre, Wilkinson	31054	Nelson, Cherokee	30151	Perkins, Jenkins	30822
McRae, Telfair	31055	Newborn, Newton	30262	Perry, Houston	31069
Meansville, Pike	30256	Newington, Screven	30446	Philomath, Rayle	30660
Medical Ctr.		Newnan, Coweta	30264	Pinehurst, Dooly	31070
Eisenhower		Raymond	32063	Pine Lake, DeKalb	30072
Hosp, Augusta	30905	Newton, Baker	31770	Pine Log, Rydal	30171
Meigs, Thomas	31765	Elmodel	31748	Pine Mountain, Harris	31822
Meldrim, Effingham	31318	Nicholls, Coffee	31554	Pine Mountain Valley,	
Menlo, Chattooga	30731	Nicholson, Jackson	30565	Harris	31823
Mercer University,		Norcross, Gwinnett	30091	Pineview, Wilcox	31071
Macon	31207	Peachtree Corners	30092	Pio Nono, Macon	31204
Meridian, McIntosh	31319	Rockbridge	30093	Pitts, Wilcox	31072
Mershon, Pierce	31551	Norman Park, Colquitt	31771	Plainfield, Dodge	31073
Mesena, Warren	30819	Norristown, Emanuel	30447	Plains, Sumter	31780
Metter, Candler	30439	North Atlanta, Atlanta	30319	Plainville, Gordon	30733
Midland, Muscogee	31820	North Decatur, Decatur	30033	Pooler, Chatham	31322
Midville, Burke	30441	North Ga College,		Portal, Bulloch	30450
Midway, Liberty	31320	Dahlonega	30597	Porterdale, Newton	30270
Milan, Telfair	31060	Northlake, Atlanta	30345	Port Wentworth,	
Milledgeville, Baldwin	31061	North Side, Atlanta	30355	Savannah	31407
Millen, Jenkins	30442	Norwood, Warren	30821	Poulan, Worth	31781
Millwood, Ware	31552	Nunez, Emanuel	30448	Powder Springs, Cobb	30073
Milner, Lamar	30257	Oakfield, Worth	31772	Powersville, Byron	31008
Mineral Bluff, Fannin	30559	Oak Grove, Acworth	30101	Preston, Webster	31824
Mitchell, Glascock	30820	Oakman, Gordon	30732	Pulaski, Candler	30451
Molena, Pike	30258	Oak Park, Swainsboro	30401	Putney, Dougherty	31782
Monroe, Walton	30655	Oakwood, Hall	30566	Quitman, Brooks	31643
Montezuma, Macon	31063	Ochlocknee, Thomas	31773	Rabun Gap, Rabun	30568
Monticello, Jasper	31064	Ocilla, Irwin	31774	Ranger, Gordon	30734
Montrose, Laurens	31065	Oconee, Washington	31067	Ray City, Berrien	31645
Moody AFB, Valdosta	31601	Odum, Wayne	31555	Rayle, Wilkes	30660
Moody AFB (official),		Offerman, Pierce	31556	Raymond, Newnan	30263
Valdosta	31699	Ogeechee Road,		Rebecca, Turner	31783
Moreland, Coweta	30259	Savannah	31405	Redan, DeKalb	30074
Morgan, Calhoun	31766	Oglethorpe, Macon	31068	Red Oak, Fulton	30272
Morganton, Fannin	30560	Oglethorpe, Savannah	31406	Register, Bulloch	30452
Morris, Quitman	31767	Okefenokee, Waycross	31501	Reidsville, Tattnall	30453
Morris Brown, Atlanta	30314	Old National, Atlanta	30349	Rentz, Laurens	31075
Morrow, Clayton	30260	Oliver, Screven	30449	Resaca, Gordon	30735
Morven, Brooks	31638	Omaha, Stewart	31821	Hill City	30735
Moultrie, Colquitt	31768	Omega, Tift	31775	Rex, Clayton	30273
Mountain City, Rabun	30562	Orchard Hill, Spalding	30266	Reynolds, Taylor	31076
Mount Airy, Habersham	30563	Oxford, Newton	30267	Rhine, Dodge	31077

423

Post Office and County	ZIP Code	Post Office and County	ZIP Code	Post Office and County	ZIP Code
Riceboro, Liberty	31323	Windsor Forest	31406	Sugar Valley, Gordon	30746
Richland, Stewart	31825	Wright Square	31412	Summertown,	
Richmond Hill, Bryan	31324	Scotland, Telfair	31083	Swainsboro	30466
Rincon, Effingham	31326	Scott, Dublin	31095	Summerville, Chattooga	30747
Ringgold, Catoosa	30736	Scottdale, DeKalb	30079	Sumner, Worth	31789
Rising Fawn, Dade	30738	Screven, Wayne	31560	Sunny Side, Spalding	30284
Riverdale, Clayton	30274	Sea Island, Brunswick	31561	Surrency, Appling	31563
Riverside, Macon	31209	Senoia, Coweta	30276	Suwanee, Gwinnett	30174
Roberta, Crawford	31078	Seville, Wilcox	31084	Swainsboro, Emanuel	30401
Robins A F B, Warner		Shady Dale, Jasper	31085	Oak Park	30401
Robins	31098	Shannon, Floyd	30172	Summertown	30466
Rochelle, Wilcox	31079	Sharon, Taliaferro	30664	Sycamore, Turner	31790
Rockledge, Laurens	30454	Sharpsburg, Coweta	30277	Sylvania, Screven	30467
Rockmart, Polk	30153	Shellman, Randolph	31786	Hilltonia	30467
Rock Spring, Walker	30739	Shiloh, Harris	31826	Sylvester, Worth	31791
Rocky Face, Whitfield	30740	Shurlington, Macon	31211	Talbotton, Talbot	31827
Rocky Ford, Screven	30455	Siloam, Greene	30665	Talking Rock, Pickens	30175
Rome, Floyd	30163	Silver Creek, Floyd	30173	Tallapoosa, Haralson	30176
Mount Berry	30149	Six Flags Over		Tallulah Falls, Rabun	30573
West End	30161	Georgia, Atlanta	30336	Talmo, Jackson	30575
Roopville, Carroll	30170	Smarr, Monroe	31086	Tarrytown,	
Rossville, Walker	30741	Smithville, Lee	31787	Montgomery	30470
Fort Oglethorpe		Smyrna, Cobb	30080	Tate, Pickens	30177
(Catoosa Co.)	30742	Main Office Boxes	30081	Taylorsville, Bartow	30178
Roswell, Fulton	30077	Cobb County Center	30080	Tazewell, Buena Vista	31803
Holcomb Bridge	30076	Snellville, Gwinnett	30278	Temple, Carroll	30179
Sandy Plains	30075	Social Circle, Walton	30279	Tennga, Murray	30751
Royston, Franklin	30662	Soperton, Treutlen	30457	Tennille, Washington	31089
Rupert, Taylor	31081	South Base, Warner		The Hill, Augusta	30904
Rutledge, Morgan	30663	Robins	31098	The Rock, Upson	30285
Rydal, Barlow	30171	South Decatur, Decatur	30034	Thomaston, Upson	30286
Pine Log	30171	Southern Tech,		Thomasville, Thomas	31799
Saint George, Charlton	31646	Marietta	30060	Thomson, McDuffie	30824
Saint Marys, Camden	31558	South Macon, Macon	31205	Tifton, Tift	31793
Saint Simons Island,		Sparks, Cook	31647	Abac	31794
Brunswick	31522	Sparta, Hancock	31087	Tiger, Rabun	30576
Sale City, Mitchell	31784	Mayfield	31087	Tignall, Wilkes	30668
Sandersville,		Devereux	31087	Danburg	30668
Washington	31082	Springfield	31329	Toccoa, Stephens	30577
Deepstep	31082	Springvale, Morris	31767	Toccoa Falls	30598
Sandy Springs, Atlanta	30358	Stapleton, Jefferson	30823	Toccoa Falls, Toccoa	30598
Sapelo Island,		Starrsville, Covington	30209	Toco Hills, Atlanta	30329
McIntosh	31327	State College, Savannah	31404	Toomsboro, Wilkinson	31090
Sardis, Burke	30456	Statenville, Echols	31648	Townsend, McIntosh	31331
Sargent, Coweta	30275	Statesboro, Bulloch	30458	Trenton, Dade	30752
Sasser, Terrell	31785	Georgia Southern	30458	Trion, Chattooga	30753
Sautee-Nacoochee,		Georgia Southern	30458	Tucker, DeKalb	30084
White	30571	Statham, Barrow	30666	Tunnel Hill, Whitfield	30755
Savannah, Chatham	31402	Stephens, Oglethorpe	30667	Turin, Coweta	30289
Bingville	31403	Stevens Pottery, Gordon	31031	Turnerville, Habersham	30580
Garden City	31408	Stillmore, Emanuel	30464	Tuxedo, Atlanta	30342
Hunter Army Airfield	31409	Stillwell, Effingham	31330	Twin City, Emanuel	30471
Ogeechee Road	31405	Stockbridge, Henry	30281	Tybee Island, Chatham	31328
Oglethorpe	31406	Stockton, Lanier	31649	Tyrone, Fayette	30290
Port Wentworth	31407	Stone Mountain,		Ty Ty, Tift	31795
State College	31404	DeKalb	30086	Unadilla, Dooly	31091
Thunderbolt	31404	Stovall, Meriwether	30283	Union City, Fulton	30291
Wilmington Island	31410	Suches, Union	30572	Union Point, Greene	30669

Post Office and County	ZIP Code	Post Office and County	ZIP Code	Post Office and County	ZIP Code
Maxeys	30671	**Warner Robins,**		**White Oak,** Camden	31568
Penfield	30658	Houston	31093	**White Plains,** Greene	30678
Upatoi, Columbus	31829	Main Office Boxes	31099	**Whitesburg,** Carroll	30185
Uvalda, Montgomery	30473	Centerville	31028	**Wildwood,** Dade	30757
Valdosta, Lowndes	31601	Robins A F B	31098	**Wiley,** Rabun	30581
Bemiss	31602	South Base	31098	**Willacoochee,** Atkinson	31650
Castle Park Sta Boxes	31604	**Warrenton,** Warren	30828	**Williamson,** Pike	30292
Main Office Boxes	31603	**Warthen,** Washington	31094	**Wilmington Island,**	
Moody A F B		**Warwick,** Worth	31796	Savannah	31410
(official)	31699	**Washington,** Wilkes	30673	**Wilson Airport,** Macon	31206
Valdosta State College	31698	**Watkinsville,** Oconee	30677	**Winder,** Barrow	30680
Bemiss	31602	**Waverly,** Camden	31565	**Windsor Forest,**	
Castle Park	31601	**Waverly Hall,** Harris	31831	Savannah	31406
Clyattville	31604	**Waycross,** Ware	31502	**Windsor Park,** S	
Moody A F B	31699	Okefenokee	31501	Columbus	31904
Valdosta State College,		**Waynesboro,** Burke	30830	**Winston,** Douglas	30187
Valdosta	31698	**Waynesville,** Brantley	31566	**Winterville,** Clarke	30683
Valona, Crescent	31332	**Wesleyan College,**		**Woodbine,** Camden	31569
Vanna, Hart	30672	Macon	31297	**Woodbury,** Meriwether	30293
Varnell, Whitfield	30756	**West Bainbridge,**		**Woodland,** Talbot	31836
Vidalia, Toombs	30474	Bainbridge	31717	**Woodstock,** Cherokee	30188
Vienna, Dooly	31092	**West End,** Atlanta	30310	**Woolsey,** Fayetteville	30214
Villa Rica, Carroll	30180	**West End,** Rome	30161	**Wray,** Irwin	31798
Vista Grove, Decatur	30033	**West Georgia College,**		**Wrens,** Jefferson	30833
Waco, Haralson	30182	Carrollton	30117	**Wright Square,**	
Wadley, Jefferson	30477	**West Green,** Coffee	31567	Savannah	31412
Waleska, Cherokee	30183	**Weston,** Webster	31832	**Wrightsville,** Johnson	31096
Walthourville, Liberty	31333	**West Point,** Troup	31833	**Wynnton,** Columbus	31906
Waresboro, Ware	31564	**Westside,** Gainesville	30501	**Yatesville,** Upson	31097
Warm Springs,		**Whigham,** Grady	31797	**Young Harris,** Towns	30582
Meriwether	31830	**White,** Bartow	30184	**Zebulon,** Pike	30295